These Things I Know

The Autobiography

of

William Grant Bangerter

Compiled by Cory Wm. Bangerter

Under the direction of Wm. Grant Bangerter

and

Geraldine Hamblin Bangerter

Voices and Images, Salt Lake City, Utah

Printed by BYU Print Services
Provo, Utah

Book Design and Layout
Kathleen M. Hughes, Voices and Images

ISBN 978-0-615-79439-6

PREFACE

Sometimes I think I was born in the wrong generation. By vicariously living through many of the experiences portrayed in this volume as well as actually participating in others, at times I have felt more like a younger brother to William Grant Bangerter than his eldest son. Truthfully, all of his sons could say the same. Many of our interests have been intertwined with his in a marvelous web, ranging from early days on the farm to a shared deep excitement and love for Brazil (which include the beginnings of the restored gospel in that great land). Certainly most of us could recite by memory many of the scenes recounted often in family home evenings, long automobile trips, and other settings where we imposed upon our father to "tell us a story."

Wm. Grant Bangerter was a magnetic personality whose intangible qualities drew people to him. He had a surety of purpose in life that seemed to radiate from his quiet yet powerful persona. His influence reached far beyond his boyhood farmhouse on 3200 West in Granger, Utah, gradually encircling the globe and touching untold thousands of lives. His faith and witness served as a bulwark to those who were trained and tutored by him.

Some time ago, I was asked to assist in the compilation and formalization of the events that chronicle the life of William Grant Bangerter. The organization of this book is chronological and the headings reflect time periods of major impact in the life of William Grant Bangerter. Some sections are longer than others due to the amount of information or the desire of Elder Bangerter to emphasize or focus on the events portrayed. Some topics of a more general nature lend to a more scant coverage.

Special thanks goes to Don Rogers of Alpine in his desire to record on video the William Grant Bangerter wartime experiences. Those taped interviews were then transcribed under the direction of Dr. Robert Freeman of the Brigham Young University Religion

Department and served as a basis for some of the material included in this volume. In like fashion, gratitude is expressed to Gordon Irving of the James Moyle Oral History Program of The Church of Jesus Christ of Latter-day Saints for his interviews and the typed transcript of Elder Bangerter's life up to and including May 1977. Luann Crossley of Alpine is to be commended for her typing of the many audiotapes as Elder Bangerter recorded his life story. Many others have likewise been helpful in reviewing, editing, and reworking the manuscript to ensure its flow, content, and accuracy, most notably Nicole Fernley and Lauren Wilde for the editing of the entire manuscript and Kathleen and Charles Hughes for the graphic design. The journals kept by William Grant Bangerter form the major impetus for the events in this work.

Credits would not be complete without acknowledging the input and encouragement of his loving wife Geraldine Hamblin Bangerter and her deep desire to see this volume come to pass. In like manner, each of the children has made valuable contributions and additions. They are in birth order: Lee Ann and Richard Lorenzon; Cory William and Gayle Bangerter; Glenda and Steven Apple; Julie and Ramon Beck; Grant Hamblin and Cleadonna Bangerter; Howard Kent and Lissa Bangerter; Peggy Brasília Bangerter and Douglas Porter; Glenn Paulo and JaLayne Bangerter; Layne Rio and Betsy Bangerter; and Duella and Lonnie Williams.

The life story of William Grant Bangerter spans the days of the horse and buggy (when the automobile was barely making its inroads into America) to the space age. His life story reflects a deeply romantic touch to the heady days of frontier living and contact with the unknown. Nostalgia and interest exude from every chapter of his life along with insights into provident and fruitful living that come alive with each page. I am honored to work with my parents and others in preparing this book for publication and distribution. In reality, Dad is more than Dad to me. He is my brother and my friend.

—Cory William Bangerter

FOREWORD

"How do you capture all that has happened in one's life in a few short pages? It's impossible!" This has always been the concern expressed by William Grant Bangerter. For one who has studied and held strong ties to history and its proper recording, the task of telling the story properly might at times seem almost insurmountable. He believed that real history, especially the history of the Church, can only truly be written by a prophet. He would hope for that same influence to properly chronicle his life.

The full story of Wm. Grant Bangerter is one of epic changes, nostalgic seasons, and golden eras. His life spanned many monumental, global changes: from the pre-penicillin era plagues of influenza to modern AIDS; from the economic collapse of 1929 and the Great Depression to prosperity of the latter 20th century; through world wars and conflicts, including "The Great War" (World War I), World War II (in which he was an active participant), Korea, Vietnam, the Gulf Wars and others. Each of these events and changes shaped and molded the world and enabled his character and attitudes to be a tower of strength for his friends, family, and followers. Nostalgia for days long past, tempered by time from the harsh realities of day-to-day existence, surge up as sweet memories to soften those difficult days. The golden eras are often seen by succeeding generations as glorious and exciting, filled with adventures and tests, all leading to a crown of respect and honor for one so deserving.

Life was hard for farmers in Granger, Utah, during the early part of the 20th century. Everyone was poor, but no one seemed to notice. Working the ground with draft animals was gradually replaced by cumbersome machinery. Elder Bangerter recalled harnessing a team of horses and planting a field of grain by himself when he was a child. As was not uncommon for the oldest son of a farmer in those days, at the ripe old age of six, he was already doing the job of a full-grown man. Eventually the farms became subdivisions and those who worked the ground adapted with the demand and became carpenters and contractors. Such was the history of Grant Bangerter's father, Wm. Henry Bangerter, and his brothers and their sons during those years. Most people grew their own food, and dependency upon the local grocer or market was minimal. It was a meager but pleasant existence, particularly for a large family where all cooperated to make life work enjoyable and full.

The children of Wm. Henry and Isabelle Bawden Bangerter, like most others in the Granger area of Salt Lake Valley, grew up, went to school, married, and had children of their own. They lived life according to the teachings of their parents and their faith in the gospel of Jesus Christ and thus served with devotion in the Lord's kingdom. The boys, their cousins, and their in-laws followed the example of Wm. Henry Bangerter and served missions for the Church. The foundation of their solid upbringing by two very mature and consistent parents gave the Bangerter children a leg-up on their peers who did not benefit from such stability and example. The collective experiences of these children made for strong individual character. Leadership in every aspect—in business, church or civic affairs—was a natural result. The sons and spouses of the daughters rose to high office in many cases. In the Church they served in bishoprics, high councils, and stake presidencies. Three served as mission presidents, and two served as General Authorities of the Church. Some served in civic responsibilities from city councils to state legislatures, and one was elected governor of the state of Utah. The daughters occupied positions in the women's auxiliaries on a ward, stake, mission, and general level, each contributing to the power, influence, and expansion of the restored gospel.

After the passing of William Henry and Isabelle Bawden Bangerter, their children began to go as well, but not before having families of their own and continuing in large measure the legacy bestowed upon them. Several beloved spouses also passed on in their season. A few grandchildren of Wm. Henry and Isabelle Bawden Bangerter preceded them in death, always accompanied by the heartache of their loss yet with reassurance in the knowledge of their spiritual condition.

But that gets us ahead of the story. William Grant, the oldest son of 11 children was accepted as a natural leader among his siblings early on. He had a natural bent toward sober things and to impressions of the Spirit. His experience and pondering taught him much about administration and the operation of organizations. His thoughtful mind, coupled with a deep sensitivity to spiritual things, inevitably led him to positions of ecclesiastical leadership at a relatively early age. Without seeking such associations, from his earliest years he rubbed shoulders with apostles and prophets, and eventually counseled with them on many occasions and became their official representative on numerous assignments. The weighty responsibilities that were given to him evidenced the deep trust the Brethren had for him throughout his life. Though serving in important callings, his humility was always foremost, never turning his position to leverage power. Many saw in him a common man invited to sit in the leading councils of the Church.

His posterity sat at his knee and heard stories of his boyhood, young adult life, early manhood, and beyond. His ability to convey the story was so refined that it became real to those who listened so that to them it seemed they had actually lived those experiences themselves. The vivid scenes are easily recalled. Each child can remember times, places, and events of settings that have since changed greatly with the passage of time. The expressions of his life overflow into the feelings and attitudes of his children and grandchildren.

This is the story of a faithful son, a devoted husband and father, a patriarch, and a patriot, as well as a committed and dedicated servant of the Lord. His story is filled with a subtle witness of the workings of the Lord in his life. To properly plumb the depths of his life experiences would take volumes. Master novelist Owen Wister said of the lead character in The Virginian that "he . . . felt himself to be a [man] whom life had made 'broad gauge.' " Wm. Grant Bangerter was broad gauge. To capture the full picture of this man, as well as that of most others who have sojourned on this earth, one will have to wait to see that great picture show in the sky. Hollywood could never do justice to the story.

—The Children of William Grant Bangerter

FOLLOWING ARE THOUGHTS

EXPRESSED BY

WILLIAM GRANT BANGERTER:

No work ought to be performed without a purpose and there must, therefore, be a good reason for composing a personal history. In my case there are several reasons—some of them compelling— that have encouraged me to launch into an involved and unfamiliar project.

There is a need to feel that we will all live for a purpose. While our lives may slip away, largely unnoticed and little recorded, the story of what we did ought to reveal some accomplishment and satisfaction, and while we believe our acts are carefully recorded in heaven, that information is difficult for our children and descendants to come by. This history is intended, therefore, to bring personal satisfaction and to provide information for those who might be interested. These will probably include our posterity, and as may be the case with Church authorities, possibly other members of the Church.

In addition, members of the Church have been directed by the President and prophet to prepare a personal history as a part of their record-keeping responsibility. Among the reasons for this assignment is the need to preserve for others the feelings of faith and incentive that have directed the course of our lives. As the stories, examples and testimonies of others have lifted and inspired us who are members of the Church, there comes a hope that in writing our own history we, too, may add faith and strength to our contribution as we witness what God has wrought in the experience of our lives. Throughout my life there has been a strong urge to proclaim the power of God, especially in the Restoration of the gospel in the last days.

On April 5, 1975, I was called and set apart as an Assistant to the Quorum of the Twelve Apostles and as a Special Witness of Jesus Christ to the entire world. I have been urged to make some record of my life's experience in order that my posterity may feel the power of faith in the Lord and the blessings of the Spirit in giving peace and assistance and in fulfillment of the promises of our Heavenly Father to those who seek to do His will (see D&C 107). My life has been a varied journey, accompanied by the blessings of heaven. I give testimony of the power of our Heavenly Father throughout my life.

The story is divided into the various episodes and periods through which I have passed, each with a heading; it is an account of what has been an incredible experience. This record of my experiences speaks of faith in our Heavenly Father. I will tell of His blessings and promises throughout my life.

In this, my 92nd year of life (January 2010), I am blessed with vigor and a sound mind, being able to carry on the activities of life in a normal manner in connection with my wife, Geraldine Hamblin Bangerter, to whom I have been happily married for 55 years. Together we continue to watch over our posterity, having 11 children and 65 grandchildren. The great-grandchildren have begun to appear with a promise of an extensive posterity. We reside in Alpine, Utah.

—Wm. Grant Bangerter

(Note: William Grant Bangerter passed away Sunday Morning, April 18, 2010.)

A MODERN DAY PIONEER

Two days prior to Grant's passing, President Thomas S. Monson came to the hospital and spent an hour visiting with him, giving encouragement and counsel. He gave Grant a blessing in which he said "You are one of the great ones in the kingdom of God. You are a pioneer, a man who goes before, showing others the way to follow. You are a pioneer in the welfare program in the old stakes of Salt Lake City. You are a pioneer in Brazil (and Portugal). You are a pioneer like the pioneers who crossed the plains."

Truer words could not have been uttered. As I think back over the many years we shared together, I see his pioneering efforts. In his patriarchal blessing it states that he would see nations born in a day. I recall that when he served as a stake president, he was assigned to be vice chairman of the Pioneer Welfare Region, where he rubbed shoulders with many of the founders of the Church Welfare Department, including President J. Rueben Clark Jr., Harold B. Lee, Marion G. Romney, Glenn Rudd, Thomas S. Monson, and many others.

But he was more than a pioneer; he was also a driven leader. While serving as mission president in Brazil (1958–1963), he led out in a marvelous way in the establishment of the Church and kingdom in South America. He pioneered efforts to open up new areas in Brazil, including large cities in the north, such as Recife, Brasília, Goiania, and others. Side by side, he and Elder A. Theodore Tuttle (who came to South America in 1960 as supervisor of the missionary work there) formulated plans for missionary work and growth in those nations. The other South American mission presidents looked to Grant for his sound advice and experience. These men, all strong and young leaders, formed the nucleus of the pioneering effort for the growth of the Church in South America. As an example of his pioneering effort in missionary work, he wrote and implemented a series of special lessons to help his missionaries become more successful in converting people to the gospel.

Also during his time as mission president in Brazil, he pioneered chapel construction in that country and supervised the building of a new mission home, which was to be the headquarters of the Church in Brazil for nearly two decades. He became a licensed contractor in Brazil, allowing him to more efficiently forward the work of construction as he dealt with the legal organs of the communities, such as architects, builders, bankers, and attorneys. He was also a pioneer in the construction missionary effort, calling local Brazilian boys to serve as construction missionaries in the early days of chapel building in Brazil, allowing these young men to learn a valuable trade. Along with these efforts, he pioneered, together with other mission presidents in South America, the transition of local ecclesiastical leadership from full-time missionaries to local men who began to assume leadership positions in the districts and branches of the mission. He called local men as his counselors in the mission presidency and established the first local district presidency in South America.

His pioneering extended beyond the mission in Brazil. Called to be the first mission president in Portugal, he once again acted as a pioneer in the establishment of the Church in that land. Through the efforts of Brother David Kennedy, who served as a Special Ambassador of the President of the United States to nations of the world as well as a special envoy of the First Presidency of the Church, the door was opened and Grant was sent to establish the mission on the ground.

When called as a General Authority, he was assigned as president of the International Mission where he immediately began to seek out those who could take hold in leadership positions in the far reaches of the world, such as Iran, Turkey, Greece, Yugoslavia, Saudi Arabia, and other places of remote access to Church headquarters. This was his third term as a mission president. He knew that priesthood leadership was needed as it was only a priesthood leader who could sign baptismal papers, call young men on missions, ordain people to the priesthood, decide who could serve in branch positions, and preside over these scattered branches of the church. William Grant started putting people in charge in each of these nations, calling men as branch and district presidents so that local leadership could flourish and the regular programs and operations of the Church could develop under the leadership of the priesthood. An example of this was Kresimer Cosic of Yugoslavia, where almost singlehandedly he worked with William Grant to establish a beachhead for the Church in that country. We saw similar examples in Greece, and Turkey.

While presiding over the North America East Area, Grant sought out Sister Beverly Campbell and established a regional "public affairs representative" of the Church (the center of truth for the world) to labor in Washington, D.C. (the center of liberty for the world). Sister Campbell personally knew many of the senators and national leaders, and she organized and revitalized the Church public affairs efforts in the nation's capital. Grant became good friends with J. Willard Marriott and had many occasions to draw on his expertise.

Under the direction of President Spencer W. Kimball, William Grant became a pioneer in his assignment with the directing of the temples throughout the world. Together with then counselor in the First Presidency President Gordon B. Hinckley, policies were established to make it possible for single sisters and wives of unendowed men to receive their temple blessings. He was at the forefront of creating visual endowment sessions for the hearing impaired. He established, revised, and smoothed operational procedures for temples throughout the world. He was not a "desk man" but rather a real field administrator. In Brazil he was a strong advocate for pioneering family history work among the members in preparation for the dedication of the São Paulo Temple. In like fashion he moved forward the ordination of men to the Melchizedek Priesthood so they could be prepared for their temple blessings in both Brazil and Chile specifically, as well as in many of the other stakes of the Church in regular stake conference assignments. In connection with the São Paulo Temple dedication, he helped pioneer the creation of a garment center in providing temple clothing for members who would be coming to the temple. In Brazil he established the first MTC outside of the United States. Today the São Paulo Missionary Training Center is the largest MTC outside the United States. Soon thereafter, he did the same in Chile and established an MTC there that is still in operation. His efforts to fill the Brazil MTC with locally called Brazilian missionaries was another pioneering effort that nearly took his life; that story and many others are all covered in this book. As a member of the Presidency of the Seventy, he helped implement what eventually became known as the consolidated meeting schedule throughout the world. Also while in the Presidency of the Seventy, he assisted in recommending aged or incapacitated General Authorities to be named to Emeritus Status. He was a wise and trusted leader and colleague of his Brethren in the Seventy and the Twelve. Though both Grant and I come from pioneer stock, I can honestly say that Grant was a true modern-day pioneer. I was blessed to be at his side for more than half a century. I had every opportunity to see weakness in him, but he never disappointed me. He was strong, hearty, consistent, faithful, wise, and true. He was the light of my life, leading me from place to place around the globe. He was my hero.

— Geraldine Hamblin Bangerter

TABLE OF CONTENTS

Period III — New Beginnings and Challenges

Period IV— Mission President Years

Period VI — Presidency of the Seventy

Period VII — Emeritus Years

Period VIII — The Concluding Years

PERIOD I —
Beginnings And Early Life

Chapter 1

FAMILY BACKGROUND
AND
BEGINNINGS

"I know that my parents reared me and all of their eleven children to be worthy of . . . any . . . calling of service. I have felt since childhood that my mother, who is a great soul, carried with her the spirit of Hannah, the mother of Samuel of olden time—that whatever else her children might become, she had already dedicated them to the Lord and to his service. We were raised to go on missions, to work hard, to pray often, and to give our lives over to service. More than all other people put together, the influence of my parents has led me to this position. William H. Bangerter and Isabelle Bawden are sacred names to me, as are, in connection with them, my brothers and sisters and other relatives."[1]

THERE ARE THOSE IN THE CHURCH WHOSE FORBEARERS WERE IN INTIMATE CONTACT WITH THE PROPHET JOSEPH SMITH AND WERE involved in the establishment of the Church from its early beginnings. My own people did not enjoy this contact but nevertheless did have connections with others of the early leaders who established

---

1. *The Collected Works of William Grant Bangerter* (Speeches and Presentations made as a General Authority of the Church of Jesus Christ of Latter-day Saints; Wilson Duffles compiler; hereafter referred to as Collected Works), p. 4

the foundation of the Church. Some of them suffered the trials and tribulations of those early days and were pioneers in coming to Utah and afterwards.

My father's father, Frederick Lorenzo Bangerter, was born June 12, 1849, in Kappelen, Lyss, Switzerland, and was the first convert to the Church among his immediate family in Switzerland. He was introduced to the gospel by his brother-in-law, Jacob Iff. Frederick was a mechanic, a blacksmith, and a wagon maker residing in Lyss, near Bern, Switzerland. He joined the Church on May 8, 1881, at the age of 31. Soon he met a young woman named Maria Elizabetha Blauer, age 23. Maria was born on April 8, 1858, in Schoren, Bern, Switzerland, and joined the Church on August 7, 1880. Frederick and Maria were married on November 18, 1881, and five days later they left Switzerland and came to the United States. Their trip to America was their honeymoon, and they settled in Utah. A couple years after their arrival in the Salt Lake Valley, they were sealed in the Salt Lake Endowment House on February 7, 1884. From the outset they established their marriage and family in Utah, and here they reared their family amidst great trial and tribulation. In addition to my grandparents, several of their family members also migrated to Utah, including Frederick's father, Friedrich Bangerter; his mother, Maria; his sister, Anna Marie, and her husband, Jacob Iff; as well as his brothers Nicolas and John. They moved around for some time trying to find a proper home. Frederick and Maria had initially gone to Manti, where their missionary friend lived, and then moved to various places in Salt Lake County.

My father's people were thought of as foreigners. Their inability to communicate well in English was a challenge. All of their deepest thoughts, prayers, and revelations were in the Swiss language. They struggled in destitution trying to locate their home in "Zion." They couldn't find a place to settle until on one occasion my grandfather had a dream. In the dream a man came to him and showed him a piece of property. It was then he saw his dream home in Zion. A few days thereafter, a man who dealt in real estate did come, and he took Frederick to the community of Granger and to the very place he had seen in his dream; Frederick had an impression that he would live there for over 20 years. He purchased the home, which was located at 3800 South and 3600 West. There Frederick and Maria reared their family, saw their children married in the temple, and in their advanced years performed the temple work for all their known deceased ancestors.

In their later lives, my grandparents gathered the names of their ancestors and began doing temple work. After my grandmother died, my grandfather continued doing this temple work. One day he returned from the temple and said to his oldest son, "I have now done all the work for my ancestors. All the names that I had have been completed." That night he had a dream. Two men appeared to him and asked, "Why didn't you do our work?" The next day he reviewed his records and found that these two men had not had a death date recorded, but enough time had passed that they could be presumed dead, and so he did their work. Soon after that he passed away. 2

Frederick and Maria Bangerter sent all of their sons on missions except one, Albert, who was drafted into the U.S. Army during World War I. The posterity of my grandparents generally followed their pattern of faith, and that posterity came to be leaders in the gospel. Through them would come bishops, high councilors and stake presidents, patriarchs, General Authorities, and civic leaders; one became the governor of the State of Utah.

My father, William Henry Bangerter, was his parents' second son and sixth child. He was born June 29, 1890, and learned to speak their Swiss dialect before he learned English. After finishing the eighth grade, he left school to help support the family through farming under pioneer conditions. My father accepted a mission call to the Swiss-German Mission, where he served from 1913 to 1914. The outbreak of World War I interrupted his work, and he completed the last few months of his mission in the Eastern States Mission.

My mother, Isabelle Bawden, came from Mormon pioneer ancestry and was born in Granger, Utah, on November 2, 1892. Her paternal grandfather, Henry Passmore Bawden, joined the Church in Devon, England, on March 20, 1848, not far from Bristol. Henry was the only member of his family to join the Church, and he soon

2. Collected Works, p. 429

migrated to Utah. He was a blacksmith as was his father before him. In 1857 he took a second wife, Sarah Freelove Howard (born August 30, 1838); they were married on March 18 of that year in Brigham Young's office in Salt Lake City and were later sealed in the Endowment House on March 1, 1860. Henry Passmore and Sarah Freelove soon settled in the Mill Creek area near 4500 South and 1300 East in Salt Lake Valley. Sarah Freelove Howard's parents, Samuel Lane Howard and Elizabeth Pack, were also early converts to the Church from England, coming from Devon and Bedfordshire respectively. The family of Samuel Lane Howard was among the first to hear the gospel message preached in England by Heber C. Kimball on his first mission to that land. Both were baptized on January 7, 1838. They lived in Bedford, north of London, and suffered through the first apostasy and period of unfaithfulness occasioned by those weak in the faith following the departure of Elder Kimball from England. They had three children: Betsy, Sarah Freelove, and a son, Samuel Howard, who passed away soon after his birth. The Howard family eventually took passage on a ship to the United States. However, a lack of funds stalled them in St. Louis, Missouri. While attempting to arrange means to move on to Utah, both Samuel and Elizabeth became ill and died in St. Louis. Their two remaining children, Sarah and Betsy, soon crossed the plains with other pioneers—walking all the way and experiencing the normal pioneer difficulties—and settled in Utah, finding their own way as youth.

My grandfather, John Howard Bawden, was born on October 10, 1858, and was the oldest of 10 children born to Henry Passmore Bawden and Sarah Freelove Howard. John moved with one of his brothers from Mill Creek to Granger, where they were some of the early settlers. He became a member of the first bishopric of Granger and served in that capacity for 30 years. He married my grandmother, Alice Jane Freestone, of Alpine, Utah. Her father, George Freestone was born on Prince Edward Island, Canada, on August 13, 1838. George was the oldest of nine children born to Thomas Freestone and Ann Fall, from Yorkshire and Suffolk England respectively. He was baptized on April 16, 1854. His parents had joined the Church three years earlier in 1851. The Freestones immigrated to Utah together as a family. George married Alice Carlisle on December 24, 1861 in Alpine, Utah, and they were sealed in the Endowment House on July 19, 1862. Alice Carlisle was born in Nottingham, England, on October 9, 1835 and was baptized in Nottingham on November 16, 1849. Her parents had joined the Church earlier that year, and the family soon immigrated to Utah.

It happened that my father's people and my mother's people lived on adjacent farms in Granger. When my mother, Isabelle Bawden, was nine years old, her mother, Alice Jane Freestone, passed away in childbirth (January 12, 1902), after giving birth to a baby daughter named Jane. Mother and baby Jane were sent to live with their grandmother, the pioneer Sarah Freelove Howard. Mother's job was to help take care of her baby sister. A year later, Jane died. During that same year my mother's father, John Howard Bawden remarried. His new wife was named Olive Smith and they were married on August 4, 1902, in the Salt Lake Temple. Aunt Olive, "Little Grandma," as we came to know her, was 27 years old and Grandpa was 43. Aunt Olive bore Grandfather seven more children. Mother continued living with her grandparents in Mill Creek. For this reason, she grew up more attached to her aunts and uncles than to her own brothers and sisters. On visits to the Bawden family home in Granger, she became acquainted with a neighbor to the south, Will Bangerter, two years her senior. Their courtship flourished at church dances, and following my father's mission they were married in the Salt Lake Temple on April 26, 1916. Because of the milling business, my father, William Henry Bangerter, became involved in raising wheat but had some setbacks, and, therefore, branched out into industrial work and other labors. He built his home on 16 acres in Granger where most of his 11 children were born.[3] At the time of my birth, my father was engaged extensively in farming, both irrigated and dry farm.

I was the firstborn son; my sister, Sarah Alice, preceded me by 17 months. My birth occurred on June 8, 1918, a hot day full of thun-

---

3. Wm. Grant Bangerter Oral History, interviews by Gordon Irving, 1974–77, typescript, James Moyle Oral History Program, Archives, History Department of The Church of Jesus Christ of Latter-day Saints, Salt Lake City, Utah (hereafter referred to as Bangerter Oral History), pp. 1–3

derstorms, according to my mother. The "hospital" in which I was born was the farm home of my father's grandparents, Frederick and Maria Bangerter. A midwife, Lettie Wilkin, my mother's aunt, assisted. They reported that I was mostly arms and legs and not very attractive except to my mother. This house was the homestead that had been shown to my grandfather in a dream as his promised home in Zion. While it is certainly true of many people, no one could have imagined what our Heavenly Father had projected for this seemingly insignificant life that began in a cottage partially built of logs.

In the year I was born, Woodrow Wilson was President of the United States. This was also the time of the great influenza epidemic that took the lives of up to 50 million people worldwide. President Joseph F. Smith was in his last year as the Lord's prophet—the flu epidemic took his life in November 1918. President Heber J. Grant was sustained as prophet of the Church at the next general conference on June 1–3, 1919. This conference was delayed from April 6 "owing to the health conditions of the communities."[4] In 1918, childhood diseases were a common threat to life—these included diseases such as smallpox, measles, diphtheria, and scarlet fever and were found in most families. Death came often, especially to children. World War I was raging, and it wasn't until November 11, 1918, that the Armistice was signed.

Life in Granger, Utah, and most of America still reflected much of pioneer conditions. Father's employment as a dry farmer included the care of horses and milk cows as well as other farm animals. Farm power was mostly horse power. Daily life was centered on farm activities. We fed and milked the cows, tended the pigs and chickens, and grew our own fruit and vegetables. We rode in buggies and used iron-tired wagons. Responsibility came early. I learned to hitch a horse to a buggy while almost a toddler. I mowed hay when I was six. At eight years of age I planted a field of wheat by myself while my father was away at work. We rode the work horses sometimes but not as cowboys. My childhood was that of farm interest and activity. Our farming activities were common in those times. Although my parents were young and had very little during my early childhood,

---

4. Conference Report, June 1919, p. 1

things did not improve as I got older. In my early youth, the nation entered the Great Depression. There were few resources, and like other families in our condition, we made do the best we could but we always had sufficient to eat and plenty to do. [5]

Although we lived in what some would consider primitive conditions, we always had adequate clothing, a comfortable home, and good food. Entertainment was simple. For example, in those trying days, great moments consisted of the arrival of the threshing machine, a summer excursion into the mountains, and happy Christmas time. The blessings of heaven were sought in sickness and in hardship. Our prayers and priesthood blessings were answered. Even though life was comparatively primitive, it was not uncomfortable. We pumped the water and used coal for cooking and heating. We used coal-oil (kerosene) lamps and lanterns and took Saturday night baths in a washtub in the kitchen. Being the oldest son, I always bathed last. Children had plenty of chores and errands to perform and lived a life of fascination with the constant activity surrounding the home and the farm as the world slowly unfolded. During that time the telephone came into use, and limited electric power gave us light and not much more. My brothers and I slept on the old screen porch year round in all types of weather. We would pile on the quilts in the winter and sleep together in the bed. Bud slept between Sam and me, and he used to say that I would take the covers and pull them in one direction, and Sam would take the covers and pull them in the other direction, and he would lie between in the open space and freeze all night.

Our lives centered on the Church, and community and social events were held in the chapel on 3200 West and 3500 South, which was a modern building for that time. The Granger Ward was part of the Cottonwood Stake of The Church of Jesus Christ of Latter-day Saints. My father was made the bishop of the Granger Ward on December 12, 1920, and later the new Oquirrh Stake was organized with headquarters in Pleasant Green, now called Magna, in 1923. Our first stake president was President George A. Little, the second was President H. Edward Sutton, and the third was President John

---

5. Bangerter Oral History, p. 2–3

D. Hill, who was Mother's cousin.[6] Father was bishop for 13 years.[7] Granger had a tradition that it was the Promised Land, being on the west side of the Jordan River. At one time it carried the name of Canaan."[8]

Shortly after arriving in America, Grandpa Bangerter set up a hand grinder to grind grain. The neighbors, seeing what he was doing, began to bring grain to be ground. Soon a mill evolved. This led to the establishment of the Bangerter milling enterprise, which for many years was prominent in Granger. The Bangerter flour mill was located on the railroad line that bordered Grandpa Bangerter's property. In addition to farming, my father worked in the mill at different times—until disaster struck and the mill burned down.

My father and his brother, Albert, purchased 32 acres of farmland from Archie Bennion located on 3200 West and 3800 South. There in 1919 my parents constructed a modern yellow brick home. My brother, Samuel, was born in the new home on November 29, 1919. The 11 children of my parents are Sarah (Sally), myself, Samuel (Sam), Pauline, Blauer (Bud), Elsbeth (Bessie), Glenneth (Glenny), Marian, Naomi, Norman, and David. David was a special child having limited capacity, but he filled our lives with great joy, appreciation, and happy understanding. Our attitudes toward the Church in our home were always of complete devotion and that of being strict in keeping the commandments and in being faithful. We believed that it was a divine mission to belong to the Church. That atmosphere and attitude was fully indoctrinated into our lives. I can say without reservation that the greatest blessing of my life was to have parents who were faithful and devoted to the gospel.[9]

Parents are the greatest of all inventions in bringing joy and expression to childhood. Over the many years people have asked: "Who do you want to grow up to be like?" or "Who has most influenced your life?" I have only one answer—my father and mother. In spite of all the impressive personalities with whom I have had as-

---

6. Ibid., p. 8

7. Ibid., p. 11

8. Ibid., p. 7

9. Ibid., p. 11

sociation, including some of the greatest people who have lived on the earth in my time, all of them put together have not had half so much influence on me as have William H. Bangerter and Isabelle Bawden, my beloved and revered parents. In our home we were sheltered and loved. Faith in the restored gospel, church activity, and regular prayers accompanied us throughout our lives. Mother was a tireless worker and deeply dedicated to the gospel; she found great satisfaction in doing genealogy or family history work. She taught the gospel and father directed us in prayers and matters of faith. We always knew that we were members of the only true Church, and we grew up to be faithful, baptized members willing to work for the kingdom. The gospel was a central theme in our home. My feelings for the gospel along with those of my family were deep and sure. I always knew that Heavenly Father was near us, and we always had personal and family prayers, blessed our food, attended Church, and reverenced sacred things. We always knew that Jesus Christ was our Redeemer and that through Joseph Smith, God had restored the fullness of the gospel to the earth.

As I've grown older, I've realized that my parents' dedication to the gospel came from their parents. When my father took me, along with my older sister Sarah, and our younger brother, Samuel, to visit his parents, I was not aware of their great spiritual stature. Grandfather Bangerter was lame, walking with halted steps because of an accident many years before, and Grandmother jerked with palsy from which she suffered in her later years. They spoke imperfect English, and though they were kindly and interested, we didn't seem to communicate too well. I never suspected then that they had lived a life of surpassing courage and privation because they had listened to the story that some young missionaries told them in their native Switzerland about an obscure and despised church located far away in the primitive western United States. They believed in the restored gospel of Jesus Christ, that it had the power of life and salvation for all people on the earth. I did not know then that Grandmother Bangerter possessed a superior intellect and a capacity to make things happen in anything she undertook. As I have learned more about them and their devotion and dedication, my admiration has expanded into reverence.

Visiting my mother's former home was somewhat more comfortable since Grandfather Bawden with his bald head and white moustache paid special attention to all his grandchildren, of which there was an endless supply. He bounced us on his knee and sang to us often. He lived until I was 18 years old. Aunt Olive adequately filled the needs of us all. The lives of each of these unusual people deserve a full history of their own. In every case, they were fully and completely devoted to the gospel and the Church and left a priceless heritage for an unusually prolific posterity.

Chapter 2

CHILDHOOD AND YOUTH

"My mother had ten children, all healthy and well-developed. Then in a more advanced age, she gave birth to number eleven, and he was a little Down Syndrome baby [David Karl]. What a terrible and discouraging condition that was. It wrenched her heart and tore her soul. But she bent to the task and loved that little boy more than all the others. She devoted the many remaining years of her life to caring for him, and developed out of that experience the attributes of humility and sanctification of the spirit and of the soul. This refinement would not have come without that special trial. The experience has been a blessing to all the rest of us."[1]

Early Family and Farm Life

My brother Sam (who was nearly 18 months younger than me) and I were often filled with projects in our playing. We loved to imitate the great threshing machine, or we imagined going hunting. We improvised ice skates or skis to be pulled behind the horse. We enjoyed going to the mountains, which we did for a few days each summer. When we went to the mountains, Sam and I began to explore and hike the ridges up to the summit of the Wasatch Range. We frequently came across small mountain lakes, and we always undressed and dove in. The water was very cold, and our swims amounted to five strokes in and five strokes back; we then got out, dressed, and moved on to the next one. Other activities included games of "Rounders" in softball where several young people participated, each working up to bat playing various positions along the way.

---

1. Collected Works, p. 433

My father kept us busy with farm work. I enjoyed it, although the many hours of weeding and hoeing in the fields were a burden. I learned to manage being tired, thirsty, and hungry in the midst of growing responsibility. Nobody ever realized how thirsty we would get with the heat and dirt. You can't imagine what it was like to lay down and get a big drink out of the ditch that flowed nearby.

Dad was a sweet companion. He often took me into the fields and usually had me ride on one of the horses he was driving. (I especially remember Snip, the grey horse.) His teachings were always on the habits and responsibilities of life. Work was the central business of living. The family needed everyone's help to make things go. Father always felt that idleness would lead to delinquency and a purposeless life. He said, "You can't expect a boy to work by himself. His father should be at his side." This companionship was the most endearing.

Dad often shared thoughts from his German background or Swiss dialect. When he wanted his boys to come and help with something, he would say, "Buba, Hermit stat bok! In Schiess keit!" which meant "Come on over boys; the town goat has fallen into the river!" (That means it's an emergency!) These sayings were common to him, and he used them frequently. He would sing Swiss songs and trained me in the verses like "Gaetzli, du Muss Hopfe Springe," or "Tru-la, Tru-la, Tru-la la," and his version of "How Much Is that Doggie in the Window" with a verse and a chorus in German. This culture seeped into our background.

Life had its routine of morning milking and feeding, breakfast as a family, cooking and cleaning, and preparing for the day's work or school. Mondays were always washday, and the women and girls strove to have some laundry on the clothesline before others in the neighborhood to signify that they had not slept in. Tuesday was for ironing the clothes and the succeeding days for the remainder of the household duties. The men and boys were usually in the fields. The labor was by hand and with the aid of machines drawn by horses. To me it was always fascinating.

Looking back on my life, I can see times when I was blessed to have unusual protection and guidance through the Spirit of the Lord. Many of those occasions happened without my knowledge or awareness but nevertheless worked for my health, safety, and personal assurance that I have been blessed and protected. I was blessed generally with good health. I had my tonsils removed when I was four. There were incidents of sickness in the family, and I was troubled with migraine headaches in my childhood and youth. At six years of age, soon after I started school, I was stricken with infantile paralysis, or polio, which kept me out of activity for about six weeks. No one knew what this disease was at the time, but I recovered without any lasting effects except some difficulty in swallowing. On one occasion, I fell from a fruit tree and broke two of my ribs. I sprained an ankle several times, and once broke it stepping on a rock in the field. I had no medical attention but it healed in due time. I also sprained my right knee, and this injury almost kept me from military service. A very serious affliction in 1977 while we were in Brazil nearly took my life (see chapter 16). Only later in life did I pass through serious medical difficulties. Others in the family sustained injuries and illnesses as well. My sister Pauline struggled with scarlet fever; Glenneth had a serious abscess that nearly took her life. Dad had several injuries—broken ribs, leg injuries, and other broken bones—of which he took almost no notice.

Mother was a strong moral influence in our lives. She resisted our fighting with associates. She prohibited evil speaking and the use of such words as "damn" and "hell." Mother also had a rule for us in how we spoke to others. Our speech had to pass three tests. First, "Is it true?" Second, "Is it kind?" And third, "Is it necessary?" This helped us keep our conversation on a higher level. She taught us not to lie and to keep our thoughts clean. Stealing was totally wrong, and one of her most frequent scriptural quotes was, "[Obedience] is better than sacrifice, and to hearken than the fat of rams" (1 Samuel 15:22). She worked in family research, providing temple work for at least 20,000 of her people.

Father was born to do physical work. His capability and willingness to labor at whatever needed to be done became the hallmark of his manhood. He had a tireless physical endowment and provided a home, a living, and the necessities of life for his family. We were always poor, but in the words of President Eisenhower: "The glory of America is that we didn't know it then." [2]

I am grateful that I had a father who was willing to leave his employment or change jobs if necessary to avoid working on Sunday. When his neighbors suggested that his hay would be ruined if he didn't haul it on Sunday, his comment was: "I don't care if it rains on my hay. I don't have to eat hay." [3]

Another great example of his commitment to honor the Sabbath occurred during the depression years when work and money was scarce. Father had been hired as a construction worker on a project, and he told his employers he would not work Sundays. He was told that he wouldn't have to. One Saturday at the close of work, his boss announced to the crew that because they were behind schedule, all would have to come in on Sunday or lose their jobs. As an exclamation point he said, "That means you too, Bangerter!" Father replied instantly, "I won't be here." The next morning his co-workers came by to pick him up, and he met them in his Sunday shirt and tie. Against their urging he refused to go. On Monday morning he showed up for work. They called roll in those days, and the boss looked at him as he called roll and said, "Bangerter, you lucky so and so." Evidently, on Sunday as the roll was called and there was no response to "Bangerter," one of his friends had said, "Oh, he's sick."

With dad as bishop we came to know everyone. We visited those who were dying and suffered with the community over diphtheria and scarlet fever. Aunt Emma died and Little Nellie died. So did Ruby Bawden, and we lived through Aunt Bashie's troubles.

Father also taught me the importance of tithing. While serving as bishop, he called me in one day and said, "I want you to pay your tithing. Here is 25 cents, which will pay tithing on all you have earned until now. You pay this and I will give you a receipt. Then whenever you earn money in the future you should pay one-tenth to the Lord in tithing."

---

2. Made in remarks at the laying of the cornerstone of the Eisenhower Foundation in Abilene, Kansas, on June 4, 1952. Quoted in *The Papers of Dwight David Eisenhower,* vol. XV. Document #681.

3. Collected Works, p. 161

On one occasion we were camping near Brighton in Big Cottonwood Canyon, and as we were by the stream, John Arnold, a neighbor in Granger came by fishing. He quickly fixed up my brother Bud and I with a short line with a hook attached to a small willow, and we rustled up some worms and started catching fish. Mother came by and said that she didn't think it was right for us to fish without a license. Bud then handed her the willow with the hook on it and said he had to get something, and quickly she caught a fish too! After that we teased her about fishing without a license.

We had no special training in sex education. Once when I was about seven or eight I heard a bad word from my associates in school, and I announced it at the dinner table. My parents were shocked and quickly admonished me; father thereafter giving me some explanation of the relationship of the sexes that was confined to marriage.

We had good, wholesome friendships that included exploring the outdoors and playing baseball and football. Close friends were Robert Hill, Henry Bawden, and Rulon Mackay (all of whom were my cousins), along with Dick Fairbourne, Stan Hale, John Eldredge, Robert Smith, and Carlisle Mackay.

There are too many happenings to remember or list them all, but they are all sweet memories of the happiest situation into which our family could possibly have been born. Some of these memories include swimming in the canal with an occasional dead chicken floating by, and in the winter improvising ice skates made by hand and screwed onto our shoes (we never had anything new)—these are all great memories.

I remember the old barn and the blacksmith shop, with Grandpa Bangerter shuffling along due to his crippled knees, and Grandma's garden south of the house. When we moved to the new home on 3200 West, we often talked of going through "The Lane" to go to Grandma's house or to the mill. We rode the buggy mostly with our horse Old Tops. I remember visiting the Monroe School in the old 59th District building. That is where Dad, as a boy, blew up the stove with a .22 bullet that he tossed into the stove when no one was looking.

Youth

The area of Granger was west of Salt Lake City and extended from the Jordan River on the east to 4800 West, a distance of about three or four miles. 4800 West was the dividing line between Granger and Hunter. From north to south it covered practically all the area that was then settled, roughly from 2100 South to about 4700 South. Childhood memories in Granger are a rich fountain of love and nostalgia. In my childhood there were perhaps eight hundred to a thousand people living in that area, and it was all one ward. Later Granger and Hunter were split into two wards west of the Jordan River, and each had approximately 600 members.[4] We knew everyone in the area. Until my late teens, I could have named every family in Granger. Certainly my father, who was the bishop, knew every family and probably every person by first name. I think those who lived in Granger during those years came to feel a closeness that would be common with other small communities. Our community ties were almost of a family nature, and the related memories build that kind of a feeling.

There were some automobiles, such as the Model T, on dirt roads. Nearby grocery stores were not all that important. Most people had limited financial resources to spend there anyway. Murray was five miles away and Salt Lake City ten. We didn't go there very often. Some people had telephones on a "party line." The operator said, "Number, please?" We answered, "Murray 534 J-1." Most homes had electric lights but no appliances or other conveniences. The standard lighting fixture was a single light bulb on a drop cord hanging from the ceiling. Housework was centered on the comfort-providing coal stove, which required kindling, coal, and taking out the ashes. Few homes had a furnace. Insurance did not play a great part in the financial resources of all the family. In the midst of what would now be considered a fragile existence, people flourished, enjoyed life, and

---

4. Collected Works, p. 442

somehow not only survived but, in a modest way, prospered. I don't believe there was a truly wealthy family in the entire community.[5]

The concept of work became a principal part of our life's effort. It has gone through a great metamorphosis during my lifetime. In the 1920s, to work meant to build or produce something—at least this was the understanding that carried meaning in our community. When a farmer worked, he produced with his own hands the actual food by which people lived. This work required muscles and long hours and demanded more strength and physical stamina than are found today in the average man. Only athletes now build that kind of physical capacity, and they use it to play games. Back then, if a man worked in an office, he was often looked upon by the farmers and other workers as something of a parasite, for he did not seem to produce anything tangible. Schoolteachers were considered a necessary public burden. There were grain binders and mowing machines, but we worked with our shovels and pitchforks to keep those machines busy. We thinned, weeded, topped, and shoveled sugar beets, and we pitched hay and grain, as well as manure (a rustic word now referred to as fertilizer). Today, there are tractors, loaders, milkers, cranes, and hoisters. Even carpenters use power equipment. They don't swing a hammer or push a saw very often; instead they pull the trigger on a machine. Farming is now more a science and an industry than a family way of life. In the past, the sons of a farmer worked at his side, becoming familiar with the out-of-doors and learning about animals. Daughters spent similar time at the side of their mothers. It isn't easy for families to enjoy this kind of association today.[6]

Granger was a farming community. The average farm would have been around 30 or 40 acres—some larger and some smaller. The crops at that time were always hay, grain, sugar beets, and potatoes. The canals served us well until the drought of the 1930s when they failed for a year or two. I think Granger grew as many irrigated crops as any other area in Salt Lake County during that period, especially grain. Farmers almost always took their own wheat to the mill to be

5. "Passing the Test," discourse given by WGB at the Thirteenth Annual Harman Lecture, BYU Continuing Education, pp. 2–3

6. Collected Works, pp. 443, 447

ground and then set in their supply of flour for the winter. They were able to sell the excess, and it was a reasonably good market in those days. The grain harvest was always exciting in Granger. The thresh-ing machines were drawn and powered by steam engines. I grew up eventually to have the high privilege of working on the threshing machine for two or three seasons near the end of their time, when combine harvesters began to take over. [7]

The Orem railroad passed through at 35th South and 18th West. The Granger station was there on the main line and went south to Payson. A branch railroad line turned from Granger and went west to Magna. The main roads were established before my childhood and were maintained in passable condition for that time—all gravel roads. There were other less-used roads or lanes into people's houses. These were not surfaced, sometimes having deep chuckholes. We did have one paved highway, which was 35th South. Our family went to Salt Lake occasionally, sometimes on the Orem railroad. Often we went to Mill Creek. We also went to Murray, which was a common shopping point about five miles away. [8]

Most families made arrangements for a supply of coal every year. I hauled coal from the coal yards near State Street and 33rd South. My father would go to work in the morning and arranged for me at the age of 10 or 12 years to meet him with a wagon when he finished work. He would load up the coal, and I would drive it home; the fol-lowing day I with my brothers would unload it and shovel it into the coal room in the basement.

George Robinson, a neighbor around my age, frequently sought out Sam and me for company. George had a .22 rifle, and we often went into the large orchard his father operated to look for pheas-ants, rabbits, or other animals. George sold us an old, single-shot .22 without a stock, so Sam and I improvised a stock. This became our only weapon for several years. To extract the shell from the gun, we had to use a nail since the extractor didn't work. Time was often long between shots.

---

7. Bangerter Oral History, p. 5
8. Bangerter Oral History, p. 3-4

Few people had riding horses, so we were limited to riding our farm horses. Will Erickson from Murray imported some wild broom-tail horses to feed to his foxes, and we decided to buy one for $15. As we looked them over, we were not impressed with the mustangs. They were unappealing and very scruffy looking with long tails and manes, scrawny and thin. But we noticed another nice, well-bred sorrel mare selling for $25. Back at home Sam and I pooled our money; we asked Bud if he had any he could throw in. We were still short, so we asked Dad if he could help out. He said he could because he wanted to have that horse as well. We came up with the $25 and bought her. She became the delight of our existence, fulfilling a lifelong dream and remaining with us for 20 years. We named her Bally. This began our love affair with horses and riding. She was a high-spirited horse and knew only one speed: full speed ahead. Since nearly everything was done bareback, she was put to work. Everyone was skillful at riding bareback. We never hauled horses, but the horses always hauled us. It took us four or five years to get a saddle for her, and when we finally did, it was an old Army McClellan saddle.

The wheat dry farms in the southwest part of Salt Lake Valley were our wilderness. The open spaces were always attractive and a place for wandering. Dick Fairbourne's father had a piece of dry-farm land that Dick and I would sometimes explore. My grandfather also had farm holdings there, and as I grew I would sometimes go with some of his family to help with plowing or tilling. To us it was a wild and a lonesome country. From that dry farm, we could see in all directions throughout the valley. Today the Oquirrh Mountain Temple sits on a portion of that land. When working the dry farm, we would travel from home and set up camp for a few days along the canal below where the temple is now located and farm during the day.

Great living experiences came in these years of childhood and youth, and in some of those experiences I was even productive. For example, one day when I was in the third grade (before I was ten years old), I stayed home from school, hitched up a team of horses to a grain drill, and planted a field of wheat.

While yet a boy on the farm, I was assigned the task of cleaning the ditches. In those days we did it with a sharp shovel, which we used to skim a thin layer of dirt from inside the ditch, removing the grass and weeds that would otherwise impede the flow of the water. I soon learned that a clean ditch meant at least doubling the efficiency of the irrigation stream. This was a backbreaking task, and often I used to speculate on better ways to clean the ditch. I would longingly look over to the corral where the cows and horses were penned up, and in my mind I would say to them, "Why can't I reason with you? I could explain to you the process of cleaning the ditch and then you could come and eat this delicious green grass. I would explain the boundaries so that you would only eat in the ditch and on the ditch bank, and you would agree not to go into the field and eat the alfalfa and the grain. I would be saved this backbreaking work, and you would not have to eat that dry old hay but could enjoy the luxury of green delicious feed." I never attempted this procedure, of course, because I knew it wouldn't work. You can't reason with an animal. I further noticed that on the farm, the bull and the stallion were placed in separate pens because they were incapable of self-control; if they were allowed to run free they would disrupt the animal society. [9]

---

9. Speech given at Ricks College Commencement, April 1977

Chapter 3

SCHOOL, CHURCH, FAMILY, AND WORK

"The traditional home has changed even among Latter-day Saints. There is a vast difference today. In my childhood it was the common pattern because so much of life among those who belonged to the Church centered around rural living, the farming communities, and there were great advantages in that the father was able to take his sons with him almost from infancy and give them the benefit of his personal influence and of his own philosophy. I don't think I can remember a single lesson my father taught, but I absorbed his attitudes and his feelings through osmosis, so to speak, by close association.

I CAN'T REMEMBER WHEN HE FIRST TOOK ME INTO THE FIELDS AND HE WOULD PUT ME ON A HORSE. IT WAS EASY TO RIDE A HORSE THAT was being driven in the harness because they had those high harnesses that looked like horns and a little boy could sit on top all day and just hold onto those horns and he was tended. Mother didn't have to worry about him, and I could sit up there and talk to my father as he was back on the plow or harrow. He couldn't hear me, but he would just give a word of, "Yes, son," or some encouragement and keep me going so that I would chatter to him from morning until noon.

I had some similar opportunity with this kind of association with my own sons. They came along when I was not in the farming business but I was in the construction business, and I was able often when they had the free time to take them with me and tend them so that their mother didn't have to tend them. It was the foundation of a marvelous association very similar to what I had with my own father." [1]

Grade School and High School

My schooling began in the Monroe School in Granger and was completed at Cyprus High School in Magna. I was a fairly good student. One notable teacher was James S. Smith, son of President Joseph F. Smith. We traveled to school in a school wagon until my junior high years. One hard winter all the west roads were drifted in. There was no attempt to plow them out for several weeks, so the school wagon shifted over to a bobsled with a cover on it, and we rode to school for several weeks in it. When I was about 12 years old, we had an epidemic of typhoid fever. The whole family was quarantined while my sister Pauline was ill. I missed several weeks of school and lost track of algebra. I finished the course, but this gap hindered my studies of mathematics for the remainder of my schooling. [2] We received a good education, for that time at least, with emphasis on English and writing, a considerable amount of history, a good introduction to arithmetic and mathematics up through high school, and fair attention to cultural things, such as music appreciation and to some extent vocal singing. [3]

After elementary school the Granger youth went to Cyprus High School. We traveled the eight miles from Granger to Magna on the Orem train every morning. There was always an interesting division of culture between us farmer people and the industrial people in the Magna area. I think they looked down on us, and we of course didn't feel that we had any particular interest in growing up in the smelter areas. Most students finished high school, but there was a considerable dropout rate, with the girls going into marriage and many boys losing interest in school. Granger was not a highly education-oriented community. Few of the young people thought in terms of higher

---

1. Collected Works, pp. 410-411
2. Bangerter Oral History, p. 2–3
3. Ibid., p. 6

education, and when the Depression came very few planned for college. [4] I always look back with a good impression on the instruction we received in high school. Our principal was Taylor Brockbank, the father of Bernard Brockbank, who served as a General Authority for a number of years. Incidentally, Taylor Brockbank had taught my mother in the Mill Creek-Cottonwood area years before. [5]

In high school, I remember how we played a certain game in some of our classes. A certain boy in the middle of the room had the facility to get someone on one side of the room to give him answers to test questions, and then he relayed them to others on the other side. It became fun to cheat in front of the teacher. I entered into the game one day and was caught, to my great embarrassment. I didn't need to cheat, and I afterward avoided the practice. [6]

After school we always went home to work, which limited many extracurricular activities. The Depression also limited those extra activities. I had no baseball, football, or basketball experience on organized teams. I did enjoy choral singing and participating in school productions. We did a production of the musical *H.M.S. Pinafore* by Gilbert and Sullivan. The Church's seminary classes held a special attraction for me, and I enjoyed Church history, Bible, and Book of Mormon studies. I always enjoyed school and did well without undue effort.

Finances were very limited, but almost every family had similar limited conditions. During these schooling years I had great associations with many cousins and friends. I never thought of them as cousins, since many were second cousins and always friends. I graduated from Cyprus High School in 1936. We had a graduating class of 105 students.

Church Ordinances and Activity

Faith and what is often referred to as a testimony were inborn in me. One of my sons [Grant] states that his testimony came with

----

4. Ibid., pp. 10–11

5. Ibid., p. 7

6. "Passing the Test," discourse given by WGB at the Thirteenth Annual Harman Lecture, BYU Continuing Education, p. 1.

him from the former estate, and I feel that the same blessing accompanied me, as I never had occasion to doubt the truthfulness of the gospel. I understood it from earliest childhood, having been taught to pray to my Heavenly Father through his Son, Jesus Christ. I always knew that Joseph Smith had received his first vision as a youth, and that he was later shown by the angel that there would be a rich restoration of divine truth, which would relate to the coming forth of the Book of Mormon as the Word of God. We were taught from the Bible and the Book of Mormon.

I always knew that we belonged to the only true Church on earth and that the Presidency and the Apostles were called of God to direct His kingdom in these last days. Jesus Christ was a reality to me; we worshiped Him as the Savior and Redeemer of all mankind. I received the holy priesthood and was dedicated through my faith to live a life of service in His kingdom. This faith was implicit in the lives and spirits of my parents and grandparents, whose forefathers had come from foreign lands to join the kingdom of God. Several of them struggled through persecution and deprivation to come to Utah and live under the direction of the Lord's anointed Prophets.

My parents were faithful and firm in their feelings about the Church and the gospel. We were always in the midst of Church activity, going to our meetings without fail every week. Sunday School was at 10:00 a.m., and sacrament meeting was at 7:00 p.m.—after we completed the farm chores of milking and feeding the animals. Father was our bishop throughout my childhood and from almost as early as I could remember. The ward meetinghouse was a half-mile away, and often we went by buggy or walked.

When I was eight years old, the morning of the day I was to be baptized I took a ride on one of our farm horses. It slipped in the muddy field and fell on its side, landing on my ankle; I was so injured that I was not baptized that day. About a month later I was baptized by Abner Fairbourne in the irrigation canal across from the chapel. Father called me while I was playing and told me it was time to be baptized, and we went over to the ditch where I was baptized without the ceremony we have become accustomed to today. Brother Fairbourne was a priest, and father had him baptize several boys that day. Our baptism costumes were the blue overalls of daily life.

Mother would often mention the time when I would be old enough to serve as a missionary for the Church. Her constant, inner thought was that we would grow up to serve the Lord. As I came of age to be ordained a deacon, I felt it a serious and important thing to hold the Lord's priesthood. I served as deacons quorum president, teachers quorum president and later as secretary in the priests quorum. By that time I was already involved in leadership and was asked to be the teachers quorum adviser while yet a priest. I was also called to be the MIA (Mutual Improvement Association) chorister.

We had various local recreational and cultural activities common to our community. It was not customary for our people to go to Salt Lake to see movies or to enjoy activities there. We made our own entertainment at home. I was 15 before I had seen two movies in my life. The Granger community was very interested in drama, and from time to time we had leaders who were very well qualified, so we'd attend ward shows. Everyone came. We lived through those homemade, home-produced dramas with emotions equal to what you would experience in the finest plays or movie productions now. Ruth and Nathan Hale began to develop drama and acting with the youth in the ward. Our ward had an active actors group, which centered on the Hales. All the family and all the community participated, and the Hales became prominent fixtures in the community; their influence grew and made a remarkable impact on drama and theater in Utah over the years.

Another prominent social activity was dancing. Dances were organized on a ward basis, and in some seasons of the year they were held weekly. Everyone of age who was interested in dancing came to these dances. The dances became the focal point of dating, and young people would come with their circles of friends. It was considered proper to circulate, so a boy taking a girl wouldn't spend the entire evening with her. He was expected to see to it that she had a good time, so we frequently traded dancing partners. Dancing was much looked forward to and thoroughly enjoyed. Abe and Will Todd played many of our dances as a two-man band. They would both fiddle. Then Abe would play a harmonica that was fastened around his neck with a collar, and William would beat a drum with his foot. They put out some excellent music and everybody really enjoyed it. We also had hired orchestras from time to time.[7]

Each year in the spring at Easter we would travel west around the point of the mountain past Kennecott, halfway to Tooele, and camp out at a place called Easter Egg Rock. Saltair Resort was another gathering place to meet, dance, and have fun. The community was full of young people. Marriages took place, and these marriages always became a community social. Nearly everyone was invited to a wedding reception, and this was another dance that lasted the whole evening. The couple would stand in their reception line, but everybody would go there prepared to dance. One of the highlights was to have the privilege of dancing with the bride, which we took occasion to do if we were able. Missionary farewells represented another special occasion. They were organized with a program, on Thursday night, which ended with a dance. The point was made of the fact that this was the last opportunity the elder would have to dance for two years. Then a welcome home party was given on the same basis and was the occasion for another dance. They were not held on Sunday, of course.[8]

In the 1930s the sport of basketball was becoming prominent, and the M-Men teams were the highlight. Young men who could qualify would get on those teams and hold their positions for years. That tradition didn't lend itself to letting the less talented have much experience, however. Granger did have a community baseball team in the Farm Bureau League for many years. Ren Butcher was the big pitcher for our team in those years.

There were a few members who were less active in the Church at that time. Perhaps there was the same percentage that you'd find today, although the distinction wasn't so great. A man might not go often to sacrament meeting, but he was still considered a good Latter-day Saint in many ways. There wasn't always the same urgent emphasis on his coming to meetings, but activity fluctuated. I felt my purpose was to be faithful and serve in the Church, to serve a

---

7. Ibid., p. 9
8. Ibid., p. 9

mission in my youth, to marry in the temple, and to be faithful to my heritage. In stating my belief, I know that I was not a perfect person. There were acts of my childhood that now bring me a feeling of remorse, but I tried to live a good life and to be worthy when the time came to receive the priesthood, to go to the temple, and to serve as a missionary.

When I was 18 years old, I received a patriarchal blessing that confirmed me in this course. Mother was anxious for us to receive our patriarchal blessings. Her father, John Howard Bawden, was our stake patriarch, and she asked him if he would give the blessings. Grandfather was in his last year of life, suffering from facial cancer and mostly bedridden, but he said to us, "Yes, you and Samuel come down to my home and I will bless you." He sat on the edge of his bed and gave me a marvelous blessing, which was unusually prophetic and inspiring and clearly marked the course of my life as a faithful member of the Church. During the blessing I did not perceive any unusual influence, but as I have read it over during the years of my life, I marvel at the vision and prophecy with which he delivered that blessing. According to my blessing, I was listed in the "Lamb's Book of Life"; I was to be called as a missionary to the land of the south and to have great influence in that work, and I was blessed to have a very effective career in service before the Lord. As these things came to pass over the years, I have been able to understand the power of prophecy and inspiration. Grandfather Bawden died a few months later, and I have always felt that it was a circumstance similar to that of Jacob giving the blessing to his sons. How did my grandfather know the things he pronounced in my blessing? There is only one answer: The Spirit of the Lord told him. Similar things can be said to each person who receives a patriarchal blessing. [9]

Family and Companions

The companions of my youth were all Latter-day Saints and active in the Church as far as going to meetings, but they didn't go on missions. As we grew a little older and started to look for dates or something to do on a Sunday afternoon, we would drift into Salt

---

9. Collected Works, p. 370

Lake City and then go to a show, not having anything else on our mind. My father suggested that that was not the right thing to do; I knew it wasn't, and so I began to resist. When the boys came to pick me up, I would ask them if they would come back for sacrament meeting. If they said they wouldn't, then I wouldn't go. I lost my friends, I thought. They began to go in their own directions. I went on a mission, and they did other things. However, as the years have gone by, I have seen that they too have found their way into a pattern of righteousness, and they have reared faithful families. They have served as bishops and leaders in the Church and sent their children on missions. So there is not a condemnation or loss of hope.[10]

Many of the boys in our community were relatives, and as I mentioned before, I became close to Rulon Mackay, Robert Hill, Henry Bawden, Dick Fairbourne, Stan Hale, John Eldredge, Carlisle Mackay, and George Robinson, who lived nearby. I had found girl-friends in high school, and with my friends I went on dates. Each summer the boys went on short fishing trips. Rulon Mackay's father had herded sheep in the Blacks Fork area of the Uinta Mountains, and in the summer of 1937 he organized a trip there with Stan Hale, Dick Fairbourne, Carl McRae, and me. This trip established a pattern of going to Blacks Fork that has remained with me throughout my life. (Carl rebuilt a cabin near the second crossing and called it his for many years.) We were close friends and active in attending church. The Depression still lingered, although employment was beginning to be available.

My Farming Career

The economy of the entire world had been affected by the Great Depression beginning in 1929. From then on, employment was dif-ficult to come by, and money became nearly nonexistent. This con-dition prevailed throughout my high school years and even until the entry of our nation in the war with Germany and Japan in December of 1941. Though work and opportunity were limited during the Depression days, we did not suffer; however, there was scarcity in clothing and any luxuries. My father reached out to operate other

---

10. Ibid., p. 385

farms on a crop-sharing basis, and in that way we gained a broad experience in farming. We were very busy as we rented and operated several farms in Granger. They didn't produce much in money, but they always produced plenty of work. I grew up in that tradition, and as Father was able to get work, I inherited the responsibility of operating the farms. By the time I was 13 or 14, I was personally and deeply involved in the farming business. We learned to operate plows, harrows, cultivators, headers, binders, mowers, and other implements drawn by horses. I would take my harmonica with me in the fields to water. In my spare time on the farm I would practice songs such as "The Strawberry Roan," "Oh! Susanna," "Roll out the Barrel," and "There Is a Tavern in the Town." Later from my Brazilian experience I learned "Sereno Eu Caio, Eu Caio," "Encosta Tua Cabecinha," and others. The hymns were also easy to play. This talent became recreational as I used it on trips or around campfires or at family night.

When I graduated from high school, our neighbor Frank Hunter, who owned 100 acres adjacent to our home, came and asked my father if we could operate his farm. Father said that he was now employed, but perhaps his son Grant would take it. So I went into business myself in farming when I was 17, operating about 100 acres on my own. I had one old broken-down horse, and I purchased another pony on a time arrangement and paid for it that fall. I used old equipment that I had learned to operate earlier, as well as an old wagon to haul the hay and grain. Looking back, I have difficulty expressing the extent of the work involved. There was constant irrigation as well as cutting hay with that old farm equipment, loading it by pitchfork, and hauling it by wagon. Dad taught me to operate the neighbor's grain binder, and I cut the fields of grain. For three years, my brothers Sam and Blauer assisted me as we cut and hauled the hay; planted and weeded the sugar beets; and irrigated and harvested wheat, barley, and oats. I worked on the threshing machine during the summers before I left for school. During previous summers, I had worked on the crew of the steam-powered threshing machine. Ted Warr was the owner and boss. Glen Warr was the engineer, and we were a crew of eight. Glen and others teased me about my goodness and called me "Bishop" after my father.

I worked the entire first year, and when I had finished and settled my accounts, I had $125 left over. This sounds small today, but I used it to go to BYU, where I lived in reasonable style for one quarter and then came back and farmed for another year. A particular aspect of this farming was the ever-present irrigation. Among the various pieces of property, the water was vital, and I spent as much as 100 hours per week on the ditches along with all the other activities of solid hard work. The second year I purchased a mowing machine and some harnesses for the horses, and I finished the sugar beet harvest in freezing weather. I had saved $150 this time and went again to BYU for two quarters. The third summer working especially with Sam, I was able to keep about half of the money for my mission. This, of course, was possible as I lived with my parents enjoying the comforts of home and good farm food. [11]

Attendance at BYU

Not yet old enough to serve a mission when I finished my first season in personal farming, I decided to spend the winter of 1937 attending Brigham Young University in Provo. I remember that while on the train to Provo, I was so frightened I didn't know what I'd do when I got there. Luckily, I fell in with one of my high school companions who had been there before. Mark Richards and Wayne Sorenson were already attending, and so I soon had friends. With the money saved from my farming effort, I spent three months boarding with a lady named Frandsen, along with five other fellows. They were LeGrand Dunkley, Max Germer, Lowell Allworth, R. J. Merrill, and Jesse Smith, the last coming from Greybull, Wyoming. Tuition at that time was $37.50 per quarter. I found it interesting that President Franklin S. Harris made a point of personally meeting each of the students attending the school. Leaving home for a week at a time was a rather traumatic experience for me. My roommate was Jesse Smith.

I met a number of new friends from distant and—to me— strange places. I met people from Dixie College in St. George, from Koosharem Junction, from Alberta, Canada, and from the Mormon Colonies in Mexico. I had never heard of these places before. I met

---

11. Bangerter Oral History, p. 13

several young men at BYU, including Max Shirts, Dan Harrison, Robert Halliday, and others who later appeared as missionaries in Brazil. On weekends I hitchhiked home for church meetings. BYU at that time did not provide for regular church activity.

The purpose for my studies was preparation for serving a mission. I joined the male and mixed choruses under the direction of Franklin and Florence Madsen, and I learned things about music that I never knew before. Classes that impressed me were English under Professor Rowe, speech under Professor Morley, religion from Guy C. Wilson, geology under Professor Hansen, and history from Meredith Wilson and Arthur Gaeyth. Among those I met at BYU were Mabel Johansen, Marjorie Merrill, LeGrand Dunkley, Ladd Cropper, and Margaret Reid, who I knew in high school. We knew Harrison R. Merrill, Robert Sauer, and other former notables.

After my second year of farming with my brother Sam, he attended BYU for a quarter, and then I returned for both winter and spring semesters. At this time, I lived with Paul Lambert, Mark Richards, Blair Sorensen, and Harry Olsen. I had been to high school with all but Blair. We lived in good but not very neat conditions. I tried to participate in track and field training; however, when I chose to go with the male chorus on a trip to southern Idaho, I lost out on athletics. We also had another trip to Blacks Fork with Rulon Mackay and Stan Hale. As I recall, we had 20 flat tires on that trip in the old Model A.

During this winter I had a job washing windows in the Education Building (now the BYU Academy and Provo Library). We had the College Building, the Women's Gym, and the upper campus with the Maeser, Brimhall, and Heber J. Grant buildings. Our classes seemed to alternate between the two campuses requiring a brisk walk between. I knew of only one student with an automobile. There were about 2,500 students. Dates were very occasional and consisted mostly of attending special evening programs, lectures, and musical presentations.

One of my schoolmates was so educated I couldn't believe it! When we arrived in Provo he said, "Yes, this is really the great metropolis of southern Utah." And I thought, "Metropolis, how did he

learn a word like that?" Soon thereafter, he taught me other important things. He said, "There is an important answer you can give in
college to any question they ask." And so he taught me to say, whenever I wasn't sure as to what I should respond, "Being inadequately
informed, but having a strict regard for the truth, I hesitate to make
an assertion for fear of propagating an error." Later, while living in
Provo and attending BYU, one of my roommates, Lowell Aylsworth,
sat down and explained to me his "philosophy of life." I'd never imagined people my age would have a philosophy of life. But here a young
man my own age had it all worked out, and he could explain to me
what he thought was the purpose for which he was living here on
the earth. Then, when he had finished, he said, "Now, tell me; what
is your philosophy of life?" I stood there with my mouth open. All
I could say was, "I don't know if I have one. My thinking has always
been religious, and I expect to follow the plan of the gospel." This
seemed to impress him, and he responded, "Well, yes, that is really
what I believe in too." I came to find out that my answer impressed
him as much as what he had said impressed me. We were learning
from each other.

When I went to English class, the professor, knowing something
of our background, would begin to read a passage from somebody's
paper and then he'd say, "Sagebrush, brother, that's sagebrush." I
wasn't sure what he meant until I realized that he saw in that verse
or that passage the evidence that the hay was still sticking out of our
hair and that we came from a rural background. Or someone might
write a passage that he thought was especially erudite, and it would
come out with all sorts of big words and phrases, and the professor
would read it and say, "Jargon, brother, jargon." So I learned another
big word.

Back and forth out of these experiences came many impressions
to my young mind. More than that, however, I began to realize—
more in later years—the powers and capacities of young people. I
have learned this so firmly that I now feel overwhelmed in the presence of young people. I now realize that there is the capacity to do
almost anything that can be conceived by the mind of man.[12]

---

12. "Living Happily Ever After," University of Utah institute fireside,
January 7, 1977

Chapter 4

TO AND FROM BRAZIL

"I did not know when I was only 8 years old that I would spend much of my life in Brazil. I only knew that my parents were planning that when I grew big enough, I would be dedicated to the Lord for two years to serve as a missionary. It was later, when I was 17 years old, that I sat at the edge of my grandfather's bed. He was soon to die of cancer, but he was our patriarch, and he blessed me by the voice of prophecy, much as Isaac and Jacob in the Old Testament blessed their sons in their old age. I was there told that I would soon be called to the land of the South, where millions of the blood of Israel were waiting to hear the Gospel, and that I would have much to do in helping establish the Lords Kingdom among them, for a nation would be born in a day." [1]

Call to Brazil

Mother and Father always assumed that their sons would serve as missionaries in their youth. The procedures for obtaining a mission call were similar to the procedures today. The bishop, knowing that a young man was available for a mission, would call and interview him. The interviews then were more apt to be held in our homes than in the church, but he would fill out the forms and send in a recommendation, and we received a call from the First Presidency of the Church. The bishop didn't always explore the possibility of sending all the young men into the mission field. [2] Bishop John D.

---

1. Collected Works, pp. 49-50
2. Bangerter Oral History, p. 12

Hill came to visit me in my family's home and said, "I understand that you would like to serve a mission."

Along with my parents, I responded, "I have always wanted to serve as a missionary."

"Where would you like to go?" he asked.

Although I had always thought that Germany was the place to go, since my father had served there, I said: "I will go where I am sent, but South America would be a special place."

I received my call from the First Presidency of the Church for me to go to Brazil in December of 1938 with the appointment to report for brief training in Salt Lake City in February of 1939. I was excited to go to Brazil. It was a thrill for me to receive the call to go to South America, and it delighted my parents, though my mother was shattered by the thought of the great distance I would have to travel. [3]

A few years before my mission call, we had in our stake conference a visit from Elder Melvin J. Ballard, who had just returned from his mission to establish the Church in South America. Elder Ballard officially dedicated South America on Christmas Day in 1925. I remember how his sermons and descriptions of his journeys in South America electrified our community. It was common talk among our people about the great things he had experienced. So it was interesting for me a few years later to sit in the office of Elder Melvin J. Ballard and be set apart as a missionary to Brazil and have him tell us of his personal experiences in establishing the work in South America. Prior to leaving I was ordained a seventy by President Rulon S. Wells. I was thrilled to learn that he had been ordained a seventy by Brigham Young. [4] I was then set apart by Elder Melvin J. Ballard. These two had officially opened the South American Mission

The work of the restored gospel in South America began with the visit of Parley P. Pratt in 1851 when he traveled from San Francisco to Chile on a sailing vessel accompanied by one of his wives and his companion, Rufus Allen. He spent a brief time trying to learn the language. He lived in Valparaiso and then moved for a period to the

---

3. Ibid., p. 17
4. Collected Works, p. 486

interior town of Quillota. He apparently had little success and returned soon thereafter to San Francisco.[5]

When I received my call to Brazil, very few people in the United States knew that the language spoken in Brazil was Portuguese. But my father knew that the mission in Brazil had first been organized in German with the missionaries preaching primarily to the German-speaking minority. It wasn't until the 1930's when the Brazilian government began fearing Nazi sympathizers, that the missionaries shifted their emphasis to the Portuguese-speaking majority.[6] Just until shortly before I arrived, the entire operation of that mission was in German. My father said, "Well, I know that it will be Portuguese. You'll probably speak Portuguese, but it may be, because of the background of the mission, that you'll have an opportunity to speak German. Would you like to have me teach you a little German?" I said of course I would. So he gave me three or four half-hour sessions. He would sit me down and have me read in German. Out of that experience I got to the point where I could sound my way through without understanding what I was reading. With that beginning, even though I was assigned to learn Portuguese, I picked up enough German through my own efforts and the contacts I made to be a reasonably effective missionary in the German language, finally presiding over the district where most of the German branches were located, conducting conferences, and giving a number of sermons in the German language, as well as in Portuguese.[7]

I had saved about $500 for the mission and my parents planned to supply the remainder of the cost. Mission expenditures were $25 a month. I was in Brazil for 33 months and spent a total of about $1,000 including clothing, and I still have the account of almost every penny to show how I spent it. We lived very well on that amount. Conditions allowed us to have board and room. We never made our beds, we never cooked a meal, and we never touched hot water in

5. June 1, 1995, re-dictation to the Historical Department, p.1

6. See *Church History in the Fulness of Times: Studen Manual* (2003), 523.

7. Bangerter Oral History, p. 15

two-and-a-half years. But as far as our physical conditions, we were
well cared for.[8]

Prior to departing for the mission field on the February 2, 1939,
I went with my parents to the Salt Lake Temple where I received my
endowments. There I felt the deep spiritual atmosphere in that sacred place and in the blessings I received. My first experience going
to the temple truly helped me feel as if I were in the presence of my
Father in Heaven and being brought as close as possible to his sacred presence. I have never gotten over that wonderful feeling.[9] I was
honored with a missionary farewell party, which in those days was
much different than what we see today. It was held on February 10,
1939. Many came and participated in the program and the dance
following.[10]

Mission preparation in those days was sketchy. I felt as well prepared as most young men, perhaps better prepared than the average
at that time. But that meant simply that I had tried to live faithfully
according to the instructions of the gospel. I had been active in seminary, which to me was a wonderful preparation in the gospel, and
I found that it had its effect over the years in my mission and the
years thereafter, giving me a basic understanding that I would not
otherwise have had. However, I don't think that I was as well prepared as young men are today.[11] We were instructed by several of the
General Authorities. Heber J. Grant was the President of the Church,
but I don't recall that he spoke to us. I do recall David O. McKay, his
counselor, and certain of the Twelve. Our mission home president
was Don B. Colton, and William E. Berrett was the instructor. He
gave us much instruction on how missionaries should act and the
basic knowledge that they ought to have of the gospel. To me it was
a fruitful, interesting, and enjoyable time. We lived in the Salt Lake
mission home during that period.[12]

------

8. Ibid., p. 13

9. Ibid, p. 327

10. See *Deseret News,* February 4, 1939

11. Bangerter Oral History, p. 12

12. Ibid.

Departure for Brazil

On February 19, 1939, I took the Denver & Rio Grande train with four companions through the Rockies and the Moffitt Tunnel to Denver. There we changed trains, going to Dallas, Texas, and the next day we went on to Houston. From there we went to New Orleans, crossing the great Mississippi River on that wonderful bridge. In New Orleans we boarded the ship Del Valle for Brazil. My four companions were James Douglas Davis of Provo, Max LeRoy Shirts of Spanish Fork, LeRoy Quentin Pia of Salt Lake City, and Woodrow Owen Christiansen of Fairview, all from Utah. I had known Elder Shirts at BYU. The train travel was a rare experience and an adventure. I had never really been out of Utah before. Arriving in New Orleans we stayed three or four days to obtain our visas in the Brazilian Consulate and to obtain our steamship tickets on Delta Line for South America. (Years later this same line would bring our family home from Brazil.) We looked over the city on the great Mississippi and visited several scenes of interest: the Old French Quarter, Lake Pontchartrain, as well as a hospital where Elder Davis had a friend studying medicine. In New Orleans we saw strange attitudes as the black people were held in segregation. We felt a new climate and saw the movement of commerce along the river.

Aboard the ship we had very comfortable accommodations and sailed down the Mississippi on a smooth surface to the Gulf of Mexico in the afternoon of February 25. As the day grew dark, the ship began to rock and pitch a little, and we knew we were in the Gulf of Mexico. The pilot left us, and we had dinner. Elder Davis was immediately seasick, but I felt well. We enjoyed the relaxing life on shipboard. We had interesting visits with our steward, good food three times a day, the chance to ride on the open deck and enjoy the sea life, and lovely moonlit nights. Our room steward, learning that we were Mormons, said that he thought having several wives was a good idea if they lived in different places. He was astounded to hear that we did not believe in that practice. We studied extensively. I read nearly all of the Old Testament during the voyage. We had some visits with passengers but felt some strangeness with people who were not of our background. Elder Pia had his accordion, which he played beautifully, and Elder Shirts had his violin.

On March 9 we crossed the equator and the ship's company sponsored a ceremony for all who had never been south of the line before. It was mostly foolishness but enjoyable. We novices were treated with showers and raw eggs and such. Our voyage lasted 19 days. On the evening of March 15 we began to see land and then majestic mountains, one with a great white cross on top. These were Corocovado and Sugar Loaf Mountain at the entrance of Guanabara Bay, where the city of Rio de Janeiro sits, and a most magnificent sight in the early evening. It had taken us nearly an entire month to get to the mission field from Salt Lake City.

Arrival in Brazil

After we docked, two young men came aboard looking for us and announcing that they were living in Brazil and knew the missionaries. It developed that they were missionaries (Elders Harmon Barton and Paul Merrill) and wanted to play a joke on us. They offered to give us a tour of the city of Rio the next day. Accordingly we spent some time walking up the main avenida, Rio Branco, and viewing the city, which was most beautiful and romantic. We saw the center of the city, the mountains, and the beaches, and we began to observe the people. These young men were playful and tested us somewhat in our devotion to our mission. In wandering about the city we passed through the red light district, which was said to be the most open area anywhere in South America, and we became aware of the seamy side of life first hand. We, of course, didn't linger in that environment, and I felt we should not have been there, but what we learned there was the ability to recognize any such place thereafter in the cities of Brazil and to stay away from them.

The next day, March 16, 1939, we sailed into the port of Santos, where we were met by the president of the Brazilian Mission, John Alden Bowers. President Bowers was a man of but 36 years. He and his wife had no children. He was really in the prime of his youth and was really a pioneer of that time. He and Sister Bowers taught us by precept and by example. My feelings and experience with President

Bowers were wonderful. He was a man devoted to his calling. He had spent much of his time, as I recall, in distant places not closely associated with the Church. Therefore his experience was related to his own missionary period, with the background of a strong Latter-day Saint home. He was a solid, stalwart leader of the gospel, and his wife, Sister Bowers, was a charming and lovely lady.

There was not too much instruction given to the missionaries. The mission president had been sent to preside over the mission without definite policies. So they didn't undertake to do what mission presidents now do, such as training missionaries in how to go out and find people and teach them the gospel. The leadership was in generalities. President and Sister Bowers also lacked the opportunity to visit frequently with the missionaries, so we seldom saw them if we were in outlying areas. President Bowers did not have a car the entire time of his presidency. During the last year of my mission I had the opportunity of working in the mission headquarters in São Paulo and of meeting frequently with my mission president, whom I loved and admired, and I tried to follow his instructions carefully. He left a great deal of the responsibility on his missionary leaders. This lent itself to a looseness of control, which allowed missionaries in some cases to be wayward and in opposition to the policies of the president, which was an unfortunate condition. I would say that the general condition in the mission was not as healthy as it ought to have been and would be now under more careful policies.[13] (President and Sister Bowers later became an integral part of the Washington, D.C., Latter-day Saint community and later served in that temple.)

Immediately upon our arrival, President Bowers took us to a Brazilian restaurant for dinner and then on to the railroad that carried us up the mountain escarpment to São Paulo, about 30 miles into the interior. It was a new experience going up the rain forest ascent and onto the plateau of South Central Brazil. The Church in Brazil at that time was established in the southern part of the country, from Rio de Janeiro and São Paulo in the north to Porto Alegre in the south. It was a distance of approximately 1200 miles, and most of the work was done amongst the German-speaking populace in that area. The

---

13. Bangerter Oral History, p. 18

missionary work among that group of people was reasonably good. The majority of the membership seemed to be women, which didn't help much in establishing a strong priesthood leadership base. Relief Society was a strong organization, however. MIA was sporadic, with few youth involved. It worked well when the young people had an interest in being part of the program. My arrival in Brazil was only four years after the Brazilian Mission had been formally organized, even though missionary work had been done in parts of Brazil since about 1925 under the direction of the South American Mission. [14]

Shortly before I arrived in Brazil, the German Hitler movement had entered Brazil among the German colonists. It became obnoxious, under the impetus of Nazism. The Germans in Brazil were pushing their culture to a point where the Brazilian government came to discriminate against it and finally to ban German activities entirely. This was before the outbreak of World War II. [15]

Brazil at that time was under the political rule of Getúlio Vargas, who had taken over as dictator. His was a stable government. The condition of the people was happy but on a low economic scale. Their standard of living didn't measure up to that of the United States, but in some respects it had a delightful quality that now is missing with the more modern and rapid pace. Cities were operated on a more leisurely basis. They were more beautiful then. The streets were often tree-lined and were not so overrun with people. Transportation within the cities was in good condition, and it enabled you to move about in an easy, inexpensive way. All this has changed in recent years.

The culture of Brazil was in some respects different from that of any other Latin American country, it being the only Portuguese-oriented nation. It still had the Catholic background and the old colonial background in common with the Spanish colonies. Brazil had a period of about 50 years of being an empire, which is unique in the Americas, and it is the biggest exception to the prophecy in the Book

---

14. Years later in the São Paulo mission office, the record kept of all missionaries called to serve in the Brazilian Mission showed that Elder Bangerter was the 72nd missionary called to labor in that mission. (CWB)

15. Bangerter Oral History, p. 17

of Mormon about not having kings on our land. But royalty didn't endure there either.[16]

Traditionally Brazil has been one of the freest areas in the world in which missionary work could be accomplished. We suffered much less persecution in reaching the people than we would have had in the United States. We had practically no official interference, certainly no more than we would have run into in the United States. At this period of time the Brazilian people were oriented toward North America. They were interested in us—they liked to watch our movies and hear what happened in Hollywood. To be a North American was to be sort of an honored guest. We found that we were generally welcome. It's surprising we accomplished so little at that time under such favorable conditions.

Brazil is by nature a Catholic nation, but their constitution allows freedom of religion the same as in the United States; it was different in this respect from Argentina, for example, which had, at that time, an official state religion. But to be a Brazilian usually meant to be a Catholic, as much socially as religiously. To be a Catholic didn't necessarily mean that you were religious, so we didn't run into serious combat with radical Catholic people who wanted to tear us down. In general the Brazilian people didn't know much about religion. There were incursions of Protestant activity—the Baptists, the Methodists, the Presbyterians, and other denominations were developing congregations in Brazil. We found them to be a little more militant than the Catholics.

In São Paulo we found ourselves in a great city of nearly a million people, and when we saw some of the dark people along the side of the road, one of the elders disparagingly asked, "My heck, do we have to preach to those people?" The city itself was beautiful and pleasant as was the climate. At the mission home in the Aclimação (Avenida Tourmalina, #78), President Bowers interviewed us and had Elder Davis and I stay with Elders Muirbrook and Gus Faust on Rua Higienópolis. We became acquainted with the many streetcars (called bondes), cobblestone streets, mule delivery carts, and the

---

16. Bangerter Oral History, p. 16

Latin aspect of the people. The boarding house, or pensão, gave us bananas and milk for breakfast, a good noon meal, and no dinner.

During the day we went to the mission home to begin our study of Portuguese, and in the evenings we sometimes accompanied other elders on visits to member families, group parties, and meetings. All of these member activities were among German people. At our first meeting in the hall near the center of town, knowing that some of the missionaries spoke German and some Portuguese, I asked Elder Davis, "Is he speaking in Portuguese or German?" He answered, "It all sounds the same to me." At that time, all the members (about 200 in the whole country) were German, and half of the elders were assigned to speak that language. We were all assigned to learn Portuguese, the first group in the Church assigned to do so. We learned our first door approach, which consisted of saying, "Mora aqui uma família que fala Alemão?" (Does a family live here who speaks German?)

I stayed in São Paulo for two or three weeks, beginning to study the Portuguese language at the mission home and attending meetings with the missionaries. The great city of São Paulo was a marvel and a mystery, but it was a fantastic experience.

Porto Alegre

After a month of limited activity Elder Shirts and I were assigned to Porto Alegre in the extreme south of the country. The trip was an adventure. We were taken to the railroad station, Sorocabana, and rode through the evening. We watched two men engage in a serious argument and thought they might become dangerous, but happily they stopped their shouting and were friends again. I was to learn that this was showing something of the Brazilian personality. In the middle of the night we were rousted from our berth (it was a sleeping car), and after quickly dressing, we dragged our baggage along the railroad track for a quarter of a mile and boarded a narrow-gauge train for the remainder of the journey. The entire trip lasted 76 hours. We wound through the flat-topped pines of the state of Paraná and the hilly country of Santa Catarina, with good-sized rivers along the way. When noontime came, the train stopped and everyone got off, entering a long wooden sort of a shed where tables were set with white cloths. Without instruction, since we knew very little of the language, we followed the crowd, sat at a table and helped ourselves to a meat dish in some type of gravy and some vegetables and fruit, with Guaraná, the Brazilian soft drink, for refreshment. We eventually entered the vast plains of Rio Grande do Sul, the Gaucho country, seeing the men in the "botas, bombachas and capas" with wide hats and large belts.

After dark on April 25, we arrived in Porto Alegre and were met by the elders of that district. We stayed for a short time in a German home, and then I was assigned to be a companion to Elder George J. Angerbauer. We lived with a family who were part black; they were very solicitous of our needs. The bathroom was out back and the shower in a board lean-to. The weather became quite cold, and I found that I would not touch hot water for nearly three years. Getting out of bed was invigorating!

As we worked, we learned that the people generally were not really looking for a new religion. They were curious perhaps, but beyond that there was no particular interest. But it wasn't difficult to find friends. Our greatest lack was in not having a well-organized, systematic presentation of the gospel. Every missionary was on his own to find his own plan to preach the gospel, and thus he did very little of it in a way that brought forth fruitful accomplishment. My experience was common. I baptized one person into the Church, but I worked with a number who did join the Church later. There were about 10 active members in the Porto Alegre branch. The meetings were mostly in German. Two other elders were serving in Novo Hamburgo about 30 miles away, and we visited that branch occasionally.

Our attitude at that time was evident in the results we obtained. We had in mind, and we often spoke of it openly among ourselves, that the great missionary movement had already taken place in the Church. I don't know how we came to this attitude. I'm sure it wasn't taught us by the General Authorities. But we looked backward and said, "In the days of Wilford Woodruff and Lorenzo Snow, the Church and the gospel went forth with power. Great numbers of people joined the Church. The kingdom of God is on the earth. We know that it is necessary to present the message before all nations, but we don't really expect that many people will respond anymore. The gathering is really over; we're doing the gleaning now. If anyone wants to come, we'll wave the message before them, and they'll respond if they have the right spirit and the blood of Israel."[17]

Elder Angerbauer had been in Brazil three months longer than I. We struggled with the language and spent our time trying to meet people. The morning after I arrived, Elder Angerbauer announced, "We're going tracting." This seemed to be a novelty for the older missionaries. He was very eager and not sympathetic with some of the older missionaries. He said, "We will show those lazy guys how to get the work done." Tracting, studying, visiting the small number of members, and learning something of the language took up our day. Elder Angerbauer didn't know much Portuguese, but he wouldn't admit it when I asked him why he didn't ask people about their feelings more often. He therefore began to enlarge his speaking, and we soon had a good opportunity to visit with the people.

Eventually, I said, "Why don't I try to talk at some of the doors?"

"Yes, you ought to speak at every other house," he responded. However, when it was my turn, he could not wait for me to compose any comments and soon took over, limiting my opportunities.

I then said, "We have two districts. Why don't we divide up? I will try the other district by myself."

"Yes, that's a good idea," he said, and with fear and trembling I went out by myself.

I soon found that it was a wonderful feeling to make some headway conversing in Portuguese, and naturally my ability increased. Our proselytizing methods did not vary much from tracting. This is how we did it. We carried a tract (or pamphlet), and that was the main approach: we wanted to hand them a piece of paper. We would introduce ourselves as missionaries of the Church of Jesus Christ and tell them that we had come to them with a message. Most of the message was supposed to be read. We tried to explain as much as was permitted. My recollection is that at that point our teaching

---

17. Bangerter Oral History, p. 17

broke down. We didn't really know how to launch into a discussion that would teach them the gospel. We could tell them about Joseph Smith, but to teach about the revelations of God and the last days and the existence of prophets and the requirement of the whole earth to listen to these messages was not well handled.

When the Book of Mormon was published in Portuguese in March of 1940, some of us made fairly good use of it. We started a lending program where we would leave the Book of Mormon in the homes of people and then call back frequently and ask them about it. I had quite a large number of copies of the Book of Mormon spread about, but I doubt they were used to any great extent. Then if someone accepted the tract or the Book of Mormon, we would say, "We'll come back in a week or two and give you another one." We would follow up, eventually inviting them to meetings. And occasionally someone would come. [18] Most of the tracts were a series by John A. Widtsoe. The first was About Myself. We'd introduce ourselves as missionaries. We followed with The Plan of Salvation and certain others. We had a few from Charles W. Penrose, Rays of Living Light. We tried to operate by the Spirit, but I think we were teaching off the top of our head. We would wait for the situation and see what happened, and then we would try to react to it, which was generally ineffective. [19]

We could organize groups in homes. We also had slide lectures that showed poor quality pictures of the Grand Canyon or Zion's Park or temples or something of that nature, but they drew a little interest. We were not skilled in turning attention from that to a discussion of the gospel, and it was slow. We did have fair success with young people when we could organize an MIA, so an enterprising missionary could develop that into some kind of a gospel discussion. I confess that my approaches to this process were not always effective. I can think of two or three families with whom we established regular visits where we were able to launch into discussions about the gospel, but those discussions were not well organized. [20]

---

18. Bangerter Oral History, p. 20
19. Ibid., p. 22
20. Bangerter Oral History, p. 21

We did find a few people to visit. One evening it was time to go home but we had another house left on the street we were tracting. The people invited us in, and we had a good conversation. They were the Schindlers, Germans, but he spoke English. Soon he said: "I have a question I have asked every minister I have met and none can answer it. Where did Cain find his wife? I think there were other people on the earth at that time." I had been reading in the Pearl of Great Price, and I opened it to the book of Moses and read from chapter 5, verse 28: "And Cain took one of his brother's daughters to wife." Brother Schindler grabbed the book and said to his wife, "Clara, look at this!" and read the verse to her. We had many good visits, and they were later baptized after I had been transferred.

Getting people to be baptized was always a challenge. Usually we would just invite them to come to church. Being invited to come to church, they would come and eventually either they would ask, "How do you get into this church?" or somebody would say, "You could become a member, if you wanted to." But it was very casual. I recall, for example, we were on an MIA outing, and a young girl who had been quite active in our group became enthusiastic and said to one of the missionaries, "How do you get into this church anyway? I guess you have to know an awful lot." His response was, "Oh, yes, you do have to know an awful lot." I overheard this, and it disturbed me a little, and I thought, "This girl would like to be baptized." So I turned around and said, "Oh, it isn't that hard. You could learn what you need to know in a relatively short time if you'd like to be baptized." She responded, and we undertook to teach her the basics about the Church; within two or three weeks she was baptized. Someone else baptized her. It wasn't me because she had been the friend of some of the other missionaries. But I just recall that incident as an example of the negativism that we carried with us in our missionary work. [21]

As you can see, we knew little about bringing people to baptism, and there was no system for teaching the gospel, so our results were small. We felt that we were not doing too much good, except to ourselves, and we were not efficient. Elder Angerbauer and I were, however, very diligent in our hours spent in missionary work. When the

---

21. Bangerter Oral History, p. 22

record was published in the monthly bulletin, we led all other missionaries. We were diligent in putting in about eight hours of tracting a day. We were then criticized, some saying, "You will make our parents ashamed of us when they see from the bulletin that we don't work as hard as you do." Elder Angerbauer would then say, "Boy, it's time someone showed them how to get off their dime."

I served six months with this driven companion, and he was then transferred to Curitiba. I was assigned to work with Elder Emmanuel Ballstaedt, who was born in Germany and grew up speaking German. I really didn't want to work with him, he being older, but he recommended that he speak in the German-speaking homes and that I try to teach those who spoke Portuguese. I never had a better companion. He was considerate and helpful, and it was a good time. I soon learned to understand much of the German my companion spoke and began to participate in the conversations.

At this time in September 1939, Germany attacked Poland, and the Germans in Brazil became very excited. Even our Church meetings in German were stopped for a time, and this was a disadvantage to the missionary work because missionaries who had been fruitful and energetic were now curtailed in their activity, and they drifted in some cases into an easygoing attitude that made missionary work unfruitful. At that point it was very appropriate and necessary that the work be extended to the Portuguese-speaking people. The destiny of the work in German had been largely accomplished and now had to go among the Portuguese.[22] Our mission president visited us once or twice, but there was little planning and instructing in teaching the gospel.

Curitiba

This assignment with Elder Ballstaedt lasted for a month, and I was then sent to Curitiba. At this point, there were perhaps 40–50 missionaries in the mission with 6–8 in each major city. I traveled with Elder Eldon Palmer by bus, and that was another adventure. We stopped in Joinville, the German-speaking area of Brazil, and I met Elder James Faust, brother to Gus Faust, whom I had known before.

---

22. Bangerter Oral History, p.17

James was new to the mission. In Curitiba, Elder Angerbauer, who was now laboring there, welcomed me, saying: "Elder Bangerter, I'm glad you came here. We will put this town on the map just as we did in Porto Alegre." My companion was Elder Wilmore Turner from Heber City. He spoke fairly good Portuguese, and we were congenial and diligent. We lived over a restaurant called Zacharias, alias "O Gato Preto." We continued our tracting with little progress. After two months Elder Turner was transferred, and Elder James Faust came to be my first junior companion. He became a lifelong companion.

Elder Faust had not been led to heavy work by his former companion and immediately asked, "How do you get so much recognition in your missionary work with the published reports?"

I answered, "We simply go out to work hard every day."

He then said, "I would surely like to have that same recognition for hard work."

I responded, "Well, let's stick together and we will see that your name is on the top of the list." He was most agreeable, and every day we would be crossing the main Praça of the city when Elder Angerbauer and his new companion, Elder Lloyd Hicken, would come bursting out of their pensão to go to their tracting district. The four of us did a great deal of work

The first day with Elder Faust, after I had clapped my hands at the gates of several houses, I said, "Now the next house will be your turn." He was somewhat reluctant to try to converse on his own, but I encouraged him, and while he clapped at the gate, I turned away to leave him on his own. When I turned back around, I saw that he was inside the gate and under the window speaking to a lady, and she was speaking English. Her name was Dedo, and she was of English descent. She later, with her children, accepted the gospel and was baptized. It has been a source of great satisfaction over the years to remember that Elder Faust, who became a member of the Quorum of the Twelve and then a counselor in the First Presidency, was so diligent and was successful with his first contact as a missionary in Curitiba.

Our district leader, Elder Harmon Barton, had rented a rather shabby hall for us to meet in near the main Praça Osorio in Curitiba and ordered materials for benches. We assembled them, painted and cleaned up the hall, and announced regular meetings in Portuguese. The first meeting came, and the two elderly women who rented us the hall were the only ones who attended. However, a man came by and inquired about the activity, and we enticed him to stay for the meeting. Since Elder Barton and his companion only spoke German, Elder Angerbauer and myself, the senior elders speaking Portuguese, did the preaching. It was not too impressive, but two weeks later as my companion and I visited with a tailor, he said: "Yes, I know who you are. I attended your first meeting, and I came away with some of the paint from your new benches on my trousers."

With our diligent work and by regularly inviting people to come to the meetings, our group increased, although we had no baptisms at that time. We held a conference in May with the mission president present and had over 100 people attend. There we first displayed the Book of Mormon. Elder Angerbauer and I became rather long-winded in our speaking since we did most of it, but it was great experience in learning the language. From this beginning in the Portuguese language in the city of Curitiba, a rather strong group of newly baptized members emerged within a year. Previous missionary work had been done in the German language, but nothing of strength remained.

During this period prior to World War II and at the close of the Great Depression, missionary work seemed to lack the vitality and forward movement of earlier days and of what was to come in succeeding years. Our approach was more in the casual sounding of "a voice of warning" with little expectation of results. I think we were not assured that the Latin-speaking people would ever accept the gospel, and we seemed to be more in the mode of "going through the motions." As a result, the missionaries were not all dedicated to earnest missionary work. There was an undercurrent of playfulness and some breaking of the rules, which was a disappointment to those of us who did follow the rules as we tried to become devoted, faithful teachers of the gospel. There was much too much playtime and not enough solid direction.

Rio de Janeiro

In June of 1940 President Bowers called me into São Paulo and appointed me as the district president of the Rio de Janeiro District. I was only 15 months into my mission and accepted this calling as some recognition for faithful service. It was always a little frightening for missionaries to go into a new area, and especially into one as unknown as Rio. But I think the difficulties were imagined. It was merely a matter of finding a place to live and then going out and knocking on doors. And as usual, there were a few people in the city who knew the Church or belonged to it. The first district president was Elder De Vere Gardner. He was sent as the first missionary to work in Brazil's capital city, Rio de Janeiro. It was at that time larger than São Paulo, so it was logical to extend the missionary work there. Missionaries had also been sent into other exclusively Portuguese-speaking areas like Campinas and Ribeirão Preto and Belo Horizonte. [23]

President Bowers informed me that my most difficult problem would be my companion, who was not happy in his mission. I found that he did not want to work much and spent much time alone. I felt ineffective and did not accomplish much among the eight elders we had in Rio. We had no branch organization and only held Sunday meetings in our quarters. We had six other elders in the city, and they were not well directed. Thus my time in the beautiful city of Rio de Janeiro was much clouded and not very productive. I became familiar with the city and we visited several people who were kind to us but made no real progress. I learned that all missionaries were not dedicated.

I was soon aware that I had been promoted away from doing actual missionary work and was now an administrator and a leader. And I took pride in doing that work, which unfortunately was not related to basic missionary work. For that reason I feel now that I lost out on the best part of my mission by being assigned to supervisory work. However, I was much involved in leadership and excited with all the activities that I engaged in. To a degree, I operated that section of the mission under the direction of the mission president.

---

23. Bangerter Oral History, p. 24

We had no meeting place. The other missionaries, Asael Sorensen, Ray Crane, Ted Neerings, Woodrow Christiansen, and Elder Freeman, met each Sunday, but we had few other regular assignments. We were allowed to go to the beach for swimming, which we did fairly often. We attended an athletic club for recreation and played some basketball. There the club team invited me to be a permanent center for them, although I had never played an official game before in my life. I felt that I could not properly give the time to that activity.

Our missionary work consisted of tracting in the Tijuca area most days and in visiting a number of people who had been contacted previously. Brother Daniel Shupe, a member of the Church who had married a Brazilian woman who he later divorced, was employed in the city of Rio where he had lived for a number of years. He and his former wife had been engaged to work on the translation of the Book of Mormon into Portuguese. Her mother, however, lived in the area of Urca. She was a lovely elderly lady, friendly and warm to the church. We visited her often and also had regular contact with Brother Shupe, who joined us on Sundays when we held a meeting of the missionaries. We had no branch center or any place to hold public meetings, and I felt that as district president I was ineffective in establishing this foundation. My companion wanted to visit the center of the city each day, mostly to obtain a newspaper in English. We visited the other elders frequently, but no one seemed to know very much about doing solid missionary work. I tried to keep the mission president informed of our difficult situation. I spent much of my time increasing my knowledge of the Portuguese language.

Living with a companion who was not dedicated to his mission, I learned how a worldly boy would think. One day as he was reading his English newspaper on the street corner, he noticed a man seemingly looking at the paper over his shoulder. In his smart-aleck attitude he slowly turned his shoulder so the man could not see the paper, and then, not satisfied with his impoliteness, he whispered to me in a fairly loud voice, "That guy was reading over my shoulder but I turned so he couldn't see it." The man then said in English, "Never mind, boy, I have already read it."

On another occasion a group of American sailors were strolling the city streets, and two of them rushed up to us and seeing that we were Americans, asked, "Where can we find girls in this city?" My companion said, "Go to the Praça Onze." A Brazilian man overhearing the direction said in English, "Boy, don't send those fellows to Praça Onze. You are sending them to hell!" Sadly this was an evil attitude for one who had been called to represent righteousness.

Rio de Janeiro was one of the most beautiful cities in the world. The scenery was unsurpassed, with magnificent mountains surrounding the large bay and harbor in addition to the outer seashore and beaches on the ocean, and it will always bring a thrill to my remembrance. A little reflection on my six months in the beautiful city of Rio de Janeiro indicates that I did not fulfill my calling very well, and that my mission was not accomplishing very much. How I wish I could live it over again.

São Paulo

Eventually President sent Elder Milton Orme to replace me in the Rio de Janeiro district, and I returned to São Paulo. I was appointed to be the district president over the largest district in the mission, presiding over 16 missionaries and five branches, most still meeting in the German language; I was not given a companion. I served in this capacity for a full year, and only occasionally did I have another elder to work with me. I did briefly work with Elder Grant Fisher, who had newly arrived, and later Elder Willard Call, but mostly I was on my own. I lived with Elders James E. Faust and Austin for a time in the Ipiranga area. Later I moved in with Elder Douglas Davis and Elder Harlow Duffin in the Aclimação district.

As I supervised the work of the missionaries, I tracted with some of them at random and tried to encourage them but spent much time attending meetings in the various branches of Mooca, Santana, Vila Mariana, and Santo Amaro. We conducted regular missionary district meetings, where our emphasis was on the spiritual aspects of our work. We didn't get far into the practical. We encouraged them to effort, but the effort achieved was somewhat of the nature that has been described. Several of those working in São Paulo were most faithful and diligent, and after our mission we became lifelong friends. They included Elders James Faust, Lloyd Hicken, Finn Paulsen, Max Shirts, Lynn Sorensen, LeRoy Drechsel, Asael Sorensen, John Rich, Norton Nixon, and Ray Duckworth, with whom I had attended high school. I felt the responsibility to watch over the branches, which were mostly gatherings of women. We would schedule missionaries to go to the sacrament meetings and be the speakers. They were the only speakers we had. Many of the meetings were Relief Society meetings, and I often accompanied Sister Bowers to these meetings. They were always held in the German language. My efforts were mainly in running administrative errands. I progressed in both the Portuguese and the German languages.

One day while I was at the mission home, a phone call came in from a young lady whom I had previously met in Rio. She had read our tract and sent me a note saying that she believed in what was written and asked me to meet her alone at the post office. She was a beautiful girl. She said that she was Israelite and that she would like to know more about the Church. We had visited her house in Rio a few times but without solid results. When she called the mission home, the president asked me to take the call; she said she was in São Paulo and wanted me to visit her. I took Elder James Faust with me, and we found her staying with a cousin. I gave a discussion about our feelings concerning the Israelites or Jews and invited her to the one meeting we were holding in the center of the city of São Paulo in Portuguese. When she came, the mission president and all the elders were astonished with her loveliness. I was thereafter accused of having a special girlfriend, although I never pursued the acquaintance. However, when I left Brazil in October 1941, she learned of my leaving and came down to the ship with the missionaries to bid me farewell. She eventually joined the Church, as did her sister, who married an American and lived in Utah. My encounter with her reminded me of something Sister Bowers used to say: "The only time a woman would not have an interest in an unattached man is when she is in the grave."

Eventually we rented space for regular meetings in Portuguese and began to gather a number of younger people to join with us. A few were baptized. I continued to visit many of the German members, who were mostly widows.

There was meager connection with home and the Church in Salt Lake City. Mail came by ship every three weeks. We had no presents or close contacts with home but generally felt comfortable with our circumstances. As war had been going on in Europe since September 1939 (while I was serving in Porto Alegre), I became aware of the intense feelings some of the German people in Brazil had concerning Adolf Hitler. Some of them fully supported him and were rabid in their feelings about "those dirty Polish people" whom Germany had invaded. By 1941 the United States was actively watching the German activity in South America, and the U.S. government began to organize surveillance of German companies and activities. As our missionaries were released to return home, a number of them were recruited by the U.S. embassy to enter into government service in Brazil. I too was approached for the same purpose and had agreed to remain there, but before my release, President Bowers spoke to me, saying: "While you would be as welcome as any other of the missionaries to enter government service, the Spirit tells me that you should not do so. You are a son of the soil, and your spirit should be in another direction." I therefore decided to return home at the conclusion of my mission. My parents were very thankful. They had counseled with President J. Reuben Clark, who had also advised me not to undertake government service.

As I consider what I later learned about missionary work, I feel that my mission as far as missionary work was largely wasted, except for the knowledge, growth, and development that came to me. I made close and warm associations with some of my companions, and they became stalwart and permanent friends in succeeding years. In reflecting on the great influence my mission to Brazil had on my life, I feel that living in that country left great impressions and made me a part of the country. Today it is a vastly different place than when I served. I remember the uncrowded loveliness of the cities and the well-kept streets and parks. My memories of the bondes that were so delightful to give easy access, the cobblestone streets with mule carts rattling on their way, the strong smell of roasting coffee, and especially the sweetness and the openness of the people always bring forth "saudades." Those feelings of nostalgia and yearning for a forgotten time are much the same as I feel for the disappearance of the way of life in Utah during the 1920s and 1930s.

As a missionary I often sought for spiritual confirmations of the faith that directed my life. My companions and I served with faithfulness and forged an association that helped us all give strength to our lives, families, progressive education, and especially our service in the gospel in the years that followed. With questions in our thoughts about what we accomplished as missionaries, the blessing of that great experience gave us personal power to move on in leadership and faithfulness. I never felt any wavering in my faith and testimony and forged a determination and purpose to be faithful in whatever circumstances, wherever the Lord might guide me.

Release and Return Home

I was released from my mission about October 15, 1941, having served nearly 33 months. I sailed for New York without companions on the Moore McCormack Line S.S. Brazil and had a pleasant voyage of two weeks. There was danger of German submarines, though the American Steamship Line was supposed to be safe. The two weeks on a steamship from Santos to New York was a time of appreciation and relaxation. A group of chorus girls and the crew of a torpedoed ship were also on board.

We experienced a thrilling homecoming in New York as we saw the Statue of Liberty and Manhattan. I was met unexpectedly by Woodrow Christiansen, who had preceded me by a few weeks. He had a sister in Philadelphia and asked me to return there with him for a visit. In New York we experienced the subways and some of the sights, including Yankee Stadium. In Philadelphia we spent several days visiting some of the historic sites of the founding of our country. A woman we had met in the LDS meeting in Manhattan had asked me to drive a new automobile to Utah from Detroit for her, so we left from Philadelphia for Detroit by bus. We found the factory in Detroit and received the new Plymouth car, leaving immediately for the west. We stopped in South Bend, Indiana, and Hastings,

Nebraska, and went on through Fort Collins, Colorado. We stayed overnight in Laramie, Wyoming and the following day arrived after dark in Salt Lake City on October 31, 1941. My family was expecting me but did not know the exact day, and it was a wonderful reunion. Elder Christiansen returned to his home in Fairview, Utah the next day. It was a great joy to be with my family again. I reported my mission in sacrament meeting shortly after my return.

It was a great joy to be with my family again. My brother Sam had recently gone to serve in the Spanish American Mission. Sarah had been married to Prescott Hardy, and others of the family were entering into further education. My brother David had been born while I was away. He had Down syndrome and was very lovable and had a deeply uniting effect on our family.

Called to the Bishopric

Several very important events took place almost immediately upon my return. Our stake presidency had just been reorganized, and our bishop, John D. Hill, was now the stake president. His counselor in the bishopric, Merrill Petersen, was called to be our bishop, and it was a great honor for me to be called as second counselor with Wendel Newman as the first counselor. I was set apart and ordained a high priest by Elder Charles A. Callis of the Twelve. I was called to be a member of the fifth bishopric that had presided over that area since its founding, so I was a member of the last bishopric that encompassed the entire area of Granger. After that bishopric, the ward was divided (see chapter 2, "Youth").[24] It was quite unusual for a single person to be put in the bishopric. I undertook the assignments with reasonable diligence; I was earnest about it, but I feel now that I was not mature. Again, the results were a benefit to me, if not to the members of the ward. I gained experience.[25]

Associations and World Events

It is interesting to realize now that I was almost totally unaware of the great, earthshaking changes that had taken place up to that

---

24. Bangerter Oral History, p. 11
25. Ibid., p. 27

time. I had limited understanding of world conditions. I knew the war was on; in fact I had been living with a German family in Brazil in 1939 when the German army invaded Poland. After I returned from my mission, I immediately found that I needed to register for the selective service. I had understood that would be necessary anyway, but I didn't have any real concept of the implications. [26]

Within two weeks of my call to the bishopric, the events of Pearl Harbor exploded on the world like a bombshell. On Sunday, December 7, 1941, my friend Margaret Ottley and I were visiting the father of one of my missionary companions who lived out in Magna, Utah. He was a superintendent of one of the mills at Kennecott Copper. He came in and said he'd been around inspecting security at the mill because of the great attack that had happened that morning at Pearl Harbor.

I still didn't recognize the nature of the disaster it was. It was very difficult for me to contemplate and understand because I wasn't aware of the threats that had been building between the nations at that time. I was told that the understanding of the Church at that time was that those who were serving in the bishopric were considered fully ordained ministers and were not subject to army service.

Having just returned from my mission, I eagerly accepted that attitude because my feelings were very spiritual and devoted to Church service anyway. But I did register for the draft and then went to take my physical examination. I got a temporary job at Winder Dairy, hoping to earn money to go back to school. The draft board sent me notice disregarding that understanding, and the First Presidency of the Church undertook to have me cleared and exempted from the draft. They lost the contest, and after a period of three or four months I was drafted into the U.S. Army.

An interesting thing occurred the evening before I went into the Army. I played a game of basketball, and I suffered an injury on my

---

26. Many of these notes are a transcript of a video interview conducted by Don Rogers of Alpine, Utah. Since the transcript is unofficial and typed by the BYU Department of Church History, no page numbers were assigned to the document. Future references to this material will be termed "Rogers Transcript." We thank Don for his efforts in this section of the history.

right knee. While I was a missionary in Brazil I injured it playing basketball, and that night, I sprained the knee again, so badly that the next morning when I went for my examination, it was about as big as a basketball itself. The examining board said, "Well, we will defer this man for six months." So I was deferred for a short period as far as military service was concerned.

During this time I worked for a time as a clerk typist at Hill Air Base and took on some temporary employment with my father. I also pursued various activities over the next few months. Margaret Ottley had been my high school friend and had taken a new interest in me and had written while I was still on my mission. Upon returning home from my mission, I resumed contact with her since we had been corresponding, and we renewed our dating. Because she had received a mission call, we didn't make any special plans or pursue the ultimate direction of where a courtship would ordinarily take you. Margaret went on her mission, and I found employment in two or three different sectors. Wages were low, but there was evidence that the Depression was easing. [27]

When Margaret completed her mission, I was stationed in Douglas, Arizona. She came through town on her way home from her mission in the eastern states. There we determined that we didn't have a basis for a future together. Eventually, my draft notice came, and I was given orders to report. Two days before that I was advised by the First Presidency that I'd better go, since they hadn't been able to resolve the problem. Therefore I knew that I was going to go in the service only two days beforehand.

---

27. This was near the end of the Great Depression (1929–1939), and annual salaries averaged just over $1700. The price for gas was 10¢ per gallon, a loaf of bread was 8¢, and a gallon of milk was 49¢.

William Henry and Isabelle Bawden Bangerter,
wedding picture.

William Henry Bangerter,
patriarch.

Isabelle Bawden Bangerter,
portrait taken for Utah Mother
of the Year.

Birthplace of William Grant Bangerter, 3600 West 3800 South, Granger (now West Valley City).

William Henry Bangerter as a missionary.

William Grant, Sarah, and Samuel Bangerter.

Maeser Building at Brigham Young University in Provo.

Threshing Machine in 1937.

Family picture 1938 prior to Wm. Grant's mission — (front, left to right) Naomi, Marian, Norman, Glenneth; (middle, left to right) Elsbeth, Blauer, Pauline, Samuel; (back, left to right) Sarah, Wm. Grant, William Henry, Isabelle

Left to right: Blauer, Norman, William Grant, and Samuel Bangerter in their backyard; about 1937.

William Grant as a farmer, with Norman on the left and Clint Bangerter, a cousin, on the right.

Sarah, Samuel, William Grant, and William Henry Bangerter.

William H. Bangerter family portrait, late 1940s — (front, left to right) Pauline, Wm. Henry, David, Isabelle, Marian; (back, left to right) Norman, Blauer, Samuel, Wm. Grant, Elsbeth, Naomi, Sarah, Glenneth

William Grant with his horse Bally in Granger, 1941.

Old Granger First Ward Building in the 1950s; located on 3500 South 3200 West.

Monroe Elementary School in the 1920s; 3500 South and 4200 West, Granger.

Arrival in Rio de Janeiro, Brazil, 1939; left to right: Elders Barton, Pia, Shirts, Merrill, Bangerter, Davis, Christensen.

Rio de Janeiro, Brazil, 1939.

São Paulo Mission Home in the Aclimação District.

William Grant on transfer day in Brazil.

William Grant Bangerter as a missionary in Brazil, February 1939– October 1941.

Curitiba, Brazil, 1939–1940.

São Paulo skyline in 1941.

Downtown São Paulo—Avenida São João, 1941.

Brazilian Mission group picture, 1941 — (front row) Unknown, William Grant Bangerter, Sister Bowers, President Bowers, Lynn A. Sorenson, James E. Faust

President and Sister John A. Bowers, Brazilian Mission, 1941.

William Grant Bangerter as a missionary in Brazil, February 1939– October 1941.

Elder George Angerbauer, first companion of William Grant Bangerter, 1939.

Elder Emmanuel Ballstaedt, second companion of William Grant Bangerter, 1939.

Elder Lynn A. Sorenson, missionary in Brazil, 1940–42.

Two pictures of William Grant Bangerter studying in his room.

Elder James E. Faust, junior companion to William Grant Bangerter in Curitiba, Brazil, 1939–1940.

James E. Faust and William Grant Bangerter in São Paulo, 1941; both were district presidents in different areas.

Grant picking up fleas to send to a former companion.

Grant shivering in the cold of Porto Alegre.

William Grant Bangerter and James E. Faust
in Curitiba, Brazil 1939–1940.

PERIOD II
The War Years

Chapter 5

You're In The Army Now

"Now, I can't yet tell you when the moment [came] in my life when I [started] to live happily ever after. I wanted always to go on a mission. I remember that I couldn't see past a mission. My parents had trained me to think in those terms, and so my life was projected to the time when I'd be 23 years old, and I would be released from my mission. I hadn't thought much beyond that at all. But suddenly the day came. 'What do you do now?' I didn't have to answer that question. The war started at that point. Someone else decided it. And I thought, 'Boy, if I could just get rid of that problem of facing the army, I could really be happy. If I just didn't have to live through that, I could go out and start to project myself into the future.' I was forced to go through four years of that experience—the most horrible that I could imagine in my life. Fortunately, I didn't become involved in war experiences, but before those four years were over I realized that I'd been doing some of the most intensive living that had ever come into my experience. Some of those things are treasured as the greatest adventures that I could imagine for myself.

"As I grew up I used to look up at those little old bi-planes that would occasionally fly across the sky. I never dreamed that I would be able to do anything like that. I could have imagined it, but I knew that wasn't for me. Suddenly I found myself in the midst of the experience of flying, doing all those thrilling things that people who fly airplanes are supposed to do. And out of it, I found other experiences. I found that as I became an aircraft instructor, I was in touch with the lives and the understandings of people.

I was teaching school two miles above the earth, and I had opportunity to extend my influence to exert leadership, to let people know that I was a member of the Church, to have them respond favorably to the attributes that they saw in the life of a Latter-day Saint. All of this took place there, and it took place in my mission, and before I finished those experiences I found myself involved romantically with a young lady. Again a whole new vista of life presented itself. Before I left the Army, we had established our home and family. I was already in the midst of life. I wasn't waiting till I finished the preliminaries to start to live. My college experience really began after that. I think I would have preferred to stay in the Army because I could see there a security that would protect me. But my wife said, 'No, you're not smart enough yet, and we're going to get you out of the service and send you to school.' And so, I re-began my college experience after I had lived a great deal of life. I managed to graduate from [the University of Utah] the day I was 30 years old. I would hate to think that the first 30 years didn't count. To me they were part of the great and fundamental experience of my entire life here on the earth—very rich and treasured. I had three children by that time." [1]

Enlistment in the Armed Forces

I dreaded the thought of service in the Army, and the reality of our nations involvement in World War II came to me slowly. I registered as required in the Selective Service, or the draft, and slowly grasped the implications of this worldwide explosion of war. I was inducted into the U.S. Army on April 4, 1942. Back then, when you were called up and enlisted they did not tell you when you would get out. They just said, "For the duration plus six months." [2]

The day before I went into the Army, I took a three-horse team and drove three or four miles up on the dry farm, where we had a little piece of property (where Kearns, Utah, now is), and I drove those three horses all day pulling a harrow with me walking behind them as fast as I could make them walk. I was wearing some pretty heavy shoes. I chased those horses all that day on a real fast walk. On the way home I thought, "I wonder if they can ever make me work that hard in the Army?" And they never did. That says something about

---

1. Collected Works, pp. 187–188
2. Collected Works, p. 199

my background and capability.

I obediently joined with another group of young men, including Lorin Simper and Joe Gunn, both returned missionaries, and went to the registry office, and then we were transferred to Fort Douglas in Salt Lake City, where, for about three days, we were processed into the Army. My serial number was 748320. None of us ever forgot our number! It developed that I was assigned to the Army Air Forces. There was no separate air force at the time, so I was always in the Army. But I felt later that I was very fortunate to have been assigned to the air forces rather than to some other branch of the service. This branch appealed to me much more than perhaps the infantry or the pioneers or some other branch.

We were placed in barracks, and after a day or two we were taken over to the clothing warehouse and were given a sack. We were told to take off all our clothes, down to the skin, and they would then outfit us with new military clothes from that point on. I was, of course, wearing my temple garments. I didn't want to be without them, but I took them off, and I put all my clothes in the sack. When I came out of the warehouse, I was dressed in a standard private's uniform; the officer who was in charge looked us over and said, "That doesn't fit too bad." But I immediately went back to the barracks into the bathroom area, took off my clothes, took off the army underwear, put on my garments, and continued to wear them, and that's the last anybody ever said about whether I should wear them or not; I just did that on my own.

We had an opportunity during those few days to have visits from our families who were nearby. I think Mother and Dad must have had a lot of anxiety about their first son going into the military, but they had been used to my absence, and our separation wasn't very traumatic as far as I remember. My bishop came and was very supportive. He said that he expected they'd be getting me out again pretty soon. All this relieved a little of the tension.

Basic Training—Tucson, Arizona, at Davis-Monthan Air Base

It's interesting to me that almost every movement during this period of my life (which now is more than 50 years ago) is as vivid to me as if I were living it again today. We spent a few days registering and then receiving Army uniforms at Fort Douglas in Salt Lake City. Following a short goodbye to my family, we were put on a bus and taken down to the Union Pacific Railroad station, where we were put on a train. We were told in strong army language that we must not reveal our destination or our movements because of war secrecy. We couldn't have revealed very much anyway because we didn't know where we were going, but this turned out to be an interesting journey. We boarded a sleeping car, since we were not a large group. Our railroad trip took us on the Union Pacific down to Colton, California, and then we changed trains and started going east on the Southern Pacific. Again, we were all guessing where we were going, and no one knew. Someone got us started singing "San Antonio Rose" and that made us suppose that maybe we were going to San Antonio, but after about a day's travel, the officer in charge divulged that we were going to Tucson, Arizona, which was a pleasant thought and a calming bit of information since we would not be too far away from our Intermountain West. We stopped at the railway station in Tucson, where we unloaded from the train. They put us on Army trucks and headed us for the Davis-Monthan Army Air Force Base.

Tucson was the second largest city in Arizona, but it was still a very small city—a small town, really. Its major feature was the University of Arizona. During my time there I could walk across that city both ways in not more than half an hour. You can't do that today. As we traveled to the base, it seemed like we went way out in the country, out through the cactus and the desert. Today, the air base is right in the heart of the city of Tucson.

We went through the gate, and the trucks pulled up in front of some two-story barracks. On the way we had seen little tent cities, and we thought, "Well, maybe we're going to have to live in tents." But as we pulled up in front of those barracks, we thought, "Well, this isn't going to be so bad." But then they moved the trucks over and parked in front of a set of tarpaper, one-story barracks, and we thought, "Well, I guess if we don't go first class, this isn't as bad as the tents." They then turned the trucks around and moved us over by the tent cities, and we said, "Well, surely, we've lost our hopes. We're going to be in tents." But they didn't even let us live in those tents. Instead, they parked us in a section of the cactus desert next to the tents, and we had to put up our own tents. So we laid out our own little tent city there.

The nights were a little cool, and they didn't issue us a whole lot of bedding, but we found a friend in the supply tent. He was a little fellow by the name of Ben Jones. As soon as he saw some of us from Utah, he came rushing up and said, "Hey, I'm from Salt Lake City. Where are you fellas from?" And we told him. He said, "Well, you're returned missionaries, are you? I've been a missionary to Hawaii." So he started to take care of us, and whenever a new comforter would come in the supply tent he'd give it to one of us. We soon found a comradeship with the boys we were with. There were a number of Latter-day Saint boys, a few of whom were from Utah who obviously weren't very stalwart in the Church. My closest companions continued to be Joseph Gunn and Lorin Simper, with whom I had grown up. The three of us were able to hold together. We soon were able to attend Sunday services on the base, though there were not any LDS services at that time.

Our practice in going to the washroom was to leave the tents with a towel draped over our shoulders with our pants and shoes on and go down to a separate little wooden building that had showers and toilets and so on to take our shower. On one of those occasions, I was going down with a towel draped over my shoulder, and one of the fellows in the group said, "Well, there comes another one of those Mormon boys." I grinned at him and said, "How can you tell?" He answered, "Well, I can tell by those marks on your tits." That's not the roughest thing that was ever said to me. But as it turned out, he also was a Latter-day Saint. Later on when we were able to hold LDS services, I remember a day when he broke down in emotion and expressed his feelings about his life and his belonging to the Church.

Our life immediately began to be centered on close-order drill and learning how to march. You wonder why that's so important in the Army, but with the movement of large groups of people, you soon find out that it makes a lot of difference in getting people from one place to another. So we'd be out on the desert forming in columns and squads and groups with a drill sergeant. He really wasn't a sergeant—he was a private like the rest of us, but he was given the authority to boss us around, which he did. We saw the difference in men who had authority there. The first day after we arrived, there was one fellow who just swaggered up and started to make some bright comments. Then he started to bark out commands, and we could tell he was just enjoying the privilege of lording it over somebody. It turned out he was nobody, but he'd been in the Army two weeks and it was just fun for him to take charge. We took about a month in this basic training. We didn't get into the handling of firearms or anything special but mostly spent our time marching. We did a march or two out in the desert that involved staying overnight and a few other marches that were not very long. Anyway, we finished this training. We'd march three times a day nearly a half a mile over to the mess hall. I think we each had about two turns at KP (kitchen police) duty in that time, so we were well fed, and we didn't have to work our heads off too much.

I still had not fully realized that I was going to war. A little later I began to catch up with it to a certain degree, but I was somewhat still in the dark. I knew we were in a war now and people were going to fight, but, of course, I was learning fast.

Interim Assignment

The day after we finished our basic training, they assigned us to permanent units, and I was assigned to a chemical warfare group dealing with contamination of chemicals at air bases and such. The day following they sent us to the dispensary, where we had a physical examination and were told that within a week, we would be shipping overseas. Joe Gunn and I determined that now that we were in the Air Forces, there was a possibility to take an examination to become aviation cadets. He said, "I want to do that." And I said, "Well, so do I." So he and I went over and applied at the office that handled the applications. They wouldn't take Joe because he was married, but I signed up to take the examination, which was to take place in two or three weeks.

When I signed up, I remember the man in charge, again a private, said to me, "Well, you can take it if you want, but it sure is hard" (trying to discourage me). I learned later that he'd flunked it. I think it was a multiple-choice exam. I turned in my card with all the answers on it and stood outside the door and waited while they checked it with the key. I heard this fellow inside say, "Tell Bangerter he passed." I thought I never had so much weight lifted off my shoulders in a long time. That was a day of great rejoicing to think that not only was I not going immediately overseas, but also that I knew this would help me for my further training. The gloom of the past took on a radiance of great promise. I knew I'd be into something that should turn out to be very worthwhile and enjoyable. So I went from there over to the dispensary where they gave me a rather thorough physical examination. It's enough to say that I qualified physically and they gave me the appointment. Joe Gunn went to Alamogordo, New Mexico, and got involved in some technical work there, and Lorin Simper got into the chemical warfare group and went to England within two weeks. There he spent the war, and that's where I would have been I suppose had I not taken the cadet exam.

In the meantime, I had many other little experiences. I started out serving in the Army receiving pay of $21 a month. After two months, they raised it to $50 a month for privates. Then, as an aviation cadet I would receive $75 a month. But I couldn't enter into my training immediately because there was a backlog of those who were appointed. It turned out that I spent four months on the base in Tucson waiting for the appointment. I had some limited duty at the Chemical Warfare Warehouse, and I handled messages for the unit and then took advantage of special opportunities that came my way.

A headquarters group at one of the warehouses had quite a lot of property to be inventoried, and our chemical warfare group was assigned this temporary duty. When our group broke up, the only man left besides myself was a fellow by the name of Hirschberg, who was headed for Officer Candidate School. He and I were both held on orders to remain in the country. There was a third man who stayed as well—a fellow from Arkansas named Atkins who didn't go because the Chemical Warfare outfit had said, "We don't want anybody with that low level of intelligence in our group." So he stayed. He was a pleasant fellow but really didn't have a very great background.

I was walking across the base with him one day, and suddenly he met a friend, a fellow he had known back home. They immediately rushed up to each other and started slapping each other on the back. The greeting he used was, "Well, I'll be a sad son of a B—." And his friend responded and said, "Well, I'll be a sad son of a B—." They spent about three minutes there and they never uttered any different words. They repeated that greeting over and over endlessly just grinning at each other and gripping each other's hand.

The corporal in charge of the Chemical Warfare Office (Hirschberg) said one day, "Why don't you come over and work with me in the property office in the Chemical Warfare warehouse. I'll act as your senior authority, and you can do little jobs like running over to the mailroom twice a day and maybe type a letter or two once in a while. We'll just tell the people in charge that you're still assigned there and you're on duty. Then they won't pick you up to serve on KP or some other duty." So very happily, I joined with him. He also told me, "Incidentally, I know how to get you weekend passes. I'll just sign it out as your officer in charge." He wasn't an officer, but he was a department head, so we had a smooth arrangement. That's about how I passed the four months of that summer in Tucson.

There were many good experiences, but in the midst of it, my brother Sam was about 75 miles away serving as a missionary in Nogales, Arizona. I went down to visit with him a couple of weekends, and I would hitchhike both ways. We had other friends in other nearby locations as well. I got a two-week furlough to come home and so just passed the time away. Tucson had two wards of the Church with a large number of LDS men, some married and in the service, and quite a large number of girls too. One girl, Alberta Payne, had come from El Paso to visit her cousin; we didn't know at the time that she would marry my future brother-in-law, Bud Schwantes. Every Tuesday night we would go to Mutual, and every Thursday night, we'd have a party—we'd all get together at somebody's home or go somewhere out on the desert. We would have a little refreshment and sing songs. We had a delightful time. It was a rich and enjoyable experience. It wasn't tough army life at all.

The War Progresses and Additional Training on My Own

There were two periods about then that bottled us in. The first occurred in early May 1942 with the Battle of the Coral Sea. The second occurred near the beginning of June 1942 with the Battle of Midway. Both were declared emergencies, and we were restricted to the base for a while because there was quite a threat as to what the Japanese might do.

I found a number of opportunities there on the base. One of our LDS men, who was a technical sergeant, said, "Well since you're going into cadet training, you'll need to learn Morse code. Why don't you come over? I'm in charge of the Code shack here on the base. Come on over and spend some time and I'll teach you how to take and send Morse code." So I went over and learned Morse code. I got fairly proficient at it after a while, at least enough to serve all the purposes I later had in my military service. I also had time to go to the library. I assumed that I might have to know a little more of the courses that I had taken or knew I needed to take at college (I had three quarters at BYU before my mission), so I studied up on various aspects of algebra and mathematics and tried to learn a little bit more about the affairs of the world, which was enjoyable.

One day I wandered down to the flight line, where the pilots trained. There they had a hangar that was filled with Link Trainers, flight simulators in which the pilots could sit and be trained in flying on instruments. The trainers were operated by enlisted men who had only been trained to run those things. As I visited with one of the operators, he said, "Well, you're going to be an aviation cadet. Why don't you come down and I'll teach you how to fly the Link." So I'd go down two or three times a week. He'd put me in the Link Trainer, and in a week or two, he said, "Well, you're doing the same problems that pilots do; you're flying this thing on instruments just the way the pilots do." Later when I was finally in flight training, our instrument phase came, and we went down and flew the Link Trainers. As the operator got me in the Link, he gave me a training pattern to fly. After a few moments, I heard him say to the other operator, "Come over here and look at this guy fly—he is flying a perfect B pattern" (the B pattern involved timed turns, climbs, descents, and changes in airspeeds; on the paper when it traced my route, it followed the design perfectly). The other operator looked at him for a minute and then said, "Oh, that's Bangerter. He's been here before."

In the meantime, throughout the summer, they brought all the candidates for aviation cadet training together and started to give us some special orientation. They ran out of subjects to teach us after about two days. They showed us what a rifle was like, for example, and then they'd take us over to the base swimming pool, and we'd swim for the afternoon. That only lasted for about a week and then they dropped it.

One day, the master sergeant in charge of my administration ran into me on the base and he said, "Say, where have you been? I've been looking all over for you." I had slacked off going over to the Chemical Warfare Department because of other activities. He then said, "I need to line you up so you can take your turn at regular duty, KP, and so on." I immediately said, "Oh, I'm already assigned to duty. I'm over at the Chemical Warfare Office." "Oh," he said, "OK." He never looked for me again. In a way I guess I passed the summer lazily being what they commonly called a "gold brick." It was not strenuous or hectic at all.

Basic Ground School Training—Santa Ana, California

In September of 1942 my official appointment as an aviation cadet came through, and I was ordered to Santa Ana, California. One of the returned missionaries with whom I became attached was Marion Evertsen, who was also slated for aviation cadet training, so we traveled together on the train. En route we saw the sites of three airplane crashes, all training planes, and we became serious in considering the hazards of our future experience.

Santa Ana was the processing point for aviation cadets, and we were given extensive physical examinations, mental and motor skills tests, and intelligence and aptitude tests. After that we were finally assigned positions. Some were assigned as navigators, some as bombardiers, and others as pilots. Anxiety ran high in the hope that we would be assigned as pilots, which, happily, became my designation. All would receive some basic aviation training prior to their specialty school. A number of men were eliminated at this point due to deficiencies in any number of areas.

There followed nearly two months of rigorous ground school rapidly covering such courses as navigation, aircraft identification, map reading and geography, and instruction on world politics and the progress of the war. We received instruction in naval operations and military principles since we were intended to become officers. We also had rigorous physical training. One of the stories that went around was about a group that was required to run around the race track area. The instructor was pursuing them with shouts of chastisement and encouragement in the Army fashion. A couple of fellows fell down exhausted, and he came up to them and said, "Well, don't just lie there, do some pushups." Well, that was all somewhat humorous.

We had good food, adequate quarters, and the standard military uniforms. Following these two months of our ground school training, we were then assigned to various primary flight training posts.

During this two-month period my parents and sister Sarah came to see me, and we had a choice visit. They did not know that my sister Glenneth was very ill at home, and by the time they returned she had nearly died. Fortunately, with great faith and many prayers, she was able to recover.

Our opportunities for church attendance were limited, but from time to time we were able to find a place to go. Marion Evertsen took me home to his mother's place in Culver City on one occasion. I was diligent in reading from the scriptures and in having my daily prayers, which always included my need for the over-watching influence of my Heavenly Father. Among my associates it was known that I had served as a missionary, and without exception my companions showed great respect for that part of my life, my habits, and my faith. Naturally there was considerable smoking and sometimes some drinking, but generally the men with whom I associated were of a sound character and had not drifted into loose habits. They were congenial and optimistic, and it was a happy association.

It was obvious to me that while I had not considered Army experience in my life, it was becoming a new and real possibility because of the way opportunities had developed. There were many moments when failure might have occurred, but I passed over them. We soon became obsessed with two major worries: one was that we would fail and be eliminated from flying, the other worry was that we were involved in a hazardous activity and might lose our lives. I had already seen and heard of numerous training accidents.

Primary Flight Training—Oxnard, California

Early in December 1942, I was sent with a group of cadets to Oxnard, California, for Primary Flight Training. We were located in a pleasant motel-type accommodation on the border of the flying field and began half a day of flight training and half a day of ground school each day. In our military organization I was named guidon (bearer or protector of the unit flag). Then, as the squadron diminished by elimination, I was named squadron sergeant. Still later the lieutenant was eliminated and I was advanced to squadron lieutenant. We were all under threat of elimination, but I survived.

I had many interesting experiences in ground school in which we were required to pay for some equipment that had been lost or damaged. On one occasion, our unit took up a collection and said, "Who will hold the money?" One of the fellows said, "We'll give it to Bangerter. He's the only one around here we can trust." He said it playfully, no doubt referring a little to my background. A little fellow from Tennessee had gone through the preliminary phases with me, and he lived with me in a tent in Santa Ana. Every once in a while he would turn over, look at me, and say, "I can't believe it." "What is it? What's the matter with you?" I asked. He said, "Well back home, whenever we saw a minister, he was so important and respected that we didn't even talk to him, and here I am sleeping next to one. I just can't believe it." I had a number of little pleasant comments and experiences like that, which led me to feel that I didn't need to hide my identity, but I didn't need to flaunt it and become sanctimonious or obnoxious about it. It was easy to have a good relationship up and down with all the fellows I associated with.

Our first flying experiences were beyond imagination. I had only been in an airplane once before in my life. It was quite an experience to see the ground fading away and to look out with nothing under you and wonder what's holding you up. That feeling of awe never left me—even after years of flying experience, I could still be out there flying and be amazed that there was nothing out there holding us up. Of course we learned something about aerodynamics and the physics of flight that helped us understand it. Charles Lindbergh described it well when he said: "The life of an aviator seemed to me ideal. It commanded adventure. . . . Pilots had the freedom of wind in the expanse of day. I could spiral the desolation of a mountain peak, explore caverns of a cloud, or land on a city flying field. . . .There were times in an airplane when it seemed I had partially escaped mortality, to look down on earth like a god." [3]

I was assigned with four other cadets to an instructor named R. L. Van Houten. Mr. Van Houten knew of my Church experience. He was married to a member of the Church. He treated me very well. He began to take us up one at a time and train us in how to manage the airplane. Things progressed pretty well with me; he seemed to be impressed enough with my ability that after about four hours of flight training he decided to send me out to get checked off for my solo flight (the normal period would have been six hours before soloing). He sent me out with the squadron commander, a Mr. Douglas Sprague, an older man of about 40. I did a poor job on my landings with him, and he decided that I wasn't quite up to standard, but if I had passed that test, I would have been the first of all the cadets to solo. After a little more training, my instructor got out and said, "Well, you go do it," which I did. It was a great thrill. Incidentally, Mr. Van Houten and Mr. Sprague were not Army officers—they were civilian pilots.

The airplanes we were flying were two-seater open-cockpit types, the PT-17, called the Stearman. Flying this plane was a delight. I soon began to grasp the ideas of flying. We had an awareness of the hazard of flying, but the experience was filled with excitement.

On one occasion while I was flying, the wind changed to a cross wind and the situation was bad. I had trouble making a safe landing. I

_____

3. *Lindbergh: Triumph and Tragedy,* Richard Bak, Taylor Trade Publishing, Dallas, Texas, 2006, cover leaf

was frightened and flew around to organize my thoughts and prayed. We were landing on a runway that had a crown in the middle like a crowned highway; as I came down and put the plane down, the wind started to pick me up, but I didn't know all the tricks to keep it down. I was about to be carried off and ground looped (a horizontal spin on the ground). I gave it the gun and went out. I came around the second time, and the same thing happened. Fortunately, it was a safe plane, or I might have had trouble because in one of my go-rounds, I had really staggered the plane off, meaning I had slowed the plane so much that didn't have enough lift to fly smoothly. I was frightened and I thought, "Here I am in the air, and I don't know how to put this thing down. What will I do?" Well, I prayed quite a bit. Then I remembered something Mr. Sprague had taught me: "Come in with a little power." So I came down with power on the next approach, but I carried it too far down the runway. I didn't use good judgment, and I landed way down the field, right at the last part of the runway. I was really a thankful boy that day. I was a very inexperienced pilot.

We came to really enjoy that phase of our training; however, it was always a nervous experience because there was a lot of pressure—pressure in ground school and pressure and fear that you might fail. If every boy there were asked, "Would you rather be eliminated, or would you rather stay in and lose your life?" they'd all say "Leave me in." Of course, early on some cadets got air sick and found that it just wasn't feasible for them to fly.

I recall one of the boys was lined up for these elimination or washout check rides, and he, being rather rowdy and a carouser, came up to me when he saw his name on the board and said, "Hey Bill, pray for me, will ya? I sure need it." And others asked the same occasionally. I was called by several names in the Army. My first name was William, but I was generally called Bill, and then later on, Bang or Bang-Bang. I thought that was better than another officer we had whose name was Bumgarner. Everybody called him Bum. I guess he'd put up with that all his life

We learned to do some aerobatics in the PT-17 such as loops, stalls, spins, and other events. Each was a thrill for us. We learned to do snap rolls and slow rolls. Slow rolls were the hardest for me. You had to synchronize your rudder pedals and stick movements just right. When a pilot got upside down, then the rudder movements were just the opposite of normal. We had one instructor who was really good with a slow roll. He even did one going straight up after taking off. Landings were graded by percentages, and I was able to get pretty good on them, eventually receiving a 110% rating.

There were always a few close calls. I had several. I came in one day when the wind was a little bad, and I nearly ground looped the plane. In the process I put my one of my ailerons [movable flap on the wing] down, and it touched the ground, which stirred a little dust. They noticed that, so they tore it apart to see if I had damaged it, and they charged the damage to me. Because of that little accident I had to go up for an elimination check ride with my squadron commander, but I was fortunate that day in that the wind was so bad that they wouldn't let the students solo. Instead he just gave me a good training ride, and I performed well. There Mr. Sprague gave me some very good counsel. He told me, "Now, you fly that plane gently and without great effort. When you go on to basic training do the same thing. You fly that airplane very easily and gently, and don't jerk it around at all." Then he trained me in how to land in a crosswind and so on, and I passed the ride in good shape. As we were landing and taxiing back to park the plane, another plane passed us. Mr. Sprague always spoke with great civility, and he was polite. He didn't curse and swear. But as this plane passed us, he didn't like the way it went by, and he did swear, saying, "Now where does that so-and-so think he's going?" We pulled in and parked the plane, and as I got out, he said, "Mr. Bangerter," which is how they addressed a cadet, "Mr. Bangerter, I'm sorry I spoke as I did back there. I forgot for a moment that it was you with me in the airplane." I was known among the squadron and the officers as a former minister and was given general respect. We all had great respect for our instructors all through our training. They were capable and well qualified in their training approach. Others who flew during the war often commented on the good training they had received from those men. [4]

---

4. See *The Wild Blue*, Stephen Ambrose, pp. 67–75, 82–84

On another occasion, our instructor had the five of us on the ground and was giving us some explanations. He was smoking a cigarette and needed his hands free to draw something on the blackboard, so he handed his cigarette to me and continued his demonstration. When he took his cigarette back he said, "Mr. Bangerter, I'm sorry I gave you the cigarette. I forgot for a moment you don't smoke. You don't drink either, do you?"

I said, "No, sir."

"Do you drink tea?"

"No, sir."

"Do you drink coffee?"

"No, sir."

He turned to the other fellows and said, "Fellows, that's the Word of Wisdom. We would all be better off if we lived that way."

I attended Church meetings whenever possible. I met a few young ladies there and also on a visit to Ventura, California. I was still in correspondence with Margaret Ottley as she served in New York on her mission. I had little association with Church groups at that time, but I did make some close associations with my companions who as a group were excellent and likeable people. I did well in my flying, gaining a good reputation, and also in my class work. My prayers were that I might succeed and that I wanted to excel. After two months and 60 hours of primary training, I graduated from Primary Flying School. I had served as a cadet lieutenant over the group.

Basic Flight School—Minter Field, Bakersfield, California

As we graduated from our primary flight training, we had a ceremony recognizing our completion of that phase, and then we moved on to our basic phase, which was at Minter Field, near Bakersfield, California. There we came under the control of Army officers. I was once again asked to be the squadron lieutenant.

We were assigned to fly heavy planes, that is, they weren't light, fabric-covered planes—they were all metal, single-winged aircraft. Suddenly we were sitting up right on top of the world and looking down the barrel of that airplane with the propeller going out in the front instead of having that wing covering us over the top. They were a Voltee aircraft, a basic trainer BT-13. They did not have retractable landing gear, but they were fairly powerful planes and gave quite a thrill.

Well, this airplane was a new experience. Of course, my squadron commander in primary training had told me that I should learn to fly it very gently and easily. I was assigned with four other cadets to the instructor Lieutenant Homer Garrett. We began to get a little more Army treatment in the language and the orders and so on but it was not unpleasant generally.

I saw the great machines of war being operated by young people. They not only operated the machinery but also directed it. They knew how to handle it, giving leadership to others. As we marched the first day to the flight area and entered the squadron ready room (about 50 of us were in that squadron), we stood in formation and waited for what came next. Various officers came in the door and stood around waiting too. They were to be our instructors. We realized they were waiting for the squadron commander to come in. After a while, one of the officers shouted, "Atten-hut!" and we all popped to. Into the room walked Captain Johnson, a tiny, sandy-haired boy—he seemed younger than our entire group. He took control with authority and energy, and I was much impressed. He instilled in us a feeling of our military devotion. He was a captain and the squadron commander, though he looked younger than we did. All of the officers seemed like they were youngsters. He had just been in there long enough to advance. But he was a good-looking little cuss. With perfect poise he stepped right up to the front, and we noticed that all the instructors paid attention, as did we, because he wore captain's bars. In a rather quiet, unobtrusive way, but with great authority, he said, "Gentlemen, I welcome you here to Squadron Seven. I want to tell you that this is the best squadron on this base. We always start our flying earlier, we finish earlier, and we fly better than anyone else. Now, if there's anyone in this room who would not give his right arm to fly for Uncle Sam, I want him to come and see me." We were shocked and impressed by the manner and control in which he gave his leadership. I've never seen leadership demonstrated as effectively as that man showed it, and the program we followed for the next two months was exactly as he had outlined it, professional in every way. [5]

I began to enjoy the influences of Army life, the military order and discipline. It was always impressive to me as I saw young men step up and take command during the war. Most of the pilots were 21 years old or younger, and they learned to master the intricacies of flying a complicated aircraft in a relatively short period of time. [6] Under Captain Johnson we went through our two months of basic flight training. Lieutenant Garrett would take us out one at a time in the planes, and we had a radio connection through earphones by now. We would ride the front seat and he would ride the back. We'd climb to a thousand feet, put our RPM at 1750, come around in a circle, enter the base leg and final approach, and then land. We repeated that traffic pattern during about four hours of training, and then he pulled over to the side, got out, and said, "Go around. I'll watch you." So I took off alone. I was halfway through the downwind leg of my traffic pattern when he said, "Watch your RPM—1750." He was still on the radio. I landed and was the first of the cadets to solo that airplane, which was an enjoyable experience.

It wasn't all that good, however. We came to formation flying phase. There they'd have three planes line up with a lead plane, and they'd say, "You don't fly your airplane—you fly that lead plane. If he bounces on takeoff, you bounce; if he lands and bounces on the landing, you bounce. You just stick with him and hold your position." But my first formation flight was miserable. I was flying the right wing, I guess, and our squadron commander was flying the lead plane. My instructor was with me in my plane, and I couldn't hold position at all. I was just fighting to get in place, and he was cussing me over the headphones, really giving me a hard time. Finally he quit talking. I thought, "He is so disgusted he won't even talk to me anymore." I found out when I landed that my earphone plug had pulled out and he was talking to the wind. During that flight, we made a turn, and I hung way out; the squadron commander up in his plane turned

---

5. Collected Works, p. 184
6. See Ambrose, pp. 110, 143, 185

around and looked at me and held his nose at me to send the message, "You stink."

Well, I went home to the barracks, and I lay on my bunk and was miserable. I thought I was really a failure and was about to be washed out. I prayed and studied and thought and wondered. I had prayed a lot about being effective and successful in flying. I had told the Lord that I had wanted to excel and to do well. Generally, things had gone along well, but here I was having a real failure, and it frightened me. As I lay there in that mood and concern, I remembered what Mr. Sprague had told me about flying a basic trainer: "Be gentle with it, just guide it, and don't try to move it around." I suddenly realized that's what I was doing—that was my problem. So I learned to fly formation lying on my bunk in the barracks. I really did. The next day when I went up to fly I hung in there just beautifully. It was just as easy as pie. That, of course, was an answer to prayer.

Instrument Flying

When it came to instrument flying, (which is where you fly by referring to your instruments when visual flying is not safe), I found that my experience in the Link Trainer in Tucson had made me adept, and I impressed my instructor. This was one of the many evidences I had that Heavenly Father was blessing me in my desire to attain excellence. The routine of half a day flying, half a day in ground school, and the constant drill continued. I acted as drillmaster from time to time. At the close of our course, I was asked to go back to my primary flying school in Oxnard and explain to the younger cadets the safeness of the basic trainer and give them a preview of that phase.

Night flying was an especially thrilling experience and an example of precise organization. In the squadron room when they told us about night flying, they said, "You'll enjoy this. The air is smooth at night generally. You'll be surprised at how you can manage it." My memories of those night flights create one of the great pictures of my life. We'd go out in that plane—an instructor with us, of course—and they had a big battery of lights that would shine on the runway to give us the landing area. The runway was marked, but they gave us extra light. We'd take off in sequence, and then they'd have a position mark. They'd have groups of three planes stacked up in that quadrant a thousand feet apart—three there, three here, and three back there—and they'd bring us all down. Each threesome would peel off and come on down to land, the lower ones first. At night the air was just soft and silky, especially in the early evenings. It was a thrilling thing.

A great wingding was scheduled at the close of our basic flight-training course, which meant a dinner with plenty of liquor. Several cadets approached me beforehand asking if I would please agree to drive their car back to the barracks after the party. Many of the men—cadets and instructors—became quite silly.

Multi-Engine School—Roswell, New Mexico

As we graduated from basic flying at Minter Field, I was assigned to go to the Roswell Air Base at Roswell, New Mexico, for advanced multi-engine flight training. I looked forward to working with a crew and to developing closeness with the men. I was more suited for bombers I suspect. I had found many friends in this close environment; it was a congenial camaraderie. One of my friends, a country boy from Oregon named Herbert Blunk, decided to go home with me for a few days. We had a few days off before we had to report, so we rode to Salt Lake City by train. We were intrigued by the attention the girls there gave to us in our flying uniforms. After three days in Salt Lake, we traveled by bus to Flagstaff, Arizona, and then by the Santa Fe Railroad to Roswell, New Mexico, arriving in late April 1943.

Roswell Air Base was a dusty place with high winds blowing over the high plains. In the spring there is a lot of wind out on those plains, so the dust of Arizona would come through in the morning, and the dust of Texas would go back the other way in the afternoon. I was assigned with four other cadets to live in a tent, which allowed a good flow of the dust and wind. The air base was for training on multi-engine flying, and it also had a school for training navigator cadets. We were assigned to fly two-engine airplanes with retracting landing gear: the fabric-covered Cessna AT-17, which did not fly fast, and the Curtiss AT-9, a metal plane that had difficult landing characteristics and was considered to be dangerous. We flew the various phases of training in twin-engine planes including transition, landings, take-offs, stalls, climbs, turns, formation, navigation, day and night flying, and instrument flying, with special caution not to forget the wheels on landing.

Our instructor, a young man named Carmen Carson, was easygoing, and he soon decided that I was his most apt student. I felt we had a good relationship. Carson was a clean-living man; he was married and religiously inclined. Later on, we attempted to get him involved in the Church after we left the Army, but as far as I know he never quite made it. He had read in my previous record that I had done well with instruments, and he commented on that. I had a feel for the twin-engine aircraft, though I was not proficient or skillful, but I managed well in the basics. Once again I was the first to solo in that aircraft. Some of the other cadets were somewhat unsure of their control, and Lt. Carson gave me the assignment of flying with the other four cadets to ensure their safety. He later said, "You trained the others for me." On one occasion he planned a cross-country flight to Denver and asked me to go as copilot. We flew to Albuquerque and then north to Denver, where I attended Church. Lt. Carson always treated me as his special student. We continued with instrument and formation flying, including day and night flying, and then worked on navigation, flying across the Great Plains at night as well as day. We covered a lot of eastern New Mexico in those planes. Our twin-engine training did not involve aerobatics but rather skills in take-offs, landings, and emergency procedures.

Roswell had a pilot training school and a bombardier training school. The bombardiers flew Beechcraft AT-11s, which were metal planes that were a bit faster than whatever we were flying. One night I was flying with Cadet Benson. We flew his course, and then I took over for another trip. I lined up on the runway just like he had and checked our direction. The runway had lights lined up, and we took off. Just as we left the ground, I felt a jar. I thought, for no good reason, "We blew a tire—I'd better land it." I was just barely off the ground, so I cut the power. The plane dropped down and tried to turn to the right, so I jammed hard on the rudder. It seemed to straighten out; then the wheels hit, and it stood on its nose and came to a stop. My copilot was sitting behind on the right side, but he could see out behind me through me the window. He said, "Let's get out! Let's get out of here!" I cut the switches for the engines, and we climbed out and saw that the whole rear section of the airplane was broken off right behind our seats. The entire tail section was folded over the right wing. We ran around the front of the plane and found an airplane engine lying in front of it. I thought, "Did I break an engine off this plane?" I looked and discovered that I still had two engines, so I looked a little further and saw another engine. And then a little fire started a little ways away, and we saw another airplane lying on its belly over there. We'd had a mid-air collision. It was a BT-7 with navigator trainees. They had overtaken our plane and mistaken our wing-tip light for a ground light on the field.

The tower saw the fire and vectored other planes away from us. Our plane was in the middle of the runway with others flying over us, so it was a dangerous situation. We soon had an ambulance on hand to pick us up. No one was injured. They loaded us in, took us to the hospital, and checked us over. The man at the hospital said, "Now will you please tell me how in the H— you ever survived that?" You can imagine how thankfully I prayed that day. We were examined at the base hospital and released. We soon appeared at an accident board but were exonerated because the other plane had overtaken us, mistaking our wing-tip light for a field light. The other pilot's explanation was interesting. He said, "Oh, when we take off, we just line up with our compass." (The whole field was covered with asphalt so you could go anywhere, and it was covered with lights too.) He said, "We just line up and pick a light at the far end of the field and aim for that and take off." The light he picked was my wing tip.

We were flying airplanes with a freedom and an abandon and an open experience that will never be duplicated. Today it's so totally controlled that it would take the fun out of it. It was also the most glamorous thing you could be involved in at that period of time. I guess airplane pilots were considered the top of the heap. We didn't have much time to attend Church meetings in either Bakersfield or in Roswell. Occasionally I did go to meetings there, and it was there I met my future brother-in-law, William Jensen.

Graduation and Officers Commission

Prior to my anticipated graduation, my instructor, Lt. Carson, asked me for my preference as to what type of plane I would like to fly. I answered, the B-17 bomber. I felt that if I could be a pilot of one of those, I would be involved with a group of 10 to 12 men and would really enjoy that association. I didn't realize then that those so assigned were to be trained immediately for service in the great air war in England, and they would become involved in some of the most vicious air battles the world has ever known. I was not aware of the danger of such a request; thousands of those crews would be lost in the air war. For many it was a death sentence. Lt. Carson, however, felt differently about me and informed me of a special opportunity available to attend Pilot Instructors School at Randolph Field in San Antonio, Texas (at that time Randolph Field was considered the "West Point" of aviation). He said, "You'd be a good one. I'd like to recommend you, if you want to go." I agreed to take that opportunity, and it changed the course of my life regarding the war.

Graduation took place on June 23, 1943, which qualified me as a pilot and an Army officer. I received my pilot wings and my Army commission as a 2nd Lieutenant, Class 43-F (this meant we were the sixth class of 1943). My sister Pauline and her friend June Carlisle came to Roswell for the occasion, and my brother Sam, still on his mission, was transferred there at the same time. Also present were William Jensen, who later married Pauline, and Milo Hansen, a missionary, who later married my sister, Elsbeth. I traveled with Sam and Pauline to Carlsbad, New Mexico, to visit the great caverns, and then we took a bus for El Paso, Texas. There I met my cousins Alden and John Bangerter. Afterwards I took a bus to San Antonio.

Randolph Field and Instructors School

Randolph Field was a permanent base—the first one I'd been assigned to. They had nice permanent buildings and a beautiful layout just like a beautiful college campus in a way. We were housed in modern dormitories, and I had another LDS boy as a roommate. He was not very active in the Church, however. I was there from the end of June into August. That was a marvelous flying experience.

During orientation, our base commander told us that we would learn something new concerning the planes we had been flying: we would be able to land the heavier planes at 60 MPH instead of 90 MPH. The lighter planes would land at somewhere near 25 MPH instead of the usual 60. Precision and control would give us a greater ability than we thought possible. My instructor, Lt. Johnny Reese, was a good-looking Texas redhead; he was quick, cocky, and intense and proceeded to carry out the program. We attended more ground school, which was a concentrated course in more precision flying as training for instructors. We were shown that we would learn to fly planes in a much more skillful way, that they could be handled under adverse conditions, and that our procedure was to be very careful. Lt. Reese taught me how to fly slowly, how to land slowly on a short field, how to fly without using the controls, and how to be alert for the conditions of the country over a large area in Texas. We flew AT-10s, AT-9s, and AT-17s, and I had a chance to fly a bomber, the B-23.

One day, Lt. Hankinson and I were invited to go on a ride in the B-23 by our squadron commander. He took another pilot up and was checking him out on how to fly this airplane. None of us had flown bombers, but he had. It was a big airplane and our first chance to get in one that size. We were up at 8,000 feet. They were going through a single-engine procedure, and this student pilot stalled it. I was standing back in the belly, when I just started to float through the air toward the open hatch in the ceiling. The plane had gone out of control. We had four parachutes lying in the bottom, so here came four parachutes floating up through the air as the plane was falling. Suddenly the pilot jerked it out of the stall, and I hit the floor with such pressure that I couldn't move, with all the parachutes on top of me. Then he stalled it again, and we went through the same thing a second time. The commander was there next to him, but since there was only one set of controls and he was sitting on the jump seat, he couldn't reach anything (he had his feet on the ceiling, and he was trying to help this guy with the controls). They finally pulled it out with 500 feet to spare. When we got on the ground, the commander said, "Hey! That would have been one of those accidents where nobody would have known what happened." The hazards of flying were impressed on us vividly.

Lt. Reese also taught us that instead of a landing roll of three-fourths of a mile, we could land within 100 yards. It was somewhat like landing on aircraft carriers. One day two of us were with him. I was doing the flying, while Hankinson was sitting in the back seat. Suddenly Lt. Reese turned the gas off on one engine. He confused me with his nervous nature, and so I searched for the trouble. The instructor often pulled an emergency on us, unawares. He said, "Whoa, what's the matter?" I said, "I don't know." He said, "Well you've lost an engine haven't you? What are you going to do now?" So I steadied the plane and tried to get it going on one engine as I went through the trouble search to see what the matter was. In doing so, I reached down and switched the valve and cut out the other engine. When the other engine quit, he said, "Well, no engines—what are you going to do now?" I was just foggy. I was totally bewildered. He then started in on me: "What do you do now? What do you do now?" He was enjoying it, and I wasn't giving him any answers and he said, "Well, it's a forced landing, where are you going to land?" I looked all over Texas, and I couldn't see a single place to land. I was that confused. He then said, "Here, I'll land it." And he dead-sticked it in and plopped it down on an auxiliary airfield, right there. He knew where it was. So we sat down on the ground, drank a bottle of pop, and laughed at my stupidity, and then Hankinson got in the seat. We went up, and he flew for a while. Pretty soon Reese reached over and turned one engine off, and Hankinson got the same confused expression and feeling that I'd had. When he went for his trouble search, he turned off the other engine, too. So here we were without any engines again. Reese just shook his head and said, "Well, that's enough for today. Let's go home."

Lt. Reese was a great pilot. He really showed me a few things. One day we were shooting these short-field landings (like carrier landings), and I was bringing in this AT-9, which was the fastest of the three types of planes that we had down there. I was bringing it down over the fence with the nose up and flying it slowly, and another fellow in a lighter plane went over the fence ahead of us, landed quite short, and was turning around when Lt. Reese said, "Hey, that guy thinks he's pretty hot. Let me take this and land it." He took over the plane, and as we went over the fence, he chopped the power and jerked back on the stick, and that plane went "flunk" just like that. He stood on the brakes and he turned that plane around a hundred yards shorter than the guy who had just made that beautiful short landing. Ordinarily you'd figure a mile run on the runway to land that plane. He did it in 75 yards. Well, those were some of the things he was teaching us.

One day as we were flying an AT-9, he turned to me and said, "Have you ever tried to fly ones of these planes without using the controls?" When I said no, he said, "Here, I'll show you. I'll take it off and land it without any controls." So he did by just giving it the throttle. He put his feet on the floor and his hands in his lap and proceeded to take off, fly around the traffic pattern, come in, and land. He did it only using the throttles, which would pull the engine from one side and then the other. Later on when I was a qualified instrument flying instructor, I took another pilot up to train him on instrument flight. After we finished the problem (he hadn't done very well), we were flying back to base with the hood still up [to restrict vision to the cockpit], but I didn't have those goggles on to shut out the vision completely. I sat there with my feet on the floor just flying the plane with the throttles; he'd never seen anybody do that. We were just sailing along, and it was just a relaxed way to get there.

He watched me for a few minutes and finally said, "Hey, if you could do that on instruments, that'd really be something, wouldn't it?"

"Oh, I could learn to do that all right. It wouldn't be hard if you practiced a little," I said.

"Like so much bologna," he replied.

"Here. Give me your goggles." I put them on and went on instruments; I jockeyed for a couple of minutes as I got the plane flying in order. I tuned in the radio range, intercepted the beam, and flew in and hit the station better than he'd been doing. He never said a word, but for three weeks I'd have pilots come up to me and say, "Hey, are you the guy that can fly instruments without using the controls?" But that's what I learned from Johnny Reese.

I was committed to obtaining excellence in my flying. I was earnest in my prayers and was recognized by my companions as a religious person; I found that my associations included many fine people. I was able to attend our Church meetings occasionally. While at Roswell at graduation time I was asked to be best man at the weddings of two companions, Lt. Baldwin (much later I learned that he had joined the Church) and Lt. Blunk, with whom I had passed through most of my Cadet Training.

War Escalates

Meanwhile, the war was progressing with Hitler's forces still in the ascendancy. We were in the midst of a very intense build-up of planes and pilots as well as the great advance of other troops in the army and the rebuilding of the Navy. The entire nation was involved in the war effort. We had controls and rationing of many items, including food. Everything in our lives was pointed to attaining a victory.

Instrument Flight School—Bryan, Texas

After finishing the month of training at Randolph in August of 1943, we were invited to attend another course in instrument flying at Bryan, Texas, near Texas A&M University. I accepted the opportunity, feeling that I could become a better flyer. Taking that course finally gave me an instrument instructor's rating. In August it was hot and muggy, but we flew every day in single engine planes, the AT-6, which was a very pleasant and versatile plane. In the movies, it's the one used as a Japanese Zero most of the time. It could do all the aerobatics, so I tuned up my general flying ability. We flew under the hood, with an observer in front, concentrating on precision through instruments and then navigating by radio also under the hood. Sometimes we would almost fly in formation with other planes doing the same problems without the instrument pilot being able to see them.

Our base commander was a man named Colonel Duckworth, who had been an airline pilot. He'd flown thousands of hours on instruments, and he was really skilled at it. One day they had a hurricane down in the Gulf, and he took his weather officer in an AT-6 and flew down into the hurricane. He said, "I just wanted to see what it was like. We found the eye of it without too much trouble." It wasn't dangerous for him. There are dangerous spots, I guess, in those windstorms, but that's what he told us.

One Sunday morning we'd finished our training, but I was scheduled to fly. So I went out with another officer, and he asked, "Hey, do you want to fly instruments today?" I said, "No, not especially." So he responded, "So, let's just go for a ride." We didn't need any more hours of training, so we headed south until we came to the city of Navasota, between Bryan and Houston. He was flying and swooped down over the town. It was a neat little town with a church steeple in the middle of it, and we zoomed up and went on further south. After a while we turned around; I was in the back seat, and for no good reason, I flipped the stick a couple of times to make the plane jump while he was flying it (which was a signal for the other pilot to take over). He thought I wanted to take over, but I didn't. As we approached Navasota again, he started to swoop down over the town again, and he went over it, lower than we'd been before, and zoomed back up and came around the second time. This time he was really low, and I thought, "I wonder if he thinks I'm flying this," and I held the stick a little so we didn't get too low. We came back up again, and he said, "Hey, why don't we go home," and I said, "Heck yes! Take it home." Nobody was flying that airplane! It had a reasonable stability, but it was in a slight curve, and it would swoop down and pick up speed, and then it'd climb automatically.

Duty Assignment—Douglas, Arizona

I finished that instrument course and now was qualified in my training to be a regular instructor and an instrument instructor. I was stationed in Douglas, Arizona as a pilot instructor in the West Coast Training Command. The organization consisted of squadrons, groups, and so on. A squadron consisted of about 54 students and about 16 instructors, and I was one of those. I was 24 years old at the time, so I was one of the older ones. I arrived there by train about September 1, 1943, and I thought I had never seen such a dry country. Little did I know that it would become much like home to me and that I would learn to love the area.

I stayed at the officers' quarters, which were in tarpaper-covered temporary war buildings. We had our meals at the officers club. I was pleased to have the assignment there, although I thought it would be nicer to be assigned somewhere closer to the temple in Mesa. I didn't know much about Douglas, but I learned that it was the third largest city in the state of Arizona at that time, though that didn't mean it was a large city. I think it had a population of maybe 20–25,000 people. They had established an air force base there for training purposes. The hills were totally brown, and the valley was called the Sulfur Springs Valley. The town of Douglas had a smelter that handled the ore from the Bisbee mines, about 25 miles away. The plume of smoke from the smelter was one of the prominent features of the area and could be seen at a great distance, so it was an easy identifying point. The taste in the air from the sulfur smoke reminded me of my high school days at Magna, Utah.

I soon learned that this was one of the most romantic areas in the entire west. A number of aspects made it especially interesting. First of all, it was located exactly on the Mexican border in the southeast corner of the state. Cochise County was in the largest cattle-producing area in Arizona and was named after the great Apache Indian chief Cochise. The territory over which he roamed was all around that country. Several famous landmarks were notable, including the Cochise stronghold, about 40 miles northwest of Douglas, in the Dragoon Mountains. The history of the west included many instances of army activities against the Apaches. One of the most famous mountain passes in the movie-making industry was Apache Pass, about 50 miles north of town. This area also had a very lively cowboy history. The town of Tombstone was about 70 miles northwest, and its Wild West atmosphere was still prevalent. John Slaughter, who became the most famous sheriff of Tombstone, had established a cattle ranch about 30 miles east of Douglas, and it was a very famous landmark in the area. So Douglas was really in the heart of the Wild West, and there was a great deal of tradition about it.

Mormon history also permeated that area. The Latter-day Saints had been through that whole country and established the colonies across the border in Mexico, some of them about 70 miles away. The members of the Church in the Douglas Ward were almost all descendants of colonists in Mexico, so there was a tremendous amount of folklore about this area and the history of the Mormon people, the Indians, the Mexicans, the cowboys, the army, the cattle industry, and the miners. It would be hard to find a more fascinating and romantic country to be in. My first impressions of course changed, and by the time I left that area over two years later, I was more personally and emotionally attached to that country than I was to anywhere else I'd ever been in the world. I was fascinated by it and greatly enjoyed my experience there.

I reported for duty at the Douglas Air Force Base on a weekend, and immediately I was assigned to be the officer of the day. That meant everyone else who went to town was off duty, but they had to have someone who would receive the telephone calls, so on that first Sunday I stayed on the air base, almost entirely alone. I remember going out on the flight line that day, and there was an AT-6 parked there. I asked the sergeant if anybody cared if I flew that airplane, and he said, "No, go ahead. Get in it, and if anybody wants you, I'll call you on the radio to come back." So I took off in that AT-6.

The next week I was assigned to be one of 16 instructors in one of the squadrons on base. Our practice was to take five students at a time and train them in the handling and flying of these airplanes. We were training the men to take off and land, and fly solo. We gave them 30 hours of dual instruction and 30 hours of solo flying with another cadet. The planes we were using at that point were the twin-engine Cessna AT-17s, in which I had had quite a bit of experience. I found, however, that going through the training course was not the same as being an instructor. I didn't have the confidence, the insight, the vision, or the understanding on how to handle the teaching of these young men. I felt that I was pretty shaky in my calling. In fact, new instructors were not allowed to send their boys up solo until they had some more experienced instructor check them out. But, after that initial period, I seemed to get along pretty well. The squadron and flight commanders were more seasoned instructors, generally a captain or first lieutenant. I gingerly took on my first five students but soon learned to schedule their time between dual and solo flight in transition, formation, navigation, and instrument flying. I was also a check pilot for other instructors in instrument flying to verify their capability and keep them current in their rating.

Along through September and October, I trained my first class of students, and then in November and December, the pace picked up a great deal as the war was raging tremendously. The air war in Europe was taking on great dimensions, and there was a tremendous need for pilots. So they began to double up on our responsibility, and instead of flying approximately 4 hours a day, probably 5 days a week, we began to fly about 8 hours a day. We'd fly our own students part of the time and then go over and fly somebody else's students at an auxiliary field. We were loaded up with tremendous activity, and I began to fly about 160 hours a month. Under that arrangement, we soon built up a considerable amount of experience in flight time. We had our share of dangers and emergencies and such. I don't think any pilot went through a week without having something of an emergency or some experience that could possibly have taken his life.

We would take a couple of hours in preparation and then finish up our duty as well. They were full days—we'd get out of bed at 5 o'clock in the morning at that season of the year, go out and fire up our airplanes in the dark, and fly to our auxiliary training field. We'd fly there in the morning, and in the afternoon we'd come back home. Often we'd switch over and fly nights because we had to give the night-training phases. The training we gave, of course, was to teach the cadets in their advanced phase to transition to become familiar with the twin-engine airplanes. It was the first time they'd flown them. They had to learn to take off and land and to handle the emergency procedures, which included turns, climbs, stalls, single engines, forced landings, and all kinds of activities. We didn't do aerobatics in those planes, but we did fly formations and navigation both day and night. When they finished this course, the cadets would graduate and be commissioned.

We didn't have a lot of association with our crew chiefs. I went out one morning to start up my airplane, and as I switched on one of the engines, one of the magnetos quit. They had twin magnetos to give double firing on the spark plug, and as part of our preflight check, we'd switch from one to the other to make sure they all worked. I called the crew chief over and asked, "Did you notice when you checked this plane out this morning that one of the magnetos wasn't firing?"

"Yes, sir, I noticed that," he responded.

"Well, how long have you been here on the line as a crew chief?" I asked.

And he said, "Three days."

"What did you do before that?"

"I was over in the mess hall. I was a cook."

So I started taking a little more care in checking out my own airplane.

The whole experience was interspersed with incidents that could have been tragic. However, in those early months, our base sailed through without any serious accidents. I think it had a record of six months without an accident. But after we'd gotten into this intense flying schedule, we suddenly had a tremendous burst of accidents. Within a week we lost six airplanes, and our commanding officers were going through the ceiling, partly in anger and partly in frustration to think that this could all happen at once.

On one occasion, one of the instructors who worked as I did had his students in two other airplanes flying formation, but he was in a third plane with another student under the hood doing instruments. He was trying to speed up his training. At the same time he was exploring the country. As I mentioned, it was a romantic area, and many of the pilots would go out around the countryside looking for points of interest. He started to fly up a canyon in the Chiricahua Mountains, a high mountain range named after the Chiricahua Apaches. It was a beautiful mountain covered in the upper reaches with forest and so on. He began to go up the canyon incline, and he couldn't make it over the top. He put his airplane into a slow-flying maneuver and pancaked it in, sliding the plane into the mountain on its belly, so that he and his student survived. The student broke his leg. The other two planes went down and killed everyone in them, with two people in each plane. After that he was persona non grata. However, he continued in his career. He was a man that had quite a personality; he weathered the storm pretty well.

I had trained two full classes, plus the extra cadets that we had at that time. It was getting to be fairly cool weather. Douglas is about the same elevation as Salt Lake City, but, of course, being further south it is not as cold. We nevertheless had some fairly interesting winter weather there. At that same time in our squadron we were flying nights off an auxiliary field, and each evening a number of instructors took off with their students. One of them just went up in the night, and we never heard from him again. There was never a trace, until about 1985. I read in the paper of an Army aircraft being discovered up on Mount Graham. That was about 100 miles north of our base. I figured that was the lost plane. I often flew night formation flights and night navigation trips, which, with students, became what we called "hairy." I trained at least 50 student pilots in that tight period. We flew much of the time from the temporary base at Hereford, over the mountain on the San Pedro River. Our training area reached from Tucson east to New Mexico and from the Mexican border north to the Gila River. With my rating as an instrument instructor I had the responsibility to check out all the pilots in my section and renew their instrument rating. We were put under some very heavy orders to tighten up on our flying and procedure.

About this time at the end of 1943, I was able to get an airplane and fly home for Christmas. They would allow us to check an airplane out and take off, so I did that. I remember I gave an LDS girl, who was a nurse there, a ride to Salt Lake too. Her name was Mash. As we flew north I knew I had to climb over some pretty large mountains, which was somewhat of a concern to me. Off in the distance I could see some pretty large peaks. As I got nearer to them, I suddenly recognized one as Mt. Nebo, another one was Mt. Timpanogos, and the third big one was Lone Peak. I was almost home!

Chapter 6

ROMANCE AND MARRIAGE—
BELOVED MILDRED

"Consider the case of a young man who returns from his mission. He stands before the stake presidency and the high council to give his report. He represents the ideal of young manhood. He is the most perfect type of young manhood anywhere. He has been through the temple and had his endowment; he has had tremendous blessings and experiences. What is the destiny of such a young man if he stays the way he is? His destiny is to become a ministering angel to those who are worthy of a far greater and a more exalted glory. He has not yet accomplished that which was pointed out in the first revelation recorded in the last days. This is one of the basic reasons why the gospel has been restored. It is necessary, for the binding together of the family of our Father in Heaven, that he go into the temple, receive a companion, and there receive another conferral of priesthood power and blessings. As he kneels together with his bride, there is organized a priesthood organization just as vital, living, and real as the organization of a ward or stake. A family is formed on eternal principles, and blessings are conferred upon that family and its leadership that will endure through all eternity. And only if those blessings are sought for and obtained by the members of this Church can the purposes for which the gospel was restored be brought to pass." [1]

Initial Contacts with Mildred Schwantes

As already mentioned, my first Sunday on Douglas Air Force Base I was assigned as duty officer, or officer of the day. My second

---

1. Collected Works, p. 177

Sunday, September 12, 1943, I had no duty and had located the LDS chapel of the Douglas Ward in the Southern Arizona Stake. There were several other servicemen attending. As I walked into the chapel, a remarkable and lovely young lady met me and introduced herself as Mildred Schwantes. Her low voice and friendly manner immediately drew my attention. I feel it's important to remember that Mildred was one of the outstanding features of the Douglas Ward, having returned from her mission in California and being eager about activity in the Church. She was a member of the presidency of the Young Women's organization and had a striking appearance and open personality that immediately drew everyone's attention. I didn't know at the time, of course, that she would become my wife, but I was pleased to have made friendship with someone like that. Mildred was an experienced secretary and was working for a colonel at the Douglas Air Base. She had also finished a course in beauticians school in Phoenix.

Mildred's mother was among the LDS colonists who had been driven out of Mexico. Her father had died recently, and she had left employment in Salt Lake City to return to be with her family. She had six sisters and one brother, who was serving in the Navy. Her father had not been a member of the Church. He was the son of German immigrants to Texas, and he had made his livelihood by operating a pool hall in Douglas, Arizona. It was the fraternal meeting place of all the men who wanted a place to stop and visit. He'd provided for his family there in selling beer and liquor as well as other things, but it was a congenial place. It was called the B&P Palace, and incidentally as of 2006 it still operates there. His partner was his wife's brother, who was a Latter-day Saint also, but not active—a fine man, nevertheless. When Mildred went on a mission, she became the spiritual leader of her family, and she began to write home letters of gospel teachings to her family. Her father had spoken at her farewell testimonial, and she wrote back to him and said, "Now, Dad, you support me on my mission financially, but you need to support me spiritually as well, so be sure you pay your tithing," and she got him in the habit of paying his tithing. Although I never met him—he had passed away six months before I met the family—he was said to be a very pleasant, congenial person, although not living up to all Latter-day Saint standards.

As mentioned earlier, we had a pretty good group of LDS servicemen, both enlisted men and pilot trainees, who attended the Douglas Ward. Over a period of a year and a half or so, it was amazing how many of the young women in the ward were picked off by these Army boys who married them. The Schwantes girls, the Huishes, the Kirby family, Gertrude Bigelow, and many others—most all of them made good marriages in the gospel and in the temple. I had been assigned as a group leader for the LDS servicemen on base, working mostly for attendance in the Douglas Ward. Kenneth Cluff was one of those LDS servicemen, and he became a lifelong friend along with Alvin Drake and many others. We attended church as regularly as our flying schedule permitted. I was able to attend meetings nearly every week and also some of the ward activities. Since I had been in the bishopric in Granger, I was a high priest and attended priesthood meeting with that quorum.

Within a short time I sought association with Mildred, but living at the air base and having no ready means of transportation made it somewhat inconvenient. I finally arranged a date with Mildred, and we went dancing at a club, the Top Hat, in Douglas. She did not seem to have other male interests at the time. I had thoughts concerning finding someone special for my life and future. I had written to a girl I met in Oxnard, and she responded pleasantly, but after seeing Mildred I didn't pursue any other interests.

Home For the Holidays—Acquiring an Automobile

I mentioned earlier that I was able to take an airplane home to Utah for Christmas and had a good visit with the family. I determined that I needed to have an automobile as I felt I was handicapped in Douglas for want of transportation, so soon after the beginning of 1944, I went home again on leave. I bought a 1937 Ford coupe V8 for about $400 and drove it back to Arizona, a distance of 1100 miles, with a wartime speed limit of 35 miles per hour. Gas was hard to come by, but there were a couple of men—my stake president and one or two others who had farm stamps—who gave me enough that

I could make it down. Once I got the car to Douglas, Arizona, we could drive across the border to Mexico and buy gas there without stamps. That was gas that they'd imported from the United States.

My intent was to have a way to get to know Mildred better. I wasn't her exclusive boyfriend, which meant there were many who were interested in her, among them non-LDS boys. She'd gone out with some of those, but was pretty discreet in her behavior. She had talked to me about how her mother sometimes baked homemade bread and rolls and had told me, "When she does, I'll give you a call." One night after I had been to the officer's club and eaten a full dinner, she did just that. Just at the moment when I'd filled my stomach, she called to say, "Momma's just baked some rolls. Would you like to come into town and try them out?" Our base was about 15 miles out of town, but I said, "I surely would." I didn't know if I could hold any rolls, but I was eager to go on that kind of an invitation, so I enjoyed that and other associations. Usually my flight schedule allowed me to have my evenings free, so we began to date and to get acquainted, and much of our dating and activities centered on the Church. At that time, they had selected a queen for the Church's annual Gold and Green Ball, and that girl invited me to be her escort to the ball. I wasn't overly enthused about that at the time, but I felt I had to respond.

Engagement

I soon came to feel that it was time for me to marry, being nearly 25 years old, and I had found the one I wished to be married to. We were often together in ward and fireside activities. I had come to a decision, and so I brought the subject to her attention. She gave me a little brush-off at first, not being sure, I guess, of what her feelings were, but within two or three days she came back and said, "I've got the answer to your question," which was a choice and wonderful moment, of course, in my life. I had brought a diamond ring back from Brazil, and when I presented it to her, it was a perfect fit. We were engaged in February, she finding in me the special one in her life.

My flight experience now became interspersed with my romance. As we agreed that we were meant for each other and that we would be married, we began to determine where we would be married. Just before our engagement, I had written to my parents in a kidding way. I asked my mother, "What would you think if I were to marry a girl who's half Mexican and half German?" (Mildred's mother having been born in the Mexican colonies and her father being of German ancestry). This worried Mother somewhat at first. A week later I wrote again, explaining the whole situation and telling them that I was engaged to be married. Wartime conditions required special arrangements for everybody. Nobody thought of traveling, so I just wrote home and said to my father—or suggested to him—"Dad, why don't you go to the bishop and get me a temple recommend?" I thought the bishop would give me one because I'd served as his counselor before I entered the service. So they sent me down a temple recommend.

Marriage and Honeymoon

We determined to be married on March 8, 1944, in the Mesa Arizona Temple. Mildred's mother had never been to the temple, though two of her daughters had been married in the temple, and she was now ready to receive her endowment. The three of us drove in my little Ford from Douglas to Chandler, Arizona, where Mildred's mother's sister lived, and Mildred and her mother stayed there. I stayed at the Maricopa Inn in Mesa.

The next day, we went to Phoenix, got our marriage license, and found her a wedding ring. On the morning of March 8 we went to the Mesa Arizona Temple for an endowment session for Mildred's mother. We were accompanied by Aunt Helen Cluff and her husband, two of Mildred's friends living in Mesa, and two missionaries we had become acquainted with. After the endowment session we went to the sealing room on the north side of the celestial room, where we were sealed together by President Harry L. Payne, temple president. He had been the stake president over Elder Spencer W. Kimball, who had served as his counselor. We took pictures, visited, and then left to spend the night in the Maricopa Inn. The day following our wedding was spent in and around Mesa visiting friends and relatives. Our plan was to drive from there to Salt Lake and meet my family. Mildred's uncle operated a dairy farm in Chandler, and he said, "Now, as a wedding present, if you want, I'll give you enough gas to go to Salt Lake." So we took three ten-gallon milk cans and put them behind the seat of our little Ford, filled them with gas, and used them for the drive to Salt Lake.

After a nice lunch with friends and family in Mesa, we left for Salt Lake. About nine o'clock in the evening, we arrived in Flagstaff to get gas. I stopped at the station of a friend of ours, Ken Harmon, whose father had served with my father in the bishopric in Granger. I knew he was there—I had visited him once or twice on my way through. So I pulled up and got gas, and when I went in to pay him, he looked out and asked, "Hey, what did you do? Did you go and get married or something?"

"Yes, we just got married yesterday," I said.

"Well, isn't that great?" he said, "You come on in." He operated a motel in connection with his gas station, and he said, "I've got a place here for you. You spend the night here."

They took great care of us. Later on, his brother served as my counselor in the bishopric and also as a counselor to my brother Norman in the stake presidency. Their family home was in Granger, but Ken had moved to Arizona. The next day they fed us a nice breakfast, and as we were leaving, Ken, who also ran a trucking business said to me, "Here's some truck stamps—I'll tell you the places where you can buy gas." So friends appeared all along the way.

Our trip through Arizona and Utah was beautiful. At this period of the year there was still a lot of snow through the high mountains of Central Arizona. The Kaibab Plateau was buried in snow, and we enjoyed the time as we told each other of our lives, our missions, our families, and our devotion to the Church and the gospel.

As we arrived at my parent's home, I introduced my wife to them for the first time. They were overcome by her friendliness and her lovely appearance. She was instantly taken in with praise for my special choice. Mother arranged a reception for us in the ward meetinghouse, and many friends gave us their blessing. We spent a week in Utah visiting before returning to Arizona and my duties in the Army. The speed limit of 35 miles per hour gave no regrets. We saw Kanab, the Kaibab, Flagstaff, Prescott, Phoenix, Tucson, Tombstone, and Bisbee as we made our way home to Douglas. I had lived on base as a bachelor officer, but immediately after marriage we rented a house.

First Home in Douglas

Our first home was on Florida Avenue, the last home next to the Mexican border. My brother Sam had finished his mission about then and stopped to visit with us. We later rented an apartment on 8th Street and lived a rather settled life with my work at the air base and Mildred's family around us. Soon after our marriage I was appointed high priests group leader in our ward, and then Mildred was called to be the Relief Society president. Even though I was regularly occupied with my duties at the base, we had what was almost a normal life in the community and in the Church.

Not too long after we'd been married—a month or so—Mildred began to feel unwell, and I didn't understand much about these matters. I was told by her and her mother that she probably had a little food poisoning or something; she didn't go to church, and I passed the word around that she was sick. I learned later that the whole ward began to snicker. They knew better than I did what was happening. She was expecting.

Back to Flying

In the meantime, I got back into my cadet training, and with two or three classes behind me, I became a fairly proficient instructor. My next class was not as high-pressure as some of my earlier ones had been, and I got almost the exact amount of time required for each training phase. I was commended for the way I'd handled my time in training by my commanding officer. The way I managed it was shown as an example of how to be effective and proficient and use the minimum amount of time to accomplish the maximum amount of training. I had been careful in scheduling my time. I found that there are a lot of secret approaches to doing a good job, as in anything else. I learned that instead of just taking off and going out into the country somewhere and then starting the training, I could begin maneuvers immediately after take-off with my climbing turns and procedures, and I planned it ahead so that every turn led me to the place and altitude I wanted to be, and then when I was at that altitude, I'd start doing the maneuvers that required altitude. By working in that way, I was able to complete all the procedures in a compact arrangement.

Following that class, there was a reorganization of leadership in the squadrons, and suddenly I was invited to become a flight commander—that meant I was to lead half the squadron. I was responsible for about 27 students and paid instructors. I carried that position for a short time, and then further reorganization brought me to the position of squadron commander. So in March or April of 1944, I took over the entire squadron, but I still had those gold second lieutenant bars. However, now I was entitled to be called "the old man" and "the commander." For a time that responsibility took me out of much personal training of students and into more supervision, which included scheduling the total activity of the squadron and so on.

Nevertheless I continued to have very interesting experiences. One night I led a flight of student pilots on a night navigation trip over the town of Columbus, New Mexico (the town Pancho Villa raided in 1916). They had an auxiliary air base over there, and we were supposed to fly over and shoot night landings, having everybody land, control them, and then take off and go back home. I flew over as the leader of the flight, intending to land and control them. I searched and searched for that field, and it wasn't there. I covered the whole territory in a big triangle. I could find Deming, New Mexico, and I could find Lordsburg, New Mexico, but I could not find that airfield, and I'd been over it a hundred times. The planes were all out there circling, saying, "Where are we going, where are we going, where do we land?" And all I could say was, "I can't find the field." Finally I said, "You'll have to return to your base." So just as they started to return to base, I tilted my airplane over and looked down, and suddenly there was the field, lit up like a Christmas tree. They'd just barely turned the lights on. We got some of the planes down, but some of them had gone back. Since we'd been circling for so long, we didn't have a lot of extra fuel, so we landed and controlled those who were still in the area, and those with enough fuel we sent back home. It was all a mistake on the part of those who made the connections from the operations office. Two or three nights later I led a similar flight over to Coolidge, Arizona, and the same thing happened. We circled and circled, and I could not find the airport. I could find the town, but no airport. They didn't turn on the lights. Well, those were interesting incidents in flying.

I mentioned previously that potentially dangerous experiences came almost regularly. One of the things we always had to worry about was teaching our students to be sure to get their wheels down. When they're circling around in heavy traffic and concerned and worried because maybe they have to line up to come in and land, they can easily forget it. As a matter of fact, when I was training as a cadet in New Mexico and flying with another fellow, we came within ten feet of landing without wheels.

My specialty was instruments. I was a certified and qualified instrument instructor, not just on a local basis, but I'd been through the air force course, so I was constantly checking out other pilots on instrument flying. Many of them were not very proficient, even some of the pilots who were being rotated back from the war. The students, of course, were just getting acquainted with it. That specialty was another distinction that gave me a little status and opportunity to exercise leadership. The average pilot would just get a standard instrument rating, which would allow him to take off under questionable conditions, but he wasn't supposed to go out in any bad weather. The card I had was much more advanced, and I was qualified to fly in bad weather. But they had another card that they'd pass out to those who kept within very close limits in their flying with very limited changes in altitude and air speed and so on; they'd give that special card to the very preferred pilots, and they said that the real value of that instrument card was that when you get in bad weather you put that card up in the windshield and the weather would get out of the way. I didn't have that one. They called that special instrument card a champagne ticket because supposedly when you went into the officers club and everybody else is drinking beer, you'd get champagne. So that was a little of the Army jargon.

In the meantime, the procedures at the air base had changed; they began to phase out some of this cadet pilot training, and they brought in a number of civilian pilots who had a lot of experience, and we were now to train them in twin engines for use by the air force. I lost my assignment as squadron commander and became an instructor again for these experienced civilian pilots being trained in air force flying. Among those who came through and received my instruction was one of the instructors I had in primary flying school, a Mr. Pruitt. So I trained him in twin engines. We were training them in the AT-9, a very interesting airplane that I had flown while at Randolph Field. It had to be flown with great precision, and when you flew it that way, it was just beautiful to handle. I developed an enjoyment, a skill, and a love for flying that airplane that I was able to transmit to my students.

I had one student named Blaine. He was perhaps 40 years old, and he had been through the course but had failed. He could fly the plane all right, but he failed because when they would give him single-engine procedure—that is, they would cut an engine and have him go through the emergency—he would become flustered and confused, and he'd lose control of the airplane. He just couldn't handle it. So they asked me to handle him and see if I couldn't get him to solo. So I took him out and trained him regularly, but I didn't give him any single-engine work; I just trained him to fly the airplane, and he learned to handle it very well. Of course, I had to go back and give him the emergencies, so I started to do that. One day we were circling an auxiliary field, and I cut an engine on him, and the plane started to turn into the field; we were at 1,000 feet and it would have been a death turn if it had kept going. I forced it and tried to control it, but I couldn't move it. Finally I kicked the rudder real hard, and it gave loose. It was then that I learned Blaine had frozen on the controls. I straightened it up, and he broke out laughing. He said, "Wait 'til I tell the boys in the barracks that Old Man Blaine froze on the controls!" Anyway, it was a dangerous moment, but we got over that. I got him trained so that he managed all right. He finally checked it out and was able to handle it.

Another dangerous situation occurred with a student who was a captain in the army but was then moving on as a pilot in the Air Force. He was one of the best students I ever had because he really learned well and followed everything perfectly. But they had us change the students from one seat to the other, and I sent him up one day in the other seat, where he wasn't familiar. He had been flying in the pilot's seat where the students always flew, and I had him move over to the co-pilot's seat with another student in the pilot's seat. When he came in, he landed hard and bounced and took off again, but in the process, he broke one of the landing gear enough that it wouldn't retract. This was an emergency on the base, and they had him fly around so they could check the airplane from the air to see what the matter was, and they couldn't solve it. So he had one wheel up and one wheel down, and everyone was wondering what was going to happen. When I went up in the tower and consulted with the control officers, we knew that he would have to land without wheels and scoot in on his belly. We assumed that this wheel would fold; if it did he'd be safe, but if it didn't he'd be in trouble. So the student retracted the good wheel and came in to land with the one wheel down. Fortunately it folded, and he made a nice belly landing right there on the runway. He was such a fine man it didn't cause us any trouble.

While in this training phase we moved into these AT-9s with other students, and it's remarkable what we did in training those students. In my first experience as a cadet, we were afraid of those airplanes, but now we were training our students to fly those airplanes and land them at night without lights, with just dim runway lights on and with only one engine. We'd take off, fly up into the black, and circle and come downwind; I'd cut an engine on the student, and he'd have to go through the procedure and control himself there in the dark and get it under steady control, flying on one engine. He couldn't leave the wheels down or the flaps down because the plane didn't have enough power to maintain its altitude on one engine, so he would leave them up until we made our final turn. Then he'd put the wheels down and give it what flaps we needed to come in, but he could only use one engine. It was always a matter of adjusting the plane because as you release the pull on that one engine, you'd adjust it to hold the pull, and then you took the power off and had to readjust the control so it didn't turn on you. It was a lot of heavy rudder pressure and then adjusting the trim tabs and so on.

When flying in the dark, we didn't want lights in the cockpit because then we couldn't see outside. So we were up there in the black. When we put our wheels down, we didn't have a visible indicator inside the cockpit. To confirm that the wheels were down, we had a little flashlight, and we'd flash it out the window and look on top of each engine where there was a little pin that would pop up when the wheels were down and locked. On one occasion, the cadet I was training was so busy, he could hardly keep track of what he was doing. So, I flashed my flashlight out the window and looked at my pin and said, "Got a pin." I then gave it to him, and he flashed it out and said, "Got a pin." And I wasn't sure whether he had one or not. But here we were coming pretty close to the ground, and I thought, "You know I didn't see my pin. I was just too quick." So I flashed out again, and there wasn't a pin. I knew what he'd done. There were two levers: first you put the selector down, and then you had to put the hydraulic pressure lever down; he had forgotten that second lever. I shoved it down and felt the wheels go in.

We had little incidents like that popping up all the time. I had another student—another of my great ones—who I was training on instruments, and we were 50 miles away from the air base at another radio range. We had directional radios that helped us find our position by the broadcasted signals. They transmitted an A and an N from the stations, and when the A and the N overlapped and fit together, we'd hear a steady hum. That was the beam. We had to learn how to fly by ear to locate our position. This boy was doing an excellent job of flying, and he solved his problem and located himself properly. When flying over the station, you could tell when you were right over it because you could hear what they call the cone of silence, so you knew your exact position. Then you'd make your turn, go into a letdown procedure, come back on the beam, hit the station again, and then be ready to pop out of the clouds and land. Of course all of this was done as a simulated situation—it was daylight, and I was observing for him because he had a hood to restrict his vision to instruments only. He located his position well and started his descent, but he forgot the essential ingredient of his procedure—he didn't put his wheels down. However, the plane contained a safety feature: if the pilot slowed the throttles while the wheels were not down, warning horns would begin to buzz in the cockpit. So they started to buzz a little bit, but this student was very intent on his flying and didn't pay any attention to them. He was just doing a great job flying. I finally leaned over to nudge him and asked, "Say, do those horns bother you any?" He looked at me quickly and said, "No, sir." He was oblivious to them! So I let him go a little longer, and then I finally leaned over and said, "Well, they would certainly bother me." So he reached over and pushed the button that turned the horns off. We came back over to the station and came down to a 200-foot level and then I put the wheels down—if it had been an actual situation without an instructor present, he would have landed without wheels.

D-Day and B-25s as a Training Aircraft

On June 6, 1944, the D-Day invasion in Europe took place, and the air force activity increased with many pilots being assigned to the war areas. I expected to be rotated overseas also. The rule was that the returning combat pilots would be put into instructor slots, and all of us who had never been overseas would be transferred out. I was therefore looking forward to that new experience. About that time they determined to use the B-25 Mitchell, a heavy warplane, as the advanced trainer, and a contingent of 15 experienced pilots—mostly war veterans—were sent to Randolph Field to train as instructors in these planes. Surprisingly, three of us non-combat men were included in the group, and in November 1944, I was sent back to Randolph to learn this new equipment. This assignment was fortunate in that it removed me from a list to rotate overseas. Most of the combat veterans had flown the B-25 in the war, and others had flown B-24s and B-17s.

The B-25 was chosen because it was one of the nicest planes to fly in the entire arsenal. It was said that only one other plane flew nicer and easier than a B-25, and that was a P-38. They said that on a P-38, you could fill out the "Form 1" (the flight report) when you were only ten feet off the ground! They said it was so easy to fly that it would land itself. The B-25 gained international fame on April 18, 1942. On that day, Lieutenant Colonel Jimmy Doolittle gave America's wartime morale a boost when he led 16 B-25s off the deck of the carrier *Hornet* for a raid on Tokyo, taking the war to the Japanese homeland. Design for the aircraft began in 1938, and over 11,000 Mitchells were built.

My first flight in the B-25 was a wonder. It felt like the whole house was going up in the air! My instructor was a former civilian flyer named Dal Zell. He was deliberate. He also drank heavily, and I was warned about him. However, he always flew very sober. This instructor took two of us up with him, and I sat in the back while he trained the other pilot for 2½ hours. This fellow he was training had been a co-pilot in B-17s, but he had already been through this training course, and he could not handle a B-25. I guess as a co-pilot he hadn't done anything but ride along. Now he was frustrated because they couldn't get him to handle it safely. Then Dal Zell put me in the seat and said, "I'll fly it around once and then you do it." So he took it off and landed it and explained what he was doing all the way along. Then he said, "Now you go ahead and do it." So I took it off and did what he told me, and he helped me with the adjustment of the controls and so on. I brought it back and landed it as he talked me through it. After we made about four landings, he says, "Well, let's go back to the main base." As we got out of the airplane he said, "Well, you can fly it as good as I can now. They say you've got to have four hours before you can take it." So, I got the four hours and took it solo. I was again the first of my group to fly the plane solo, ahead of all the combat fliers. The reason was simply that we followed procedure. We were schooled in doing it right, and we immediately learned what to do and handled it and checked it out. It was a real thrill to fly that plane.

We spent that month in all the phases of B-25s in emergencies and then cross-country flying. We took off one day for Albuquerque, an overnight, cross-country flight. The other kid, who didn't fly very well, started the flight; halfway up we changed over, and I took it. He cut an engine on us, and we flew on single engine for about half the way over, and it flew very well. It was an ideal trainer. The instructor on this flight was a little slow on the uptake. I'd been to Albuquerque before, and as we moved over the mountains to the east, I saw the lay of the field and noticed the way the traffic was landing. Since we were in perfect position to drop down and come in, I cut back on the power and asked him if he wanted me to go ahead and land it, and he said, "Well, huh, what do you mean?" And I said, "Well, there's the traffic pattern. They're landing this way. So should I get into the pattern and go ahead?" And he was still a little confused. And he said, "Well, yeah." By that time I was on the base leg ready to turn on the final approach, and he was still catching up on where we were. I just dropped down gently and swooped in, coming around putting the wheels down, and made the final approach. When you go into a strange field you don't always know your distances quite the same. I carried just a little power on it, which we ordinarily didn't do in training, but doing so gave a lot more control. So I managed it quite easily over the fence and then down on the runway. It was one of those landings where you can feel the tires just brushing the gravel on the runway. We rolled to a slow turn for the parking area, and he looked at me and said, "Blankity-blank! That was a blankity-blank grease job." So I knew he was pleased about it.

Later on Dal Zell was transferred to our base in Douglas. He came as a maintenance officer. He had to have his instrument card renewed, and because I was an instrument pilot he asked, "Hey, will you give me a check-out on the instruments?" He wasn't too sharp on them. So I took him out, and we worked a problem or two and I gave him his rating. I said to him, "Okay do you want to take it home?" He said, "No, you take it. I learned a long time ago to keep my hands off when you're in the air." That was kind of a pleasant comment to get. He remarked to me one day when a couple of other fellows were around, "I've always thought you were the best military pilot I've ever worked with." Well, I don't know if that was true, but what it meant to me was that I had prayed and desired that the Lord would bless me to be able to manage this phase of my life well and to excel, and I felt it an answer to my prayer that I had achieved something of proficiency at least. In a month I returned to Douglas as a B-25 instructor and instructed for a full year in B-25s. The B-25 was a noisy plane. Even today if a B-25 flew over I'd know what it was. The AT-17s and other planes we had been using were phased out.

Because I was designated as an instrument instructor I flew most of my time with my students under the hood. We would take cadets out and train them on instruments after they had learned to manage the airplane, and an interesting part of that procedure was that they had to have a certain number of single-engine landings to complete their training, but they were not allowed to land it without an instructor. So, for that year 95% of all the landings I ever made in that B25 were on one engine. I was expected to give them single-engine landings on nearly every flight, cutting off one or the other as they approached the field. During that time, one of my good friends had an engine catch on fire, and the plane crashed. The hazards were still there. In all my years of flying I logged about 2,300 hours. I spent 700 hours in the B-25. I remember saying once, "I've spent more hours flying than I have in a car!"

Birth of Lee Ann

During the summer of 1944, with Mildred showing the evidence of pregnancy, we were still both in leadership callings in the ward. I was released as the high priest group leader and made president of the MIA and Mildred continued serving as the Relief Society president. I was also still the group leader of the high priests. Then my younger brother Blauer was assigned to our air base as a meteorologist. We spent 10 months together, he living, of course, on the base. We did a lot of things together, both flying and entertainment. Mildred became very ill with morning sickness and stayed with her mother at times. This problem soon abated, however. We had time to go with ward members on outings and also to explore together some of the desert that surrounded Douglas. We went on a camping trip to the Chiricahua Mountains and occasionally visited people we knew and explored the surrounding areas. My brother Sam completed his mission in Nogales and spent a day or two with us. Some of our close friends in the Army included Kenneth Cluff and M. J. Rudd.

Just before Christmas, Mildred went into labor. We took her to the hospital in Douglas, and on December 21, 1944, our lovely daughter, Lee Ann was born. We had been living in an apartment, and while Mildred was in the hospital I moved our residence to a small cottage on B Avenue not far from her mother's home, and she went home there with me. Life with its involvements and responsibilities had quickly descended upon us.

The war had been raging both in Europe and in the Pacific, with the Allies making substantial progress. We learned how awful the air war was for the flyers in Europe from those who returned as instructors at the base. My flying was now over a larger area in the B-25. I was mostly instructing on instruments, not having a set group of cadets. I also flew with returned combat men so they could keep up their qualifications. For a period I flew with Chinese students who did not understand English. I'd line them all up in the ready room and I'd give them a sentence of instruction, and the interpreter would talk for five minutes on what we just told them, and then I would give them a little more. I'd explain what they were supposed to do, and then I'd take them out and point. Most of the training we were giving them was navigation. Almost every night I would go out on a night flight. One night I might go east to Big Spring, Texas, and the next night I might go out to San Diego, California.

I remember I was approaching the base one day, and I heard someone on the radio say, "Airplane with an engine on fire, what is your position?" And somebody said, "Right over the airfield." I looked over the air base, and there came a B-25 with a big stream of smoke behind it. Then a ball of fire burst out on the wing, and it started into a slow turn right over the field. I just sat there in my airplane. I thought, "Please get out of there." I saw one parachute come out, and then the plane went in and crashed. That was terrible luck right there. That's the only real bad crash I saw. The other fellow didn't get out; it turned out to be a fellow named K. D. Daniels with whom I had trained and flown for quite a while. The fellow that parachuted out injured himself and died on the way down. This was near the end of the war.

End of the War

I continued to expect to be rotated overseas. Just prior to being named for transfer overseas in April, Germany surrendered. This reduced our training considerably, but I still flew a lot. Of course it was a great relief that we had Hitler down and out, one of the great evil influences of the world. But I had a strong feeling that we were not through yet, that the enemy was still there. I never did trust Russia, and I always felt like we hadn't won this thing because we hadn't been able to put Russia down. In the 1930s we used to hear horror stories about Russia and the communists, about the experiences of people who were gobbled up by that secret police system and persecuted and killed and so on. Suddenly those stories stopped because Hitler came on the scene, and we started getting horror stories about him. Nobody talked about Russia any more. But I knew that Russia's government was an evil one, as bad as Hitler's. It astounded me—I never could understand why Roosevelt and Churchill were not facing the facts. I lamented that for 25 years after, with the feeling that if they had played their cards right, they could have restricted Russia and put the clamps on them. They didn't necessarily need to fight them, but they didn't have to give them part of Germany and freedom all over Europe. This was confusing to me, and I just felt like we had not ended the problem when Hitler caved in. I eventually came to understand through my study of history that if we got out of tight spots we'd always get into another one anyway. If we had solved our problem with Russia at that time, we would still have been back in some hot water with some other problem. But at that time we were still fighting Japan. We didn't have much sympathy for them. It was a fearsome thing because we were facing terrible challenges with the fanaticism of the Japanese as we moved into Iwo Jima and Okinawa, with the prospect of eventually invading Japan proper. I expected to eventually be rotated to the Pacific Theater.

We learned of the death of President Roosevelt and of the surrender of the forces of Hitler in Europe and the fact that once again the lights of that continent could be turned on. My thoughts come back to the feeling I had—that all of us had who are old enough reflect on what we were doing when the news burst upon us of the attack on Pearl Harbor in 1941—that day the lights began to go out in our country. It was a terrible feeling. The lights had already largely gone out throughout Europe, and subsequently we all passed through a period of terrible travail before the lights came back on again. We used to sing a song in those days, "When the Lights Come on Again All over the World." [2]

However, when the lights did come back on, they revealed an unspeakable destruction of many of the cities, the horror of suffering among the populations, and especially the barbaric attempt to eliminate the Jews by the Nazi regime. Japan was still fighting, and we looked for a great struggle to overcome their empire. Thus the war in Europe ended in April 1945. In July of that year there was a notice in the newspaper that a big ammunition dump had exploded in Alamogordo, New Mexico. It was so big they said that people over in Arizona had even seen the lights from the explosion. The meaning of the event became evident when an atomic bomb was dropped on Japan in August. A second bomb finished Japanese resistance, and suddenly the whole world was at peace. When they dropped the bomb on Japan, we wondered, "What kind of a world are we in?"

Victory Flight

In October 1945 a great victory flight was scheduled with airplanes from many bases, including ours. We were to fly over Los Angeles as a victory armada. We trained for it for a few days, and I really enjoyed the flying. On the day of the big flight, I took off, as did many others, in a B-25 with a copilot. Soon after we were airborne we received the word by radio that the great demonstration had been canceled. As I returned to land I noticed the plane landing ahead of me had aborted his landing and decided to go around for another try. I knew that his giving full power to take off again would create heavy turbulence as I followed. However, I judged that by coming in low I would miss the rough air. I had just flared out for my landing when we hit the turbulence. The only recourse I had was to give full power to keep from being upset in my landing. We staggered across the entire runway, barely avoiding a crash. Happily we survived the

2. Collected Works, p. 120

turbulence and regained our momentum, which allowed us to make another attempt at landing, which I accomplished easily enough. This was my last flight while on active duty in the Army and was one of the closest calls I ever had.

Determination to Leave the Military

With the surrender of Japan in August 1945 training activity dropped again. I was now a first lieutenant. I considered continuing in the Army, which I had begun to enjoy. I had no promise of income outside of the military and thought this could bring security and adequate income for my family. However, Mildred didn't accept the idea of remaining in the army. She said, "No, sir. We are going back to Utah, and you are to finish your college education." I knew she was right, and we submitted my request for separation from the service. With the war over, soldiers would just take the uniform off, go home, and get a job. We left Douglas and the ward members with some regrets, including Mildred's family, the Huishes, Marvin and Vadna Follett, the Kirby family, and many others. The soldiers who had passed through Douglas had done a good job of marrying the local Douglas Ward girls. Most of them were fine LDS boys. We started for Utah about November 15, 1945. Our drive took us through Clifton, St. Johns, Gallup, Cortez, Monticello, Moab, and Price. After nearly four years in a southern sunny climate and open skies, we felt like prairie dogs going down into our hole to spend the winter. The skies were more cloudy and the temperature much cooler. We were welcomed by my family. We stayed with my parents for a short time and then moved into the home of my sister Sarah since her husband, Prescott, had been transferred away temporarily.[3]

We had the purpose to return to Utah where I would then pursue my education. On December 19, 1945, I was given my discharge. We drove through Utah and on to Boise, Idaho, where I was officially separated from military service. After I was discharged, I continued in the reserves for about five years, but I was only active for a year.

---

3. The economy was improving with an annual salary in 1945 being nearly $2400. A loaf of bread cost 9¢, a gallon of gas was 15¢, and a gallon of milk was 62¢.

During 1946 I was still enlisted in the Air Force Reserve and played "hooky" from university classes to go to Hill Field where I was able to check out an AT-6, a single-engine aircraft. This continued into 1947, and I spent two weeks in the summer on active duty at Hill Field. At that time I was deeply involved in school, and I was very earnest and active about my Church responsibilities. They began to organize units in the reserves, but their meetings were all on Sunday, and I thought, I don't want to do that. At that time I definitively ended my military involvement. When I left the reserves, I was promoted to captain, a rank I had operated in for many months while in active duty but had never received.

PERIOD III
New Beginnings and Challenges

Chapter 7

STARTING OVER

"I have always known that the gospel is the same for me whether I serve in positions of responsibility or not. In my childhood and long before I was called to leadership, I knew through the spirit of the Lord that I was a person set apart to live by the covenants of the gospel throughout my entire life. This is true for each of you and your families before, during, and after your service and call to leadership. The gospel is the same for the members of the Church as it is for the Apostles." [1]

University of Utah

As we settled into this changed program of our lives, I registered at the University of Utah to pursue a bachelor's degree, financed by the government's Servicemen's Readjustment Act of 1944, commonly known as the G.I. Bill. My service in the U.S. Army entitled me to 45 credit hours of advanced military science and shortened my time in school, even though I took a lighter course load in order to support my family. I had finished three quarters at BYU before my mission, so I already had some done. I transferred to the U of U in December 1945 and took courses in many of the basics such as English and biology, but I settled on a study of history and languages. I focused on

---

1. Collected Works, p. 158

courses in German, Spanish, and Portuguese and in history, where I covered both ancient and modern history with some higher studies in Western history. I studied German under Llewellyn McKay and Professor Wyler and History under Dr. Dahlgliesh and Dr. Leland L. Creer, the head of the department.

Prescott and Sarah had a cow that I milked twice daily, and then I walked 1/4 mile to the Orem interurban train, riding to Salt Lake and taking the streetcar to the University. I was earnest in my desire to be blessed in my schoolwork, and with our busy Sunday activities I determined that Sunday would not be a day for study because I felt that would be the same as working. My brother, Samuel, attended the university with me much of the time. Sam always seemed to know more about each subject than I did. There were many former servicemen in school, and I found a number of former companions from high school and from my mission as well as associates in the military. The university was becoming crowded, and classes began to occupy temporary Army buildings adjacent to the campus. I spent most of my later classes in these buildings. As I studied through the fall, winter, and spring quarters during 1946, 1947, and 1948, I did well in my languages and tended to excel in history.

My university days were not all easy. As I neared the time for graduation [June 1948], I had a mountain of work to complete before the specified time. I worried that I would miss the deadline. Over the years of college training, I had been earnest in my prayers and had constantly asked that the Lord would bless and guide me. But I was not aware of any special help received, even though I had made good progress. One Sunday, about a week before graduation, as Mildred and I visited with Dick and Bonnie Platt, Dick asked if I were ready to graduate. I told him that my work was still incomplete and that there was some doubt whether I could complete it. "Oh," he said, "you'll make it all right. Let's look in the newspaper. They just published the list of graduates." He began by reading the names of those who would graduate with honors, and he included my name. Of course, I knew he was only teasing, and I laughed as I said, "You can't fool me with your jokes." Then he said, "Well, isn't this your address?" and he read out our address. I said, "Let me see the paper."

As I read my name among those who were to receive honors, my eyes filled with tears, and an inward light filled my whole being with understanding. As clearly as in a vision I saw how, over the years, in quiet, unseen ways, God had been listening to my prayers and had overshadowed me with his blessed influence to bring me through triumphant![2] I was shocked and humbled with the assurance that due to my prayers and attitude, Heavenly Father had helped me overcome what had been finally a great struggle. Only Mildred attended my graduation; my family was not able to come. The ceremony was held outside in the University Stadium. I graduated with a BA degree in history from the University of Utah. The next year in the winter I undertook the beginning of a master's degree in history. I pursued this study for another two quarters, but I finally desisted because of my employment and, in part, because of my being called as a bishop of our ward. The change in education plans helped determine my career course in home construction.

This period of three years of university study required great effort, especially since I was working too. Mildred and I were also deeply involved in our Church assignments. All this activity was very rewarding to both Mildred and I, and we felt great growth in our lives in the gospel. We attended the temple frequently, performing ordinances for family ancestors whom Mother had assembled in her extended search.

Establishment of Home and Economic Struggles

The return from the Army and the project of attending the University was a fundamental change in both my life and Mildred's. I was greatly impressed with her willingness to go through privations and extra efforts to begin a life, almost without resources, in a new kind of world after World War II. We lived on a limited income as I worked part-time in carpentry with my father. I began to work one-half of each day and go to school the other half. We went from jobbing to remodeling and eventually to home building. By the time I had finished school, he and I had made a partnership, and we

---

2. Collected Works, pp. 491–492

worked together to develop some land and build homes on it. Over the intervening years our business continued to advance as opportunity afforded.

Mildred never complained about our limited circumstances and was always happy and positive, and I was gratified that she who earlier had lived more comfortably was able to assume the "pioneer attitude." We lived comfortably but very frugally. She was a devoted mother and a most capable housewife. Because during the war household appliances were not to be found, we worked with coal stoves for cooking and heating. We were able to buy a refrigerator and finally a washing machine, but it was the type that required rinsing and then hanging up the clothes to dry.

Our home life was tranquil and happy. When Cory, our first son, was born on February 1, 1947, we began to feel the beauty of parental responsibility. When I first saw him I was greatly shocked with what seemed to be a stretching out of his features, obviously a normal result of his birth. But all was well. Mildred had decided to have him at the LDS Hospital rather than the Cottonwood Maternity Home due to a cold she was struggling with at the time. Mildred generally enjoyed good health but had some trouble with morning sickness and a back disorder of a minor nature. I was always comforted by the ready acceptance she showed in living on limited and sometimes primitive circumstances.

These years were loaded with many other special activities. We were fully busy with family activities and Church responsibilities. We lived in the Granger 2nd Ward, and my former bishop, Merrill Petersen was our bishop once again. I was called to lead the teachers quorum, and Mildred was soon called to the stake Primary board. I was visited one evening by the stake Young Men presidency and asked to take charge of the men's athletic program, which I did for several years, first in the Oquirrh and then the North Jordan stakes.

We were at home among our former friends and many relatives and began numerous activities. Several of my former missionary companions were all recently married, so we began meeting with them and their wives in a social association nearly each month. These included Finn Paulsen, Lynn Sorensen, Richard Platt, John

Rich, Jim Faust, Lloyd Hicken, Ray Duckworth, Glenn Erickson, and later some others. This was a very dear and close association that these dear friends have held together since 1939.

My father gave me a half-acre of land near his home, and Mildred and I decided to build a residence on it. I had saved about $2,000 while in the service, and we undertook the construction of one of those basement homes that were then common. I dug the foundation with a team of horses, formed the walls and poured the concrete. With a top on it we moved in. We had coal stoves, not much furniture and a rustic way of living. We had one bedroom, a living area and a kitchen and bath. I finally took out a loan of $6,000 to build the upstairs of our house. I did the work myself with Father constantly on hand to help. With a mortgage on the home I feared such a burden since I had never had a debt before. Glenda, our second daughter, was born on July 14, 1949, and we were crowded in our quarters. We eventually sold the house and rented a home on 3500 South.

After graduating from college I decided to continue in the building business. I purchased a lot on Granger Drive and, with Cory at my side, began to build another home. We were able to buy a few necessities with our income. I bought Mildred a good washing machine and a gas stove, and she handled the home very well along with her frequent pregnancies. I finally decided to finish the house on Granger Drive and sell it, again to be free of debt. Then I built another house near my father's home and sold it as well, and finally decided to build our permanent residence on 3835 South on Father's property. With these struggles we were mostly free from debt.

A rather cute incident occurred when Cory was a little boy. I had him accompany me while I killed a chicken for our dinner. As I chopped off its head, and Cory, seeing that it was dead where it had been alive moments before, he looked up at me and asked, "Did you bweak it daddy? Is it bwoken?"

Church Service

While Mildred was serving in the stake Young Women organization, our stake was divided and she was called to preside over the

Young Women in the new North Jordan Stake. She had a wonderful association with the women and girls. I was also called as secretary of the stake Aaronic Priesthood and supervised the M-Men activities for a few years. There I organized and operated a very extensive basketball program.

In the meantime I was also appointed to the stake Aaronic Priesthood committee and had some excellent training under three men. One was my father, who was on the high council. The second was Owen Jacobs, who was also on the high council, and the third was Alvin Barker, who was in the stake presidency. These men had a concept of Church leadership that was not common. They wanted to get down to business about it. Their influence, I think, had a strong effect in setting my attitudes about Church activity and leadership and what ought to and could be done. So for that period of a few years, I viewed myself as being in training and was quite active about it. We attempted to visit in the wards and quorums of boys and see what their leadership was like and then give their leaders special training, setting up their goals, and pointing out the specifics of working with boys, how you can reach this boy or that boy and bring them in. In some cases we saw good success.[3] All this activity was very rewarding to both Mildred and me, and we felt great growth in our lives in the gospel.

The work in the Aaronic Priesthood program was a little different than it is today. The majority of leaders, bishoprics and advisors in quorums, didn't have a very clear insight into going after every boy. We knew, even at that period, that there was a way to do it and that it could be taught to leaders. I think what we were trying to teach them would be almost exactly the way we teach now. You see, that was the period when LeGrand Richards was the Presiding Bishop, and he had come forth with a revolutionary approach to getting hold of these boys. He didn't necessarily to do things differently, but he told stories such as, "Of this quorum of 24 teachers, 22 of them have gone on missions, and of that quorum of 15 priests, this is the 14th of them to go on a mission." Part of our problem was that the base of

---

3. Bangerter Oral History, p. 30–31

acceptance of these ideas wasn't great in the Church. If a stake president, for example, didn't have this insight and if he wouldn't make it go, nothing effective would happen. So sometimes the knowledge wasn't able to reach its destination.[4]

4. Ibid.

Chapter 8

———◆———

CALLED AS BISHOP

"I was approached soon after I was called to be a bishop by a man in a stake presidency in Salt Lake City. He said, 'I understand you have been called to be a bishop.' As I answered that I had, he didn't say what most people said when they come to compliment a new bishop. The usual conversation we had was, 'I feel sorry for you. You now have the most thankless job you will ever have in the Church.' But this great man of understanding said, 'I don't feel sorry for you. I congratulate you. If you ever wanted to be in a position to be on the firing line to give service to the Lord and touch people's lives you now have that privilege. It is one of the greatest honors that will ever come to you." [1]

A New Calling

In December 1950, our stake president, John D. Hill, asked me about my plans on building a new home. A division of the Granger Ward was planned, and he wanted to know on which side of the division I would be living, since I was being considered to be the bishop of one of the wards. I told him that we planned to stay on 3500 South for the present time. I was soon given the calling to be bishop of the Granger Ward. I was installed on the occasion of the division of the Granger Ward into the Granger First and Third Wards, and I was made the bishop of the First Ward. The two wards then continued to meet in the old chapel on 3500 South and 3200 West. When I was sustained, there were some who were challenged by the movement of the ward boundaries, and a small group of individuals did not sustain me as the bishop. It was a temporary thing, and later many

---

1. Collected Works, p. 294

of them became my most ardent supporters. As counselors I named Maurice Harmon and B. Orson Goddard. They were excellent men and performed their assignments very well. We were set apart, and I was ordained in the office of bishop by Elder Spencer W. Kimball in March 1951. My uncle, Marwood W. Bawden (Uncle Mike as we called him, though he was younger than me), was made the ward clerk. There were over 800 members of the ward at the time, and attendance was between 25–30 percent. Wards were much bigger in those days than they are now. There didn't seem to be as many problems with members, but then we weren't reaching all the members either.

We had little trouble filling positions in the ward. We would prayerfully decide who should serve in the various positions, and the Lord would bless and direct us. We did have some supervisory role over the Melchizedek Priesthood. This situation fluctuated over the years in the Church. When I was a young man recently returned from a mission and assigned as second counselor in the bishopric, the bishop assigned me to supervise the elders quorums. We had two of them in our ward. I understood the emphasis there to mean that I was to be active in it. So I worked as a sort of an overseer of the elders quorum presidencies and visited in their meetings, and I neglected the deacons quorums, where I should have been. By the time I was bishop the emphasis had changed again, and we were told in those days that the Melchizedek Priesthood quorums were to have nothing to do with the bishop. There was no good method to correlate with them. They would come to the same priesthood meeting, and we would assign them rooms to meet in, but that was all. So it was kind of a swinging of the pendulum. Now things are under a different arrangement, which I'm convinced is according to the basic and doctrinal intent of the gospel. [2]

As a bishop, I felt a need to prioritize my assigned responsibilities. I did so in the following manner: number one, general secretary of the Aaronic Priesthood; number two, MIA superintendent; number three, Sunday School superintendent (I didn't concern myself much with the Melchizedek Priesthood); number four, chair-

2. Bangerter Oral History, p. 38

man of the ward teaching committee, which was our business at that time; number five then, of course, was the women's organizations of Relief Society, Primary, and MIA.[3] We directed our attention to the Aaronic Priesthood and organized the auxiliaries. The stake presidency was available to us, but they assumed that a new bishopric had watched other bishops do it, and they should know how to go ahead. They held their regular leadership meetings and tried to train us in Aaronic Priesthood work and so on. My father, who was on the high council, tried to give me special attention without overstepping his assignments; I think I was reasonably well oriented. We had handbooks, and my predecessor was called to the high council, so he was available. I think we knew about what was expected of us.[4]

I tried to pay close attention to the Aaronic Priesthood and then the senior Aaronic Priesthood. At that period Thorpe Isaacson was in the Presiding Bishopric, and he gave a strong emphasis to that work. As a bishopric we undertook to do much of the work in what is now called the prospective elders program. In our ward we had a fair amount of success. I feel that I was not adequately prepared and didn't have sufficient understanding, but the little effort that we made brought good results. We still have men in that area and some who have moved elsewhere who began their activity in the Church at that time. I remember I decided that I should bring all my adult priests—I had nine of them in the ward—together and hold a meeting. I went personally and invited them all. Seven of the nine came. That was a revelation to me that these men would respond and that they had an interest.

As mentioned earlier, one of the major focuses of our labors in the bishopric at that time centered on the Aaronic Priesthood and the Young Men's MIA. We weren't getting all our boys. We had a handicap during the period in which I was bishop—the Korean War began, and we were not able to send the boys on missions. (My brother Norman was drafted and spent a year in Korea himself.) So to some extent we were frustrated in bringing them a crowning glory, a capstone of priesthood responsibility. I think we sent only two

---

3. Ibid., p. 37
4. Ibid., p. 32

boys on missions while I was bishop. They were, incidentally, the only two boys who were eligible to go under the government restrictions, so we obtained 100 percent in that regard. We were present every Sunday in our Aaronic Priesthood quorum meetings. This is different from what I indicated was the case while I was a counselor earlier in the bishopric. As bishop I took personal charge and responsibility of the priests quorum, but I had advisors to assist me. They carried out the detail that was outlined by the bishop and generally gave the instruction to the quorum. [5]

We also had a focus on youth activity. At the time we had a youth organization that operated as a separate auxiliary, known as the MIA or the Mutual Improvement Association. The program was successful; however, we didn't pay enough attention to those who were not involved. It was a day when the program was more important than the individual. Scouting was moderately successful. I have seen it done better. [6] Awards for attendance were offered to the youth, and this had a way of maintaining their interest. The young men and young women upon reaching age 16 or 17 would often remain in the organization, but there was always some fallout. Often they would organize their own activities and gather in groups as they desired. The M-Man and Gleaner programs were also coming into focus during those years as well. This was the forerunner to the young single adult program of today. There was not as much permissiveness and transgression amongst the youth at that time either. Bishops were not instructed in ways to assist the youth in trouble as they are today.

The Sunday School received great emphasis as President David O. McKay had been over it for many years. We always had a good selection of teachers, and the program was run very professionally. In some cases, members felt that Sunday School was more important than sacrament meeting, and since they could receive the sacrament during Sunday School, they felt they did not need to go to sacrament meeting. This contributed to a lower percentage of attendance at sacrament meeting.

---

5. Bangerter Oral History, p. 40
6. Bangerter Oral History, p. 41

We dedicated a lot of time to accomplishing a high result in our ward teaching (which is much like home teaching today). We quickly organized for solid improvement, moving in one week from 25 to 75 percent. We encouraged the brethren to "Just get it done!" Shortly we were achieving 95 percent in our efforts. Some men did excellent work as ward teachers. The older men would take the younger Aaronic Priesthood boys out with them, and each companionship would have 4–5 families to visit.

The Primary organization worked well. The families seemed to expect their children to be active in Primary, so we had most of the children attending. We seemed to have good success in getting our people to respond to callings in the Primary. In those days, turnover in Church callings was minimal.

The Relief Society president worked closely with the bishop and was very helpful in administering the welfare needs to those requiring assistance. She was heavily involved in leading the women of the ward, and they were always the backbone of the work force. There was a much stronger emphasis on canning and food storage then than there is today. They had sewing projects and other assignments, which they filled capably and well. They also were much more successful in their visiting teaching than most of the men were in their ward teaching.

With regards to our sacrament meetings, we worked hard at making them interesting and vibrant. Sometimes we would have people from outside the ward speak. Our fast meetings were quite good but often less effective than we would desire. They seemed to have a good spirit to them and were much improved over the spiritual flatness that I had observed in my youth.

In those days the collection of tithing was not as structured as it is today. We probably only collected between a fourth and a fifth of the amount that should have been collected. Full-tithe payers were not reported, but the leaders were all faithful in that regard. Fast offerings were collected from door to door much the same way we do today. Each bishop did his best to protect the sacred funds of the Church; these funds were not given out freely, but many people were assisted—many of them were not fully worthy members.

Each ward was also involved in welfare assignments. Our stake had a welfare farm, and the bishops were given responsibility over getting the people to work on the farms. This was a big responsibility for the bishops. At times the bishop would simply ask everyone to show up, and sometimes there would be a good response. During some periods, we had assignments every week.

There were some inconveniences presented by the old Granger Ward building. Our system of interviewing members was not well defined, and calls made to leaders in the organizations were done much more casually. We didn't have an office where we could close the door and get down to business. I didn't have an office in the chapel or in my home. After I had been released as bishop and was stake president, I undertook to build a new home, and I had it in mind that the one thing I had to have in the new home was an office, a place where I could sit down with people and close the door so I wouldn't have to chase my family into the bedroom while I met with people. The ward clerk would receive the tithing in the meetings and do his business at home. We had no filing cabinets, no typewriters, no duplicating machinery, and no telephone.[7]

We knew that the old chapel was obsolete and that it was on the site that should go for a business, so we knew we had to rebuild. I helped procure the new site, but I was released before we built the chapel. We had two wards operating in the same building. There was room for two groups by good scheduling. We didn't have any trouble. We had had the experience before for a time with the Second Ward. Everyone was prepared for it.

During those years, not too many new people moved into the ward. We did have some German and Dutch immigrants who joined us in our community, but growth was generally slow. New people were accepted whole-heartedly into our midst. At that time there might have been a half dozen nonmembers living in the ward area. There were few bad feelings amongst ward members. Any fractions and disputes of the old days in Granger were never brought up, and peace and harmony reigned. The widows and single members were often watched over by the Relief Society, and each organization

---

7. Bangerter Oral History, p. 35

would try hard to include them in their activities. Ward socials were held regularly throughout the year, and many people would participate. Also by that time, with several other wards in the area, community activities became more and more localized, rather than including everyone in the community. Some of that activity later did not have any Church affiliation. Church discipline was fairly infrequent. Some of it centered on teachings and some on transgressions. We did not investigate things as deeply then as we are expected to do today. Generally it was a united ward.

We had a very good relationship with the stake and the stake leadership. My attitude in becoming bishop was that the stake president was my presiding officer and that I was there to carry out his wishes and to cooperate with him in every way I could. I found that by having this attitude, enduring warmth developed between the president and me. It gave him strength. He felt that he had the support of the bishops. I had been in bishops' meetings where there was opposition to the stake president, and it was a good feeling to be able to stand up and defend him. I gained a testimony of the virtue in that attitude. I think it had some influence in my being selected as the succeeding stake president. [8]

My feeling about my service in the bishopric is tempered by various conditions. I feel that it was another of those training episodes in my life, where I knew more about how to do it after I was released than while I served. I don't mean that I was ineffective. I think I served with at least average ability. [9]

Family Tragedies and Blessings

I entered my calling as bishop with complete devotion. However, we did not foresee the trials that would soon beset us. I had scarcely gotten oriented to my calling, when Mildred delivered our fourth child. Mildred Elizabeth was born on April 13, 1951. She lived but a few moments; we had our first great family sorrow, and I had my first funeral as a bishop. With the help of many friends and my family, we secured a burial site in the Taylorsville Cemetery. Mildred recovered

---

8. Bangerter Oral History, p. 47

9. Bangerter Oral History, p. 48

from the birth and the sorrow, but she did not seem to return to the same vitality as before. On July 4 of that year she had a fainting spell, and we had her examined. It was found that she had leukemia, which suddenly meant to me her eventual passing from this life. This shocking and humbling condition led me to a feeling that if we had sufficient faith she could be healed. As I fasted and prayed, attended the temple, and saw the faith of my family, Mildred seemed to rally and passed through her next year with many high and low points. We never discussed the threat to her life, but she lived valiantly throughout the year, generally doing most of the household chores and managing the children. We had several treatments to reduce her enlarged spleen, but eventually her condition continued to fail. Dr. LeRoy Wirthlin gave her good attention. I had several special prayers and much fasting and some promise of her well-being, but no final healing. I often blessed Mildred as I left for necessary appointments, and these gave her comfort. She did not suffer great pain. We had great support and loving expressions from our family, members of the ward, and special neighbors. Through this trial the Holy Spirit often comforted me, and I had a remarkable moment when I knew the Savior was near and blessing us.

At this time I had a powerful reconfirmation of the truthfulness of the Book of Mormon. Too many Latter-day Saints have read the Book of Mormon and have never asked the Lord if it is true or not because they think, well, why should I, I believe it already. I don't believe that is good enough. There will come a time when each individual will have to have more than that to stand on as faith and testimony; all will eventually be under an obligation to make a covenant about the Book of Mormon with our Father in Heaven, who promises that on certain conditions He will reveal to us the truthfulness of that book. [10] If we desire to know the truth of those things, there is a process by which it can be made known to us by the power of the Holy Ghost. I think most Latter-day Saints have heard of that promise. At that time in my life I had filled a mission, served in the armed forces, married, and served in a bishopric, and I had never proved that promise because I simply felt that it did not apply to me.

---

10. Collected Works, p. 231

I did not question the Book of Mormon. I believed it. I thought I understood it. But the day came when I had to have a little stronger evidence and strength; I reached out for that promise, and the Lord answered my prayer and redeemed His promise to me. I feel that any member of this Church who does not have that testimony of the gospel has not kept the commandment. It is our duty and our obligation to seek for the testimony that will give assurance that God really lives. When we have that, we won't have any problem reconciling our secular ideas with our religious faith because we will know the truth as it relates to what the Lord has given us. The Lord requires that we get a testimony. It is not simply a matter of reading the Book of Mormon through. [11]

My strengthened testimony of the Book of Mormon gave me great comfort at this time. Our lives were filled with fasting and earnest prayer, and the endearment Mildred and I felt grew into a celestial nature. Many blessings and comfort came to us at this period, and we recognized the choiceness and greatness of each other. I cannot express the struggles I passed through during that period, but I received many spiritual assurances that blessed my testimony. Her tragic passing occurred on August 11, 1952, at my parents' home. She too was buried in the Taylorsville Cemetery next to our baby daughter. In my sorrow, as I carried Glenda from the funeral, together with Lee Ann and Cory, I made a resolve that while I did not expect or appreciate this experience, I would bear the sorrow and the burden and prove to my Heavenly Father that I would be true to my faith and that I would pass this test.

I continued to serve as bishop and received wonderful support from the members of my ward and total help from my family. Not knowing what my situation would be like, I was able to move into the new home on 3835 South at the time of Mildred's passing. At the time of the funeral, my brother Blauer with his wife, Bessie, came to me and explained that he had considered leaving his teaching position in Murtaugh, Idaho, and entering the University of Utah to obtain a master's degree. They suggested that they would like to move in with me in our new home, conserving their resources and assisting me

---

11. Ibid., p. 216

with the children. This arrangement seemed to be a blessing to us all, and we followed through with it for about a year. I was able to continue serving as bishop and our family life became more or less normal.

Shortly after the passing of my wife, our son, Cory, contracted polio in October of 1952. At that time it began to be rampant throughout the United States. As a great favor of our Heavenly Father, Cory recovered within a few days, but during my period of leadership both as bishop and stake president, large numbers of members contracted this dreaded disease, and we dealt with people who were suffering from polio under various difficult conditions. Several of them passed away, and some became crippled to the point that they were handicapped throughout their life. There were other sicknesses of course, but this was one of the most dominant and trying experiences in the matter of health at that time. Much consideration was given to this problem in the direction of the LDS Hospital in Salt Lake City, of which I was later a member of the board.

About this same time Lee Ann broke her leg playing at the school and quickly became accustomed to moving agilely on crutches. When she about two years old, she had also been found to have lost most of her hearing. Mildred had undertaken to have her treated and to begin speech therapy, but she was unable to hear all that she needed in her schooling. On taking note of all this Cory said disappointedly one day, "Dad, Lee Ann has a cast, crutches, glasses, and a hearing aid, and I don't have ANYTHING!"

Working with my father, our home building and construction continued with a reasonable income. However, with my responsibilities as bishop and attending to the family, my hours at work were somewhat restricted. There were various times when financial problems seemed beyond my ability to handle, but we never entered our work without daily prayer, and the companionship and support of my father and mother brought some unexpected blessings even in financial ways that could not be explained other than as direct blessings from our Heavenly Father. The arrangement with Blauer and Bessie in our home greatly relieved my mother. My sister Glenneth who lived nearby with her husband, Lowell Wilson, was always on hand to assist with the children. I cannot forget or repay all the love and kindness and service that came to us during this difficult year, especially from my parents. They were always with me in spirit, and our lives continued in a somewhat normal vein. The membership of the ward and especially my counselors in the bishopric lifted us and blessed us in countless ways. In the bishopric we concentrated on helping families who were less active and directing them to receive their proper priesthood. We had intense activity in the temple, attending nearly each week. Thus the second year of my bishopric passed as I sought to serve well under the pressure of personal problems.

The Blessing of Geraldine

As my brother Blauer finished his master's program at the University of Utah, he was invited to the BYU Physical Education Department, and with his wife (who had given birth to their first son, James), moved to Provo. I now felt forlorn and wondered how I would be able to manage my life and family. As I prayed for help the answer came: "Now you are under no great problem at this time. What are you worried about?"

Eventually friends and relatives began to mention someone they knew who might be interesting to me in making acquaintance and finding companionship. I was totally uninterested, being much in love with the sweet memory of my marriage to Mildred. However, my brother Sam and his wife, Gloria, had made contact with a former acquaintance of Gloria's who worked as a nurse in the St. Mark's Hospital. They arranged for an evening together, and I met Geraldine Hamblin at her home in Murray. Sam and Gloria accompanied us to dinner and a visit to the county fair. I was immediately impressed with this young lady, and we had succeeding dates together. Within a week we both had the assurance that we would build our lives together. I found myself in love with Geraldine. She was 29 years of age, and the Lord had reserved her and approved of our relationship. She decided to leave her opportunity for higher education in New York City in nursing, which was her profession, and establish herself as a mother and wife. I had been moved with the feeling that regardless of how I felt about Mildred, it was right for me to reorganize my family and continue with our lives. We had what we considered a fairytale courtship. I was always involved in my ward duties, but I managed to see Geraldine every day. What a lovely, remarkable, educated, and trained person she was. Her family was connected with Jacob Hamblin, and she had a great faith and testimony, as did her parents. Geri's parents were protective of her. Her mother wanted to see the ring and thought that all I wanted was a mother for the children. So Geraldine and I arranged a meeting with them wherein we announced our intention to marry, indicating that we did not really need their approval as we were of age but that we were nevertheless asking for their blessing. This changed the relationship to a most warm association.

I had counseled with the children before announcing our plan to marry and asked them if they thought it a good idea to find a new mother. They accepted the thought enthusiastically. I asked them who we should find, and they immediately answered: "Let's get the lady who went with us swimming and picnicking." So it was unanimous at once. I took the children up to St. Mark's hospital where, as Geraldine came out of the door with some of her friends, Glenda ran up to her and shouted, "You're going to be our new mother!"

Marriage

My family and hers, along with all our friends and the membership of our ward, were greatly impressed with this wonderful happening in our lives, and we were married on October 14, 1953, in the Salt Lake Temple. Geraldine had not received her endowment until that day. President Robert Young performed the marriage. Our parents were present, and we had a small reception at my parents' home following the temple experience. As we left our reception, we found Glenda hiding in the back seat of the car expecting to go with us. Not being allowed to come along greatly disappointed her. Geraldine and I took a trip to Lake Tahoe and then drove to Yosemite and Los Angeles, where we visited her brother Ivan and his wife, Ramona, and Geri's cousin, Jay Eyre, and his wife, Afton. On this honeymoon journey, Geri asked about plans for the children, and throughout our trip we established our goals for our family and children. They included learning to play the piano, education through college, Church faithfulness and missions, the kind of manners and culture we would foster, and the type of language that would be the pattern of our home. This planning and conversation had lasting consequences. We visited Las Vegas, Hoover Dam, Kingman, and the Grand Canyon before returning home to enjoy our children, who were thrilled with the happy arrangement.

I felt the children had passed the difficult times of Mildred's illness and passing without great mental difficulty. I had helped them to know that she was with Heavenly Father, and in most situations they remained happy. Lee Ann's hearing loss at age two caused us great concern. Geri made valiant efforts to have her treated, and then to give her special training. Lee Ann began to read well before going to school. Her speech was somewhat garbled until we obtained hearing aids, which greatly helped her. She was given piano lessons and soon played lovely music, enjoying it thoroughly. Glenda had not remembered her mother too closely but was always a happy gem in our midst. Geri took immediate care and with wonderful love kept the children progressing naturally.

Geraldine was surprised after we were married when she inquired as to how we paid our mortgage. I told her that we had no mortgage; it was all paid for. This was a revelation to her as she had been hoarding her savings for the payment each month, expecting a bill to arrive, but it never did.

Before we were married, Geri was called into the stake Young Women organization as the stake speech director. She gave me unfailing support as bishop, and we had a close circle of friends, wonderful families (hers and mine), and the entire ward giving their support and love. We were constantly at the home of my parents and also at the home of Dad and Mom Hamblin. With all the difficulties and big changes in my personal life, I felt at times that as a bishop I had not given my best.

Chapter 9

———◆———

CALLED AS STAKE PRESIDENT

"The implications for us of the restoration of the gospel are as follows: first, we can really know that God lives; second, the gospel will guide us to a richer, happier, more purposeful life on earth; third, we can know that God watches over us; and fourth, we have assurances that we will live again after death and renew our association with those loved ones we have lost. We have received the promise of a life so rich and happy that its wonders have only been hinted at." [1]

Introduction

During the month of June 1954, Geraldine and I took our children to a ward "young people's" outing to Moab, Utah, where we camped three days in the park and enjoyed the associations and a visit to Arches National Monument. There were several adult leaders in the company with us. My first counselor, Maurice Harmon, who carried the responsibility of this activity, was not able to go because his wife's mother had passed away two days before, and he, of course, remained home. Geraldine and I enjoyed this break and association very much, even though she was progressing in her first pregnancy.

As we left the outing, instead of returning home with our group, we proceeded up the Colorado River, enjoying the scenery, and on through Grand Junction. Thereafter, we followed the Colorado River to the Summit of the Continent and passed over the Great Mountain Pass, which led down to Denver, the capital. We were driving Geraldine's 1951 Studebaker Champion, and fortunately it did not use a great amount of gas. Arriving in Denver, we went to

---

1. Collected Works, p. 193

Aurora, where my sister Marian and her husband, Richard Lindsay, were living. We spent two days and had a happy visit with them. Following this visit we returned home, going northward, passing through Rawlins, Wyoming, and on to Salt Lake. During our journey we discussed the situation in which I had been serving as bishop, and I told Geri that I was not fully satisfied with the leadership and service that I had provided, even though the Lord had blessed me in many ways. Because of the preoccupations of my wife's sickness and passing, and then the subsequent experience of finding a new companion and spending time getting acquainted with her, I felt that I had not adequately fulfilled my calling as bishop. As we traveled, we determined that from that time on we would fully devote ourselves to the calling that I had received and that I would try to serve as a real bishop should serve, being fruitful and productive.

Upon arrival at home, my father, who was a member of the stake high council, reminded me that a stake conference was scheduled for that weekend, and that I was requested as a bishop to meet with and be interviewed by the visiting General Authorities, Joseph Fielding Smith, President of the Quorum of the Twelve Apostles, and Mark E. Petersen, also of the Quorum of the Twelve. All bishops and high counselors were to be interviewed by them. As I met my appointment with those Brethren, I noticed that their attention to me indicated some interest in considering me to be the stake president as they were planning to reorganize the presidency. I returned home in the afternoon and made final arrangements for the sale of a house we had recently finished to Brother and Sister Leonard S. Kennard.

We had just finished supper when the stake president, John D. Hill, knocked at our door and asked that I go back to meet with the General Authorities. I realized immediately that I was on the threshold of something very serious that would vitally change our lives. I hastened to make preparations to return, and there, under a very intense personal interview, Elders Smith and Petersen investigated in detail my life and my spiritual nature. One thing in particular impressed me in Elder Petersen's questioning. He asked me if I believed in the gospel, along with many other questions. My response, of course, was that I did as far as I understood it. Then he pressed the point by saying, "But what I mean is, do you believe the gospel as it is taught by President Joseph Fielding Smith?" At that time such a question might have been a stumbling block to some people because President Smith had been considered a very strict interpreter of the doctrine. I was able, however, to respond with a full assurance of the Spirit that I certainly did so believe, that if I had gained any deep understanding of the doctrine of the Church, it had been through the teachings, over many years, of President Joseph Fielding Smith, largely through the writings that he had developed and presented to the Church, such as *The Way to Perfection*, *The Progress of Man*, and *The Doctrines of Salvation*. These books became prominent, and I felt wholeheartedly in accord spiritually with the teachings that he had given. It has been a pleasure to reflect over the years since and realize that I was able to be in harmony with what some might consider being strict interpretations and fundamental principles of the gospel. I have found it a great blessing to have that feeling of harmony with President Smith and the great teachings he has given. I have been similarly in harmony with the General Authorities of the Church as a body. This experience helped me in teaching and strengthening others.

They then told me that I was being called to preside over the North Jordan Stake. This was a fearsome thing because I was at that time less than 36 years of age and felt myself young and incapable of assuming a responsibility that I had felt was almost beyond human capacity. I think I passed through some of the most difficult moments of my life at that time, which came near to making me physically ill. But having no way to escape, I accepted and was invited to select counselors. In the previous interview they had asked me whom I would recommend as the new leader of the stake, and at that time I gave them the names of Wayne C. Player and Merrill L. Nelson. Brother Player was the bishop of the Taylorsville Ward, and Brother Nelson was the bishop of the ward in Kearns. As I was being called to preside over the stake, they inquired as to whom I should like for counselors, and I again gave them the same two names. I feel like I had been impressed and inspired from the beginning to remember these two brethren who were called thereafter to serve at my side.

I was to be sustained the following day, Sunday, June 6, 1954, as the new president of the North Jordan Stake. I was very concerned and troubled about the immense responsibility that had come to me and felt totally inadequate and very young for this position. After the morning conference meeting, I returned home to have dinner with the family knowing that the reorganization would take place in the afternoon, but I was unable to join the family in the dinner that Geraldine had prepared. Cory, our young son, asked his mother what was wrong with Daddy. He asked, "Is he sick?" She said, "No, he is excited." Cory then responded by saying, "Oh, maybe we shouldn't have told him that we were planning to go Lagoon for our recreation." When Geri told me of his response, I laughed so much that it relieved all the tension. As I returned to the stake conference and went through the process of being sustained as president of the North Jordan Stake, I was able to do that with a rather happy and pleasant spirit. In the presentation of the new officers, a few men raised their hands in opposition to my calling. President Joseph Fielding Smith simply said, "Well, brethren, it looks like you're outvoted." He later told me that I should visit with each of them to determine their feelings, which I did. It turned out that they just did not want the former president released. I was set apart by President Joseph Fielding Smith, assisted by Elder Mark E. Petersen.

The Dimensions of the Stake

The overwhelming responsibilities of being stake president were amplified in our case by the excessive size of our stake. At that time the North Jordan Stake was by far the largest stake in the Church. It had well over 11,000 members and 14 wards. The three main areas of the stake—Granger, Taylorsville, and Kearns—were already assuming proportions of development that indicated they needed special and separate attention. Within three years my two counselors each presided over separate stakes. I remember Carl Buehner, who was in the Presiding Bishopric, saying to me one day, "Oh, you're the new stake president. I understand that you preside over half of the Church out there in Granger." Our stake consisted of the aforementioned communities of Granger, Taylorsville, and Kearns, as well as

Bennion, Hunter, and the Redwood area. It was a diverse gathering of people. Some had longstanding roots there, and others were moving into the rapidly growing subdivisions.

The High Council and Bishops

The following Sunday, according to the order of organization, I met for the first time with members of the high council. I immediately obtained an awareness of the power of this body of men. All had had responsibilities in leadership ahead of me in the gospel. They were an interesting group. The first man, H. Earl Day, had been in the stake presidency ever since I was a child. Henry Hintze was over 70 years of age. Marcus L. Bennion held me in his arms as a member of the bishopric when I was blessed. My uncles Willard and Richard Bawden were further down the line, as was my father, William Henry Bangerter. There were others on that high council who had formerly presided over me, such as Dennis Dial, Boyce Labrum, Herman Nielsen, and Clyde Barker. I felt overwhelmed by the magnitude of experience among those brethren. But the first day we met, at the conclusion of the meeting those men seemed not to just casually saunter out to take care of their responsibilities and assignments—they dashed forth to accomplish the assignments that had come to them from the stake presidency. In breaking the ice with them, I began by saying, "Well, they have hitched up the team with the jackass in front and the thoroughbreds behind." I felt an overwhelming power in the strength of those men, who in many ways were exceptional and unusual to high councils because normally the makeup of a high council was apt to be of younger men of less experience. The way they responded to our leadership and carried out instructions was a great strength. I felt that even though some of them were advancing in age, they were among the strongest leaders we ever had, with experience and ability that surpassed that of many high councils today. They were a working group. They were not tradition-bound, even though many of them had considerable age. I found that they wanted nothing more than to be given direction and leadership, and then they would proceed to fulfill their callings.

We met every Sunday morning at 6:30 a.m. This was something

of a new proceedure, but it gave us an opportunity to handle our business, send out our assignments and instructions, and have these men available to be in the various wards by 8:00 a.m., when most of the priesthood meetings were being held. This required me, of course, to be at the stake office by 5:30 to 6:00 in the morning. I would usually arrive at that hour, finding opportunity in the beautiful setting that had been provided in our high council room to feel the great spirit of the gospel and of the leadership and presence of the Savior. I had the privilege of kneeling alone in prayer before we entered the activities of the day. Then my counselors would come and we could have a few minutes of organizing and setting ourselves in the proper frame of mind before the high council arrived. Those were precious experiences, and they went on regularly over the period of four-and-one-half years that I served as stake president.

Plans to Divide the Stake

Over the next few weeks I made great effort to visit each of the wards in our stake. This, of course, was rather time-consuming, but I found that I was well received in every case. Soon thereafter, when visiting with Elders Mark E. Petersen and Spencer W. Kimball of the Quorum of the Twelve Apostles, I learned that it was definitely their plan to divide our stake rather soon. Elder Harold B. Lee was also involved in the plans for the division. I spent three or four months getting acquainted with the people in the stake and felt very close and united with them. I had a choice and happy relationship with my two counselors, Brothers Player and Nelson, and their wives.

Within weeks we were into the project of dividing the stake. At the succeeding stake conference in September, the North Jordan Stake was divided and became the North Jordan and Taylorsville Stakes. We were located in the fastest-growing area of Salt Lake County, and I think in the entire Church. Kearns at that time was expanding rapidly. We had the opportunity of dividing the Kearns Ward for the first time. It grew into several wards, and then a year or two after the organization of the Taylorsville Stake, Kearns was divided off of that stake and made into a stake of its own. It was a separate community. Therefore, after just three months, I lost both my counselors to the Taylorsville Stake: Wayne C. Player became the President of the Taylorsville Stake, and he chose Merrill Nelson, from Kearns to be one of his counselors. I selected as my two new counselors Vern Breeze, bishop of the Hunter Ward, and Dennis Dial, who had been on the high council and was formerly the bishop of the Granger Ward. Reed Arnold had served as our stake clerk up to that point and had served many years with President John D. Hill. He was released, and we selected Ruel Bawden as our stake clerk. We also called a number of new brethren to the high council. This greatly reduced the area and the number of people and wards in our stake.

I recall thinking in terms of what parts of the stake I would like to retain. I wanted to keep it all, really. I had a feeling of love for all of it. The Redwood area (the area formerly called Chesterfield) was in a rather poverty-stricken condition. It was a difficult area to administer to or to find leadership. I gained a feeling that I must love and appreciate those people, and I came to the conclusion that I would rather keep them than all the rest. My feelings were strengthened by contact with Elder Harold B. Lee, who had been president of the Pioneer Stake at the time when that area belonged to his stake. He knew the people there intimately. I was happy that they were retained in our stake. It became one of our projects and one of our great privileges to work with the two Redwood wards, helping to give them leadership and development and to watch the emergence of many wonderful people who had their roots there. One of them was the Pedersen family. This family was remarkable. The father, Oliver Cowdery Pedersen, had raised his children from their youth without the help of the mother, who had passed away. There were seven boys and two girls. All the boys were great young men, and all went on missions. One of them was Herschel Pedersen, who later served as a Regional Representative, a mission president, and a counselor in a temple presidency[2]

Calling People to Serve

In calling people to serve in positions of responsibility in the stake, I came upon an example mentioned by President Kimball

---

2. Bangerter Oral History, pp. 54–55

when he served as a member of his stake presidency regarding the way in which people had been selected to serve. As they were being called appropriately in the proper setting, he taught that they needed to realize that the Spirit of the Lord had directed their calling and that they were expected to pray earnestly before giving an answer. In this manner, most everyone we called was very responsive and willing to assume the positions that were selected.

I remember two remarkable experiences in calling leaders. We had sought for a president over the Young Men of the stake and decided to call a certain brother to this position; however, he was a neighbor to my counselor, President Breeze, who said, "I don't think he will accept because he and his wife like their Sundays for recreation, and they may not have a full desire to serve." We, having consulted with the high council and having prayed about it, nevertheless called Brother Clark. I announced to him his calling as president of the stake Young Men organization. His response was as President Breeze had expected, saying that he did not feel that he ought to serve. I then told him that we felt that the Spirit of the Lord had called him and that we had the confirmation of all of the presidency and high council; we asked him to go home and discuss it with his wife and then pray about it and I would call him later in the week and hear his response. When I called him, he was somewhat unhappy as he agreed to respond to the calling that was given. However, he became a very capable and stalwart leader and eventually became a member of the high council. The same thing happened with my cousin Henry Bawden, who was called to be president of the stake mission. He was reluctant to accept this calling for various reasons, and when I told him that the Lord had called him and that I promised that he would have great joy and satisfaction in his service, he agreed to accept it. He served with great effect and his experience led him to become the bishop of his ward and a great patriarch over his family.

Growth of the Area

Granger, in particular, was burgeoning with the building of subdivisions. We had ward divisions coming at a rapid rate, and families were moving into the area in tremendous numbers. It was pleasant to see them come because by and large they were young families with many children and were faithful and active in the Church; they made ideal material for leadership and strength. I remember President Lee said, "Now, President, we'll divide your stake if you'll promise to develop leadership." Developing leadership became one of the enjoyable and interesting projects of our stake. We could find multitudes of leaders. It was a gold mine. The makeup of our wards was sometimes curious. We had in one ward nearly 300 children in Primary and two people in Mutual because of the young age of the families. This of course changed as time went on. Our activity included working up new organizations, calling new people to bishoprics, drawing people from bishoprics to go into the high council or vice versa, organizing quorums of elders, and keeping our stake auxiliary organizations strong and intact. We felt in nearly every case that we had strong and powerful leadership. It was a time of vigorous growth in the Church. [3]

In the process of time, as our stake continued to grow rapidly, we again reached the number of 8,000 with 10 wards. It was decided in 1957 to once again divide the North Jordan stake. Elder Mark E. Petersen came as the General Authority in charge, and with the new division, President Vern Breeze was called to preside over the North Jordan Stake. The new Granger Stake was organized in 1958. I chose as counselors Iris Morgan and Franklin Kennard, as Dennis Dial had moved out of the stake. Previously, I had asked Leon Miller to serve for a time as a counselor in the North Jordan Stake. This reorganization set up the new Granger Stake, of which I became the first president. The responsibilities I carried in this great assignment included that of organizing and dividing a number of new wards because our area was growing rapidly in population with the building of many homes. During the period of four years I served as stake president, we installed at least 25 bishoprics, which were required because of division or new organization. It seemed we were adding or changing a bishopric nearly every month. Very few of these people were ever released, since they were needed in a new ward or in an additional capacity. I should mention the names of a number of those who

---

3. Bangerter Oral History, p. 55

were called as bishops during this period. They included Maurice Harmon, Raymond Coates, Wallace Bawden, Alvin Wilkinson, Ray White, Robert Barber, and others. We met monthly with our bishops, providing training and instruction in regular interviews. We also had monthly training meetings with the bishops and bishoprics. This helped engender great harmony and unity amongst the bishops and bishoprics of the stake.

Building Needs

Regarding our building needs, at the time I was stake president we just barely began to move into the construction phase. We had a relatively new stake center, and three or four ward chapels were being constructed while I was stake president. But much more was required to be done afterward. We were under the necessity, of course, of dividing wards where we didn't have all the chapels we needed. But we moved to install at least two and frequently three wards in each chapel. We had on occasion almost abandoned certain chapels—the old Granger Ward and the old Bennion Ward, for example—but they were quickly repossessed and reoccupied due to the need for buildings.

We had a very active property procurement program. A member of the high council watched over it and reported each month so that we planned to have a church building site on almost every quarter section of land in our community. We didn't achieve this during the time I was there, but we did obtain a number of sites that were eventually used for chapels. Our policy moved very strongly in the direction of having all wards share and assist in whatever chapel was to be built. Those who were to occupy it would generally carry the major burden, but we developed a practice of asking each ward to make a commitment to help those we were going to build. (Most buildings at that time were built by the members themselves.) It's always difficult to raise building funds, but with good strong leadership and faith, people made contributions in the spirit of sacrifice and almost invariably testified that they were blessed.[4]

---

4. Bangerter Oral History, pp. 62–63

Assignments as President

The numerous assignments that I received as stake president of the North Jordan Stake included the presidency over the stake's board of education, which had direction of the seminary program that operated at Cyprus High School in Magna. Later on, with the organization of the Granger Stake, we had a new seminary for our stake operating adjacent to the Granger High School. For a while I served as chairman of the board of education for both seminary programs.

I was also assigned to be a member of the board of trustees of the LDS Hospital and later to be a member of the executive committee of the board of trustees, in which capacity I also met weekly or biweekly to consider the problems in the administration of that hospital. This was a new proceedure for the LDS Hospital at that time. It had formerly been under an appointive board not necessarily composed of stake presidents. But our new group first met with the Presiding Bishopric, who were of course "ex officio" members of the board. At that time the Presiding Bishopric was made up of Joseph L. Wirthlin, Thorpe B. Isaacson, and Carl W. Buehner. We met with them frequently during much of the time I served in that capacity. Eventually the conducting of the hospital program was left in our hands. Our chairman was Harold H. Bennett, President of ZCMI, and the vice-chairman was Virgil Smith, President of Beneficial Life, but the rest of us were stake presidents—Lincoln Hanks, Elmer Christenson, George Nelson, and myself. Clarence Wonnacott was the hospital administrator at the time, and Brent Goates was his assistant.[5]

Welfare Program and Stake Farms

Our stake was deeply involved in the welfare program with our center in Welfare Square in Salt Lake City. As I attended one of the regular meetings in connection with the welfare program, Elder Marion G. Romney announced that I had been chosen as assistant to the chairman of the Pioneer Welfare Region, who was President Alex Dunn of Tooele. I served with him and Howard Allen, president of

---

5. Bangerter Oral History, p. 67

the Granite Stake, for two years until I was called to preside over the mission in Brazil [in 1958]. This calling led me to have close contact with the true nature of the assistance of the poor and the efforts that were being made to provide for them in various projects through-out the stakes in the Salt Lake Valley. One of the prime leaders was Glenn L. Rudd, who was the director of Welfare Square. Through his experience and background and close contact with Elder Harold B. Lee, who directed the Church program, he had a very powerful, inspiring spirit concerning those who needed assistance and help. It gave me an understanding of a new dimension of the gospel that I had not fully appreciated heretofore. I felt these men were among the most knowledgeable in the entire church.

At the time, the Pioneer Region had 12 stakes in it and admin-istered to about half of the welfare in the entire Church. This area included everything on the west side of the Salt Lake Valley and Tooele County to Nevada. There were also a Salt Lake Region, a Sugar House Region, and a Jordan Valley Region. Some of the asso-ciations we had then have been remarkable in the years since. There I first became acquainted with Bishop Rudd, as I have indicated, and Elder Thomas Monson, who was a counselor in the stake presiden-cy to Percy Fetzer. I also became acquainted with a future mayor of Salt Lake, Adel Stewart. Fred Schwendiman was one of the stake presidents, as were Lewis Elgren and Alex Dunn, the father of Elder Loren C. Dunn of the Seventy. It also gave me close contact with President J. Reuben Clark Jr., and Elders Harold B. Lee, Henry D. Moyle, and Marion G. Romney.[6]

It was evident early on that Brother Rudd and President Dunn loved the poor. They communicated that spirit to me, and I felt an awakening in my heart of what the Savior meant when He talked of the less fortunate. I learned to help people first and ask the questions later. That brought a Christ-like relationship with those with whom we worked. We were involved in numerous large projects: the opera-tion of the storehouse and of Welfare Square, the overseeing of many stake projects, the development of the milk plant, and the running of the cannery. All these things were handled by Brother Rudd, but we

---

6. Bangerter Oral History, pp. 55–57

supervised and controlled them, and it was interesting to be involved in these activities. In our own stake I understood that it was our responsibility to obtain another welfare project.[7]

In meeting with Elder Marion G. Romney, the managing director of the Welfare Program, about our responsibilities, he advised me that we were expected to obtain a stake farm since the properties that we previously held had been allocated to the two stakes that had been divided from us. Our former stake president, President Hill had been vigorous in providing welfare projects, so of course we were interested in developing that work. I tried to make excuses due to the fast growth and limited resources of our members. He would not budge but insisted that we could do both concurrently. I informed him that it would cost us over $100,000 to get a project, which I felt was quite high. He replied, "That won't matter. My stake never got a project. They've paid out a quarter of a million dollars helping people with money out of their own pockets. They don't have a thing to show for it now. Go ahead and spend your $100,000." I came out of that meeting realizing that as a young man, almost a boy, I had to think in bigger terms. In consultation with one of my counselors, Brother Leon Miller, he came forth with the idea that we should call 100 men of our stake to a special priesthood meeting and invite each one to contribute $100, which would amount to the $10,000 we would be expected to pay. We followed through with this plan under an influence of earnest prayer and desire, and as a result our brethren responded with great faithfulness and contributed not just $10,000, but $18,000 to our project. A number of men who had not been invited to make contributions came forward and asked why they had not been included. They felt it an honor and privilege to make this contribution. Therefore, along with my counselor, Vern Breeze, we studied areas where we might find a farm. We located some property on the north bench of Lehi that was not too far away and that could be purchased at a reasonable price. I counseled with Clifford E. Young, a General Authority and a resident of that area, about buying this farm. We eventually purchased about 300 acres of excellent farmland in a very lovely location. About the same time we

---

7. Bangerter Oral History, pp. 55–56

located a small farm in Alpine, which Geri and I purchased for our own family needs.

I often thought of those days when our children were small and we were struggling. My wife said: "You are the stake president. You shouldn't drive the oldest car in the stake and the ugliest one." But it was a good car. That is why I married her. She had this new car then. It was a Studebaker Champion. It didn't have much zip, but it sure went a long way on gas. We drove that for five years, and she said we needed to get a new car. The springs were coming out of the seat, the tires were bald, the paint wasn't very good, and it used a lot of oil, but it always started. We determined that we would go back to Chicago where my brother-in-law lived. He said he would help us get a good deal on a new car, but just then we got a call to go on a mission to Brazil, so we didn't go to Chicago. Instead we saved the $2,000 (that's all a car cost then), and we put that down on a piece of land where we live now [in Alpine]. That little sacrifice got us 30 acres of land—our little old car was the reason for it. You couldn't buy that today, but we did it then. Our building lot of 30 acres cost us $15,000, and it took us a long time to pay for it.[8] Our experience in raising our family had been somewhat different, and we have sought to do things that cost us an awful lot in personal gratification. I expressed to my wife the feeling that I went most of my life without having enough change in my pocket to buy my lunch when I went to work. Why would I do that? Because I didn't feel entitled to take away the funds that otherwise would be used for the clothing, feeding, and caring of our children.[9]

Our stake had a heavy responsibility in taking care of the operation of this farm. In close association with Elder Marcus L. Bennion, a member of the high council and a semi-retired farmer, along with his brother, Leo Bennion (who became the operator of the farm), we worked diligently to bring to fulfillment the program of this welfare effort. These two great men, through much devotion and sacrifice, spent much extra time in establishing our farming business. In providing sufficient labor to operate the farm, a member of the

8. Collected Works, p. 416–417
9. Collected Works, p. 251

high council was given the responsibility to organize work teams to serve on the farm every week or so. First, Brother Walter Brock of the high council carried out this duty with faithfulness. Later, after the division of our stake to the Granger Stake, we called Brother Owen Grant to this position. These two men were extremely faithful and diligent in accomplishing their assignments. One of the activities that we instituted with the procurement of the new stake farm was an annual stake outing on Labor Day of each year when members of the high council would arrange a special breakfast for all of the members of the stake in honor of the service that they had given in helping operate the farm. This became a tradition that was very enjoyable to our people.

Access to General Authorities

At the time I served as a stake president we had almost total access to the General Authorities, and principally to the members of the Council of the Twelve. They did not seem to be so overwhelmingly scheduled as they are now. It was simple, common, and easy for a stake president to call any of them on the telephone, to get a response or an answer to a question, or to make an appointment and have a visit. I profited very much from numerous visits of this kind. In addition, General Authorities came more frequently to our stake conferences. It seems that the policy was generally for General Authorities to come to each stake conference during the time I presided, although I believe there were occasions when they were not able to do so. Of course with a smaller number of Assistants to the Twelve we had more frequent visits from the members of the Twelve and from the Presiding Bishopric. Those Brethren gave explicit instruction that pertained to the work of the stake presidency and to the work of the bishopric. [10]

As a child, as a missionary, as a friend, and as a stake president, I have been privileged to associate with almost all of the General Authorities who have lived during my lifetime. The combined impact of my experiences with the General Authorities, who are among the choicest spirits the Lord has ever sent forth on the earth, has been

---

10. Bangerter Oral History, p. 60

overpowering. With great humility, I acknowledge the unusual privilege that has been mine to feel their influence, to look up to them, and to appreciate their great qualities.[11]

Summing Up

I have described how it was on the farm and in the farm home and how it was in my profession when I was out building and could take my boys with me. I didn't have to pay them very much. I was able to give them a little for encouragement, but the main thing was that they knew they had to work, and they all liked to work if we did it right. They learned to enjoy their work, and so I have five sons now who are carpenters. One of them [Grant] still works at it, but the others don't. But they enjoy work—I suppose up to the limit that most men enjoy work.[12]

Throughout the period of my service as president of the stake, realizing that I held a position of recognition among the members of the Church, I felt very humble in my lowly economic condition to make an adequate contribution to my calling. My sweet wife, Geraldine, had given birth to our daughter Julie in 1954 and a year later to our son Grant. In 1957, another son, Howard, was also born. We now had six children, which was a substantial family. I continued to earn my livelihood by building houses and was able to build and sell two or three houses and to construct the one in which we were living. Two years later Geraldine and I joined together and built another home in the same neighborhood and were able to enjoy a fully comfortable place of living to take care of our family and to properly agree with the responsibilities, contacts, and meetings of being the leader of the stake.

Geraldine and I truly fell in love with all the people in our stake, including those in the stakes that had been divided away from us. We felt a rich association with the countless number of people who were our close, beloved friends and associates and whose influences have continued to be with us throughout our lives. Little did we know of the change our lives would take after but four and a half years of service as a stake president.

---

11. Collected Works, p. 487
12. Ibid., p. 412

Grant on moving day at Santa Ana, California, 1942.

Grant as the guidon, marching with others of his squadron, 1942.

Grant in flight gear, 1942.

The PT-17 was the first plane Grant learned to fly. He described this plane as very enjoyable and maneuverable and felt he could do just about anything in it. He learned to fly this aircraft at Oxnard, California.

The BT-13 was a fixed wheel trainer and one Grant flew early on. It was much more powerful than the PT-17 and was said to be like riding a strong horse. The Army air forces pilots flew formation with it. Night flying was also done in this aircraft. He learned to fly this aircraft at Bakersfield, California.

The AT-17 was the first twin-engine aircraft Grant learned to fly. It could be flown very slowly with a 25 MPH landing speed as well as a low take off speed. It was a very light plane, and he flew it at Roswell, New Mexico.

The AT-9 was originally built as a fighter. Grant described it as very fun to fly. It took off and landed faster than the other aircraft he had flown up to that point. He flew this aircraft at Roswell, New Mexico.

The AT-10 was a bigger aircraft and made of metal. Grant flew this airplane at Randolph Field, Texas.

The B-32 was a big bomber. Grant only flew it once while at Randolph Field. Each instructor had to fly it once on an animation flight

The AT-6 Texan was a popular trainer. Grant described it as a fun airplane with lots of power and speed and requiring a little more finesse to fly. It was also used as a trainer for fighter pilots. He flew this aircraft at Bryan, Texas, in Instrument School.

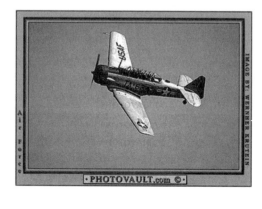

The AT-11 was the airplane Grant flew to Salt Lake with some of the men from the air base. When asked how many times he had flown it, he said, "Oh, this is the first time." They used it to train bombardiers. He flew this at Douglas, Arizona.

The B-25 was Grant's favorite and the one he flew until the end of the war. They were a powerful and classy looking aircraft with sleek lines and good speed. When he first went up in it, Grant said he thought the whole house was going up with him. He felt it was the best-designed airplane he had ever seen, and it was easy to land, and was extremely powerful. He flew this out of Douglas, Arizona.

Bomber Training Squadron 11, Randolph Field, 1944.

Flying Group at Minter Field, Bakersfield, California, March 1943 — Instructor: Lt. Garrett (with hat). Grant is at the instructor's right. (Aircraft is PT-13.)

Training group. Grant is second from right, back row.

Grant in the cockpit of an AT-6, 1944.

Instructors group showing off; Grant is tallest in the middle (AT-6 aircraft).

Grant as a commissioned officer, second lieutenant.

Mildred as a missionary, 1942–43

Mildred and Grant in front of the Schwantes home in Douglas, Arizona, 1944.

Mildred and Grant, formal wedding picture, March 8, 1944.

Mildred and Grant preparing to leave on their honeymoon, March 1944.

Grant and Mildred outside the Mesa Temple on their wedding day, March 8, 1944.

Grant and Mildred at Bryce Canyon on their honeymoon, March 1944.

Grant and Mildred in the Utah snow, March 1944.

Mildred and Grant in front of their Douglas, Arizona, home near the Mexican border, 1944.

Mildred and Grant outside the Salt Lake Temple, 1946.

Mildred as the Base Beauty Queen.

Grant and Mildred at the time Grant was called as bishop, 1950.

*Grant, Lee Ann, and Mildred, Utah
1945–46.*

*Mildred and Grant with their three
children: Lee Ann, Cory, and Glenda,
spring 1950.*

Mildred, about 1944.

Mildred, 1952.

PERIOD IV
Mission President Years

Chapter 10

EARLY EXPERIENCES

"I offer you my testimony of the knowledge that God has restored the truth to His people in the last days; that we represent those who have been called out of the world to help in bringing salvation to all mankind; and that we are on a mission of service and devotion that requires us to live differently from the way people live in the world. That ought to make us the happiest people alive. There couldn't be a more blessed situation than the one we have at the present time on the face of the earth. God bless you to appreciate and enjoy what you have." [1]

Introduction and Call

In the summer of 1958 my wife, Geraldine, commented to me on the pleasant and comfortable situation in which we found ourselves. We had proceeded well in the growth of our family. Howard was one and a half years old, and Geri was expecting another child to be born in December. We had completed the building of a comfortable home six months previously and felt satisfied with our situation. With my calling as president of the Granger stake, Geri felt we occupied a position of respect and enjoyment. I continued my occupation of home building. I recall we were building a home for Brother Pete

---

1. Collected Works, p. 296

Thompson not far from our own when Geri sent word to me that I had received a telephone call from President Stephen L. Richards of the First Presidency and that he would like me to return the call. I immediately felt impressed that I might be called to Brazil to serve as the mission president.

As I returned to the house, Geri asked, "What does a member of the First Presidency want to talk with you about?"

"Well, I don't think that's especially unusual. I am the president of a stake, and the Brethren occasionally make calls to one or another," I responded.

"What is it he does in the First Presidency anyway?"

I replied, "I think he often speaks in connection with those who are called to preside over missions."

"Ohhh!!!" was Geri's reply.

I returned the call to President Richards, and he asked if I would make an appointment with him. I had more than a premonition that he would talk to me about presiding over the mission in Brazil because I knew that there was not a large number of former missionaries from the Brazilian Mission who might at this time be considered. The night before the appointment, Geri did not sleep well and had the assurance that we would be spending our next five years living in Brazil. On September 26, 1958, I met with President Stephen L. Richards in the Church Office, and he talked with me about a call to be president of the Brazilian Mission. I, of course, was eager and willing to accept because I had a great desire to someday return to my mission field. We talked about Geri's condition, and I expressed the opinion that it would be better if we moved to Brazil before the birth of our child since otherwise it could cause a rather long delay.

Naturally, this news and decision put our lives into an uproar. I announced my calling to the presidency of the stake and the high council, and they were surprised and excited. Parties were arranged in our honor, including one by the presidencies and high council of both the Granger and North Jordan Stakes. I received an expensive wristwatch as a gift, and Geri received two beautiful pieces of luggage. President Leon E. Miller, my former counselor, and his wife gave a dinner for our previous group in the presidency, and they presented us with a new camera, a most expensive piece. The combined families of Geri and me had a party in the Granger Ward to which all the descendants of Father and Mother came along with my in-laws— it was one of the few times we had all been together. Gary Weaver, the husband of my sister Naomi, had just returned from a year in the Far East with the Navy, and it was a great occasion. The family's gift to us was a movie camera with much equipment to go with it. They also gave us a copy of all the scriptures in one volume, beautifully bound. The group of our close friends from the Brazilian Mission also honored us and gave us other luggage and their blessings at the home of Jim and Ruth Faust.

We made arrangements to put the conditions of our home in order. We had a large stock of preserved fruit that Geri had worked on, and we arranged to pass it around to members of the family. We also decided to sell our home, which gave us a reasonable financial resource that allowed us to make the change in our life.

All these affairs were followed by our farewell testimonial at the Granger 8th Ward. Elders Spencer Kimball, Mark E. Petersen, and George Q. Morris of the Twelve were present and spoke, as did President Alex Dunn, Bishop Rudd, President Faust, President Breeze, President Morgan, and Bishop Harman. Their tributes were flattering and kind and made us feel very humble. An open-house reception was given in our honor at the Pioneer Region on November 11. Elder Romney and his wife attended, along with many of the presidents and workers in the region. At a meeting of the executive committee of the LDS Hospital on Friday, November 14, I was extended the best wishes of the board of trustees. [2]

Elder George Q. Morris of the Quorum of the Twelve and Henry D. Taylor of the Assistants to the Twelve came to visit our stake to reorganize the presidency, and President Iris B. Morgan, my counselor, was called to be the stake president.

We had very little training at that time to be mission presidents. We were invited to attend sessions in the missionary home with all the missionaries, but nothing specific was given to us. We had

---

2. Wm. Grant Bangerter Mission President Journal, Vol. 1:18–19; hereafter referred to as WGB M.P. Journal

opportunities for interviews with various offices and leaders of the Church. I had a brief interview with the First Presidency—that is, the Counselors; President McKay was in the hospital at the time I was set apart. And so President J. Reuben Clark (who set me apart) and President Stephen L. Richards (who set Sister Bangerter apart) gave me opportunity to ask questions, but the interview was brief. (Lee Ann, Cory, and Glenda accompanied us to the setting apart.) I felt President Clark's blessing to me was very spiritual and prophetic and to some extent congratulatory on the service that I had given theretofore; it was rich with encouragement and with promise of a successful mission, with much counsel to depend on the Spirit of the Lord. President Clark also gave me pointed instructions about being cautious with the Church's money. [3]

The Brazilian Mission was a strong and thriving mission. I had been informed that President Asael T. Sorensen had been extremely vigorous and outstanding among the mission presidents of the Church in organizing the proselyting work and developing the mission. I found this to be true. He had developed the use of the lesson plan. It had been very effective. The convert rate had moved from somewhere around maybe 4 or 5 a month up to 40, 50, and 60 a month. They were gaining 300–400 converts a year. I felt that I inherited a very healthy and vigorous mission directed by an outstanding mission president. [4]

History of the Mission in Brazil.

The Brazilian Mission was organized officially in 1935 with Rulon S. Howells as president. President Howells only spoke German. Previously the work among the German-speaking people in Brazil was directed from mission headquarters in Buenos Aires, Argentina, beginning in 1928. Brother Reinhold Stoff, a native of Germany was called to preside over the mission after Elder Melvin J. Ballard's departure. President Stoff began to search out colonies of German-speaking people both in Argentina and Brazil, and soon German-

---

3. Bangerter Oral History, p. 68
4. Ibid., p. 84

speaking missionaries were sent to some of the areas in Brazil where Germans had congregated in large numbers. The most prominent of these colonies was Joinville, in the state of Santa Catarina. There were also large groups of German-speaking people in the states of Rio Grande do Sul, Santa Catarina, Paraná, and São Paulo. The first two missionaries assigned to labor in Brazil were Elders Fred Heinz and David Ballstadt. In the beginning the work was carried out almost exclusively among the German people. Very few of those early missionaries spoke any Portuguese. The preaching of the gospel to the Portuguese-speaking people commenced in late 1938. Elders Melvin Morris and Grant Brooks were the first assigned to do so. As a young missionary, I had arrived shortly thereafter, and my group was the first group assigned to learn and preach in Portuguese (see chapter 4). We began our efforts to learn Portuguese and to perform our work as missionaries with almost no materials in Portuguese. We had the Bible, of course, but the Book of Mormon was not published in Portuguese until 1940. Most church meetings were held in German, but we began to hold meetings in Portuguese in the major centers such as Porto Alegre, Curitiba, Rio de Janeiro, and São Paulo. It should be recognized how miraculous and impressive the hand of the Lord was in providing vision and revelation for the establishment of His work throughout the earth. [5]

Impressions about Brazil

My overall impression at the time I returned from Brazil as a missionary was that it was a wonderful experience for me and that I'd had a mission that I prized, but I didn't feel it had been rich in the experiences of teaching the gospel. I had the attitude, which I carried for years afterward, that posed the questions: "Is Brazil one of those places where the Lord really plans to establish a branch of his kingdom with firmness and power? Will the Church ever really amount to anything in Brazil?" I had these reservations partly because of the heavy black African mixture and the freedom of intermarriage there. These feelings were common to most missionaries

---

5. Excerpts taken from the June 1, 1995, narration to the Historical Department, pp. 2–4

as the Church hadn't yet issued the Official Declaration stating that all worthy males could hold the priesthood. This open questioning about the destiny of the Church there wasn't dissipated until after I'd been called to return as a mission president.[6]

As Geri and I petitioned the Lord concerning our call to Brazil, a revelation opened to my mind. While studying the scriptures in the Book of Mormon and Doctrine and Covenants starting with 1 Nephi 13:42, we read that the Lamb will "manifest himself unto all nations." Mosiah 3:13 indicated that the Lord had sent prophets to every nation. Alma 13:21–22 showed that the voice of the Lord was to "all nations." Alma 29:8 said that the Lord granted to all nations to teach His word in their own tongue. Alma 37:4 indicated that the records would "go forth unto every nation." 3 Nephi discussed the Three Nephites going to every nation (see 3 Nephi 28), and John the Beloved was assigned to prophesy to nations, kindreds, tongues, and peoples (see D&C 7:3). D&C 64:42 told us that people would be gathered out of every nation and that they would come to Zion. Of course, D&C 133:7–8 said that we were to go to all nations. These scriptural clarifications gave us comfort and strength to move forward in the charge given us.

I might mention two specific items about which I prayed very earnestly before I left to go to Brazil as a mission president. The first was: "Father in Heaven, do you really intend to organize and establish a strong branch of your Church and kingdom in Brazil? Are we really serious about it down there?" Before I could finish the prayer—immediately on asking the question, in fact—He answered it to me in my mind and vividly, almost with words, directed me to turn to the Book of Mormon and read many passages that I wouldn't have been able to recall without that flash of inspiration. For instance, in 3 Nephi 28:28–29 I found that the gospel, as stated in the Book of Mormon, was directed to the Gentiles and to the lost sheep of the House of Israel. Many passages came to my mind concerning the message to the Gentiles, and I was immediately informed by the Spirit that it didn't matter whether they belonged to the house of Israel or not. The gospel was for them. When I arrived in Brazil

---

6. Bangerter Oral History, pp. 25–26

as mission president, I found that everyone already understood the answer. The missionaries and the mission president were working in that direction with power. They were moving and having real success. My second question was rather a thoughtless one, but in my anxiety I said, "Heavenly Father, I'm willing to go on this mission, provided you'll go with me." It's humorous to me now to think of it. Again I received the answer immediately, before I could finish my prayer. It seemed that He said almost out loud, "My boy, I'm already there."

Those two experiences had a profound effect on my attitude when I returned to Brazil and saw how conditions had developed since I had been a missionary and how the work was now advancing. It gave me a sense of testimony and a feeling of destiny that has never been questioned in my life since. And the developments have borne out the testimony. Where I had thought up to that point that Brazil would be the least responsive of all the nations in South America, it turned out in fact to be the most responsive. The present-day developments are a fulfillment of those personal testimonies and revelations to me at that time. I felt that personally my mission was a great fulfillment. It laid foundations within my experience that have been beneficial ever since. I think that I personally obtained a fullness of the spirit of the gospel and of the missionary work, according to my limited understanding, and that I returned with devotion, with a reasonably broad knowledge of the gospel. I believe that the experiences I had in leadership helped to prepare me for other assignments that came at other times. [7]

Departure from the U.S. and Arrival in Brazil

The following is an excerpt from a record kept regarding our departure on November 17, 1958:

"We now arrive at the day before our scheduled departure. We are packed and prepared both in spirit and in physical arrangements. Our parents have been wonderful to us, and we can never repay them except by living as we should. We have fasted and prayed about

---

7. Bangerter Oral History, pp. 25–26

this mission and have had many problems answered to us; some by instruction, some by impression, and some by the inspiration of the Holy Spirit. We pray that we can fulfill this mission pleasingly before the Lord. We have great ideals and examples before us and hope to lead out in a great unfolding of the blessings of the restored gospel to an unknown host of people in Brazil where they may be discovered to us by the promptings of the Spirit of the Lord. We have met a few of the missionaries as they have left for Brazil and many of their families. We know that this can be a glorious experience, and we are truly devoted to it. We are delighted to be able to take our family who are most sweet and precious to us and who have entered into the spirit of the mission so well along with us. May God bless us to remain close together and receive joy in the experience before us and to obtain the vision and the knowledge of the work to do is our constant prayer." [8]

The day of departure for our mission to Brazil arrived. We had slept at Mother's home and then had an early breakfast and left for the train station. We drove the old Studebaker to the railroad station, and there my wife sold it to her mother for $1. Her mother thought she could get a little out of it, but the radiator leaked, and it was a cold November day. Her mother drove it home, and that night the temperature plummeted; the engine froze, and it never moved again. We always claimed that it died of a broken heart. [9]

Our families and a number of people from the ward, stake, and the Pioneer Region were there to see us off. We made the departure very well, considering the implications, and soon were happily en route to Ogden. We all rode the dome car most of the way through the mountains and enjoyed the luxury of the train and the grandeur of the scenery. We were fortunate to be able to spend 10 minutes with Geri's brother Dale in Green River, and from thence we moved across the plains. An accident ahead of us just before Rawlins delayed us three hours, and no one was there to greet us. We settled the children for bed and all retired early. We had our meals from the lunch box. It was a most interesting day but we missed so much

8. WGB M.P. Journal, p. 19.
9. Collected Works, p. 417

of the plains in our travel through the night. We arrived in Omaha about daylight, four and a half hours late, on November 18.[10] We traveled by rail through Chicago and on to Washington, D.C., and eventually to New York City where we would take a flight for Brazil. This was an exciting and interesting journey for all of the family, and we were comfortable as we traveled across our native land. Arriving in Washington, D.C., we met with my former mission president, John A. Bowers, and his wife. They were very cordial and helpful in helping us find our way around Washington. We also met with some of my former missionary companions who lived in that area. After touring some of the nation's capital, we then proceeded by train to New York City, established ourselves in the hotel, and saw many of the sights of that city. From there we made arrangements for our flight to Brazil. It must have been about November 25 when we were transported by bus to Idlewild (now JFK) airfield to board a large, four-engine propelled plane (a DC-7) all the way to São Paulo, Brazil. We made a stop en route at Caracas, Venezuela, to refuel. We arrived in Rio in the morning where we changed planes to go on to São Paulo.

Shortly after takeoff we went over the Atlantic Ocean southward and for seven hours steadily parted the sky until like an arrow we landed without any apparent effort in Caracas and were in an instant in South America. We considered that perhaps we were among the very first of the mission presidents to fly to their assigned fields of labor with their families, and we were aware of the great progress of the air age. The day before we stood on the edge of our native land, and suddenly we were setting foot on a new continent, almost a new world as it were. The marvelous things of this earth were thrilling to contemplate, and yet we knew they were almost insignificant compared to the glories of eternity. As we flew over the vast continent of South America, and Brazil in particular, I wrote down the following impressions:

"As the dawn breaks forth in splendor above the clouds at 20,000 feet, a mighty river appears far below. I guess it to be the São Francisco in eastern Brazil. The past night contained many grand ex-

10. WGB M.P. Journal, p. 17.

periences and feelings as we sat and watched the great engines draw us swiftly through the sky. I have never ceased to marvel at the way such a great plane can be sustained above the earth, and I watch it with fascination. Our thoughts are deep as we know that shortly we will enter fully into our work. We realize somewhat how great is our responsibility to preside over a land, one of the largest of the earth, with all the power of the restored priesthood. We know wonderful things await us, and we have felt the power of God upon us to make our way smooth as He did the day before yesterday when it appeared we would not be able to receive visas for Brazil because of baggage complications. Now in the midst of clouds there is nothing to be seen of the land below, and we have been able to see very little of Brazil throughout the seven or eight hours of our flight across the land. Even airplanes cannot altogether dwarf such an extensive territory." [11]

Housing and Mission Tour

In São Paulo we were met by President and Sister Asael T. Sorenson, the outgoing mission president. They took us to the mission home located in the Bela Vista section of downtown São Paulo on Rua Itapeva 378. The living situation was rather uncomfortable and not easily congenial since the Sorensons had planned to remain for about two weeks before returning home. Geri was crowded in the facilities, and the Sorensons still occupied one of the rooms. This put a special burden on Geri and the family. She was within days of delivering her baby and was most uncomfortable. There was some arrangement made for Thanksgiving, but it was a confusing time.

Much of the discomfort had little impact on me, however, since President Sorensen had arranged to tour me throughout the entire mission and visit the branches and the missionaries in order to orient me. I enjoyed the experience and the companionship with him. Our tour led us through all the branches around the city and into the interior of the state of São Paulo, as far out as Rio Claro, Ribeirão Preto, Araçatuba, and Marília; from there we went on to the state of Paraná, seeing Londrina and then Curitiba. In the state of Santa

---

11. WGB M.P. Journal, p. 117

Catarina we visited Joinville near the coast and then Ipoméia in the interior, which was a very primitive area with a newly constructed chapel. Finally we moved into the far south, visiting branches in Porto Alegre and Novo Hamburgo, one of the original branches organized by the German-speaking missionaries. We finished our tour by going to Rio de Janeiro and on up into the state of Minas Gerais, where we stopped at Juiz de Fora and the city of Belo Horizonte.

In each of these places we met the missionaries and had a very happy time with them; we also met with the membership in different branches, which were small throughout the mission. Most of the branches had a membership of from 15 to 25 people, met in rented rooms, and were presided over by missionaries. We had a membership of about 3,000 in the mission at the time. The mission had not expanded much more in numbers of cities than when I was a missionary. Most of the work was done in cities of 100,000 inhabitants or more. As we traveled about, I was expected to speak to each of the branches. While the Portuguese language came back very slowly to me, I was able to make a suitable impression, which brought a good response from the missionaries.

Birth of Peggy Brasília

On December 5, 1958, I took Geri to the Samaritano Hospital where she gave birth to our second daughter, Peggy. We named her Peggy Brasília in honor of our residence in a new country and in recognition of the projected new capital for that country. Two of the sister missionaries took personal charge of Sister Bangerter. One of them, Sister Carol Wheeler, was a nurse and helped her in some early orientation. Geri had full confidence that she could go through the experience of a birth in a foreign country without difficulty.

Departure of the Sorenson Family

By mid-December the Sorensen family had a farewell and met with many of the members at the Santos dock as they returned to the United States. Having them leave the mission brought a great relief to my sweetheart, who, while under pressure to handle responsibilities in a new language, in a new country, and with a new baby was now not under the pressure of another family.

Geraldine met with unusual conditions and circumstances in this new country. She had two maids working in our home who did not speak English. They had a vacuum cleaner that did not function. The washing machine did not work, nor did the dryer. It was in the midst of the rainy season. She now had two children in diapers, and it was a difficult thing to have dry clothing and surroundings. All of the children were bewildered with the new country and culture, and they were all beset with fleas. The home was run down, and the equipment was by and large faulty. The cooking, under the direction of the maids, was an unusual experience to her. The home was very busy with the mission offices downstairs, which included several missionaries doing secretarial, translation, and auxiliary work, along with the printing, distribution, and general management of a large mission. Understandably Geri felt moments of discouragement and frustration. One day I found her in distress, sobbing in the bedroom and worrying about her conditions. We had a wonderful conversation together, and I helped her see how these hardships were going to be the things that would be the subject of our future conversations and would bring us great happiness and joy. We discussed how we should now settle down to enjoy these difficult times in the same way we would enjoy them when we later told about them. This brightened Geri's attitude greatly, and we adopted the motto "Enjoy it!" and thereby faced forward in all circumstances of our new life in Brazil.

Responsibilities of Sister Bangerter

I felt that Geraldine was the ideal mission president's wife and mother. Her primary responsibility was with the family. When she married me, I already had three children; three more were born to us before we went to Brazil, and three would be born while we were there. That would seem to indicate more than a normal load for any mother. She had adequate maid service in the home so that she was not confined to the various chores of homemaking, although she gave intense and personal attention to the children. Geri's responsibility consisted of taking leadership of the women's organizations.

Our children seemed to accept the attitude that they were also on a mission. Lee Ann, even with her hearing weakness, never failed to intermix with any group of Brazilians and soon became famous. Cory felt from the beginning that he was a missionary and loved to associate with the elders. Glenda took over the leadership of the younger children, and Peggy Brasília was almost immediately the special pet of all the members who never failed to give her the utmost attention. Geraldine took a full interest in our missionaries and in sustaining and helping me as the mission president. She was always concerned and alert to the missionaries' problems. She also had an active interest and responsibility in the construction program, especially in helping with the furnishings. When we built the new mission home, she spent a tremendous amount of time in working out the furnishing arrangements and the organization of the home.

Geraldine developed what I consider an unusual interest and ability to give direction to the Relief Society and advisory leadership to other women's and children's organizations as well to our staff. The Relief Society was in the embryo stage at that time, but with the assistance of one of the sister missionaries and by choosing two women who had some ability to speak English, she began to devise and formulate a program for carrying the Relief Society program forward. She began almost from nothing since there had been very little done previously. In her leadership with the Relief Society she moved ahead without having any knowledge of the language. She worked first through interpreters but soon began to communicate with the women in their own language. Out of it all she developed a real skill. Without being polished in the use of the language, she became very proficient in communicating and took full responsibility for leadership. She even held some of her leadership meetings from her hospital bed while she was confined with her children.[12] Women leaders arose under the leadership of Sister Bangerter as the Relief Society grew. One of the most outstanding of those leaders, perhaps, was Flávia Garcia Erbolato, who joined the Church in Campinas in its beginning and became indispensable in translation and in other Church leadership positions. She died in Provo, Utah, in 1998.

---

12. Bangerter Oral History, pp. 114–115

Office Arrangements

The office facilities for the mission were in the basement of our mission home. We had about six to eight missionaries serving part-time as secretaries and assistants and performing many functions, such as translating and printing, because everything in the Church had to be produced in our own office. We were deeply involved in translation. We had the responsibility of finding and dealing with all real estate matters, including the renting of chapels and the purchasing of places in which to meet. A new mission home had been projected in Salt Lake City before I left, and an architect had worked on the plan in Brazil. His name was Max Ouang, of Chinese extraction. Very gradually we developed the plan together, and over a period of about a year we entered into the building of a new chapel on property that had been purchased in São Paulo on the corner of Avenida Rebouças and Avenida Iguatemi (later changed to Avenida Faria Lima).

All weekends involved branch or district conferences in various places in the mission and meetings with the missionaries. I, thus, became closely associated with the missionaries between those who were worthy and faithful and those who were less devoted to their work. Sister Carol Wheeler gave great service in the office as a helper to Sister Bangerter. Later we had many other wonderful sister missionaries such as Sisters Royle, Walker, and Sorensen. Other missionaries had special talents. For example, Blaine Morgan was gifted with the ability to type 80 words per minute, and he accomplished great things in preparing material for publishing. He later became a mission president. Elder Drew Day did a wonderful work keeping the finance in order, making the accounting, and taking care of the banking. He was a special assistant and later also became a mission president.

Conditions in Brazil

When I arrived as mission president, Brazil had been for several years under complete civilian control. Juscelino Kubitschek was the president. His great project was the development and building of Brasília as the new capital. We felt that the government was reasonably stable, although they were experiencing considerable inflation, partly due to expenditures of the government in connection with Brasília. Also certain social legislation had begun to tax the country. But Brazil was a peaceful, quiet, and pleasant place to be. In Brazil we felt that it didn't matter much what the government did. The people were concerned, and some things happened that affected them very much economically, but as far as their interest in missionaries and the message of the gospel, we had an even time of it. Brazil had grown rapidly since I had previously been there. São Paulo had developed as the great industrial and population center of the country. It was growing at a rate faster than any other city in the world. The large cities of São Paulo, Rio de Janeiro, and Porto Alegre had become great metropolises. Previously they were not so crowded. There had been room for people. But now the streets were jammed. It was difficult to drive a car because pedestrians would fill the entire street. This was a new impression to me of people being crowded together.

At that time Brazil had become almost completely integrated. Most of the vestiges of nationalism among minority groups had disappeared. The children of Germans, Poles, and Japanese all learned Portuguese. They left aside their culture and accepted the Brazilian culture, and it became almost the same kind of melting pot as it is in the United States. We never needed missionaries who spoke Japanese. We felt that they could reach the Japanese people in Portuguese. In the German areas during my presidency we still maintained some minor activity in the German language because some meetings were still held in German. Some missionaries who spoke German labored in those areas, but they also spoke Portuguese, so they were not exclusively a German group.

The Spirit of the Adversary

The changes since my mission dealt with a greater apathy toward the Catholic Church. The Catholic Church was still the dominant church, with perhaps 95 percent of the people being Catholic. I saw a tremendous growth in religious interest outside of the Catholic Church. People were not being satisfied religiously with what they had, and they turned to other pursuits, which were in a sense semi-religious, some of them philosophical. A very prominent part of this was the movement towards Spiritualism. People could be Catholics nominally and participate in Spiritualism without apostatizing from their church or being excommunicated, so many people in Brazil were involved in Spiritualism, which became their active religion.

Spiritualism then and now has a wide variety of manifestations. Some of it was on a high plane of intellectual activity where people united to build hospitals and do social work. The Spiritualist movement covered the spectrum from the altruistic attitude all the way down to low forms similar to African voodooism. Brazilians then and now became involved in the Spiritualistic philosophy. We noted that Spiritualism brought them into contact with the powers of the adversary. His activity there was real. It was apparent to every missionary in our mission that evil spirits were abroad in the land, that they made contact with people. People unthinkingly invited them into their homes and into their lives and associated with them, learned how to speak with and communicate with them. On many occasions our missionaries had contact with them, and in the first year of my presidency this was a serious problem among our missionaries. It seemed that sometimes our missionaries became so preoccupied with Spiritualism that they interpreted this as being part of their own spiritual experience, and we would hear missionary testimonies relating to their experience with evil spirits, which brought a depressing and troubled atmosphere.

After a number of personal experiences with this influence and feeling the attitude of the missionaries, I came to the conclusion that this attitude was completely improper for missionaries of the Lord. I counseled with my assistants, and we determined that our missionaries were doing wrong in concentrating so much on these experiences with evil spirits. We thought the problem through and under inspiration came to the assurance that while we knew that the adversary was active and had great power and that his representatives were abroad in profusion in the land, this did not pertain to our mission and our work, and it was wrong for us to center our thoughts and attention on it. If the encounters with Spiritualism had any significance whatsoever for us, it should simply be that they were another indication that the spiritual powers were true, but that the spirit with which we should be concerned was the Holy Ghost, the Spirit that came forth from God. We knew that we needed to devote our missionaries to finding that Spirit and working with Him and to having testimonies of the Holy Ghost rather than testimonies of evil spirits. We explained that in the event the elders were under necessity of being in contact with evil powers, they had the right and the authority to remove those evil influences from their path. Otherwise they were to seek for the power of the Holy Ghost and to work with it and to draw it close to them and enwrap themselves in that great influence and to bear testimony of the Lord Jesus Christ.

This matter of Spiritualism came specifically to the attention of Brother Harold B. Lee when he visited our mission and divided it in 1959. As I explained what our attitude was, he gave us his enthusiastic blessing and later referred to our policy on many occasions, including one occasion in a general conference talk. We had experiences that would be much like those received by Heber C. Kimball when he went to England. I knew that the powers of the adversary were seeking actively to destroy the work and sometimes to combat me personally and to combat our missionaries. In recognizing that, I feel that we eventually gained a tremendous strength in coming to the conclusion that we would labor with the Spirit of the Lord to overcome the adversary.

In connection with this evil influence, I felt that much of Brazil in our early days was under a cloud of darkness. I could feel the forces of darkness that moved across the land. It was a spiritual feeling that was evident with me. Often when I went into new areas I could feel that these clouds of darkness were obstructing the entrance of eternal light. I had a strong impression of that obstruction when I went north to Recife with the intent to explore that area as a new field of labor. Over the years that we were in Brazil, where we introduced the Church and the gospel, I could feel the dispersion of those dark clouds and the feeling that the rays of light were coming forth with great power into the land of Brazil. I was aware of waves of powerful efforts on the part of the adversary to destroy us. They would come in different forms. I never knew how to anticipate them, but

I learned they would come. For example we had a period when numerous branch presidents—I think six of them in one week—sent in word that they were resigning. We then undertook to go back to the branches and put them back together. Some of the presidents were salvaged; others left the Church. On another occasion we had a serious uprising of homosexuality among some of our young men. We were able to learn about it, to reach to the roots of it, and to resolve it. Then other waves of opposition would come. Perhaps all over Brazil missionaries would have impulses to kiss girls. Then we would give them strong instructions and set that in order. Then something else would come. But I was aware of these rolling waves of opposition that seemed to attack us with the hope that they could destroy the Church. I had numerous requests to cast out evil spirits, and I officiated in this way many times. [13]

This feeling of being opposed by the adversary had genesis in an experience on June 1, 1959. I received a phone call from Odair de Castro to come to his home because his brother had an evil spirit. I took Elder Day, and we found the man all distorted and semi-conscious. As I attempted to anoint, he suddenly struck the oil from my hand and with a horrible wild look attempted to attack me. He was restrained with great difficulty. We could do absolutely nothing with him, and finally Elder Day, Odair, and I bowed together in prayer and in our authority called on the spirit to leave him. This only acted to arouse him more, and he attempted more than once to attack us. We took turns praying and commanding the spirit to depart. After a considerable time I continued to be mouth, and after each prayer Odair said, "Keep praying, President, it is going," and so it was. Odair was finally able to catch and hold his brother by the hand without his strong resistance, and as we prayed again the spirit left him with a lingering struggle; he opened his eyes again as sane and normal as anyone, not knowing that anything had been wrong and wondering why we were there.

The feelings of horror in the presence of this evil influence are almost impossible to describe. It was as if we had to fight it or succumb to its influence, and only when we were actively calling on the Lord

---

13. Bangerter Oral History, pp. 69–73

did we feel the absence of fear. The spirit definitely recognized us and abhorred any approach to the man, fighting us with a superhuman frenzy. The change after the evil spirit had departed was almost unbelievable. The man was the friendliest of people, embracing us and inviting us to sit down, take coffee, and visit. Odair with his parents were left in sobs of gratitude, and we embraced all around in the feeling of comfort and thanksgiving that entered among us.

Elder Day and I soon left and drove home with feelings of weakness and humility. As I left the car, I felt the evil influence start to overcome me, and hurrying into the house with Elder Day, we stood by the door and commanded the evil power not to enter our home, which was an abode of the priesthood. The remembrance of the incident did not leave me at peace, however, and after greeting Geri, I returned to the elders' room, roused all six of the brethren sleeping there, and knelt in prayer with them. I felt moved to speak for all of us and to call upon God to put His influence around every missionary in Brazil, for I realized at that moment just how much we were surrounded with an unknown evil and how completely the land was cursed with evil deeds and practices and how rampant the forces of Satan were. We felt the need to call upon the Spirit of God to preserve us in the mission home and all the missionaries in the field. I felt the spirit of discernment come over me, and I understood how much our work was hated and opposed, and I felt that perhaps we were more successful than even we realized. After leaving the elders and going upstairs, I still did not feel satisfied and knelt by Geri's bed to call forth more protection upon our house and family. After that I went to the bedside of each of the children and blessed them in their sleep that no harm could disturb them and that no evil could come into the house. Following all this I had no desire to sleep but lay awake reflecting on the marvelous power with which we had striven and fearing it, but wondering again at how it had finally left in our presence and how we had been delivered. I continued to thank God for his blessing and protection. [14]

There were many other occasions where the adversary attempted to disrupt the work involving minor transgression and temptation

---

14. WGB M.P. Journal, p. 54

among the missionaries, especially in relation to their conduct in meeting with and associating with young women. We re-emphasized the standards of the missionary program to offset these difficulties. I was most earnest in trying to find the spiritual influence that would impel our missionaries to move with increasing success.

Challenges Faced by Missionaries

There were other challenges in missionary work. Some involved dealing with common-law marriages, as divorces were very expensive in Brazil. We also encountered a fair amount of illiteracy, but in general the Brazilian people worked hard to overcome that challenge by taking evening classes and seeking to improve their education. By so doing, they improved their economic situation as well. One of the positive aspects of our time in Brazil was the favorable attitude the people had towards North Americans in general. Following are some of the specific challenges faced by our missionaries.

The Police

In the early days of our experience in Brazil, we heard stories of missionaries being threatened by the police for their proselyting activities in Santo Andre. When I learned of this situation, I made an appointment with the chief of police in that area. He threatened me and declared that our missionaries were acting unlawfully. I was able only to assure him that I would be fully responsible for their actions. However, I was uneasy that police power would threaten our missionary work and therefore called our attorney, Dr. Renato Veras, asking if we could not find a remedy. Dr. Veras advised me that his brother was a high official in the police organization of São Paulo and that we should arrange an interview with him. In a few days we met, and the brother of Dr. Veras said that he felt that the problem was already settled. He had mentioned to the head of the police force the problem in Santo Andre and this head man said: "No, that can't be a problem. I have been to Salt Lake City and know something of those people and of the missionaries. They are perfectly honorable." That was the end of the problem. On another occasion the missionaries in the interior city of Rio Claro were likewise threatened by police action. Dr. Veras arranged for a letter to that city from the São Paulo Police Department, and we never heard further of objections to our missionary work from the police.

Challenges from Other Churches

It happened that a local Catholic newspaper, possibly prompted by the local Catholic bishop, published a report that the Mormons were racist and opposed to receiving those of African lineage. A local editor called me explaining the report and offered me the opportunity to refute the negative article. This caused me great concern, and in earnest prayer I asked our Heavenly Father to assist us in avoiding widespread publicity that would limit our effectiveness in teaching the gospel. I felt blessed to visit the local editor and answer him that we would make no statement concerning the accusation. It developed that nothing of importance resulted in the threat to accuse the Church of racism. Some of the missionaries were concerned about provoking the Catholic Church by our efforts. I told them that we were so small that the Brazilian society didn't pay much attention to us. I said: "The Catholic church doesn't even know we are here. They don't even care. There are more Catholics born in São Paulo every day than we will baptize this year. We really don't amount to much in their view. Don't get excited about how much they may hate us because most of them don't even know we exist. We are not that prominent yet."

Teaching People of Other Races

One of the great problems in our mission was the policy of the Church regarding those who had any lineage of the black race—they were not eligible to receive the priesthood. President J. Reuben Clark had emphasized this to me when I was called to be president of the mission. All matters of ordination were specifically placed in my hands, and I was required to make the decision as to who could receive the blessings of the priesthood and who could not. Thus, the missionaries in their proselyting followed a policy of discreetly determining whether their investigators had any African ancestry. This policy, of course, had been carried out for many years in the mission and was one of the major preoccupations of the operation of the Brazilian Mission. In approving the ordination of men to the priesthood, I very earnestly sought the guidance of the Spirit of the Lord, and because of the mixture of African ancestry among Brazilian people, it was always very difficult to determine who would be eligible to hold the priesthood. As I made these decisions, I prayed to Heavenly Father and told Him that in the various cases before me I had decided to ordain them to the priesthood and that if it was not approved, He should let me know in order that I would not make a mistake.

Communication Concerns

We found that presiding over the mission in Brazil was unique in that we were far removed from Salt Lake City. We had no regular communication, either by telephone or by postal service, and we were pretty much on our own to direct the affairs of the Church in a country larger than the United States. Telephone calls were very expensive and mail service took 14–20 days each way. Telegram service was our preferred means of communication, both within the country and with Church headquarters. For communication mostly within the city, we did use the telephone. Our telephone number at that location was 33-67-61. When we arrived, our mission consisted of about 40 small branches and about 170 missionaries, nearly all of them North Americans, and two or three Brazilian missionaries. Being somewhat alone as the presiding authority of the Church in a nation of 85,000,000 people, I repeated my tour of the mission following the departure of President Sorenson, becoming better acquainted with the missionaries. I had many occasions to address members in the Portuguese language and felt in the beginning that I could hardly put two phrases together. However, through forced effort and the answer to many earnest prayers, I weathered through this beginning experience. My past ability with the language began to return, and I soon found that the missionaries were impressed. The gift of tongues was evident in a most natural and practical manner.

At that time there was no particular supervision over individual missions. We corresponded with the Quorum of the Twelve or the First Presidency about our problems. But it was somewhat like this:

"You go out there and take care of things until someone comes to relieve you." It had been three years or more since the last General Authority had visited the Brazilian mission. Even after General Authorities began to visit us, we were still in a rather autonomous situation, as the mission president was on his own to make decisions and develop policies. At the time we went, there was a need developing over the Church to project the districts toward stakehood. I noted that my call was similar to that of many other mission presidents of that period who had served in Church leadership positions. I was called out of a stake presidency as were many others. Some were called out of bishoprics whereas previous to that time many calls to be mission president had been made to men with little experience in Church administration and leadership. It was very appropriate for the time because we could see that the membership needed leadership and organization.[15] Later on, President A. Theodore Tuttle became involved in supervisory efforts from Salt Lake City, but eventually he moved to Uruguay with his family to render closer assistance and supervision.

Conversion of Three Ministers

We had an interesting situation transpire just prior to our arrival in Brazil. In 1957, the missionaries had found three men who were ministers in various Protestant denominations and who had been affiliated with the ministerial college in São Paulo. One of them, Hélio da Rocha Camargo, was asked to provide information on some other Church. He had heard vaguely of the Mormons and decided to see if they would like to make a presentation to the seminary. Two elders went. Eventually three of these students, now ordained as ministers, found contact with the Church and all three joined. They were Hélio da Rocha Camargo, Saul Messias de Oliveira, and Walter Guedes de Queiroz. With their education and understanding, all three became outstanding leaders. I ordained each of them to the Melchizedek Priesthood. Brother Camargo served in the first district presidency; later he served as a bishop and stake president, then as mission pres-

---

15. Bangerter Oral History, p. 89

ident in Rio de Janeiro and all of the north of Brazil, and as a regional representative. In 1985 he was called as a General Authority and later served as a patriarch.

It was remarkable to see the development of these men as they were given responsibility. When we first called a district presidency in São Paulo, they floundered for a period of a few weeks. Then Brother Camargo, who was a counselor, came in to me and he said, "I would like to be released. I'm not doing anything of value here."

"Why?" I asked him, "What would you like to do?"

"I'd like to go back to my branch and be a teacher. I could be a good teacher," he said.

I asked him then if he could teach over in Santo Amaro too, and he said, "Well, not very well if I taught in Vila Mariana."

I asked, "Do they need you in Santo Amaro like they do in your own branch?"

"Yes, perhaps even worse," he answered.

"Who is going to provide the teachers over in Santo Amaro?" I asked.

"I don't know."

Then I said to him, "Maybe you can get some insight into the reason why you're in the district presidency. Then who is going to provide those teachers? It will not be me or the missionaries. They are going to be people like you."

He left my office with no further questions about what a district presidency was for. Within weeks that presidency assumed full leadership over the branches. Within a year they were presiding over branches as extensive as most stakes in the Church. Their district went from Santos on the coast to Campinas in the interior, and they spent their Sundays traveling. They would release and install branch presidencies under my general approval and supervision and give those presidencies instructions that were equal to those from any stake president I have heard. It was marvelous how the Lord blessed them and enabled them to fulfill their calling. They were blessed also in other ways. Where they couldn't afford a bicycle in the past, suddenly they were able to buy an automobile and travel. They were helped to do their work by blessings that came to them from the

Spirit of the Lord so that the Church could grow.[16] I think that in the matter of giving public instruction it would be difficult to surpass Brother Camargo, who had an extensive religious background, in addition to having graduated from the Brazilian military academy. He was a man of fine education and culture and had an unusual ability as a public speaker. People listened to him with intense interest, both in and out of the Church. Saul Messias de Oliveira also became a bishop, then a mission president, a stake president, and a regional representative. Walter Guedes de Queiroz followed the same pattern, becoming a stake president, a mission president, and a regional representative, as well as a temple president in Porto Alegre.

Air Travel and Centers of Strength

During our service I found myself traveling extensively by air from our headquarters in São Paulo to the southern extremities of Brazil, and later on I made frequent visits to the far north of the country. It was an area probably equal to at least two-thirds of the area of the United States. We saw the building of the new capital of Brasília in the interior and watched the missionaries undertake the organization of the Church in that special place. The main centers of our mission were in São Paulo, Porto Alegre, Curitiba, Rio de Janeiro, Belo Horizonte, and then outward to Recife, Goiânia, and further extension into the interior of the states of São Paulo, Rio, and Minas Gerais. We visited many of the distant places of Brazil, including the interior of Mato Grosso and Cuiabá and all the southern areas of the nation.

Family Growth and Progress

Our family progressed beautifully. Our older children were enrolled in the São Paulo Graded School and were given adequate training and leadership. The younger children, as they attained the proper age, followed through as well. Peggy, as mentioned, was born 10 days after our arrival in Brazil in 1958. Glenn Paulo was born on July 14, 1960, which was on the birth date of our daughter, Glenda,

---

16. Bangerter Oral History, pp. 87–88

who was then 11 years old. Layne Rio was born two years later on April 11, 1962. The family growth proceeded normally and happily with our children in excellent condition. Geri had arranged for all the older children to take piano lessons and found an excellent piano teacher with good qualifications in São Paulo. We encouraged our children in piano, and in Cory's case, he was later allowed to drive as a reward for learning hymns. Our daughter Julie was baptized in our São Paulo chapel and felt herself a real Brazilian Latter-day Saint.

Family Activities and Travels

I was able to take some of the family with me when I drove the mission car. On one occasion I took Glenda (she was about 10 years old at the time) with me to Sorocaba for some Sunday meetings. On the way she asked me, "Daddy, what are you going to talk about in the meeting?" I replied that I hadn't decided yet. She then said with a sly smile, "Talk about me!" At other times I took others of the children, mostly into the interior of São Paulo. We enjoyed our time together, visiting and recounting stories and experiences of times past. Cory always enjoyed being close to the missionaries and often palled around with them when occasion would permit. Early in our time in Brazil I took Cory with me on a trip to Rio de Janeiro. It was a pleasant visit shortly after the Sorensons' departure. He also accompanied me to Curitiba, Videira, and Ipoméia during a school break in July of 1959. We enjoyed the picturesque valley of the Rio do Peixe and the lovely chapel on the hill in Ipoméia. That evening we had a lovely German dinner at the Bauer home. Cory had to speak in either Portuguese or German to get some food to eat. It forced him somewhat to spread his wings and learn a little more of the language. Geri went with me from time to time in my movements to Rio de Janeiro or Belo Horizonte or to other conferences and to the far north in Recife.

Chapter 11

———◆———

THE MISSIONARIES

"The gospel is faith in the Lord, Jesus Christ. This implies a willingness to accept His doctrine and take upon us His name, being obedient to His commandments. The gospel is repentance and a cleansing from all iniquity. It is baptism whereby we have the covenant and promise. It is the right to have the companionship of the Holy Ghost, which, when we have a correct frame of mind, will teach us as we go through the temple. The gospel is the scriptures. The answer to almost any appropriate question about the temple will be found in the scriptures for those who seek it. The gospel is prayer, humility, teachableness, charity. It is commitment and it is covenant and ordinances. It is also blessings. Now may I give some counsel to teachers, bishops, and stake presidents? No one, of course, will learn all about the temple by only one experience; but if you want to prepare your people for the temple, teach them the gospel." [1]

Missionary Organization

Upon our arrival in Brazil and meeting with President Sorenson, I realized that he had been the first of all the presidents in that mission to establish patterns of intensive missionary work and to follow the organized procedure of teaching the gospel according to planned lessons. Thus he had developed a well-ordered mission with faithful and devoted missionaries. His impact on the founding of the gospel in Brazil had been significant. Most people who are called to positions in the Church wonder why they are given responsibility in a particular place and at a particular time. As I reflected upon the

———

1. Collected Works, pp. 88–89

reason why I was called, I realized that the time had arrived for the full order of the Church to be established. Until that time, foreign missions, as well as those in the United States, had been directed somewhat informally. Missionaries labored faithfully. They made contacts and preached the gospel, but the full order of organization of the Church was lacking. Individual members were baptized and then watched over by the missionaries, but the priesthood was not well established among the members. In the case of Brazil, few men were found among the members of the Church. In 1958 there were approximately 3,000 members of the Church in Brazil. The number of men who held the Melchizedek Priesthood was very small.

Even though I was young in years, I had previous experience in Church leadership, having served as bishop and as the president of two stakes in the Salt Lake Valley. This gave me insight into the administrative responsibilities of ward and stakes, the realization of the value of high councils, and the necessity for men to be called and ordained to the priesthood.

Not knowing what purpose I should serve, soon after I became president, the Holy Spirit began to unfold concepts and insights about the mission to my vision. Although I was not well versed in the individual work of the missionaries, I perceived that the way they went about teaching the gospel was different from what we had done when I had served previously. They were, of course, much more effective, teaching with an organized presentation of the gospel. However, the Lord helped me to see that the missionaries were in charge of everything, including the leadership of the districts and branches. There had been so few men baptized and ordained to the Melchizedek Priesthood that few had been called to leadership. The same thing was true among the women's organizations. Missionaries were still giving direction to the Relief Societies. Elders and sisters of the missionary force were doing most of the teaching not only of the gospel but of the programs of the Church. The Spirit of the Lord, therefore, helped me see that we needed to break out of some of these old patterns.

For example, those missionaries called to be district and branch presidents had been assigned a lesser amount of missionary work than the average missionary. The mission standard for proselyting time for a missionary was supposed to be 50 hours of actual proselyting per week. Those who were called to leadership, however, were advised that they could reduce this time to 35 hours of proselyting. This did not ring true in view of the experience I had in the administration of wards and stakes. I knew, for example, that a bishop who presided over his ward and did so with great effectiveness was at the same time fully employed for at least 8 hours a day in his profession. He also had the responsibility of his family, and he took care of the incidentals of his home, yard, garden, automobile, and various other tasks. All of this he did on his own time and still accomplished a very effective and powerful work in his Church leadership. I tried to show the missionaries this concept. The missionary leaders, however, resisted this counsel. [2]

The mission at that time was organized with four of the leading elders being called as traveling supervising elders (TSEs). Their mission was to circulate among all the other elders of the mission every two months and check up on how well they were presenting the discussions and teaching the gospel. They did not personally enter into any proselyting but merely served as "check-ups." While they were faithful in their efforts, their visits were not well received by the missionaries because they did not teach them how to do better missionary work. My experience as bishop and stake president had impressed me with the capacity of men called to serve in leadership positions, bishops in particular. I believed that the governing of Church organizations should be taken care of in their spare time.

I began to teach the missionaries these concepts and met with considerable resistance because they felt the importance of their callings as leaders and administrators rather than being fully devoted to full-time missionary work. This being the case, I called the four TSEs into my office one day and asked, "Brethren are there any missionaries in this mission who really know how to find investigators, teach them the gospel, and bring them to baptism?"

When they responded that they were not sure but that there were many fine, effective missionaries, I asked them if this was in the ca-

---

2. June 1, 1995, dictation to the Historical Department, p. 4–5

pability of any that they knew. They couldn't respond, and so I said, "What about you, brethren? Do you know how to convert people to the Church?"

They responded, "Well, President, we don't do that anymore. We are in leadership."

I then announced, "Elders, we are changing your assignment as of now. If we're not sure if we have missionaries who can convert people to the gospel, I want you four elders to be the ones to experiment and find out how it's done. You have had vast experience. You were out in the field proselyting before your present assignment. No one is better qualified to solve this question than you. You will go two in one area and two in another, and you will go out to find investigators on your own, teach them the gospel, and bring them to a commitment to be baptized."

With that charge in place, I sent them out to determine if in reality that could be done. Within a short period of time, they reported back that they indeed could do it! Elders Rasmussen and Gary Anderson were two of those who experienced early success. They undertook this assignment with great desire. After a period of two or three months the experience of these two pairs of elders was not dramatic, but they were learning and finding some inspired principles in their teaching.

When Elder Rasmussen was released, I said to Elder Anderson, "Now out of the four who were so assigned, you are the only one left. So you are to take Elder Kay Hamblin, a younger elder, and work with him until he understands all the ways by which you can find people and effectively bring them to conversion. When you have Elder Hamblin well trained, we will give him another companion, and we will provide you with another younger elder, thus doubling the number of effective missionaries. As you work among the other missionaries, you will become a spiritual force to infuse the vision into them." This became the basis for tremendous changes that began to take place in the spirit, direction, and feeling of the mission.

Outline of Missionary Work

As we examined the success of these missionaries in their efforts to bring new converts into the Church, some additional adjustments were made in mission policy as outlined below.

Leading missionaries were to move forward in proselyting in spite of incidental responsibilities such as presiding in branches and districts. This principle was taught and emphasized by Elder Kimball in his visits. District and branch leaders were told that unless they could outperform those under their direction, they would be released from their leadership positions.

A special period of devotion was instituted wherein the missionaries were asked to meet a very high standard of hours in proselyting. We began with what we called "Week of Devotion" and asked missionaries to totally rededicate themselves to commitment to achieve the goals we had set. One pair of missionaries spent over 100 hours a week in proselyting activities.

Missionary branch leaders were to be replaced with members and the eventual organization of mission districts would be presided over by members. In some instances this met with resistance among our missionary leaders. They were hesitant to make changes in a system that had been in place for many years.

Attention was to be focused on bringing the Spirit into missionaries' teaching. Following the desire to obtain greater success and in answer to many prayers, it was given me to understand the surpassing power of the Holy Ghost in the teaching of investigators. I was able to show individual missionaries how in their teaching the Spirit of the Lord could command the attention of the listeners and convey knowledge of what they taught. I spent many hours with individual missionaries in rehearsing this principle. I was led by the Spirit to envision and write certain examples of how the Holy Ghost touched the lives of investigators, and the missionaries bore powerful, personal testimonies. By these examples they were able to change listeners into believers. These examples were not my invention but were taught to me by the Holy Spirit. They became known as "Lessons of Faith."

These ideas began to catch hold with the missionaries, and we began to see marvelous changes take place in the mission. It became a turning point in our missionary work. Later on we called it "New Era" of missionary work in Brazil. The power of the Spirit of the Lord began to be felt all over the country and in my personal deliberations specifically. Our missionaries began to believe in their ability to see the blessings in the work. There came a feeling among the missionaries that they simply could not fail. With these feelings being manifest, our training focused on how to answer concerns expressed by investigators, and even how to handle their rejection of the message and the missionaries. Then, in order to retain our new converts, we established "Integration Classes," which served to instruct and solidify new converts in the mainstream of Church activity. Each of these policies and approaches will be discussed in more detail later on.

In addition I made a couple of changes to the rules operating missionaries (rules in those days were not standardized—each mission president set his own):

"I never want to hear another memorized presentation. The gospel is three simple stories: the Godhead, the plan of salvation, and the Restoration. Be prepared to tell it short or long, but it better come from your heart."

"No more Preparation Days. You are on your mission for two and a half years. If you need to write a letter, go write the letter. If you need to go shopping, go shopping. If you need to do your laundry, do your laundry. But if a person or family presents themselves to be taught, teach!"

The overall power by which the mission proceeded came through the revelations that came to us from the Holy Ghost, which caused us to make adjustments and movements to receive the power to teach by the Holy Spirit. I can never forget when early in my experience, I felt the influence and strength of the Holy Ghost descending upon me and upon the mission, endowing us with an unusual power.

We had other involvements that are not common today. At that time we did almost all of our own translating into the Portuguese language in the mission office. We had the responsibility for publication of *A Liahona*, which was the official Church magazine in

Portuguese. We handled all of our printing problems and the production of material for leadership and study in the different organizations and throughout the Branches. We also had the full responsibility to provide buildings for our people. This necessitated a great and continued search for real estate and sometimes involved the purchasing of land, which we handled on our own initiative but with approval from Church headquarters. We also had full responsibility for the construction of two chapels before the Building Committee became active in our area. I therefore supervised the building of the São Paulo and Campinas chapels, and after that the building of the new mission home, which to some extent we worked on in design and fully supervised the construction. [3]

Visit of Spencer W. Kimball

In the midst of this early transition in the mission, in March of 1959 we had a visit from Elder Spencer W. Kimball of the Quorum of the Twelve, who stopped briefly on his way to Argentina and Uruguay; he then later returned to spend three weeks visiting our mission. At the time there were only three missions in South America. We had a youth conference in progress, and he spoke briefly with the youth who had gathered. He never wasted a moment and was busy all the time, even setting up an office in the back seat of our car and typing on his typewriter as we drove.

This visit proved providential in our approach to teaching missionaries a new approach to their work. We visited all the branches and met with all the missionaries; his emphasis was on the absolute necessity of keeping their proselyting time sacred and not allowing other functions, including branch leadership, to interfere with their work. From this teaching we established a policy that we presented to the missionaries, as mentioned earlier. If they were to occupy positions of leadership in the branches or districts, their first requirement was to be leaders in the amount of proselyting they did. Thus, our leading and most capable missionaries who had been somewhat released from proselyting were now required by the policy of the

---

3. Bangerter Oral History, pp. 113 (with added inclusions from WGB M.P. Journal)

mission to be the leaders in proselyting in their areas. If they did not perform in leadership and example, they would not be able to maintain their calling as presidents of branches and districts. Through Elder Kimball's influence we developed a much higher level of proselyting. Thereafter, we projected the missionaries into a demonstration of full devotion to see how many proselyting hours and visits they could accomplish in a week's time. They extended themselves generally in a way that was inspiring, and we felt a wonderful response to their work. As Elder Kimball outlined this condition, I had a renewed vision of what I had brought out of my experience with Church leaders who operated in the wards and stakes, and I said to myself, "These missionaries will never overwhelm me again with the idea that they cannot do a full measure of missionary work." More on the visits of Elder Kimball will be mentioned later on in connection with the visits of other General Authorities.

Teaching Challenges Faced by the Missionaries (Development of the Lessons of Faith)

At the same time the Lord blessed me with other influences through His Holy Spirit. I was made to see that most missionaries, in their day-to-day work would have some success in returning to the homes of their contacts but that almost invariably the time would come when the father or mother would meet the elders as they came for a return visit and say to them, "Well, we have decided not to continue our studies with you."[4] I asked the elders how often this happened, and they mentioned that it was a very common occurrence, that it happened hundreds of times and resulted in a feeling of being fully disappointed that their best investigators had fallen by the wayside. This was usually a moment of great discouragement for missionaries and a common experience of nearly all of them. The Lord helped me to see that this was a normal situation and that during the absence of the missionaries between visits, other influences came into the investigators' lives. Perhaps people had spoken to them against the Church, or maybe they had considered what it might mean to make a change in their religious life, and the

---

4. June 1, 1995, dictation to the Historical Department, p. 8

easy way out was to tell the missionaries not to come back again. The Lord blessed me to see that this was a way to take this discouraging moment and turn it into a moment of power. The Spirit of the Lord rested upon me in such a way that I could understand the solution to this problem, even though I was not skilled in teaching the substance of the discussions. Elder Kimball had suggested that we might in some way shorten our discussions and move a little more effectively to involve our investigators. The old practice was to make one visit a week. I felt impelled to tell the missionaries that they should visit their investigators as often as possible, every day if they were able, so they would be able in a short time to bring them to an understanding of the gospel because after seven sessions only once a week, most of the investigators had lost the influence of inspiration that had first attended their meeting. Heavenly Father helped me to understand that when the missionaries met a family who had been friendly and now decided contrary to hearing more of the gospel, the missionaries should recognize this as an opportunity and that they should expect their investigators' condition to develop positively.

We taught them that an experienced and wise missionary would go back to the home where he had previously taught expecting that there would be a negative response. If he anticipated this moment, he would thereby be prepared and would say in substance, "Oh, I'm sorry that you have decided not to continue studying with us. However, that is your decision and we do not wish to force our religion upon you. We want to tell you how much we have appreciated your kindness to us, and the enjoyment we have had in telling you things that are important about the gospel. Without imposing on your time, could we come in and give a greeting to your family? Then we will not press you unduly to go further in the discussion of the gospel."

Since the missionaries' attitude was friendly, the family would naturally respond with a friendly invitation to enter for a brief period, and then the elders would say, "Now you, of course, do not have to accept our teaching of the gospel, but before we leave, we need to tell you how much the gospel means to us. We want to tell you how we have been called by the Spirit of God, and He has told us how true the experience of Joseph Smith was when the angel Moroni appeared to him. We know that this is true as if we had stood in the presence of the angel ourselves. Now you do not have to join the Church, but we feel you should not refuse the knowledge of the gospel until you have knelt down and asked God what he wants you to do about the message we are bringing."

Almost invariably this would cause the individual or the family to kneel and pray and receive the answer that the Lord wanted them to hear more of the gospel. This and other inspired approaches allowed the missionaries to overcome the objections and the refusals that constantly beset them. This was a revelation to me of power from on high, and I spent many days rehearsing these concepts and this revelation of power to the missionaries. Our supervisors captured the vision and began to have almost daily success. [5] With this concept, we developed a number of common objections and taught the elders a series of what we called "Lessons of Faith" by which they would overcome objections and meet with the power of faith and testimony to bring their investigators to a happy response.

The New Era: Growth in Baptisms

The number of baptisms in the mission had been somewhere around 25 per month, and we wondered how it could be improved. A new spirit of devotion began to disseminate among the missionaries, and their efforts to proselyte were greatly increased. Among those who responded and gained a special influence in teaching the gospel were Elder Gary Anderson of Provo and Elder Larry Memmott of the colonies in Mexico. These brethren, along with others, began to set a standard that raised the level of service and faithfulness among all the missionaries in our mission.

At about this time, missions all over the world were moving forward at an accelerated rate. Those who had previously a rate of 25 baptisms a month were now moving up to 150 or more. We heard of this sort of thing happening in England and in France, and we thought, "Why doesn't it happen in Brazil?" We began to earnestly seek for keys to find how our work could grow. This was the beginning of what came to be known in our mission as the "New Era." At

---

5. June 1,1995, dictation to the Historical Department, pp. 8–9.

that point, with a great deal of study and earnest prayer and looking for what was being done in other places, the Lord came to our help and gave us understanding that I consider to be clear revelation on how our missionaries could be directed, and I was able to instruct our leading missionaries, our supervisory group, in ways that they could overcome obstacles among investigators—the aforementioned "Lessons of Faith." Since these principles were pointed out to me clearly in a spirit of revelation, we taught them to the missionaries, and they gained a sense of power that was different from what they had enjoyed in the past. In the middle months of 1959 and the early months of 1960 there seemed to come an unfolding, an awakening, and a new dawning of understanding and spiritual strength among our missionaries that was remarkable. For example, we had a gathering of our district leaders and supervising elders in a regular leadership meeting in March of 1960. We had been in the mission a little more than a year. There we asked these elders to report on the number of baptisms they expected to have that month. And instead of it being the normal 20 or 25, they suddenly counted up to 75 and 80. It was amazing to all of us to see what was happening. The next month they did have over 70 baptisms, and the following month they jumped to 150.

From that point on, our mission went on to a level of growth that was almost ten times what it had been when we arrived. That year (1960) we saw more than 1,000 people join the Church, where the best year before had been about 500, and the previous year was less than 400. The following year (1961) we had over 2,000 join the Church. This, of course, infused a spirit of success among the missionaries, but it was achieved mostly through the sense of power that they gained in their teaching, which related to how well they could work in companionship with the Holy Ghost. We were able to develop certain instructions and a certain type of lesson approach that would help them at the right moment to reach people and to bring them to respond to the gospel. It is difficult to explain the change that came over the mission, both in its spirit and in its function.

Because of these efforts, we suddenly found that a little house that had been rented to accommodate 25 or 30 people as a branch chapel was completely inadequate. We needed places that would hold 200. We began searching for places of this type and found several, so we were able to expand the size of the branches to the point that they looked like a ward. Many branches in our mission blossomed overnight. Under this kind of explosive growth we were under the necessity of doing what was evident, and that was to fully organize the Church.

Our missionary program continued in a more or less rhythmic way throughout the remainder of our mission. The missionaries had strong supervision. We sometimes had as many as ten pairs of supervising elders. They didn't just travel through the mission—they were sent by special appointment to certain areas where they remained to work for as long as we wanted them to with the other missionaries. They could go into a branch that was disheartened and open it up, with prior assurance. I remember one branch, in Penha, as an example. The senior companion was discouraged and had taken his new companion who had been on his mission but one day out to look over the city. As they stood on a hill, the senior companion uttered a dismal prophecy. He said, "Elder, you're new here, but I want to tell you that the people of this part of the city are not worthy or prepared to receive the gospel. And very soon you'll see that the president of the mission will call us out of this branch so that it can be closed down." He didn't know that that very week we decided to send two of these traveling supervisors out. They came into that branch, and within two weeks' time they had helped baptize 20 new members into that branch. The elder who had uttered the negative prophecy had to assist in the baptism of some of those people. The missionary work came to take on the aspect that nothing was impossible. It became the basis for the establishment of a Church that when we arrived had less than 3,000 members and when we left had two missions and over 14,000 members.

I think our missionaries under the previous leadership had worked with devotion and dedication under strict rules and order, but I think we were able to find some new dimensions. And when the missionaries saw that people were responding to their message, that naturally lifted their spirits to the point where they couldn't wait to do more. We were blessed with an outstanding—and, I might say, a very unusual—group of supervising elders, young men who blossomed to a stature that is still amazing. I'm sure that many of these young men would measure up as being among the very best in the entire Church. They continue to be that kind of men today in their continuing activity in the Church. [6]

Integration Classes for New Members

We developed a process by which we were able to integrate the numerous newly baptized members of the Church. This integration was accomplished in every branch as the missionaries organized what we called integration classes. These were usually held on Wednesday evening, and as new people were baptized into the Church, they were all enrolled in these classes. They met for a period of 12 weeks for instruction regarding what the purpose of the members of the Church should be. It was then followed with a program of preparation and introduction to keeping the commandments, meeting the leadership that was established, and understanding their true position as members of the Church. They learned to pay tithing and fast offerings, to attend meetings, and to be qualified and prepared to receive the holy priesthood.

Feelings about Missionaries—Elders and Sisters

The individual work of the missionaries was the force that carried the mission to ever increasing growth. Their devotion and obedience was a marvel testifying to their faith. Among those who served as missionary counselors were Darwin Christensen, who has since served as a mission president, temple president, and a General Authority; Harold Mickel, who has since served as a stake president; and Larry Memmott, who has since served as a mission president and a temple president. Elder Memmott had a remarkable impact on the mission when he was asked to lead the Rio Claro District. He was suffering from the effects of amoebas and in poor health. He took the assignment to lead his district in proselyting under these adverse conditions and gave me the knowledge that other missionaries were

6. Bangerter Oral History, pp. 84–85

without excuse in their effort. His example had great effect in our mission.

Many others, elders and sisters, gave great support and special leadership including Donald M. Jones, Lawrence Mauerman, William Choate, George F. Richards III, Bruce King, Wilford Cardon, Duke Cowley, Larry Storrs, Bruce Christensen (later to become Dean of Fine Arts at BYU), and Gary Garner, among others already mentioned. One of the greatest of our missionary leaders was Frederick G. Williams III, later a mission president and temple president. There were so many great missionaries that it seems almost unfair to single out only a few.

I would like to mention something about our missionaries. As the atmosphere advanced in the mission, many of the older group began to be released and returned to their homes in the United States. I must mention the wonderful feeling that developed among our missionaries and the closeness with which we felt united to them. It gave us an overwhelming impression to have these young men and young women come in their youth, seemingly without much capability, and to watch them advance in control of their lives and directing the development that was necessary to learn to speak and be effective in a new language, and then to take over the responsibilities of priesthood leadership and power. I perceived that those who would be considered merely boys, after a number of months, developed the capacity to serve to the full measure of their ability and be equal in their responsibility to the capability of the older men with whom I had association as members of the high councils and bishoprics while I served as the president of a stake.

We had an unusual experience with our lady missionaries as well. There was a time when most of our sisters were being released, and suddenly the Church sent a new group of young women to replace them. These, of course, had no ability to speak the Portuguese language, and it was difficult to know how to assign them. We reached out to call a number of young Brazilian women with whom we had had experience and acquaintance. Among them were Cleonice Carvalho, Cleri Pereira, and Marli Pimentel from Ribeirão Preto, and Yone Guarani from Petrópolis. These, and others, became companions of the new sisters who could not speak Portuguese. These teams of women joined together to become very powerful and inspiring in their enthusiasm.

On occasion some of these new lady missionaries came to Sister Bangerter and asked if it was necessary for them to dress in drab apparel and have the appearance of older women. We arranged to have a conference for these sisters. Under their initiative and with the guidance of Sister Bangerter, they developed thoughts and plans of composure, capability, appearance, and loveliness, which made them outstanding young women. As an example of their influence, we had a young lady from American Fork named Jeanette Royle who was especially qualified and capable in her education. She was an example of several others who set a wonderful tone of appearance and spiritual power among the young women of our mission. We enjoyed a delightful experience with the sister missionaries. Generally they were very intelligent and deeply devoted to their work. A number of them served part of their mission in the mission office, usually spending part of their time there and the other half in proselyting activities. We will always remember Sisters Bodily, Burningham, Crook, Daines, Gygi, Huerkens, Olpin, Ovard, Royle, Petersen, Sorensen, Stanley, Wheeler, and others, including Brazilian Sisters Guarani, Pereira, and Pikel. They became an outstanding influence in the mission.

We thoroughly enjoyed the presence of missionaries, a few of whom had living quarters in the mission home and ate meals with us. We always had others coming in on transfers or for a visit, and they joined with the family in a very congenial and happy arrangement.

Without fully realizing what could be developed in our missionary experience, I learned that because of my background in leadership and understanding of the priesthood order of organization, we would be expected to establish and organize The Church of Jesus Christ of Latter-day Saints in its order. In the past, missions seemed to operate merely as groups of missionaries who went out to preach the gospel and convert a limited number of people and then left them on their own. In Brazil we found ourselves deeply involved in the establishment of the Church, much in the same pattern that was followed by the prophet Joseph Smith as he drew on the capabilities of newly called members of the Church and gave them responsibilities in organization by which eventually wards and stakes and priesthood and women's leadership were established.

Chapter 12

——◆——

VISITS FROM AND WITH DIGNITARIES, LOVED ONES, AND GENERAL AUTHORITIES

"The people of this world need you. They need the message that you can give them. They need it more than they need anything else that they can find in this world. Don't ever question the need that people have to know that the gospel has been restored in the last days. When you think of some of the evil conditions that exist around us today, you will see that people are headed to their doom, as it were, if they don't change their course and recognize the power of God in their lives and repent of their sins.

"Repentance is still a valid principle. Some people think that it ought not to be mentioned in polite society, that repentance is just one of those little words that we find in the scripture that we don't want to insult people with that they may have something in their life that they need to repent of, but they do. They really do need to repent and to call upon God. This message is the burden of the gospel of Jesus Christ since the beginning. Adam and Eve cast out of the Garden of Eden spent many years—it says many days, but I think it meant many years not knowing what their course would be, feeling hopeless no doubt that they had no means for their salvation. The great promises they had thought of living eternal life and in the presence of God when they were in the Garden of Eden had all been taken away, wiped out.

"Adam was offering sacrifice to the Lord. The 'angel of the Lord appeared unto Adam, saying: Why dost thou offer sacrifices unto the Lord? . . . I know not, save the Lord commanded me. And then the angel spake, saying: This thing is a similitude of the sacrifice of the Only Begotten of

the Father, which is full of grace and truth. Wherefore, thou shalt do all that thou doest in the name of the Son' (Moses 5:6–8). In those beautiful words the Father set up Jesus Christ as the High Priest by which his children could find their way back into his presence. 'Wherefore, thou shalt do all that thou doest in the name of the Son, and thou shalt repent and call upon God in the name of the Son forevermore' (v. 8).

"As Adam revealed this great message to Eve, the Holy Ghost fell upon Adam and said to him that because thou hast repented 'thou mayest be redeemed, and all mankind, even as many as will' (v. 9). It is a message of eternal life and salvation to which I testify with all my heart knowing that God has restored it in these days."[1]

As part of our assignment, from time to time we enjoyed visits with people of distinction and, at times, political influence. When President Hugh B. Brown came in 1963, we made an appointment to meet with the governor of the state of Guanabara, Dr. Carlos Lacerda. On one occasion two of our missionaries in Brasília obtained an appointment to meet with the president of the nation, João Goulart. They met with him, discussed the Church, and presented him with a copy of the Book of Mormon. On a few other occasions, official contacts of this nature were made, but they had no particular influence in advancing or retarding the proselyting effort. Really we could work in our normal rhythm with or without the knowledge of the leaders of the nation and of the states, but it was always interesting to meet them and inform them of what we were doing.[2]

President Dwight D. Eisenhower

In connection with the arrival of President Eisenhower to Brazil in late February 1960, Brother Gary Neeleman of United Press International (a former missionary to Brazil and later a counselor in the mission presidency) asked that some of the missionaries be invited to give coverage and help to their staff. He therefore arranged for Elder Memmott and me to fly at their expense to Brasília to assist

1. Collected Works, pp. 405–406
2. Bangerter Oral History, p. 84

the United Press there. Inasmuch as I had been seeking a chance to visit Brasília for some time, this was a fine opportunity.

On arrival the pilot gave us a good air tour of what is undoubtedly the most modern city in the world. Situated on a plateau of low rolling hills, the city springs from the vastness of the undeveloped Brazilian interior. The great rolling country is covered by good grass and sparse to heavy tough Brazilian bush. The city has a most agreeable climate and a wide-open, expansive view. The aspect seemed to me in great measure similar to that of the North American West, giving a feeling of freedom and primitive potential. The city was constructed in every way on monumental lines with modern concrete and plaster and is laid out on the shore of a man-made lake with great sections of buildings rising in separated spaces for government, commerce, and residence. Modern connecting highways were already developed. We saw that everything was new, but nothing was finished, and an overlay of red mud blanketed the footing everywhere inside and out.

We arrived in the afternoon and went to town seeking the United Press offices. I was assigned to work with Carl Cramer, head of photography, helping him with interpretations in order that he could give immediate treatment to the first films and transmit them by radio photo to the United States. During all the excitement of the arrival of President Eisenhower, I was occupied in the press room. I enjoyed the chance to see a big news operation on one of the biggest assignments of the year. The men were most grateful for our help. About 5:00 p.m. I went back to the airport and took the return flight to São Paulo, during which I had a long visit with Maria Wickerhauser, who operated an English-speaking broadcast from São Paulo. She was much interested in the Indians and ruins of all America and we had a fine visit. [3]

Governor George D. Clyde

In 1960 the governors of the United States were on a tour to Brazil, and Governor Clyde of Utah was part of that group. Brother David Evans was his advisor and companion, and of course they

---

3. WGB M.P. Journal, pp. 124–125

made contact with the mission. Brother Evans invited my wife and me to attend certain functions in honor of the governors. We attended a reception that was held in the palace of the governor of São Paulo, Carvalho Pinto, and met 15 or 20 of the governors from the United States. We also met and had our picture taken with the governor of the state of São Paulo.

Visit of our Parents: William Henry and Isabelle Bawden Bangerter and Henry Marcene and Duella Hamblin.

In mid-December 1960, we were honored by a visit from my parents. The children were delighted to see them following a two-year absence. Almost immediately they settled into the normal activity of the mission experience, traveling with us at times to various branches for meetings and seeing points of interest as time permitted. Father was able to use his German from time to time as we met with members who spoke that language. Early in their visit, Father gave patriarchal blessings to the three oldest children. I recorded them on the Dictaphone, and they were typed up by our mission secretary. Our outings took us to the interior of São Paulo and to Rio, where we enjoyed touring the city and sights nearby and attended meetings with members and missionaries. They experienced much of the settings in each place we visited, including torrential downpours of rain from time to time. I enjoyed several conversations with Father. On one occasion he told me something of the need he had for strength in his calling as a patriarch; the power of his spirit always showed through in his firmness to serve the Lord and keep in touch with His Spirit.

After a long absence, Geri's parents also paid us a visit. They arrived in October 1962 and stayed with us until January 5, 1963. Their visit was a delightful and happy time for us all, especially for the children as they had time to enjoy the attention of loving grandparents. The family all remember the incident of Father Hamblin walking into the kitchen area, going to the refrigerator, and looking for some cold water to drink. Geri and her mother were meeting there with several sister missionaries. Father found a bottle of cold liquid, tipped it up, and took a healthy swig. Suddenly he gagged, spewing it out and uttering an oath that surprised all present. He then ceremoniously dumped the entire contents of the bottle down the sink, much to the consternation of Geri and her mother. It was the carefully preserved wave set brought from the U.S. as a special treat for Geri to use in her and the girls' hair!

Often we took Mother and Father Hamblin with us on short trips into the interior, visiting places like Ribeirão Preto, Campinas, Juiz de Fora, Bauru, Americana, Santa Barbara, Piracicaba, Araraquara, Santos, Rio de Janeiro and other locations in and around the city of São Paulo. They took a side trip to Iguaçu Falls, which they enjoyed tremendously. Of special note were preparations for Thanksgiving and Christmas, where intense effort and delightful preparations added to the enjoyable atmosphere of the season.

Visits from General Authorities

Various Church leaders also visited the mission during our time there. I think universally they were impressed with Brazil. No doubt they were impressed with situations wherever they went, but I felt that it was important for them to see Brazil as one of the largest nations of the earth in territory and in population. Invariably they recognized Brazil as one of the giants among the nations, with a tremendous potential. I believe that before this period there had been a tendency to feel that the destiny of the Church in South America lay more in Argentina or Uruguay. But these visits seemed to turn the attention of the General Authorities to Brazil as the real heartland of South America, the place where great things would inevitably happen. Of course, I don't want to appear to downgrade the importance of any other country. [4]

Elder Spencer W. Kimball

Elder Kimball visited in March 1959, and this was a period when we developed a strong system for missionary work in the Brazilian Mission. The lesson plan when I became mission president consisted of seven lessons more or less standard throughout the Church. But there had been widespread experimentation with these lessons. The thing that became most popular in progressive missions in the

---

4. Bangerter Oral History, pp. 97–110

Church was what they called a "three-in-one" lesson, which to some degree condensed the first three lessons of the seven-lesson plan into one lesson and allowed for much more rapid teaching. Missions that began to use this type of lesson seemed to get baptisms much faster. They brought people into the Church in a shorter period of time, of course, and increased their baptism rate. So we immediately began to study it, and my supervising elders thereafter wrote a three-in-one lesson, which allowed us more versatility. This was one of the factors that helped things to go faster in our mission. Of course many missions then began to feel at liberty to recompose their lesson plans according to their own ideas. [5]

As Elder Kimball spoke to the missionaries, he told a story of a boy who went to the university to obtain his education. In order to augment his resources, the boy undertook a side employment of chopping wood to be sold to the people who lived nearby. The income he received was so rewarding that he devoted more and more time to chopping wood and lost the vision of why he had come to the university. The question came to the missionaries: "Are you a wood chopper or a missionary?" "Wood chopper" became a byword describing those who did not devote full time to teaching the gospel.

During our visit to the city of Juiz de Fora, we had had a full day of meetings with members and missionaries. Elder Kimball suggested that we sleep in a bit later the following morning since our schedule had been heavy. The next morning I arose and checked at Elder Kimball's hotel door at about 7:00 a.m. Sister Kimball informed me that Elder Kimball had left about an hour before to go over to visit the elders at their branch. I hastened over there, saying: "Brother Kimball, you deceived me!" He answered, "Well, you looked a bit tired last night, and I thought I would allow you to sleep in." From Elder Kimball's comments after having interviewed most of the elders at that conference, I learned that he had found several conditions in their lives that had escaped me, and as a result he had given very emphatic and effective counsel. At the conclusion of our travels together, we gathered at Iguaçu Falls with the other two mission presidents in South America.

---

5. Bangerter Oral History, pp. 101–102

Elder Harold B. Lee

Brazil being such a large country and the number of branches and districts having extended considerably, it had been understood for a long time that eventually the Brazilian Mission would be divided. Before I left for Brazil, Elder Henry D. Moyle had spoken to me about it and said, "While you are there the mission will be divided." And so it was not a surprise. President Asael T. Sorensen returned with his family, in company with Elder and Sister Harold B. Lee in September of 1959. In the process Elder Lee and his wife toured the mission, and we were with them for a period of nearly three weeks, which was about the term of a mission tour by a General Authority in those days. Those occasions with President Lee and President Kimball and later with President Joseph Fielding Smith and President A. Theodore Tuttle were outstanding in their personal effect upon us. To be able to associate from day to day for that prolonged period with these men and their wives was an unusual and very treasured opportunity.

President Lee, of course, in his visit did similar things to what President Kimball did as he strengthened the missionary work and encouraged us. He taught us constantly about the spirit with which we should work, gave instructions about leadership and Church government, and counseled us to move in the organization of districts with local leadership and branches under local presidencies.[6] Meetings were held in Rio de Janeiro with members and missionaries. He told of the reasons for the visits of the Apostles to the missions of the Church, mentioning that the priesthood is a positive power in foreign lands that needs to be increased. He mentioned how the leaders of the Church need to know more about South America personally, how he had instructions to see every missionary personally, and how visits from the headquarters of the Church guard against apostasy. Quoting from the Doctrine and Covenants he also showed how men are called at the right time to preside and fill missions, and that such calls were the Lord's business.[7]

---

6. Bangerter Oral History, pp. 90–91
7. WGB M.P. Journal, pp. 75–76

Elder Lee had a habit, I think, with his companions, whoever they happened to be, of tending to confide in them. Many of the things that he talked about were personal stories, stories of an inspirational nature. One thing we discussed that is vivid with me was his relationship with President J. Reuben Clark. President Lee had been trained as a member of the Twelve under the tutelage of President Clark, working with him closely in the Welfare Program. As I commented to him about this relationship he said, "I suppose that no father was ever closer to a son than President Clark has been to me." Other incidents—and they were too numerous to mention in full or even to recall—would include some personal stories of the testimony of various members of the General Authorities. One that is vivid was his recounting of the time when Heber J. Grant was supposedly on his deathbed, and those who would probably succeed him were Reed Smoot and Rudger Clawson. These men had already passed the time when, because of extreme age, they could be effective in leadership in the Church. It was of great concern to the First Presidency and to the Twelve, and they were anxious to know what the Lord wanted them to do. President Grant was in the hospital in Southern California at the time, not expected to live, and was attended by members of his family, some of whom left Salt Lake periodically to go down and spend the weekend with him.

President Lee's story indicated that one of the sons-in-law of President Grant had been doing legal work for the Church and was about to depart for Southern California when he asked President Grant's counselors if there was anything particular to discuss with the President. They said, "Well, we are greatly concerned about what would happen if he should die." They requested President Grant's son-in-law to ask him, if he had an opportunity, what the Church should do. And so it happened that the son-in-law, sitting with President Grant in the hospital throughout one of the nights found that they could converse together, and he said, "Now Grandpa, the Brethren are very concerned about what will take place if anything should happen to you. Do you have anything you want to tell them about it?" He said President Grant considered the question for some time, and then he said, "Well, I think the Brethren could very safely leave that problem in the hands of the Lord." He then thought a little longer and finally said, "But I will tell you one thing: it won't be Brother Clawson, and it won't be Brother Smoot." He then proceeded to recover and outlive both of them. President Lee told us that story as an indication of how the Lord is in complete control and directs the succession to the Presidency of the Church. I think this subject was always of great importance to President Lee. He was assured as to the manner in which the Lord selects the President of the Church.

Regarding the correlation program, Elder Lee made no particular reference to a readjustment in Church order at that time, but of course he had, years before, fixed his mind on attitudes that indicated that the Church already had the structure to give it proper leadership and that we should not expect to form new patterns of leadership and organization. He always understood that the priesthood was the proper organization and governing agency and that the structure was established by the Lord. I heard him say that in those days and before and since. To have experiences of this kind, walking and living personally by the side of men of this nature, was an opportunity very rare to people on earth. We prized it very much. We had another experience that I recall of having family home evening with Elder and Sister Lee in our home. To have them sit and visit with our children and talk with them and to hear him bear his testimony about how he knew that he had been called of God when he was named one of the Twelve Apostles was a very inspiring thing. Under these circumstances, each of the visiting General Authorities in some degree took on the aspect of a real father to me in the training, instruction, and leadership they gave and in that personal association. [8]

After touring the mission with me, Elder Lee divided the mission in a conference in Curitiba, forming the Brazilian South Mission, which included the three southern states of Brazil. This change gave us a new beginning.

Elder Ezra Taft Benson

Elder Ezra Taft Benson of the Quorum of the Twelve came to Brazil in his official capacity as Secretary of Agriculture in the

8. Bangerter Oral History, pp. 90–93

Cabinet of the President of the United States. Elder Benson arrived in Rio on Friday, October 21, 1960. He came from Brasília in company of the Brazilian Minister of Agriculture, along with his son Reed, his wife, May, and his daughter Bonnie, as well as his secretary, Miller Shurtleff. They were met at Galeão Airport by the U.S. Ambassador Cot and others of the U.S. and Brazilian Departments of Agriculture and by me, the president of the Brazilian Mission.

On Sunday the 23rd, Elder Benson gave his whole time to the activities of the Church and met with the combined branches of the Rio de Janeiro District in the building of the Brazilian Press Association. Two meetings were held, one being a sacrament meeting with more than 200 people attending and featuring the members of Elder Benson's party as speakers. He spoke about the prophecies pertaining to the house of Israel and the various phases of the gathering, explaining how in his numerous travels he had found good people throughout the world, including the people of Russia, and how he had been especially impressed in his visits to the Holy Land to see the great progress being made in the return of the Jews to that place. He emphasized that among many of the Jews of Europe, Zionism is the great motivating factor in their life. In the afternoon meeting he spoke of the promises of blessing and protection to the inhabitants of the American continents; he also spoke of the great progress of communism during the last 40 years and of the evil it represents in the destruction of freedom for mankind.

Between the two meetings, Elder Benson's party had lunch in the Alta da Boa Vista with President and Sister James A. Wilson, first counselor in the mission presidency, and Sister Bangerter and me. Both President Wilson and I spoke in the afternoon meeting. A short meeting was also held with 27 missionaries who had gathered in the city. Elder Benson gave words of encouragement and advice, outlining three things he considered to be always necessary to successful missionary work: testimony, humility, and love for the people. All were told to be true to their companions and to the mission president and to sustain each other with prayer. Following this meeting the party of Elder Benson returned to their hotel on Copacabana Beach.[9]

Elder Benson, departing from Rio de Janeiro, went to São Paulo, where he had requested the privilege of visiting the mission home. This he did in our absence, and he spent one night there and enjoyed some time with our children. He reported to us later on that when he arose in the morning he found himself under the necessity of waiting in line to use the bathroom because of our children.[10] The story is also told that little Peggy slipped into bed with him during the night!

President Joseph Fielding Smith and Elder A. Theodore Tuttle

President Joseph Fielding Smith of the Quorum of the Twelve, accompanied by his wife Jessie Evans Smith and Elder A. Theodore Tuttle of the First Council of the Seventy, also visited about the same time as Elder Benson (October/November 1960). Generally mission tours were made by only one General Authority at a time, but President Smith was advancing in age, and I think the Brethren felt that he ought not spend that much time without someone to accompany him, so Elder Tuttle was assigned to accompany him. This trip prepared Elder Tuttle for his assignment as the resident General Authority for South America. He was ideally suited to the assignment. He was, incidentally, the only member of the First Council of the Seventy who received an assignment of this kind. All others who were so assigned were Assistants to the Twelve, called to Europe or Australia or elsewhere. This, of course, was a forerunner to the program that is again in vogue in the Church, wherein area supervisors (area presidencies) are now working throughout the earth.[11] (Elder Tuttle was indeed a pioneer in regard to the pattern later established for area presidents. He was a member of the First Council of the Seventy—He directed the work for all of South America, but he had no keys of authority and had to request approval from Salt Lake. In light of future organization in the Church, his mission was truly remarkable.)

---

9. WGB M.P. Journal, pp. 179–181

10. Bangerter Oral History, p. 98

11. Bangerter Oral History, p. 101

They arrived by ship in Rio de Janeiro on October 24, 1960, and were met by a large group of missionaries and members from the nearby branches. It was truly a royal welcome, headed up by João Dias who later became the district president in Rio. President and Sister Smith and President Tuttle each responded that coming to South America was the fulfillment of a lifelong dream and that they could see that the spirit among the Latter-day Saints in Brazil was the same as among the Saints in the world over. From there they drove to the international airport for a brief visit with Elder Ezra Taft Benson before his departure for São Paulo. This meeting was the first time in modern history that two members of the Quorum of the Twelve and more than one General Authority had been in South America at the same time. With Elder Tuttle present there were three General Authorities of the Church. [12] The following day a missionary meeting was held in Rio de Janeiro. President Joseph Fielding Smith gave instructions on the purposes of the work and the qualifications and preparation for people to be baptized into the Church. Following that meeting, the official party (the Smiths, A. Theodore Tuttle, Geri, and I) left for similar meetings in Recife, staying at a lovely hotel on the beach in Boa Viagem.

The next day another missionary meeting was held and the elders each gave their testimonies, which emphasized the unity and happiness they enjoyed in Recife and the privilege it was for them to work under the special conditions encountered there. In the evening a general meeting was arranged for the members and friends of the Church in the meeting hall of the Caixa Econômica in the center of town. Several of the members had arrived early and were decorating the place with floral arrangements; they had made a most careful preparation. We found that the meeting had been fully advertised and that once again men of the press and television were present to report the occasion. About 120 people attended, many of them investigators, which was a remarkable crowd considering that the branch has only 30 members and was only six months old. Short talks were given by Sisters Bangerter and Smith, and then I, Elder Tuttle, and President Smith spoke in that order with special musi-

___

12. WGB M.P. Journal, pp. 179–181

cal numbers being presented by Sister Smith in between. The spirit among the members was marvelous in that they couldn't express themselves enough in the happiness they felt to receive the first visit of General Authorities to their city. Elder Tuttle spoke on the possibilities of development for members of the Church and how it is an advantage to live under the blessings of the priesthood of God. President Smith followed with a discussion of the testimony of the Book of Mormon and bore a strong witness to its divinity and the connection he has with it through his family and his position as the historian of the Church.

Leaving Recife, the party flew to Brasília where they toured the new capital city before continuing on to Belo Horizonte. A special conference had been arranged in one of the government buildings downtown with a large and well-appointed auditorium. Once again, all of the party spoke. Elder Tuttle spoke of the necessity to maintain the peculiarities of the Church and showed the value of the Book of Mormon as a new witness and accompanying book that clarifies the doctrines of the Bible, with emphasis on the story of the true baptism. President Smith followed with a brief but emphatic presentation of the true doctrine of baptism especially as it relates to little children who have no need of it and gave a forceful testimony of the doctrine of the Church. There were in attendance at the meeting about 120 people, many of whom were investigators of the Church.

The following day we met with the missionaries in the Belo Horizonte area. Presidents Smith and Tuttle then gave some initial instructions and followed them by holding personal interviews with each of the missionaries. The meeting concluded with remarks from Sister Smith telling of her feelings in the special welcome and attention of the members and missionaries and with instructions from Elder Tuttle who explained the various phases of a missionary's life, past, present, and future. President Tuttle also taught that we were now of the leadership of the Church. He showed how little the Catholics had accomplished for the moral strength of man in the last 400 years and admonished the missionaries to follow the Master and study him. Finally a question and answer session was conducted by President Smith, including explanations of the following questions:

"Who is God's Father?" "Who atoned for the fall of Adam?" "What causes physical deformities?" "Will we progress more slowly without our bodies?" "Are sins of children the responsibility of parents?" and "Who is the God of the Old Testament?" He admonished the missionaries never to forget section 4 of the Doctrine and Covenants and said that revelation will always come from proper authority. From there, the official party departed for Rio de Janeiro.

Following a delightful morning drive with President Smith and Elder Tuttle to Corocovado, where we enjoyed the view and took pictures, we met in the Tijuca Branch, where we attended a district priesthood meeting, attended by approximately 25 members and 24 missionaries. The next day, a Sunday, a special conference was held in the Rio de Janeiro District in connection with the visit of President and Sister Smith and Elder Tuttle. The Theater of the Brazilian Associated Press was the setting, and meetings were held at 10:00 a.m. and 2:00 p.m. A special feature of the conference was the organization for the first time of a district presidency among the members of the Church. The district was adjusted to include the Branches of Tijuca, Ipanema, Niteroi, Petrópolis, and Meier. I made the presentation of the proposed organization, and installed as district president was João Antonio Dias Jr., and his counselors were Merrill Boyce Asay, president of the Ipanema Branch, and Jorge Mauler, a counselor in the Petrópolis branch presidency.

Both meetings featured the discourses of President Smith and Elder Tuttle as well as talks from Sister Jessie Evans Smith, who spoke to the people with such a warmth and love that she captivated their hearts. She also sang in each of the sessions. There were about 190 people in attendance at each of the sessions, most of them members of the Church but also a number of investigators invited by the missionaries and members. There were also representatives of the cities of Teresópolis and Novo Friburgo, which had recently opened to missionary work, and several members visited from the branch of Juiz de Fora in Minas Gerais.

On October 31 we left Rio and flew to São Paulo. The new edition of the Book of Mormon had just been completed and the first copies delivered. A press conference was arranged at the mission home in the late afternoon, which was attended by representatives of the principle newspapers of São Paulo as well as Television Station 2-P. Papers represented were the *Folha*, the *Diários* (*Associated Dailies*) and *Última Hora* (*Latest Hour*). The interview covered the range of activity and beliefs of the Church in general and was a friendly and agreeable meeting. Questions were posed by the reporters to President Smith and Elder Tuttle and were answered with me as the interpreter. The interview was arranged by Brother Gary Neeleman of the United Press International São Paulo Bureau.

The next day consisted of a tour of the new chapel being constructed in São Paulo, following which a meeting was held with the missionaries serving in the mission office. In the afternoon, we all left for Campinas where we looked over the new building project being constructed there and then repaired to the hotel in preparation for the meeting that evening with the members of the Church in Campinas. The meeting was an outstanding success with 175 people present to enjoy the singing of Sister Smith and hear the messages of President Smith and Elder Tuttle.

After spending the night in Campinas, we left by car and drove to Rio Claro. A group of 46 missionaries had gathered from the districts of Campinas, Rio Claro, and Bauru. The day was spent in missionary meetings, beginning with interviews by President Smith and President Tuttle. During this period Sister Smith and Sister Bangerter met informally with the missionaries in an extemporaneous talent show and entertainment program, which was most enjoyable for all the missionaries. The program was highlighted by the happy, congenial spirit of Sister Smith, who also sang several numbers for the group. In the more formal meeting which followed, several of the missionaries gave reports of their work, following which President Smith opened the meeting to questions about the gospel and gave response according to the scriptures. He answered such questions as "Was Christ married?" "What is the Adam-God doctrine?" "What about Paul's statement that by faith we are saved?" "What is the proper method of administering in the priesthood?" "How best to handle evil spirits?" "What is the work of the gospel in the spirit world?" and

"Which of the Godhead speaks by revelation to man—the Father or the Son?"

In the instructions given by President Smith and Elder Tuttle, President Smith set forth the duty to warn the nations and to bear testimony to all men, leaving them without excuse, and spoke of the great value in the present missionary program of working through referrals. Elder Tuttle's remarks spoke of the great joy it is to study the gospel. He instructed missionaries on becoming organized and living for the blessings of the Spirit, which can be counted as extra blessings, explaining that even revelations may come when needed and they should learn to commune in prayer with the Lord. He taught that missionaries should exercise faith, and senior companions should bear down on juniors, who are expected to respond, all in the proper spirit. In the evening the members of the Church from many branches in the interior of São Paulo gathered. They represented Rio Claro, São Jose do Rio Preto, Aracatuba, and Bauru. There was a gathering of more than 250 people, by far the largest member gathering ever assembled in Rio Claro. The Church was jammed beyond capacity. Special seats were set up in the open area outside, and this space was also filled beyond possibility of further standing room. We returned to São Paulo late at night.

The next day we went to the Vila Mariana Chapel, where all the missionaries of the districts in and around São Paulo had gathered for a special missionary conference. Once again President Smith and Elder Tuttle carried out personal interviews with each of the missionaries, during which time Sister Smith and Sister Bangerter had another interesting program with the missionaries who were not involved in interviews. Then followed a meeting in which President Smith again gave answers to many questions presented by the missionaries in what was an enjoyable session and an outstanding opportunity for all of us. Some of questions presented were as follows: "Was the Melchizedek Priesthood taken away with the departure of Moses?" "Did anyone hold the Melchizedek Priesthood between Moses and Christ?" "What were the keys held by Elijah?" (The answer was, "To open and close the heavens.") "What were the keys of the dispensation of Abraham?" (The answer: "The keys of Noah.")

"Where did John receive the authority to baptize?" "How can we discern spirits?" (There followed a full discussion on spirits.) "Can a Mason be baptized?" "Did the Nephites have the Melchizedek Priesthood?" (Answer: "That's the only Priesthood they had.") "Why couldn't Adam and Eve have children in the Garden of Eden?" "Do all spirits have physical bodies?" (Answer: "Yes, but this does not mean bodies of flesh, they are bodies of spirit.") "Who wrestled with Jacob?" (The answer: "It was some being of mortality, although perhaps in a changed state.")

We then heard the inspiring reports of a number of the missionaries who told of their success and enthusiasm in working in the new era. Elder Tuttle then spoke, giving a most animated and inspired talk, teaching the missionaries to be prepared in all things and showing the vision that has come to the Church through the prophet in the new era. He taught of the necessity to organize and perfect each missionary. He showed that companions should be united and taught them how to love and be a little blind toward each other, explaining that you can't give away what you don't possess. He showed the necessity of testimony, faith, and knowledge. In the study of the gospel, he counseled not to go in over our depth but to find the answers when we don't know them so that we will not always be in ignorance of the truth of the gospel.

The following morning we held a special meeting of the mission presidency in which we covered a review of the organization of the mission and the direction of the work among the members and among the missionaries, including programs of leadership, proselyting, and integration of new members. We received instructions from President Smith and Elder Tuttle especially on the power of working through referrals. That evening we had arranged for a special reception to be held in honor of President and Sister Smith and Elder Tuttle, and beginning at about 7:00 clock about 75 or 80 people came to the mission home, consisting of the various leaders of the mission, the São Paulo District, and the branches in the district, with their wives and husbands, and a number of the professional people—the lawyer, school teachers, architect, and contractors—who worked for and with the Church. They came leisurely and were able, each one, to spend considerable time pleasantly talking with the General Authorities and getting well acquainted with them. It was a pleasant and enjoyable experience and one that greatly thrilled the members in leadership in the Church.

The following day was spent in and around São Paulo. A baptismal service was held at the mission home during the afternoon for 19 people. Four others also joined the Church in São Paulo that day but were baptized in another place. In the evening a special music festival was held in the new and as yet uncompleted São Paulo chapel. It was presented by the Mutual Improvement Association of the São Paulo District and consisted of a series of musical numbers of all kinds, with many of them being framed by living figures in still pose with lovely costumes and interesting decorations. The program lasted about two hours, and there were between 400 and 500 people in attendance.

On Sunday a special district conference of the São Paulo District was held under the direction of President Smith assisted by Elder Tuttle in the unfinished São Paulo Chapel and consisted of a priesthood meeting held at 8:30 in the morning, followed by two general sessions at 10:00 a.m. and 5:30 p.m. A special leadership meeting was also held at 4:00 p.m. with a short special meeting with branch and district presidencies prior to the priesthood meeting. Special talks of instruction were given by President Smith and Elder Tuttle to the assembled leadership and priesthood. Five priests were presented for ordination to the office of elder, and several men and boys were presented to receive various ordinations in the Aaronic Priesthood. In the report of the priesthood it was noted that the Aaronic Priesthood had increased 25 percent in number in the last six months, and the Melchizedek Priesthood had increased 33 percent in six months. There were 11 branches represented, and the attendance in the morning meeting was 671; in the afternoon it was 732. Special musical numbers were given by Sister Smith in each of the general sessions, and a missionary quartet furnished music in the morning. Besides President and Sister Smith and Elder Tuttle, other speakers included me; the counselors in the mission presidency, Presidents Wilson and Hamblin; the district president, José Lombardi; and the second counselor, Hélio Camargo.

A mid-day luncheon was served at the mission home after which President Smith and Elder Tuttle gave a special blessing to Lee Ann because of her difficulty in hearing, which gave her a feeling of comfort and joy.[13] President and Sister Smith and Elder Tuttle also visited with the family around the dinner table, discussing various questions in the scriptures, especially those pertaining to the resurrection from the Book of Mormon and from section 88 of the Doctrine and Covenants.

President Smith took a particular interest in this discussion and in a very sweet and humble manner explained the pride he has always felt in belonging to the family of the Prophet Joseph Smith. He then gave his opinion on the Prophet as a man of mighty stature before the Lord and explained his testimony of the position Joseph Smith occupies in the work of God among his children, feeling that he towers among the very greatest of the faithful of the Lord's servants. It was a thrilling and impressive experience, coming as it did from the heart of this sweet and profound student of the gospel. After we had finished this discussion and had seemingly run out of comment, President Smith again spoke and referred to the fact that he was a close relative of the Prophet Joseph Smith. He said, "I don't feel that it happened just to do me honor. I don't feel that I'm better than anyone else. But I have always counted it one of my great blessings that I have been a member, a close member, of the family of the Prophet Joseph Smith." Then he referred to his grandfather, Hyrum Smith, who was the brother of the Prophet. He said, "I think it would be a privilege for anyone to have that close relationship." He then gave us a testimony of the Prophet Joseph Smith that was unusual, and perhaps unique. "I have come to know," he said, "that Joseph Smith was one of the greatest of all the men who have ever come forth out of heaven to work on the earth for the salvation of mankind, perhaps the greatest excepting the Savior, but at least one of the very greatest of all the spirits that ever have come." Then he said, "I feel that I have been distinctly blessed and honored to be a part of that great family."

---

13. WGB M.P. Journal, pp. 181–188

I felt that we were listening to one of the great testimonies of my experience, from a man who had the knowledge, the understanding, and the ability to make that special reference to the Prophet Joseph Smith. It was an occasion that I shall never forget and that I treasure as one of the greatest testimonies that I have ever received. [14]

In conclusion he told us we better get better acquainted with the scriptures if we expected to get into heaven. Geri told him that on account of her being busy and trying to bring up the children behind to make a favorable presentation on me, she did not always have time to study as she would like and asked, "Do you think there is any hope for me?" He responded by pulling his glasses down over his nose, looking her in the eye, and saying, "I suppose so, if you will make him a cherry pie once in a while."

It was a day of monumental activity and progress in São Paulo and one of special experience for all of us who had contact with the visiting these Brethren. The following day the Smiths and Elder Tuttle left for Curitiba to spend time in that mission with the missionaries and members. During this whole period of the visit of the General Authorities I was sustained immeasurably by my dear wife who made all things move for me so that my attention could be undivided in the responsibility of caring for them. She expressed a marvel of love and sweetness for me that never is properly repaid to her in expression, although it is perfectly felt in all times and places. [15]

Elder A. Theodore Tuttle

When Elder Tuttle arrived to preside in South America residing at Montevideo, Uruguay, in 1961, he made regular visits to all the missions. In those visits he dealt with the supervision of most matters that were being handled in the Church. He was not specifically authorized, as I recall, working with the Building Committee program, but he did attempt to correlate it. Our missions were still administered through direct contact with Salt Lake City because the department in Montevideo didn't have the facilities to do all the things that we needed. But in policy, in instruction, and in guidance

---

14. Bangerter Oral History, pp. 98
15. WGB M.P. Journal, p. 189

and leadership Elder Tuttle was our leader and, of course, advised us on procedures that should be followed. We appreciated and loved him with all our hearts and accepted his instructions and the wisdom of his leadership without reservation.

Elder Tuttle had a great ability to see into the missionary process. He could relate himself to what a missionary faced from day to day. His ideas were very practical. He could pick up points of inspiration from individual missionaries and project them for the benefit of all others. He also kept us centered on the main goals of missionary work, including the need to build for strength, the need to find men, and the need to bring families into the Church. These concepts are still valid and are being taught with increasing urgency, but they were well projected at that time by Elder Tuttle, who I think had a profound insight into the nature of the way missions should grow. I have always felt that he was among the great missionaries of all time in the Church because of his vision, ability, and general understanding. He saw the value of numbers. He felt, as we did, that if we baptized many people and lost 10 percent in apostasy we would grow much faster than if we baptized few people and lost 10 percent in apostasy. So we didn't feel too distressed that there was some fallout among the membership of the Church. Of course we didn't want to have many people baptized and have a 50 percent apostasy; we worked hard to avoid that, and I think we were successful. [16]

Elder Milton R. Hunter

Elder Milton R. Hunter of the First Council of the Seventy visited us in July or August of 1961. He was conducting a tour for members of the Church in areas that were called Book of Mormon lands and throughout other parts of South America. He had had considerable difficulty with his transportation arrangements, and I went with him to the head office of Real Airlines, which had failed in some of their commitments, and helped work out some of the difficulties that their tour had encountered.

One special incident relating to this visit occurred while he and his tour group were in Rio de Janeiro over Sunday. We therefore ar-

---

16. Bangerter Oral History, pp. 104–105

ranged for the group to visit in the branch in Jardim Botánico. There the time was given to Elder Hunter to speak, and I interpreted for him. He undertook on that occasion to bear his testimony of the Book of Mormon, he being perhaps one of the most qualified men to do so in terms of demonstrating the external evidences of the Book of Mormon, to which he had devoted a great deal of study. But as he spoke of these evidences and then began to talk of the internal evidences and then of the great testimony that was available, I noticed in the midst of his speech (though I was unable to concentrate on it fully because of the pressure of translation) that we were witnessing an unusual experience. He was being especially inspired to give the spiritual side of his testimony. Following the talk Brother Hunter turned to me and said, "You know, I'm so weak I can hardly stand. While I was speaking I felt an experience that I have had only once before in my life. It seemed that I was being lifted out of my body almost, that I was standing almost off the floor. It was of such a nature that I was physically weak. But I knew that it was a manifestation of the Spirit of the Lord, that He approved of what I was saying." And he continued, "I had a similar experience a number of years ago in New England, but I would advise you not to talk about it. Let's just keep this to ourselves. It's a sacred thing to me." I think that since he has passed away it wouldn't be out of order to make mention of this special manifestation. He indicated that Elder S. Dilworth Young was present on the former occasion. I don't know whether that experience has been recorded, but I mentioned it to Elder Young following my return from Brazil, and he said, "Yes, I was there on the other occasion. I know what it was." [17]

President Hugh B. Brown

President Hugh B. Brown, a Counselor in the First Presidency, came to Brazil in January of 1963. He was there at that time on a tour of all the missions in South America, and it was a short visit. He was accompanied by his daughter, Zina Lou Brown. We met them in Rio de Janeiro and held conferences in that city and then went on to São Paulo and held a large mission conference there. On both occasions

---

17. Bangerter Oral History, pp. 107–108

we held a conference with the missionaries and another one with the members. Nearly all the missionaries in the mission were invited to those two meetings. Because of the brief nature of his visit, we didn't visit other cities. President Brown was of an advanced age at the time, but very vigorous, although we were careful to safeguard his health.

I can remember the impressiveness of his instruction, especially to the missionaries. In São Paulo during the conference with the members his speech was interpreted by Remo Roselli, a Brazilian who had formerly filled a mission in Brazil and who was not a particularly active member of the Church. However, he had an unusually fine ability to translate or to interpret. President Brown there told his special parable of the currant bush. Brother Roselli was able to interpret for him in such a way that the interpretation seemed to enhance the presentation and the testimony that was attached to it. It was a very spiritual occasion. President Brown's method of speaking lent itself to an easy interpretation, and the spirit and the understanding of his message came through in a very powerful way, impressive to everyone. The spiritual level at that meeting was something almost unequaled in our experience. The same was true in the meeting he held with the missionaries, where he projected a spiritual influence to them that was unequaled in my experience with other General Authorities. We felt very much the closeness of the Holy Ghost in the meeting. He was able to uplift and inspire the missionaries. He made a comment that I understand he may have made on other occasions. He said near the close of his remarks that there were those in the group who would someday be in bishoprics and in stake presidencies, and he said, "There also will be some of this group who will be among the General Authorities of the Church." I don't know whether it was out of a brief moment of ambitious thinking or whether it was a true touch of the Holy Spirit that said to me, "You might be included in that group."

Later, after these wonderful meetings, we persuaded President Brown to take a little drive with us down into the center of the city. He had not been able to go down into the business center, and I felt that he ought to get a picture of what was there. Immediately as we entered that section of the city, his eyes began to sparkle and pop, and he said, "My goodness, I never dreamed there was anything like this in South America." It was a true eye-opener and an impressive experience for him. [18] Elder Brown was given our master bedroom to stay in while he was in São Paulo. The following morning we found him in the room with many of our children, who had come in to greet us and found him there instead. He was delighted with the experience.

The emerging areas in the Church up to that time had been Europe and England. Then Mexico began to develop, and solid growth was occurring in Japan. There was also an awareness of South America. I think following the visit of these men, there was a realization that South America was one of the great areas of the earth and one of the productive areas as far as the growth of the Church was concerned, so that it has ever since been considered one of the central areas. Awareness came to them concerning the Portuguese language, for example. Before we went to preside many people thought that Brazil spoke Spanish like the rest of South America. The General Authorities, however, have always known the difference.

18. Bangerter Oral History, pp. 97–110

Chapter 13

GROWTH IN BRAZIL

"Heber C. Kimball undertook a mission, and in less than a year had established the preaching of the gospel in England and had gathered many thousands of people to respond to the message of salvation. I often think it must have been rather difficult for people to join not only an obscure organization but also almost a nonexistent one and then proclaim that it is the only true church and that its destiny is to fill the whole world and to bring to fulfillment the prophecies of Daniel that in the last days a stone would be 'cut out of the mountain without hands' and would roll forth and fill the whole earth. (Daniel 2:45; see also D&C 65:2.) We can comprehend that a great deal more right now when we see a body of wonderful people like yourselves ready to go than we could have in imagining what must have passed through the mind of Heber C. Kimball and many others like him, but the work is moving now with great power." [1]

Land Purchases and New Chapels

The Church had authorized the building of a full-sized modern chapel in São Paulo. The property had been purchased on Praça Italia along Avenida Rebouças. With the help of Dr. Max Ouang, we negotiated a contract for the building with an Italian-Brazilian firm. I was expected to give supervision to the construction. We organized the local membership to do some of the initial work in preparing the site, but there was little they could accomplish and the giving of any substantial contributions was not realistic due to the small membership and their limited resources with a depressed economy. The building progressed well and was finally finished far enough for

---

1. Collected Works, p. 393

a conference to be held during the visit of President Joseph Fielding Smith and Elder A. Theodore Tuttle in 1960. It was finished in 1961 with impressive ceremonies.

We were also authorized to build a new mission home, which we did, adjacent to the chapel in São Paulo. It was a lovely structure, having adequate accommodations for the family and for visitors, with the office area downstairs giving appropriate work space for all those who came in to carry forward the leadership responsibilities. We were quite comfortable in these quarters and felt content to stay there as long as the Church wanted us to continue.

Being responsible for all matters of real estate, and without an agent, I began to look for properties in which to meet. In some places we rented houses with adequate facilities. In a few cases, we purchased houses that had the means to expand. These are only a few examples of the various places where we felt the need for more facilities, more expansion, and more growth.

The following year (1960), we made a contract to build another chapel in Campinas. In the meantime I had purchased a house in Ribeirão Preto, which we decided to remodel and which served as a chapel for several years. In Penha in the city of São Paulo, we purchased a modern home that served well, giving room for adequate church activity as the membership grew. We rented larger homes in Santo Amaro and Pinheiros that allowed attendance for as many as 200 people. In Rio de Janeiro in the Jardim Botánico area, we also purchased a house, which later was demolished to make room for construction of a chapel. These arrangements were to accompany the great increase in membership and the accelerated rate of baptisms. In many ways I saw the vision of a growing and expanding Church in Brazil. Thereafter, the Church eventually established a building program, calling on native young men to serve as building missionaries. Several other chapels were developed in different parts of the country.

Northern Expansion—Recife and Brasília

With the Brazilian Mission area reduced after the division of the mission and the loss of the southern areas, especially Porto Alegre and Curitiba, we renewed our emphasis in the north. The building of the new capital in Brasília drew our attention, and we expanded to begin proselyting in that area. We also sent missionaries into the state of Goiás in the city of Goiânia and opened a few new areas within the state of São Paulo. This led, of course, to our interest in some of the more distant parts of Brazil. We had never done any work in the northern areas, which were composed of a somewhat heavier mixture of people who were of African descent, but I felt that we needed to explore and understand the possibilities in these areas. We, therefore, made a journey to Recife in the far north of Brazil, where I saw a great and thriving city. We made visits to some of the other northern cities as well, such as Salvador, São Luíz (where we had an American member family living), and Belém. I also visited the cities of Cuiabá and Campo Grande in the state of Mato Grosso.

In consultation with my missionary leaders, we determined to expand our mission and especially to open the area of Recife by send-ing a group of missionaries to that area. Recife was about 12 hours or 1500 miles away by air from our mission headquarters, and it was a rather significant departure in the function of our mission. That would mean administering someplace like Chicago from Salt Lake City. But we had good airplane flights, and it was a matter of merely getting on a plane and arriving. Eventually, I chose four elders to go there and begin what appeared to be almost a second mission. Elder Michael Norton was designated to be the leader of this group of four. The others were Elders Stanley Dunn, Joseph T. Williams, and Gary Kidman. They went forth with great vision and understanding. The opening of Recife was the most impressive and meaningful advance in the mission, but we also moved north from São Paulo into oth-er areas of the state of Minas Gerais, sending Elder Kay Hamblin to Uberaba and Elders David Hibbert and Craig Shiner to the city of Goiânia in the state of Goiás. This made it possible to consider the new city of Brasília. In São Paulo, missionaries were sent to São Carlos near the city of Araraquara, and before the division of the mission they were sent to the city of Maringá in the state of Paraná.

With regards to Brasília, the president of Brazil, Juscelino Kubitschek, had launched the effort to construct the new capital of the nation in a wide open area of endless plains in the interior of the state of Goiás. There were no railroads and only primitive highways to supply the vast construction of such a monumental city. Brasília was nothing but a construction camp in 1958 and 1959. It was officially inaugurated in 1959. It took another year or two to finally establish a population that was stable there. Of course there were many thousands of construction workers, but we were there from the beginning. On the occasion when President Eisenhower visited Brazil he stopped in Brasília to help inaugurate the new capital. As soon as we found it practicable, we sent missionaries there to proselyte. We had two or three families of the Church who were already living there and who had made contact with us, so we were able to establish a small branch right away. Angelo Perillo and Jason Sousa, who had moved from Campinas, were some of the early leaders. I visited Jason when he was working as a government official, and he quickly determined to resume his activity in the Church. It eventually became a thriving branch. In Brasília we were able to have the government donate a parcel of land on which to build a chapel. Eventually the population there became stable, and we were able to contact people on the basis of their connections with other parts of Brazil. It was a pleasant place to work. [2]

Our missionary work in Recife was immediately successful. Within a few weeks our first missionaries contacted and converted key families who became the stalwarts among the leadership of our branch and then later our district there. These included the Milton and Irene Soares family and later the João Dias family, who moved there from Rio de Janeiro. Milton's son Irajá served a mission and later was called to Church leadership as bishop, then as stake president, and eventually as regional representative. He also served as an Area Seventy. Another son, Mozart, was also a leader of prominence who served as a bishop, stake president, and Area Seventy. Opening Recife turned out to be a thrilling and enjoyable experience.

Brazil is so expansive that it has great regional cultural differences, perhaps greater than what you find in the various areas of the United States. Transportation was not yet developed to the point

---

2. Bangerter Oral History, pp. 93–95

where they could amalgamate the whole country. Northern Brazil is different, but it's still Brazilian. This had been one of the interesting aspects of the missionary work in Brazil. Even though we thought about and foresaw problems with the mixture of races, they almost never developed. I was pleased to see how easily the people of the country and the members of the Church adjusted to the existing policy of the Church. Where I thought this would be one of the great difficulties to the progress of the gospel in Brazil, during our time and since, Brazil has been the leading area of Church growth in South America.

Local Leadership in Brazil

When I first arrived and became mission president, the mission presidency counselors were both missionaries. One of them was assigned to watch over the missionary activity and the other to give supervision over the members in the branches and to help develop leadership programs, all of which emanated from our office. After about a year or year and a half, I called Brother James A. Wilson, who had recently arrived as a representative of General Motors, to be my counselor. Brother Wilson was heavily involved in business and didn't give a dynamic influence to leadership, but he was interested and effective in many areas and eventually was asked to watch over the member activity. Even with a local member as a counselor, we still needed a missionary to follow through because the work became more intense, so we had an assistant to the president to help out with items associated with the missionary work. The other counselor continued to be a missionary for some time. However, with the rapid growth among the members, I eventually called a second member, Hélio da Rocha Camargo, to be a counselor. Our member counselors took assignments to conduct special leadership training and to preside in some cases at district conferences and often to accompany me to these special meetings. At that point I organized what I called a "missionary council" of three elders, who supervised the missionary effort under my direction, without being themselves members of the presidency. I had a series of missionary counselors: Darwin Christensen, William S. Reich, Lynn Leigh, Kay Hamblin, and Don

Jones, among others. At the time I was released (in 1963), the new mission president called two Brazilian men to be counselors, Brother Camargo and Brother José Lombardi, who by then had served as a district president. Brother Wilson was released at that time. [3]

The training of members and local leaders was carried on with ever increasing effectiveness. In 1959 we organized the first district presided over by members. It may have been the first such district in all of South America. Brother José Lombardi was called to be the district president. His counselors were Hélio da Rocha Camargo and Lionel Abacherli. President Lombardi bought a car so he could visit the branches from Santos to Campinas. He was imbued with the Spirit of the Lord, and he interviewed and called leaders to preside over branches. This presidency prepared men to be ordained to the priesthood. We began to add members to the district council. Women were called to Relief Society boards, Primary boards, and MIA boards.

We demonstrated graphically how sacrament meeting should be conducted. We taught the various programs of Church activity, such as home teaching, welfare, and genealogy. We eventually had seminars to train these groups of leaders and help them understand what the Church should really look like and how it should fulfill its purpose when it was properly organized. All this training became the foundation for the future organization of stakes. The first stake in all South America was organized in São Paulo a short time after we left the mission. [4]

We found these early leaders came from a variety of backgrounds. The controlling factor was their faith and devotion to the gospel. Thus I think of Brother José Lombardi, who became the first district president, the first bishop, and the first patriarch in South America. He was a rather humble man, without an education, who had built his own business as a television repairman and made it pay well, but almost his entire experience in leadership was what he had in the Church as a branch president and in the other offices. Later he was made a regional representative and was sent to Portugal as a

---

3. Bangerter Oral History, p. 115
4. June 1, 1995, dictation to the Historical Department, pp. 9–10.

patriarch. He also served in the presidency of the São Paulo Temple. I don't believe I have seen a more effective leader. His effectiveness centered in his spiritual nature and in his general understanding of what a leader or a father ought to do to train those under him. He did it earnestly.[5]

The Lord blessed many men and women with tremendous power as they accepted leadership in the Church in Brazil and became a mighty force in its establishment and its growth. Over a relatively short period of time, there was a great flowering of leadership amongst the local members of the Church. These men surged forth and became great leaders of the Church. Brother Jason Garcia de Souza became a strong branch leader in Brasília. Over the succeeding years he became a mission president in Porto Alegre, then a stake president in Curitiba, and then a regional representative and a temple president. Antonio Camargo, one of our earliest native Brazilian converts had lived for a time in Utah and was an ever faithful and capable leader, also becoming a regional representative. Brother Walter Spat, one of the earliest members in São Paulo, worked without ceasing in the early days of the mission. He served in the district presidency and was called to be the first stake president in South America. He was also a regional representative and eventually served in the presidency of the São Paulo Temple. He operated an impressive furniture factory in Caxingui, near the future temple and has been much honored as one of the pioneers of the Church in Brazil. Brother José Benjamin Puerta, one of the early members in São Paulo, served as stake president, as regional representative, as temple president, and as president of the Brazil Florianopolis Mission. There are many other notable leaders among those early members of the Church, but I cannot recall and mention them all in this history.

Developing Strong Leadership in the Branches and Districts

With the increasing rapid growth of membership in our mission, it became obvious that we needed to do more to establish and organize the Church. My experience had been that of organizing wards and presiding in stakes, so I began to look about in all of the

5. Bangerter Oral History, p. 121

branches of the mission for men who could be called and given leadership assignments. I eventually came to the decision that the poorest member called to be a branch president would probably be equal to or superior to the best missionary who did not have any unusual background in Church administration himself.

There were two phases to our efforts to accomplish this. First of all, we needed to remove missionaries from branch and district leadership positions. We emphasized to them that in order for them to be effective in leadership with members, they had to be effective missionaries in their proselyting efforts. The second phase was to seek out and call local members to assume leadership responsibilities. We, therefore, began to organize branches with local men called to preside. In so doing, many who were not well acquainted with the procedures of leadership in the Church did not know how to proceed. I remember on one occasion I had organized six branches under local presidencies, and in one week three of those presidents resigned and left their calling. Two of them left the Church, but I proceeded in reorganizing with others and called some of the men back to their positions and began to get a little more firm foundation in leadership in the Church.

It also became apparent that missionaries presiding over the districts would not be adequate for leadership, and I was led to organize the first district leadership among members in the São Paulo area. We organized another member-led district in the city of Rio de Janeiro. The Rio de Janeiro area had been opened in 1940, and as a missionary I had served as the second district president. The work then was quite slow. By 1960, we had a large group of fine men available and were able to organize the district presidency. Brother João Dias, an army officer who had been a faithful Church member for several years, became the anchor man, and we made him the district president of that area. Over a period of two or three years we added counselors and members of the district council. He and his counselors followed through with great interest and close attention to their responsibilities.

We had two main centers in the state of Minas Gerais—Juiz de Fora and Belo Horizonte, which was a large city. We expanded sometimes experimentally into other towns, but I think we weren't always successful in being permanent. Our progress in Belo Horizonte was limited because of a lack of good men in leadership. During this period we did find a fine man who became our leader—Walter Cardoso. He took over the responsibility of the branch and eventually of the district and did a great deal for the establishment of the Church in that area. It wasn't as rapid there as it was in São Paulo, of course. We did not consider a district there immediately because the cities were a great distance apart. But we eventually did have a district in Belo Horizonte, and it had supervision over Juiz de Fora and the new branch in Brasília. Missionary work is usually more productive in the large cities because cities are where the people are. We tended to concentrate within the city and then to reach into the suburbs, which are of course an integral part of the city.

We had an interesting situation in Campinas. We had a fairly large number of longtime members of the Church there, but for some reason some of the most promising leaders and young men had fallen into disrepute or general inactivity. This communicated a rather strange spirit to the branch. Sometimes they could be extremely enthusiastic, and other times they were difficult to manage. Depending a little on the attitude of missionaries, we would have periods of fast growth and many baptisms and other periods when things seemed to go slowly. But we were handicapped by the lack of one good, strong personality to hold leadership, and this restricted the development of Campinas for some time. We did have other large centers in the state of São Paulo, such as Ribeirão Preto. Ribeirão Preto was one of the larger interior cities, and the Church did fairly well there. In the interior of the state of São Paulo, the progress was more gradual. Frequently good leaders would move away, often into the metropolitan area of São Paulo, so it wasn't always possible to keep the branches expanding at a rapid rate. Often we did not have the answers to finding strong leaders in some of those areas. Sometimes the Spirit of the Lord seemed to move in unusual ways. We had a good leader named Brother Carboni in the city of Araraquara, for example, who moved out to another city called Araçatuba, and we thought we could count on him for leadership there. But he almost immediately went inactive, and he remained dormant for a period of 12 or 15 years. He later reawakened his interest in the gospel and became a fine leader in Araçatuba, so even though he didn't contribute much during our time, his influence was effective later.

The bulk of leadership still came from those who were converted to the Church, but there was a rapidly increasing number of people who grew up in those convert families and eventually became leaders. An example is Brother Osiris Cabral, who served as stake president and was later appointed a regional representative of the Twelve. He was a boy while I was mission president and later served a mission. Increasing numbers of young men joined the Church in their childhood and became powerful leaders.

Most of our new converts were interested in having an opportunity to exercise their faith, so we focused on calling them to positions of leadership and then training them to give proper service. I think that if we truly understand the concept of growth, more people should add more strength. I think that growth in and of itself need not be a weakening factor. It ought to be considered in fact as a strengthening factor. I feel that this is the case in the mission fields as well as in established stakes of Zion. For example, an elders quorum presidency frequently looks on their less-active brethren as a burden. They ought to see them, and must eventually see them, as a great resource, a great building material, out of which their quorum can become stronger. If they'll take that attitude, these men can become powerful in developing the strength of the Church.

Our tracking of activity rates helped us see our growth potential. President Kimball had helped us to see that when you have 60 percent activity, that's wonderful in terms of comparing it to 20 percent, which may have been the case years ago. But then he said, "This is terrible when you think that four out of every ten are not fully active. For Latter-day Saints that's inadmissible." In our experience in the mission I felt that the branches generally were performing at a level somewhat equal to what I had observed in my stake experience— sometimes a little better, sometimes not so good. But it was not discouraging to me. They seemed to be doing well, relatively speaking.

That meant about 30 percent activity at that level, which was not a bad standard throughout the Church.

I felt that our local leaders came through in a marvelous way. It seemed to me that calling them to positions and giving them basic instruction was about all that was needed, and they would then shoulder the responsibility and go forward. There were always those who didn't understand that to be a member requires activity. Many converts to the Church never realize that they have to do things personally about their religion because they have often left most things up to their pastor. There are exceptions to that, of course, but in Latin America this was often the case. Most of our converts had never done anything except attend church, and many of them had never even done that. So in a sense it was converting them to a new type of society, as well as to the gospel. I thought they responded well. When they received responsibility, they accepted it.

The new members had no problem with changes or modifications in Church programs. The only pattern they had to follow was what we showed them, so they did that. In the case of Brother Hélio Camargo, he had been a Methodist, and he had a number of preconceptions. They were not troublesome to him. I think where he found himself under the greatest difficulty was trying to get the members of our church to live their religion as strictly as his Methodist ideals had led him to believe it should have been lived. And sometimes we were a little more relaxed than he liked us to be.

All kinds of personalities can be found in a mission, as well as in stakes. Sometimes a man is bound by his preconceptions. He may be domineering. We sensed this with some of our leaders. But usually they took the responsibility with humility, and adding to that a certain vigor, they were able to assign their work out in a reasonable way. In general I think they did a good job. This growth came on gradually, and most of them were not heavily involved in large administrative responsibilities. The mission tended to control the purse strings through the period I served. [6]

The purpose of our establishment of leadership in Brazil was to direct our leaders towards the eventual organization of a stake. We

---

6. Bangerter Oral History, pp. 117–121

took special care in the training of our leaders, which was closely monitored by the mission presidency. We eventually added members of the district council and others in branch leadership positions. We were careful to train them in many sessions focusing on the specifics of their efforts.

Schedule and Administration of a Mission President

The schedule I had in a regular workday varied, of course. Developments frequently took place that made necessary rather heavy adjustments to the daily program. However, my activity was centered largely on the necessity to travel. The mission was of such a size and the distances involved were so great that I spent a considerable amount of time on airplanes. When I first arrived, the highway system was not highly developed. We used the automobile to go short distances into the interior of the state of São Paulo, but nearly every other trip was made by air. At that time we had the southern areas of Brazil (which later were divided off into the Brazilian South Mission), and since that was also an extensive area, I traveled frequently to Curitiba, Porto Alegre, and smaller centers in that part of the country. I made calculations that indicate that I averaged about 20 journeys a month throughout almost the entire period that I was mission president. That would indicate that two days out of three I would be going somewhere. Some of these trips of course were out and back the same day by automobile. And in the last two years of our term we did a large amount of travel by automobile centering in the state of São Paulo.

My general pattern of administration called for a district conference in each of our districts every three months. During the district conferences I planned to interview each of the missionaries. I also planned to visit each of the branches with some purpose or other between the district conferences, and this allowed me to see each missionary once every six weeks. One contact would be at the district conference, and the other would be in his normal missionary setting. I felt that this contact on the basis of every six weeks was necessary to keep closely in touch with the missionaries.

A mission president's day is a little difficult to describe as a standard thing. When I was in the office I would have a large amount of paperwork and correspondence to take care of, and I handled much of this by Dictaphone and through my staff members. We had weekly reports from each of the missionaries, and they were always reviewed, and in many cases notes or letters were written in answer to the problems of the missionaries. Frequently missionaries would come into the office for various reasons, many of them being transferred from one area to another, and on most occasions I would interview them. Our mission also, being of a large size, had many changes. Almost monthly we would receive a new group of missionaries, and at the same time, or at times roughly corresponding, we would release others. These changes required special training sessions, and I attempted to handle almost all of these personally, but naturally I had the assistance of members of the staff. I attempted to receive all of the incoming missionaries at the airport by meeting them personally, and with a few exceptions we tried to take our departing missionaries to the airport and give them a personal send-off as they left the mission.

There was, in spite of the constant travel, a surprising amount of time when we found ourselves at home. I felt close to my family. We spent many evenings together. We were not involved with the normal recreational pursuits that are common in the United States. We didn't have television, and family life had a deeper and closer meaning than we've found it possible to maintain since we've returned. [7]

Of course I found it difficult to keep up with all the paperwork. I think this is true of almost any administrator. There are times when you fall behind. I noticed that if I gave intense attention to the missionaries, within a month or two my attention to the members and their organization was slipping. Then I would perhaps take time off from the missionary interest to concentrate on leadership among the members and their developing organizations. But things seemed to move ahead in a rhythm that kept us in touch with practically everything.

---

7. Bangerter Oral History, pp. 111–112 (with added inclusions)

Revision of the Portuguese Scriptures

We had a constant program for reviewing the scriptures. We had Brazilian young women called who were serving in the office to try to refine the wording of the Book of Mormon and the other scriptures. I reviewed all of their corrections and adjustments, and during the time we served in Brazil, we published two different and somewhat revised editions of the Book of Mormon and the Doctrine and Covenants.

Mission Presidents' Seminars and Meetings

During our service as mission president, we had several occasions to meet with mission presidents from the various missions in South America as well as one occasion where all the mission presidents in the world met together in Salt Lake City. In March of 1959, a short mission presidents meeting was held at Iguaçu Falls under the direction of Elder Spencer W. Kimball. Present were Sister Bangerter and me, President and Sister Pace of Argentina, and President and Sister Jensen from Uruguay. Our efforts focused on the organization of branches and districts and encouraging missionaries to proselyte full time. The sisters also met to discuss items of common interest. In June of 1959, we met with President and Sister Arthur Jensen of the Uruguayan Mission in Livramento, on the border with Brazil and Uruguay. In this encounter we discussed mutual concerns relative to finances, missionary methods, and even the possibility of their mission taking over the work in Livramento.

At the end of September 1959 on the occasion of the division of the Brazilian Mission, Elder Harold B. Lee met with us, President and Sister Asael T. Sorensen, and President and Sister Arthur Jensen of the Uruguayan Mission. The meetings centered on construction needs and concerns, the baptism of people with African ancestry, and baptizing people who are unable to obtain a divorce. The sisters took time discussing needs of the Relief Society. Sister Bangerter then began to look at serious issues of health and to diagnose general causes for health problems of the missionaries. She wrote a health manual that was distributed to the missionaries describing how to avoid common health problems. She gave regular talks to the missionaries and counseled them on ways to avoid difficulties. The number of hours lost to illness in the Brazilian Mission dropped significantly. After Geri discovered on her own how to respond to hepatitis with gamma globulin shots, she talked about her program at one of the regular conferences held with the other mission presidents. All the missions were having similar health problems, particularly hepatitis. Elder Tuttle instituted a similar program of gamma globulin shots for all the missionaries throughout South America.[8] Much of the information in her health manual was used in a Church-produced health manual for missionaries until 2007, when a new revision was made.

Several times during 1960, President and Sister Jensen from the Uruguayan Mission visited us on assignment relative to construction in our mission. As he had experience in the building of churches and other large structures, several problems were solved through his instrumentality. In February of 1961, several changes had taken place in mission leadership in South America, and a meeting of all mission presidents and wives was held in Buenos Aires, Argentina. Present were Geri and me, the Sorensons of the Brazilian South Mission, the Sharps of the Andes Mission, the Fyanses of the Uruguayan Mission, and the Snelgroves of the Argentina Mission. We met under the direction of Brother Wendell B. Mendenhall, the chairman of the Church Building Committee. This was an historic meeting in which was implemented the building missionary program, with building supervisors sent from the United States to administer the program in South America. The details of the administration of the program were discussed and agreed upon by all the mission presidents attending.

In April of 1961, we met again in Montevideo, Uruguay, with the same group as mentioned before. This conference, however, was under the direction of Elder A. Theodore Tuttle of the First Council of the Seventy soon after he had been called to preside over all the missions in South America. The focus dealt with publication of materials for use in our missions. It was at this meeting that the an-

---

8. *A Land of Promise and Prophecy,* Mark L. Grover, 2008, Brigham Young University, p. 123

nouncement was made of the forthcoming release of President and Sister Sorenson of the Brazilian South Mission.

We attended the Worldwide Mission Presidents' Seminar held in Salt Lake City in June of 1961, leaving for the U.S. on June 23 and returning to Brazil on July 12. That seminar was the first of its kind, the only one up to that time in the history of the Church, wherein the mission presidents from all over the earth were invited to Salt Lake City to review missionary practices and policies. Certain presidents were not included if they were about to be replaced, of course. Many newly called presidents were there. We spent about eight days together. Our meetings were held in the Relief Society Building under the direction of the First Presidency.

Sister Bangerter and I almost missed being invited to this historic seminar because we had been in our mission about two and a half years at the time the conference was held, and it was questionable whether we had passed the limit of our term. Finally President Henry D. Moyle sent us a telegram that invited us to the conference and indicated that we would thereafter return to Brazil. This was a turning point in a way in our mission because it relieved us of the anxiety that naturally came when we thought we were about to be released and felt that we had not yet finished our mission. That circumstance allowed us to continue for another two years, and this resulted in our being in the field nearly five years.

At this seminar a new standard lesson plan was presented, and we were all required thereafter to abolish our own individual plans and use the new standard plan, which, incidentally, we felt incorporated most of the practical and important ideas of our own experience.

We learned at this seminar that the growth of the missions was of such a nature that many missions were under the necessity of organizing the members for their own leadership, with the intent that stakes would eventually be added in those distant areas. We had already contemplated this to some extent in our meetings in South America. President Thomas Fyans, who presided over the mission in Uruguay, had begun to develop a plan that he called "Six Steps to Stakehood." There were presentations given at this seminar that pointed out appropriate ways to organize our mission membership into districts and branches. We had of course already made some moves in this direction. President Fyans's approach to organization of districts in preparation for stakes was an inspiring concept to all of us. We hoped to model our growth after the "Six Steps to Stakehood." I thought by the time I was released in 1963 that we had enough members gathered together that they could operate a stake if they were properly organized. I knew it wouldn't be a strong stake, but I felt that they could probably do as well as they were doing under mission leadership. I suppose my enthusiasm caused me to be a little premature. I think the organization of a stake, for which we waited about three years following my release, was more in order at the time it finally took place. We did undertake in the closing months of my mission presidency a very powerful effort of leadership training, pointing out the need for our people to prepare themselves for stake leadership and going through a series of special orientation courses. The depth of leadership in the Melchizedek Priesthood was not sufficient by 1963. Their experience level was not adequate. We had men in the district presidency in São Paulo who were very well qualified, I thought, but to reach down from there to high councils and bishoprics would have been stretching it a little. [9]

Our meetings took place in various locations, and instruction was given by nearly all of the General Authorities. The focus was on proselyting work and the various options for accomplishing this effort. I made a presentation on holding street meetings, which was well received as a means of finding investigators. We were one of the few missions in the Church conducting street meetings at the time. Often we broke into smaller groups to discuss various aspects of our work. The new lesson plan was rolled out and discussed in deep detail. I also had opportunity to explain our integration classes, which was enthusiastically received. Other presentations dwelt on the mechanics of running a mission, including everything from automobiles to building programs, Relief Society, and genealogy. Eventually all of the auxiliaries made presentations that were very helpful in our developing mission. In other sessions we discussed Church history, welfare, finances, membership records, office staff, and the Aaronic

---

9. Bangerter Oral History, pp. 102–104

Priesthood programs. Elder Lee gave a powerful presentation on Church administration in the missions, and Elder Howard W. Hunter gave an excellent presentation on handling transgressions. Some areas were of less impact on us, such as the Servicemen's Program, Boy Scouts, and issuing temple recommends. Many presentations were powerfully moving and deeply insightful in helping us raise the level of commitment and gospel understanding in the mission. A special temple session gave us a deep spiritual feeling to our efforts as well. We had several meetings under the direction of Elder Tuttle as we applied the various directives to our situation in South America.

Our experience in this Worldwide Mission Presidents' Seminar was powerful and very helpful to us in our mission. It was also a great thrill for us to reunite with members of our family whom we had not seen for over two and a half years. Our involvement allowed us to meet many missionaries assigned to our mission in the mission home prior to our meetings. On July 4 we met with many of the parents of our missionaries and some former missionaries from our mission.

Most of our evenings were open, and we were involved in many visits and associations with family, friends, and associates. Our Brazilian missionary group gathered for a delightful evening at the Fausts' home. Often different family groups would have us in their homes for a meal or an event of some sort. On Sundays we often met in our home ward or were invited by our home stake to participate in special meetings and events. As the meetings drew to a close, we had acquired a large amount of material that needed to be packaged up and shipped to our office in Brazil. Finally after all the goodbyes had been said and packing taken care of, we boarded a flight to Chicago and then to New York and on to our mission, home, and children in São Paulo. It had been a refreshing and highly motivating experience to be gathered with all the mission presidents worldwide to be instructed by the leadership of the Church in our duties in the mission field. [10]

In November of 1961, a mission presidents' seminar was held in Montevideo, Uruguay, under the direction of Elder A. Theodore

---

10. WGB M.P. Journal, p. 252–258

Tuttle. Present at this seminar with me were Finn Paulsen of the Brazilian South Mission, President Sharp from the Andes Mission, President Snelgrove from Argentina, President Delbert Palmer from Chile, and President Fyans from the Uruguayan Mission. We discussed publicity and leadership approaches for local members. We also covered language study and proselyting approaches, as well as construction concerns, genealogy, and other policy matters. In December of that same year, we met again in Montevideo this time with our wives. The focus was on missionary work and how to move it forward. We also discussed publications, maintaining records, and administration procedures.

A mission presidents' seminar was held in São Paulo in March of 1962 with the following missions represented: President and Sister Sharp of the Andes Mission, Lima, Peru; President and Sister Palmer of the Chilean Mission, Santiago; President and Sister Laird Snelgrove of the Argentine Mission, Buenos Aires; President and Sister Fyans of the Uruguayan Mission, Montevideo; President and Sister Paulsen of the Brazilian South Mission, Curitiba; and Geri and me of the Brazilian Mission. It was directed by Elder and Sister A. Theodore Tuttle of the First Council of Seventy, who presided over all of South America with headquarters in Montevideo. The emphasis of the conference was building and leadership and administration.

Another seminar was held in Lima, Peru, at the end of June of that same year. Our experience there was fascinating with our trip to the ruins in and around Lima, Cuzco, and Macchu Picchu. We felt a powerful spiritual influence as we met together under the direction of Elder Tuttle. At the conclusion of our meetings, it was announced that President and Sister Sharp were being released and that the Nicolaysons would be taking their place.

Statistics and the End of the Mission

After nearly five years of service, we felt that the Church had become fairly well established in Brazil. The missionaries were working effectively and having success in drawing many people into the Church. In the year of 1962, for instance, over 2,000 people joined the Church. Districts were organized in Belo Horizonte, Rio de Janeiro, and in São Paulo, and we had some stronger branches among the 40 or 45 branches scattered throughout the nation. By the time our missionary service was completed, we found that we had a body of 14,000 members in all of Brazil (both missions) instead of the 3,000 that was the number upon our arrival. Among them there were branches functioning somewhat on the level of wards. They were under the leadership of district presidencies who were local members, having been ordained and given the authority of the priesthood to carry forward the leadership and organization of the Church. I had taken opportunity to organize special instruction groups among the members, teaching them the basic principles of priesthood leadership and the functions that were necessary in the operation of the Church and kingdom of God. These included priesthood responsibilities, women's activity, organization of welfare responsibilities, and the pattern of maintaining contact with the membership through the authority of the priesthood and the visiting teachers of the Relief Society.

In June of 1963, we received notice from Church headquarters that our release was forthcoming and that our presidency would be replaced by President Wayne M. Beck. We felt that we had brought considerable growth and development and good order into the Church and that it could be turned over with a possibility for expansion and constant growth. We had wonderful meetings among the members in the cities of São Paulo, Rio de Janeiro, and Belo Horizonte. We left with a feeling of deep love and appreciation for so many of the members of the Church.

Journey Home on the Boat

Our journey home by steamship took about 15 days and was very enjoyable for us and our nine children. We had adequate rooms, and our family was comfortable and had a happy time on the steamship. We stopped en route at Curacao in the Dutch West Indies and continued on to Houston, Texas, where we landed. The ship carried about 40 passengers, so with Geri and me and our nine children, we almost formed a majority.

It turned out that there were three other ministers on board, and within a few days each of those three approached me and inquired how we could get together and visit about what the Mormons believe. They didn't seem to be unusually interested in what they believed among themselves, but they all wanted to know what we believe. With a little hesitation, because my experience had not been that of having contact with ministers of other faiths, we arranged an interview where all four of us sat down together. It turned out to be very congenial and consisted primarily of them asking questions and me giving the answers. I had supposed that they would come out with strong arguments supported by scriptures that would make it difficult for me to hold my own. But in their friendly, congenial way they just asked questions, and it turned out that I knew the answer to each question. I didn't realize beforehand that I was that well informed. Within a few minutes, as we visited, they began to turn to each other and make comments like this: "Isn't it interesting? He has an answer for any question you can ask." They repeated that comment over and over again, and we ended our discussion on a very friendly basis. One of these men, however, two or three days later, engaged me in conversation and said, "I have been thinking of what you told us the other day, and I wonder if it is right to know everything. I think maybe you know too much. I don't believe the Lord wants us to know it all." I could tell that he was offended. A day or two later he spoke to me again. He said, "I've been considering what you told me, and I have come to the conclusion that what you teach is very dangerous heresy."

General Impressions

As I reflect on our mission, several thoughts come to mind. My experience has been that as people join the Church they tend to devote themselves to keeping the commandments. It usually takes a period of time for them to learn exactly what their duties are in family prayer, family home evening, and in doing away with coffee and other practices that they may have had. They are supposedly taught these things at baptism, but they don't understand them well, and it takes a little time. But faithful members of the Church in the mission field seem to me the same as members of the Church everywhere. In our well-established wards and stakes we have people fully devoted and people only partly committed. The same thing, naturally, is true in the mission field.

People who go on missions are engaged in an activity from which they will never recover, no matter on what basis they serve. Having served with my family for five years in Brazil, the nature of that experience was so fully ingrained into our lives that we will never be free of its influence and interest. The experiences that we enjoyed are constantly brought back to us in our conversations and remembrances, by the pictures we brought back home, and by the constant flow of people in our lives—both missionaries and members who come from time to time from Brazil.

We have kept contact with the majority of the missionaries with whom we served. My wife at the present time (2009) has the addresses of probably 400 out of the 450 missionaries we worked with, and it's unusual to have a week when we don't have some contact with some one of these missionaries. And naturally everything that we talk about when we get together relates to our experience in the mission field.

The same thing is true with our children. We constantly refer to those great experiences that we had together. Most of our children are fluent in Portuguese, and the language itself crops up in our conversation. We have special family songs we learned in Brazil, and we frequently sing these songs in our family home evenings or at other times. Two of our children have returned to Brazil as missionaries. Cory served in the Brazil South Mission, and Glenda served in the Brazil São Paulo North Mission. A second son, Grant, served in Spain, but he has a vivid remembrance of his time in Brazil. The remainder of our sons, Howard, Paulo, and Layne all served in the Portugal Lisbon Mission. Of course the fact that we went to Portugal for eight months and took our younger children with us was a sort of an extension to the Brazilian experience. Many of our grandchildren have also served in Portugal and Brazil on their missions. But we feel very much in our hearts a spiritual, personal relationship with the missionaries and with the members of the Church in Brazil. We have said facetiously at times that having been so closely in touch with that country so long, we feel in a sense as if we own it. All that goes on seems to be a part of us, even though we may not have direct contact with those things at the present time.

I think the Missionary Department and the General Authorities who had contact with us felt good about the progress in Brazil. The Brazilian Mission was showing a more extensive and rapid growth than any other mission in South America and was comparable with some of the leading missions in the Church. I feel that our report was acceptable in many respects. Although we didn't feel that we had performed a perfect mission, we thought that it had been effective. And I think this attitude prevailed with the leaders of the Church. [11]

As a concluding thought about our experience: I have witnessed the entire process of the work grow in Brazil, as there are now well over 1,000,000 members in that country (2009). We have witnessed from the beginning the roots of the Church in Portugal, as well as witnessing the same growth in other countries of South America where we later served, including Chile and Argentina. When you consider what has happened in my lifetime from the northern border of Mexico all the way south, truly the prophecy to me in my patriarchal blessing from the hand of my grandfather has been fulfilled (see chapter 3). When I left for my mission you could name on less than one hand the number of people in Utah who could speak Portuguese.

---

11. Bangerter Oral History, pp. 127–128

Chapter 14

NEW AND EXPANDED CHALLENGES

"We are called out of the world to live in Zion. Here in America we live in the land of Zion. But what is intended is that we will establish a spiritual Zion, that we will become in fact a Zion people worthy of all the blessings that were given to the original city of that holy name. A people pure in heart, set apart from the world in the way they live their lives. A people to be a light on a hill; worthy to abide in the presence of God. . . . I want to say something about family prayer. Again, this relates to our home evening and the training of our children. . . . Family prayer means gathering your family together every morning and kneeling down together while someone leads in a family prayer. You can't do this by merely sitting around the table and asking a quick blessing on the food. The same process should be followed in the evening. Where members of the family cannot always all be together at the same time, family prayer requires that the individual members should kneel down at the close of their day and offer up their earnest prayers to the Lord. We should go with our younger children into their bedroom and see that they are trained in this practice. They should, also, be trained in the practice of going privately in secret prayer before the Lord each day. Every true Latter-day Saint should be afraid to face the day with its problems and the chancy happenings of life if he has not knelt down to ask the Lord to send His special protection and guiding influence upon the activities of that day. Furthermore, they must be taught to the Saints, and that is your responsibility. In the midst of our affluent society, those who have taken upon themselves the name of Jesus Christ cannot continue to live spiritually in Babylon. Zion is our spiritual home. We will never attain Zion if we dabble with Sodom and Gomorrah."[1]

---

1. Collected Works, pp. 159, 161–162

Returning Home and Re-establishing Our Situation

My parents met us at our landing in Houston, Texas, and accompanied us back home. We purchased a station wagon in Houston and drove across Texas to Arizona to visit my sister, Naomi, and then on to Albuquerque to visit the mother of my deceased wife, Mildred. On our arrival home, we were happily received by our ward and stake. A stake conference was in process in a newly built stake center. Elder Henry D. Moyle was the visiting authority, and he gave very impressive comments about the service we had given in our mission.

When we arrived home, we were able to move into a house that had been recently finished by my father, and we rented that until we were able to build our own. I made arrangements for a loan to build a new house at 2822 West 3875 South, on property obtained from my father. With the help of Cory, my father, and Geri's father we were able to finish it and move in at Christmastime in 1963. That was the year Santa filled only the stockings at our home. It was a big disappointment to the children until we looked into the stockings and found a note. The note informed us that Santa was confused as to where we lived, so he filled the stockings here and left Christmas at the new house—all was resolved happily from there.

At this season we saw our first snow in five years. Snow falls silently, and I came home from work shaking the snow from my clothes and informed the children it was snowing; until then no one had noticed. We were blessed with about a foot of snow in this first snow storm, and the children watched it fall into the night.

The business in which I had been involved before going to Brazil had shifted to other members of the family, and I did not have employment. Upon leaving Brazil, one of the children asked me what I was going to do for a job when I got home. I was approached by several people to join with them in different activities. One of these was Art Jensen, former mission president in Uruguay, who invited me to help develop his construction program. He made arrangements for an adequate income ($1,000 per month), and I began working with him, which I did for three years.

General Church Service

Upon our return from Brazil as mission president, I found that the Church was in the midst of an extensive project in correlation and was working to get the various activities and programs aligned and assigned under proper leadership and effective training. I was invited to participate in a study of certain missionary activities. I felt that the Church made a serious error in the notion that new members should come totally under the direction of the bishop and that missionaries would thereafter have no activity or responsibility. This decision affected the Church adversely for 20 years, until fortunately it was determined that missionaries should give follow-through lessons after the baptism of their converts.

Also shortly following our arrival home, I was invited to Church headquarters and asked to take an assignment with the General Home Teaching Committee of the Church. The Church was in the process of careful correlation of the activities of the priesthood, and I was asked to serve under Elder Marion G. Romney of the Council of the Twelve and Alvin R. Dyer, one of the Assistants to the Twelve. The work of this committee was a part of a great correlation effort to establish uniformity in training the leadership of the Church. In addition to many instructional meetings, I was assigned to attend stake conferences in the place of members of the Quorum of the Twelve Apostles. Beginning in the year 1964 I began to receive these assignments to go to stake conferences, generally in the state of Utah, and to accompany General Authorities as we worked to foster the program of proper home teaching in the Church. As I followed through on this assignment, I visited many of the stakes throughout Utah, including some of my own home stakes.

Sometime later my responsibility was expanded to include participation in the Melchizedek Priesthood Committee of the Church, and there I had additional assignments and responsibilities to teach priesthood principles to the leadership in the stakes to which I was assigned. We also had many conferences and training sessions under the direction of Elder Harold B. Lee and were deeply schooled in the processes of leadership among the stakes and organizations of the Church. Finally, I was asked to sit as a part of the Church Correlation

Committee under the leadership of Elder Marvin J. Ashton. These functions gave me opportunity for further experience in the overseeing of the work of leadership in the Church.

Developments in Family and Finances

The conditions in my employment did not develop to any great extent, and we were struggling to have success the first three years following our return from our mission. In the midst of these problems, Brother Jensen suddenly passed away, and I was left without a means of employment. At that time a neighbor called and asked if I would like to build a home for them, which I agreed to do with my brother Samuel. We built our own construction program between the two of us, taking on numerous small jobs and etching out some sort of a means of surviving for our family.

My wife, Geraldine, worked valiantly to manage the family and took on the job of selling lingerie. Here she became the top sales person of LeVoy's—a company started by James Sorensen. She was also an expert in food preparation and in using the resources of Deseret Industries. Geri would take our daughters to lingerie parties in the evenings, and I would stay home with the boys. It was my practice to read novels to them as they cleaned their room and prepared for bed. When they would stop working, coming up to lie with me on the bed, I would pretend to close the book. When they asked why I stopped, I would say, "I guess you don't want me to continue—you have all quit working." At this they would all jump down and begin again to straighten their room. I would read them some of my favorite novels: *The Virginian, Where the Red Fern Grows, Recollection Creek, Call of the Wild, Star of the West*, and others.

Lee Ann went to BYU, and our eldest son, Cory, was called to serve as a missionary in the Brazil South Mission at this time. We were not sure how we would be able to sustain him, but things worked out to make it possible. I often thought that when your son is called on a mission, the Lord would bless you; we waited and waited for the blessing, but it did not happen in such a way that we could discern it until he was about ready to come home. Geri's parents were very kind and supportive, and we enjoyed the companionship and attention with them. We especially enjoyed the support of my mother, who was very attentive to all of our family, especially the children.

In early April 1966 my father, William Henry Bangerter, passed away due to a heart attack. He had a happy spirit, and his conversations were usually filled with fun and interesting comments. He had a wry sense of humor and enjoyed funny little stories like Mike and Pat, referring to them often while working on the job. He loved the mornings and, as is common in agrarian communities, he was an early riser and would sing his morning songs as he worked. In his youth he was assigned to feed the coal-fired potbellied stove in the school. He had a .22 rifle cartridge in his pocket one day and wondered what it would be like if he threw it in the stove. He knew that if it went off right away, everyone would find him the culprit. So he began making a spit wad and put the shell inside. The next time he fed the stove, he threw it in. He said it seemed like forever! Then he heard it explode. It seemed that the cartridge went one way and the bullet the other—round and round inside the stove. The result was that all the stovepipes fell down, and the room filled with smoke. School was let out early, and he didn't tell anyone for years that he had been the cause. In his later years he served as a patriarch in the stake and as a temple worker in the Salt Lake Temple.

Just prior to his passing, he was working on a chapel in our stake in Granger, and as he finished that Friday, he gathered up his tools and announced that he would not come to work anymore. The next day he suffered a heart attack and was taken to the hospital. He passed away the next day, which was Easter Sunday, April 10, 1966. He had earlier said to his grandson Steven Jensen that he felt that dying on Easter Sunday would be the ideal time to pass away. About midday on Easter Sunday, while the Tabernacle Choir was singing "Still, Still with Thee" over the radio as part of general conference, he quietly passed away. I was listening to the music on the car radio before coming into the hospital to pay him a visit. He left Mother with sufficient means from his business and savings to take care of her throughout her life.

My brother Sam and I were building our business in construction and carpentry, but our resources were very limited. Property that we had been studying for a development in Arizona before the death of Brother Jensen came forward as a possibility. With Delbert A. Palmer, a close friend and former mission president in Chile, we arranged other associates to finance this project, which would be 150 apartments adjacent to Arizona State University in Tempe. The finance officer of the loan company, Warner Stevens asked to join us to carry the project forward. I had signed personally for a million dollar loan to complete the project.

We began in July of 1967 and completed the work by January of 1968. I was assigned to supervise the construction of this building, which required me to visit Arizona, and in one year I made the trip by car at least 20 times. We were stretching every possibility of our resources, but in 1968 we finally completed the building, and the rental to the students of Arizona State University became almost a guaranteed process. The project became an immediate success. Thus, I found that after three years of struggle and concern and wondering when the Lord's blessing would come, He had finally brought to fulfillment a wonderful accomplishment and had endowed us with income that made us capable of supporting our family and carrying on the assignments given to me in the Church.

We enjoyed this association in Arizona very much and took the family with us on several trips. To them it was a vacation, and we always had a place to stay in our apartment project, which we kept for about five years. The income from the building compensated us and repaid us for some of the frightening investments we had made to make it possible. The returns established my financial base as if I had not gone on a mission. I realized that Heavenly Father had given us everything we had achieved and allowed us a measure of prosperity for which we had not dreamed. As I traveled there, we frequently visited the building site, where Warner and I would offer prayer. Later he commented to me that he thought that it was the first development in Arizona approved by prayer and built on our knees.

Call as Regional Representative

In 1966, while attending a conference with Elder Spencer W. Kimball, he advised me that a very important adjustment was being made in Church leadership. This developed with the announcement at general conference that there would be a number of men called to serve as regional representatives of the Quorum of the Twelve, and my name was listed among 67 of these men. This gave me a new responsibility, and I was assigned to conduct stake conferences in lieu of General Authorities at certain times.

This assignment of the regional representatives was the beginning of specific training for the stakes. It developed into the eventual calling of men into the various Quorums of the Seventy. The Church entered a new phase of leadership organization. My assignment was the Coalville Region. The stakes were Heber City; Coalville; Kamas; Evanston, Wyoming; and Rock Springs, Wyoming. I began traveling to the wards and stakes in this area almost constantly during the weekends. I undertook to be very close to the stake presidencies and in time visited all the wards and branches in these stakes. I thus formed a close relationship with the memberships and leaders, which continued over many years. After three years I was reassigned to the St. George Region with the stakes of Kanab, Enterprise, St. George, Bloomington, and Hurricane. I followed the same procedure as in the Coalville area and had a wonderful relationship with the people and leaders.

Move to Alpine

Sadness once again befell us in a short period of time. Dad Hamblin passed away in September 1969 from a heart attack. We had Mom Hamblin move in with us in Granger as her health was failing. She passed away in January 1970, the same week as her mother, Mary Alice Eyre. President David O. McKay also passed away that same week, so our time was spent in mourning the loss of these great souls.

With Glenda at school at BYU, Geri and I felt it was an opportune time to consider moving our residence to the small farm we had purchased many years earlier in Alpine, Utah County. In the meantime the family was growing. Lee Ann was at BYU, Cory had returned from his mission, and Glenda was preparing for school. She later was called to serve a mission to the Brazil São Paulo North

*Grant as a graduate of the University
of Utah with honors, 1950*

Grave of Mildred Elizabeth Bangerter, 1951.

*Geraldine Hamblin in her
nursing uniform, 1950.*

*Grant and Geri Bangerter, wedding day,
October 14, 1953.*

*Grant and Geraldine Hamblin on a date in the
canyon, August 1953.*

*Wedding reception at the Wm. H. and Isabelle Bangerter home. — Left
to right: Henry Marcene Hamblin, Mary Alice Eyre, Duella Hamblin,
Geraldine H. Bangerter, Wm. Grant Bangerter, Isabelle B. Bangerter,
Wm. Henry Bangerter. October 14, 1953.*

Bangerter children: Glenda, Cory, Lee Ann,
October 14, 1953.

William Grant and Geraldine H.
Bangerter family, October 14, 1953.
Front: Cory, Lee Ann, Glenda; rear: Geri
and Grant.

Grant and Geri Bangerter.
October 14, 1953, Granger, Utah.

Part of the former bishopric of the Granger 1st Ward Left to right: Verne Breeze (counselor to Grant in the stake presidency), Grant Bangerter, Dennis Dial (counselor in the bishopric).

Stake presidency of the North Jordan Stake: Wayne C. Player, 1st counselor; Wm. Grant Bangerter, president; Merrill L. Nelson, 2nd counselor

Former stake presidency and high council of the North Jordan Stake. The high council remained the same when Grant was made the stake president.

Front, left to right: Edwin K. Winder, 1st counselor; John D. Hill, president; Alvin Barker, 2nd counselor; Reed S. Arnold, clerk

Back, left to right: Brother Merrill, Floyd N. Bendixon, Wm. H. Bangerter, Herman C. Nielsen, Owen Jacobs, Hiland Kent, Clyde Barker, Willard G. Bawden, Boyce Labrum, Marcus L. Bennion, Henry Hintze, H. Earl Day

Special Presentation to President and Sister John D. Hill following his release as stake president by newly called President William Grant Bangerter, 1954.

President Alex F. Dunn, Chairman of the Pioneer Welfare Region (father of Elder Lorin C. Dunn of the First Quorum of the Seventy) and mentor to Wm. Grant Bangerter.

Glenn L. Rudd, secretary to the Pioneer Welfare Region and later a member of the First Quorum of the Seventy

North Jordan Stake Center on 4200 West in Granger

Family picture in Granger Home (3011 West 3835 South) — Left to right: Glenda, Grant H., Wm. Grant, Julie, Geri, Cory, Lee Ann, 1956.

Cory and Wm. Grant building model airplanes, 1956.

Wm. Grant Bangerter as stake president, 1954

Geraldine H. Bangerter in 1985

Bangerter family portrait prior to departure for Brazil — Clockwise from the left: Wm. Grant, Cory, Lee Ann, Glenda, Julie, Geraldine, Grant H., Howard, 1958

Boarding Pan American Airways flight in New York City bound for Brazil, November 1958 — left to right: Geraldine, Lee Ann, Julie, Cory, Glenda, Grant, Howard

Arrival in São Paulo, Brazil, November 1958 — left to right: Elder Nelson Baker, Wm. Grant Bangerter, Julie, Geraldine, Howard (back of head), Grant H., Ida Sorenson, Asael T. Sorenson, Cory, Lee Ann, Glenda

In front of mission home on Rua Itapeva 378 in São Paulo, Brazil. Left to right: Asael Sorensen, Ida Sorensen, Elder Crandall, Geraldine Bangerter, Wm. Grant Bangerter, Elder Nelson Baker, 1958

Old mission home and office located at Rua Itapeva 378, Bela Vista, São Paulo, Brazil

Baptismal service behind mission home in São Paulo, Brazil. Wm. Grant Bangerter speaking.

Elder Spencer W. Kimball addressing Saints in Brazil with Wm. Grant Bangerter translating, 1959.

Picture at Iguaçu airport May 1959. Left to right: Sister Camilla Kimball, Elder D. H. Jacobs, Elder Spencer W. Kimball, Elder Michael M. Norton, Geraldine Bangerter, Peggy Brasília Bangerter, Wm. Grant Bangerter.

Visit of Elder Harold B. Lee to Brazil, September 1959. Left to right: Cory, Elder Harold B. Lee, Sister Fern Lee, Geraldine Bangerter, Wm. Grant Bangerter.

Elder and Sister A. Theodore Tuttle in Recife, Brazil, 1961. Left to right: Elder A. Theodore Tuttle, Sister Marne Tuttle, Boyd Tuttle (Baby), Wm. Grant Bangerter, Geraldine Bangerter, unknown members.

President and Sister Joseph Fielding Smith in São Paulo, Brazil. Left to right: Geraldine Bangerter, Elder A. Theodore Tuttle, President Joseph Fielding Smith, Sister Jesse Evans Smith, Peggy Bangerter, Grant H. Bangerter, Wm. Grant Bangerter, 1961.

President Hugh B. Brown in Rio de Janeiro (Jardim Botânico), 1962. Left to right: Sister Marne Tuttle, Elder A. Theodore Tuttle, President Hugh B. Brown, Zina Brown (daughter of President Brown), Wm. Grant Bangerter, Geraldine Bangerter.

Family Portrait behind old mission home in São Paulo, Brazil — front, left to right: Julie, Peggy, Howard, Paulo, Grant H.; middle: Geraldine Bangerter, Wm. Grant Bangerter; back: Lee Ann, Cory, Glenda

South American mission presidents' seminar at Macchu Picchu, Peru. Left to right: Pres. Thomas Fyans, Sister Helen Fyans, Pres. Vernon Sharp, Sister Faron Sharp, Marne Tuttle, Elder A. Theodore Tuttle, Pres. Finn Paulsen, Sara Paulsen, Pres. Delbert Palmer, Sister Mabel Palmer, Pres. Wm. Grant Bangerter, Sister Geraldine Bangerter, Sister Edna Snelgrove, Pres. Laird Snelgrove.

Brother Hélio da Rocha Camargo, counselor to Wm. Grant Bangerter and later a member of the Second Quorum of the Seventy, standing by Wm. Grant Bangerter.

New mission home in São Paulo, Rua Henrique Monteiro 215

Mission leadership gathering at the São Paulo District Chapel next to the mission home. Avenida Rebouças and Avenida Faria Lima.

Family picture in the new mission home. Front, left to right: Peggy, Howard, Paulo, Julie; middle, left to right: Grant H., Geraldine, Wm. Grant; back, left to right: Cory, Glenda, Lee Ann, 1961.

Sixty-nine newly called regional representatives, 1967. Wm. Grant Bangerter is on the back row, third from the right.

Mission, where she met the young man (Stephen Craig Apple) whom she eventually married. While at BYU, our daughter Lee Ann fell in love with and soon married a returned missionary, Richard Albert Lorenzon, on June 29, 1969, in the Salt Lake Temple. He was from Philadelphia, Pennsylvania. In December 1969, our son Cory was married to Gayle Bishop in the same temple. We made all the necessary arrangements and began the construction of our new home by June 1970. In the interim period, Cory left for his military training in New Jersey and Maryland. He returned in time to help with the finishing touches of our home. This home became the focal point of family gatherings and many years of enjoyable associations and sweet memories.

At this period my brother Sam and I did some extended home building in Murray and Cottonwood in partnership with M. Paul Mertlich, with whom I had a happy experience. Together, we developed the Creek Road Terrace subdivision and built many homes there and in other neighborhoods. I also served on the Alpine City Council about this time.

Travels and Assignments as a Regional Representative

My first assignment as a regional representative was to the Coalville Region where I met frequently with the stake presidents and members of the wards from Rawlins, Wyoming, on the east to Heber City, Utah, on the west. I had interesting and inspiring experiences with members of the Twelve, especially Elder LeGrand Richards, in calling and setting apart new stake presidents in the area. In the reorganization of the Coalville stake, as we interviewed the various leaders under Elder Richards, he asked me if I felt the inspiration of calling a new stake president. I indicated a certain man who had not been previously come to our attention, and Elder Richards immediately said, "That's my man!" We knew the Spirit of the Lord had directed this choice.

I now wish to review what is to me one of the remarkable episodes in the growth of the Church, one of the outstanding, inspiring events in all Church history took place in April of 1974. It was brought about through the leadership of President Spencer W. Kimball, who became the President of the Church in December 1973. I had been serving for seven years as one of the first group of regional representatives since 1967. My assignments had been in the regions of Coalville, southern Wyoming, southern Utah, and west Texas. I enjoyed these experiences greatly and became closely acquainted with the leaders in nearly all the wards and especially in the stakes. The regional representatives met with the General Authorities in their regular leadership meeting on April 4, 1974, prior to general conference. President Harold B. Lee had recently passed away and it had been a great shock to the Church, inasmuch as we had expected that he would preside over the Church for an extended period. We never had envisioned Spencer W. Kimball as being the president of the Church, and we all felt that this was a burden almost too great for him to assume. Our anxiety and our prayers in his behalf were very strong.

As we met on that April morning, President Kimball came forward for the first time in his position as the Prophet and President and gave instruction on the course that we should take in Church leadership. This became one of the most remarkable and powerful meetings of my entire experience. Soon after President Kimball began to speak we lost track of the feeling that he was inexperienced and incapable. We felt the Spirit of the Lord rest upon him in a mighty way and felt the power of God speaking through him as he held forth to our view the exciting, expanding place of the Church and the growth of the gospel. He seemed to be opening the curtains that allowed us to view into eternity. It was on this occasion that he announced various impressive concepts that had not previously received much attention. He said, for example, "We will open doors. We are not going as far in teaching the gospel as the Church has done in previous times and we must reach out to the world." He also said, "Every boy should become worthy to serve a mission, including those outside of the United States, in Latin America, and in Europe. They should all be called to go." He announced, "It is time for the Church to lengthen our stride." These great declarations became principles or watchwords by which the Church began to move forward under a new spirit of driving and concerted effort. [2]

In my regional representative assignment I realized that this order of leadership far superseded the previous visits of the General Authorities in the haphazard and the undirected approach to training. Elder Neal A. Maxwell called this type of leadership "MBWA" or "managing by wandering around." Many opportunities came from this. Stake presidents with whom I worked felt the personal influence and direct teaching I was able to give, and many of them reported that they looked back on these experiences as some of the best training they had received. I felt all the stake presidents paid very close attention to my leadership. I don't think all regional representatives were as intense in contacting their stakes as I was. The leaders in the stakes where I served never forgot the close association and the things that they had learned. We would be sent out with programs, and whenever they came, they were often not well received unless personalized in a way that members became excited about the new direction. I think there were many regional representatives whose presence in their visits was felt in lesser effect. The calling of regional representatives was new territory, and no priesthood keys were given. Some men felt to ask approval about almost everything and were frequently denied. I sought to keep a low profile and do as the Spirit directed me. As a result we had some marvelous experiences and felt the hand of the Lord in the work.

Later I was assigned to the Sandy Utah Region and thereafter to the Cottonwood Region, where I enjoyed close association with each of the stake presidents. My activity usually centered on visits almost every Sunday to one or more of the stakes. With the opportunity that these assignments afforded for travel, especially in Utah, I was able frequently to take members of my family with me and enjoy the great experience of travel throughout the western part of the United States with them. Sister Bangerter attended with me on many occasions and developed a close friendship with the presidencies and their wives. All the stake presidents became very closely united with us

---

2. June 1, 1995, dictation to the Historical Department, p. 2 (see also general conference talk, *Ensign,* May 1975, p. 39).

in friendship, and frequently for many years thereafter, they would comment on the particular value they received in the training from the regional representatives. It was a busy time as I had two regions at the same time. I also had the West Texas Region following the Sandy Region.

I served in this calling for seven years, and the indication came that regional representatives would be released after seven years. Instead of being released, however, I was assigned to the stakes in Brazil, which had been formed after our term as mission president. Elder Monson suggested that they may want to hide me a little longer than the normal time of service for regional representatives.

In my visits to Brazil, I became very much obsessed with the need for calling native Brazilian young men to serve as missionaries because visas for the North Americans were very difficult and slow to obtain. The missions in Brazil—by then there were four—only had a staff of 65 or so missionaries each, or about half the number they needed to carry on an effective proselyting program. With the calling of President Spencer W. Kimball to lead the Church, he injected so many ideas of forward movement and development that it almost revolutionized the movement of the Church, especially in growth and in missionary work. Being inspired by the spirit of his instructions, I received a spiritual assurance of the importance of calling native Brazilians to serve missions. Shortly thereafter, infused with the things President Kimball had projected, I paid my first official visit to Brazil and met with five of the stake presidents who were now under my direction. I could hardly wait to tell them what President Kimball had declared. I told them specifically that we were expected to call the native young men of Brazil to go on missions. To my surprise, some of them resisted this concept. Their response, for example, was, "Oh no. That principle doesn't apply to Brazil. That is for the United States. In Brazil we do not have the resources to support missionaries. Our young men cannot interrupt their education like they do in the United States. They don't have family support to carry out their calling." I was frustrated by this negative attitude. I said, "What are you going to do then about the words and declarations of the Prophet of the Lord?" They didn't know. They looked down toward the floor with a spirit of discouragement, but no real vision.

How could I overcome this negative spirit? The answer came a few days later as I rode with Brother José Lombardi, serving as the first patriarch in a stake in South America. We went together in his car down the mountainside to Santos on the seacoast. On the way he talked to me about his experience as a patriarch.

He said, "You know, Brother Bangerter, I don't know how to be a patriarch. I have had no previous experience, and I know of no other patriarchs. I'm the first one in South America and no one has really instructed me on how to give patriarchal blessings. The only thing I can do under these circumstances is to say in the blessings the things the Lord tells me to say."

I thought, "What a marvelous attitude or response to the Spirit of the Lord." I told him I thought he would do very well as a patriarch.

Then he added, "You know, as I give blessings to these young men, you would be surprised how many of them are told that they are to go on missions."

Suddenly I saw a vision and felt revelation, and I knew what to do about the stake presidents who were reluctant to move forward. I held another meeting with them and I said, "Brethren, this is the circumstance that we face in the calling of missionaries. The Lord has already called these young men to serve. I know it because he has revealed it to the patriarch. It is not the will of man or the work of human beings. The Lord has already called them to be missionaries and the President of the Church has announced the will of the Lord. Now, certain leaders in the Church (referring to some stake presidents) are standing in the middle of the road telling the young men they cannot go on missions. Brethren, is there anyone here who lacks vision? Is there anyone here who is impeding the work of the Lord?" This comment made some of the brethren very uncomfortable, and, maybe somewhat grudgingly, they agreed that their young men should be called on missions. A slight beginning came forth. There had been, of course, over the years a certain number of Brazilian young men and some young women who had been called to serve as missionaries, but this had not been the general pattern. But now, at least, the attitude began to change among these brethren, although the number of native missionaries did not increase very much. A newly opened mission in Portugal transformed their attitudes completely.

Our Calling to Preside in Portugal

When President Spencer W. Kimball announced that "doors would be opened" and we were to advance the missionary work and to move forward in teaching the gospel to new nations, little did we realize that we would be the vanguard effort to opening the doors to the nations of the Earth. The first door opened was to Portugal. One evening in August of 1974, I received a telephone call at home from President Nathan Eldon Tanner, counselor to President Kimball. He inquired about the possibility of me, because of my former service in Brazil, going to Portugal and opening a mission there. He was concerned that my resources were not adequate to take care of it and supposed that they may have to look to someone else. I told him, however, that our conditions were moving forward well, and about a week later he called me the second time, formally calling me to preside over the mission in Portugal.

This, of course, was a very exciting prospect for both me and my family, and we began actively to organize our affairs to go there. As the regional representative to Brazil, I went to President Ezra Taft Benson, then President of the Quorum of the Twelve, and said, "What should I do now, President, with my assignment as regional representative?" He responded, "Well Brother Bangerter, your mission in Portugal will not be very large, and you won't have very many missionaries for a time. Probably you will have as much time to be a regional representative while you're in Portugal as if you were at home, so why don't you continue both assignments and work out your Brazilian responsibility from Portugal." I was very pleased to do this.

Visiting the leaders in Brazil before our move to Portugal, I announced to them that I had been called to open the mission in Portugal. They were transformed with enthusiasm. They felt the spirit of the Prophet in the possibility that Brazil was now going to be responsible to convert their mother country. I reminded them that President Kimball had said missionaries from Latin America should go across oceans to the nations of Europe, so we would expect that Brazil would furnish missionaries to go to Portugal. These local Brazilian leaders were excited about the possibility. On one of my visits to President Kimball, I said, "President Kimball, you said that the Latin Americans would help in preaching the gospel to the European nations. May I propose that one half of all missionaries called to Portugal be sent from Brazil?" He responded, "Yes, that is what we said in our announcement, so we will establish this as a policy.[3] Half of the missionaries to Portugal will be from Brazil.' "[4] I pursued a program of calling missionaries from Brazil for about four years, by which we were able to call many Brazilians to fill up the quotas necessary to fill up the various missions.

Brother David M. Kennedy, who represented the First Presidency as Special Ambassador for the Church, had gone to Portugal and met with the government officials. He had arranged with the Minister of Justice, who controlled religious affairs, to allow the Church to move into Portugal and for us to organize the mission.

About this time our son, Grant, received his mission call to Spain. His call came by way of phone, from Ned Winder of the Missionary Department, to his apartment at Ricks College. Ned explained to Grant that he could wait for his letter to open later with the family or, since I was headed on one of these trips the following day, he could have the information now so that I would not need to wonder about it in my travels. As it turned out our call took the thunder out of Grant's call as we left before he did. We did attend the Salt Lake Temple with him on October 21 when he received his endowment.

I made some preliminary trips to Portugal to set up a home and office and generally scout things out. One night I was by myself and found out what it means to suffer "jet lag." I went to sleep at 10:30 p.m., being tired, but I woke up at 1:30 a.m. and couldn't go back to sleep. It was a wonderful opportunity for me to do some reading because usually when I read it puts me to sleep. But I had the experience of reading extensively that night.

---

3. June 1, 1995, dictation to the Historical Department, pp. 2–3
4. Collected Works, pp. 546–548

Out of the eleventh chapter of 3 Nephi, the Savior in his visit to America declared: "And this is my doctrine, and it is the doctrine which the Father hath given unto me. . . . And whoso believeth in me, and is baptized, the same shall be saved; and they are they who shall inherit the kingdom of God. And whoso believeth not in me, and is not baptized, shall be damned. . . . And whoso believeth in me believeth in the Father also; and unto him will the Father bear record of me, for he will visit him with fire and with the Holy Ghost" (vv. 32–35).

As I read those passages, I felt the truth of them by the power of the Holy Ghost, which came to me and bore witness to me that this was truly the doctrine of our Father in Heaven and Jesus Christ, his Son. [5] This began to open up to my mind the vision the Lord had for our work in Portugal. The country had been under a 50-year dictatorship and had just entered a revolution to form a new government. During the period of our call, there was a powerful effort on the part of Russia to capture Portugal with a communistic regime. This agitation assumed massive proportions, and the country and the economy were in great turmoil. Portugal has a fascinating history, having had a great power in colonizing many areas of the world. Their tradition was that of seafaring and discovery. They were a Catholic nation, and we had concern that we would find great opposition. This never did develop. The people were warm and friendly and easy to approach.

We had arranged for the rental of a home in the town of Estoril, a suburb of Lisbon. It was Thanksgiving time, and we made speedy arrangements to move into the home in Estoril and establish quarters for the missionaries in Lisbon. Geraldine, with our five accompanying children, came a little later.

In the beginning, I took four missionaries: Elders Perisse, Camargo, Topham, and Thompson—two Brazilians and two Americans. I had recruited them from the Brazilian missions during my visits to that country. And so we began our missionary work. This was an unusual and outstanding experience. President Kimball had instructed me to move with caution to avoid opposition. In meeting with the missionaries, we studied the country and our prospects.

---

5. Collected Works, pp. 128–129

We settled the missionaries in Lisbon and undertook getting them started in their missionary work there. We were under caution and restraint to be very careful about not making waves or causing disturbance and antagonism because we were not fully authorized legally to be in Portugal. However, we found that there really was very little opposition in evidence, and our missionaries began to reach out to find people who would join the Church. Printed materials in Portuguese and other items were supplied from Brazil.

At first we held our church meetings in the home of American members Brother and Sister Ray Caldwell, where they had been meeting as a family branch. We established the Portugal Lisbon Mission and organized the Lisbon Branch with Brother Caldwell as Branch President. A Brother Lindsay who worked in the U.S. Consulate had converted a Portuguese girl, and I was asked to perform their marriage.

We sought for a larger place to hold meetings and eventually found a nice spacious hall in a prominent hotel in the city of Lisbon. This allowed us to meet under circumstances that were pleasant, open, and impressive. The American family of members, the Caldwells, sponsored the beginning of the organization, and we asked the missionaries to be sure that every Sunday they brought people to attend our meetings. Thus our beginning was strong. We never had a small, struggling branch, but almost from the start had a large number of people coming who had the feeling that this was a moving, dynamic organization. They realized that it had a strong foundation in Brazil, and they were not reluctant to join the Church.

At first the members did come slowly, but within a short time we had 150 or more people meeting together. Little by little they were baptized, so the branch grew, with Brother Ray Caldwell as branch president. Over a period of time the mission in Portugal grew by leaps and bounds. The mission continued to grow, and for a period of ten years or more, about half of all the converts to the Church on the continent of Europe were in Portugal. [6]

Our approach to proselyting was to take references from members in Brazil who had connections in Portugal, and the missionaries

---

6. June 1, 1995, dictation to the Historical Department, pp. 4–5

made some early contacts with some of these people and were effective in drawing a few of them to the Church. We soon found that the country was really wide open to missionary work without any objection or resistance. As such we had the missionaries begin contacting in the homes and among other persons who came into our circle. The Catholic Church was not a factor in opposition. We established missionaries in the city of Lisbon and two months later had four of them go to the city of Porto in the north of the country.

Among the people who joined the Church, we were fortunate that the elders found Brother and Sister Amaral, who accepted the gospel and were baptized. Also, Sister Bangerter had joined in the leadership of the American Boy Scout troop that had been established among Americans in Lisbon and there she made contact with a Brazilian couple named Leme. He was an airline pilot. Sister Bangerter had missionaries go to their home, and this family eventually joined the Church. They were delightful and wonderful leaders. It is interesting to note that these two men, Brother Amaral and Brother Leme, eventually rose to leadership and both were ordained to be patriarchs before they died. We also found success in our labors and association among those at NATO. Also, there was a period of unrest in Angola and many Portuguese people came back to Portugal as refugees. These people have proven to be a fertile and powerful group as they came into the Church.

Our days in Portugal were intriguing. We drove about the country as much as possible and found two or three members scattered about who had joined the Church in other areas. We flew to the Azores Islands, where we had a branch among the U.S. servicemen stationed at the United States Air Force Base at Lajes. We also visited the island of Madeira. We purchased a Ford Station Wagon as the mission vehicle. I also made bedsteads for the family to sleep on. We found a piano on Christmas Eve and began to feel at home. Sometimes we would play and sing our "homesick" songs. Another happening was the idea that came to us to go Christmas Caroling among our neighbors—this at first startled them, but several received us well. About the first of the New Year, 1975, we began to receive additional missionaries, most of them newly called from Brazil.

Our children were enrolled in an English school (Saint Columbans) and carried on their education. With our automobile we traveled as far as possible throughout the land of Portugal. I visited the city of Porto in the north with Howard, my son, who stayed close to me and was a great support. With the family we also visited many different areas including Setúbal, Évora, and Beja and came to appreciate the country. We had a delightful time with our children in becoming acquainted with the land and the people.

Call as a General Authority

Towards the end of March 1975 a telegram came asking Geri and me to attend general conference in Salt Lake City. The feeling came that a new adjustment was intended by the Church leaders, and we traveled there to attend the conference. Geri and I soon met with President Kimball in his office, and he then presented to me the new calling to serve as an Assistant to the Quorum of the Twelve Apostles and to represent the Church in the entire world. It was a most solemn moment. We were informed that we were to return to Portugal for a brief time and then report for service in Salt Lake City. We were told to share this information with no one until it was announced in general conference. Nevertheless, we invited many of our children to be in attendance as well as my mother and some of my siblings. At the opening session of the April conference my name was presented along with three others to our new calling. They were Robert D. Hales, Joseph B. Wirthlin, and Adney Y. Komatsu. In retrospect, this action was very historic in nature, as we were the last four called to be Assistants to the Twelve. I was called upon to address the conference in one of the sessions.

Following the Saturday afternoon session, Geri and I were asked to meet with the First Presidency and the Twelve in the Salt Lake Temple, where I was set apart to my new calling by President Spencer W. Kimball. All the members of our family who had been endowed were invited to be present. These were Lee Ann and Richard Lorenzon, Cory and Gayle Bangerter, Glenda Bangerter, and Julie and Ramon Beck, who had been married the previous December.

All of them had their recommends in hand and were able to witness that setting apart.

Immediately following the conference, a dedication ceremony for the new Church Office Building was held in the patio between the Church Office Building and the Administration Building. Within a few days I was assigned an office on the 20th floor next to Neal A. Maxwell and Franklin D. Richards. Before leaving for Portugal I was called to preside over the International Mission, succeeding Elder Bernard P. Brockbank. After our return to the U.S. in July, I was called by President N. Eldon Tanner to receive the other half of my responsibility, which was to serve as a managing director of the Genealogy Department, working under the direction of Elder Theodore M. Burton. I soon moved to that department but continued the dual responsibility of my calling.

Returning to Portugal we were concerned about the first great election to be held in there in late April, and because of our anxiety over the possible result, I asked the Brethren in Salt Lake City if it was appropriate to call Elder Thomas S. Monson, who was then in Sweden, to come to Portugal to officially dedicate the land for the work of the gospel. He responded immediately and came along with his wife, Frances. We had a great meeting at a spot in the rocks and crags near Sintra selected by our committee for the dedication of Portugal. The date was April 25, 1975. The nation was very much in turmoil during this time. The communist party had made a tremendous effort to capture the interest of the country, and other more democratic parties were not allowed to take part. However, when the election came, the Portuguese people came forth after 50 years of no elections and registered their votes. The communists obtained only 13 percent of the votes. This immediately terminated their activity, and they disappeared from the country. Here we felt the power of the Lord's hand in the affairs of the nation. In the meantime the country had reached a period of stagnation, and the people were suffering with a partially dormant economy.

Brother Kennedy, who had been very instrumental in clearing the way for the Church with the Portuguese government, was very anxious that I remain in Portugal because of the rapid and strong beginning we had found there. However, in June 1975 Elder Lynn Pinegar came to preside, and we were released. About that time, some of our former missionaries—Duke Cowley, Kay Hamblin, and Elijah Cardon—came for a visit as some of our wonderful associates from the early days in Brazil.

We left Lisbon driving a car across Spain, stopping in Madrid and Barcelona, where we visited our son, Grant. From there we drove into Switzerland through France where we visited with the mission president in Geneva, from whom I would assume some areas under his direction in my new calling as the president of the International Mission. We also attended the temple in Switzerland. We stopped in Stuttgart, Germany, to visit our nephew Terry Hansen and family, then we traveled across France to Paris where we visited Owen James Stevens, one of our former missionaries in Brazil, and his wife before going to Calais to cross the English Channel.

In passing through France, I asked our children to take advantage of their French classes, and to our disappointment they couldn't even figure out how to ask for water. In Paris, Paulo felt bad about this, and while in the park near the Eiffel Tower, he found a Frenchman who was kind enough to practice with him. In the end the man asked Paulo, "Where did you learn French?" Paulo told of being in a class in Portugal. The man said, "That is interesting because your French has a Chinese accent to it." Paulo replied, "Well, our teacher was Chinese." Paulo was so adept at picking up the nuance of languages that the training had affected his education. At this point the family threw out the French language experience. We spent two days in London, but the children were anxious to return home, so we flew back in a 747. We returned to our home in Alpine, where I commuted to the Church Offices each day. During this period, however, the Church administration was on a summer vacation, and this gave us time to readjust.

PERIOD V

General Authority Years

"To all of you of whom I have made mention—unbelievers; nonmembers; members of the Church, both faithful and those not so devoted—and to the leaders and all who bear the holy priesthood, I declare as one who knows and has authority, that Spencer W. Kimball, President of The Church of Jesus Christ of Latter-day Saints, is the prophet of God to all the inhabitants of the earth. He is the direct successor to Isaiah; Malachi; Peter, James, and John; and to Joseph Smith and others in between. He is the chief Apostle of Jesus Christ on the earth and is authorized to announce that the gospel has been restored to the earth in these, the last days, in preparation for the Second Coming and that these are the days to prepare. His is a voice of gladness in the glorious news he bears and a solemn warning to us all. I so testify." [1]

Chapter 15

———◆———

OVERVIEW OF
EARLY ASSIGNMENTS

"I commend to you the principles that have been restored in the last days, that should and must guide your lives to do what you are doing now, reaching outward and onward for more knowledge and more ability.

---

1. Collected Works, p. 77

What for? So that you can be ready for the next thing. And the next thing, in almost every case, certainly in the eternal sense, will not be static. It will become dynamic and onward going. More than anything it will involve you in the great mission that the Savior has ordained for this world—that of the redemption of all the sons and daughters of God in such a way that they can enjoy eternal life." [2]

"Now, the Book of Mormon is evidence, testimony, and proof that Jesus is the Christ and that the gospel has been restored to us in the last days. And so it becomes our purpose to hold fast to the knowledge that we gain in a testimony borne by the Holy Spirit. These Brethren and Sister Bangerter have spoken and have told us how they have that testimony. The Holy Spirit has revealed to them that the gospel is true. The Holy Spirit has revealed that to me by the power of the Holy Ghost. I have been called and ordained to be a witness of Jesus Christ. That is my major purpose as a General Authority of the Church. I am able to do that because the Lord has revealed that to me through the teachings of his Holy Spirit, that Jesus is the Christ, that the gospel is true, that the Book of Mormon is the word of God. So I know that. I don't know it because of logic or because of teachings of wise men. I know because the Lord has told me so through the power of his spirit." [3]

The Mission and Responsibility of a General Authority

When the summer period ended, the regular General Authority activities centered on stake conferences, with an assignment nearly every week. My first assignment was to the Tooele Stake. I had been there before as a regional representative, and the procedure was somewhat familiar. In addition to the conferences, there were constant meetings—we met nearly every day with those of our departments and regularly with all the General Authorities. We reported personally on our activity in stake conferences and were instructed by the Twelve on our responsibilities. Special assignments and appointments were given from time to time to speak in devotionals at BYU and Ricks College and in certain conventions relating to our department.

---

2. Collected Works, p. 189–190

3. Collected Works, p. 425

In September of 1975 I attended my first meeting with the General Authorities in the Salt Lake Temple. This was an unusual and a very impressive meeting with the First Presidency and the Quorum of the Twelve all seated in their places in the council room; others of us who were Assistants to the Twelve and members of the Presidency of Seventy were also in attendance. Later on that month I was impressed with the General Authority training under the direction of President A. Theodore Tuttle. I was asked to speak during the priesthood session of the general conference on October 4, 1975. I spoke concerning home teaching and emphasized some of the principles that I had learned over the years in working with that leadership program.

The International Mission

As already mentioned, I was assigned as the new president of the International Mission shortly after my call as a General Authority. Elder Howard W. Hunter first served as my advisor, and later Elder Thomas S. Monson replaced him in that function. An additional valuable advisor was Elder David M. Kennedy, Special Ambassador of the Church. The International Mission had authority over all members who lived away from organized stakes and missions worldwide. Many of the nations under the authority of the International Mission were transferred from the Swiss Mission, including Poland, Czechoslovakia, and Hungary. There were also several thousand members around the world, located in Greece, Lebanon (which soon was closed due to political problems), Egypt, Saudi Arabia, Turkey, Iran, Pakistan, India, Iceland, Greenland, Afghanistan, and other individual locations, including remote areas in Africa (excluding the areas supervised by the South African Mission). We maintained contact with them by correspondence and received their tithing, gave temple recommends, and performed other official functions. Upon early examination of the situation in the International Mission, we determined that it was important to have a more formal mission organization established in order to facilitate our efforts and maintain an easier flow of information to and from those living in such areas.

Returning from our first visit to the Middle East, I considered some of the needs of leadership in this responsibility and determined that I should have counselors. I had Percy Fetzer and Ted Cannon cleared through my advisor, Elder Thomas S. Monson, and they were called to work with me. We met weekly. Rex Reeve and later Len Harmon were called as executive secretaries to our presidency. We soon established leadership in the various areas and called men to be district presidents. In Greece, Brother James Nackos, a Greek member of the Church from Springville, Utah, was asked to take over the responsibilities as a district president. In Egypt we appointed Lynn Hilton, and in Saudi Arabia we appointed a man who had considerable experience there, Brother DeVoe Heaton. We also asked Ivan J. Barrett to be responsible for watching over the members of the Church in Israel, although they couldn't proselyte.

While my assignment in the International Mission was part of the Church's missionary activity, I was told by President Kimball that I should operate independently of the Missionary Department. I did meet with the department and advised them as to what I was doing for those two years. In addition President Kimball assigned me to be responsible for three missions: Portugal, which was new; Yugoslavia, which did not yet permit missionary activity; and Iran. President Kimball also asked that these missions be kept confidential for the time being. In Iran there were about 1,500 Church members from the U.S. and elsewhere, and it was determined to organize a regular mission there. The Iran Mission was eventually organized with Elder Dean Farnsworth as president with about seven elders assigned to serve there. Geri and I visited Iran on two or three occasions along with Elder David M. Kennedy to arrange the legalization of our work. We had interesting visits to Tehran and to Esfahan, meeting with members and the missionaries with the hope of eventual success. Within two years, however, the Moslem hierarchy took over the country, and our efforts came to an end. We maintained contacts with Portugal, of course, visiting several times. Later on our son Cory, with his family, was assigned to organize the Church Educational System there and in Spain, and we enjoyed seeing them. President Gustav Salik from Brazil had been called to preside in Yugoslavia. However, missionaries were not permitted to go there, and he lived with his family in Austria, visiting his mission area on occasion. With him we visited Serbia, Bosnia, and other locations, seeking to prepare the Book of Mormon in those languages. In Zadar, we were able to establish contacts to begin the translation. Later efforts led to calling missionary couples to pave the way in the nation of Ceylon (now called Sri Lanka), and the Mauritius Islands in the Indian Ocean.

We began to receive letters from groups in Ghana and Liberia telling us that many thousands were anxious to join the Church. Under instruction from the First Presidency, we could not give them encouragement. Many members of U.S. origin were living in several African nations, and we attended their needs when they visited us in Salt Lake City.

In February of 1977 I was asked to make a presentation to the First Quorum of the Seventy about the scope and impact of the International Mission. In this meeting, I outlined the history of the mission and the major participants in its direction and supervision. I then outlined the efforts we had made since 1975. The main effort was to acquaint the Brethren with the need to seek out and serve the scattered members of the Church around the world and to appeal to those members to assist us in furnishing information that would assist in expanding the gospel to new lands. At that time, our responsibilities served a population of about 1,200 members and about 2 billion nonmembers. I informed the Brethren about our efforts relating to methods of proselyting in each of those areas, our organization, how we maintained contact and distributed materials to them, and our procedure in issuing temple recommends to worthy members living in those areas. I was able to explain the position of the First Presidency regarding Black Africa and asked that all communication from those areas be directed to the International Mission. We encouraged the Brethren to develop contacts with visitors and foreigners coming to Utah to assist in making a favorable impression to be taken back to the home nations. I concluded with a feeling we had regarding the special spirit we felt in nations behind the Iron Curtain and other remote areas of the world. In many ways, we felt our efforts were a pioneering experience to reach out to the nations of the earth not yet serviced by the Church.

During this period the problems in the country of Lebanon were getting international attention. There was an uproar of antagonism against the government. Lawlessness was common, and we found that a number of members of the Church in Lebanon were trying to find a way to get to the United States. We did some things to help facilitate their exit and their travel to the United States. I carried this responsibility for two years before I was assigned to Brazil.

The Genealogy Department

Working in harmony with Theodore M. Burton, I began to understand how members of the Church were finding names of their people for temple work. A process of 26 checkpoints was required to clear names, which would almost make progress unfeasible for anyone. There was a beginning of the study of the use of computers, but the department was not greatly involved. Elder Packer and some others of the Twelve were anxious to develop a better process. The old Temple Index Bureau was not effectively correlated, and the Church was still marking time to develop technology. The department held annual seminars at BYU to bring members and interested workers up to date. Most member activity in genealogy was being done by those who used the libraries in personal effort. Several large libraries had been established, such as at those at BYU and in Ogden and other locations. As a positive step it was decided to rename the Genealogy Department the Family History Department. During this period I felt that we were not making great advances in this fundamental part of the gospel. I had visits with Elders Packer and Burton to consider further activity with the Genealogy Department in how research might be more effectively carried out. Elders Tuttle and Burton gave me some guidance as to what was taking place in the Genealogy Department and what the activity ought to include.

Yearly Summaries

1975

On August 20, 1975, I performed the sealing of our daughter Glenda to Steven Apple in the Salt Lake Temple. As far as I remember, this was the first time I performed that special ordinance with members of our family. Later in the year of 1975, I received a letter from the Alumni Board of the University of Utah asking that I accept the assignment to serve as a member of that board. I called President Tanner concerning this responsibility, and he advised that I should accept it and represent the Church.

In October of 1975 I received an assignment to attend a stake conference in the Zurich Stake in Switzerland. I enjoyed the conference with the stake president and his associates, who spoke English to me. I gave my leadership instructions in English but understood somewhat what was taking place as they spoke in German. It was interesting to notice that when they met in council meeting among themselves, they spoke the Swiss dialect. But when they spoke in public in the general meetings of the conference, they used regular High German. I also determined to include in my trip to Europe some visits wherever possible in locations that pertained to the International Mission and the Near East.

During this period we were able to arrange another trip in the International Mission. I had an invitation from the leader of the branch in Doha Ram in Saudi Arabia. We also visited Brother Salik, who was presiding over the Yugoslavia Mission. Brother Salik, who had grown up near Hungary, had a relationship with people in Hungary, and so we made another tour through that area of Europe. Brother Salik had found success in teaching the gospel in Hungary and arranged the baptism of some people. However, we eventually found out that the person who was promoting the Church, having spent time in Australia and gotten acquainted with the Church, was very unreliable in his approach, and the beginnings that he made were of no value.

We flew to Greece and met with a number of members of the Church who lived there and a group with the American air base established there, holding a Sabbath day meeting with them under the direction of Brother Nackos. We visited Mars Hill and the Acropolis. Someone arranged for a morning meeting with the members, giving us an opportunity to visit some of Athens later in the day. We were taken on an extended journey to the south along the seacoast and saw some of the ancient ruins that were part of the Grecian culture.

From Greece we moved to Cairo, Egypt, and there I met with Lynn Hilton, the district president. He instructed me somewhat in how to get a visa to go from Egypt to Saudi Arabia because I had not been able to make full arrangements before we left home. It was a rather trying experience, but I persisted in asking officials at the visa office, and finally they issued our visa to go to Saudi Arabia shortly before our airplane was scheduled to leave. We flew across eastern Egypt and the Red Sea and then into Saudi Arabia, a vast desert country, and landed at Dhahran on the Eastern border. It was a very large oil installation, directed mostly by companies from the United States. The district president, Brother DeVoe Heaton, had arranged for a group of 200 or 300 Latter-day Saints to gather together in a facility in the area of Dhahran for a series of meetings. On the day following the meeting, the group arranged a tour to the south of Arabia to visit what they called an oasis by the name Hofuf. We went there with intense interest and found that the oasis consisted of a large number of canals surrounded by date palm trees and lots of vegetation, something very strange in the midst of the desert. We enjoyed this visit and picked up a souvenir or two before returning to Dhahran. From Dhahran we flew to Tehran in Iran and met President Dean Farnsworth and the seven elders in that mission. While they were not authorized to proselyte among Muslim people, there were many other religions in the country and especially a large body of members of the Church from the United States who were employed mostly in military activities in support of the government of Iran.

In a subsequent visit to the Middle East, we went in company with Elder David Kennedy. On this occasion we traveled together to Greece, Egypt, and Persia (or Iran), where we met with legal counsel to provide a legal foundation for the Church in that country. On the second visit to the Near East, we also stopped in Istanbul on our way back to Greece. One of our missionaries was serving in the military in Turkey, and we were invited to attend a conference with him and the group with which he was affiliated.

While in Tehran we received notice that I had been asked to go to San Diego and dedicate a flagpole at the Mormon Battalion installation there. So Geri and I took our plane from Tehran and flew almost nonstop halfway around the world. We stopped briefly in Rome, England, and New York. It seemed like the longest day of our lives. When we arrived in New York, we were so tired that we went to a hotel and stayed the night. The next day we flew across the United States to San Diego. We met briefly with President Frank Bradshaw, the mission president, and some of his missionaries and then attended the ceremonies held at the Mormon Battalion monument before we finally returned home from this prolonged journey.

At Utah State University in Logan, a large number of foreign students from Iran had taken up residence. The Latter-day Saint students there had taken an interest in meeting with them and trying to fellowship them. They had made them very welcome. However, since these people were Muslims they were unable—because of their religion—to do anything about joining the LDS Church, and this situation caused them to have a negative attitude towards members of the Church everywhere. We counseled with these students as to how they should smooth their relationship. At this time Poland was also placed in the International Mission. I did not have the opportunity to go there, but I counseled with several members of the Church who lived in Poland. In connection with the genealogical activity in the Church, we were able to arrange microfilming for the religious records in Poland, which was carried out largely through the agency of the Polish Catholic Church. They did this because we provided them with a copy of the valuable information that was gathered.

1976

Following the New Year activities we once again were involved with stake conferences, our first being to the La Crescenta California Stake. We also participated in a missionary conference with Presidents Brent Goates and Frank Bradshaw, which turned out very well. At the end of the month I was assigned to the East Los Angeles Stake conference. Interspersed with all of those were regular meetings with those involved with the International Mission. David Kennedy also reported to me on various circumstances in countries around the world.

Later on we met with several of our former missionaries in the Phoenix area, being housed by Duke and Alice Cowley, as I participated in the Phoenix North Stake conference and dedicated a chapel in that stake. Our efforts through May were much the same with seemingly endless meetings, stake conference visits, sealings, and more meetings and interviews. Our time was spent in meetings with one or another of the General Authorities dealing with genealogy needs, often with Elder Packer and Elder Hunter. I was assigned to speak at the Regional Representatives' Seminar on April 5, and the following instruction I gave is reminiscent of that which I received from a young captain in the military: "When you make your own presentation in this section, we hope it will be a highlight. This is your moment to perform in genealogy. It is expected that you will function during your appearance with the high priests as if this work were your greatest interest. We hope that you can reflect a deep personal involvement and an overriding faith and testimony in that which you are presenting." [4]

In the office we continued our meetings with the Genealogy Department and the Melchizedek Priesthood Committee. We also enjoyed regular General Authority meetings in the temple where special information was given and special prayers offered. I toured the massive vaults in Little Cottonwood Canyon as part of my assignment. Meetings continued most regularly for my assignments in the Genealogy Department and the International Mission. We met with Dr. James Mason as he was interested in writing up what Geri had prepared for our missionaries in Brazil on health issues. I also met with several Africans who were seeking membership in the Church. We determined in our International Mission presidency that Brother Percy Fetzer should make a special journey through Eastern Europe

---

4. Collected Works, p. 131

determining how many members of the Church there were outside the wards and stakes in Germany and where they were located in East Germany and especially in Poland.

In June of 1976, I was assigned to attend a stake conference in American Falls, Idaho, and while we were there we received news of the disaster of the Teton Dam break upstream on the Snake River. We learned it had destroyed the town of Sugar City, above Rexburg, Idaho, and had flooded Rexburg and threatened certain other parts of Idaho. Eleven people lost their lives in that tragedy.

In other assignments, I spoke at the Provo MTC and was later assigned to supervise the stakes and missions in Nevada and Colorado and tour the missions there. We had an enjoyable time going through all the stakes in Nevada and covering the country, which was mostly desert. In Colorado I went with the mission president and his wife to several meetings with missionaries. In Denver I consulted with a missionary who was having problems and advised the president on how to work with him to help him be successful in his mission. We then traveled to Cheyenne, Wyoming, and then east to Grand Island, Nebraska. From there we turned south going through Hayes and Dodge City, Kansas, and on to the border towns of Oklahoma, where I dedicated the chapel. We returned to Denver across the Great Plains. To me these areas held a deep fascination.

About the middle of the year we made another visit to the Near East; we stopped in Austria and met with President Salik. He drove us through various parts of Yugoslavia, going through the towns of Croatia, particularly, where we met with the mother of Kresimir Cosic, the BYU basketball player who had joined the church. We talked to some who were considering helping in translating the Book of Mormon. We went to the town of Zagreb and then to Belgrade, the capital of Serbia, where we had a pleasant evening and enjoyed some of the entertainment in one of their restaurants. While in that country, we offered a special prayer that the nation would open up to the preaching of the gospel.

I was assigned to attend the regional conferences in Great Britain and Scotland. Geri and I went to England, stopping in London and then traveling on to Manchester, where we had a large gathering of

Latter-day Saints. From there we drove by bus in company with Elder Ezra Taft Benson, a member of the Twelve. He showed us where he had lived in London following World War II and the place in Carlisle where he had served as a missionary and where he had been threatened with persecution. We arrived in Glasgow, Scotland, to attend the conference in that area. I gave addresses in Manchester on June 20 and in Glasgow on June 22. I was interested especially in Scotland to find a difference in the dialect of the people. President Kimball also spoke at the Glasgow conference and made some prophetic statements, which have yet to be fulfilled. In my remarks I said: "I hope everyone who attended yesterday realizes that we heard at least two prophecies by the President of the Church. I have listened to him frequently in the last year and a half, and I rarely hear him make such specific statements; in fact, I can't recall when he has been so explicit in making an expression of prophecy as he did yesterday. Do you remember what it was? He mentioned specific countries where the gospel would be carried by people from your country; the other one was to tell you that you will have a temple here someday. Like all prophecies there are two parts—one is the inspiration that brings it to us, and the other depends upon our performance, and he made that condition yesterday as well. I felt that he spoke by the power of the Holy Ghost when he made those two prophecies yesterday." [5]

While we were attending the conference in Glasgow we received word from home that my sister Glenneth Wilson had passed away in Arizona. Her husband, Lowell, was most attentive to her in her failing years. As soon as we were finished with the conference we flew back to Salt Lake City and from there drove our car to Arizona, where we attended her burial in the cemetery at Glendale, west of Phoenix. Glenneth had been weakening for some time. She was a very cheerful and delightful sister and much beloved by us. But she took an attitude of sweetness and understanding up to the time of death on June 21.

In September we flew to Australia and then to New Zealand where we visited the temple. I had a stake conference in the city of Brisbane and enjoyed very much the chance to associate with the

5. Collected Works, p. 38

Saints there. In New Zealand we got acquainted with the Maori members of the Church, noting the great capacity they have for singing beautifully together.

In September of 1976 the leadership of the Church determined that they would organize the First Quorum of Seventy and that those who had been called as Assistants to the Twelve would become members of that quorum. The quorum was formally announced at the October general conference. This organization proved to be fulfillment of the charge given in section 107 of the Doctrine and Covenants that the Seventy take their place as the third governing body in Church leadership, and the transition placed the Seventy in a prominence not entirely understood in previous decades. It also became the impetus to disband stake seventies quorums and to encourage these men to return to the elders quorums or high priest groups in their respective wards.

Assignments inside the United States found us involved in an interim mission presidents' seminar for those missions in the states of the Intermountain West. This was an opportunity for us to become better acquainted with those leaders. During this time we also toured the Nevada Mission. We also obtained permission to call a couple, Brother and Sister Harames, to serve in Greece as our representatives there for the International Mission.

I had another assignment to Switzerland and was asked to attend the district conference at the Church building adjacent to the temple in Switzerland. We attended the sacrament meeting there, and I was asked to speak. Before I spoke, we were told that all the people on the first two benches were relatives of my family living in places near Bern, Switzerland. None of them were members of Church, and therefore I made my remarks concerning the great number of the Bangerter family who had left Switzerland and settled in Utah and what type of people they were. Following the meeting we met with these relatives and became acquainted with them. We met with some of them again in subsequent visits to that country.

Our travels during this trip also took us to Iran, where with a small group of members we offered a special prayer over that country. During all this period of my early experiences as a General

Authority, I was called upon to attend stake conferences almost every weekend. I am unable at this time to recall the names of the various stakes, but they were very impressive, and I had the responsibility of giving many addresses and having council meetings with the leadership. I also performed several temple marriages, as was normal for a General Authority.

1977

In early January of 1977, Brother George Durrant came into the office to begin his service as the director of priesthood genealogy. I spent much time with him and Elder Packer, giving Brother Durrant an overview of the assignment and reviewing basic principles. I felt that he was a great brother and would be a valuable addition to the department. During this time, I also spoke at the University of Utah Institute devotional on living "Happily Ever After." I later met with Brother Dennis Neuenswander about his forthcoming visit to Poland to negotiate for copying of genealogical records there.

During our priesthood board meeting, President Benson gave impressive instructions on how we should appear and perform as General Authorities. In a subsequent meeting, Elders S. Dilworth Young and Hartman Rector reviewed material we were preparing regarding the local seventies quorums in the stakes. Much of what I had presented earlier was acceptable to them.

In visiting stake conferences at various locations, I was always surprised to run into some of our former missionaries, such as Elder Mauerman in Louisiana; Elders Peters and Matsen in the Los Angeles region; Elders Turner, Morgan, Moore, and Mickleson in the Denver region; and Elders Hamblin, Cowley, Cardon, and Rose in Mesa and Phoenix. All of them were dear to us for their service in Brazil.

In many of these conferences I came away deeply impressed with the caliber and depth of many called to speak. They brought such a tremendous spirit in their presentations. In like manner I was also blessed with a special spirit of inspiration in many of these meetings. One example of this took place in the Dallas North Stake. During my remarks in the general session, I called on a young elders quorum president to assist me in the demonstration of how to teach tithing.

It developed that he had recently had a very serious interview with the stake president about how to be closer to the Lord and how to get along better with his wife and family. He had not been paying his tithing until recently. Because of our demonstration, he and his wife were overwhelmed. The stake president felt it was a miracle that this young man had been chosen to participate in the demonstration.

In February of 1977, I went to Greece to hold meetings with members there. I arrived a bit early, and soon Brother Jim Nackos, the district president, and Brother Hein, the branch president, picked me up and took me to a lovely hotel overlooking the great bay near Athens. After a half hour of consultation about our time in Athens, I was left to get two hours of much needed rest. In the afternoon we spent much of our time discussing the affairs of the Church in Greece. According to President Nackos, Brother and Sister Harames, the couple who had been called to represent the International Mission in Greece, had been extremely rebellious to his authority, doing many foolish things and spending considerable amounts of money. This was one of the urgent problems I needed to resolve while in Greece. There also seemed to be an unusual interest in the Mormons with several articles appearing in the paper, most of them erroneous and misleading. The problem with Brother and Sister Harames was most concerning to me, and I studied and prayed about what we could do to resolve this difficulty.

After a tour of some of the important landmarks of that area of Greece, including the Temple of Poseidon on a mountaintop over-looking the Aegean Sea, I returned to the hotel for a couple hours of rest. As I revived for the remainder of the day, Brother and Sister Harames came to the hotel and we had an important meeting to-gether. I found that Brother and Sister Harames's feelings concerning Brother Nackos had been developing for quite some time. It was ev-ident that Brother Nackos had taken a rather dominant attitude over them, and their feelings had built up to a point where they felt un-able to cooperate. I explained to them the need to have harmony and to avoid contention. Sister Harames began to soften in her feelings, and I realized that it would be possible to overcome the difficulty. As Brother Nackos came a little later, I had a meeting with him and explained his need to be more understanding and less domineering. He was surprised to realize that Brother and Sister Harames had felt offended, and he was quick to apologize to them. They were all overcome by the spirit of repentance and forgiveness and understanding, and I believe we came finally to resolve the whole problem.

As a special event in connection with my visit to Greece, we arranged to meet with Brother Nackos; Brother Harames; Brother Hein, the branch president; his two counselors, Brothers Adams and Morgan; and several others of the priesthood leadership, including those from Thessaloniki and surrounding areas. We all went together by automobile into the center of Athens to Mars Hill. There we had Brother Nackos read, in Greek, Paul's speech concerning the unknown God as it appeared there on the plaque that is embedded in the rock. We then mounted the summit of Mars Hill, and with the Acropolis towering above us, we surveyed the view of Athens and the temple-crowned hills of ancient Greece; the ancient marketplace ruins that were spread beneath us are probably the area where Paul gave his discourse.

Being relatively alone, our group then sat on the rocks, and I explained to them my desire to take a few sacred moments to review and contemplate some of the great events that had taken place in the area under our view. We talked of the great cultural heritage that had descended from ancient Greece. Brother Nackos spoke of the great sea battle between the Greeks and the Persians that had taken place not far below us. We then reviewed the story of Paul's journey as he traveled to Athens from Northern Greece. Brother Bradford then read to us the entire 17th chapter of the book of Acts, including Paul's sermon concerning the unknown god. I then asked the brethren there assembled to join with me as I offered a special prayer to bless the land of Greece and to raise up people who could assist in establishing the gospel in that land, that the people of that country might also receive redemption from their sins through the blessings of the gospel.

We thereafter descended from the mount and drove back to Brother Hein's home in the outskirts of Athens. Thereafter, some of the members, including the branch presidency, Brother Nackos, and

Brother and Sister Harames, went to the home of Brother Nebeker, where a special meeting had been arranged to meet with the members and friends of the Church who were Greek. Brother and Sister Boubalos and their two children were present. They were eventually responsible for the latest revisions of the Book of Mormon in the Greek language. Brother Nackos conducted this meeting, having various people there to interpret the remarks of those who could not understand English. Then I was called upon to speak. I compared the similarities of our time and our message with the time and message Paul brought to the ancient Jews, explaining that in the midst of teachings about Christ there was a necessity for people to hear the truth and be called to repentance because the churches of the earth were not capable of teaching His gospel effectively. Several investigators were present who responded with expressions of appreciation for what we had told them. It was a most inspiring visit.

From there we went to Egypt and finally to Persia (or Iran), where we met with legal counsel to provide a legal base for the Church in that country. We also stopped in Istanbul on our way back toward Greece. In Turkey we visited at Ankara, Adana, and Smyrna. One of our missionaries was serving in the military in Turkey, and we were invited to attend a conference with him and the group with which he was affiliated in the midst of Turkey. From there we went back to Greece; from Greece we went to Germany and then to Austria, again touring in Yugoslavia.

Another of my assignments was to visit the Churubusco Mexico Stake and the Church school at Benemerito in Mexico City. At this conference, the stake president was being released to become a mission president, but he had arranged for all the senior graduates of that school to sign up to be called to go on missions. There were 100 of them who were lined up to go from the Benemerito school as missionaries to various parts of Mexico. I was impressed with this stake presidency. The president had considerable experience as a counselor before being named president three or four years earlier. In our leadership meetings I took most of the time, with my brother Blauer, who was a mission president in Mexico City, helping me with the board. I had an unusual freedom of expression in Spanish during this meeting, and I felt very much strengthened and able to present my instructions to the brethren who were assembled. I think the Lord truly helped me in this effort. However, in the general session I again spoke for over a half an hour in Spanish without feeling the same fluency, although I believe my remarks had better effect than if I had tried to use an interpreter.

I later met with Blauer and got more acquainted with his mission operation, learning of his attitude and policy in developing the missionary work. He reported that while previously they had baptisms at the rate of 600 to 700 per month, he had reoriented the missionaries to work closely with the members since most of the baptisms in the past came through tracting contacts, and the retention rate was not strong enough. As a result of that shift, he felt they were able to retain nearly all those who came into the Church, and they would therefore be able to build their baptism performance on a much sounder basis and at the same time increase their numbers.

In March of 1977 I was assigned to reorganize a stake presidency in the Albuquerque East Stake. We went directly to the stake center, and Elder Petterson, the regional representative, and I began immediately to interview men and to prepare ourselves to handle the assignment to reorganize the stake presidency. By the time we had concluded, it was clearly apparent to us both that Bishop Jay Richard Payne should be appointed as president of the stake. It was interesting again to me to notice that he and no one else was pointed out to us through the Spirit of the Lord as the one who should take this position. Having come to this conclusion, we invited him and his wife in for consultation. He accepted the appointment and then named his two counselors.

Prior to April general conference in 1977, the General Authority meeting was of significant impact to us; we spent two hours bearing testimony following a review of new assignments to the various Brethren. It was a spiritual feast for us to be strengthened by each others' witnesses of the restored gospel. Early in the meeting President Tanner announced that the Presidents of the Seventy who had been serving overseas were being called home, and that they, along with others of the First Quorum, would be assigned as advisors to the

Area Supervisors, thus replacing the members of the Quorum of the Twelve. This necessitated several other adjustments in assignment, and I immediately noted on the assignment sheet that I was assigned to replace Brother Faust in Brazil. While this was not unexpected, it nevertheless caused me sufficient mental turmoil that I did not pay complete attention to the further proceedings of the meeting.

Following conference, we moved ahead with plans to wrap up our current assignments. We were able to set apart Brother and Sister Matthew Ciembronowicz as special representatives of the Church to Poland, which would ease our concerns there regarding the International Mission. Their calling was a most historic moment, perhaps the first time to send those who could carry the gospel to that great country.

A highlight of conference occurred in the seminar for regional representatives where, under the direction of Elder Boyd K. Packer, we made a presentation of the genealogy program. We had worked several weeks to make this a dramatic and impressive presentation, and it came off in a truly inspired manner. I had outlined a scriptural presentation to begin with, which was put to sound and music, and it was most impressive. I am sure no one went to sleep. All who were there evidently felt that it was the best genealogical presentation they had seen or heard.

Following general conference, Geri and I visited Scotland for a stake conference, after which we flew to London and then to Vienna, Austria, where we met with President Salik to review the conditions of Yugoslavia and Hungary. There were a number of people prepared for baptism in those two nations. Included in our conversations was the possibility of having material translated into those two languages. From there we flew to Greece as part of our attempt to wrap up our assignment with the International Mission.

In mid-June, we had a Melchizedek Priesthood board meeting, where I was greatly impressed with the enthusiastic reports given by Elder Hinckley concerning the Far East Area, by Elder Monson concerning the Europe Area, and by Elder McConkie concerning South America. Taken in context, the overall growth of the Church seemed phenomenal. The projections for future growth were much greater than we had seen in the past. We also brought to bear the initiation of a new Sunday School course on genealogy, which would focus more on the notion of a workshop rather than simply a period of instruction.

Our son Grant came home from his mission to Spain on January 2, 1977, where he had served a very successful mission in many capacities of leadership. Among other things, President Stevens called Grant to serve six months with him in the office in Madrid as Mission Commissarian (materials manager), and later he was able to meet President Hugo Catron as one of the first assistants to the Seville Mission. The Spain Madrid Mission was divided into three missions, including Barcelona and Seville, six months before Grant came home. As a final event prior to our departure to Brazil, we held our annual family outing to the High Uintas in July, spending some time at Black's Fork with the family.

Chapter 16

BACK TO BRAZIL

"What we see today is only the seed for the things which must soon come to pass. In the likeness of the people of Zion many people have been richly blessed with the gospel since it came to South America. I can see something of the panorama which is taking place in the lives of the members of the Church. Brother Lombardi, a television repairman, seemed to have no great destiny before he joined the Church. Now he together with Brothers Spät, Camargo, Cabral, and Oliveira meet with the Priesthood Leaders from all around the world. I can see a young bishop named Paulo Puerta with five beautiful children and a devoted wife, along with scores of others like him guiding the growth of the kingdom of God. His father presides in the temple of the Lord. Several months ago we watched 12 young Brazilians returning from their mission in Porto Alegre on the same airplane. They were greeted by a hundred members of the Church, including parents, relatives, former companions, many already married, with their wives and some of the wives already big with child. And we saw many lovely young ladies. I wonder why there were so many young ladies.

"Zion is not what we see in the Church in Brazil. It is much greater and more perfect. Can you see what the Lord sees and what President Kimball sees? Think about the potential. I can see 1,000 Brazilians serving missions in 1979. In 1981 they will be ready to organize 1,000 Zion homes. We will have 1,000 potential bishops and quorum presidents. We will have 1,000 happy young women with a man worthy to take them to the temple. We will begin to see 10,000 more babies born in the covenant of God with the privilege of growing up protected from the errors of the world. I can see 100,000 Brazilians joining the Church in a year. That means 10 missions. It means 25, 50, or 100 stakes in Brazil. It means more temples because this temple will be too small to hold us. We will see enough faithful members paying their tithing that the Church in Brazil will be financially inde-

pendent. We will begin to give the ordinances of the gospel to this nation of 120,000,000 and then take it to those who have died. We have the vision of the salvation of a mighty nation and we know how to do it." [1]

Area Supervisor for Brazil

In April of 1977 I was named as the area supervisor to Brazil. I was to exchange places with Elder James E. Faust, who would assume the International Mission responsibility while I took over in Brazil. Before assuming this assignment, I made a quick trip to Brazil and met with Elder Faust. We went to Brasília, where we met with government officials who consulted with us on the possibility of easing up the visa arrangement for missionaries coming from the United States. Certain promises were made, which were not kept.

While in Brazil, I visited overnight with Elder and Sister Faust in their home in São Paulo and met Sonja Wosnjuk, who lived with the Fausts and was their cook. We discussed the various circumstances of my assuming the responsibilities for the area of Brazil. He had prepared an excellent outline of the conditions, and I enjoyed the chance to become better acquainted with the problems in the area and with the progress of the Church. The São Paulo Temple was under construction at the time, and we walked over to visit the site, which was just a short three blocks from their home. We inspected the construction site and walked through the temple, which was advancing well, the steeple being in the process of construction and the basic structure being practically complete. I surveyed the building with the intent to understand how the dedication ceremony could best be handled because there had been some question about whether the dedication ought to take place inside the stake center that was being constructed adjacent to the temple. We finally came to the conclusion that we would recommend that in each of the three days of dedication, the first session ought to be held in the temple, and the two succeeding sessions with the First Presidency could be conduct-

---

1. Collected Works, pp. 50, 54

ed from the stake center. Of course the temple would be filled in each of these sessions and televised to give everyone a view.

Considering what President Kimball had expressly announced about the calling of missionaries from the various lands of the world, I studied the membership in Brazil and found that there were probably 2,000 young men of an age to go on missions, and that if we could call a certain number of these, we could fill up the complement of missionaries in all the missions in Brazil. I knew that I would need special authority because of the previous experience with negative attitudes among Church leaders. So I went to President Kimball before going back to Brazil and said, "President, I need help when I go down there. I wish you would give me ammunition by which I can direct the leadership, especially in the area of calling native young men to go on missions. I have studied the possibilities, and I think there are 2,000 young men who could serve a mission. If we could call 360 of them at once, we should have enough to fill up our missions. Would you please give me a direct order, or commandment, so to speak, to the leaders to immediately call 360 young men to serve as missionaries?"

President Kimball responded, "Elder Bangerter, if there are 2,000 young men available, why do you only want 360?"

I perceived the driving force of his purpose, and then he saw the dismay I must have shown in my countenance. He said, "Oh, I suppose you mean you want to begin with 360, is that right?"

I responded, "Yes, President, that's really what I had in mind."

He then said, "All right. You go down and tell those brethren who are in leadership that they must immediately get those 360 missionaries called so that we can carry forward the work of the gospel in that land."

President Kimball's vision and impulse were fantastic. I then outlined to him the need we had to ordain many more men to the Melchizedek Priesthood. Some stakes in Brazil had as many as 1,000 prospective elders, and I knew the gospel could not be strong with this number of men not qualified to lead in the Church. President Kimball fully agreed with this attitude and said, "Yes, they must be ordained. They must be carefully prepared for their callings in the priesthood." We then talked of the importance of having every member becoming involved in the missionary process so the Church could grow with great strength and power. He again gave his assent in this urgent directive to the accomplishment of this great responsibility. Even though it was a brief interview, it gave me the authority and direction I needed to begin some of the important projects in my new assignment.

Shortly thereafter, I met Elder Thomas S. Monson in the elevator in the Church Office Building. He said "Grant, I wish you well in your assignment. See what you can do to straighten out the visa problem for the North American missionaries."

I felt I had a different direction in the calling of missionaries in my consultations with President Kimball, and I felt within myself that the Lord had allowed the restriction of visas of North American missionaries to force the calling of native missionaries. So I responded, "Brother Monson, I'll do what I can in the direction of visas, but I don't think that is the answer any more."

"Oh," he said, "What is the answer?"

I said, "It is to do what President Kimball said and call the native members of the Church to serve on missions." So he added his blessing to me that I might be successful in that purpose.

We made adjustments with our son Grant and his future wife, Cleadonna, and our daughter Glenda and her husband, Steven, to move into our home in Alpine. On July 7, 1977, we departed. Geri and I with four of our children—Peggy, Paulo, Layne, and Duella—flew to São Paulo, Brazil. We were met at the airport by Elders Hatch and Duffles, who took us to our residence, formerly occupied by the Fausts. Within a short time we were at home. Sonja Wosnjuk, who was the maid and cook, took good care of us, and we soon realized that she should join in our family and be a part of our regular activity.

Home and Office in Brazil near the Temple

As already mentioned, the home was within walking distance to the São Paulo Temple construction site. The decision to build a temple in São Paulo had been made in 1975 while we were in Portugal. Since then construction on the building had proceeded, and our two sons Paulo and Layne often helped in the construction of the temple, performing minor tasks. Our home saw a constant stream of visitors from Church headquarters, those representing the Temple Department, the Presiding Bishopric's Office, mission presidents, and others coming through Brazil for various reasons. Several of the Brethren stayed with us as they came through, including Elders Marvin J. Ashton and wife, Franklin D. Richards and wife, Dean Larsen, Royden Derrick, Mark E. Petersen, and even President and Sister Kimball. We even began an MTC experience in our home for new Brazilian missionaries before we set up a Brazilian Missionary Training Center in the old mission home on Rua Itapeva 378. Layne and Duella entered school at the São Paulo Graded School. There we found Lee Ann's name on a plaque as one of the first graduating class of that school.

The Church had reserved a large number of apartments across the street from where the temple was being built to house those who would come as temple workers. They were not being occupied at that time, and I decided to move my office from the home where we lived to one of those apartments and made that the headquarters of our activity and responsibility.

Shortly after our arrival, I met with the Governor of the State of Rio de Janeiro in a very congenial interview wherein we were able to share some of our purposes in the growth of the Church in Brazil. He received us warmly and favorably.

Within a few days I was able to hold a meeting with the presidents of the four missions in Brazil and outline for them the goals we had. I found some very interesting conditions existing in the missions. First of all, the rule had been given out several years previously that after members of the Church had been baptized they were no longer the responsibility of the missionaries, and the missionaries must not visit them anymore. It then became the duty of the bishops to fellowship them. The bishops were overwhelmed in trying to take care of the new converts because they were new and had a small, less-than-perfect organization in their wards. As a result, these new members were often not being taken care of. I immediately told the presidents that we would change that policy and henceforth the missionaries were expected and required to visit all those who had been baptized and to follow through on those who had been brought in and had not been properly fellowshipped. Often this would require frequent visits for up to six months.

I spoke with my two assistants, Elders Hatch and Duffles, and asked them if they were successful in their missionary work. They said that they had had some people join the Church, and when I asked if they visited them anymore, they said "No, no, we don't do that."

I said, "Well, you will do it now. From now on it is your policy to follow through and teach them."

Then I asked why they didn't work with members, and they said "Of course, as is everywhere in the Church, members won't help."

I said, "Yes they will. But you don't know how to help them. You don't know how to show them how to do it."

And so we outlined a study program of how they'd go to the members and have certain leaders introduce them to possible prospects to join the Church. This soon became a strong and solid effort to increase the numbers in convert retention, and the results began to show success in a great increase in baptisms. Within a few months, most of the missions in Brazil were working with members, and the policy was solidified that missionaries should follow through after baptism with sustaining visits to their new members for up to six months. After some discussion, we suggested a process on how to work with the branch mission leader, which would produce referrals. I also put the missionaries in touch with my wife, Sister Bangerter, and they quickly found several people to whom she could give them introductions. We followed this program through for a matter of about a year, and the missionaries who served as my assistants stated that at the end of that time they had at least 100 members join the Church in our own branch in Vila Sonia.

Geraldine and I had wonderful times visiting the stakes and each of the five missions. We went from Porto Alegre and made a complete visit of the state of Rio Grande do Sul. We also visited Curitiba in the state of Paraná as well as Florianopolis in Santa Catarina. We were constantly in contact with all the areas in São Paulo, Rio de Janeiro, and Minas Gerais. The Church was well organized in Brasília and in the north, which gave us the opportunity to visit Recife, Belém, and Manaus as well as Fortaleza. I was given the responsibility to divide and organize stakes under the direction of headquarters in Salt Lake City. We met with great numbers of missionaries and their presidents. I felt a lack in capability for good and effective missionary effort and soon arranged by recommendation for the calling of some of my former missionaries to be mission presidents who would be able to set the pace and lead the way.

Construction on the São Paulo Temple was scheduled for completion in 1978. There was still much to be done, however, and I consulted closely with the builders so that it could be dedicated in 1978. I soon had concern about the lighting in the construction of the temple and met with the supervisor and the contractors, and I felt some urgency about the problems we were facing in the construction. We were somewhat disappointed in the progress that they had been making. In connection with the temple work we arranged to establish a garment-making facility in São Paulo to support the needs of the temple when it should be opened. Brother Harmon was instrumental in this issue. I met with the construction supervisors to assess the various construction projects currently in operation throughout in the country.

I felt that we needed to organize the Melchizedek Priesthood and to follow through on the ordination of many men to be elders. The temple in São Paulo, the first in all South America, was being prepared for dedication, and unless we had more Melchizedek Priesthood and their wives to go to the temple worthily, we would not be able to make good use of it. I told the leaders: "We are under a time pressure to organize the members of the Church to come to the temple, which will open within 18 months of this meeting. We need to have more men ordained to the Melchizedek Priesthood. The second problem is the lack of missionaries. Our missions are functioning with 50 percent of their complement of missionaries. We do not see a great prospect in increasing the number of North Americans, so the answer, as the President of the Church has announced, is to call native young men and women to serve as missionaries in Brazil."

Soon after our arrival I held a meeting with the regional representatives in Brazil. I told them of the responsibility to call local missionaries. I met with some of the same attitudes I had encountered during my service as a regional representative (see chapter 14). Some of these brethren resisted the idea, stating that they didn't believe that should happen in Brazil, that it was a program for the United States. I emphasized what President Kimball had told us to do. I felt it important to make a beginning in projecting our direction, and we spent two and a half hours studying the principles relating to the need for calling an additional number of missionaries. We established an assignment schedule and an arrival schedule so that a certain number could be called from each stake; the schedule was intended to assist stake and ward leaders to bring this result to pass. Eventually we got their agreement that we would begin to call Brazilian young men to be missionaries. I assumed that task as one of the primary responsibilities for my assignment to Brazil. Almost immediately there was resistance. Not all of the regional representatives resisted, but it was obvious that the attitude of some was not positive. One of the brethren, my dear friend Walter Spat, announced openly, "Frankly, brethren, I'm not in favor of this program." I was a little bit shocked, but I responded, "Brother Spat, you don't understand. You are not required personally to support all these missionaries. There will be means provided by which they can be supported in their work. But they are to be called under the authority of the President of the Church, having been foreordained by the Lord to take this responsibility."

I reviewed with them once again the spiritual assurance that I had received about the service of native missionaries. I said, "If we do not call these native young men and women we will face several overpowering problems. First of all, there will not be adequate leadership for the rapid growth of the Church, which is now taking place. Secondly, the calling of local missionaries will provide a fountain of men from which we can draw future leaders. We cannot preach the gospel to this nation of 120 million people unless we have the force to do it. Therefore, we must move forward. Thirdly, we have a need to increase the genealogy work on the part of the local members." A fourth activity we discussed was to call these newly ordained men to be home teachers. At that time, home teaching was very weak in the country. Brother Spat relinquished his opposition, but it took a little time for him to fully come to the realization of what the Lord intended.

So the word went out that the young men should be called to go on missions. Nothing happened. Very few, a trickle really, of young men had continued to come over the months, but the 360 did not materialize. I began to worry. We met with stake presidents. We encouraged them to seek out young men and call them on missions. They didn't accomplish very much. I began to realize that the stake presidents and bishops did not know how to recommend and call missionaries to serve. Finally we suggested that each stake president relieve one of his counselors of all other responsibilities and assign him, along with a member of the high council, to go among the wards and search out young men who could be called to serve missions. We saw that there was really no comprehension of how missionaries were to be called. Bishops didn't have the forms to recommend them. Stake presidents lacked experience in processing them.

Brother Osiris G. Cabral, one of the regional representatives, was very enthusiastic about this purpose. He had served years before as a full-time missionary in the Andes. He went to the stake in Porto Alegre, which was his area. He held a special meeting in which he asked all the young men who were available to be brought forward to be recommended as missionaries. When he returned to São Paulo, he said, "I asked for 40 missionaries from that stake. I really should have asked for 75 because there were enough to make up that number!" So we anxiously waited for the recommendations to come from that stake, but they didn't come. Nothing happened. We were disappointed. Similarly not much happened from any of the other stakes. We did have in the Bosque Stake, however, a positive result. Brother Harry E. Klein, one of the high counselors, in company with a member of the stake presidency began to visit the wards and meet the young men. They personally presented the call to these young men to go on missions. They had success with a certain number, and in the process they began to gain the spirit of their mission and gain enthusiasm. I had thought that within a matter of three months we would have all those missionaries called, but it didn't work that way. We still found that there was apathy among the bishops to call young men to go on missions, but they very slowly began to get some interest and a little more enthusiasm in accomplishing this work.

In late July I determined to meet again with each mission president to review a number of subjects, including the circumstances of their mission, prospects for growth, division of the mission, problems with visas for U.S. missionaries, raising more native missionaries to serve, and so forth. I began in the Rio de Janeiro Mission with President Hélio da Rocha Camargo. I was also able to hold similar meetings with the two São Paulo mission presidents (President Saul Messias de Oliveira and President Roger Beitler) as well as the Porto Alegre mission president, President Jason Garcia de Souza. Each mission president in Brazil appeared to me to be sound and capable. The work indeed was in good hands. I encouraged each mission to continue in their devotion and instructed them about gaining skill in their work and obtaining a true, spiritual testimony of the gospel through a careful and prayerful reading of the Book of Mormon. In further meetings with the regional representatives and the Temple Executive Committee, we found that there was a lack of knowledge as to who would be invited to the temple dedication and that no concrete plans had been worked up as to who would be seated in certain areas as well as how the people would be permitted to come. We asked that they work to answer these questions immediately.

We presided at the first stake conference held in the newly constructed stake center adjacent to the temple. Though it was practically completed, there were still aspects of the electrical and plumbing systems that still needed finishing as well as the landscaping and sidewalks. Nevertheless, it was a great moment to enter this magnificent, new building, probably the largest LDS meetinghouse in all of South America, and to meet under conditions that are equal to those in the stakes in the United States. It was filled to capacity with nearly 33 percent of the stake in attendance. This was double the attendance of any previous stake conference held. Almost every day brought another milestone or historic moment in the Church in Brazil.

In September 1977 we returned to the United States for general conference. Geri came ahead of time in order to visit with our children and especially to review the arrangment of Grant's marriage to Cleadonna Webb. Lee Ann had just had a baby daughter, Alisa Dawn, on September 3, and it was nice to see the new addition to the family. In the general conference of October 2, 1977, I was called to be one of the speakers. I had prepared an address concerning the calling of President Spencer W. Kimball, which became very impressive to the members of the Church and to those who understood the problems concerning its background. It was also the first time I was introduced to the teleprompter in giving a speech. In the temple meeting prior to general conference, we announced that we had set a goal of calling 500 young men in Brazil to serve missions within the next few months. This was received with excitement and approval among the General Authorities. Little did we know how the efforts of the adversary would attempt to hinder this movement.

On October 6, shortly following conference, I was privileged to attend a temple session with Jack and Ruth Stricklin, my sister-in-law in the Schwantes line and her husband, as they received their endowments. Afterwards I performed their sealing with many of the Schwantes family in attendance at the Provo Temple. It was a special and impressive family gathering. The next day I was honored to perform the marriage of our second son, Grant, and his bride, Cleadonna, in the Salt Lake Temple. I believe the Spirit of the Lord was with us to make it a sweet and wonderful moment.

In November 1977, after returning to Brazil, we inaugurated a Missionary Training Center in São Paulo so that the new missionaries who were being called would have at least some minimum amount of orientation before they started on their missions. We held our first meetings in the garage of our home, giving some of the instruction ourselves and calling on local leaders to assist. It did not seem possible to locate them in the stake center nearby, and therefore I asked Brother Osiris Cabral Sr., who was in charge of physical facilities, to take the old mission home where we used to live on Rua Itapeva 378 and remodel it with bathroom facilities sufficient that they could handle both elders and sisters there, and a place for a director to live. By this means we were able to organize a fully capable Missionary Training Center for the missionaries called to Brazil. The day following this assignment to Brother Cabral, we participated in an outing in the Serra Region with several members. It was perhaps on this occasion that I contracted the dreaded disease that almost took my life.

Serious Illness

On November 14 I spent some time at the office but returned home because I felt I had the flu. The next day I tried to do some more work but felt incapable of carrying on, even though we attended a lovely function in Santana that evening. I was still not improved. The next seven days I continued to struggle, not improving in my health, but trying to continue with appointments from time to time. I thought at first that it was scarlet fever, and we had several visits to the doctor and constant attendance at home, but I didn't get better.

On November 22 I had an interview with President Darcy Correa. My wife worked for about an hour to get me propped up in a chair so that I could properly sit and talk with him. He came, and I reviewed with him the urgency of calling the missionaries because he had seemed not to have a great enthusiasm about it. I was very anxious about the ability of his stake to call full-time missionaries and felt that President Correa had not seen the vision of this work nor did he have the understanding as to how it could be developed. I therefore outlined to him a method that I thought would be effective, asking if he were willing to release his second counselor from all other activity, together with Brother Werner Sporl, a member of the high council, and send them on a month-long mission to go to all the wards and seek out the young men and work with the bishops to have them interviewed, recommended, and called to go on missions. President Correa grasped the concept and said that he would go forward with this assignment immediately. It later developed that he became very effective in sending his assistants to bring young men to missionary service. Within two weeks of our meeting, his own son had accepted a call to serve a mission. During our meeting, President Correa seemed very concerned at my physical condition.

In the afternoon, Geri and I went again to the doctor's office, where he checked me over. I was so weak that I could hardly sit up. The doctor, at this point became quite concerned with my condition, realizing that there was some problem with my liver and kidneys, and he recommended that I should enter the hospital. I was not satisfied with the arrangement, having gone through nine days of ineffectiveness; as I returned home, I telephoned Elder James E. Faust, telling him that I had decided to return to the United States. We checked the airlines to see if there were some flights available that evening. But finding it impossible to go to the United States, I went with Geri and the missionaries to the hospital, where I was admitted. Immediately my condition turned very serious. I suppose that had I boarded the airplane to the U.S., I would have passed away en route. As soon as I arrived in the hospital, I became less and less capable to think and to feel and became very uncomfortable. Geri stayed with me in a private room during the first night, but I was almost beyond thinking. President and Sister Beitler also came to spend some time in helping Geri watch and comfort me. I felt myself becoming a little irrational and incapable of sustaining constructive thought. Geri determined during the night that I was in serious condition and had me moved into intensive care where they gave me oxygen.

At the hospital they gave me numerous tests and checked my heart and found that I was afflicted with what is called leptospirosis, a loathsome disease that is transmitted through the urine of rats and can infect humans when contaminated water comes into contact with the eyes, breaks in the skin, or mucous membranes. It was not common among people who lived in healthy surroundings. Almost as soon as the doctor discovered what I had, I was stricken to the point where I could not function. I was vague and confused in my mind, almost delirious. It developed that I was afflicted in nearly every part of my body. My skin was afflicted, and I was attacked in my kidneys, in the brain, and in the digestive system with encephalitis, nephritis, myocarditis, and meningitis—all of these things hit at once. My digestive system ceased to function, and it seemed almost certain that I could not survive.

I had lost my ability to speak by this time, and when I was lucid enough to think, I came to the conclusion that I had suffered a stroke, which was very upsetting to me, and I felt extremely discouraged and almost abandoned. At the same time the doctor would always come in and reassure me that I was just fine and that everything was all right. This kind of comment almost made me furious because it seemed nothing more to me than a flat lie, and I felt that I was being treated as a baby.

Entering intensive care, I felt that they gave me some of the most unusual treatment that I could ever imagine. They wheeled me all around the hospital for special tests and stood me up (in a condition where I had to be held upright) to take x-rays, which to me was actual physical torture, when I thought I should be given special attention and care and some help to be comfortable. During this period I felt like I lived through an eternity with the fantasies of delirium going through my mind. All of it was uncomfortable, even horrible at times, and I came to the conclusion that I was no longer living. At times between deliriums I would yearn for an ice cold drink of water from the spring on Box Elder Peak in Utah, where our family frequently took horse rides.

The disease was usually very damaging and often fatal. For a week or more there was question of my survival. Our family was very earnest in their special prayers. Our young son Layne, 15 years old at the time, called the family together with great urgency and said, "We have to pray that the Lord will spare Dad's life." In like fashion, the extended family in Utah was very devout in petitioning the Lord for my health and protection.

While there was great fear that I might not live, Geraldine determined to put forth every possible effort to preserve my life. She got on the telephone to Church headquarters and spoke directly to Elder James E. Faust, who was a member of the Presidency of the Seventy, saying, "Please send a doctor down here. There's Dr. Lloyd Hicken, who used to be a mission president in Brazil. Can't you get him to come down? The expense is not so great but what it would offset one of Grant's visits to a stake conference. Please do something or he will die!"

Elder Faust, with great energy, arranged for Lloyd Hicken to leave his medical practice in Bountiful and travel to Brazil. When Dr. Hicken said, "I don't have a visa," my wife had prompted Elder Faust to say, "I know you can get a visa in a short time." He arranged his passport and came down to Brazil, arriving on Thanksgiving Day in 1977.

Dr. Hicken's attention was constant over me. He consulted with the local doctors, and they determined that I needed massive doses of penicillin (20 million units), which hopefully would destroy the effects of the spirochete that had caused my problem. This medication was administered in such doses that my wife said I even seemed to smell moldy. I was given dialysis to rid my body of the toxins that had accumulated. I was delirious much of the time. I had in mind that the dialysis was a means that the doctors wanted to perform an autopsy on my body after my death, and I vigorously refused to give them permission. Geri finally convinced me of the need, and I was able to receive the dialysis.

In the evening (November 22) I felt that they had abandoned me as a person already dead—this of course being one of the fantasies of my mind. I could not remember when there had been anyone in to attend me in the past period. I had imagined that my family was leaving Brazil since I had passed away, and I wanted to go to the window to catch a glimpse of the airplane as it left for home. Without realizing what I was doing, I sat up and got out of bed, being completely unclothed, and tore the intravenous apparatus out of my arm as well as the other connections that they had. I walked out onto the balcony, trailing blood behind me and just wondering what was going on. Suddenly the nurses and doctors came charging into the room, realizing that something serious had happened. They led me back to the bed and began to take care of my bleeding. But suddenly I found myself more lucid than I had been and had come to a decision that I wanted to take charge of my condition. I told the doctors and nurses what I wanted them to do. They were concerned about my mental state no doubt and undertook to be very attentive to the things I was telling them. I told them that I wanted my wife to come in, and shortly thereafter she came, being the most beautiful presence that I could ever remember in my entire life. I suddenly found that I had regained the power of speech. She told me that I had not had a stroke but that the toxins in my body had so affected me that I was unable to use my faculties. She gave me every comfort and reassurance, and I spent a long time chattering and talking to her although in a very thick and rather drunken manner. But I was suddenly happy, reassured, and feeling certain that whatever it was that was bothering me would be overcome. It was as if the Lord had completely cleared my mind of any apprehension about my sickness. From that time forward, I felt encouraged.

Previously I had received administrations of the priesthood. Before leaving home, Elder Hatch and Elder Arndt administered to me, and before I went into intensive care, President Beitler and the elders gave me an administration and a blessing with great promises. On one or two other occasions, Brother Osiris Cabral and Frederico Herve came in and blessed me. Dr. Hicken, with the assistance of Osiris Cabral, also gave me a blessing soon after he arrived. Most of the organs in my body had been attacked. I was still in a very precarious condition.

My recollections of those hard days were that Dr. Hicken was constantly by my side, checking on my condition. He even made arrangements to take me back to the United States on a special flight; reservations had been made, but at the critical moment, it fell through. Even then I might not have survived the journey. Frequently with Dr. Hicken was Brother Osiris Cabral. It seemed they were there almost every morning at my bedside, placing their hands on my head and giving me further blessings. President Beitler also took special care to be close in attendance. He was permitted to be at my bedside often. He represented himself as a doctor; though not a medical doctor, he did have a PhD in law. He had free entry and often brought my wife to my bedside. I remained in intensive care for a number of days with Dr. Hicken and others attending me. Geri was by my side almost continuously.

At one point, both Dr. Hicken and Geri were greatly concerned that I was not improving, and they both had spent considerable time fasting and praying and asking the Lord to indicate to them that I might be able to recover. As they came to see me early in the morning in the hospital, I had suddenly taken on an aspect of brightness and improvement that very much encouraged them. That seemed to be the turning point, and I was on my way to recovery.

I learned that great numbers of people had become seriously concerned with my condition and that so many people had telephoned our home that our bishop had sent women to alternate in attending the telephone and receiving the messages of many people. Knowledge of my affliction had soon become known among the members of the Church, and they began to offer special prayers in my behalf. Groups throughout the Brazil Area had fasted and prayed for my well-being. I learned that the General Authorities, in their Thursday meeting had made special mention of my need in prayer. Our family in the United States had been in constant touch with us on the telephone, and they and the members of our home ward had also devoted themselves to fasting and prayer for my well-being. I knew in some part of the hazy mental state under which I had labored that the Lord had truly determined that I should recover, and I felt no concern about my condition but realized somehow in my mind that I would pass through a period of recovery and would be restored to full health and strength. With that assurance, Dr. Hicken returned to the U.S., and we continued monitoring my progress over the coming days.

The prayers of members, family, friends, and those of the General Authorities who knew of my serious condition reached forth to heaven. In my faint moments of full consciousness I had an assurance that the Spirit of the Lord would bless me, that I would recover, and that I would not suffer any evil effects from this affliction. Even friends we had met who were not members of the Church reached out in their faith and prayers and their best wishes that I would recover. One woman we had met on one of our journeys paid her priest in the Catholic Church to have a special mass said in my behalf. The result of this combined effort was that the power of God came forth through the faith and prayers of many people and rested upon me, and my recovery began. I had total awareness that the adversary had taken this as an occasion to destroy me and move me out of my calling thereby thwarting the effort to move the gospel forward through the missionary effort.

Slowly I began to respond to treatment following several episodes of sweet administrations of the priesthood and the constant care of my wife Geri. Finally I recovered with no residual problem. However, during my sickness Geri continued to meet with our leaders along with Brother Osiris Cabral, and the group began to make progress in calling missionaries. We felt that my sickness and the prayers and concerns had moved upon the brethren to make continued efforts. Eventually the children were allowed to spend time with me in the hospital in a more comfortable room and this greatly encouraged them in their desires for my well-being. On December 4 I was discharged from the hospital to recuperate at home.

Elder Dean Larsen of the First Quorum of the Seventy had arrived to attend the São Paulo North Stake conference and was staying in our home. After his conference activity, he returned, and I enjoyed a visit with him. I was in bed but was able to converse with considerable strength. Elder Larsen reported that my condition had been pointed out to the General Authorities. They all felt greatly concerned. He, in his concern, had climbed to a favorite spot on the mountainside near Kaysville, Utah, where he had asked the Lord to give me a blessing. He said that at that time he received such an assurance as to remove any concern about my well-being, knowing fully that I would be healed and restored to health and strength. Nevertheless at that moment he asked the privilege of giving me a special blessing, which I readily granted and very much appreciated knowing that his heart and spirit were devoted in a great feeling of love to bringing the gifts and blessings of the Spirit of the Lord. Over the next few days I continued resting in bed, although I was able to get up and walk around to a certain extent. I went to see the doctor, who felt that I was improving although my blood was very weak. [2] The following month I rested at home a great deal, and I limited my time in the office until I recovered. It took several weeks for my blood to build up its strength, and gradually I improved. We had a happy holiday season with our family constantly expressing gratitude for

---

2. WGB M.P. Journal; taken from the dates indicated in the record.

my miraculous preservation. After Christmas my daughter Julie and her husband, Ramon, visited us for a couple of weeks.

More Native Missionaries

In the meantime, the meetings for the calling of local missionaries continued. My wife Geraldine met with Brother Cabral because I had told her, "I cannot get these missionaries called. What purpose will my assignment here serve if I can't bring these leaders to recognize the importance of this great effort? I might as well go home." I sensed that the adversary had taken the occasion of my illness to destroy me and thus thwart the efforts that we had undertaken. My wife and Brother Cabral met repeatedly with the stake presidents, and they emphasized the great urgency that I felt in this project. As they met together, President Darcy Correa explained to them the feeling that he had obtained in relation to calling missionaries and the method that he had installed in his stake to make it effective. He gave a very powerful testimony. I think it was evident that he had been very much touched by the Spirit of the Lord, partly because of my serious illness and the instruction I had given him before going to the hospital. This had a powerful influence on him and the others, and they all, being concerned for my welfare, had humbled themselves and determined to listen to the voice of the Lord in the calling of these missionaries. The presidents were touched by the fact that there had been an effort to destroy my life through this evil disease. All seemed to recognize that the adversary had taken an active position to remove me from the place to which I had been called so that the work of the missionaries could not be accomplished. Therefore, an organization developed that gave promise of bringing many missionaries forward from the various stakes that had done very little to arrange for new missionaries.

I was soon able to meet with leaders and carry on the project of calling missionaries. I found that in the Santo André Stake, the members of the presidency and the members of the high council had interviewed many young men and called them directly to missions. Then, in an interesting sequence, they would take the young man immediately to a doctor and say, "Give this boy a physical examination. He's going to serve the Lord." Then they would take him to a dentist and say, "This young man needs a checkup on his dental condition." Thus, professional services were given without previous appointment and without charge. Then they would take him over to the airport and have his picture taken in a photo machine. They would fill out the missionary recommendation immediately and send it in. In a short time, they had several young men who responded to go on a mission. Brother Harry Klein did the same thing in his stake, and so the flow began and our missionaries began to come forth. Brother Cabral, being disappointed in the response of the stake in Porto Alegre, made another trip there. With him he took a photographer and a doctor and the missionary forms. They had another meeting, and they interviewed the young men and called them on missions. They had the examinations and the pictures taken and the forms completed. About 30 young men from the Porto Alegre Stake were prepared to go on a mission in a very short time.

Still, of course, there were leaders, stake and mission presidents, bishops, and others who did not fully understand the process of carrying out this assignment. After my recovery, we arranged on a certain Sunday to go to the stake in Sorocaba. With me were Brother Antonio Carlos Camargo and Brother Harry Klein, the high counselor from the Bosque Stake. We arranged a meeting at 7:00 a.m. with President Genaro to meet with all his bishops and elders quorum presidents. President Genaro said, "President Bangerter, I know that you want more missionaries, but we have worked hard to get missionaries in our stake, and we have found 7. You state that you want 35 from our stake, but there aren't any more. We have called all who are available." I responded, "Never mind, President Genaro. Let's go ahead and hold the meeting before making any decisions."

So we met together, and there I explained to the bishops, elders quorum presidents, and the stake presidency that the calling of missionaries was absolutely essential and directed by the Lord. I emphasized again the reasons we must have men who could assume leadership in the Church because of the growth: "We must have men who will preside over families through the temple marriages that will be forthcoming with the dedication of the temple this year. We must have missionaries preach the gospel to the great numbers of people here so that we can increase the number of missions and carry the word of the restored gospel throughout the land. That is why we must have the missionaries."

Then Brother Camargo, a regional representative, stood and spoke, and he told of the great value that would come to the missionary as the missionaries were called and the influences that they would reflect on the members of the Church. Incidentally, he had been a missionary many years before in the early days of the Brazilian Mission and had been one of the outstanding leading members in the priesthood ever since. Then Brother Harry Klein next stood in the meeting and said, "Brethren, I'm going to tell you how we will do this work. We're all gathered here, the bishops and elders presidents, and we're all going to kneel down around this table, and we will pray. We're going to pray silently, but we will stay on our knees and pray that the Lord will bless us with the Spirit to realize the power that comes through the calling of missionaries. Everyone is to remain on his knees until he feels the spirit of this calling come upon him and the Holy Ghost directing him. When you feel that the Lord has blessed you with that spirit, then you may rise up quietly and the bishop and the elders president will go together out into your ward and you will find a young man and bring him here to the chapel."

So we all knelt and silently prayed. I prayed, and I felt the spirit of this mission. This special purpose came upon me, as I knew it did for the others too. Little by little they began to arise and depart, the bishops and elders presidents together. We waited for about 45 minutes with the stake president. Eventually a bishop returned, and he had a young man with him. The stake president said, "What will we do about him, President Bangerter?"

I said, "President Genaro, I think you're supposed to interview him to go on a mission." He took the young man into his office, and in 15 minutes he came out waving a recommendation for him, almost shouting, "I have one! He's ready to go, and he has no problems!" Within another hour we had every room in that chapel filled with a bishop and a young man being interviewed to go on a mission. [3]

---

3. Re-dictation to the Historical Department, 1995.

The first young man I interviewed agreed rapidly that he would like to go on a mission and made arrangements to adjust his employment so that he could leave within two and a half months. I interviewed a second young man who had been inactive for at least five years. He also said he would appreciate going on a mission and felt his family would give him full financial support. I interviewed a third young man who said he was not in any condition to go on a mission because of the nature of his life. He had many problems, but as we conversed he said he accepted the concept that he ought to go on a mission and even though he was engaged to be married, he studied very carefully how he could prepare himself to eventually go on a mission. I interviewed another young man who said his life had not been appropriate for the gospel but was willing to consider preparing himself for a mission. Others had been interviewing almost constantly during the morning. The results of our contacts indicated that at least six were ready to go immediately and that we would probably obtain another four or five in short order. We did the same procedure in Campinas in the afternoon, and between six and ten more were available for immediate missionary service. It had been a most productive day.

Because of the scattered condition of the stake, not all of the bishops were there, but we made further contact with them, and that day we gathered up 15 more missionaries in that stake with a promise of more to follow. It was a thrilling and inspiring experience. Soon thereafter, Brother Walter Spat went to Curitiba, where he was assigned as a regional representative, and he held a similar meeting with stake presidents in that area. He had arranged also for a doctor, a dentist, and a photographer. He came home on Sunday night, and he couldn't wait to call me. He said, "I've brought back 25 missionary recommendations!" He was overflowing with the spirit of this great purpose. Similar experiences began to attend the other brethren, and we had an ongoing flowing response so that within six months' time we had achieved our objective of 360 added missionaries now from their own native country called and ready to serve on their missions. [4]

4. Ibid.

Shortly following the temple dedication later in the year, Elder Allen Ostergar, one of our former missionaries and later in charge of training at the Provo MTC, arrived to assist in setting up a more permanent and extensive Missionary Training Center in São Paulo. He was met by Brother Leon Michaelson and his wife, who had recently been called to head the work in the place of Brother and Sister Osiris Cabral Sr. Elder Ostergar and I had many occasions to counsel together about the Brazil MTC. We were projecting for an expanded training program to begin on the first of January. We worked over the curriculum and made plans for the proper course, including listing prospective teachers who would make up the faculty. Argentina would also be sending us missionaries for training, which necessitated having Spanish instructors as well. In early 1978 we had recruited enough new missionaries to fill out the number needed in each of the missions. The effort to call native missionaries finally brought to pass not only the calling of sufficient local missionaries to fill out the missions, but also provided later leadership for future families and for the Church. As these young men and some young women began to arrive for their missions, Geri and I determined to begin a small start of a missionary preparation class until the Brazil MTC was in place.

Visit of Elder Mark E. Petersen

In February of 1978, Elder Mark E. Petersen of the Quorum of the Twelve came to hold conferences, view the progress of the temple, and review the progress in our missionary effort and the training done by the regional representatives. He stayed with us in our home for about ten days, during which time he did much writing about the prophets of the Old Testament and attended two stake conferences. One of the assignments of Elder Petersen was to select and call patriarchs. I assisted him with the language as well as the ordaining of the two brethren selected. We had a special home evening with him as we devoted it to our son Paulo, who would leave soon for missionary service. Paulo did some impersonations, showing some of his talents in self-expression. He was 17 years old and would need to leave Brazil before he turned 18 to avoid the risk of being called up in the military since he was born in Brazil. (He received a special dispensation to serve a full-time mission at age 17, so we had arranged for him to serve a short-term mission in Londrina.) Following the discussions and presentations, I ordained him an elder, and Elder Petersen set him apart to be a missionary in Brazil. Though he was but 17 years old, he had completed his schooling, and Elder Peterson extended to him a local call soon to be followed by an official call from the President of the Church. Elder Peterson made some very warm and impressive comments about our family home evening. He said that it was the best home evening meeting he had ever attended in his life and that he felt that our family was one of the very choice families living on the earth. These were touching comments and deeply appreciated, and we felt especially grateful to have such a lovely and enjoyable family.

At the reorganization of the Curitiba Stake, Elder Peterson and I met with the leaders and their wives. Elder Peterson asked that I give them instructions, which I did, outlining the pattern the leaders in the Church and their wives must follow. I discussed the operation of a presidency between the president and his counselors, the necessity of keeping confidences, the importance of being exemplary in all things, and the importance of being teachers of the gospel and preparing themselves through study. The entire conference was most impressive with over 800 people attending the leadership session, more than any other stake around the world. There seemed to be a firing enthusiasm in the stake about this conference. Over 2,500 attended the general session. This represented over 50 percent of the membership of the stake. The music was impressive and the discourses most appropriate and insightful.

Our good friends and long-time acquaintances Finn and Sara Paulsen were called to be the new president and matron of the São Paulo Temple. They arrived in March of 1978 and soon were engaged in calling and preparing workers. They were choice companions and friends, and we often went together to visit stakes and missions, assisting in the preparation for the temple dedication.

Returning for April general conference brought about interesting feelings of living on two continents. We would leave one that we missed extremely, but arriving in the other we found ourselves suddenly at home with everything seeming normal. We took Paulo with us to Salt Lake City since he was shortly to enter the Missionary Training Center in preparation for his mission to Portugal. During our time at general conference we visited with many family members, attended special meetings, and greeted three newly called mission presidents to serve in Brazil.

Returning to Brazil on April 10 following general conference, Finn and Sara Paulsen accompanied us in attending several stake conferences, where they encouraged members to prepare for temple attendance. At this time I also prepared an article to be published in the Church News about preparation to go to the temple. We worked closely with priesthood leaders to increase the number of young men called to serve missions, which need we reiterated in a mission presidents' seminar held in April.

Geri and I went to Brasília, which gave us time to review the Church situation there with President Stewart Burton, a North American who was serving as the district president. He was employed with the U.S. government and had good contacts with the Brazilian government. We hoped that his influence would help with the North American missionary visa problem. We also visited and toured the Porto Alegre Mission with President and Sister Jason Sousa, followed by a tour of the Rio de Janeiro Mission under the direction of President and Sister Hélio Camargo. At that time, the mission included Brasília and all of the northern regions of Brazil. Our visits took us to Recife, Fortaleza, Teresina, São Luiz, Belém, and Manaus. Later in May, Elder and Sister Faust paid us a visit, and we discussed in detail the calling of more local young men to serve missions.

About this time we looked forward to the return of our son Howard from his two-year mission to Portugal. He had been able to serve as the first companion to our son Paulo as he arrived on his mission. He returned to Brazil even though he had been called from our home ward in Alpine, and he reported his mission to the stake presidency and high council in São Paulo. Prior to our Brazil assignment, I had supervision of the mission in Portugal, and Geri and I visited there once and had the chance to spend some time with Howard. He became an outstanding leader and assistant to the president. Upon his return, he spent a few weeks with us and then returned to the United States with our daughter Peggy. They had an interesting adventure during their journey, having to go through Argentina due to Peggy's visa concerns (she had been born in Brazil).

We held a special mission presidents' seminar with all the presidents in Brazil in anticipation of the changeover of three of them in the coming July. We gave instruction on how the old mission presidents could make preparations for an easy transfer. We also discussed in some detail the program of finding converts to the Church through the assistance of members. I was convinced that this process had to be based on powerful leadership from the full-time missionary force and would require the mission president's complete attention. This activity initially developed slowly in some of the missions but was being felt in its effectiveness in others. We also discussed how to improve our importing of North American missionaries so as to expand the work in Brazil.

Developments in Church leadership in Brazil came in the form of a call from Elder Bruce R. McConkie, advising me that two of our Brazilian brethren who had formerly served as mission presidents were now approved to serve as regional representatives. They were Hélio da Rocha Camargo and Saul Messias de Oliveira. It was a thrill to see these men assume additional responsibility.

Special Telephone Call

June 9, 1978, proved to be a momentous and historic day. I returned home from visiting the MTC to find that Elder Bruce R. McConkie had been attempting to reach me for several hours. When I made contact with him, he gave me the most outstanding news I ever expected to hear: the President of the Church had received a revelation that had been approved by the Twelve to the effect that all worthy male members could receive all the blessings of the priesthood and the temple, including those of the black race. I was so much touched by this information that I was scarcely able to function for the rest of the day. However, I hurriedly called a meeting of our principal leaders—the regional representatives, the mission presidents, the temple president, and a few others—so that I could make the official announcement. It was a long-anticipated day and will always be remembered by members of the Church. By early August, Marcus Martins, the son of Helvécio Martins from Rio de Janeiro, arrived to serve his mission. He was the first of our missionaries of the black race to serve a mission.

Later, on the occasion of the dedication of the temple, President and Sister Kimball were staying in our home, and he related the story of the coming about of the revelation. Since it was Monday evening, President Kimball said he did not want to miss the family home evening, so we joined together. I explained to President Kimball how we had enjoyed using the scriptures in our home and told of the experience we had with President Joseph Fielding Smith many years ago during his visit to Brazil. I then suggested that he might wish to make some comments about some of the things that had been added to the scriptures during his period of presidency.

He immediately began to talk to us about his experience in receiving the revelation concerning the priesthood going to all races. He told of how for several weeks he had been considerably concerned about this great problem and had spent many hours going to the temple almost daily and asking the Lord to help him to know what the course should be. He made himself available to the Lord, stating that he would leave conditions as they were for the rest of his life and defend the position of the Church if that is what the Lord wanted, but he felt impressed that the Lord was moving him to do something else. In consultation many times with his counselors and the Quorum of the Twelve, they all agreed that they would sustain the President in whatever decisions the Lord gave him. One of these meetings was held on June 1, 1978; a second meeting of the General Authorities occurred on June 8 when, after having met with the Seventies and the Presiding Bishopric, they were dismissed, and the Twelve continued with the First Presidency for another session and another prayer circle. President Kimball offered the prayer, and it was during this prayer that he received the information that the Lord's desire would be for the priesthood to be extended to those of all nations, races, and colors. The Twelve felt the influence of the Lord's Spirit and gave complete assurance that they knew the information had come from the Lord. Accordingly, a second meeting was held with all General Authorities early the following morning, June 9, and the statement that had been prepared was then sent to the press—first to the Deseret News and then to the entire world. We felt that hearing this story from the lips of President Kimball was one of the special privileges that we enjoyed in our life, especially as he told us of his struggle to obtain the will of the Lord and his assurance that it had come.

On July 27 I received a phone call from President Ezra Taft Benson requesting me to send him some ideas of the concept of freedom in Latin America and the evidences of divine direction the Lord had given to this part of the world. As a result, at a youth conference in our stake, I spent time working on a four-page outline concerning the story of freedom in Latin America. In other matters, several visits with Harry Klein, director of the Seminaries and Institutes in Brazil, brought us to the determination that with the successful advancement of the program in Brazil, constructing seminary buildings in Brazil might be a possibility in certain areas. We also anticipated the change of two mission presidencies. President Roger Beitler was being released with Wilford Cardon to succeed him, and Saul Messias de Oliveira was to be succeeded by President Maxwell from Rexburg, Idaho.

During the months of June to September of 1978 our time was filled with several powerful projects. First of all we continued in the great effort to have local Brazilian young people called into the missionary service. This effort had by this time succeeded in bringing the missionary force in each of the missions to nearly 150 missionaries each. Efforts to further the calls of Brazilian young men and women continued throughout the year. On August 4, 5, and 6, Geri and I went on a special visit to the Porto Alegre Mission with President and Sister Jason Sousa to tour the interior of the state of Rio Grande do Sul. We went through the northwest and on to the western border, visiting São Borja, Uruguaiana, and the cities along the frontier of Uruguay. Our final purpose was to study the organization of a stake in Alegrete, where we found members from several distant towns, including places on the Uruguayan frontier. We had an excellent conference with good prospects for a new stake. The mission presidents' seminar began on September 11 under the direction of Elder Howard W. Hunter. It was held in the Hotel Das Cataratas on the brink of the famous Iguaçu Falls. This event continued for two full days.

Prelude to the Dedication of the São Paulo Temple

A major thrust during this time was the completion of the temple in São Paulo, and we worked with President and Sister Paulsen in arranging for the workers and completing the facilities. The forthcoming dedication scheduled for the first of November required much attention. The construction was coming along, but slowly. With the supervisor, Brother Ross Jensen, we visited the contractor, trying to get a little more effort on the project. Brother Emil Fetzer, the Church architect, also came to give some further preparation.

One concern we had in connection with the forthcoming completion of the São Paulo Temple was the fact that the number of men holding the Melchizedek Priesthood was limited, there being only about 2,500 of them in Brazil. These with their wives would limit the number eligible to attend the temple to 5,000. We moved in council to increase the number of men ordained according to their condition and worthiness. I also discovered in visiting high priest groups in the Santana area that there was nothing being done to prepare for temple recommends, and I felt we had not done enough to prepare our people for the coming of the temple. Other evidences, however, gave us a better assurance that we had been making some progress. We added an emphasis to the goal that 10,000 men must be ordained to the Melchizedek Priesthood in Brazil and that the members should be prepared to have 100,000 names of deceased relatives prepared to be brought to the temple.

Later on that month we had a very spiritual meeting with President and Sister Paulsen and most of the stake presidents, along with several brothers and sisters who had been called to be temple workers. The group included several missionary couples, and we made a careful review of the arrangements for the visitation of the new temple and our expectations for its dedication thereafter. We held several important meetings with the temple dedication committee in preparation for the upcoming temple dedication. We also continued to stress with local leaders the importance of preparing more and more people to go to the temple when it was completed and dedicated.

In the midst of our activity concerning the temple and visits to some of the missions, Geri and I traveled to Buenos Aires to attend a stake conference. There we were met by our nephew Ralph Hardy, with whom we stayed. We met with Elder G. Homer Durham of the Presidency of the Seventy, also on assignment, and with Elder Robert D. Wells. The stake president was Robert Frederico Lindheimer. As a former race car driver, he helped us make exceeding rapid travel around the city to meet our appointments. In the meetings of the stake I made a strong attempt to speak in Spanish, which I accomplished with the assistance of Ralph Hardy. Returning to Brazil, we visited some areas with President Maxwell and gave him some direction. This all took place just prior to the dedication of the São Paulo Temple. Also the week prior to the temple dedication, I was able to give blessings to each member of the temple presidency at their request. They were President Finn Paulsen, José Benjamin Puerta, and Angel Miguel Fernandez. President Fernandez was from Argentina. It was a most enjoyable and sweet moment for us all.

Progress towards the Temple Open House

In May, Elder James E. Faust came for three days to visit us and to review the progress of the temple. It had been his pride and joy during the two years he was stationed in Brazil as the Area Supervisor. Together with President Paulsen, it brought together the three of us who were formerly missionary companions and lifelong friends. We told each other stories of our families and reminisced about our wonderful association together. Elder Faust was very impressive to me in the way he related to people. He had a genius for obtaining friendships and for remembering people's names and something about their lives. This was a side of him I had not been well acquainted with in times past. Together we discussed matters pertaining to the temple and various options available to bringing more North American missionaries into the country prior to his departure. Efforts included having them register as students, thus avoiding a work contract program.

We continued to work on the upcoming mission presidents' seminar in mid-September, and the effort was nonstop to make everything ready for the public open house of the temple. Those called to be temple missionaries were a happy group of mostly Americans, and they met in our home for a lovely social in mid-August. Shortly thereafter Geri and I had another assignment that took us to Montevideo, Uruguay, for a stake conference. We stayed with the mission president, President Robinson and his family. The stake president was President Viñas, who several years later was called into the Seventy, and it gave me ample opportunity to continue speaking in Spanish. Immediately following that conference, I was assigned to attend another stake conference in Curitiba the following week in company with Elder Saul Messias de Oliveira. We were to reorganize the stake presidency. Following experiences with Elder Mark E. Petersen earlier in the year, we decided to call on Bishop Alfredo Héliton de Lemos to preside over the stake. Another momentous event was the calling of José Lombardi as a regional representative.

As preparations continued toward the dedication of the temple, the meetings of the temple committee took on added import. On one occasion we met together and knelt in prayer, each in turn offering up the prayer of their heart to God. These collective prayers, lasting for about 25 minutes, contained petitions for special blessings on the construction, on the presidency's preparations, on arrangements for the dedication, and on the conference to bless the people to have the Spirit and to really prepare them to attend the temple. I thought that it was impressive to us all and that the Lord would certainly hear us. Following the reports of the committee, I met with several brethren to organize the genealogy board to visit all the stakes and train them in preparing themselves with recommends, names, and forms to enter the temple.

With 50,000 members in Brazil and only 2,500 men with the Melchizedek Priesthood, we had a great urgency to awaken the membership of the Church and help them understand what they must do and how important it is to go to the temple. In July the workmen took down the scaffolding around the tower so that it could stand forth in its entire splendor. The remainder of the palms for the front garden arrived, and in the evenings they turned on the floodlights and the fountain. Many of those going into the stake center would stop and gaze in astonishment at the building. On one occasion Geri and I were in the drug store across the street, and the druggist could hardly attend to business for looking out at the lighted temple. Still we felt we were far from being prepared for the opening of the temple, at least as far as the members were concerned. We felt very much that we should have 10,000 to 12,000 people at the temple dedication and that 10,000 members of the Church should arrange for their temple recommends.

The end of August brought about the long-awaited day of the open house of the temple. On August 29 we had one final meeting of instruction for the temple workers, and on the 30th we began the open house for the São Paulo Temple. It continued for about a week, giving access to the public and including in the cultural hall of the adjacent stake center a very extensive display of the Church and its activities. Geri and I had spent the night before until midnight with a number of temple workers seeing that everything was in order. In the morning we went to the temple, and it was sparkling and beautiful in every respect. Immediately upon our arrival, we found people arriving who represented the press and television stations. In each case I had an interview with them and in some cases, a televised interview, explaining in brief words what the purpose of the Church is and why we built the temple. I had seven or eight of such interviews, including a team from the Church that was filming the opening of the temple.

Many distinguished people came to view the temple, as did members of the Church in São Paulo. Several General Authorities were visiting, including Elder Gene R. Cook and Robert Wells from Argentina. Elder and Sister Faust later arrived along with Elder

Howard W. Hunter. With the arrival of Elder and Sister Faust, we went immediately to the temple, where they experienced the great joy of seeing the culmination of their efforts of two years in Brazil, where they had laid the foundation for the building of the temple and watched through certain stages of construction. They were deeply impressed and moved with what they saw in the finished product. In connection with the opening of the temple, several stake presidents in Argentina and Uruguay also came. Special guests included long-time friends such as Mr. and Mrs. Max Oaung, a former architect for Church buildings in Brazil, and Dr. and Mrs. Renato Veras, the lawyer who had been so helpful in years past.

The first time we went through, I noticed a tall Japanese man, a journalist, who as he entered the celestial room stood so much in awe that he scarcely dared raise his eyes off the floor. But as he eventually lifted his face upwards to the chandelier and beautiful mirrors, he caught the spirit of the room, his eyes welled up with tears, and he suddenly brought his hands together in the attitude of prayer. This impressive spirit seemed to touch everyone who went into this beautiful building. On the first day of the general open house, over 3,000 people came, and each of us took turns hosting the visitors. As we took them through the temple, they were deeply impressed and spent more than half an hour afterwards asking questions, trying to learn more about what the temple is for and what Mormons believe in. The open house continued for several days, and many people enjoyed the opportunity to view this magnificent structure. The written comments of those who went through the temple were inspiring and touching. I know we all felt the Spirit of the Lord as we entered this sacred building. Eventually we found that over 75,000 people went through the temple during the open house, which was less than we had wished, but we felt that an excellent job done was done in publicity and that it was probably the circumstances in São Paulo that limited us.

Call to the Presidency of the Seventy

Geri and I prepared for our semiannual visit to Salt Lake City to attend general conference. We left on September 23, flying to Los

Angeles and then on to Salt Lake. From there we journeyed to our home in Alpine. We visited many of our family before the conference.

As we prepared for conference, I went to the temple meeting held in the council room for the First Presidency and the Twelve. We were fasting, and I felt that it was a treasured and blessed experience to be in the room with so many wonderful people. An announcement was made that certain of the older and less capacitated Seventies would be advanced to the status of emeritus members of the First Quorum of Seventy. Those named included Sterling W. Sill, Henry D. Taylor, John H. Vandenberg, James A. Cullimore, and S. Dilworth Young. It was a little sad to see this step taken, but it also seemed to be an answer to relieve these brethren of the tremendous burden that they carried over the years. It would also make room for younger and more vigorous men to occupy their positions. Along with many others, I was called upon to bear my testimony in the meeting and spoke in gratitude for the assistance and support I had received during my illness, telling the Brethren how, at one point, I thought I was dead, but that the main reason why I knew I wasn't was that nothing happened that was supposed to happen when you die. I expressed my gratitude that I had known through the influence of the Spirit that the directions we receive are from the Lord.

After attending several other meetings, I was asked to report to Brother Haycock, the secretary to President Kimball and was invited into President Kimball's office. I immediately went in, and there he advised me that one of the Presidents of the Seventy would be called to fill a vacancy in the Quorum of the Twelve and that I had been designated to replace this member in the Presidency of the Seventy. He embraced me and made many compliments on my service, including back to the time when I had served as bishop and my wife Mildred, had passed away. President Kimball commended me for what he thought was outstanding leadership and work in my assignments. I felt weak as water in meeting with President Kimball; it was always a fearful thing that something unusual might happen. I told him that I was frightened and concerned about the responsibility, but in answer to his question, I told him that of course I would serve wherever he wanted me to, and thanked him for his confidence.

President Kimball especially thanked me for the supporting dis-course I made last October in telling the story of how we received the blessing of the Holy Ghost that confirmed upon us the knowledge of his appointment to be President of the Church. He said that speech of mine had been very effective and helpful in educating the mem-bers of the Church to the facts surrounding the prophet of the Lord and in giving them a knowledge that the Lord really does send His Spirit upon his servants and confirms upon them the knowledge that He is guiding them. He said this is very important for members of the Church to learn. For me it was a sweet moment and an honor to have received that new assignment. This call indicated that I would be asked to leave Brazil soon. As it turned out, Elder Faust was called into the Quorum of the Twelve, and I replaced him in the Presidency of the Seventy.

Following general conference, I immediately began meeting with the Presidency of the Seventy. I was assisted in the transition with in-terviews with President Tuttle and Paul H. Dunn. We also received instruction from the Quorum of the Twelve on how we should think and act in the great responsibility we carry. The next few days were filled with meetings of various sorts as well as interviews with what seemed to be a constant stream of people.

All too soon it was time to return to Brazil and family and re-sponsibilities there. In late October, Elder and Sister Faust came once again to São Paulo to visit the temple prior to the dedication, and in the process he suggested that he give special blessings to the mem-bers of the temple presidency and their wives. In the process, Geri asked Elder Faust to give me a blessing as she was concerned about my health. He gave me an unusually sweet and powerful blessing, blessing me with health, giving me counsel to be cautious and care-ful, and blessing me with renewed conferral of all the powers and responsibilities that I bear.

Dedication of the São Paulo Temple

The preparation and dedication of the temple was a most inspir-ing experience with the association of President Kimball and the other General Authorities. It was filled with pageantry beforehand

and solemnity during each of the sessions. It was indeed a spiritual high point for all involved. The culmination of the entire celebration of course was the dedication itself, which took place October 30–November 2 with special sessions in the temple and later with more public sessions in the adjacent stake center. President Kimball and President Tanner and others of the General Authorities came for the event. President Kimball stayed in our home with his wife, Camilla.

The dedication proper began at 4:30 on October 30. Because of the small size of the celestial room, the First Presidency and three members of the Quorum of the Twelve, Elders Hinckley, Packer, and Faust, with their wives, sat there. Elders Stone and Cook sat in one ordinance room, and Elder Robert Wells and I sat in the other to be in touch with the various members who were attending the dedication. The service took over two hours. Those in the celestial room explained that the music from the 18-voice choir was perhaps the most sweet of any they had heard, as they softly and sweetly blended in singing the sacred hymns and numbers they had prepared. President Tanner was the opening speaker, followed by Elder Faust, then President Paulsen, and finally President Kimball, who spoke for about 25 minutes. He then offered the dedicatory prayer, which took another 25 minutes. We then all together joined in giving the Hosanna Shout. The choir sang the Hosanna Anthem, and we joined in singing "The Spirit of God," after which the closing prayer was offered, closing the session.

The following days we continued with the dedicatory services, holding them in the stake center adjacent to the temple. Each session was completely filled with members invited to participate. The talks were outstanding, and the Spirit was extremely strong, to the point of overcoming many of us with emotion at various times in the proceedings. I spoke in one session, telling the story of my grandparents coming from Switzerland as an example of our roots and the interest our ancestors have in the saving ordinances of the gospel.

The entire celebration was concluded by a marvelous area conference held in the Pacaembu stadium. Several stake presidents spoke, as did some of the regional representatives and of course the General Authorities. Elder Faust and President Kimball gave especially inspirational and touching talks, Elder Faust centering on his love for the people of Brazil and his connection with it. President Tanner spoke of many of his experiences in the background that brought his family and himself into the Church. The entire conference was a spiritual feast for all who attended. Finally we took President and Sister Kimball to the airport. The entire group of people, in company with the General Authorities, was there and we visited for approximately an hour before they were called to board the plane, after which Geri and I relaxed our spirits and drove home. We supposed that we might not see another such experience of equal intensity in our lifetime.

The next day, November 6, the temple opened for ordinance work, and it was interesting to see how smoothly everything functioned. I was so deeply impressed in watching everything taking place. I sat in the projection booth and looked down on a session in process, noting how smoothly and pleasantly it functioned. We went into the baptismal area and saw the smoothness with which that operation moved forward. I was greatly impressed with all that was taking place. The opening day was a marvel. They had three endowment sessions and sealed a considerable number of people. I performed sealings from time to time, which was a very enjoyable experience to have in that new temple.

In mid-December, I was anxious to find a special time and place to think, pray and meditate, inquiring of the Lord about our work in Brazil, my new calling in the Presidency of the Seventy, and problems with the family. I entered the temple, which was closed for the holidays, dressed in my white suit and spent about two hours reading the scriptures, thinking, and especially praying. I prayed about my new calling, my preparation and worthiness, our work in Brazil with the Brazilian leaders, and missionaries obtaining visas for missionary service. I prayed earnestly for the success of President Jason Souza in his efforts in Brasília to allow more North American Missionaries to enter the country. I also prayed for my wife and children, remembering some of the struggles they were having at this time. I prayed for Paulo in Portugal. I felt I communicated a little with the Lord, more than normal in my prayers. I certainly felt the sacred influence of the holy temple. I read from Doctrine and Covenants sections 88, 107, 110, and 112. It gave me great comfort to have that sacred experience.

Our concluding time in Brazil seemed to rush forward more quickly than we had hoped. Soon after our return from conference, we met to organize a new stake in Araraquara. The Spirit of the Lord was manifest in the selection of the stake president. This was my first experience at presiding in the organization of a new stake. We met with each group—the new presidency, bishops, high councilors, and auxiliary leaders—to give them specific instructions and to set them apart. It was a marvelous manifestation of the Spirit of the Lord. I later divided the stake in Porto Alegre, creating the Novo Hamburgo Stake. We interviewed several men during the day and in the evening, and after interviewing more than 40 men, it suddenly became apparent to President Jason Souza and me that his counselor, Brother Paulo Grahl, should be the president of the Novo Hamburgo Stake. He was outstanding among all the other brethren, and we felt certain that the Lord would approve of our appointment. We therefore advised him of his calling, which he accepted with humility, and we directed him to make the choice of his counselors. He was soon able to make this decision after prayer and thought. We then proceeded to reorganize the Porto Alegre Stake and in the process of our interviews felt impressed to call Brother Silvio Geshwandtner to be the new stake president in Porto Alegre. Both of these new presidencies quickly organized their respective high councils and also indicated who should be the bishops of the newly created wards. The conferences were excellent in their presentation and spirit. Afterwards we set apart each new presidency and left them with our blessings.

Family Visits

According to arrangements we had worked out with our daughter Julie and her husband, Ramon Beck, they came for a visit at the conclusion of my illness and confinement in late 1977. Julie was expecting at the time. Shortly thereafter (in the late spring of 1978) we arranged for a visit with our daughter Glenda and her husband, Steven Apple, who both served as missionaries in Brazil. They had a delightful visit to Jundiaí where Glenda had served as a missionary many years ago. These were happy times. We wanted to have all our children visit us, but many of them missed that opportunity. Grant and Cleadonna were making plans to come when we were called home. In early December 1978 our son Cory and his wife, Gayle, paid us a visit as Cory was on assignment with the Church Educational System to meet with distribution centers throughout Latin America. It was delightful to have them in our home for a few days. They left just prior to our returning to the United States. Others who paid us a visit included our nephew Harlan Bangerter and a family friend from Alpine, Clark Burgess. Some of them took an extensive drive in our car to the interior of the state of Paraná to visit the great falls of the Sete Quedas on the western border.

PERIOD V —I
Presidency of the Seventy

Chapter 17

ADDED DUTIES

"If you understand the gospel and if you understand what temples are for, you will know that going to the temple is not optional. … We need to understand that the temple is really the gospel. The temple is not a superficial, superimposed, higher-level part of the gospel. It is basic and fundamental to everything we know in the Church and in the gospel.

"If you understand the first principles of the gospel, we come first of all to faith in the Lord Jesus Christ. If we really understand that and accept it and follow it, that means we have taken upon ourselves the name of Jesus Christ. All members of the Church have not fully understood this nor analyzed it. They have said: "Oh, yes, we believe in Jesus Christ," but they have not appreciated what it means to be able to take upon ourselves the name of Christ. . . . That means that we have repented of all our sins, doesn't it? That means that we are humble. We are obedient. We are teachable. We have accepted the scriptures as being the word of God. We have accepted the priesthood as being the authority of God. We acknowledge that the Church of Jesus Christ is His organization on the earth. All of those things we have automatically included in our acceptance of Jesus Christ, and so now with that background we go to the temple and we don't know what is going to happen there, but we can very confidently say: "Heavenly Father, I don't know what the temple is really for. I don't know what I am going to see here. I don't know what I am going to learn here, but I know it is the House of the Lord. It is the place where I am to be taught some things that

I may not understand, but whatever you want to tell me is all right with me." Isn't that a good attitude to take to the temple?

"What do you do then? Live the gospel! . . . That is required of anyone who wants to get into the celestial kingdom. . . . You had better work on it and so the answer is there. It must be there for those who have found faith in the Lord Jesus Christ.

"Brothers and Sisters, these principles do relate to the fullness of the gospel of Jesus Christ, and I hope it has been clear to you that the temple is richly referred to in the scriptures and that you cannot understand the gospel of Christ unless you know about the temple and appreciate its purpose and what takes place there and how that all relates to the total, the sum total of the gospel.

"My first experience going to the temple truly helped me feel as if I were in the presence of my Father in Heaven and being brought as close as possible to his sacred presence. I have never gotten over that wonderful feeling. I earnestly pray that you will always revere the temple and the sacred things that have happened to all of us as we have gone there." [1]

New Changes

Following the dedication of the São Paulo Temple, our lives moved into a frantic pace to complete all we needed to accomplish before returning to the United States and assuming my new responsibilities in the Presidency of the Seventy. Prior to our departure for home, I spoke with President Franklin D. Richards, and he informed me that in a meeting just concluded with the Quorum of the Twelve and the other six Presidents of the Seventy, that certain vital changes had been approved that gave almost total supervision over the departments of the Church and the ecclesiastical areas to the Presidency of the First Quorum. The seven of us, therefore, would become, in effect, the leadership and correlation committee of the Church. This change added urgency for us to return early to Salt Lake City. Returning from Brazil, we traveled through Iguaçu Falls, then by car to Asunción, Paraguay, and then by plane to La Paz, Bolivia, and Lima, Peru. We spent New Year's Eve at Cuzco, making

---

1. BYU Married Students Fireside, October 19, 1983

a visit to Macchu Picchu. We then flew through Mexico City to Los Angeles. The New Year's holiday traffic was so great that we could not find a flight to Salt Lake City, so we rented an automobile, to the delight of our son Layne, and drove from Los Angeles to Salt Lake.

As soon as we were able to establish ourselves, I reported to President Franklin D. Richards, the Senior President of the Seventy and began to meet weekly with the Presidency of the Seventy in the Salt Lake Temple. I was always impressed with the earnestness and expressiveness of the prayers offered by these men. Constantly I had feelings of their greatness and capacity and in consequence feelings of frustration at my inabilities. We also held meetings with other members of the Quorum. As a part of my responsibility I was assigned with Elder Paul Dunn to work with the Missionary Department. In a later meeting with the leaders in the Missionary Department, we developed the understanding that it is the obligation and responsibility of the Quorum Presidency and members of the Seventy to project the missionary work and carry it forward. The Missionary Department is a service agency that provides the background and backup, but it must be the ecclesiastical line of the Church that moves this great effort forward.

Our presidency also directed to some degree the members of the quorum. New members began to be added, and some were assigned to areas around the Church. All General Authorities continued to fill assignments to stake conferences and to visit missions. We continued to work toward the growth of the Church and in so doing presented a new program on governing the Church through councils, which meant that the Area Supervisors (later called Executive Administrators and eventually Area Presidencies) would preside over councils and all functions within their area, including the functions of temporal affairs, though they would not direct personally the temporal affairs. The former Presiding Bishopric area supervisor would become the director for temporal affairs, and the General Authority previously called the Executive Administrator would be called the Area President. This structure ensured a unity in the administration of all phases of the Church program. The Presidency of the Seventy was invited to meet with the Quorum of the Twelve each week. The first meeting consisted of the Presidency of the Seventy explaining the process undertaken to provide leadership for the members of the quorum and taking charge of the various departments of the Church. I also had responsibility in the Genealogy Department.

In early January we said our farewells to Elder Ted Brewerton, on his way to Brazil to replace us. Various other responsibilities came along as well, including counseling, the restoration of blessings, speaking to various groups, and speaking from time to time at the Missionary Training Center. The first time I was privileged to officiate in the restoration of blessings was a special experience. Following a long interview with the couple involved, I felt that they were indeed prepared and worthy to receive the restoration of their blessings, which had been authorized by President Kimball. I could sense the great joy and appreciation that they had in returning to full fellowship in the gospel and something of the intense suffering they had experienced during the period when they had been out of touch with the Church. I found myself invited to perform marriages in the temple, mostly for members of our family or other relatives.

The members of the quorum Presidency also supervised the various departments of Church leadership. In our weekly Presidency meetings, we covered a number of items, ranging from operation of the quorum, to reports from the various major departments of the Church, to solving problems that arose, such as giving instructions to mission presidents who were involved in what we called hasty baptisms. We sent out a letter to all mission presidents instructing them to avoid abuses in missionary activities. There had been concern expressed by some of the Brethren of looseness in converting principles.

Stake conference assignments came almost every week. I began at the Mount Olympus Stake and thereafter went to Brigham City. These assignments were always filled with a deep spiritual presence and involved reviewing the condition of the stakes and leaving some message of inspiration. I often reviewed with the presiding men their roles as priesthood leaders and pointed out the method the Lord had used to establish his Church, quoting particularly from Doctrine and Covenants sections 20 and 124. Other assignments took me to

Vancouver, B.C., to a young adult conference, stake conferences in the Bountiful Heights and Weber Heights stakes. I was assigned to speak at the BYU devotional on April 10, at more stake conferences in Orem, and at the Winslow Arizona Stake. We took several of the family through all the well-known early Arizona pioneer areas on the Little Colorado River. My next assignment was in Mexico City, where I had a chance to visit the mission where my brother Blauer presided. It forced me to continue my development of speaking in Spanish. I visited the Torreon Stake and the adjacent mission.

Later I had assignments in the Cumberland Stake in the Shenandoah Valley in West Virginia because the stake president had passed away. It was a sobering experience to meet with his wife and then proceed with the reorganization of the presidency. I had some time for a quick tour of the Washington, D.C., area during that visit. I then went to Pensacola, Florida, and then to Albuquerque, New Mexico, to reorganize the stake presidency there. This was a sad occasion as the new president, a Brother Payne whom I had installed just a few months earlier, had died of a heart attack while jogging. David Larsen was chosen to replace him. In such cases of the reorganization of a stake presidency, we interviewed several of the local leaders, and our feeling always was that the Lord had decided who should be the president and that our business was to find out who it was He had chosen to serve as the stake presidency there.

Other events seemed to fill up the hours and the days. We met with the General Authorities to discuss the use of councils in the leadership of the Church. This was the forerunner to the establishment of Area Presidencies throughout the world. At another meeting of the General Authorities in the temple, Brother Jeffrey Holland, President of the Brigham Young University at the time, gave an outstanding report of a visit on assignment to the Holy Land. Several of the Brethren later participated in the Logan Temple rededication. The meetings of the Quorum Presidency continued as well as the meetings with the Twelve. These coordinating council meetings became a standard of operation in Church administration.

My time in the office was occupied with interviews and meetings with various committees, including those of the Curriculum,

Priesthood, and Missionary Departments. One of the major thrusts of these meetings dealt with the need for the Church to reduce and simplify much of the material going out through our distribution centers. This series of meetings was most interesting and far reaching. The Presidency of the Seventy met with the Quorum of the Twelve, and Elders J. Thomas Fyans, Neal A. Maxwell, and A. Theodore Tuttle presented to them an unusual demonstration of the magnitude of the programs of the Church as represented in printed and published materials, including visual aids. The Twelve were overwhelmed by what they saw. The work of printing and publishing was so well orchestrated and developed that no one really realized the magnitude of all the work that was being done. Immediately following that presentation, it was determined that the First Presidency would like to see it, so the presentation was repeated to them and was so impressive that the decision was immediately made to proceed in showing this presentation to all departments of the Church with the directive that we drastically simplify and reduce the published works of the Church. Soon the dramatic reductions proposed in the printed material of the Church were presented and accepted by the Brethren. It embodied the simplification of the structure of Church programs and a reworking of the scheduling done by the Curriculum Department.

We also met in council to discuss the need for implementing a consolidated meeting schedule for members of the Church. It later came about and was implemented worldwide. We held the annual seminar for mission presidents in late June at the Provo MTC as well as in Salt Lake. It was impressive to see the leadership of President Spencer W. Kimball in those meetings.

In my association with the Missionary Department, I was asked to assist one of the Twelve in the assignment of missionaries to their missions. It was an inspiring process to be a part of and made firm my testimony that surely those calls are inspired of the Lord. Also in connection with the Missionary Department and visitors' centers of the Church, I was assigned to dedicate the visitors' center at the Liberty Jail, which had recently undergone a major renovation. This was my first experience in visiting these interesting parts of

Church History. I was especially impressed with the display of the reconstruction of the Old Jail, since only a portion of the wall and foundation of the jail remained. As we looked at the display and saw the dungeon with its hard stone floor and the upper level where the Prophet did some of his writing and wrote out some of the revelations he received in this place while imprisoned in 1838 and 1839, I was deeply impressed and felt the sacred atmosphere and spirit that pertained to this great place and the events that took place there. The building had actually been the headquarters of the Church for about four and a half months. I felt my remarks and dedicatory prayer were well received.

After the dedication, I was also privileged to tour some of the other nearby sites of Church history. We visited the Far West Temple site, which was a very impressive place to me. As we imagined that there were probably more than 5,000 members of the Church living in this town at one time and then looked across the contemporary countryside at nothing but vacant farm land with an occasional farm installation, we were moved as we thought of what they had there once upon a time. The cornerstones of the temple are still plainly visible, and the site has been surrounded by a lovely fence and is well landscaped so that it is a very impressive place. We drove to Adam-Ondi-Ahman, past the site of the battle of Crooked River and other settlements nearby, including the city of Seth. I was impressed with Adam-Ondi-Ahman in remembering the great, mighty events that transpired in this lovely place. We also contemplated what may happen in the future. We returned through Gallatin, where an altercation between the Saints and Missouri citizens took place in 1838. It was all so impressive and inspirational to me.

Occasionally I was able to break away for a short outing on horseback with my sons into the mountains surrounding Alpine. As I celebrated my sixty-first birthday, I felt approximately the same as I did on my twelfth or twentieth. I have often remarked that I think I am still the same person as I was back then. It seemed strange to be able to reach up well over sixty years, but life has been rich and very deep, and those reflections make it seem appropriate to continue going forward hoping that I may attain other much more extensive milestones and enjoy the health and vigor that had attended me to that point. We always looked forward to the summer break during the month of July where we could spend time with family in the High Uinta Mountains, taking horses and much gear, all supervised and organized by Geri. It was a delight to relax in those glorious mountains, fishing, camping, and being with the family. We also took time to work on our Alpine property and enjoyed the Mormon Miracle Pageant in Manti. A highlight of our summer was the sealing of Geri's brother Ivan to his wife, Betty, in the Provo Temple. All of his brothers and sisters were in attendance at the sealing, and we all felt the joy they found in this action.

As July progressed, we became aware of the illness of President Finn Paulsen, President of the São Paulo Temple. He had returned to the U.S. and was interned in the hospital. Our entire Brazilian group gathered for a special meeting of fasting and prayer on his behalf, as it had been reported that he had a malignant tumor. Geri and I went to the LDS hospital to visit him. He had been carrying on reasonably well but with some difficulty. As we went into his room, President Kimball came in from the next room where he too had been hospitalized for a minor procedure. He seemed very pert and chipper, and he walked up to President Paulsen to give him his greeting and blessing. Much fasting and prayer was offered in President Paulsen's behalf. Sadly, on August 1 we suffered the tragic loss of this great friend and associate, as he passed away after a lingering illness. We sorely missed his leadership.

Early in August we attended a lovely reunion for the early Granger residents. Soon we were back into the normal schedule of events at the office as August placed us back into a routine. Of special note was the assignment of our son Cory and his family to begin the Seminary and Institute program in Portugal and Spain. This was a marvelous opportunity for them. Our son Grant was able to complete his education and graduate from BYU. I suffered an unfortunate accident with our horse, Babe, as she reared up and fell on me, breaking my pelvis and putting me on crutches for six weeks. I had to get help from Geri to get into the house following the accident. Another accident occurred in our family later in September wherein my brother

Sam was seriously injured. He fell through an opening in a home he was working on and broke his back. In spite of these setbacks, we continued to move ahead with family activities and projects. We held a special family picnic at our home for my brothers and sisters and their spouses, which was a most pleasant affair. As a family we went to Aspen Grove for a few days. My brother Sam continued to struggle in the hospital with his back injury, and we paid him regular visits to buoy him up and strengthen him. In the fall I was involved in getting the boys outfitted and off on the annual deer hunt in the mountains near our home.

October general conference was an inspiring time. We had special training provided for the Seventy centered on a stronger organization of the quorum. I had been asked to speak in the general conference and struggled over several months as to what and how to present my topic. Following my remarks, Elder Ezra Taft Benson commented favorably on what I had said. President Spencer W. Kimball then turned to me and said, "I really enjoy how you preach!" I was overwhelmed during the delivery of the speech when people began to pay special interest, even finding humor in some of the things I had not intended to be particularly humorous, but altogether they seemed to feel an alertness and awareness that was unusual for my talks. I was similarly overwhelmed by the expressions of appreciation from people who seemed sincerely to think it was a very special treatment of an important subject. [2] The announcement was also made to the General Authorities regarding the new consolidated meeting schedule for ward meetings throughout the Church. During that conference we had a lovely gathering of people at our home, including several from Brazil. Shortly after conference, Cory and his family left for their assignment in Portugal with the Church Educational System.

About this time I was assigned to be the Executive Director of the Missionary Department. This was a very enjoyable situation for me as I felt close to missionary work through much of my life. I continued to perform marriages in the temple nearly every week and also attended stake conferences in nearby stakes. Of special note

2. See Collected Works, pp. 73–78

were a couple of stake conferences. One was to Obregon, Mexico, where Duke Cowley flew us in his airplane to attend that conference and where once again I worked to perfect my Spanish speaking. Another was in Ithaca and Elmyra, New York. Even though I still struggled with crutches, I was able to visit Cornell University; I was also privileged to visit the Peter Whitmer Farm and the new construction going on there, which proved to be a sweet experience for me personally.

Other conferences took us to BYU and Santa Rosa, California. I returned home from a conference in Clearfield and found that Geri had gone to the LDS Hospital with a blood clot. There were several anxious days surrounding her condition until mid-December when she was cleared of any further complications. The aging process seemed to stop for no one. In early December a special meeting was held with the Twelve in the Temple. I was asked to give a presentation on "What Think Ye of Christ?" I focused on four points: 1) Our relationship with the Savior; 2) How far He is above normal mankind and how He stands in our view; 3) A development of who He really is as He taught in the discussion of the bread of Life sermon found in chapter 6 of John; 4) The difference between being a Christian and being Christ-like. It was almost frightening to think of giving instructions to men like Bruce R. McConkie, President Benson, and others who have been students and scholars of the gospel as well as Apostles of the Lord.

With the frantic preparations for Christmas came also the preparations for the marriage of our daughter Peggy Brasília, which took place on December 27. She received her endowment a week previously. It had been a most interesting and eventful year for us. We felt it had been a good year for us. Our children had worked through some rather serious and severe problems. All together, we felt it had been a year of accomplishment. We could do none other than thank the Lord with a great feeling of appreciation for His multitude of blessings.

Year-by-Year Account: 1980

Soon after the New Year of 1980, we began some special meetings with the Presidency of the Seventy. We had already been discussing a new and revised schedule for ward meetings, looking to combine them into a three-hour block, which would include sacrament meeting, Sunday School, and priesthood and Relief Society meetings, with Primary overlapping two hours. The program needed serious study by the Twelve, and it required two or three months to settle it. This schedule represented a radical change in the system of holding regular Sunday meetings and had the benefit of permitting three and perhaps four wards to schedule their meetings in the same building. It had been approved in the October 1979 general conference and was implemented in March 1980.

Other major concerns covered in these special meetings dealt with the service of General Authorities on assignment overseas who did not speak the language of their area. I continued to have regular assignments that included supervision of the Missionary Department as well as the Curriculum Department. We were in need of recommending that more missions be opened due to the increase in the number of missionaries being called. I still performed temple marriages on occasion as people would request them and of course for family members.

In matters regarding the dedication of temples, Sonia Johnson, the apostate, was discussed and we were given instruction regarding how to handle similar situations. Sisters Barbara B. Smith and Beverly Campbell appeared on the *Phil Donohue Show* to defend the Church in the Sonia Johnson case. They both did an outstanding job and received much praise for their efforts. About this time, President A. Theodore Tuttle was called to preside in the Provo Temple, and Robert L. Simpson was assigned to the Los Angeles California Temple. These assignments foreshadowed a change in the Presidency of the Seventy with four of us eventually being released, those being Presidents Tuttle, Hanks, Dunn, and Bangerter. I was informed of my release from the Presidency by President Romney, and he acknowledged in a very kindly and pleasant way the service I had rendered and the esteem and good feeling he held for me and the work I had done. I had served in the Presidency for two years.

Continuing in my calling as member of the First Quorum of the Seventy, I was informed that I would be appointed as the Executive Administrator over the South Salt Lake Area and advisor to the mission in the southern half of Utah. I visited many of the stakes in my assigned area. We emphasized more faithful paying of tithing and the ordination of many more men to the Melchizedek Priesthood. To assist us, we also directed the work of regional representatives. I continued to take members of my family with me since many of the assignments were in Utah. I continued to have stake conference assignments, starting in Rapid City, South Dakota, where Lonnie Nalley presided as stake president. While there I interviewed a man proposed to be the stake patriarch and felt to approve his ordination. I was also assigned to Midwest Area, covering Colorado, Nebraska, Kansas, and Oklahoma. Here I visited the stakes and toured the missions. I had many interviews with missionaries and advised their presidents. Other stake conferences took us to Columbia, South Carolina; Nampa, Idaho, under the direction of President Beus; and Hemet, California, where they had recently experienced a bad flood. We also went to the Cerritos Stake in Southern California. Ivan and Betty Hamblin attended with us in a sweet reunion. While there I was asked to give a priesthood blessing to Brother and Sister Ed Graham. I also received a new assignment that included the supervision of southern Utah beyond Salt Lake County.

My business activities continued and included our development in Sandy, Utah, and a farm in Clawson, Emery County, in partnership with Paul Mertlich. Regarding our family, our son Howard became engaged to Lissa Harrison, a lovely girl with whom he had limited association on his mission where she was also serving. Her mother is a Brazilian from the São Paulo area and her father a missionary associate of mine in Brazil many years ago.

Called to Chile

With members of the Presidency of the Seventy, we discussed the possibility of supervising overseas areas from Salt Lake City. I knew I could do that in Brazil but soon learned that I was assigned to Chile, which would be separated from Argentina, and that I would supervise that area from Salt Lake City. We would have several visits to that nation. This left me with two areas to supervise, one in Utah and the other in Chile. Originally I thought that if the Brethren would assign me again to Brazil, the supervisor who was currently there could go to Chile because he spoke Spanish, and I could supervise Brazil along with my responsibility in the U.S. without having to move back to Brazil. To my surprise, in two weeks I received the assignment to be the Area Administrator over Chile along with my other assignments. Thus I would not need to move to Chile but would commute from Salt Lake City. In Chile at that time there were about ten stakes and four missions and two regional representatives. I had forced my use of the Spanish language as I had filled assignments to Mexico and other areas in South America. Thus, with the strength of the Spirit of the Lord I moved quickly into the use of that language.

In anticipation of our assignment to Chile, I met with Ed Howard and Charlie Lewis, regional representatives to Chile. I also set apart Delbert and Mabel Palmer as the MTC President in São Paulo. Since I had been scheduled to speak in general conference during the Priesthood Session on Saturday, April 5, I spent much of my free time working on an appropriate speech. On Wednesday, April 2, seven new temples were announced, including one in Chile. This brought an added excitement to our assignment in Chile and also set me busy to regain some ability in the Spanish language, since I would be sent to several stake conferences in Latin America. This general conference was a special one as we celebrated the sesquicentennial anniversary of the organization of the Church. Portions of the conference were broadcast from Fayette, New York, and all participated in the celebration worldwide.

Prior to going to Chile, one of the interesting assignments we received was a rather extensive visit to Alaska and Canada. I was assigned to a stake conference in Vancouver, British Columbia, where President Biddulph presided, and to another stake conference in Nanaimo, British Columbia. Between these two conferences, Geri and I had been asked to tour the Alaska Mission under the leader-ship of President Snarr. In our travels we visited Ketchikan, Juneau, Wrangell, Petersburg, Sitka, and then Whitehorse, Canada. We returned by train to Skagway and Haines. It was a delightful visit and filled with marvelous scenery seemingly at every turn. On our way home, we stayed with my sister Elsbeth and her husband, Milo Hansen, in Seattle. I participated in other stake conferences in the Sandy Utah Crescent Stake; another in the Eugene Oregon Stake; an-other in Indianapolis, Indiana; and one near home in the American Fork North Stake.

Around our home our Arabian mare delivered a colt. These events were always a time of interest and enjoyment. We welcomed home our son Paulo, who had completed his mission in Portugal. He served with distinction in his mission and in leadership positions, having success with a number of converts. He gave a wonderful re-port of the growth of the Church there. We were also able to visit him there once during our travels. He entered BYU where our children Howard and Peggy were also enrolled. Peggy graduated from the BYU Nursing School on April 20. Three days later, our son Howard was married to Lissa Harrison, and I performed that ordinance.

All too soon we made preparations for our first visit to Chile. We flew to California and spent a day visiting in Walnut Creek with Jim and Trelva Wilson, dear friends from our mission presidency days in Brazil. We then flew from Los Angeles to Santiago, Chile. Soon after our arrival I met with two regional representatives, Ed Howard and Charlie Lewis, and Brothers Cifuentes and Richard Sabel, both em-ployees in the Area office. We also met with the mission presidents at various times. They included Presidents Gibson, Stott, Packard, Walker, and Day. The Walkers were from Lindon, Utah. We went with President and Sister Gibson and his wife on several occasions to branches and areas within driving distance from Santiago. The land of Chile was very extensive—it stretched from the north where it touched Peru to the south at the Straits of Magellan. The two region-al representatives were eventually released, and I arranged for Elder Delbert A. Palmer and his wife, Mabel, close friends and former mis-sion president in Chile, to come and be my assistant. They rented an apartment in Santiago where Geri and I could stay with them whenever we had to go there. We developed arrangements where we would leave Salt Lake on a Friday evening about 5:00 p.m., fly to Los Angeles and catch a plane for Santiago at 8:00 p.m., arriving there after an all-night flight able to begin our efforts and visits to stake conferences during the weekend. We would then spend the next week or two visiting the missions before returning to Utah.

The country of Chile had been taken over in the years before our assignment by a strong communist regime. The economy of the country had been decimated, and when the government was rescued from the communists, the country was stagnant, business was stumbling, and the people were generally very poor. We spent much effort in helping young men to find employment and arranged for the Church to send a large amount of clothing for member use at little cost. In addition to the assignments I had in Chile, I continued to fill appointments elsewhere in the world, often in Mexico and Argentina as well as Brazil.

Since President Kimball had announced the building of a temple in Santiago we began searching for an appropriate site. It was finally determined that the temple could be built on the property where the headquarters of the Church had been established. We also realized that if Chile were to justify a temple, there would need to be a strong increase in the number of men who held the Melchizedek Priesthood. We therefore set the goal of 10,000 elders in the country by the time the temple was completed. We also knew that in Brazil, before their temple was built very few members had moved forward on their ancestral genealogy. Therefore, we established a goal of 100,000 names of the deceased of our members to be ready for temple ordinances. Sister Mabel Palmer was given the responsibility to receive these names. Our effort also included the calling of native Chilean young men and women to serve missions, and we followed the practice we had begun in Brazil to greatly increase the number of missionaries. Delbert and I decided that it was a good idea to organize an MTC in Santiago because he and I realized that the expense of sending all of these missionaries to Brazil to the temple would be prohibitive. The new MTC advanced the calling of Chilean young men as missionaries to a large measure. In other matters, I sought to organize my office with proper procedures for administering the affairs of the Area. We also set out to visit several of the nearby districts in anticipation of organizing future stakes.

Our training and discourses throughout our time in the country focused on proper temple preparation, ordaining of men to the Melchizedek Priesthood, and strengthening the leadership in anticipation of the forthcoming temple. We held an interim mission presidents' seminar, which provided us with valuable insights into the operations and efforts of missionary work in the country. I had constant stake conferences throughout the country, and we visited from Punta Arenas in the south to Arica on the north at the Peruvian border. My assignment in Chile was often interspersed with conferences in other South American countries as well as others in the United States, including a pleasant time in Afton, Wyoming. My use of the Spanish language was mandatory, and I felt I developed a fair amount of fluency in it. Back in Utah I continued to watch over the Utah South area with stake conferences interspersing my schedule.

Chapter 18

THE TEMPLE DEPARTMENT SUMMARY

"One of my assignments as a General Authority is to be the Executive Director of the Temples. This is to supervise the operation of all the temples in the Church. I don't do it all by myself. We have four other General Authorities who are associated with me, but it is a very exciting and inspiring activity to be engaged in." [1]

Managing Director of the Temple Department

In the midst of what had become a full schedule with many appointments, on May 29, 1980, President Nathan E. Tanner called me to his office and advised me that Elder O. Leslie Stone was being released as the head of the Temple Department and that I had been selected to replace him as the Executive Director. This overwhelming assignment left me without expression. He made some explanation about the reason for my appointment, including some very complimentary statements about my background and past service and the qualifications that should help me properly manage this great program.

The responsibility suddenly placed upon me was cause for feelings of wonder, apprehension, and weakness. Like all faithful members of the Church, I had looked on the temple as a place so sacred that it was almost untouchable. I had felt that those who presided were specially endowed, and now I was expected to oversee the op-

---

1. BYU Married Students Fireside, October 19, 1983

eration of all the temples of the Church, numbering about 25 at the time, with many more being built. President Kimball visited with me, explaining that he considered the temples as the special responsibility of the Presidency of the Church and that he planned to be very close to them.

This assignment was made without releasing me from my other assignments. It was later considered in meetings of the Quorum of the Seventy whether or not I could manage all three assignments—the Temple Department, the administration of Chile, and the supervision of the Utah South Area. It was decided that I should continue in all three for the present time. Soon, however, I was replaced in my Utah assignments. In meeting with Elder Packer, we considered the need to unite efforts between the Temple and Family History Departments. The future extent of temple work was a major consideration. I entered into the workings of the Temple Department, learning much of my duties and responsibilities there. In a meeting with Elder Stone, he communicated to me the responsibilities he held in the Temple Department. He was very warm and cordial, explaining that his health was not good and that he looked forward to a chance to relax and rest from his labors.

My calling in the temples continued for 10 years, during which time I was able to visit all of the current functioning temples and all of those being constructed. While I was an advisor in connection with the construction of new temples and also in their maintenance, I was especially responsible for their operation and organization and for the procedures of the ordinances, as well as any and all superficial and deep responsibilities relating to temples their function and operation. These responsibilities included the production and procedures for the temple garments and clothing.

1980

I continued to serve as the Executive Director of the Temple Department during our assignment in Chile and in that function visited temples that were in my course of travel. Geri generally went with me, and we found many conditions that needed attention. For example, in the Logan, Ogden, and Alberta temples, some procedures were not being performed correctly. The Manti Utah Temple was being renovated, and I spent long hours with President Cox there over a period of nearly two years to make certain that the restoration would be authentic and historically correct. Some of the temples had been remodeled in such a way that their original historic construction had been lost. President A. Theodore Tuttle and his wife were called to preside in the Provo Temple and they worked with me to review procedures and establish uniformity in all temples.

I became acquainted with most of the key personnel in the Temple Department, including Brothers Metcalf, Ashby, Fullmer, and Wray, as well as Elders Durham and Cuthbert, who were the General Authorities assigned to work with me. Shortly we were involved in participating in the reorganization of temple presidencies, mainly the Salt Lake and Ogden temples and eventually the São Paulo Temple, where President Benjamin Puerta was named as temple president, filling the vacancy in the temple presidency following the death of Finn Paulsen. President Walter Spat was called as second counselor.

We were present in Santiago for the groundbreaking of that temple. President Kimball came, and we had ten thousand people stand for hours in the rain. We left Chile for Brazil, where I assisted in some special work done by President Kimball. Geri and I were invited to attend the dedication of the temples in Mexico City, Buenos Aires, Denver, Boise, Chicago, Frankfurt, Freiberg, Stockholm, and Tokyo. I was called upon to speak to the congregations in each of these areas as well as in Samoa and Tonga. We also visited in Tahiti, Johannesburg, and all other temples that had been constructed. Several members of the Seventy were called to assist me in the direction of my responsibility, including G. Homer Durham, Rex C. Reeve, and others. President Kimball frequently called and asked if I could come to his office to discuss various concerns. This direct contact tended to remove me from working closely with the Twelve Apostles, and eventually the unifying of church responsibility placed the Temple Department under their direction. President Kimball began to fail in health, and I did not have the same relationship with the

Presidency thereafter.

The month of July was spent largely at home with incidental meetings in the office to cover various matters. Geri and I had several excursions on horseback up into the mountains. I also enjoyed a pleasant ride with my brother Blauer. As was common, we spent a week at our favorite camping spot in the High Uinta Mountains on Black's Fork.

All too soon our vacation time was over, and at the end of July we returned to Brazil to reorganize the São Paulo Temple presidency. From there we flew to Santiago to continue our efforts in that nation. We found ourselves on a tour of the north of the country, a desert area of very infrequent rains. I presided at a conference there, organizing a stake in Antofagasta, in the far northern regions of Chile. I felt very blessed in my ability to speak Spanish. I do not claim that my skills were perfect, but I am fully aware that I frequently had the gift of tongues to strengthen and assist me in my official responsibilities.

Following that marvelous experience, we enjoyed a special mission presidents' seminar with all of the mission presidents in Chile. An interesting aspect of our assignment dealt with senior missionary couples who did not speak Spanish but were charged with the responsibility of teaching genealogy work to the members. With the goals we had set for obtaining names for the temple to be constructed in Santiago, they were frustrated in not being able to move forward in their assignment. I sat with them one day and pulled out a family group sheet. I instructed them to go to the stake president, hand him the sheet, and then point to lines that he could fill out. I told them that if they could point, they could fulfill their assignment. It worked. I also spent time with President Walker in the Concepción Mission, traveling south to Los Angeles and then to Argol where we held member and missionary conferences and a stake conference in the Villa Alemana Stake. Following that visit I spent some time in the Viña del Mar Mission. In meetings with the area council, we felt that ten more stakes needed to be created in the country to manage the growth experienced in various areas.

Upon returning to the U.S., I visited several temples nearby and also worked on the details of the future completion and dedication of the Jordan River Temple. We were heavily involved in the remodeling of the Manti Temple, which was being restored to its original condition. Along with my assignment in the Temple Department came the responsibility of overseeing the manufacturing of temple garments in consultation with the presidency of the Relief Society.

The fall season brought a flurry of activity relating to the dedication of the new Seattle Washington Temple, as well as fortifying the presidency in its operation. They had endured many attacks from people opposed to its construction, and elaborate demonstrations were planned but did not interfere with the dedication on November 17. I was also able to visit the Cardston Alberta Temple. In the meantime, we had another visit to Chile where we attended the Nuñoa Stake conference. We then continued north to La Serena a Copiapo and Ovalle with President and Sister Day. At the end of that week we reorganized the Quinta Normal Stake. Within a few days we on our way back to the United States. Our efforts with the temples and stake conferences continued to press on us constantly. We had stake conferences in Monticello, Utah, and in Provo at the Sharon West Stake. One of my former assistants from our Brazil days, Wagner Camargo, and his mother paid us a visit and spent several months with us. I spoke at the MTC on the Prophet Joseph Smith. At this time some concerns began to arise regarding Elder George P. Lee of the Seventy and some questionable experiences, some in connection with the temples. During the events surrounding general conference in October, a special meeting was held with the First Presidency to give instruction to the temple workers in the new temples. Other meetings on temples took into account problems associated with the dedication of the Tokyo Temple and housing for patrons in the São Paulo Temple. Also under discussion were the new temples in Australia and Argentina.

October 1980 consisted of several diverse activities, including getting Paulo and Layne out on the deer hunt. They had a very difficult time with the heavy snow, almost losing their horses and the deer in the process. I had a stake conference in Heber City and was not able to pay close attention to their needs. At the end of the month we paid a visit to the Hawaii Temple and then continued on to Tokyo for the temple dedication there on October 27. There were several sessions and other activities including meetings, dinners, and special ceremonies surrounding the dedication. I then attended a stake conference in Tokyo. Geri and I returned to the U.S. and immediately traveled once again to Chile. While there we visited the Osorno Mission with President and Sister Stott. We visited Ancud on Chiloé Island and then Punta Arenas on the Straits of Magellan. It was extremely windy and cold where we held a stake conference in Temuco.

We returned to Utah and proceeded to Seattle where they held their temple dedication on November 17 without any interference from opposing factions. It was a sweet and powerful experience for all involved. We held a stake conference later that month in Orem and finished out the year by returning to Chile where I presided at a conference in Arica. By that time I had visited all of the stakes in and around Santiago and made many adjustments in several of the stake presidencies. Before leaving for home, I, together with Brother Delbert Palmer and Brother Ed Howard, felt it would be appropriate for us to kneel down and have a very earnest and sincere prayer about many of the circumstances that related to our callings. In offering the prayer, I asked for special guidance and blessing upon the land and for the influence of the Lord to be with those who were called to leadership; I asked the Lord particularly to strengthen Brother and Sister Howard and Brother and Sister Palmer in the great responsibilities they had assumed. We prayed very earnestly that the Lord would help us as with the rapid progress that was taking place and that we would be able to assimilate the members and to give them leadership and guidance. We also prayed that the political conditions of the country would continue to be favorable. It had been a fulfilling and eventful experience in association with Chile. Geri and I returned home to Alpine for Christmas and the holidays.

1981

1981 proved to be a most interesting and definitive year in many respects. Our assignment with Chile continued to bear fruit. Instrumental to our efforts were our dear friends Delbert and Mabel Palmer who assisted in our work. In early January I was given an assignment in the Temple Department from the First Presidency allowing me to make decisions concerning sealings for the dead in an attempt to streamline some of the process for these sealings. I felt that my report was well received, although there were serious questions about whether or not I was able to give adequate attention to the Temple Department with so much absence. I was later called on to give a report on Chile and how my leadership was working out while based in Salt Lake City.

I spoke at the funeral of President John D. Hill, our former stake president. It was a very lovely occasion. I think all the people there were lifted up in the remembrance of President Hill and the great work he had done, and although the feelings were somewhat tender, the spirit was one of deep appreciation and enjoyment.

Shortly thereafter, we drove to northern California and spent several days with President and Sister Richard Sonne of the Oakland Temple. We visited our son Howard and his wife, Lissa, and family as they lived nearby. In these visits we had time set aside for special meetings with the ordinance workers. I felt the meetings were very spiritual in nature.

Our efforts also included visits to the Ogden and Salt Lake Temples, taking advantage of the time in reviewing their procedures and operation. It also gave us occasion to get acquainted with the personnel and the manner in which this great work was being carried out. We felt the Spirit of the Lord strongly and found that the presidencies were moving forward on a sound basis. We were also in the final stages of preparations for the dedications of the Jordan River Utah Temple and of the temples in Samoa; Tonga; and Sydney, Australia. President Kimball would be heavily involved in each dedication. We did a review of the St. George Temple, and it was my first opportunity to see this temple since it had been remodeled a few years previously. The facilities were exceptionally fine, especially with the construction of the extensive new annex. As we proceeded on to Los Angeles to visit the temple there, we held a stake conference in Long Beach under the direction of President Lufkin. Being in Southern California offered us an occasion to visit with several of our former missionaries who live in the area.

At the end of January, Geri and I once again flew to Santiago, Chile, where we stayed with Brother and Sister Palmer in their two-bedroom apartment. This was a better arrangement than always depending on the mission presidents. We were involved in a division of the Valparaiso Stake and enjoyed the company of President and Sister Day of the Viña del Mar Mission. In the division of the stake, it developed that most of the leadership would be in the new stake, and we were put to a severe test to determine who could preside over the old Valparaiso stake. For a while I almost despaired of finding someone. The leaders in the stake were so new as members of the Church. One branch president had only been baptized four months. We finally determined on Brother Armando Gula, formerly a bishop and then serving on the high council, and invited him to accept the responsibility. We had been in most earnest prayer and felt that he was the only possible candidate. He accepted with the utmost reluctance, feeling entirely incapable of carrying out such a heavy responsibility, but finally in a very humble spirit with tears he sought the Lord in prayer and found that he had no other answer than to accept. He then selected two counselors, one of whom had been a bishop and a member of the Church a year and a half, while the other had been a member for two years. We were surprised that the leadership was so inexperienced. However, once we put them together they appeared very much like a presidency should, and we began to have confidence that they would carry the responsibility.

After returning from the conference, we were invited by the Santiago North Mission under the direction of President and Sister Packard to participate in a special family home evening for investigators. They had 12 or 15 people present and presented to them some of the attitudes of Latter-day Saints on family home evening and asked Brother Palmer and me to speak. We invited them to understand and accept the gospel as it was being presented to them. One lady who was present had been baptized six weeks earlier and had brought 16 people, mostly relatives, into the Church.

Later we toured the Santiago South Mission, which took us to Peñaflor, Melipilla, and San Antonio along the west coast. We also visited Rio Loa and Cartagena as well as Rancagua, Los Leones, and

Graneros. All of these places held a charm and distinction of their own. We held a stake conference in the Andalien Stake and proceeded to visit the Concepción Mission under the direction of President and Sister Max Willis. Upon our return to Santiago, we held a large area council meeting in which it was determined that we would have 30 stakes in Chile before the year was out. Our return to the U.S. necessitated that we proceed through São Paulo as there was an emergency need concerning the temple recorder, Gustav Salik.

Geri and I returned to the U.S., and soon I was in Rexburg, Idaho, where I spoke at the devotional at Ricks College. We were hosted by the president of the college, Bruce Hafen, and members of his staff, including Rex Bennion, a lifelong friend from Granger. Also included were several relatives—my brother Norman's son Jordan and his wife; two of our nieces, Carrie Wilson and Tammy Shirley; and Lee Hamblin (our nephew on the Hamblin side) and his wife—so it became somewhat of a family reunion. In the process we were able to visit the Idaho Falls Temple and review their operation. Three days later I was speaking at the University of Utah Institute of Religion devotional, so opportunities to bear witness were frequent. About this time we also had several meetings on temple clothing and the temple physical facilities committees.

I had an interesting interview with Stan Weed and Cyril Figuerres of the research team attached to the Presidency of the Seventy. They wanted to discuss methods by which we could increase the rate of growth through baptisms and conversions into the Church. I enjoyed the experience with them and reviewed my feelings, which centered on the three principles of finding, teaching, and fellowshipping people into the Church. My comments centered on a method whereby every pair of missionaries could have enough investigators to keep them fully occupied in teaching if they would just follow the available instructions. These instructions, however, did not appear to be widely known or understood and were really only given lip service by leadership in the majority of the missions. The key to finding these investigators is, of course, to work through the members. Very few missionaries seemed to have the knowledge and skill to make this principle operative. We then discussed effective teaching and reviewed the methods by which missionaries can be effective in converting people to the gospel. We finally reviewed fellowshipping, which I emphasized must be carried on jointly by the missionaries and the membership, especially in areas where the growth of the Church is rapid.

In March we joined our son Layne as he received his temple blessings prior to his departure to serve as a missionary in the Portugal Lisbon Mission. We were thrilled with his desire and attitude and enjoyed the experience very much. It also gave me an opportunity to become a little more familiar with the Salt Lake Temple. Shortly thereafter we found many events rushing in upon us. We considered with the First Presidency the names of brethren to be called as temple presidents. Our travels took us to the Atlanta Temple, where President Kimball performed the groundbreaking ceremony. The temple president, President McDougall, was there as was Governor George Busbee.

Shortly afterwards, Geri and I left for another trip to Chile and our assignment there. Our efforts with humanitarian aid were demonstrated in the presentation of several pieces of equipment donated by the Church to a Catholic hospital in Santiago. One of our major concerns during our visit in Chile was to focus on improving the fellowshipping of new converts in the wards and branches, which continued to be a major challenge. We visited the Concepción Mission under the direction of President and Sister Willis and held conferences with the missionaries and coordinated our visits with a stake conference assignment in the Republica Stake. Elder Boyd K. Packer was the presiding authority at the stake conference. We learned to our dismay that Brother Sabel of the area office had been imprisoned in connection with some former problems he had experienced in Argentina. This situation took some time to properly work through.

We returned to the U.S., stopping in Mexico City to check on the temple there. Brother Emil Fetzer, the temple architect, had made some suggestions, and we wanted to see them firsthand. Among the features of this temple is the provision made to avoid the uneven settling of the building since almost any building in Mexico City settles because the city was built over an old lakebed. There were special provisions made in the foundation to set up compartments in the footings and to drive pilings down into those areas so that, as the settling continues, the building itself may be anchored from time to time to the various pilings to bring stability to its position—a very ingenious arrangement. We returned to Salt Lake after a rather whirlwind trip.

Shortly thereafter we participated in a meeting in our own Alpine Stake in which wards were created and boundaries were realigned. We also participated in the Highland Stake conference. Following the conference, we went to a dinner held at the home of President and Sister Larson. At the dinner, Brother and Sister Harmon, stake clerk, told of an experience five years previous when they were in Magdalene, Sonora, Mexico, and had visited the grave of Father Eusebio Kino. Sister Harmon recounted how, as she stood near the grave, she heard Father Kino's voice in her mind telling her that he needed his work done. She explained how she was uncertain as to the meaning, but it was repeated to her three times with such emphasis that she knew that the spirit of Father Kino was calling to her that he needed the blessings and ordinances of the gospel, and she related that she got the information and presented it to the Genealogy Department and that the work had been done. This was a matter of great interest to us.

As April general conference drew nigh, we held several meetings regarding future plans for temple building, and, indeed, during conference President Kimball announced nine new temples soon to be constructed. As members came from all parts of the world to attend conference, we had several of our great leaders from Brazil and Chile participate with us in a special meeting in our home prior to their departure and return to their countries. The remainder of the month was taken up with stake conferences in Magna Central under the direction of President Charles Canfield, a dear friend, and in Casper, Wyoming, under the direction of President Warr. We visited the Mesa Arizona Temple and viewed the possibility of installing a fourth ordinance room as recommended by President Junius Driggs.

The end of April saw our daughter Julie Beck graduate from

BYU and our son Layne depart for the MTC to serve his mission in Portugal. Throughout the month I performed several temple marriages, as always seemed to be the case for General Authorities. The Temple Department was also being moved to the sixth floor of the Church Office Building.

In May we accompanied President Kimball to St. George to install a new temple president. President Bowler was released and President Russon was installed. There was an indication of a threat to President Kimball's life; therefore, security had been very carefully arranged in St. George. We disembarked from the airplane in the hangar instead of at the terminal. We had a police escort as we proceeded to our meetings.

Following that experience I left for Chile, this time without Geraldine. Together with Brother Howard, we organized the stake in Curico. We called a bishop, Brother Luis Ferreira, to preside over the stake. In each of the stake reorganizations I participated in, I felt the powerful influence of the Lord in making our selection of leaders. It was interesting to see how a few hours earlier, we didn't know if there was anyone capable to preside over the stake. In a brief period the Lord raised up someone, and suddenly when he was appointed, he looked and acted like a real stake president. We felt this on many occasions.

We stopped in Talca and Molina and also met with President and Sister Willis of the Concepción Mission. Returning to Santiago, I met with Brothers Palmer, Sabel, and Howard, and we consulted over a multitude of subjects. My specific preoccupations in coming to Chile dealt with the feelings of inspiration and impressions that we needed to make more definite, positive steps in the direction of preparing our people to receive the new temple. We broke down the things needing to be done into various activities. For example, we felt that there should be 100,000 names from the four-generation activity so that people could do the work for their own kindred dead and have a beginning at least, in preparing this work. Secondly, we felt we needed to have 10,000 people prepared with temple recommends, which would require of the members a greater attention to paying tithes and keeping the commandments. We also broke down these objectives to make clear what would be required from each ward or branch of the Church in Chile. I gave considerable thought and care to the preparation of a program whereby the Chilean members could handle the names they had provided for themselves and could oversee the checking and processing of these names so the temple would be provided with enough names to begin work. We found that there were approximately 90,000 names already prepared in Chile by extraction for use in the temple, but we still felt the need for the additional 100,000 names of the families of living members.

Brother Palmer and I also checked out facilities and furniture in order to establish a new MTC in Chile. During the time there I attended stake conferences in Puerto Montt and then visited with President and Sister Stott in Osorno. We also held stake conferences in the Andelién Stake and the Talcahuano Stake and organized a new stake in Penco. Part of our time was spent with President Day on ways he could improve his mission.

At the end of the month, President Kimball arrived from Lima, Peru, with several people in his group. We were escorted by two motorcycle policemen each time we took to the streets, moving from one venue to another. These policemen were both members of the Church. I had never imagined we could make our way through the city of Santiago as smoothly and rapidly as we did with these two men guiding us. Together we paid a visit to Admiral Merino, an assistant to General Pinochet. Much of our time with President Kimball surrounded the preparations for the temple groundbreaking ceremonies. The evening prior to the ceremony was delightful and pleasant. When we met the next morning with 10,000 Saints, it began to rain and continued throughout the ceremony. It was a great day for the Chilean Saints to have a temple begun in Santiago. It was at that time that I was informed that I would be released from my assignment to Chile. The entire group seemed shocked by the news of the change in my assignment. It brought to a close a delightful era in our efforts to build the kingdom in that nation. Elder Gene R. Cook was assigned to replace us in Chile. We traveled with President Kimball to São Paulo, where he asked me to assist him in some special blessings and in the arranging of sealers for the São Paulo Temple.

June came with a much slower pace than we had been involved with previously, though our time was certainly well occupied. We visited extensively with our son Paulo and his girlfriend, JaLayne Garlick. We bid our son Layne farewell at the airport as he departed for his mission to Portugal. On my birthday I treated myself to the privilege of answering an ad for an American Saddler horse and her filly colt. Thus we acquired Little Jewel and her colt Topaz. We learned that our son Cory had been called as second counselor in the Lisbon Stake presidency, organized under the direction of Elder James Paramore. In Salt Lake we met with the three new temple presidents selected by the First Presidency. They were Harold Brown for Mexico City, Donovan Van Dam for Jordan River, and Stan Reese for the Bern Switzerland Temple. In my remarks to them, I outlined the theory, philosophy, and doctrine concerning the work of the temples. Others of the Brethren gave outstanding counsel and advice as well. Towards the end of the month we participated in the mission presidents' seminar in Provo. I was also assigned to supervise the Ogden Area.

With the advent of summer, we relaxed a bit and enjoyed our family and surroundings. I had a delightful visit with Mother in the Church Office Building cafeteria. She continued to be bright and alert and constantly interested in her family, in spite of her advanced years. We spent a couple of days with Dale (Geri's brother) and Lois Hamblin and their family in the mountains at their cabin, where we enjoyed a lovely sacrament meeting with members of our families. Later in July we made our annual trek to the West Fork of Black's Fork. My cousin Rulon Mackay and his family were also camping nearby. He was the impetus that brought me to Black's Fork beginning with our outing in 1938. We spent many delightful hours riding horses, fishing, and holding special gatherings around the campfire with our family. During July Geri and I also took a couple of short excursions on horseback into the mountains near our home. I also met with Jay Garlick, our son Paulo's future father-in-law. A couple of short visits to the office during the month allowed me to meet with temple workers in the Salt Lake and Ogden Temples. During this time Elder S. Dilworth Young passed away; he had been a dear and close friend and great mentor to me in my assignment as a General Authority.

August became a time for gearing up again to shoulder new responsibilities. I got acquainted with the Ogden area by attending meetings with welfare agent Larry Whiting and touring the installations, and viewing the activities of the storehouse, cannery, and milk plant in the area. We visited the employment center office and the Welfare Services office, as well as the Deseret Industries, which opened my eyes and gave me considerable insight into what was going forward. I also had meaningful discussions on the Kaysville Bishops' Storehouse.

We attended stake conferences in Kearns and Ogden Terrace and met with other special groups along the way. One meeting consisted of viewing the video of the endowment produced for the deaf. We had several temple visits interspersed along with meetings with Emil Fetzer, the temple architect. Brother Val Greenwood and I studied problems involving the sealing of deceased persons, and President Kimball asked me to take care of the arrangements for the cornerstone ceremony of the Jordan River Temple, which took place on August 15.

As we began preparations for general conference in October, I visited the site of the Chicago Illinois Temple and met with the chairman of the temple committee before going to the Washington D.C. Temple for the first time. It was a most impressive view in the evening hours with the lights on it. We reviewed with the ordinance workers the principal purposes, the doctrine, and the spirit of temple work and counseled them on what they should be alert to and how they should encourage the members to do the work. It seemed to be a moment of great inspiration, and I was uplifted by the experience.

Other temple matters dealt with the upcoming dedication of the Jordan River Temple and a future temple in Australia. We discussed the needs of the Oakland Temple and its declining attendance. I participated in a stake conference in Shelley, Idaho and visited the Idaho Falls Temple with President and Sister Harris. I also continued to perform sealings for friends and family. I was asked to deliver a special presentation to the Quorum of the Seventy on better understanding the purpose of temples and temple activity. I visited the Cardston Alberta Temple as I attended stake conferences in Helena, Montana, and I was able to tour through Yellowstone Park in the meantime. The following week I was in Kaysville, Utah for a stake conference.

In response to several ministers of other churches who had been somewhat critical of our church, President Hinckley met with them at the open house of the Jordan River Temple and held a very open discussion with them, which greatly alleviated many concerns. He did all of this in a very capable way. Others who later visited the Jordan River Temple included Utah Governor Scott Matheson, a less-active Latter-day Saint. Prior to general conference, President Kimball had been in the hospital but was able to attend most of the conference. During this month I spent a considerable amount of time studying the new edition of the scriptures following an impressive lecture delivered by Elder Bruce R. McConkie. He showed us the marvelous advantages of the new scriptures with their cross-referencing and other study aids over the old ones.

The middle of October brought the formal engagement of our son Paulo to his sweetheart JaLayne Garlick as they toured the Jordan River Temple. Geri and I celebrated our 28th wedding anniversary on October 14. Later on I participated briefly in the deer hunt with Grant, our son. In my concern over our business affairs, I arose early one morning to pray about them and ask for special guidance. I felt that there was a good solution to many of our projects. I therefore set out to visit with various individuals and parties, which put an entirely new face on our projects. I felt it was a clear answer to my prayers.

Stake conference assignments took me to South Ogden Stake and also to the 14 stakes at BYU, where I worked with Elder Bruce R. McConkie. In one meeting, Elder McConkie gathered the leaders of these 14 stakes and enumerated a number of special concerns and principles wherein he tried to calm the extreme attitudes of some. He talked about maintaining a balance between studies and Church activity, emphasizing that Brigham Young University is a house of learning. He talked about studying on Sunday, how to obtain answers to gospel questions, the appropriate approach to special blessings, and whether prayers should be held on dates; he gave special attention to the question: "What should be our relationship to the Savior?" The outcome of his discussion seemed to be that we should establish a relationship with our Father in Heaven through prayer, and the other relationships would then work out appropriately. It was a most impressive teaching opportunity. Other items of import during the month included an interesting discussion with the First Presidency as we reviewed the temple ordinances and minor adjustments they needed. We finalized those minor adjustments of temple procedures under the direction of President Kimball and the First Presidency.

With the forthcoming dedication of the Jordan River Temple, I had several consultations with long-time friend Brother Carl Pederson, who served as chairman of the dedication committee. The dedication took place on November 16 with President Kimball presiding. We were deeply impressed by the remarks and inspired by the choir, the singing of the congregation, and the Hosanna Shout. The dedicatory session lasted several days.

Other temple matters covered November included a visit to the Ogden Temple and special services held in the Salt Lake Priesthood Room and in the Salt Lake Tabernacle. I had a meeting with President Tuttle of the Provo Temple as we corrected some procedures in the initiatory ordinances. In another meeting we went into detail on temple clothing. We reviewed matters pertaining to the Mexico City and Salt Lake Temples. We also considered new temples and the ability to finance them, including those in Guatemala; Korea; and Dallas, Texas. Stake conferences took me to Layton, Utah; Declo, Idaho; Kearns, Utah; and Phoenix, Arizona. I later attended a meeting with the Quorum of the Twelve where I made a presentation entitled "A Review of Temple Activity in the Church." There I presented the condition of the members of the Church regarding their own living temple work and presented some figures about the number of members who carry temple recommends and those who use them. Elder Peterson later commented on how impressed he was with the information.

As the holiday season came around, we enjoyed the time with

family. A major event involved the marriage of our son Paulo to his sweetheart, JaLayne Garlick, on December 17. I performed their ceremony, and it was an enjoyable and exciting moment. They were certainly a beautiful couple. The events of the day were completely filled with this celebration, including a wedding breakfast and a reception in the evening. Our holiday season was interspersed with minor visits to the office for interviews and meetings. It was a most enjoyable and relaxing season, spent with family and loved ones.

1982

The year 1982 seemed to be a constant flurry of activity with little let-up from start to finish. Our efforts consisted of concentrated concerns with the operating temples and with additional new temples and their locations. Of particular note were visits to the Jordan River, Ogden, and Tokyo Temples, the last under the leadership of President Duane Anderson. Other concerns dealt with proper artwork to be included in temples, temple garment problems (in consultation with Elder Mark E. Petersen), as well as a study of the schedule of the Salt Lake Temple. In meetings with the Temple Department and other General Authorities, arrangements were made to eliminate the special assignments from wards and stakes for initiatory and sealing ordinances so that the local priesthood could be relieved of this responsibility.

Early stake conferences included one in East Murray where President Bronson presided with Weston Daw and Denzil Watts, two of my cousins, as counselors. It was an excellent stake conference. I felt good about the presentations that were made, and in the priesthood leadership meeting, again I felt that the teachings we had given over the years needed to be reemphasized and reinforced. The meetings had an excellent spirit and there was good response. The general session was outstanding, one of the best of all stake conference sessions I remembered. Each speaker seemed inspired and spoke pertinently and effectively. Another conference led me to Mueller Park in Bountiful and later the Bountiful East Stake. Several Bangerter relatives were in those stakes.

In late January I was requested to go to the LDS Hospital to visit

Dennis Nelson, a policeman who had been shot earlier in the week by a criminal being apprehended. On the occasion of this altercation, Brother Nelson's fellow officer, Ron Heaps, was also shot, and he had died at the scene. Officer Heaps's family is from Alpine, and this incident was of great concern to the community. Brother Nelson, in the midst of the trouble, shot and killed the criminal. As I visited with Brother Nelson, one of his police department colleagues was there, and we conversed for about 15 or 20 minutes about the protection and blessing the police force gives to our citizens and how the Church and the doctrines of the gospel support their activity and that his part in this lamentable experience was altogether honorable and in keeping with the doctrine and principles and teachings of the Church. His wounds seemed to be healing, although he was still in great pain. He indicated that he would appreciate a blessing, so his colleague, who also held the priesthood, and I gave him a blessing to be restored to health and strength.

In early February we attended a meeting with Elder Mark E. Petersen in which we determined to reduce the number of patterns of temple garments being made in order to reduce the cost of manufacturing. I also had an opportunity to explain some of the reasons why I thought members of the Church who have received their temple endowments do not always wear their garments as they should. I was asked to speak at various functions, including a Boy Scout leadership meeting, the Los Angeles Interstate Business Meeting, and a faculty gathering at the Ogden Institute of Religion. Later I spoke to the faculty of the Northern Utah Seminary and Institute program. We talked about temples and how the doctrine of temples relates to the basic doctrine of the gospel, which is not always well understood. I reviewed the attitude that develops about asking too many questions outside the temple and presented the thesis that preparation for the temple is found in the gospel. I emphasized that members of the Church should be well founded in this understanding, and then they will know what the temple is all about.

We soon left for an extended visit to Europe, including England, Portugal, Germany, Denmark, and Switzerland. We flew from New York to Gatwick in England where we visited the temple under the direction of President Jonkees and his wife. My impression about the London Temple was that the workers and temple missionaries were doing a major part of the temple work that should be done by the members of the Church in the local area. From there we flew to Lisbon, Portugal, where our son Cory resided with his wife, Gayle, and family. He was serving as the associate area director for the Church Educational System, as the country director, and as a counselor in the Lisbon Stake presidency. We enjoyed some time with their family, visiting sites dear to us and recalling wonderful events of years past when we presided in that land. Much of our time was spent in stake conference with Elder Owen James Stevens, one of our former missionaries in Brazil who was serving as the regional representative. The conference was held in the Roma Theater near the location of our first meetings in Portugal. It was a great enjoyment to meet large numbers of members, some of whom we had known for several years, and to feel the strength of the stake and see its ongoing progress. Our conference was followed by a mission tour under the direction of President Harold Hillam. Our visits took us from Lisbon to Coimbra and then to Porto, followed by a southern sweep to the Algarve and Sagres. We were so tightly scheduled that we seldom had time to sit down and have a bite to eat and were quite exhausted when we finished. We did meet with our son Layne, who was serving his mission in Porto at that time. Many remembered our sons Paulo and Howard as well as our daughter-in-law Lissa who served in that mission.

We departed Portugal en route to Frankfurt, Germany. There we studied some possible temple sites, and I was able to recommend one in Friedrichsdorf where the temple was eventually built. We attended a stake conference in the Stuttgart Servicemen's Stake. We made a slight adjustment in the stake presidency due to members leaving for other destinations in the military. We proceeded to Stockholm with a later stop in Copenhagen as we sought additional temple sites. We flew back to Zurich and drove to Bern, where we visited the mission and the temple in Switzerland. President and Sister Bishof of the Switzerland Zurich Mission accompanied us through the Alps and other portions of their mission. In Bern we met once again with members of our extended family, some of whom had met with us five years previously at a stake conference in Zollikofen. It was good to visit again with them. The Swiss temple was busy and well organized. We also made a change in a counselor in the temple presidency. We returned to the U.S. through Boston and arrived in Utah in time to attend a stake conference in Midvale.

In our monthly temple meeting, President Kimball attended and seemed stronger than in the past. We enjoyed hearing from him as he expressed his testimony and his thanks for the faith and prayers of the members of the Church. President Gordon B. Hinckley read a memorandum outlining an adjustment in the administration of the Church, which would proceed through three councils, one dealing with missionary work, one dealing with the priesthood, and one with temples and genealogy. I was named to be a member of the latter council along with members of the Quorum of the Twelve and two of the Presidents of the Seventy, as well as President Romney, who was to be the chairman. Other stake conferences followed, right up until general conference time. I attended one in the Wells Stake in Salt Lake, followed by another in the Val Verda Bountiful area, and another in Delta, Utah, where I was accompanied by Elder A. Theodore Tuttle. In an Area Council meeting in Utah county we took the opportunity to review methods for how to bring greater achievement to the stakes, how to have more men ordained to the priesthood, how to get more young men to go on missions, how to get more of our members to pay a full tithe, how to prepare them to go to the temple, and so forth. These were topics I had focused on in many stake conferences. I attended the dedication of the Spencer W. Kimball Tower on the BYU Campus. Other activities took me to meetings with my brothers Sam and Norman, held at Norm's office in the state capitol where he was Speaker of the House. I also performed several marriages during those months.

General conference brought with it some excitement as temples were announced in Boise, Denver, Ecuador, and Taiwan. Meetings were held in connection with conference, including a meeting of all General Authorities in the temple and another special meeting with stake presidents. In that meeting, it was announced a new approach in the building program of the Church. Now local units receiving a new meetinghouse would only make a minor contribution in funds, providing there is an element of tithing faithfulness. I was also asked to speak in general conference and focused my remarks on temples.

The week following conference, we had a special family home evening with our adult children. We felt that we should bring to their attention certain of the things taught us in the recent general conference. We talked extensively about work and how it was time for their children to be trained by their fathers and mothers in the patterns they need to follow. Other family activities also took up some of our time during those weeks following conference. I took a trip to Clawson, Emery County, and picked up a beef.

Also in April I was asked to speak at the dedication of the Caroline Hemenway Harman Continuing Education Building on the BYU campus. Sister Harman had been one of our Granger neighbors. I spoke for about ten minutes in which I reminisced about the circumstances in which we lived in Granger when it was one ward. Several of our close friends and members of the Harman family were there. Other activities included clearance of several names of men to be temple presidents as well as meetings discussing the sealing in the temple of people who could not be married legally in their home country. At the office, there seemed to be a never-ending stream of visits, interviews for clearance of missionaries, restorations of blessings, and temple marriages.

Our assignments continued to move us around the country. In April we took our son Paulo and his wife, JaLayne, with us to New Mexico for a stake conference in Las Cruces and Silver City. Harold Daw, my cousin, was the stake president. It was an excellent conference, with split sessions, one in each of those two locations. In Silver City there was a serious concern about employment inasmuch as the mining companies had largely closed down, and the people were not sure what they would do. Some were already planning to leave the area. I felt impressed to promise them that if they would keep the commandments, they would be able to find employment and a means of carrying on their responsibilities in their lives. Many commented that this expression was a source of encouragement that they deeply appreciated.

Afterwards we drove through Deming, New Mexico and then on to Dublan, Mexico, where we enjoyed the company of one of our former missionaries, Larry Memmott, and his wife. We returned through Douglas, Arizona, and visited relatives there. Following that we paid a visit to the Mesa Temple where we carefully reviewed the proper administration of the sacred ordinances, in some cases making adjustments as necessary. We also visited my brother-in-law Lowell Wilson, who lived in Scottsdale. Items at the office took up much of my time between travels. I returned to New Mexico in May for a stake conference in Farmington. Before the summer break I also attended other conferences in Columbia, South Carolina; Cuautla, Mexico (where I noticed that I was the only gringo in the crowd!); Spokane, Washington; Oklahoma City, Oklahoma; and Medford, Oregon. While in the Cuautla conference in Mexico, I experienced the Lord blessing me with the gift of tongues in making me equal to my assignment. I was able to visit the temple site in Mexico City with Harold Brown. While in Seattle, I visited the temple there and also spent time with my sister Elsbeth. Other duties of my calling involved an area council meeting in Ogden as well as regular meetings in the temple with all the general authorities.

As the summer approached, our son Cory and his family returned from their three-year CES assignment in Portugal, and he went to work in the Church Office Building as the director of CES material production. It was wonderful to have them back home with us. July found us in Randolph, Utah, where we attended the funeral of one of our former missionaries, Elder Norman Dale Rex, a noble and faithful man. He was still a young man of 44 and had already reared a fine family. I can truly say he accomplished the essentials of his life's mission on earth. We later spent time with our family at our retreat in Black's Fork. We also took my mother with us on a short trip to Jackson, Wyoming, which she enjoyed. We enjoyed being home, riding horses, and sharing time with the family. At the end of the month, we had a delightful reunion with our missionaries. We found about 80 of our former missionaries had gathered together with their families. It was an outstanding event and thrilling to see how they had progressed both in their family lives, in continuing faithful in the Church, and in receiving high appointments as well as how they had grown in their professional activities. Several had already achieved positions as doctors, lawyers, teachers, and other specialists. Others were in business, and all appeared to be doing well. About this time our son Howard graduated from the BYU.

As August dawned upon us, we returned to the hectic schedule of our lives, attending a meeting in the Oakland Temple with President Hinckley as we reorganized the temple presidency. I met with Elders Hunter, Ashton, and Perry in discussing the need to have a temple presidents' seminar that included all General Authorities. I explained that it represented an unusual opportunity to concentrate our attention on the work of the temples and to give specific training to all of them and especially to the Area Executive Administrators. I also spoke with the temple workers in a meeting at BYU. Much of my time was filled with interviews, council meetings, and an occasional family problem.

Towards the end of August we had two stake conferences in the South Pacific, one in Tonga and another in Samoa. In each location we were treated royally with large feasts and native dance programs. It was always a sumptuous affair. We even participated in the dance numbers when invited, to the delight of the members. Other programs were presented by students of the Liahona College, which were most enjoyable. We visited the temples, noting their progress in construction and met with the missionaries. We were impressed with the great harmony of the Tongan singing voices and felt that there is probably no group in the Church who sings with more power than those Tongan people. They sang in nine-part harmony and were excellently trained. Attendance at conference was about 79 percent, and there was such a happy spirit throughout. We were given a marvelous tour of the island by President and Sister Muti, including a visit to the Liahona College. In Samoa, we visited the temple construction and met regarding other concerns relating to housing and so forth. From there we flew to New Zealand, where we reviewed the operation of that temple. We loved traveling through the countryside, seeing the many flocks of sheep and horse ranches everywhere.

We attended the stake conference in Hamilton, and it was a positive experience. It seemed that at almost every stop we were showered with gifts, tapa cloths, sheepskins, and other significant offerings.

Upon our return, we noted that President Call of the Provo Temple had been ill, and he later passed away. Prior to October general conference we met with the new temple presidents in a seminar. We were able to give excellent instruction to the newly called presidents and the Executive Administrators who would be working with them in their various locations around the world. I was involved with setting apart several of them. I also had an assignment to the Anchorage Alaska Stake conference. While there we visited the stake farm in Palmer. It was a delightful experience, and the farm appeared to be a valuable asset to the stake.

Following October general conference, we had meetings on the operations of temples and on how to improve missionary work. I was invited to speak at the MTC, where we enjoyed the presence of over 1,900 missionaries. It was an inspiring sight, and I felt impressed to say a number of things guided by the Spirit. We participated in the BYU homecoming parade by riding in a special car. From there I proceeded directly to a stake conference in Payson, Utah. The next week was followed by a trip to Canada, flying to Great Falls, Montana, and then driving to Cardston, Alberta, to visit the temple there. Following that visit, I went to Raymond for an excellent stake conference. I returned by car to Great Falls and flew home.

On the first of November I joined with the family in commemorating Mother's 90th birthday. Many family members and friends came from large distances to honor her on this special occasion. That month took Geri and me to South America once again, starting in Santiago, Chile. There I met my cousin Henry Bawden. It was a most pleasant visit as they drove us to Church headquarters. We visited the temple and noted the structure was complete with the interior walls in place. The other buildings were also coming along, including temple housing, an MTC, and office space for genealogy and other functions. We had a stake conference in Mendoza, Argentina, and another in San Juan. At times the stakes seemed a little weak in leadership and we noted instances of lack of confidence in stake leaders, but our conferences were uplifting and worthwhile. We traveled to Buenos Aires to consult on the temple there.

A visit to São Paulo brought us in contact with three of our former missionaries in a mission presidents' seminar. Darwin Christensen, John Hawkins, and Duke Cowley served under us many years ago. Other presidents in attendance were Lynn Sorensen (one of my missionary companions), Osiris Cabral, Paulo Puerta, and Danilo Talanskas. I was asked to speak in one of the sessions, and I felt impressed to speak about being united and avoiding criticism, which is designed to break down the influence and authority of those who are called to this work. Later we visited with the Bronze family and Brother and Sister Lombardi, dear friends from years past. We then flew to Porto Alegre and on to Livramento to hold a stake conference in that city under the leadership of President Radke. We visited Santa Maria and Alegrete, both areas where our son Cory had labored as a missionary many years ago. We returned to the U.S. through Miami and arrived home in time to greet our son Layne returning from his mission to Portugal. He spoke in sacrament meeting and gave an enjoyable, lovely presentation about his mission. Thanksgiving time was spent with family, and we enjoyed the time together. The holiday was saddened by the passing of President N. Eldon Tanner, one of the great men of the kingdom and one who contributed so much to the order and operation of the Church.

As the year drew to a close, we made one last trip to Hawaii, where we visited the temple in Laie and viewed their proceedings. We held a stake conference in Honolulu, presided over by President Ho. It seemed that at each meeting we were presented with beautiful leis, which added to the warmth of the hospitality of the Hawaiian Saints. We enjoyed the strength and spirit of those lovely people. I had another stake conference in Pleasant Grove, Utah, and one more in Des Moines, Iowa, with some of the meetings in Ames. We decided to take advantage of driving to that conference so we could visit our daughter Peggy and her family in Omaha.

We enjoyed a delightful social with the General Authorities at the close of the year and then relaxed with family as we celebrated the Christmas season and the coming of a New Year. As I reviewed

my journals of the past several years, I was amazed at the frequency
of interviews with various people seeking counsel, hope, and peace.
Often I was assigned to interview people prior to the restoration of
their blessings or prospective missionaries who needed special clearance. It seemed to be almost a never-ending stream of interviews
coming at least weekly if not daily. Our involvement with meetings
and consultations with the leading Brethren in various circumstances was similar: constant and all part of the ongoing operation of the
Lord's kingdom.

1983

1983 began with a spurt of good weather, which was welcome
for any outside activity on the farm. Our son Layne brought his girlfriend, Betsy Cryer, to get to know the family. She was a delightful
girl and was quickly drawn into our circle. Layne also took upon
himself the duties of a sheep rancher as he acquired several sheep
and placed them in our farm. Soon lambs began to be born to them.
We found a greater need to build stronger fences to keep the sheep
in. Later in March I took Mother back to Alpine to spend a few days.
During the week I did several jobs and chores to take care of the
home and farm. In April I disked a piece of land on the farm where
we intended to plant barley.

We soon found ourselves involved in the midst of our church
assignments, including a meeting with members of the Twelve as we
reviewed the temple presidents' handbook, which had been undergoing reorganization for nearly two years. Elder Marvin J. Ashton had
carefully gone through the handbook during the holidays and in our
meeting spent two and a half hours covering all the items, making
slight adjustments, but in a large measure accepting the work carried out by our staff in its preparation. We attended to several details
concerning the operations of temples in various parts of the world.
We were saddened by the passing of Elder LeGrand Richards, whose
funeral we attended on January 14. His passing brought back vivid
memories of experiences with him and the influence and impact he
had on the Church. As we met in our quorum meeting, I was invited
to make a presentation on the activity that should be provided for

new temples. I felt strengthened by the Spirit in the things I taught. We showed pictures of all the new temples being constructed, as well as the floor plans. I outlined the principles surrounding temples and the teaching that needs to be provided for members where the new temples are being built so as to properly organize the members to receive their blessings. In our temple meeting that month, President Kimball appeared to be quite weak and feeble. It was hard for us to see him in such ill health.

In early January, I was assigned to the Manila Stake in Pleasant Grove, presided over by President Fugal. It was a good conference, and we enjoyed being close to home. Other stake conferences were held in Centerville, under the direction of President Layton, and in the Maeser Stake in the west side of Vernal, under the direction of President Johnson. Duella and Geri attended with me on that occasion. At the end of the month we drove to the Oakland California Stake for a conference and were also able to spend a day or two visiting with Howard and Lissa as Howard was employed by Bechtel Corporation in the area. They lived in Novato, across the bay. We also visited the Oakland Temple and made some adjustments in the procedure they had been using to accommodate large sessions. We had a delightful experience with the workers and leaders of that temple. In mid-February we had a stake conference in Springville, Utah. The next week was the North Ogden Ben Lomond Stake, held in the Ogden Tabernacle. I felt an unusually fine influence in our meetings as the spirit of our teaching came forward with great impulse. I thought those who spoke properly conveyed the principles of the gospel.

I was invited by the Young Women general board, under the direction of Sister Elaine Cannon, to speak to them about the temples. It was an unusually fine experience, and I think these women were able to discuss questions about the temple and what should be taught to Young Women in a very open way. I tried to impress upon them the idea that the temple is something that should be taught about and that it should not be a mystery. I noted that, of course, we do not talk of the things that take place there, but a better understanding should be arranged. The women were somewhat troubled that at times bishops are not sympathetic to the needs of young women and young men who go to the temple.

We next made a journey to Mesa, Arizona, to visit the temple and its operations. We spent the first portion of the week in the temple and then had stake conference in the Maricopa Stake. On the return trip we stopped in Snowflake and visited with Ray and Judy Caldwell and their pig farm, which was a big operation for them. In the middle of all this we continued our efforts in the Temple Department, including a review of plans for the East German temple with the architect, Emil Fetzer.

The March temple meeting once again showed the continuing physical weakness of Presidents Kimball and Romney and displayed the heavy responsibility resting upon President Hinckley as a Counselor in the First Presidency. In other matters we had meetings to discuss proper use of councils in the Church. In a meeting with Elder Faust we discussed Elder Farley Lee, an Indonesian of Chinese descent who lost his leg while serving as a missionary in South Brazil. He was completing his education at BYU. As usual I was heavily involved in performing sealings in the Salt Lake and Jordan River temples for family and friends. At the end of the month I traveled with Elder H. Burke Peterson to Manti, where we gave serious attention to the remodeling and refurbishing of that temple with the anxiety that there would be no changes in the building as it was originally constructed.

Stake conferences took me to the Ogden Farr West Stake, the Provo Edgemont Stake, and the Pleasant Grove Timpanogos Stake. In these conferences, a number of additional meetings were held including visits with bishoprics, missionary leadership, and so forth. Other conferences later on took place in the San Diego Stake. We returned from California by making a roundabout trip, stopping in Mexicali and traveling the byways all the way back to Salt Lake City, with visits at Panaca, Nevada, and Minersville, Utah. I was assigned to a stake conference in Buffalo, New York, with President Cooney as the president, and Geri and I took time to visit Niagara Falls.

I had been assigned to speak at a 14-stake fireside at BYU, and in preparation for that, I spent several hours studying the scriptures.

I was reading in the Book of Mormon and felt very impressed with what was written in chapters 13, 14, and 15 of 1 Nephi. I concentrated on those chapters as I developed my topic, "How to Enjoy Life in Service in the Gospel."

On April 1 a special meeting was held in the tabernacle with regional representatives and stake presidents to announce adjustments in the welfare program. It involved the re-evaluation of each project, with a number of them being reduced to meet the production needs of the Church. Stakes would no longer be required to raise cash funds for the budget to help the needy, but fast offerings were encouraged. This changed showed the increased financial stability of the Church. All of this preceded the general conference. We enjoyed a visit with Brother and Sister Hélio Camargo of Brazil, who were in town for conference. In other matters there were some concerns about the Manti, Mexico City, and Oakland Temples that needed the input of Brother Emil Fetzer to help us resolve the issues. In the middle of the month, Geri and I made a trip to visit the Los Angeles Temple and traveled by way of St. George. While there, we reviewed the operation of the temple in St. George and felt it was in excellent condition. We were able to do the same in the Los Angeles Temple.

The spring of 1983 had been a major struggle for the state of Utah due to the heavy runoff from the mountains. Early in May, I went with Brother Bush of the regional welfare office and Lt. Gary Clayton, who was responsible for emergency preparation in Utah County, to view the effects of the landslide in Spanish Fork Canyon. He took us in a county vehicle to the top of the landslide above Thistle. There we observed the extent of the earth movement that had closed off Spanish Fork Canyon and made a lake at Thistle. The scene was beyond imagination. Huge amounts of material had slid down Billy's Mountain, and the canyon is blocked to a height of between 200 and 300 feet. They had large numbers of heavy equipment moving dirt in order to put it in the right position, but they seemed to be doing almost nothing compared with the massive movement of the earth. We then drove to the Provo Boat Harbor and the State Park area and saw how all that had been flooded. From there we drove to Lehi where the lower end of the valley was largely under water.

Stake conferences led us first to the Vernal Stake. We visited with the families of Glade Southam and George Day, former missionaries of ours who had both been killed in an airplane crash a short time previously. I was assigned to a stake conference in the Buenos Aires Godoy Cruz Stake. Geri and I flew from Miami to Buenos Aires. The stake was not performing well with spotty attendance at the meetings. We left Argentina for Santiago, Chile, to check on temple items there. Leaving Chile, we returned by way of São Paulo, visiting there and reviewing quite extensively the São Paulo Temple operation. We held a meeting with the missionaries under President Darwin Christensen and President John Hawkins, two of our former missionaries serving as mission presidents there. We also enjoyed renewed association with Lynn and Janet Sorensen, a former missionary companion who was the director for temporal affairs in São Paulo. Our many meetings included time with the missionaries at the MTC and with the staff of the area office, many of whom were close friends, established over the years. We left São Paulo to return to Buenos Aires for another stake conference in the Litoral Stake and for meetings with the Buenos Aires North Stake. We stayed at the home of President Lindheimer, a North American who presided over the north stake. In an executive council meeting of the Temple Department, President Hinckley joined us to consider patron housing at the various temples.

At this time our son Layne and his fiancée, Betsy Cryer, were in the midst of planning their marriage, which took place on May 19 with all the adornments and activities. I performed the ordinance in the Salt Lake Temple. It was such a wonderful opportunity to have all our married children there, and I spent some time giving them all a sermon about the requirements of the gospel in living their lives according to the covenants. It was a most choice experience. Through all of this, Layne's sheep became an increasing problem around the farm.

On June 1, Dr. Richard Call, a regional representative in our area passed away. He and his wife, who was a close friend of Geri's, had asked me to speak at his funeral. He was also the administrator of the Utah Valley Medical Center in Provo. In other duties we held a meeting in the temple concerning the cancellation of sealings. Visits to stake conferences included one in Rupert, Idaho, which allowed for a visit to the Idaho Falls Temple. We later visited the Atlanta Temple and consulted with President and Sister Winston who presided there. They were just beginning the opening activities of the temple. We had meetings with all of the workers and felt the greatness of their spirit in being involved in temple work. From there we left for a stake conference assignment in Monterey, Mexico. President Renteria of the Monterrey Libertad Stake presided. I fulfilled my assignment using Spanish, with which I had a reasonable facility. Next we had a conference in the Springville Utah Kolob Stake and finished out the month with a stake conference in Salem, Utah. In a personal note, I celebrated my 65th birthday on the June 8. In the middle of the month we drove to Emery County to bring back two of our horses that had been pastured there. Our good friends LaMont Smith and his wife had cared for them.

As normal, the month of July was mostly a vacation for the General Authorities. On July 1 I took a horseback ride up the mountain with Geraldine. We did similar excursions with various family members throughout the month. We went to Black's Fork for several days of camping with the family. We took several horses with us. I visited the American Fork hospital to see Sister Stewart, the wife of a stake president in Lehi, who had suddenly developed cancer that threatened her life. We administered a blessing to her and spoke comfort to her family. We then proceeded to Pleasant Grove where President Lyle Thacker had developed a condition the doctors told him would be fatal. I felt impressed to tell him that he did not necessarily have to die as he thought, but that it was possible for the Lord to heal him, that he might be restored and be able to continue on. On July 5, by assignment of Pres. Hinckley, I flew to Dallas, Texas, to meet with the temple president, Brother Ivan Hobson, to consider construction problems with the Dallas temple. It took two or three hours, and I returned home that evening. On July 17 we had a serious discussion with President Hinckley about the design and construction of the temple in Chicago. On July 31 I spoke at a leadership session of the single adults conference, so there were many activities to fill the month.

In August we drove to San Francisco and stayed overnight with Howard and Lissa in their home in Novato. The next day we left for Honolulu, Hawaii, and continued on to Pago Pago in American Samoa. From there in a light plane we flew to Apia in Western Samoa, and we met with President and Sister Sampson of the Samoa Temple. They had just completed the open house for the new temple and reported great success, with perhaps a fourth of all the people in the Samoan nation coming to visit the temple. We carefully toured all aspects of the building, reviewing audiovisual needs, security, and other items needing attention. Later we met with the ordinance workers in a training and information session. President Sampson told of his early missionary experiences in Samoa. When he got off the ship, the mission president took him directly to a far end of the island. He put him on a little boat, pointed to another island off in the distance, and said, "When you get there, there won't be anyone to meet you, so take a path to the left, parallel to the beach for five or six miles. When you get to a little village, you will find an old shack. It will be padlocked. Get a tool and break the padlock." So he did what he was told. When he got there and was in the process of breaking the lock, he ran into a big Samoan with a machete who said to him, "You must be one of our new missionaries!" It was a delightful start to his mission. He said: "I wasn't afraid or worried! I just enjoyed it!"

We spent several days visiting with the temple presidency and workers in Samoa. On August 4 the Apia Samoa Temple was dedicated under the direction of President Hinckley. A cornerstone ceremony included placing a copper box with various articles in it into the building itself. The subsequent meetings took up the following four days. Because of the large crowd, the dedication sessions were generally held in the adjoining stake center. All the sessions were inspiring and beautifully presented.

On August 7 we departed for Tongatapu, Tonga, where we participated in the dedication of the Nuku'alofa Tonga Temple. There were many celebrations and activities associated with that temple dedication. The festivities in Tonga were very involved. In each case all of the participants were provided with more food than we needed, all very delicious and well presented. After the first session, President Hinckley returned to Utah as he felt it necessary to avoid long absences from the Presidency. The others of the Twelve continued with the remaining sessions, most of which were held in the high school auditorium. The choirs and speeches in both settings were excellent and inspiring. We found that following the dedication, Brother Derek Metcalfe was most helpful in providing assistance in the technical areas, aiding the transition for the newly called temple workers.

We left Tonga to go to Auckland, New Zealand, to visit the temple in Hamilton, reviewing the activity and procedure in that temple. We toured some parts of New Zealand, including a marvelous sheep dog demonstration in the town of Rotorua. Those dogs were phenomenal. We also saw several magnificent Maori buildings. From there we flew to Sydney, Australia, where we visited the construction site of the new temple there. It was progressing very well. After a day in Australia, we flew to Tahiti where we visited the temple site. The building was nearing completion. We met with the members of both stakes in Papeete. The translation was from English to French to Tahitian. From there we flew to Honolulu and the next day on to Los Angeles and then home.

Also during August I reviewed with President Hinckley certain modifications of the Santiago Temple and then met with President Wilbur Cox of the Manti Temple. I had a stake conference in Lindon, Utah, presided over by President Greenwood. Later on we attended the Bountiful Utah Orchard Stake conference. In other matters, I was involved with a discussion of the temple in Frankfurt, Germany, where certain restrictions were being imposed on the building site. On August 28, we attended the dedication of the Lindon Bishops' Storehouse. We participated in the open house ceremonies, and with the presence of Bishop Victor L. Brown and Brother Glenn Rudd, I gave one of the speeches and offered the dedicatory prayer.

September had its share of conferences and additional assignments. First was the Schaumburg Illinois Stake conference. I flew to Chicago, and President West met me there. Later we drove to Phoenix where we had a missionary reunion in Tempe at the home of Duke and Alice Cowley, following which we visited the Arizona

Temple, discussing the conditions with President Wright. Duke Cowley and Wilford Cardon delivered me back to the airport to fly on to Hermosillo, Culiacan, and Guadalajara. My assignment in Guadalajara was to reorganize two stakes, one stake on one weekend and the other the next. We first met with the Independencia Stake. In our interviews, we felt strongly about Brother Espinosa, who had been a stake president in Mexico City before moving to Guadalajara. About two-thirds of the way through the interviews, I stopped what we were doing and said to Brother Rojas, the regional representative, "I don't think we can find out any more than we already know. Who do you think should be the president?" He was quick to say that he was impressed with Brother Espinosa, and I confirmed the feeling. We proceeded to call him and approve his selection of counselors. The conference sessions went well and were inspiring in content and participation. I stayed in the home of Brother Rojas. I then left for Guatemala City to check on the construction of the temple there, following which I flew back to Salt Lake.

Later that week I flew back to Guadalajara for the second stake conference. We reorganized the new stake leadership under the leadership of Brother Ontiveros. He was indeed the man chosen by the Lord for this assignment. Upon extending to him the call, he informed us that the past week he had been placed in various difficult situations, very unusual to him, as if the adversary were struggling to give him problems, even in his own home and family. He indicated that he had been able to surmount these obstacles and to find peace and reassurance, and he was then given to know that he would be asked to participate in the new presidency. It became so clear to him that he had already made his decision as to who should be his counselors. We accordingly called these men and the conference went forward very smoothly.

On September 29 we had a meeting in the Salt Lake Temple with all of the General Authorities in preparation for general conference, which were the first two days of October. On September 30 I attended and spoke at the funeral of Aunt "Noni"—Ione Smith Bangerter, Uncle Albert's wife. She had lived a long and productive life.

October found me heavily involved with temple operations. I

visited Manti and had a tour through the entire temple. The next day I flew to Seattle to visit that temple and meet with the workers. Over 1,200 of them attended the outstanding, special meeting filled with the Spirit of the Lord in the discourses and instructions given. I also met with Milo and Elsbeth Hansen, my sister and her husband. Elder Thomas Fyans was appointed Senior President of the Quorum of the Seventy with the release of President Franklin D. Richards to be the President of the Washington D.C. Temple.

I later spoke at the MTC in Provo. I struggled to know what I should speak about, but the night before I suddenly felt impressed to speak on personal revelation. I was able to outline the principles and doctrines relating to the topic, outlining clearly the various ways in which we receive revelation and how we can distinguish between what is true and what is false as well as who has authority to receive these impressions. Following the speech, President Bishop said that my remarks were a direct answer to his prayers. Evidently there had been several circumstances in which many of the missionaries in the MTC were in danger of being deceived by what they thought was the Spirit of the Lord.

Family events came along as well. On October 13 the family went to the Salt Lake Temple to celebrate our 30th wedding anniversary, which came the following day. Shortly thereafter I had a horseback ride up the mountain with Elder Robert Wells and later did the same with our son Paulo. In November I took a nice ride with Drew Day, one of our missionaries from Brazil.

In October Geri and I participated in the BYU homecoming parade and breakfast. It was an enjoyable day for us. We then left Provo for Price, Utah, where I had been assigned to preside at a stake conference. We had to go through Duchesne since the road through Spanish Fork Canyon was still under repair following the slide earlier in the year. Later on that month I was assigned to the Ashley Stake conference in Vernal. The final stake conference of the month involved an interesting set of circumstances. I went deer hunting on the mountain with Layne, and we then drove to Salt Lake where I took an airplane to Missoula, Montana, for a stake conference; Elder Kikuchi joined me on the flight as he was going to Salmon, Idaho.

Also in October I participated in family sealings under the direction of my cousin Neslin Bangerter, who had gathered many family members to perform sealings for ancestors from Switzerland. I sealed 57 couples, and afterwards Neslin asked the group if anyone had seen anything during the session. He indicated that he had noted the presence of each of the couples as they were called forth to be sealed to each other. This gave us a feeling of the richness of this operation as we were called to perform these activities in behalf of those who had died.

Stake conferences in November took me to the BYU 1st and 13th stakes. President Rolfe Kerr was president of the 13th stake. He later became a member of the Seventy. The general meeting was conducted by Elder Monson on Saturday. The first conference was held in the field house under the direction of President Bushnell, and the 13th stake was held in the Fine Arts Center under President Kerr. The next week we met in the Duchesne Stake under President Howard Todd.

In the middle of the month Geri and I flew to Santiago, Chile. I had a stake conference in Quilpué, near the coast. President Perez was the stake president there. We focused on the need to pay a full tithe and to qualify for a temple recommend, as these items seemed to hold many members of the stake back from full activity in the gospel. We met with the presidency of the Santiago North Mission and with President and Sister Olson of the Santiago Temple. We drove up the canyon to a ski resort, almost to the dividing line between Chile and Argentina. The mountains surrounding us were as high as 22,000 feet tall. All the mountains were solid rock with absolutely no forest on them, just high mountains. The next day we spent in the Santiago Temple, reviewing their procedures and meeting with the workers.

November 24 was Thanksgiving Day, and we spent part of the day in the Santiago Temple. We flew from Santiago to Concepción with President and Sister Roland Hamblin of the mission there, he being a relative of Geri's. They took us touring to certain areas, and we found and purchased some good blankets. We finished out the month with a stake conference with Brother Jaramillo, who was the regional representative. I tried to communicate in Spanish, but the stake president was very self-centered and paid no attention to the visiting General Authority and spent the entire time visiting with the regional representative. He would not listen to me at all but felt he had to take his own lead.

We returned to Santiago by train and then flew to Argentina, where we visited the temple site. From there we returned to Miami and then back to Mexico City as that temple was about ready for dedication. Beginning December 2 the preparations were in order for the dedication of the Mexico City Temple, which lasted through the 4th. Each session was inspiring and powerful. The temple itself was a rather large temple in comparison to others that had been recently dedicated. President Hinckley and President Benson both gave outstanding talks that applied directly to the Saints in Mexico. I also spoke in two sessions and felt the Spirit of the Lord accompanying me in my remarks. Immediately following the dedication, ordinance work commenced for members who had come long distances to attend the dedication. At the dedication of the temple in Mexico City a member of the Quorum of the Twelve told me that while participating in this heavenly exercise in the celestial room he looked upward and seemed to see a balcony above the congregation, filled with countless people of the Mexican race, looking on with expectation at the great promise that was being unfolded to them. He said, "I didn't really see them, but it seemed that I was seeing them." As he told me of this experience I said, "This confirms exactly the same experience that came to me as I had an assurance of the presence of countless souls beholding the means of their redemption." On a later visit there I entered the celestial room and looked up to remember the marvelous impression I had experienced when the temple was dedicated. [2]

I wrote the following to President Hinckley after the dedication:

"Dear President,

"The events of the dedication in Mexico City and some of the comments relating to that special moment have impelled me to

---

2. Collected Works, p. 458

set forth a few of my own thoughts and feelings.

"First of all I am grateful to have been a witness of what took place, and I am gratified by the great effort and cooperation which contributed to the smooth flow of the dedication, in spite of the many assurances that the temple would be ready. The first miracle was that (speaking generously) it was. You could not have been fully aware of all the items which were put in passable condition at the latest possible moment. Another miracle was that the temple was able to function the day following the dedication. Many workers and miracles, in fact, combined to build and finish the temple.

"The overshadowing feature, of course, was the surpassing evidence of the spiritual presence which pervaded the dedication itself. I am confident that all who were present sensed the richness and power of the Holy Ghost in the various sessions. To me, the high moments of feeling were in the first session when the choir sang the Hosanna Anthem. Again in the last session as the inspired choir from the Colonies lifted us to a level of feeling which seemed to be of a heavenly order.

"The most impressive of all, however, was during the last session when you were touched and lifted even beyond the usual excellence and power of your expression. It seemed to me that the thoughts you expressed came flowing out of eternity. The impression was that they were circulating all around us, self-evident and ready to be spoken. As you referred to the children of Lehi, I could feel them and almost see them, vision-like, pressing forward to claim the blessings prepared for them. I truly believe that a nation was present to accept and rejoice in the great redemption promised in the dedication.

"Furthermore, as you spoke of President Kimball and his forceful leadership, based on his vision of the course the gospel must take, I felt that he too, was present in spirit to savor the fulfillment of the things which he had projected to be accomplished under the inspiration of God. It was a great testimony of the power of his ten years of presidency, following the many years of his striving in behalf of the Lamanites.

"I remember how, at the dedication of the São Paulo Temple the prayer petitioned for an extension of his life to accomplish the work he knew should be done. Now, five years later, although he has lacked the strength to personally perform, he is still in place to represent the high aim and vision of his prophetic calling."

December 6 we flew to Los Angeles and then on to Salt Lake City. December found us winding down a little bit. On December 8 we had a General Authority meeting in the temple. In the afternoon I flew to Washington, D.C., and was met by President Franklin D. Richards. We visited in the temple and flew together to hold a meeting in Jackson, Mississippi. I then flew to Lexington, Kentucky, for a stake conference on December 11. The next week I was in Bakersfield, California, for a stake conference in that city. On December 23, our son Cory announced at a family gathering that he and his wife, Gayle, had been called as a mission president by President Gordon B. Hinckley to serve somewhere in the world. It was a wonderful opportunity for them to develop their experience in the gospel.

1984

We continued to have much involvement with temple work, particularly regarding the leadership of the Boise and Provo Temples. There were several meetings with the executive council of the Temple Department to resolve issues. I continued to have area responsibility over southern Utah, and we held many area council meetings. We had consideration of cities where new temples might be established. I was invited to participate in a special Young Women training activity in the Marriott Center at BYU. Stake conferences in Utah led us to Mapleton, Provo Oak Hills, and Manti. At the Oak Hills stake conference, I found the stake extremely well organized with a greater load of talented people than I have found anywhere in my experience. They responded to my instruction on leadership with more compliments and appreciation and with a better understanding than any other stake I remember. I don't remember when all the speeches in the conference were so inspirational and full of good, sound principles.

Also in January, Elder Mark E. Petersen passed away and left a vacancy in the Quorum of the Twelve. His funeral called forth many sweet remembrances of our long association with him and the influence he had in our personal lives and in the Church. He would be sorely missed. I attended the Orem Stake conference followed by another conference in the Spanish Fork Utah Stake, and then I presided in Huntsville, Utah. President Marlin Jensen was the stake president and later on became a member of the Seventy. We went to Boise and visited with President and Sister Redford of the Boise Temple. In other assignments during the month, we had a meeting of the Seventy in the Salt Lake Temple. I also gave the annual report of the Temple Department to the First Presidency.

In family matters, we found ourselves involved with various activities throughout the month of January. My brother-in-law, Garland Bushman, passed away in late January. His passing was quick; he suffered some discomfort before going to the hospital, where he received emergency treatment but soon expired. The services and burial were held in Snowflake, Arizona, and I spoke at his funeral. Scott Webb, brother-in-law to our son Grant, reported his mission to Brazil in his home ward, which we attended. Cory and Gayle received their assignment to serve as mission president in the Brazil Rio de Janeiro Mission. On the farm we did a lot of fencing, riding horses, and preparing the ground for seed.

Towards the end of February we went to the Granger Ward and enjoyed the renewal of feelings of members in connection with the celebration of the Granger community centennial. Many people came together in a sort of a reunion. Don Bennion was the stake president. We also attended a nice dinner at BYU under the presidency of Jeffrey R. Holland. On a rather negative note, the General Authorities were shown The *Godmakers*, a movie that attempted to demean the sacredness of temple ordinances. We discussed it to some length.

In our March temple meeting with the General Authorities, Presidents Kimball and Romney were both quite feeble and did not participate. We flew to Atlanta and visited the temple there for two or three days and reviewed their procedures. From there we went to Raleigh, North Carolina, for a stake conference. President Weed was the stake president. We returned to Atlanta and went on to Santiago, Chile. There we visited with the temple presidency and noted the death of Brother Cifuentes, who had been an outstanding leader and strong support of the Church in Santiago. We were involved in many activities there, including the setting apart of counselors in the temple presidency. From there we flew to Lima, Peru, and visited the temple there and then traveled back through Santiago to Buenos Aires.

We went from Buenos Aires to Resistencia on the Parana River for a stake conference and a change in the stake presidency. I felt I communicated well in Spanish, being sustained by the Spirit. It came to me as an expression of the gift of tongues. It was difficult to understand everything others said, however. The stake in Resistencia was weak. Brother Fernandez was the regional representative. We prayed earnestly to be directed in the selection of a stake president. Brother Fernandez and I met again at noon and prayed again and discussed our feelings. He was inclined towards Brother Regnet but felt the assurance, as did I, that the Lord had called Brother José Toledo, a bishop in Corrientes. This was confirmed through prayer, and we invited him to come in. The new presidency accepted their calls, and we felt our major purpose was accomplished. We spent considerable time in leadership sessions, training the new presidency. During the conference we also met with about 55 missionaries.

From there we flew to São Paulo and met with Darwin Christensen, one of our former missionaries serving as a mission president, as well as President Benjamin Puerta, the temple president, and Lynn Sorensen, the director for temporal affairs in the area office. We also visited several close friends in the São Paulo area. We left on the 16th for Montevideo, Uruguay, and on the 17th drove north through the beautiful countryside to the city of Melo. The pasture land was full of cattle, sheep, and horses. Our first meeting was to be held in the city of Treinta y Tres. The name of the city commemorates 33 war heroes of the last century. The stake president's home was very modest, but they provided us with the best accommodations possible. Brother Call drove us about 60 miles west from Melo to the Brazilian border. There we met Roy and Alice Ruth Drechsel at the town of Rio Branco in Uruguay, and they drove us northward to Porto Alegre. The scenery all along the way was captivating as we imagined the gauchos moving across the rolling plains on horseback. We flew from Porto Alegre to Rio de Janeiro and met President Danilo Talanskas, whom Cory and Gayle would replace in July. They took the time to show us the facilities Cory and Gayle would have when they arrived. We flew overnight to Miami and separated at that point so that Geri could visit with Peggy in Omaha; I continued on to Salt Lake.

Upon returning, I spent extensive time doing business in the office due to my prolonged absence. Later on, we had an interesting meeting of the First Quorum of the Seventy. Remarks by President Hanks focused on our calls to serve. I also spoke at the Orem Institute of Religion upon invitation. I visited with President Hinckley concerning the operation and administration of temples and the calling of temple presidents. Prior to April general conference I attended a conference in the Grandview Stake in Provo. President Robinson was president, and the stake was well organized. This was the stake of my brother Blauer. In other activities I spoke at the monthly devotional of the Temple Department about honesty and trustworthiness. I interviewed Ian Mackie of Sydney, Australia, and Bo Wernerlund from Stockholm, Sweden, concerning the projected temples in both locations. I was assigned to speak in general conference during the Saturday afternoon session, and in my preparations I struggled earnestly to obtain the proper spirit and be blessed by the Lord. I was blessed in my delivery. In connection with conference, President Hinckley announced the construction of five new temples in San Diego, Las Vegas, Portland, Toronto, and Bogotá. The two vacancies in the Quorum of the Twelve were filled by Elders Russell M. Nelson and Dallin H. Oaks.

Following conference I met with Hugo Catron from Buenos Aires, a regional representative who had some matters to cover with me. He had been one of our son Grant's mission presidents in Spain. I later met with President Whitaker of the Cardiff Wales Stake about his stake and with Elder Adney Y. Komatsu about the Tokyo Temple. I had a review with Elder Hales on the problems connected with the opening of the temple in Freiberg, East Germany. We also hosted an evening with my former companions of our Brazilian missionary group. I met in Alpine with Elaine Cannon, recently released as General Young Women President of the Church. She had been very vivacious and effective.

We left on a trip to visit the temples in Idaho Falls and Cardston, Canada, coupled with a stake conference in Edmonton. I invited Lloyd Hicken, a former missionary companion born in Canada, and his wife to accompany us, and he was pleased to have an opportunity to visit the areas of his childhood. The extent of the farming operation in that part of Alberta, Canada, was enough to stagger the imagination. We drove through about 500 miles of wheat farming territory with the farms stretching in every direction. We held a nice stake conference in Edmonton that weekend and visited one of our missionaries, Elder Schilling, then living in Edmonton. It was a long drive up and back, but it was most enjoyable with the Hickens.

Later in April we met to discuss the best means of handling the singles wards in Orem and Provo. Our daughter Duella left at the end of the month to spend the summer employed at Jacob's Lake in northern Arizona, which was a marvelous experience for her.

In early May we had a meeting of the General Authorities in the Salt Lake Temple. Elder Dallin H. Oaks was there for the first time, and we were able to witness his ordination as one of the Twelve Apostles and to hear the charge to the Twelve. I joined with Vaughn Featherstone in administering the sacrament. Of special note is the opportunity that sometimes came to us of administering the ordinance of the restoration of blessings. This ordinance is a sweet moment for members who have put their lives back in order, and it was our privilege to administer it.

Layne and I did some incidental work on the farm, using the horses and the tractor, planting some grain in the fields, and riding the horses. On a sad note I attended the funeral of Mary Santos, who had been weakening in health and whom we had visited in the hospital. Her husband, Claudio, was very distraught. They were long-time associates from Brazil. May 21 we drove to Emery County to retrieve two horses that had wintered there, again under the care of LaMont and Nellie Smith. On the 28th we had the annual birthday party for my brother David, held at Marian and Richard Lindsay's home in Taylorsville.

We soon departed on our journey to Europe, stopping in Denver and New York and arriving at Dusseldorf, Germany. From there we proceeded to Hamburg. President Back was the stake president there, and we stayed in their home. I made some remarks to the conference in German and promised the congregation I would qualify myself to be able to speak their language. I felt the instruction on leadership to the stake was particularly effective. The conference was excellent and the speakers inspired. This city held a special charm for me as my father had served here as a missionary in 1914, presiding over the branch at that time.

We then traveled to Zurich, Switzerland, and were taken by President and Sister Hurst on a touring drive to see parts of Switzerland. We enjoyed the area around Zurich and then traveled on to Interlaken and the mountains surrounding it. The scenery at every turn was spectacular and impressive. Everything seemed so well ordered and flourishing. We enjoyed the scenery around Lauterbrunnen as well as that in the next valley of Grindelwald with ski resorts and waterfalls coming from glaciers higher up. We returned to Bern and spent the night with President and Sister Rees of the temple presidency. We met with President Rees and discussed needed changes or refinements in the temple. President and Sister Rees drove us around areas where the Bangerter family had originated, basically Lyss and Aarberg. The country was overlaid almost throughout with little villages and the large Swiss farmhouses that we see nowhere else in the world. They include housing for the family, all the animals, the storage, garage items, and so forth.

We returned to Zurich and flew to London where we spent considerable time with President and Sister Hampstead in the London Temple reviewing their operation. With them we drove to Bristol on the western coast of England. It only took two hours to cross England. We met in Bristol with the missionaries of that mission and then left by car to cross the Severn River and go to Cardiff in Wales. President Whitaker of the Cardiff Stake was our host for a stake conference in that city. After conference, we took the long drive back to

London with Brother and Sister Hempstead.

From there we flew on Lufthansa to Frankfurt, Germany, where we took the underground train into the city of Frankfurt. We visited Friedrichsdorf and a possible site for the temple at an old factory location that had been torn down. We recommended that it be considered as the site for the Frankfurt Temple.

We went with Brother Henry Haurand to cross the border into the DDR (Deutsche-Demokratische Reupublik, or East Germany). We arrived at the crossing point and waited in line for three hours while the guards took their time to check us out. There was a long line of trucks and cars waiting to cross. The region we passed through was full of interest and excitement. Our route took us past the city of Eisenach where the composer Bach was born and the Wartburg Castle is located. The Wartburg Castle is where Martin Luther translated the Bible nearly 400 years earlier. We passed through Leipzig, Zwickau, and Freiberg and drove on to Dresden where we stayed the night. We toured through Dresden, which had been heavily bombed in WW II, and returned to Freiberg to visit the temple site, where we met Brother Henry Burkhart and Brother Manfred Schutze. The structure of the temple was finished, the chapel was nearing completion, and they were in the process of finishing the interior of those buildings. The guides provided us by the government were very courteous and attentive and showed interest in what we were accomplishing. Brother Schultze drove us north to Berlin, and we crossed the Elbe River and saw much of the forest in the region. In Berlin we drove through the city and saw the Berlin Wall, the Avenue Unter den Linden, and the Brandenburg Gate. We pulled up to Checkpoint Charlie and crossed into West Berlin without much delay and stayed in a hotel in West Berlin. We climbed a platform and looked at East Germany across the Wall. From Berlin we flew home, arriving in Salt Lake City before dark.

A couple of days later I flew to Boise in preparation of the temple dedication there and returned to Salt Lake City the next day. At the end of May I went with Brothers Bush, Walker, and Harvey to Elberta at the south end of Utah Lake, where I had been assigned to offer a prayer of dedication on a grain facility installed there by the General

Church Welfare Committee. I flew to Montreal, stopping in Chicago. President and Sister Kurt Wynder of the mission met me there. They were kind enough to give me a tour of the city, which was impressive to me. We had two general sessions of conference. I spoke in Spanish in the second session for the Spanish branch. It was a new experience to be interpreted from Spanish to French for the benefit of the rest of the congregation. Geri and I flew again to Boise in preparation of the dedication of the Boise Temple. The next day I spoke in the first and second sessions of that temple dedication. We felt the richness of this experience and rejoiced in the chance to spend this time with the Saints in the Idaho area and to have some opportunity to meet with the temple presidency. That evening we returned to Salt Lake.

June 3 was a solemn assembly in the Salt Lake Temple, held in two sessions. I was invited to speak and felt it was a very spiritual meeting. President Hinckley and Elder Maxwell were most inspiring in their comments. Shortly thereafter in a general announcement to the Church, Area Presidencies were assigned throughout the world in an attempt to place leadership closer to members of the Church. I was assigned with Elder Rex Reeve to the Northeast Area of the U.S. We also had meetings with the temple administration.

On June 8 we had a Schwantes family reunion at our home in Alpine. We attended Cory and Gayle's ward in Sandy the next day, where they were honored prior to their departure for Brazil to serve as mission president. I was asked to give some remarks. Shortly thereafter, Elder Bruce R. McConkie asked me to join him in setting Cory and Gayle apart. Later on I drove to Logan where we had a detailed review of activity on the Logan Temple. We then drove to Burley and on to Twin Falls. President Nelson of the Filer Idaho Stake accompanied us. We drove around the Snake River Gorge, the Shoshone Falls, and the Twin Falls and had a good stake conference in Twin Falls. Cory and his family were in Alpine prior to attending the mission presidents' seminar in Provo. We participated in portions of that seminar with them. Towards the end of June we sent Cory, Gayle, and their family off to Brazil where they were to preside over the mission in Rio de Janeiro. About the same time my brother Norman was nominated as the Republican candidate for governor of the state of Utah.

In July we had several family activities and periods of relaxation. We visited Jacob's Lake, Arizona, and with John Rich we reviewed the area to the east in House Rock Valley and then south to the Grand Canyon. We returned to St. George where we stayed with President and Sister Russon of the temple presidency. On another occasion we took the horses and rode up into the mountains above Alpine. Later we had a family reunion with the Hamblin family in Alpine. Following Pioneer Day we made preparations to go to the High Uinta Mountains and camp at Black's Fork with members of the family. We had a delightful time, staying until July 30. Also in July, President Hinckley asked me to assist in setting apart several new temple presidents: Brother Garth Andrus was to go to Manila, Ream Jones to Idaho Falls, and Glenn Rudd to New Zealand.

August found us once again in a flurry of activity. I went to Boise, Idaho, to review the activity of the temple there and stayed with President and Sister Redford. From there we went to Idaho Falls and did a similar review. We participated in the reorganization of the temple presidency later that week under the direction of President Hinckley. We met with the widow of President Harry Maxwell, former mission president in Brazil. She was struggling with physical problems. Later we had a meeting in the Provo Tabernacle with workers of the Provo Temple. President and Sister Priday of the Provo Temple and President and Sister Cox of the Manti Temple also came. In the middle of the month we had a temple presidents' seminar, which was very successful. President Hinckley, Elder Hunter, and I addressed those in attendance.

I then flew to Toronto to review the mission operation there. President and Sister Bacon of the Toronto Mission met me. We flew north to the city of Timmons, stopping at North Bay and visiting Brother Scott, a patriarch and leader in that area. He was troubled with his health problems, so we administered to him. We went from there to Sudbury where we looked at a site for a church building. We returned to Toronto and drove to Burlington, near the city of Hamilton. We looked at several different places around the city of Toronto for possible temple sites. The next day I flew to Baltimore,

Maryland, and President Duane Peterson, a counselor in the Columbia Maryland Stake met me. I met with President Franklin D. Richards of the Washington D.C. Temple, and he joined me in the reorganization of the stake presidency. We called President Peterson to be the new stake president. Brother Ensign, one of the new counselors, grew up in Magna, Utah, and I had known his family for many years. Geri knew his wife, who was a former Catholic from Cheyenne, Wyoming. Elder Lawrence Mauerman, a former Brazilian missionary of ours had been called to be a bishop and lived in that stake.

Toward the end of the month I met with Elders Wirthlin and Hales to consider problems about temple clothing in East Germany. I also met with Brother Seastrand from Las Vegas, formerly of American Fork and chairman of the Las Vegas Temple committee, to discuss some energetic and interesting approaches to the dedication of the temple in Las Vegas. Later on in the month we traveled to Toledo, Ohio, for a stake conference. I was impressed with the depth and strength of the leadership, although there were many scattered branches. The next week I was in Saskatoon and Regina in Canada for a stake conference. The sessions were split between the two cities and we felt a good spirit in our meetings. Our involvement with the temples took us to temple dedications in Sydney, Australia, and Manila, Philippines. In Sydney the process worked very smoothly, and we were uplifted by the power and strength of the speakers and participants. We found ourselves in the middle of a hotel strike, so for two days our meals were scanty at best. I spoke in two of the sessions and felt the power and influence of the Lord in my remarks. The Manila dedication was a special time for President Hinckley. He was quite emotional due to his heavy involvement of opening the work in the Philippines. He had dedicated the land 23 years previously for the preaching of the gospel, and at the time of the dedication there were nearly 90,000 members. We were sobered by the visit to the American Cemetery, where 17,000 U.S. servicemen were buried and over 35,000 more had their names on the walls of the monument. President Hinckley once again was particularly moved by the experience, as were we. We located the name of Geri's cousin,

Spencer Hamblin, who was a pilot lost at sea during that conflict. We returned through Tokyo and visited that temple before moving on to Hawaii, where we held a temple review with the leaders of that facility. From there we traveled to San Francisco and Oakland, California, visiting the temple there as well. Howard and Lissa hosted us while we were in that area.

In the fall we had our annual Labor Day breakfast with our family. The weekend before, we drove with Duella to Rexburg, Idaho, where she was to enter college. We were saddened later on in the month when our horse Babe was hit by a car and needed to be destroyed. In November we met as siblings to celebrate our mothers 92nd birthday, with Geri serving as the major force behind the celebration. We ended the evening with a special prayer in behalf of Norman, who was facing his election as governor of the state of Utah. It was with a feeling of elation for all of us that on November 7, Norm won his election. We had a nice diversion in riding the horses into the nearby mountains with Wagner Camargo. Layne also went with us. We also learned that our son-in-law Steve Apple had been called as bishop of his ward. We participated in his ordination and setting apart, his father ordaining him an high priest and I ordaining him a bishop. We had several of our family to visit for Thanksgiving, and many of the younger children enjoyed riding horses and jumping on the trampoline as part of the festivities. After a delightful Thanksgiving Day, we drove to Ferron and checked on our property and animals there. We delivered a pair of horses at that time.

Following the October general conference we visited the Montreal, Quebec, area of Canada, and a week later were assigned to the Pittsburg, Pennsylvania Stake conference, where we were blessed with a good spirit in our meetings. The stake president was especially appreciative of our participation. We continued on to Boston for a mission presidents' seminar, allowing us to see some of the Revolutionary War sites in Lexington and Concord. Elder Neal A. Maxwell presided and gave outstanding counsel to us in our meetings. His scriptural insights were a special treat for all. Geri and I flew from there to Washington, D.C., where we participated in a temple review prior to our holding an area council meeting. We had a good discussion about the Hill Cumorah Pageant and later were able to agree on accepting goals for ordaining more men to the Melchizedek Priesthood, calling more young men to serve missions, and increasing tithing faithfulness among the members. While in Washington, D.C., one of our former missionaries, Bruce Christensen, took us on an extensive tour of the capitol, including the Supreme Court building and areas in the Smithsonian. We proceeded from there to a stake conference in Richmond, Virginia, an area rich in Civil War history and events. The conference was especially inspired and I felt blessed in my own remarks. Geri gave an excellent talk on that occasion.

In our assignments with the Seventies, I was asked to present an approach on how to prepare missionaries. Later on we met to discuss cottages for temple workers to be housed near the Manti Temple. I continued to perform marriages and participate in stake conferences. We traveled to Akron, Ohio, and stayed in the home of President and Sister Stanley Smoot, who was the mission president there. While there we were able to visit the Kirtland, Ohio, area. Brother Karl Ricks Anderson escorted us around Kirtland, and we visited the temple, the Whitney Store, the Isaac Morley farm, and the Johnson Farm in Hiram. We then held the evening meetings for the stake conference. I felt very strongly the influence of the Spirit of the Lord as we bore testimony to the Restoration of the gospel and the great progress that is being made in the work of the kingdom.

Geri and I then flew to Washington, D.C., and on to McLean, Virginia, where we met with President and Sister Swinton and their missionaries in the Virginia Mission. We participated in the training of district and zone Leaders in an excellent meeting. We also visited the Antietam Battlefield of the Civil War period as well as the site of the two battles of Bull Run. It was a solemn moment for me due to my interest in history. We continued with more conference meetings in Silver Springs, Maryland, and also in the Annandale Stake Center.

After our meetings in the east, we flew to Dallas, Texas, to visit the temple there—my first time since its dedication. We met with President and Sister Hobson and a large number of missionaries and workers. I later worked out some temple housing arrangements. From there we flew to Atlanta, Georgia, where we met with the temple presidency and reviewed their operation. We had a stake conference in Jacksonville, Florida, and were met there by President and Sister Bone. I participated in the Primary program of priesthood preparation. I later went with President Bone to the priesthood leadership meeting and also had an excellent visit with President and Sister Stubbs. President Stubbs was a chaplain for the Navy. We returned to Salt Lake after many days on the road. In the office, we spent much time working on the plans for the San Diego Temple, and President Hinckley approved the revised plans for the temple. I also met with Elder Haight and Richard Lindsay on public affairs in the Washington, D.C., and New York City areas. At the end of the month we flew to Phoenix, then to San Diego, and back home through Los Angeles on assignment with the Temple Department. I also had a good visit with Malcolm Warner of CES on their needs and also with President Benson in our executive council on temples.

December had many activities but also reflected a slow-down due to the holiday season. I continued to attend stake conferences, beginning at the Olympus Stake in Salt Lake. It was a particularly inspirational conference. Brother Vernon Sharp was in that stake, and we enjoyed renewing acquaintances with him. We also attended several functions related to the Christmas season, including one for the Temple Department and another for the First Quorum of the Seventy. The Osmond family and Sharlene Wells participated in the entertainment, which was most delightful. I met with the architects of the San Diego Temple, and our recommendations were well taken. Elder Boyd K. Packer spoke to us, giving us some inspiring remarks concerning the influence we should feel in our work under the guidance of the Holy Spirit. I had a meeting with President Hinckley for an hour wherein he reviewed his impressions about the temples and what should be done. He was disturbed that the remodeling of some of our temples had been done by people who were not authorized to be in temples and the temples would therefore require rededication. This was especially true in Manti. He gave me some impressions about changes and remodeling in the temples, which caused me to think we could modify our approach to some of the various projects being proposed. I attended the monthly temple meeting for the

General Authorities and was one of those invited to bear testimony. Elder McConkie spoke at some length on the conditions of the Savior's birth as he had studied them in outside material. President Hinckley spoke to us, and we had the sacrament and the prayer circle.

There was some evidence that conditions in Guatemala were not altogether in order for the temple dedication that was to take place within a week. Geri and I flew to New York City to meet President and Sister Boyd Christensen. There we met with the missionary leaders and discussed in detail the proper use of the teaching time. While there we toured a bit around Manhattan and enjoyed the movement of that bustling city. Shortly thereafter we flew to Bermuda and spent two days with the members of that isolated branch before returning to Washington, D.C., where we met with Richard Lindsay and Don Ladd regarding public communications in the East, including the Hill Cumorah Pageant. In other meetings I met with Elder Monson as he outlined the program for the Freiberg Temple and then in council with the First Quorum of Seventy on missionary preparation. Geri and I drove to Idaho Falls, where we reviewed the temple operations, and then on to Rexburg, where we spent some delightful time with our daughter Duella and brought her back home for the Christmas break. I also performed several sealings for family and friends as the holidays approached. We held our annual Hamblin Christmas party, with our family involved heavily in the preparation and execution of it. We enjoyed a special time with our daughter Duella in reading of the birth of the Savior. We took a day to drive to Ferron to check on our animals and pick up some meat from a beef we had butchered. In family activities we put our old bobsled into commission under the direction of Layne and set it up for the ponies to pull around the farm in the snow. My brother Blauer needed bypass surgery, so we gave him a blessing prior to his operation and he came through in excellent condition. We continued to be active in speaking and with other functions during the holiday season, including being master of ceremonies at the Temple Department Christmas social, speaking at an event featuring the American Fork Civic Chorus, and attending the Christmas broadcast in the Tabernacle. On Christmas Eve we went caroling with members of our family to various friends and neighbors. Christmas day was filled with the normal visits to family and enjoying the presence of our children and grandchildren around the farm. During the break Geri and I drove around Utah Lake to enjoy the winter scenery. We had my mother visit us on New Year's Eve as we issued out the old and welcomed in the new.

1985

Early in January, my brother Norman was inaugurated as governor of the state of Utah, and we were privileged to participate in some of the activities associated with that event. We toured the governor's mansion and enjoyed a lovely brunch with other invited guests, including their children. There were four former governors in attendance at the ceremony: Herbert Maw, J. Bracken Lee, Calvin Rampton, and Scott Matheson. We enjoyed visiting with each one of them and also with our congressional delegation, including Senators Hatch and Garn and Representatives Hansen and Nielson. Mayor Ted Wilson was also present. Governor Matheson made some excellent complimentary remarks that left a good feeling, and Norman's inaugural address was an excellent announcement of his view of the aims of government and the course his administration should take.

Also in January we were invited to Washington, D.C., to participate in the inauguration of President Ronald Reagan, and even though we made the trip, several of the activities were cancelled due to the extreme cold. We kept warm in our hotel room and watched the major proceedings on TV. While there we did participate in an area council meeting with the regional representatives and other officials on the eastern seaboard as well as a mission presidents' interim seminar in Washington, D.C. We later participated in a stake conference in Norfolk, Virginia. It was an enjoyable time with the members of that stake. We left in a blizzard but had little trouble making connections to return home.

Other stake conferences included one in the Salt Lake Parley's Stake; they met in a large cultural hall, giving a good feeling to the meeting. Another conference took place later in the month in the Annandale Maryland Stake. On that trip we visited Chicago and Rochester, New York, where we participated in a mission tour.

Following visits to some Church history sites in Fayette and Palmyra, we proceeded to Syracuse and on to Washington, D.C. In many cases, it was my first experience in those areas. Almost at every stop we encountered people we had known in years past—missionaries who had served with us in Brazil or friends from the early days of living in Granger. Earlier in the month I flew to Atlanta to check on things regarding the Atlanta Temple.

We sadly said our farewells to Elder G. Homer Durham, of the Presidency of the Seventy who passed away. The funeral was outstanding in its content. President Hinckley, a lifelong associate, directed the proceedings. Later on my brother Norman invited all of his brothers and sisters and their spouses along with our mother to enjoy an evening of dining together in the governor's mansion. Geri and I took Gloria and Gene Bowers with us to Arizona as we visited the temple in Mesa. They had an opportunity to visit with Elsie Fern Bushman and Ruth and Jack Stricklin, who lived there. Bud Schwantes was also in town for a visit, so it was a real family reunion.

February took us to more stake conferences, including the Wellsville Stake near Ogden. We also spent time in the Ogden Temple. I recall in that stake conference that the Lord sustained and blessed me in an adequate way, at least in my responsibilities. Geri gave an excellent brief talk, and President and Sister Johnson from the Logan Temple added measurably to the spirit of the meeting. Later we determined to visit the Manti Temple and examine the remodeling efforts there. On our way to the Cedar City Stake, we took a rather circuitous route through Manti, Salina, Elsinore, Hurricane, Las Vegas (to check on the temple there), and St. George (where we also visited the temple), finally arriving in Cedar City; we returned home by passing through Geri's parents' hometown of Minersville as well as the town of Kanosh.

Later in the month we attended the Morristown New Jersey Stake conference. The general session of that conference turned out to be one of the outstanding meetings of our experience. The speeches given by the participants were very inspiring. I was able to see the Statue of Liberty on that trip and traveled through various portions of New England that were significant to Church history and

U.S. history. That trip took me through several states and included visits with missionaries in the Boston mission region as part of the mission tour.

Of special note was a meeting with President Hinckley in which he informed me of my reassignment to the Presidency of the Quorum of the Seventy to take effect in April conference. It caused me many reflections, and Geri and I had considerable conversation about it and some serious and earnest prayer. President Hinckley also approved a yearly temple presidents' seminar and determined the length of service for temple presidents—he felt that it would be best for them to serve less than five years, to which I agreed.

March took me on a quick trip to Seattle regarding temple matters and to a stake conference to the Boise Idaho Weiser stake. We also visited the Boise Temple during that visit. Towards the end of the month I flew to Toronto, Canada, for a stake conference. Cory and Gayle returned from Brazil to attend the mission presidents' seminar in Provo and Salt Lake. All mission Presidents from around the world were gathered together so that a new approach to teaching the discussions could be introduced. The sessions of the seminar were electrifying and insightful as increased emphasis was given to the missionary program of the Church. Elder Packer made a presentation that captivated all, including a choir from the MTC of missionaries going to various locations in the world. The mission presidents' seminar concluded with a special sacrament meeting in the Salt Lake Temple. I was asked to officiate at the table along with others. It was a wonderful time to be with Cory and Gayle for a short visit until they returned to their mission in Rio de Janeiro.

I was once again called into the Presidency of the Seventy during April general conference, and those responsibilities matched up better with my assignment as Managing Director of the Temple Department. I was asked to speak in conference and had been greatly concerned about my speech. I felt it was a fairly weak speech, but the Lord greatly blessed me to be able to make it effective in delivery, and there was good commendation about its effect. The conference also gave us one final experience with Elder Bruce R. McConkie, who delivered what was to be his farewell address as he was suffering from cancer. He passed away a few days later. During the conference, our lifelong friend from Brazil, Hélio Camargo, was called to the Second Quorum of Seventy. In our meetings following general conference, I was asked to speak briefly concerning my new appointment as one of the presidency, and I made comments on the authority and power that has been conferred upon us in our calling as members of the First Quorum and as General Authorities.

Following general conference I was assigned to a stake conference in the Monterrey Cuidad Victoria Stake; I flew in and out of Texas, where I also visited the temple in Dallas. I felt blessed in my ability to speak in Spanish during that conference. A week later we left for the Boston area to participate in a multiregional conference, where President Benson presided. The elements of the conference were all outstanding and most appropriate. We then traveled into New Brunswick and Halifax, Nova Scotia, touring the mission and addressing many missionaries before returning the next weekend to the Roanoke Virginia Stake conference. Once again we met many of our former missionaries and friends from times past. In Washington, D.C., we met with many senators and congressmen as part of the public affairs meetings, receiving VIP treatment in our associations and interviews. Another major event in April was the graduation of our son Paulo from BYU, where we were invited as guests of honor for the convocation and other ceremonies. It was a delight for us to participate with this wonderful son in his accomplishments.

In May we had an extensive trip to Honolulu, Samoa, Tonga, New Zealand, and Australia, where we reviewed the operations of each of the temples in those lands. In each place we felt the sweet, peaceful, pleasant spirit of the workers and members who came. We were treated in royal fashion at each stop, and the leaders and members were most gracious in their expressions. In New Zealand we found everything was being carried out in a sweet and decorous manner. We were impressed with the order and organization that President and Sister Glen Rudd brought to the temple and the spirit with which they related to all the members and workers. President Rudd had spent his lifetime in association with New Zealand and made it a point to know everyone and to be able to greet them in the warmest way. Sister Rudd had gained a similar approach in her expressions. After a stop in Sydney, Australia, where we had time to spend with our nephew David Weaver and his wife, Linda, and their children, we flew back to Los Angeles and on to Mexico City where I presided at the Chalco Stake conference before returning home. I enjoyed the stake presidency in Chalco and particularly the display they had to show how they take care of the information on the membership and setting up their goals. It was one of the best arrangements I had seen anywhere. President Flores and his counselors seemed to be excellent men, and I thought they were in good control of the work of the stake. I spoke throughout in Spanish and thought I did reasonably well, having asked the Lord for special help and support. Upon returning home, it seemed like we had spent a long time in airplanes.

June found us involved with a seminar for new temple presidents. President Hinckley and others gave inspirational instructions to the new temple presidents. I was also able to visit the temple in Manti early in the month to ascertain its readiness for rededication. I visited the Meridian Idaho Stake conference and then returned to Manti for the rededication of that temple. I was called upon to address one of the sessions, all of them being under the direction of President Hinckley. These sessions were held in the priesthood room occupying the upper floor of the temple, with overflow seating in the various rooms throughout the temple so that it was not necessary to hold too many sessions.

At the end of June we traveled with a large entourage of General Authorities to Switzerland, where we reviewed the temple operation. We flew on to Berlin as a group and then traveled by bus to Freiberg, East Germany, for the temple dedication there. It was a marvelous event. The dedication was one of the most impressive at which we had ever been present. The German Saints were so orderly and thorough in their preparation, and they evidenced a tremendous spirit of excitement and gratitude due to the fact that they would have a temple to bless their lives. They had prepared two choirs with two different conductors, and their performances were in every way outstanding. I felt that there would not be found more expert and well-trained choirs anywhere in the Church. We were thrilled and over-come by the beauty and power of their music as they sang many of the well-known hymns of Zion. Over the years of my life I have come to know many of these hymns, and I felt an affinity to these people because of my somewhat limited ability in German.

In the third session I was called upon to speak. I had prepared a talk to be given in German and, following a great deal of effort and a lot of prayer and desire, I gave my remarks in a way that seemed to be acceptable and perhaps impressive. I was able to enunciate in the German language with considerable effect and received many com-pliments afterwards. The experience of nearly a lifetime seemed to come full circle as I thought back on the beginnings of my under-standing of the German language and the people with whom I had affiliated in Brazil in 1939.

Following the dedication we returned to Berlin, where we had to wait over an hour for the process of crossing back into the free world. All of us were impressed with the tremendous blessings of freedom that we enjoyed in the West, freedom that was not under-stood by those behind the iron curtain. There did seem to be, howev-er, a tremendous movement back and forth across the border among the German people, so there was evidence that the policies of inter-course between the two countries had been relaxed a great deal.

We then made our way to Stockholm, Sweden, where we par-ticipated in that temple dedication. It was remarkable to us how President Hinckley moved through these activities in a calm and un-ruffled way, always ready with appropriate and inspiring comments at each of the moments when he was expected to respond. The first two sessions were in Swedish. A different group of members came to each session and the temple was full with between 500 and 600 people, filling all the rooms. We were much impressed with the dé-cor and special features that surround this temple, which is similar to the temples in the Philippines, Taiwan, and Korea. Its situation is unique and very beautiful, about 20 kilometers out from the cen-ter of Stockholm and located in a wooded area. Access is very easy as train and bus lines run right to it. We returned through London where we visited that temple as well.

On a personal note, later in the month, I spoke at the funeral of my cousin Alice Green. The funeral was held in our old ward in Granger, and it was choice to see so many members of the family present, including all of Alice's brothers and sisters. Some of them were becoming quite aged and feeble. We began to see that most of the old generation was passing on, and now the inevitable toll was reaching into our own generation. Alice was only three or four years older than I. In mid-June we were with the Hamblin family in the Uinta Mountains at a family reunion. We were also able to participate with the family in the annual camping experience in Black's Fork in the mountains. Geri and I also enjoyed a day in Park City.

Though July was generally a month of lesser activity in my calling, I was assigned to visit the Chicago Temple open house in the middle of the month and then to visit Denver to examine the construction towards the end of the month. August was historic for us in many ways. I spoke at a BYU Fireside followed shortly by the temple dedication in Chicago. The speeches and choirs were outstanding and contributed greatly to the strong spirit that pervaded the ceremonies. In my remarks I remembered Walter and Pat Cryer, Betsy's parents, who had been converted to the Church in Chicago, and I also spoke of President Hinckley and his great dedication. In my last talk I spoke of Michael Kennedy and Gracia Jones, the descendants of the Prophet Joseph Smith who are now members of the Church, and the promise made to those descendants to enjoy the blessings of eternal life. The middle of the month brought about a celebration of the 50th anniversary of the organization of the Church in Brazil. We gathered as a group of former missionaries to commemorate this event. Meeting with these dear friends was always a delightful and stimulating event. It had been celebrated in grand style in Brazil at the end of June. We attended the Blackfoot Idaho Stake conference towards the end of the month. I was impressed with the leadership of this stake and the high level of activity among the members. The afternoon meeting with the priesthood leaders turned out very well, and the evening meeting went according to plan with speakers giving excellent treatment to the theme "The Atonement, Justice, and Mercy."

September took us once again to Manti, where Geri and I reviewed the temple operation. We then held stake conferences in Mountain Home, Idaho; Washington, D.C.; and Mariana, Florida. We also reviewed the temples in the locations near those conferences. In the Mountain Home conference we had an interesting event. Early in the meeting I was much concerned because of the serious economic problems of the farmers in the area and elsewhere in Idaho. We found the same conditions all over the state in the past several months, and many were losing their property because of their debt, high interest payments, and low crop yield and prices. I felt impressed that we might interrupt the conference and have a special prayer for the blessing of those choice and special people. Therefore, as I was announced as the last speaker, I arose and invited President Jones, the patriarch, to come forward and offer this kind of prayer. He did so under great emotional stress and offered a beautiful prayer, calling forth the Lord's blessings upon the people and their circumstances. After the meeting he told me that he had been impressed that he would be asked to participate in the conference, but when the meeting proceeded to the final speaker and he had not been called upon, he thought his impression was incorrect. Then when I asked him to come forward, he was so emotionally touched that he had difficulty in controlling his feelings. This, of course, was a confirmation to me of the influence of the Spirit in directing us in the conference.

While in Washington, D.C., for the Frederick Maryland Stake conference, I was taken by the stake president to Gettysburg. There we viewed the scenes of the tremendous battle that took place there during the Civil War. The stake conference itself was blessed by the Spirit of the Lord. It seemed we were on airplanes much of the past few months.

October general conference once again showed the weak physical condition of President Kimball. In our meeting prior to conference, President Benson spoke to the General Authorities at length about our duties and the responsibilities of our office. He advised us strongly to teach from the Book of Mormon and to take time to meditate and pray. He reminded us that we are agents on the Lord's errand and that we represent the Lord. He told us that there was a need for repentance and occasional rebuke and that we should be willing to accept counsel and reprimand as occasion required. We received excellent instruction on procedure and protocol. For instance, we should not pre-empt the time of those who are senior to us. We should conform to the standard time restraints in our meetings, conferences, and marriages. Our testimonies should be extemporaneous and brief. We were counseled to accept our appointments as given. In our stake conferences, our interviews should have the support of the stake president. Much of what he shared with us dealt with the need to conform to policy.

Following conference, we flew to Lima, Peru, where we reviewed the construction of the temple there. From there we flew to Buenos Aires and attended the Bayfield Stake conference. It was more than the usual stake conference, with each speaker being inspired in what he or she said. The choir began with a group of children marching up and singing a special number and the intermediate hymn was "The Spirit of God like a Fire Is Burning," but the music director had timed the singing at such a slow pace that the feeling came through in a way that I had never experienced before. It was a very impressive, spiritual moment and filled the building with an influence that was most appropriate for this special meeting. We were warmed by the greetings of the people following the conference. I felt that my own remarks were blessed in that I was able to speak Spanish with a clarity and influence that was not often possible. Geri spoke a few lines in Spanish and then had her speech interpreted, but it was very impressive.

We left there and flew to Iguaçu and then to São Paulo, where we took time to visit the temple there. While in São Paulo, we visited many friends and associates of years past. Our feelings about being back in the midst of familiar scenes of so many years of our lives in São Paulo were often very poignant and touching, especially as we met the many people who had become precious to us. We knew that we could not relive all the experiences we enjoyed together, but we realized that we have a huge box of memories and special feelings that we hope will never be left behind. We returned to Santiago, Chile, to observe their temple operation. I bought a billfold at the airport and presented it to Geri as a wedding anniversary present. She immediately remembered that she had not given me a gift, so she presented it to me, and I had what I wanted. She then went across the way and bought a copper bell and presented it to me, and I was able to give it back to her; thus we satisfied our gift problems for the moment.

We returned to Buenos Aires and then traveled to Bahia Blanca for a stake conference there. From there we flew to Rio de Janeiro and enjoyed a visit with Cory and Gayle for a couple of days as we attended zone conferences and relaxed with the family. One day at noon, three departing missionaries came to the home for a farewell luncheon, following which we all went to the old Tijuca chapel, which is now the headquarters of the Rio Andaraí Stake. There we had a meeting with many of the missionaries of the nearby zones. Cory gave some excellent instructions, and Gayle and Geri also spoke. I was then asked to speak in the way of inspiration. It turned out well and was a great, enjoyable experience for us. We prepared to leave for Bogotá, and as we arrived at the airport to check in for our flight on Avianca, we were informed that our flight had left the day before. Evidently there had been a schedule change. However, some problem had developed, and it turned out the flight had not left yet, but it was going that day and was in fact ready to leave immediately. The airline attendants took special care of us, issuing us boarding passes and helping carry our baggage directly to the plane and putting us on board. We were told that there was no room in first class but that we could ride in tourist class. However, when we got on the plane, we found that first class was nearly empty. They seated us there but said that there were no first class meals for us, but when they served the meal, it was all first class anyway, so it worked out very well. We felt it was a special blessing of Providence in providing such ease and comfort on our journey.

In early November I drove to Ferron to check on our animals there. Our son-in-law Richard Lorenzon had been recommended by his stake presidency to be ordained a high priest, and I was privileged to perform that ordinance under the direction of President Jon Huntsman Sr., who came to their home for the ordinance.

On November 5, President Kimball passed away, bringing to an end a marvelous era. He was a dear friend and mentor to me over the years. The funeral was held a few days later. President Benson was sustained as the new prophet according to established procedure. Prior to his appointment, in a temple meeting with all of the General Authorities it was evident that there was no question about him assuming the presidency of the Church.

Later that month I was blessed to participate in the ordination of another son-in-law, Ramon Beck, to the office of a high priest. He was ordained by his father, and I then set him apart as a member of the bishopric of his ward. I was assigned to a stake conference in Springfield, Missouri, where we reorganized the presidency. As I had two regional representatives with me in our interviews, I asked them to reflect upon those with whom we had met. I had been impressed even before I met Brother Banner, a bishop of one of the Springfield wards, and when he came in I felt that among all those who had been considered, he was the one indicated. These brethren agreed, and one of them said "I had a very strong impression as I watched him and a group of other men that he was to be the next stake president." We finished our interviews and then consulted with Brother and Sister Banner. It developed that they had the same impression, and Brother Banner was immediately prepared to submit the names of his counselors. We felt the arrangement was directed and guided by the Spirit of the Lord. Our Thanksgiving was celebrated somewhat quietly with various families visiting us during the day following their feast at relatives home. We did have some of our immediately family to join with us.

Early in December we moved the remains of Mildred and baby Mildred Elizabeth to the Murray Cemetery because the one in Taylorsville was being deactivated. Another reason for this move was that we had no close family connections in cemeteries on the west side of the valley, and we reasoned that probably most of our family would not be buried in that area. Additionally, all four of my grandparents were buried in the Elysian Gardens in Murray, as were both of Geri's parents. The disinterment worked very smoothly. Mildred's remains were inside a concrete vault, and it was a simple process

THE TEMPLE DEPARTMENT SUMMARY

to uncover and raise the vault onto a truck. The infant, Mildred Elizabeth, had been buried in a small casket that been placed in a wooden box. Over the 34, years since her death, the wooden box had disintegrated and there was not much left of the casket. We took what was there encased in soil and placed everything inside a small concrete box, placed a lid on it, and then transferred both of the caskets to the Elysian Gardens. We watched them reset Mildred's vault in the grave in Murray, and then the baby's vault was placed on top of hers so that they are now buried in the same plot.

I participated in the Salt Lake Wilford Stake conference that weekend. I left shortly after that conference to Durango, Colorado, to speak at the funeral of my brother-in-law Jack Strickland. It was an emotional time for the children, especially Jack Jr. On our return, we went through Mesa, Arizona, and spent a couple of days reviewing the temple operation there. Our Arizona missionaries and the temple president loaded up our car with lots of fruit to enjoy over the holidays. We returned home via a circuitous route, which was always enjoyable to us. I spoke at the MTC in Provo and at the close of the year visited the Manti Temple once again.

We enjoyed the holidays with the family at our home in Alpine, making the rounds to visit each of the families in turn and enjoying the spirit of the season. As we enjoyed the last of our holidays, spending the time at home rather quietly and giving some reflections to the blessings that we had enjoyed during the past year, Geri and I also reflected somewhat on our experiences and accomplishments during the year. Much of what we did centered on the various extended journeys we made. During the first half of the year we were frequently in the east in Washington, Boston, New York, and eastern Canada. Other long journeys included the trip to various temples in the South Pacific, the trip to Europe for the dedication of two temples in Freiberg and Stockholm, and the trip to South America in October in which we visited all the temples and the temple sites. The year 1985 also saw the launching of our son Paulo into law school and our son-in-law Rob into medical school. Layne was blessed in the special employment he received to work with the wildlife services, something that thrilled him perhaps more than anything else.

Each of our family had similar protection and blessings. Howard and Lissa moved to San Diego and were able to purchase a home, much of that done through our support, but we were glad to be able to assist.

1986

January of 1986 was filled with conferences, first in the Grant Stake in Salt Lake, where we renewed acquaintances with Dennis and Arlene Dial, a former counselor to me in the stake presidency, followed a week later by the St. George Washington Stake, where we once again encountered many friends from days past. The growth in the Washington area was amazing, with many members coming in from other locales as they retire and settle there. We finished the month with a conference in the La Crescenta California stake, stopping on our way in Las Vegas to review progress on that temple site and then in Los Angeles to review the temple operation. In each conference we often had additional firesides and special meetings with groups to address needs perceived by the stake presidency.

February took us to the Cardston Alberta Temple in company with President Hinckley where we installed a new temple presidency. In mid-February we flew to Honolulu and on to Manila, Philippines, where I presided at the Angeles Stake conference. Our flight over was in a huge 747, and we were able to take advantage of the bunks provided for us. I did not sleep well, but Geri had a comfortable night's rest. We landed in Honolulu and took off without even getting out of bed. In Manila we spent quite a bit of time reviewing the temple operation before going to our stake assignment. From there we visited the temple in Taipei, Taiwan, our first visit there in nearly a year. President Gifford and I spent most of a morning checking out the method by which temple records are processed and recorded. There was a great difficulty in insuring accuracy if the names of people had been placed in Roman lettering. The only true security was to maintain the Chinese characters. From there we flew to Tokyo, Japan, where the temple was scheduled to take care of missionaries who were leaving to go home and also some native Korean missionaries who had not yet received their endowments. They were doing very few sessions for the dead. Gradually they were working towards this goal, and President Slover had drawn enough people together to operate the temple and was giving them excellent training, moving gently and cautiously so that they would not be overrun before his workers were ready. We moved on to Seoul where we attended another stake conference, which was very well organized and directed. We returned to Hawaii where we visited the temple there before returning home after a 14-day journey.

Assignments took us to various parts of the globe. In March I was assigned to the Medford Oregon Stake, where we also visited the Portland Temple site. The week following we attended the Granger East Stake conference. The end of the month took us to the McGrath Canada Stake conference just the week prior to general conference. We drove our car through Montana and spent some time in the Cardston Temple before continuing on to McGrath. It was an exceptional conference with many opportunities to give blessings to those in need and also to restore blessings to repentant members who had strayed in the past. Performing that ordinance was often an assignment we received in connection with these visits. In general conference I had no special assignment except to preside at the Marriott Center during the priesthood session. In our quorum training meeting we received excellent instruction as a summary of conference in the following areas: 1) Attention to the Book of Mormon; 2) The invitation for less-active members of the Church to come back into activity; 3) Greater attention to missionary work; 4) Coming up to date with the principles of the welfare program; and 5) Personal righteousness.

April took us to the Fairfax Virginia Stake conference, where I also viewed some sites relating to the Civil War. The sessions of conference proceeded well with an excellent spirit and fine messages. In May we attended the León Mexico Stake conference and checked on operations in the Mexico City and Guatemala City Temples. I felt sustained and strengthened in my ability to teach and speak in Spanish. I am sure the Lord came to my rescue and helped me according to my needs and prayers. I also participated in the Colorado Springs Stake conference and later visited the Manti and St. George

Temples, reviewing the operations in each and making adjustments as necessary. June brought conferences in the Salt Lake Holiday Stake, the Coalville Utah Stake and the Idaho Falls Lincoln Stake. In the Lincoln stake conference, we were assigned to make a change in the stake presidency. I had a strong impression early in our interviews that Brother Weldon Pressley Bowman should be the man appointed. All the comments from those with whom we visited seemed to lead us in this direction, and about noon, Brother Hillam and I along with President Olson knelt together in prayer and asked the Lord to confirm to us the assurance that Brother Bowman should be the stake president. Brother Hillam felt very strongly, as did I, that Brother Bowman was the man, and we therefore arranged for him to come. We continued our interviews with bishops and others, more to get a feeling about the stake than to confirm our opinions about the new stake president. Later in the month we participated as much as possible in the new mission presidents' seminar held in Provo at the MTC.

In family matters, in late April I met with my brothers and sisters and our mother and enjoyed reminiscing, reaching back to our childhood and early family experiences. It seemed amazing to realize that in the brief period of my lifetime, from the times that I could remember, the family had grown from Father and Mother, sister Sarah, and myself to the following dimensions at this time—11 children, 10 husbands and wives, 72 grandchildren, and somewhere near 180 great grandchildren, with the first great-great-grandchild just recently born. Mother seemed cheerful and alert, being 93 years old, and we thoroughly enjoyed the chance to be with her. While in St. George in May, Geri and I participated with several of my brothers and sisters in a relaxing time together. Earlier in the month we rededicated the grave of my wife Mildred and our daughter Mildred Elizabeth. We had moved them from the Taylorsville Cemetery in December 1985, and many of the family gathered for the rededication. Mother; my sister Sarah and her husband, Press; my sister Pauline and her husband, Bill; and most of our children were there. We had a pleasant graveside service. Lee Ann spoke, leaving remembrances of her mother, and Glenda talked briefly about thoughts of her baby sister, who would now have been 35 years old or so. I then rededicated the grave, and we had a pleasant family gathering. Two of Mildred's sisters, Gloria and Beth, were also on hand.

We had the normal farming duties to care for, caring for horses and the land. There is a theory that General Authorities take July off as a vacation period. This of course does not take into consideration the need to be responsible for all of our assignments, and I had quite an ongoing responsibility in the Temple Department. The regular meetings are not held however, so July was much less active due to our vacation period. During the springtime, I would often take time to be with Layne in various locations as he would set traps for his work in animal damage control. In July we enjoyed a week with the family at Black's Fork in the High Uinta Mountains. We spent much of our time at the Millcreek Ranger Station with our son Layne. We were also with our son Grant's family in Fruitland, where they were looking to build a cabin. Geri and I spent some time on the road visiting the Oakland Temple to review their operation and driving through some of the back roads of California and Nevada back into Utah. While there we enjoyed contact with Jim and Trelva Wilson and Dan and Marina Harrison. Later in the month we drove to Chicago, stopping in Lyman, Wyoming, for a Pioneer Day fireside and then traveling on to Omaha for a visit with our daughter Peggy and her family. We read much of the travels and travails of the early Saints as they made their way west in the mid-1800s. We toured Nauvoo and Carthage and enjoyed very much the sensations associated with those special places in Church history. We appreciated the chance to review the operations of the Chicago Temple. Both trips were fairly extensive. We also enjoyed a missionary reunion in Farmington, Utah, with many of our former missionaries.

Our family gathered around us in mid-August and we had a marvelous evening discussing principles surrounding the family, beginning with the financial and economic aspects of family life and then discussing the upbringing and control of children. I think they were all delighted with the experience and didn't seem to wish to go home. September also brought its share of interesting events, besides the annual Labor Day breakfast with the family. There was a special commemoration at Camp Williams featuring the Governor's Day celebration, which was an honor for my brother Norman. We also enjoyed another reunion in Heber City at Norman's cabin with my brothers and sisters. Later on that month my high school class at Cyprus High School celebrated their 50th reunion. It seemed as though everyone had gotten quite a bit older as the years passed by.

August had me assigned to only one stake conference, that being the Murray West Stake, where we enjoyed time with Darlene and Noel Anderson, Geri's sister and her husband. We also participated in the reorganization of the Provo Temple presidency. Our temple presidents' seminar went very well. We also drove to Clarkston, Utah, for a special commemoration of Martin Harris. While in the area, we reviewed operations in the Logan and Ogden Temples. Two stake conferences prior to general conference occupied some of our time. One was to the Menlo Park Stake in San Francisco and the second was to the Jardin Stake conference in Torreon, Mexico. The second trip took me through Los Angeles, Mexico City, and then Dallas and Denver on the return trip. Temple visits were also included in these travels.

October general conference included the naming of Elder Joseph B. Wirthlin to the Quorum of the Twelve Apostles. Following general conference, Geri, Duella, and I drove to Boise, where we viewed the construction of the addition to that temple. Upon our return I visited the Pocatello Idaho Central Stake for conference, which was a delightful occasion, many remembering Milo and Elsbeth who used to live in that area. This conference was followed by the Lethbridge Alberta Stake conference, which allowed me to visit the temple in Cardston as well. At the end of October the Denver Temple was dedicated. It was a satisfying and rewarding time for Geri and me as we participated in those remarkable sessions. I was invited to speak at the opening session. I had struggled hard to prepare my address and was unsure of its acceptance. However, the Spirit of the Lord came to me in such a way that I was able to effectively present my remarks, which centered on the comment in my patriarchal blessing that "your name has been properly recorded in the Lamb's Book of Life never to be erased therefrom except by your own consent." I developed the theme behind this by recounting the experience of the Nephites in Zarahemla as King Benjamin brought them together to receive a new name that would never be blotted out except through transgressing. I received many commendations for the expressions I was able to make. At the end of the month, many changes were made in the leadership of the various councils of the Church, moving Elder Ashton from the chairmanship of our council to the chairmanship of the Priesthood Executive Council. Elder Perry was moved from our council to become the chairman of the Missionary Executive Council. Elder Faust remained as the only other member of our council. Elder Boyd K. Packer was named the chairman of our council and Elder Dallin H. Oaks would join him.

November proved very busy. I participated in a stake conference in Minneapolis. The meetings were very well planned, and the speeches were excellent and inspiring. I felt blessed in all my responsibilities and hoped that my visit had a good influence. I returned to help the extended family celebrate Mother's 94th birthday. It was pleasant to be with family members on such a memorable occasion. The 6th of November found us flying to Brazil for various meetings with the temple presidency and then a stake conference in the Santo Andre stake in São Paulo. I had a chance to visit with President Roger Call of the São Paulo South Mission and learned that his wife had a problem with cancer that was being overcome and that the mission was going forward well. Our travels also took us to Lima and Santiago as well as Buenos Aires to review the temple operations in those cities. We stopped in Rio de Janeiro for a few days to visit with our son Cory and his family while he was presiding over the mission there. It was a delightful and welcome break from the hurried life we led. Our grandchildren Jed and Nathan were very loving and attentive. In fact, they all were. They seemed to hang on us and were delighted with our being with them. This four-day respite from travel was much appreciated, and we relaxed and rested a good deal. All too soon we were on our way to Johannesburg, South Africa, to check on the temple there, then to Frankfurt, Germany, to observe the construction there, and finally to London to review the temple operation under President and Sister King prior to returning home for Thanksgiving Day. It was a profitable time for us.

As the Christmas season came upon us, we had several occasions to be with family and friends, sharing the spirit of the holidays, including a family Christmas party held at the home of my brother Sam and his wife, Gloria. I was assigned two stake conferences, one in Yuba City, California, and at the end of the year another one in the Palm Springs Stake. While in the Sacramento area, I also met with the missionaries of the Sacramento Mission under the direction of President and Sister Norman White. At the end of the year we flew to Phoenix to view the Mesa Temple, and from there we went to the San Diego and Los Angeles Temples in our travels. We enjoyed some time with my son Howard and his wife, Lissa, on that trip. It had been a full and rewarding year.

Passing of many friends

The year brought several sad events as people near and dear to us passed away. In March we attended the funeral in Evanston for one of our missionaries, Lee S. Barker, and members of his family, who had been killed in a tragic accident in Provo Canyon. Several of his missionary companions attended as well. During the month of April we bid farewell to Elder O. Leslie Stone, a faithful emeritus General Authority who had served for many years in the leadership of the Church. He presided over the Temple Department before I was given the assignment. It was not a sad experience due to his deteriorating health. It had been a year since his wife had passed away. We had fond memories of his life and association. In May we attended the funeral for our missionary Rodney Price, who had passed away with cancer. June brought the passing of Elder James A. Cullimore, an emeritus Seventy. His funeral allowed us to review his outstanding life. Also that month President Childers from Tahiti shared with us the passing of his daughter-in-law six months previously and her appearing to him twice shortly after her passing. He said: "I was sitting with my wife in our living room in Tahiti. We had just received word from our son that his wife had passed away, and we were, of course, anticipating that this would be the result of her illness. But as we sat there, suddenly across the room there she stood, and she spoke to me saying, 'Dad, I am all better now. Please take care of my husband and children.' And with an evidence of happiness she disappeared." September brought the sudden passing of our friend and relative J. Paul Beck, father of Ramon Beck, our son-in-law. He passed away in his sleep while he and his wife were attending an overnight outing with their ward at Strawberry Reservoir. The funeral of Brother Beck was well carried out. While the feelings of the family were tender, there was a spirit of appreciation for his life and comfort in the realization that his health, particularly the condition of his heart, was such that he could not have lived much longer. It was a blessing that he enjoyed good health and regular activity throughout his last weeks. He and his wife and his sister and her husband had recently completed a long trip to visit the historic sites of the Church. In our First Quorum of Seventy meeting in October, Elder A. Theodore Tuttle gave a most marvelous and inspired presentation concerning the Atonement of Jesus Christ. All of us were greatly and deeply touched. Brother Tuttle was not well, having been stricken with cancer, and he had been suffering and fighting with this disease. He seemed to be slipping in his physical strength and powers, and we were very worried that he might possibly not recover, which indeed was the case. He bore a marvelous spiritual testimony and seemed to carry a happy and sweet attitude about his circumstances. I felt that his teaching had been unsurpassed. In December we paid a fond farewell to him, our long-time friend, leader and colleague. The funeral was an outstanding occasion of great spiritual value. I gave the closing prayer.

1987

As 1987 dawned on us, we continued our time with Howard and Lissa and their family in San Diego prior to a stake conference in Palm Springs. From there we moved on to Los Angeles, where we visited the temple and reviewed their operations before returning to Utah. Mother had needed someone to be with her, which resulted in a lady living with her to give her constant care. I found myself constantly marveling at the busy time in which we were living. We continued to be involved with stake conferences, one in the Midvale

Fort Union Stake, where Geri and I spoke in all sessions, and another in the Pachuca Mexico City Stake, where I did my best to communicate in the Spanish language. We finished out the month with a visit to the Tahiti temple, followed by another visit to the Hawaiian temple in Laie before returning to the U.S. While in Hawaii, the temple president, President and Sister D. Arthur Haycock, took us to visit Pearl Harbor, which we had not seen before. They also took us on an extensive tour of the Polynesian Cultural Center, including the buffet they serve there. Speaking assignments took us to the Provo MTC and later to a devotional at Ricks College in Rexburg, Idaho, under the direction of President Joe J. Christensen. I had stake conference assignments at the Lynwood Washington Stake and the Poway California Stake, where I felt impressed with the direction of President Lance Wickman and the spirit of the leadership of the stake. We also attended the Orem North Stake conference later in the month. Intermixed with these travels were visits to the temples and sites in Oakland, Boise (where we held a special meeting with the temple workers, who were addressed by Elder Reeve, Elder Faust, and me), Idaho Falls, San Diego, Las Vegas, and St. George.

The month of February brought a degree of sadness with the sudden passing of President Harlan Clark of the Johannesburg South Africa Temple. Later that month Elder Henry D. Taylor, an emeritus member of the Seventy, also passed away. He had been ailing for some time. His funeral was a very impressive memorial to this dear brother.

March was a calmer month, giving me an opportunity to prepare more fully for my general conference address. In a meeting with the General Welfare Committee, we received some interesting information concerning the continued indebtedness of the people of the United States and the decline in personal savings, which were ominous statistics. Geri and I thought we ought to review these circumstances with our family. We visited the Manti Temple where we reviewed their operations, and I later attended stake conference in the Sandy Crescent Stake. I had an interview with a sister from Pittsburg who had written of some serious questions she had about the temple. She and I met in the Salt Lake Temple for an hour or so, and I believe

I was able to assist her in giving her reassurance and understanding about the things that take place in the temple. She was most grateful for the chance to visit and said that it was a shame that other women who don't understand the temple couldn't have a similar opportunity. We were able to speak quite frankly about the ceremony and the ordinances since we were meeting inside the temple.

April conference came with an assignment for me to address the membership, and I had spent extra time studying and preparing for it. I was not very much impressed with my speech, sometimes feeling even quite discouraged. We went to the office early and then attended the opening session. I was called upon to be the speaker immediately following the intermediate hymn and felt great freedom in presenting what I had prepared. I used the teleprompter but felt very comfortable in giving the address with no particular nervousness, although I had a lot of anxiety about how the speech would be accepted. Following the session I was immediately approached by nearly everyone nearby with the expression that it was the best speech I had ever made and very impressive to those who heard it. This, of course, was a great satisfaction, but I felt that somehow the Spirit of the Lord had touched me in ways that I had not understood to prepare the thoughts I presented and then lifted me with the power of the Spirit to make the presentation effective, for which I was most grateful to our Father in Heaven.

After conference, Geri and I flew to the Atlanta Temple to review their operation and proceeded on to attend the Dayton Ohio Stake conference. Later in the month Geri and I flew to Guatemala and visited the temple there, following which we returned via Mexico, eventually participating in the Mexico City Zarahemla Stake conference as well as reviewing the temple there. In the stake conference, we reorganized the stake presidency of this young adult stake. We advised the counselors, of course, that they would not be automatically considered in a new stake presidency. We proceeded to interview various leaders, members of the high council, and bishops, as well as others who did not belong to the stake. We interviewed a Brother Serrano, who served as a counselor in a nearby stake, and were definitely impressed that he was the one indicated by the Spirit to assume the leadership of the stake. We proceeded accordingly. Just prior to the general session, the former stake presidency had arranged for us to meet with about 100 young men and some young women who were recommended to serve missions. It was a tremendous gathering of young people, and Geri and I were impressed with this effort.

My brother Norman, serving as governor of the state of Utah, invited us to the Governor's Ball, which was a delightful experience. Prior to our journey to Mexico, I severely wrenched my shoulders in an accident with the pony cart, and the injury caused me some distress throughout my travels. Our son Grant completed his involvement with the Granada Corporation about the same time and began to do business on his own. I also rode out into the west desert with our son Layne on one of his jobs with the Animal Damage Control. I also had a delightful interview with Drew and Loraine Day in their preparation for their mission in São Paulo. I presented to them some principles by which they could enjoy more of the influence of the Spirit of the Lord. In May I checked on our holdings near Ferron, Utah. On Memorial Day we visited the cemetery in Millcreek, where we left some flowers at the grave of Mildred and the baby and also Geri's parents. These graves were located very close together. We also visited the graves of my grandparents interred there as well. From there we drove to the family reunion, which commemorates David's birthday held every year on Memorial Day. Mother was there and rested quietly throughout the period. Geri and I had a trip to Seattle where we visited that temple at the end of the month.

The month of May found us busy with conferences in LeGrande, Oregon, in company with Elder George R. Hill; in Calgary, Canada, where I addressed a considerable number of Spanish-speaking members coming from nearby stakes for a special fireside; and then later on in the Altoona Virginia Stake in company with Elder Lynn Sorensen. During this time I also visited the Boise Temple construction and the Seattle and Washington D.C. Temples. At the end of the month we presented the annual report of the Temple Department in the quorum meeting. Elder Scott spoke about the teaching of the doctrines of salvation, and then I took over to make a presentation that I had been preparing for several weeks. It consisted primarily of a review of the principles by which members obtain eternal life, and since we were going to discuss in some detail certain blessings and ordinances that are performed in the temple, our meeting had been arranged to be held in the Salt Lake Temple itself. We met in the women's ordinance workers instruction room. I felt I was blessed to be able to make the presentation appropriately and effectively. I received many compliments thereafter.

June found us attending stake conferences in Preston, Idaho, the Ogden East Stake, and Paul, Idaho, in company with Elder Glenn Rudd. I thought Elder Rudd and I teamed up well, and we had a good experience and response from the brethren. At the end of the month we participated with many of the Brethren in the annual mission presidents' seminar held in the MTC in Provo.

July was the happy reunion with our son Cory and his family as they completed their mission to Rio de Janeiro, Brazil. He had great success as a mission president. We gathered members of the family at the Salt Lake Airport to welcome them home. They all looked wonderful and happy to be back. We took them with us to Alpine and stopped at our home. Cory suggested that we find a place where they could settle down and spend the night. At that point we said we had better go and look at a proposed rental home, which we did. They were overwhelmed to see that the house was all organized and the furniture in place for them to move into immediately. We then returned to our place for a cookout evening of hot dogs, hamburgers, and so on, with the special enjoyment of having the family together.

Other activities during July included a temple review at the Provo Temple as well as a special event with my former Brazilian missionary companions. Practically all of them were able to come, and it turned out to be a delightful evening. We arranged to have the horses saddled, and several of the men went out for a brief ride through the fields. Shane, Cory's boy, gave me support with the horses. We noted that it might rain, so we stretched a large tarp over the table area of the lawn and continued to hold the event outside. I presided over the cooking of the chicken, and even though it did rain, we were comfortable under the tarp. We appreciated many of the girls of the family who helped out. We adjourned to the family room downstairs and heard the report of various members of the group, including the Drechsels, who had just returned from presiding in Recife; the Becks, who were leaving to preside over the São Paulo Temple; as well as a report from Lynn and Janet Sorensen. He had recently been called as a General Authority, and they were to return to Brazil as a member of the Area Presidency. It was an outstanding opportunity to be together.

Towards the end of July we enjoyed some time at Black's Fork in the High Uinta Mountains. We were involved with many activities, including hiking, horseback riding, and fishing, along with campfire stories and horseshoes. A fairly large tent city sprang up with Lee Ann, Cory, Glenda, Julie, Grant, Paulo, Layne and Duella and families. About 40–50 people had assembled in our camp.

We took an extended road trip from our home through Heber City and Vernal and then into Colorado, passing through Rifle, Vail, Denver, Littleton, Colorado Springs and returning through Montrose, Grand Junction, and Ferron, Utah. This allowed us to view the progress of the Denver Temple. It was an enjoyable journey. In August we enjoyed the annual Alpine Days events. Following a nice family breakfast, we provided various members of the family with horses to ride in the parade. Many of the grandchildren were riding different horses in the event.

August also brought a change in the name of the Church's Genealogical Department to the friendlier sounding Family History Department. Geri and I visited her cousin Clara Carter and her husband Jack. Clara was afflicted with cancer and did not feel she had much time left. Her husband, Jack, was featured in the *Church News* as being the son of one of the 1856 handcart pioneers. It seemed almost incredible that a child of one of those pioneers could still be living. Jack, of course, was over 80 years of age. We also held a temple presidents' seminar in August, which was very profitable for those couples leaving to serve in various temples around the world.

Towards the end of August, Geri and I left for an extended trip to Europe where we visited the temples in Switzerland; Frankfurt, Germany (the temple was dedicated during this trip); Freiberg, Germany; Stockholm, Sweden; and London, England. I was called upon to speak in the second session of the Frankfurt Temple dedication. I had prepared my speech to be read in German and accomplished it satisfactorily; at least there were many who commented on how well I was able to handle German. I felt comfortable and thought that my pronunciation was better than some others.

As part of the dedication experience, many of the General Authorities were able to move about, taking short tours or proceeding on their way for other assignments and destinations. We decided that Brothers Metcalf, Foster, and Marshall would accompany us on a drive to Wiesbaden and then north to the Rhine River gorge. It turned out to be a beautiful day, and we thoroughly enjoyed driving through the countryside. I had been there years before with Elder and Sister Wirthlin, but I again felt it was one of the beautiful sights in Germany. As the river winds through the mountains, there are castles at nearly every turn and a tremendous amount of river traffic in barges and passenger and sightseeing ships. We stopped along the way to do a little souvenir shopping. We drove past the Lorelei Rock, and I recited to the group the legend of the Lorelei, which they had never heard before. We drove all the way through the gorge to the city of Koblenz, which is an expansive and spread out industrial city. We returned on the freeway to Frankfurt, taking about an hours' time.

On our way back to the U.S., we participated in the organization and conference of Setubal Portugal Stake. Elder Harold Hillam joined us, and we came ultimately to the conclusion that President Melo, the district president, should be called to preside over the stake. We extended to him his call and asked him to select his counselors. We later met with the new stake presidency and worked with them over the selection of members of the high council and bishops. This worked out very well inasmuch as practically everyone who had been serving in the district and branches was called back again to similar service, although many of the positions had been adjusted. President Melo was a convert of about eight or nine years; he had lived most of his life in Angola and was back in Portugal as one of the "Retornados," or those who migrated back to Portugal after the takeover of Angola and Mozambique by native governments.

Early September took us to the Gillette Wyoming Stake conference. Sadly, Sister Camilla Kimball passed away in late September. Prior to general conference, we attended a four-hour training meeting under the direction of the Quorum of the Twelve. This was one of the most impressive and historic meetings I have attended. We were given some marvelous instruction concentrating on the concept of what a Seventy was rather than what he did. I think we were all deeply inspired. Shortly after general conference we participated in the preview of the Church-produced movie *How Rare a Possession*, the story of an Italian convert and his quest to find the truth. It was an impressive presentation, and we thoroughly enjoyed the experience as well as the association with members of the quorum and their wives and children. Lee Ann and Richard came, and inasmuch as the film featured the experiences of an Italian man, it was especially attractive to Richard, whose ancestry is 100 percent Italian.

Geri and I flew to Bogotá, Columbia, and attended the mission presidents' seminar there. We entered Brazil via Manaus and went on to Porto Alegre, where we participated in the regional conference and the Porto Alegre North Stake conference. We also participated in another mission presidents' seminar at the Iguaçu Falls. This meeting was carried on in a room in the hotel just above the main stairway, which happened to be the very same room where the first mission presidents' conference in all of South America was held (Geri and I attended that conference in 1959 with Elder Spencer W. Kimball and his wife). We enjoyed a good visit with Drew and Loraine Day, who presided in the São Paulo North Mission and who had been close to us over the years. President Day told us how he had tried to make some adjustments in having his missionaries visit the new members in order that they would not be lost, but there had been some objection on the part of the Area President to this process. I reassured him that it would all be worked out in the seminar, and this turned out to be true. Elder Ballard made some strong comments about the necessity of having the missionaries follow through on visits to new members and then asked me to make a further exposition of this concept, which I did for about 30 minutes, emphasizing that the missions have finally joined the Church and that missionaries are one of the great resources to strengthen the wards and stakes and to carry the members across to full activity after baptism. I explained that it was foolishness for missionaries, mission presidents, stake presidents, and others to stand and argue whose responsibility it was when a poor new member was being left to languish and dwindle in unbelief because nobody would agree to take the responsibility for them. This instruction was very well received by all the mission presidents and I think by the Area President as well. He could not have missed the emphasis that was given, and I was sure that President Day felt reassured and vindicated in his wise program to strengthen the Church.

We concluded our trip to São Paulo for another regional conference. We were touched with the enormity of the crowd and the tremendous advance that had taken place in Brazil over the years of our experience respecting the growth and strength of the Church. We were overwhelmed by the great number of people who reached out to us as our former associates and companions, our former missionaries, and the former missionaries who served under Cory, all of whom were so anxious to give their greeting and make contact. It was a glorious time to be together.

At the end of September I also attended the Lovell Wyoming Stake conference. We continued to attend stake conferences throughout the closing months of the year. We went to Wilmington, Delaware, where we focused on the concepts of working with less-active people and recognizing the worth of their souls. We also reviewed in some detail the difference between administration and ministering and the importance of all members of the Church going to the temple for their ordinances. We met a large number of people with whom we had acquaintance and felt the affinity of being with these choice members. A conference in Thatcher, Arizona, brought us close to President and Sister Layton of the temple presidency and whose son Robert and son-in-law Darrel Bethea had served with us in Brazil. We felt very much the affinity of this family. At the Concord New Hampshire Stake conference, we reorganized the presidency. We soon came to recognize three of the brethren who should be considered. After some earnest prayer and consultation together, the regional representative and I agreed that the Lord seemed to be guiding us to the appointment of Brother Gary S. Carter as the president. We invited him and his wife to come, and he accepted the appointment and his wife sustained him. She was the stake Relief Society president and a lovely wife and mother. My last conference of 1987 was in the Dallas East stake. We also visited temples in Washington, D.C.; Mesa; Chicago; Dallas; Manti; and Provo.

Thanksgiving Day came upon us with the usual celebration and enjoyment. We had prepared two turkeys, and I helped Geri stuff and put them on for roasting, one in the oven and one in the roaster. She and the girls spent the rest of the morning working diligently while I seemed to relax. Lee Ann and Cory came with their families, as did Paulo, and this gave us a sizeable group with which to celebrate. Some others of the family dropped in during the evening, so we had a houseful all day long. In other activities, we gave our daughter Lee Ann a special blessing regarding her hearing concerns, and it proved to be a sweet occasion. We enjoyed a delightful evening with my brothers and sisters and their spouses. Mother was also present. We had an evening of visiting, feasting, and then listening to Mother's counsel and advice. Her voice was failing and she had a hard time speaking, but she exhorted us all to remain faithful to the principles of the gospel and to bring up our families righteously. We had been told many times that we have one of the greatest mothers to be found in the world. She has frequently been recognized as one of the truly noble women of this dispensation. Several years ago Elder James E. Faust made specific mention of her in an address he gave at Brigham Young University, which has been widely remembered and quoted.

The end of the year brought another loss with the passing of our dear friend and colleague Franklin D. Richards. His funeral was a fine expression of his life of dedication and service. December brought a slowdown of activity as we enjoyed time with the family during the holidays. I did speak to over 500 temple workers in the Manti Temple. It was a beautiful setting. The workers were all dressed in white, and a most spiritual atmosphere permeated the meeting. I spoke of the Savior in connection with the principles of the gospel and the doctrines of salvation provided by Him. I made reference to His birth, reading extensively from the scriptures, quoting from the first and second chapters of Luke and then concentrating on the fifth and sixth chapters of the Book of Moses which have so much affinity with the temple endowment. I referred then to the vision of glory in the 76th section of the Doctrine and Covenants and concluded with references for the redemption of the dead in the 138th section of the Doctrine and Covenants. In some ways it could have been considered a rather heavy presentation, but I thought it was appropriate to the subject and to the period of the Christmas season. I believe those assembled accepted it well, and I felt blessed in my delivery.

Evidently someone in the Alpine community felt it to be a badge of honor to knock over the Bangerter mailbox as it had happened with great frequency. Duella helped me repair it a couple of times. Our Christmas was a joyful and delightful occasion. Many of our children paid us visits, for which we were grateful. Our time was taken up with riding horses and visiting around the fire, mostly enjoying one another's company.

1988

Early in January we met with the leadership committee of the Twelve, including Elders Faust, Maxwell, and Ballard. Regular meetings with this committee developed into a choice spirit of unity and harmony between the Presidency of the Seventy and members of the Quorum of the Twelve, surpassing anything we had felt over the years. Our deliberations and decisions were powerful and were carried forth to the First Presidency in regular fashion. We soon became involved with a flurry of stake conferences, beginning in the Orem Central Stake, where we found very strong attendance. This was followed by Geri and me driving to the Kirtland New Mexico Stake, where a large number of Indian branches formed a portion of the membership. The members of these branches did not attend in great numbers. Our third conference was to the Fremont California South Stake adjacent to the Oakland Temple. Close friends in attendance included my missionary companion, George Angerbauer and his wife and Jim and Trelva Wilson, who had served with us as a counselor in the mission presidency in Brazil. We also reviewed the operations of the Oakland Temple prior to this conference. At the end of the month we met with the Salt Lake Mount Olympus Stake.

In February we attended more conferences, including the Salt Lake Hunter West Stake, where we reorganized the presidency. Richard Winder, the regional representative, and I entered into the process of interviewing to become acquainted with the leaders of the stake. The outgoing stake president had some very definite ideas about those who should be considered and included all of the high council and the bishops in the interview process. I asked him if there were any others outside of that group who ought to be included, and he said, "No, there are no more." As we talked with the various brethren, however, one of them in particular mentioned a former bishop, Theron Rose, with a good report, and I sent word out from our interview room that we would like to have him come in and visit with us. Later on, various others of the brethren we were interviewing mentioned others who might be included. I consulted with the stake president on those others who had been mentioned but did not do so about Brother Rose. In each case, the president pointed out obvious reasons why these other brethren would not be considered, and so they were not invited to come. I am confident that if I had consulted with him before inviting Brother Rose to come, he would have given me reasons why he should not have been interviewed as well. In any case, Elder Winder and I came to the conclusion that the first counselor would be the appropriate man to be the stake president. Brother Rose came in for an interview after we had fairly well come to our conclusion. We were, however, impressed with him and checked up a little on his record as a seminary teacher and received a good report. I was now somewhat undecided about how we would make the decision, but we determined to pray to ask the Lord for confirmation in our selection of the first counselor. As I prayed, I had no special impression and had suggested to the Lord that it was our intention to appoint him unless we were told otherwise. Elder Winder then offered a prayer. During his prayer, the surging impression came very strongly to me that Brother Rose should be the stake president; as we arose from our prayer, I said to Elder Winder, "It is Brother Rose who should be sustained." Elder Winder agreed with me. We therefore called him in to advise him of his appointment.

He then told us that about two weeks earlier he had felt impressions of the possibility that he would be called to be the stake president. These feelings he had tried to submerge, but he accepted his calling with great humility. We met with his wife as well and found her to be a very capable and impressive person, both of them with strong testimonies.

Geri and I next went to the Eugene Oregon Stake conference, visiting the Portland Temple construction along the way. In that conference I was impressed to call on a young man who had recently returned from his mission in Germany. His name was Elder Singer. It developed that he was a convert to the Church of about three years. He had served his mission as the only member of his family. He had a great insight into the responsibilities he carried for his family and for accomplishing his purposes in life. It was very impressive to all who were there. Towards the end of the month, Geri and I attended the San Diego Temple groundbreaking ceremony, stopping in Las Vegas to review the temple operation there as well. In San Diego, we enjoyed a magnificent choir at the ceremony. The meeting itself was rather brief, consisting of short remarks by myself and Don McArthur as well as remarks by President Monson and President Benson. President Monson was then asked to give the dedicatory prayer, and then we joined in the groundbreaking exercise with about 20 shovels being distributed to the various stake presidencies.

March took us to the Tucson East Stake, at which time Geri and I visited the Mesa Temple and then enjoyed a short diversion to Benson, St. David, and Tombstone, then over the mountains to Elfrida and Douglas before returning to Mesa and home. It was a time to recall nostalgic days of my time in the military. Much of this trip was in company with Roland and Mae Hamblin, relatives of Geri who lived close by. The next week found us in Washington, D.C., visiting the temple there and attending the Philadelphia Stake conference. It also gave us an opportunity to view some points of interest regarding the early foundation of our nation. We returned via Omaha and Winter Quarters, where we visited our daughter Peggy and her family. The following week I had an assignment to the Matamoros Mexico Stake conference, once again giving me an opportunity to use the Spanish language. In other affairs I was asked to speak at the Provo MTC and was delighted to once again rub shoulders with the missionaries. We spoke for about 45 minutes, and my remarks centered on the importance of having a testimony. In meetings with the First Presidency and the Twelve, it was determined that women married to non-member husbands could receive their endowment if their husband gave his consent. This was a major policy adjustment.

In personal matters, our little pony Spook escaped through the fence and was hit by a car, losing his life and causing sorrow among the family members. About this time, my brother-in-law Prescott Hardy passed away following a lingering illness. His funeral was a sweet remembrance for all. My brother Norman once again invited us to the Governor's Ball, which was a delightful experience for Geri and me. April conference brought about some changes and adjustments normal for the growing church. One included the call of our former missionary Wilford Cardon as a regional representative. In the evening following Sunday's sessions, we gathered all of our married children who were in the area and had a discussion and review of the teachings that had been presented in the conference. We gave particular attention to our concerns over problems in the families of our children. They seemed to rejoice in this experience and the opportunity to be together and to talk of spiritual things. Later on that month our son Paulo graduated from the BYU Law School with the honors associated with that marked accomplishment.

The stake conference assignments continued throughout the month of April with a conference in Gunnison, Utah, followed by another in Manassa, Colorado. I took with me our son Cory and his son Chad. We spent the night in Bayfield, Colorado, with my two sisters-in-law, Ora Mae and Ruth. The drive over the mountains of Colorado were exhilarating both going and coming. President Bagwell of that stake operated a fairly substantial cattle ranching program. The people in that stake are generally rural in their outlook and activity. They were mainly descendants from immigrants from Georgia who came in the 1880s to settle the valley. The general session was very well attended with 54 percent of the membership in attendance. This was the highest attendance I remember. Towards the end of the month I had another stake conference in the Idaho Falls Ammon Stake, and we took advantage of our visit to review operations in the Idaho Falls Temple. In our quorum meeting we had an outstanding experience as we listened to Brother Arnold Friberg, who presented to us the new painting he created of Joseph Smith praying in the Sacred Grove. His remarks were profound and very reassuring about his faith and testimony and the purposes he achieves in the magnificent pieces of art he produces. He talked of the truth that his paintings represent—how they offset the adverse influences of irreverent people and carry a great element of faith and testimony. It was a moving experience for all of us and a great reaffirmation of Brother Friberg's testimony and faith in the gospel.

In May, Wilford Cardon came in for an extended visit. He wanted to discuss his responsibilities as a regional representative, and we focused on the basic principles taught in the mission field. Later I visited the Lafayette Illinois Stake conference, followed by another in the Arvada Colorado Stake. We felt that this stake was accomplishing more in the right direction than most any stake we had visited. They were certainly following through in trying to bring more people to prepare for the temple. They seemed to be on top of every part of their assignment.

Also during May we received word that President Marion G. Romney, a great mentor and friend, had passed away. His funeral was beautiful and most appropriate for this choice man. We had some excellent experiences with him, and the funeral brought us many memories and much appreciation for his great and inspiring leadership.

Interspersed throughout the month were visits to the Chicago, Denver, Ogden, and Mesa Temples. We found that it seemed to be the habit and pattern of many leaders in temples, missions, and such that as soon as they arrive, they want to reorganize and refurbish everything. The attitude we were trying to promote was that the temples should be accepted as they are and that those who are called to work with them adapt to conditions as they exist rather than trying to reconstruct the temple. In meetings with the Temple Executive Committee, with the wives of the General Authorities present, several comments were made concerning the wearing of fancy bridal dresses in the temple. Adjustments to policy were formulated therefrom.

Also in May we made preparations to honor my brother David's 49th birthday, and a family party was held at the Granger Stake Center. Mother was able to come, and we all gathered around to visit with her. David was there, of course, and most of our children joined with us. It was a pleasant and happy occasion.

June saw us in the Kearns Western Hills stake and later to the Huntington, Utah stake. We spent some good time on the road during these events. Around my 70th birthday a large gathering of our children provided a presentation of various episodes of my life, including some of my childhood escapades and precocious experiences, my call to serve a mission, my experience in the military, my marriages to Mildred and also to Geri, and various episodes of family life including the experiences in Brazil and in Portugal. It was at times touching and often hilarious, and I deeply appreciated the interest and feeling of devotion that the family presented. Julie and Ramon had provided a video or slide presentation picturing various circumstances in our long history. It was a little shocking to be reminded that I had reached the age of 70, which is said to be three score and ten years and by some standards the expected term of mortal life. I, however, had come this far in good health and strength—not able, of course, to do all the things I could do in my youth, but I still felt in command of my faculties and physical powers to be able to carry on a rather normal life. To be surrounded by such a great swarm of children and their companions and the grandchildren brought an overwhelming feeling of fulfillment and satisfaction. Towards the end of the month we enjoyed participating in the annual mission presidents' seminar at the Provo MTC.

With July reserved mostly for vacation and family time, such as the annual Fourth of July breakfast with nearly 50 people coming, we nonetheless did occasional assignments such as moving our offices form the sixth floor to the fourth floor in Church Office Building and making them more presentable. I participated in the dedication of the Jordan Park Peace Gardens and also spoke at a special sunrise service on the Logan Temple grounds for the Alpine Stake youth conference. Many of our family participated in that conference. While in Logan we reviewed the temple operation there. On July 24 I spoke at the LDSSA fireside in Salt Lake City. The next day we took to the road again and drove south through Kanab, Jacob's Lake, and on to Mesa. We enjoyed the Mesa Temple and also had a reunion with some of our missionaries as part of the trip. We returned through Las Vegas, visiting the temple site there, and through St. George, where we also visited that temple. At the end of the month I spoke at the multiregional single adult conference in Provo.

We also enjoyed a special time with the family in the High Uinta Mountains with all the accompanying activities. One day as we were making our way up the canyon in the truck through the rocks, I bounced over a rock and hit the gas tank, which then sprang a leak. We were prepared to put a container underneath to catch the gas when Geri suggested that if we rubbed soap in the crack it would seal up. Cory immediately took a bar of soap that Geri happened to bring along and rubbed it in and the leak stopped. This was something of a miracle for us all. Later on during our stay, Cory and Grant decided to put up a swing between two trees. They mounted a cross pole between the trees and then tied a rope to it. I was assisting them. After we got it well installed and tied a cross piece on the bottom to sit on, Grant decided to test it by holding on with his two hands. As he swung out over an edge, he lost his grip on the cross piece and fell about six feet, somewhat out of control, landing heavily on his side, arm, and head. We were worried that it might have caused him some damage. Cory and I rushed to him. He seemed to be knocked out and began to groan and moan. We turned him over on his back and Cory cradled his head. We found that he had hit several places on his head. He soon opened his eyes however, and we realized that he was not totally unconscious. It took him 15–20 minutes to reorient himself. Cory and I gave him a blessing. His injuries did not seem to be unduly critical, but Cleadonna, his wife, was very concerned and wanted to rush him down the canyon to the doctor. We assured her that the best thing he could do was to rest and recover from the shock rather than dashing about in an automobile, so we spent the rest of the day taking care of him. He recovered pretty well and was up and about in the evening, but it took him some time to get over the shock. He had a fairly comfortable night's rest. Geri patched up the scratches and cuts in a satisfactory way and gave him aspirin and other pain relief. It put a real damper on the day's activities although we continued our activities in camp.

Part of the normal events in August consisted of participation in Alpine Days. Several of the boys were involved in a "Ride and Tie" race, where two runners alternate between riding a horse and running. Unfortunately some of them got lost on the track and ended up arriving at the destination two hours later. Other events included a five-kilometer run and a two-and-a-half-kilometer walk for the girls. August also took us to the Boise Central Stake for a conference and then a delightful seminar for new temple presidents.

September took me back on the road with a conference in the Bountiful Heights Stake, where several of the extended family participated with us. This was followed by a journey to Guatemala City, where we reviewed the temple operation there, and then to a stake conference in the Mexico City Churubusco Stake. It kept me practicing my Spanish. I later attended the Fredericksburg Virginia Stake conference and visited the Washington D.C. Temple as well.

As a prelude to general conference, the international Area Presidencies gave reports during our meeting. My impression was that they had made tremendous progress in adjusting to their leadership over the past two years. They appeared to be in touch with the special needs and concerns of the Church and were in a position to carry forth with power the progress of the gospel in all its phases. This led up to general conference, in which I spoke. My feelings about giving a conference address were always anxious and reserved. I often felt that the substance was not strong and was most anxious that the Lord would bless me. Of course I prayed earnestly that He would allow His Spirit to touch what I had to say. I felt that this request was fulfilled with great effect since following my address, President Monson and President Benson both shook my hand and commended me. Following the conference many people commented on how well it was received. Elder Hanks gave me a special expression of commendation, which I felt was unusual coming from him who gives so many outstanding speeches.

In October I had a couple of stake conferences, one in Portland Oregon and another in the San Antonio East Stake. I visited the Seattle Temple on the first trip. I also accompanied the engineers of the Salt Lake Temple as we inspected various portions of the temple, including its construction, the foundation, and the towers. It was an interesting experience for me.

On October 14, Geri and I celebrated our 35th wedding anniversary. I reflected on what a marvelous period this had been—half my life married to Geri. I felt that our experiences and achievements had been fabulous. The way in which we built our family together is one of the miracles of our life, and we felt richly blessed by them all. We reminisced about the wonderful memories we had of that day 35 years earlier when we were married in the Salt Lake Temple, when my mother and father hosted a little afternoon luncheon including her parents, and when we departed on our honeymoon leaving the three children with my mother and going for a week's vacation to California.

On October 30, Duella and her boyfriend, Lonnie Williams, sat down and told us of his desire to marry Duella and asked for our approval, which we readily gave. We then spent a little bit of time discussing the arrangements for their marriage, which they expected to hold near the middle of latter part of December.

November opened on a sad note as our dear friend and Granger neighbor Iris B. Morgan passed away. He had served as my counselor and had followed me as stake president many years ago. His funeral was a pleasant gathering with many close friends and former associates. Shortly after this event, my brother Norman was re-elected as governor of the state of Utah. In participating with him in this event, Geri and I went down to the Little America Hotel, where all the faithful supporters and party members were gathered, and we watched the returns coming in for a while on the television. The reports were almost absolutely even between Ted Wilson, the Democrat, and Norman. We returned home, and at 2:30 we arose and listened to a news announcement that indicated that Norman would win. This of course left us with a very comfortable feeling. Later in the month we enjoyed some time with Norman and Colleen in their apartment in St. George with other good friends from our years in Granger. Our Thanksgiving feast brought several of our children together, and we had an enjoyable time.

I attended stake conferences in Naperville, Illinois, where I felt a powerful spirit and warm atmosphere, better than usual in my experience. I later attended the North Hollywood California Stake conference. We also paid a visit to the Los Angeles Temple and spent some time with our son Howard and his family in San Diego. As we began to close out the year, we attended the Las Vegas Sunrise Stake conference, taking some of the back roads to and from Las Vegas, visiting friends and family along the way. In a temple meeting we were informed by the First Presidency that stake presidents would no longer be invited by the Church to attend general conference. They were still free to come, but would have to do so on their own. Regional representatives would attend conference each April in connection with instruction given to all General Authorities. I was asked to speak at a BYU MBA fireside as well as a fireside in our former stake in Granger. We also took a couple of trips in the car to Strawberry and then to Ferron to check on our holdings there. The major event of the month for us was the marriage of our daughter Duella to Lonnie Williams of Vernal, Utah. They were a sweet, happy couple, and I was honored to seal them in the temple.

We enjoyed the Christmas season surrounded by loved ones. It gave us occasion to reflect on some of the achievements of the year. First of all, no doubt, was the marriage of our daughter Duella and the privilege of having all of our family together with us in the temple. We felt that they were generally going in the right direction and were faithful and devoted to the gospel, and we hoped our leadership had been effective in their behalf. We had not traveled overseas to visit temples this year like we had in the past, although I had been to Mexico several times and also to the Guatemala Temple. We had, however, visited many of the temples in the United States and had choice experiences in visiting stake conferences. Geri went with me whenever it was possible to drive, and on some occasions we flew together. We gathered at various family members' homes to celebrate the coming of the New Year.

1989

The year 1989 began with the inauguration of my brother Norman as the governor of the state of Utah for his second term, which was a source of satisfaction for our entire family. I thought Norman did very well in his address, and everyone seemed content that the election was over and he was still in the governor's chair. Two days later I was in the hospital following a violent allergic reaction to some medication. It caused difficulty in breathing, and I was taken to the hospital in an ambulance. I was released the next day. On another personal matter, we arranged for Duke Cowley and Wilford Cardon to assume the Sandy Subdivision financing, which greatly relieved us of that pressure.

In ecclesiastical assignments, I attended a stake conference in Albuquerque, New Mexico, where we reorganized the stake presidency. After several interviews, it became evident that the second counselor, Brother Pixton, would be an excellent leader. We also felt comfortable with two bishops we had interviewed. We felt it was wisdom and approved of our Heavenly Father to call Brother Robert Pixton, so we proceeded to interview him and his wife, extending to him the calling. He nominated as his counselors the other two strong candidates we had interviewed, which brought us great satisfaction. Our next conference was in Mission Viejo, California, where Geri found a dear friend from her nurse training days, and we renewed acquaintance with Burt Yancy, one of our missionaries from Brazil.

Our final conference for the month was in Pocatello, Idaho, where we encountered our former missionaries Wayne and Ruth Millward who lived in that stake. We also reviewed operations in the Idaho Falls Temple. As we departed from the Millward home, which is on a high hill southeast of town, we made a sharp turn on the loose gravel and sand on the road, and I was unable to avoid a pickup truck coming up the other direction. We bumped into the truck, which damaged the hood and headlight of our car. It took us an hour to straighten out the difficulties, including a visit from the sheriff to work up the accident report. The man whose truck we hit lived just around the corner, his name being Winterbottom, and we spent some time visiting in his home. Wayne Millward came down from his home when he learned of the accident and assisted us in getting everything cleared. We later learned that his wife felt that our accident was providential in that the Winterbottom family was inactive in the Church and this gave them an entree into their home. The Winterbottoms were impressed with the ways in which we responded to the problem, and altogether we felt like we had made friends for Ruth and Wayne.

Later on we were able to attend our own stake conference in Alpine. Each weekend was filled up with the associated meetings, one of which was with Earl Monson and Allen Erekson on a discussion of new temples that could eventually be announced. We had a sweet, spiritual moment talking about the design of temples and the beauties of those that had been built. Our comments centered on the idea that the most striking of all the temples in the Church were the temples in Salt Lake; Washington, D.C.; Manti; Arizona; and Hawaii, the latter being largely because of its beautiful setting.

February took us on another series of interesting visits around the globe. I began with a stake conference in East Millcreek in Salt Lake City, where I felt we were richly blessed by a good spiritual experience in the conference that showed the Lord was interested in us and assisted us according to our need.

Shortly thereafter Geri and I departed for the Orient. We stopped in Tokyo and then went on to the Philippines, where we held a regional conference on the Bataan Peninsula at Dagupan. We then visited Taiwan, where we carefully reviewed the temple operation and were shown some of the interesting points in the city by the temple president and his wife, President and Sister Hyer. From there we proceeded on to Tokyo again and to Osaka for a mission presidents' seminar and a regional conference there. Elder Ballard asked me to lead out in the priesthood leadership meeting where I covered three major concerns: 1) The missions and stakes needed to work well together, but they were not taking care of the new converts nor ordaining brethren to the priesthood; 2) There was a tremendous backlog of prospective elders and very little progress made to prepare them for the priesthood; 3) There was a need to do more to prepare people to go to the temple. Following the regional conference, Geri and I flew to Seoul, Korea, where we reviewed the temple operation there. We returned to Honolulu and Laie to visit that temple and enjoyed being hosted by my brother Blauer and his wife, Bessie, who were teaching at the college. They even took us snorkeling for some recreation. We returned home via Los Angeles. It had been a lengthy but eventful trip with much interest in these foreign lands.

March seemed to continue with the same pace. I attended stake conferences in Torreón, Mexico, having an opportunity to visit the Mexico City Temple en route. We held two sessions of conference in Torreón and felt a sweet spirit with the members gathered together. Geri and I traveled to the Denver Arapahoe Stake by driving through meaningful places in Wyoming such as Ft. Bridger, Lyman, and Rawlins and returning through Grand Junction, Colorado; Green River, Utah; and Price, Utah.

The next week Geri and I flew to Guatemala City, where we reviewed the temple operation there, then to San Salvador and to Camayaguela, Nicaragua, for a stake conference and to reorganize the stake presidency. In this experience, we interviewed brethren over a period of three hours. Certain men came to our attention, including Brother Sierra of the high council and Bishop Duarte of one of the wards. We felt impressed to call Brother Duarte, and upon extending to him the calling, he selected as one of his counselors, Brother Sierra, who incidentally was a brother to the retiring stake president. We were somewhat surprised and almost shocked to learn that President Duarte, who had been a bishop for five years, was only 27 years old. He was very highly spoken of and appreciated by the members of his ward and those in the stake who knew of him. Our daughter Julie later reported the following about President Duarte:

"Elder Duarte told a story of Daddy traveling to Honduras and calling Elder Duarte to be a stake president when he was 27 years old. He said he had a hard time thinking that he was the president, and Daddy said he definitely had the call to be the president. Once he had received his call, Daddy told him he needed to go in a room and pray for counselors. He said, 'I have the names of your two counselors in my pocket.' Elder Duarte said, 'Well, just give them to me and I will tell you if they are men I like and can work with.' Daddy said, 'No, you have to go get your own counselors.' He said he went in a room and prayed. When he came out he said, 'I have the name of two men, but I'm not sure if they are the same ones you have.' He gave Daddy the names, and when Daddy pulled out his paper, he said, 'These are exactly the same ones,' and told him that was a sign that he really was the stake president. He said it was very empowering for him. It changed his life and the way he operated as a priesthood leader."

At the time of his call to be stake president, he and his wife were poor students, and his wife was in the hospital having a baby. Elder Perry released President Duarte after he had served for 14 years. The stake had been divided twice, and President Duarte was always moved to the new stake, so his time for release never showed up on the computer. When he was released as stake president he was called as a mission president. Later he was called as an Area Seventy. He and his wife were both successful attorneys and have four grown children now. We returned home through Houston. Towards the end of the month we received the new *General Handbook of Instructions*, an item that had been in process for several years.

April general conference developed into an outstanding conference with great inspiration. The Second Quorum of Seventy was organized due to the growth in the Church. I was sustained once again as a member of the Presidency—both quorums come under the same Presidency. My brother-in-law Richard Lindsay was called as a member of the Second Quorum and assigned to South Africa in the Area Presidency there. I assisted President Hinckley in setting apart some of those newly called, including Richard. We were very proud of him.

The day following conference, we visited the rest home where mother had been staying for the last several weeks. We visited with her, although she did not respond very well and could scarcely speak at all. We helped her sit up, and she eventually went to sleep in the chair. After two hours or so we left. Geri and I returned a little later and found Mother sleeping quietly and beautifully and felt her special, angelic spirit, not knowing that this would be our last moment to view her while she tarried on this earth. The next evening we received word that our mother, Isabelle Bawden Bangerter, had just passed away. She was in her 96th year and had been without Dad for 25 years. It is hard to express the feelings one has at the loss of a parent. I did not attend the training meeting the next day but went to the mortuary where I met with Sarah, Pauline, Richard Lindsay, and Sam to make arrangements for Mother's funeral. We were honored that many dignitaries participated in her funeral service, including her son Norman, the governor; a son and son-in-law General Authorities, Richard Lindsay and myself; as well as President Gordon B. Hinckley of the First Presidency. The speakers included Mother's four sons and President Hinckley. William Jensen sang a closing solo, "O My Father," and prayers were offered by Richard Lindsay and Gary Weaver. The service and interment were sweet and rewarding to all members of the family. While we were subdued in our thoughts and feelings, the members of the family did not feel any deep sense of sorrow. We recognized that Mother's life had been rich and full, that she had lived the full measure of her days and had worn out her body to the point where she was unable to speak with any force, although we were able to maintain communication with her until the final moments before she died. All of us felt the deep need she had to be released from her physical weakness, and her passing away left us a feeling of peace and well-being as well as an attitude of rejoicing that she had finally returned to the realms of eternal life and had rejoined our father, her own mother from whom she had been separated for nearly 90 years, her daughters Glenneth and Mildred, and so many others with whom mortality had bound her with wonderful experiences and tender loving feelings.

Two days after mother had passed away, another brother-in-law, Victor Milo Hansen passed away as well, leaving my sister Elsbeth a widow. Following mother's funeral, we all left for Washington State, where we participated in remembering Milo. We arrived after dark, and Elsbeth of course received us with very tender feelings. Milo had been ill for a year and a half, suffering with serious problems with his back and legs, finally developing a rapid cancer that carried him off in a matter of two months. The funeral service included remarks from the bishop, and I became the concluding speaker. I attempted to relate our close association with this family to events in connection with the gospel and the history of the Church, referring to the deep and devoted background of Milo's family, including that of his grandfather, an immigrant from Denmark and a pioneer in Utah and Idaho. Milo and Elsbeth's sons offered the prayers at the closing of the casket, the funeral service, and the dedication of the grave. The children were deeply touched in his passing as he was only 67 years old. I felt that they were an outstanding family with devoted and faithful lives and real accomplishments in their education and careers. Since we had rented a Church van to carry many of my brothers and sisters and spouses to the funeral, we visited the Seattle Temple, reviewing their operations and doing the same in the Portland Temple. Returning home, we felt fairly drained due to the passing of these two great people in our lives.

Later in the month we enjoyed some time with Norman and Colleen in their apartment in St. George with other good friends from our years in Granger. Our Thanksgiving feast brought several of our children together, and we had an enjoyable time.

The last three weeks of April found us again in stake conferences in Hermosillo, Mexico (Pitic Stake), followed by the South Bend Indiana Stake conference, where I was accompanied by my brother-in-law Richard Lindsay, recently called as a Seventy. The stake president there was Gabriel Kemeny from Brazil, and we had known each other for many years. He had moved to the U.S. several years ago and had recently been called as the stake president. The Kemenys eventually moved to Alpine and became our neighbors. (He had been one of the first branch presidents called in Brazil when we served as mission president there.) My last stake conference of the month was in the Fairmont West Virginia Stake. The speeches were outstanding, and in the midst of my remarks, as we were dealing with the topic of the love of the Savior and the Atonement, I asked Brother Flannigan, who had conducted one of the choir numbers, if he would sing the song "How Great Thou Art." He did this with great ability and beautiful interpretation, and it left a strong spiritual impression on the congregation. I also spoke at the MTC at the end of the month. I

felt blessed in my remarks, and Geri made some excellent preliminary remarks, which I think helped to introduce us. We attended
the graduation of our son Layne from BYU and were invited to the
graduation banquet along with Elder and Sister Robert Backman,
who also had a daughter graduating. Duella graduated from BYU in
August ceremonies.

In May we participated in the Ashton Idaho Stake conference
and visited the Idaho Falls Temple in connection with our journey.
We then left for Brazil for a regional conference in Brasília, visiting
the temples in Buenos Aires and Santiago on the way. It was a delight
to be back in our beloved Brazil once again. While in Brazil, we were
informed of my pending release from active General Authority status
effective in the October conference. At that point I would be named
an emeritus General Authority. Dean Larsen was assigned to replace
me in my assignments. This portended a change in our lifestyle that
we had not anticipated. All of this, of course, was kept confidential
by Geri and me. It was nevertheless something of a letdown for us to
have word of our release. I was informed later on that I would remain
in my position until the first of October.

We went with Brother and Sister Hélio and Nair Camargo to visit Brother Walter Spat, who was critically ill in the Albert Einstein
Hospital. We knew he was suffering from cancer. His family had
requested that we come, and all members of his family were there.
Brother Spat was breathing very heavily through his mouth and
struggling with great discomfort. We did not think he recognized us,
but Elder Camargo and I administered to him, feeling as we did so
that he probably would not survive this illness. The next day Elder
Camargo and I went back to the hospital, where we gave another
blessing to our dear friend Walter Spat. He continued to struggle
for breath and seemed uncomfortable. We felt he recognized us as
we gave him the blessing. We thereafter gave a blessing to his wife.
Our feeling was that he would not recover, and so we blessed her
with comfort and peace in her heart. We learned the next day that
he had passed away in the night. I called Elder Faust, advising him
of Brother Spat's death, and received the responsibility to convey
the greetings of the First Presidency, the Quorum of the Twelve,

and others to Brother Spat's family. The funeral was brief, consisting of remarks by the bishop, reading of an obituary and a life story by Oscar Erbolato, and then remarks from me. I gave a resume of our experience with Brother Spat and of the great achievements he had made as a pioneer of the Church in Brazil, being the first stake president in South America, a patriarch, temple worker, sealer, artist, furniture maker, loving husband and father, and a great follower of Jesus Christ.

As we concluded our visit in Brazil, we were invited to the Campinas Mission under the direction of President and Sister Sheldon Murphy, where we spoke to many of his missionaries. We also had a delightful fireside in the São Paulo chapel near the temple where we once again met with a large number of choice friends and associates. We returned through Lima and went on to Guayaquil, Ecuador, for another regional conference before returning home. I had prayed earnestly that I might be blessed with the ability to speak well in Spanish, and my prayer was answered as well as on any occasion I remember. I spoke in connection with the nature of our Eternal Father and his Son Jesus Christ and concerning the callings we receive as we become witnesses to His holy name. It was an effective conference with nearly 5,000 people in attendance. Visits to temples along the way were part of our intention. The end of May took us to the St. George and Provo Temples, where we reviewed their operations. Those of us who were being placed on emeritus status on October 1 were given some instruction by the Human Resource Department. We concluded the month by celebrating David's birthday before going to the Valley View Cemetery to leave some remembrances on the graves of my parents.

In June, I had a good meeting with President Hinckley where I presented some concerns in the Temple Department. He then told me how much my work in the temples had been appreciated over the last many years and spoke of how I had been placed in many difficult situations but that things had worked out for our best good. Later on I went with Elder Richard G. Scott to Monterrey, Mexico, where we met with the regional representatives in that area. Later Geri and I drove to the Turlock California Stake conference. Geri spoke for

15 minutes and gave an excellent address, reviewing again the conversion story of her sister-in-law Betty and the re-conversion of her brother Ivan. She was very intent on having an impact on Ivan's three sons, who were soon to join us in a family reunion in Alpine. We returned by passing through several less known communities along the way. It was always delightful for us to become more familiar with the less traveled roadways of our country. We also enjoyed participating in the annual mission presidents' seminar at the Provo MTC.

July brought a flurry of family activity, including our annual trip to the High Uinta Mountains. On our return trip, once we reached the paved road, Shane was there telling us that Cory's old International Travelall had a flat tire, and he was getting it fixed at the service station. We followed them towards Evanston, and once again they needed to repair the flat tire, so we unloaded our horses for a rest, and Geri opened the trailer and fed everyone lunch while Cory and I went into town and purchased another tire. We moved on from there home, over Parley's Summit. It was another memorable Black's Fork experience.

We visited the Manti Temple and were asked to participate in the Pioneer Day celebration in Snowflake, Arizona. At the conclusion of the parade, we sat in the shade and watched the rest of the parade come by. There were six floats proposing a future temple in Snowflake. I knew beforehand that there would be a lobbying effect to try and convince me, and through me the leaders of the Church, that a temple should be built in Snowflake. I of course, had very little influence in this matter. On that occasion we enjoyed a leisurely drive through southern Utah and Northern Arizona. On the return trip we passed through Ganado, Chinle, and Many Farms and then crossed the Colorado at Hite Crossing before continuing on to Hanksville then Torrey, Gunnison, and home. Later that month we flew to Mesa for a nice reunion with our missionaries from that region. Wilford Cardon and Duke Cowley had provided their airplane to ferry us back and forth to Utah. On the way home, the pilot, Ron Adams, invited me to try my hand at managing the plane, which I did for about half of the trip, the first time in perhaps 40 years that I had tried to fly an airplane. I was able to do a good job in keeping direction and altitude, and it was interesting to be involved once again in this endeavor. The basic procedure to keep a plane flying was not so different, but the equipment had changed dramatically with many innovations and instruments to give security and stability to flight. There was some stormy weather en route, which we managed to fly through without problems. We were flying at 25,000 feet. As we arrived at the Provo Airport after dark, I was interested to see that the pilot could press a button and turn on the lights of the airport by himself.

August began what one might consider the beginning of the end of our service as a General Authority. We visited sites and temples in Las Vegas and Portland, where we participated in the dedication of that temple. At the cornerstone-laying ceremony, I was invited to make a brief address of five minutes, in which I mentioned the methods of construction used in the past and in modern times and the symbolic placing of the cornerstone, which carries the inference of the place of the Lord Jesus Christ in our lives. In the dedication itself, I was invited to participate in the second session as a speaker, talking about the holy ground in the temple and how it can be carried forward into our own homes. Prior to our departure, we viewed the temple operation as the first endowment session proceeded, as well as viewing a sealing of a young couple.

I later had an assignment to attend the Glendora California Stake conference. An interesting event took place during this conference. On Saturday evening, just ten minutes after we had left the building, intruders entered the building, disconnected the gas line in the closet where the water heater sits, and then set a candle down the hall anticipating that the building would fill with gas and eventually explode. By fortuitous circumstances, and no doubt through the protection of the Spirit of the Lord, according to recent instructions, a man assigned to patrol the building came by within ten minutes of the setting of this potential disaster. He immediately summoned the fire department who came and turned off the gas, snuffed out the candle, and ventilated the building.

We enjoyed an excellent temple presidents' seminar in the middle of the month. In a meeting of the Temple Department, Elder

Robert L. Simpson referred to his youthful employment in being a caller for bingo games and how he was offered an opportunity to go to Reno to be involved in the gambling operation there. Instead his bishop called him to go on a mission, and his employer contributed to his mission. When he returned from his mission, he found that his employer, Bill Harrah, had become one of the great casino owners in Reno.

At this time continuing problems came to the surface with two general authorities. One was excommunicated, the first time such action had been taken in nearly 50 years. It was a sad time for us all. It was determined that the other would be placed on emeritus status in hopes of deflecting some of the attention that might be directed to the Church.

In September I was assigned to attend the stake conference in Toledo, Ohio, visiting temples in Dallas, Atlanta, Toronto, and Chicago during the travels. I concluded my stake conference assignments by attending the Kaysville Stake conference. Our elder grandson Ricky Lorenzon received his mission call to Ecuador, and we participated in his farewell sacrament meeting, I being the concluding speaker. President Jon Huntsman Sr. invited me to set Ricky apart, which I was entitled to do as a General Authority. As general conference approached, we met with the First Presidency and Quorum of the Twelve in a lengthy meeting where we were instructed by the leading Brethren. Strong counsel was given concerning the attitudes of members of the Church in being ostentatious and proud. We were cautioned not to overdo our comments about the growth of the Church, realizing that this brings criticism from various directions. A farewell banquet was held in the Temple Department for those of us being placed on emeritus status. Elder H. Burke Peterson conducted the session, which he called a funeral service, but he filled it with sparkling humor and a happy atmosphere. We were then asked to make comments and each received the gift of a framed picture of the Salt Lake Temple with the signatures of all those in the Temple Department on the back. Our wives came and joined with us on that occasion. We felt deeply honored that the people of the department as well as those in the Special Projects Division would feel so warm towards us after our years of service.

On September 30, in general conference, we were released and placed on emeritus status, bringing to a close many years of fascinating service in the highest councils of the kingdom of the Lord. On that day Geri and I went to the office early to prepare for the traditional meal between sessions for members of the family and friends who would participate. We then went to the Tabernacle for the opening session of conference. In the afternoon session I was released from the Presidency of the Quorums of Seventy and was placed on emeritus status along with seven others: Robert L. Simpson, Victor L. Brown, J. Thomas Fyans, Paul H. Dunn, Royden G. Derrick, Rex C. Reeve, and Theodore M. Burton. Many expressed their sorrow in this change but recognized it would bring many other opportunities.

Sunday after the last session of conference, many of the family helped us clear out my office of the remaining books and pictures. That evening we arranged for all adult members of the family to come to our home for a review of the conference. I invited each one to consider the messages and explain what the messages meant for them. George and Jeanette Oaks joined us and added greatly to the occasion. He had served as one of our leading missionaries 30 years ago in Brazil. I was impressed by the depth of feeling of each of the adult children. We were blessed to have them all so devoted to the gospel and living in righteousness.

For those General Authorities who were made emeritus, it was not an easy transition. Many, including me, were still young, healthy, and vibrant and filled with valuable insights that could have contributed still to the growth and development of the kingdom. Though I was involved in the initial recommendation as a new member of the Presidency of the Seventy in 1978 to provide emeritus status to elderly or health-challenged General Authorities, little did I know then the impact it would have on my own life and service in the kingdom.

Bangerter family picture, 1966, clockwise from bottom left — Duella, Geraldine, Howard, Julie, Glenda Cory, Lee Ann, Grant H., Wm. Grant, Layne, Paulo, and Peggy in the middle.

Picture of Bangerter Family shortly after their arrival in Portugal, December 1974 — Left to right: Peggy Brasília Bangerter, Glenn Paulo Bangerter, Wm. Grant Bangerter, Duella Bangerter, Geraldine H. Bangerter, Layne Rio Bangerter, Howard Kent Bangerter

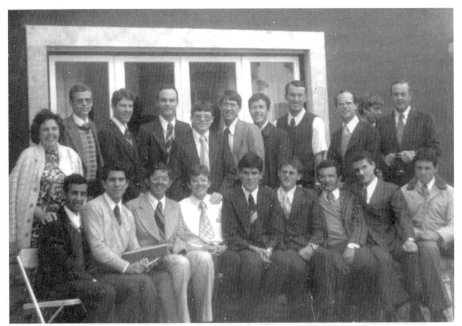

Group of missionaries serving in the Portugal Lisbon Mission, May 1975 — Sister Geraldine Bangerter, far left; President Wm. Grant Bangerter, far right back

Wm. Grant Bangerter at special meeting to offer a prayer near Guincho Beach, January 1, 1975.

Portugal dedication site near Sintra. Left to right: Wm. Grant Bangerter, Geraldine H. Bangerter, Sister Frances Monson, Elder Thomas S. Monson, April 1975.

Dedication of Portugal with Elder Thomas S. Monson surrounded by members and missionaries, April 1975.

Wm. Grant Bangerter on beach at Nazaré, Portugal.

Early baptism in Portugal held in the stairwell of the mission home in Estoril, Portugal.

April 1975 General Conference. Sustained as Assistants to the Twelve—Wm. Grant Bangerter, Robert D. Hales, Adney Y. Komatsu, and Joseph B. Wirthlin (off picture).

Wm. Grant Bangerter speaking in general conference.

Wm. Grant Bangerter in his office.

Wm Grant and Geraldine Bangerter at the time of his call, April 1975.

Family portrait, fall 1977. (Howard was on his mission in Portugal.)

Wm. Grant Bangerter speaking in general conference.

São Paulo Brazil Temple

Wm. Grant Bangerter in his office in São Paulo, Brazil, 1977.

Wm. Grant Bangerter speaking in Brazil, 1977.

President Hinckley, Elder Hélio Camargo, Presidents Kimball and Tanner, Wm. Grant Bangerter, and David M. Kennedy review São Paulo Temple plans, 1977.

Elders James E. Faust and Wm. Grant Bangerter with the São Paulo Brazil Temple presidency, Benjamin Puerta, Finn B. Paulsen, and Angel Miguel Fernandez, 1978.

Geraldine and Wm. Grant Bangerter outside the Manti Temple.

Elders Marion D. Hanks and Wm. Grant Bangerter confer after general conference

Elder M. Russell Ballard shaking hands with Elder Marion D. Hanks with Elders Dean Larsen and Wm. Grant Bangerter looking on.

*Wm. Grant Bangerter and President Gordon B. Hinckley
conferring over models of temples to be constructed.*

*Wm. Grant and Geraldine H.
Bangerter, December 1981.*

*Wm. Grant and Geraldine H.
Bangerter outside the Freiberg,
Germany Temple*

Cornerstone ceremony for the Portland Oregon Temple. Left to right: Pres. Gordon B. Hinckley, Pres. Ezra Taft Benson, Elder James E. Faust, Elder Wm. Grant Bangerter, Pres. Thomas S. Monson.

Wm. Grant and Geraldine H. Bangerter outside the Papeete Tahiti Temple.

Picture of the Quorum of the Seventy with the Presidency of the Seventy seated in front, 1988. Wm. Grant is seated in the center.

Jordan River temple presidency and staff, 1991.

Wm. Grant Bangerter as a sealer in the Mount Timpanogos Utah Temple.

Wm. Grant and Geraldine Bangerter outside the Mount Timpanogos Temple.

Wm. Grant and Geraldine Bangerter outside the Mount Timpanogos Temple following the marriage of a grandchild

Duella and Wm. Grant Bangerter with a new colt.

Wm. Grant Bangerter on horseback with grandson Greg Lorenzon

Birthday celebration. Grandson Garren Apple helps Wm. Grant blow out the candles.

Neighbor Conrad Teichert and Wm. Grant Bangerter on the tractor at the Alpine farm.

Wm. Grant and Geraldine Bangerter near Horsetail Falls above Alpine, overlooking Utah Valley.

Wm. Grant and Geraldine H. Bangerter on horseback after fishing in the High Uinta Mountains.

Wm. Grant Bangerter loading up the truck in the High Uintas, taking the family upstream for a fishing expedition.

Horseback riding with family members up Dry Creek Canyon above Alpine, Utah.

Reunion of Brazilian Mission companions. Left to right: Wm. Grant Bangerter, Max LeRoy Shirts, James Douglas Davis, James E. Faust, Lloyd R. Hicken, Lynn A. Sorenson, Hap P. Johnson, Asael T. Sorenson, Joseph Glenn Erickson, LeRoy A. Drechsel, Raymond B. Duckworth, John P. Rich, Benjamin R. Platt, Norton B. Nixon (insert)

Family portrait, February 2009, in celebration of Geraldine H. Bangerter's 85th birthday. Photo taken at Ashton Cabin near Sundance Resort in Provo Canyon. Front, left to right: Betsy Cryer Bangerter (Layne), Julie B. Beck (Ramon), Duella B. Williams (Lonnie), Geraldine H. Bangerter, Wm. Grant Bangerter, Gayle B. Bangerter (Cory), JaLayne G. Bangerter (Paulo), Cleadonna W. Bangerter (Grant H.), Lissa H. Bangerter (Howard). Back, left to right: Layne Rio Bangerter, Ramon Paul Beck, Lonnie Dale Williams, Steven Craig Apple, Glenda B. Apple, Peggy B. Porter, Lee Ann B. Lorenzon, Richard Albert Lorenzon, Cory William Bangerter, Glenn Paulo Bangerter, Grant Hamblin Bangerter, Howard Kent Bangerter.

Wm. Grant and Geraldine Bangerter with Julie B. Beck at the time of her call as first counselor in the general Young Women presidency. Four years later Julie was called as general Relief Society president.

Wm. Grant and Geraldine Bangerter at a family Christmas party 2001.

Wm. Grant and Geraldine Bangerter at a wedding reception held at Grant H. Bangerter's home in 2008.

Wm. Grant and Geraldine Bangerter as he is honored by Brigham Young University as a distinguished alumnus, 2008.

Wm. Grant and Geraldine Bangerter in their kitchen with "the quints"—five grandchildren born within six weeks of each other. Back, left to right: Jayne Dowse (Peggy), Josh Apple (Glenda), Suzie Bangerter (Layne), Rachel Bangerter (Grant), Luke Bangerter (Cory).

Extended family picture in the High Uinta Mountains on the West Fork of Black's Fork.

Wm. Grant Bangerter at 91.

Partial family photo on board a cruise ship, 2008 — left to right, Paul, Glenda, Cory, Lee Ann, Howard, Peggy, Grant H., Layne, Wm. Grant and Geraldine in the foreground

Casket of Wm. Grant Bangerter, April 2010.

Wm. Grant Bangerter

PERIOD VII —
The Emeritus Years

Chapter 19

TEMPLE PRESIDENT, JORDAN RIVER TEMPLE

"Members of the Church sometimes think about temples as the place where old people go to do work for the dead. The day will come when you young people won't think that they are so old. But it is a place where young people should go too, and the first thing we should do is obtain our blessings. The Lord has revealed to us great blessings and promises. . . . Some people who are a little bit skeptical about what may happen in the temple say, "I don't know what they are going to do in there. I'll go there and see if I like it or not and decide afterward." Obviously, they have not put the first principles of the gospel in place. Faith in the Lord Jesus Christ requires that you have full confidence in what he teaches. You have accepted him as the Savior of the world, the Son of God. You understand that He is the one who has organized the Church and kingdom. He is the one who has given us the scriptures. The scriptures are the word of God. He has restored the Church in the last days and established His priesthood. If you are going to go to the temple as one who has put the first principles in place you will say, "It is the House of the Lord. I don't know what they are going to teach me in there, but it's His house, and whatever it is, it's all right with me." Then you will be all right too. If you don't have those principles in place, somebody may be troubled.

"Of course we do work in the temple for those who are dead. We also do our own work. We also need to go to the temple as often as we can to worship the Lord in that special way, because more than anywhere else in the world He said, 'My presence shall be there, and my people need

to be there so that they can grow up in the Lord, and obtain a fullness of the Holy Ghost, and then be organized according to my laws.' All of those things take place in the temple. Those who have analyzed the ordinances and blessings of the temple know that you are not required to live any new commandments after having gone to the temple that you did not already have in your life before. No member of the Church is expected to live better after going to the temple than he should have been living before, but the promise to keep the covenants is given with much deeper emphasis and those who go are expected to be even more faithful than those who have not been to the temple. It is not a new gospel. It is the same presentation of the plan of salvation, the fall and redemption, and it all takes place according to the basic principles of the gospel of Jesus Christ."[1]

Emeritus General Authority—1989

At the conclusion of the October general conference, a new era began in our lives. Without the daily assignment to report to the Church Office Building, we began to get a taste of what retirement was like. We began to tackle several projects, a major one being the locating of room for all the books and files accumulated over the years in the office at Church headquarters. In connection with the move, we also found a need to respond to many notes and letters of people expressing appreciation and thoughtful remembrances of our service. I certainly missed having a good secretary to assist in the accomplishment of that task. We enjoyed a continuance of association with many of our former colleagues in occasional socials and meetings with them. These included a final meeting with the Seventy where those of us retiring were given a chance to express ourselves. On another occasion we enjoyed an evening with the Presidency of the Seventy. We also enjoyed a social held in our home with many of my former missionary companions, whose association had remained strong over the many years since our service together.

As a continuance of our previous assignment, we responded to requests that we speak at firesides, sacrament meetings, and other functions as people would ask us to share some of our experiences. Included in these functions were BYU football games as well as a spe-

---

1. Collected Works, pp. 357–358

cial recognition of my brother Blauer by the BYU Physical Education Department. I also continued to perform sealings for family and friends on an almost weekly basis. Towards the end of October, I accepted the calling to serve as the gospel doctrine instructor in our ward. We continued to enjoy the farm, having time to repair some failing equipment and inviting our children and grandchildren to participate in the continuous task of gathering rocks that appear on the farm. They called the rock-gathering activities "rock parties," and they seemed to derive a certain enjoyment from those events. We also enjoyed having family and others come over to ride the horses as well. It was a sweet blessing to have many of our grandchildren close by. We enjoyed helping our sons and a few of our grandsons prepare for and execute the annual deer and elk hunt. They returned with some success. Geri and I enjoyed traveling to the Uintas for the start of the hunt. We considered entering into a partnership with our son Layne in acquiring several sheep to winter on Charlie Danzie's range and eventually proceeded with this venture, though it did not make us much money. We sold some lots in Creek Road and purchased another from Grant in Layton, which helped us with some of our cash flow. Later on we were able to pay off some of our debts through the blessings of the Lord to us.

November brought us enjoyment with family around the farm and in anticipation of the holiday season. We remembered with fondness the birthday of my mother, who would have been 97 years old. Our events with the family included a family sealing session in the temple, where most of our children participated in the work for many of our deceased family members. I performed temple marriages as requested by family and friends through the end of the year. I continued to teach my Sunday School class, and we spoke at several functions, such as funerals, firesides, seminary morningsides, and special gatherings as requested by those who had an acquaintance with us. Our attendance at the BYU football games was always a highlight for us and for those who joined with us. BYU seemed to come out victorious. Around the farm we continued to ride the horses as often as we could, winterized the equipment, and took special care in canning tomatoes and juicing apples to add to the enjoyment of the season. We helped Layne with some repairs on his home, which turned into a major project. We had several of our children over for Thanksgiving. As November came to a close, we purchased a nice Christmas tree and began our preparations for that holiday.

Winter came with a good snowfall in early December. This did not dampen efforts to ride the horses or ride out into the west desert with Layne on occasion. It was also a season of car failures with some of our children, and we found ourselves in the automobile-lending business for some of the time. When the weather cleared and dried out somewhat, we had another project of gathering rocks around the farm and dumping them into the gully by the pasture. I still spent a considerable amount of time catching up on correspondence, which seemed to maintain its pace from day to day. We continued our preparations for the Christmas season with Geri coming up with a large amount of gifts for family members acquired from various parts of the world on our numerous travels. We celebrated the season with my missionary companions in the Jordan River Temple with a meal and a temple session together. We held the annual Bangerter/Hamblin Christmas party as well and participated in many other social events connected with this time of year. Christmas day found us visiting each of the children in turn and enjoying their happy expressions. Later they all came to our home to pay us a visit as well. As the year drew to a close, we mourned the passing of Elder Theodore M. Burton, who had been ailing for some time. Nevertheless, we rejoiced in the goodness of the Lord to us in many areas, including the reduction of our debts and the prosperity of our children. Each child was doing well, and we felt to express appreciation to the Lord for His blessings.

1990

Though we had been released from active general Church responsibilities for four months, our lives continued to be extremely busy with many events to occupy our time. Our time was filled with a host of temple sealings for family and friends, averaging about one per week, sometimes more.

Geri and I took a two-week trip, heading first to St. George, where we spent a couple of days with my brother Norman and his wife, Colleen. We attended the temple with them and then later drove to Las Vegas, where I performed the sealing for one of Geri's extended family. We continued after a day or two to Mesa, via Kingman and Wickenburg. In Mesa we had a lovely time with former missionaries and family members. We also did a sealing in the Mesa Temple. Often we encountered people with whom we had labored in the Temple Department, and they were always glad to see us. We left Mesa with the Cowleys, who drove us south through Tucson, Benson, and Tombstone and into Douglas, where we crossed the border into Mexico. We made our way east and then south to Nuevas Casas Grandes and Colonia Dublán, where we settled in with our former missionary Larry Memmott and his wife. We enjoyed the hospitality and the wealth of Mexican food, which was always tasteful to us. While with the Memmotts, we arranged to have an airplane ride and flew over all the mountain colonies, seeing them from the air, including Colonias Pacheco, Garcia, and Chuichupa. The following day we returned to the U.S. via Antelope Wells, New Mexico, and then to Lordsburg, Tucson, and Phoenix. We enjoyed a visit with Lowell and Cora Wilson before proceeding on to Miami and Safford for a lovely visit with Roland Hamblin and his wife. From there we drove north into Pleasanton, New Mexico, and then Alpine, Arizona, where Jacob Hamblin is buried. We went through St. Johns, Holbrook, and Flagstaff before traveling through Page and spending the night with Geri's brother Ivan and his wife, Betty, in Kanab. From there we drove home through Salina. All along the way we had been treated most kindly by family and friends, much more than we felt we deserved.

In other events during the month of January, I continued teaching the gospel doctrine class in our ward as well as enjoying most Sunday evenings in the company of family, both children and grandchildren. The farm also took up much of our spare time, though the weather prohibited much activity in that area. We rode the horses, took day trips with Layne into the mountains, and also spent some time searching for goats to provide a family project for some of the grandchildren. Our previous connections with the General Authorities provided special invitations to events such as a luncheon at the Harman Building at BYU, where we enjoyed renewing friendships and acquaintances with past Granger residents, seminars and presentations at BYU, as well as the annual General Authority dinner, and a basketball game. We also enjoyed a tour of the new Beehive Clothing building open house.

February continued at the same pace with much taking place. We had heavy involvement with family; grandchildren frequently stayed with us as parents had events taking them away from home or as they just needed help in tight situations. Our children helped around the farm as best they could, doing small chores and keeping themselves occupied in their free hours. I made repairs on farm equipment and fencing, and towards the end of the month I did some plowing since the soil had dried sufficiently. We also had a chance to spend a couple of days in St. George with my brother Blauer and his wife, Bessie, enjoying some golf and visiting. I continued to perform sealings on a regular basis and was also asked to speak at the funeral of Ora Pate Stewart, a gifted writer and author. A special event for us was the open house and dinner celebrating the opening of the new Primary Children's Medical Center. We enjoyed the evening seated next to Jim and Ruth Faust, who had been great friends and associates over the years.

We celebrated Geri's 66th birthday with grand festivities with the family. All expressed their love and devotion to her for being such a marvelous person. I reflected on what a truly outstanding wife and mother she has been. We also participated in a farewell for our grandson Shane prior to his mission to Portugal. I was also able to spend some time with Layne in the west desert area with his employment. We concluded the sale of a lot in our subdivision in Sandy, which made for more financial liquidity. My spare time was filled with working on the farm, plowing, disking, drilling, harrowing, and the ever-present rock parties. In ecclesiastical areas, I continued to teach the gospel doctrine class in our ward and accepted speaking assignments in various places. Geri and I spoke at the Richfield Seminary morningside and on another occasion to a high priest fireside in

Loa. I continued to perform sealings for family and friends weekly. Towards the middle of the month, we attended a lovely reunion with our Brazilian missionaries at the Rodizio restaurant in Salt Lake. I also paid a visit to my former mission president, President John A. Bowers, who was in failing health. Towards the end of the month, Hélio and Nair Camargo paid us a visit as they were in town for general conference. It was a delight to spend time with them. We enjoyed hearing the latest news from Brazil from them and others who paid us a visit during conference time.

In early April we were invited to a special meeting in the temple with all the General Authorities and temple presidents. It was a special moment for us to participate with this group in such a setting. I continued to perform sealings weekly as well as speaking in various locations such as Spanish Fork, Hunter, and in Salt Lake City. There always seemed to be some event that demanded the presence of someone from the Church. We enjoyed participating in the Governor's Ball as well. Our involvement with the family centered around events on the farm such as riding horses, working the irrigation, or making repairs of various sorts. We finally located some goats, which we were able to place in Cory's pasture for his boys to learn some skills with animals. In other family matters, we saw lots of changes coming with our children and their employment: Howard was in the process of moving to Highland; Peggy, and her husband and family were soon to finish Medical School in Omaha; Paulo left his law firm to strike out on his own; and Layne was preparing to accept advancement in his work, which would take his family to the Boise area.

Temple President—Jordan River Temple

May brought with it the beautiful springtime and the joy of being on the farm. Our grandsons and Layne took special delight in irrigating the place, often holding all-night events to be together, playing games and visiting between shifts with the water. One of the great delights was meeting with my brothers and sisters as we settled our mother's estate to the happy satisfaction of all in the family. At the end of the month we once again all joined together to celebrate

David's birthday party with the extended family in attendance. This celebration had become an annual reunion.

We took an extended trip to Omaha to be with Peggy and Rob as Rob received his MD degree from Creighton University. It was a marked accomplishment for the two of them. We stopped in Rawlins, Wyoming, and paid a visit to Dale and Lois Hamblin on the way out and also spent some time in Winter Quarters before following the Oregon and Mormon Trails as we came back.

We participated in a meeting with temple workers in the Provo Temple, which was a special occasion. We shortly thereafter received an invitation to sit down with President Thomas S. Monson in an interview wherein he extended to us the calling to serve as president and matron of the Jordan River Temple. We gladly accepted, knowing that for the next three years, our activity and freedom to be involved with many family and other activities would be somewhat restricted.

June came upon us with the full measure of the springtime. We enjoyed the baptisms of three of our grandchildren, all in one meeting—Heidi, Rachael, and David. We worked around the farm, cutting and bailing hay, with the grandsons doing the irrigating. Many of the family would drop by to ride horses on or near the farm. We had a Schwantes family reunion in Holladay and then in early July an Eyre Family Reunion at Mutual Dell campground in American Fork. I continued to speak at various locations for different groups. President Bowers, my mission president, passed away, and I spoke at his funeral. As the month drew to a close, our son Layne and his family moved to the Boise area to accept a job assignment with the government there.

In July we drove to Boise, where we helped locate Layne and his family in Middleton. We also planned and executed our annual family outing to the High Uinta Mountains. We spent about a week together, with more than 50 of our family there at any given time. We enjoyed hiking, riding horses, and fishing as well as the grand association with our children and grandchildren. I continued to perform sealings and to speak with Geri at several functions, often on a ward or stake basis. Towards the end of the month we harvested the oats, and Layne returned to Utah for that event. The oats nearly filled our granary and were a pleasant addition to our needs for the stock. As we completed the month, we met with the newly called counselors in the Jordan River Temple presidency, President Rex Reeve and his wife and President Morris Rowley and his wife. We found that working with them made a very enjoyable and smoothly working presidency.

August brought a flurry of events in preparation for our assuming the presidency of the temple. Prior to making that move, we enjoyed the time with family in the garden and on the farm, canning corn and filling the barn with hay. The third crop had given us more than we had expected. I continued to perform sealings regularly; one session was memorable in that we had our entire ward come to the Provo Temple for a session.

Also in August we were set apart as president and matron of the Jordan River Temple by President Thomas S. Monson and then attended the temple presidents' seminar. It was enjoyable for me to be able to sit quietly and not have to make a presentation as we had done so many times in the past. The Brethren, especially the Twelve, gave us valuable instruction. We held a luncheon for the retiring president and supervisors in the Jordan River Temple, which was a delightful transition. A sad note at the end of the month occurred with the passing of my business partner, Paul Mertlich, who died suddenly of a heart attack. I spoke at his funeral.

With the start of September came also the change of leadership in the Jordan River Temple. Prior to our first day, we met with over 40 former Brazilian missionaries of our era to celebrate the 55th anniversary of the organization of the mission. The next day, a Sunday, we met in the Jordan River Temple in a formal transferring of responsibilities from the old presidency to the new one. We enjoyed the sweet spirit of President Larsen and his counselors as they made that transition. The next Tuesday was our first day. We were there early, and all went smoothly as the previously scheduled events had been well established. We found that one of the enjoyable events in the temple is giving instructions to those who come for their own ordinances. Soon we were in the midst of heavy temple activity, involving sealings, endowments, and other ordinances in the temple. Many friends and former associates would come to the temple to be with us, and we enjoyed their association.

In other areas, we continued to maintain as best we could a regular involvement with family members, including riding the horses, either up the canyon, to Lake Hardy, or around the farm. We had other events with members of our extended family, including visits and dinners. Geri and I also spoke in many ward and stake functions, hopefully adding to the faith and unity of the members. We were able to close on three lots in the Willow Creek Subdivision, and then Geri and I attended the 55th anniversary of my high school graduating class. There weren't as many of my classmates around as there used to be.

October brought another general conference. We attended a couple of sessions, enjoying the chance to sit in the audience rather than on the stand. We also enjoyed the association with Hélio and Nair Camargo, who were released from the Quorum of the Seventy as they assumed the presidency of the São Paulo Temple. Our son Layne and some of the grandsons decided to participate in the annual elk hunt, and we helped them prepare, even going up one day to Black's Fork to be with them. We settled our account on the sheep investment we had made several months ago and felt fortunate to break even on the deal. In our temple activity, we continued to perform many marriages for family and friends. We also continued to speak at funerals, firesides, and other events. A major thrust we made as a temple presidency was to invite stakes to come to the temple and spend the entire day there, performing all of the ordinances and filling the temple to capacity and beyond. This program was extremely well received and began to show fruits almost immediately.

One of the joys we experienced in early November was to have several of our children and their spouses come to the temple, where we performed a number of family sealings. I continued to perform sealings for family and friends in the Jordan River, Salt Lake, Provo, and even Manti Temples. Also that month we had the singular experience of having a large group of Navajo members come to the temple, where we held the first session entirely in their language. Our stake temple day program continued to receive enthusiastic response from the stake presidents with whom we met. Geri and I also accepted many opportunities to speak to groups, quorums, wards, and stakes at firesides and other functions, which helped promote temple worship. On our time off, we rode horses, repaired the roof on the barn, or did some plowing. These activities served to refresh me.

December brought a sad event in our temple efforts. We discovered that the manager of the temple cafeteria had been taking money from the proceeds of the cafeteria and going to Wendover to gamble, supporting a vice he had struggled with for a number of years. This was sad for the entire Temple Department and showed that the evil one can still enter the temples through various means. I continued to perform many temple marriages, some in English, others in German, Portuguese, and Spanish. Often they were for people with whom we had associated over the years in various locations. The Jordan River Temple registered near record numbers for ordinances for the year, and we felt blessed by those events. Christmas also came upon us with all of the preparations and festivities. We had a delightful evening with my brothers and sisters and their spouses in Granger and enjoyed other Christmas events with our own family. Christmas day again found us visiting nearly all of the children, and then they came to visit us. We enjoyed the snow, pulling the grandchildren on the sleighs behind the horses. It had been a marvelously inspiring year for us all.

1991

Our efforts for the New Year consisted of entertaining many of our children who came by to wish us well. We returned to full temple activity following the holiday break. Many stakes participated in special stake temple days with varying success, mostly depending upon the emphasis provided by the stake leadership. We carried this emphasis throughout the year. There were other special groups who came to the temple to participate in the ordinances. I performed marriages and sealings nearly every day as family, friends, and missionaries who served under us asked to have that blessing for their children. We held regular meetings with the supervisors and ordinance workers at the temple, all of which were inspiring and sweet in their nature. We sorrowed at the sudden passing of Brother Reed Brown, our executive secretary. I spoke at his funeral. Eventually we were able to have Brother Keith Bergstrom called to serve as his replacement.

February was a continuation of requests for me to perform sealings and marriages nearly every day. I was asked to participate in two regional stake conferences in Murray and West Jordan, which were insightful. We also spoke in other settings to various groups. We made a quick trip to Kuna, Idaho, to visit Layne and his family. At home, when the weather permitted and schedule allowed, we rode our horses to keep them used to our involvement with them. We bid my brother Blauer and his wife, Bessie, farewell as they prepared for a mission in Spain.

In other activities we enjoyed having our children and their families over for a meal from time to time. On our days off, we tried to relax and recoup as much as we could with the constant demands of a large property to care for. We rode horses as often as the weather permitted. One of our projects was to repair the downstairs bathroom, which needed attention. We enjoyed the visit of Duke and Alice Cowley from Arizona. Our son Layne and his family also spent some time with us visiting from Idaho. We spoke in sacrament meetings and in stake conferences by invitation. Towards the end of the month we watched with deep interest the progress of the Gulf War, brought on by the invasion of Iraq into Kuwait. This war effort was basically culminated with great success by early March.

Early in March we traveled to southern Utah. Geri and I had been invited by her brother Ivan and his wife Betty to speak at a Relief Society conference as well as a fireside in Kanab. It was a delightful time to be with Ivan and Betty. Throughout the month we seemed to be involved in speaking assignments—firesides, sacrament meetings, or other affairs—almost on a weekly basis. We had continued involvement with the farm, including some plowing, leveling, and planting oats. Several of the children came at various times to assist. Often these interactions included riding and caring for the horses. Our son Howard had surgery on his neck, fusing some vertebrae due to an earlier injury. He came through it well. Geri and I had medical check-ups and found all to be well with us, except for a nagging problem with my sciatic nerve. Our involvement in the temple was constantly bolstered with several stake temple days, wherein many participated in all the temple ordinances. Involvement with sealings and marriages of family and friends continued at a steady pace. We had a special meeting with President Hinckley as we reviewed several changes in the temple film, which was soon to come out.

With April came general conference and the attendant activities, including missionary reunions, mainly with our missionaries. Our temple efforts continued with sealings of family and friends. I also performed the sealing of a family from Chile. Our stake temple days continued with good attendance and participation. We held regular meetings with ordinance workers, sealers, and others who participated with us in the temple. In other areas we enjoyed the annual Governor's Ball hosted by my brother Norman and his wife, Colleen. Several of our siblings attended, and we enjoyed the evening together. Geri and I were asked to speak at a Boy Scout Jamboree as well as at firesides in stake and ward functions in many locations. We also participated in regional meetings upon invitation. Peggy and Rob and their family came to visit us, as did Layne and Betsy and their children. Our farm continued to take up much of our spare time with irrigation and care of the animals. We participated in the graduation of Milton Camargo, Hélio and Nair's son, as he was the valedictorian in the BYU MBA program. We said farewell to our grandson Greg, Lee Ann and Richard's son, as he left for a mission to Russia.

May brought showers with little chance to work the farm. We participated in the marriage of Ana Wosnjuk and David Baldwin. She had been somewhat adopted by us, as were her sister Sonja (our housekeeper and cook while we were mission president in Brazil) and brother Tony. We also traveled to Phoenix to perform the marriage of Duke and Alice Cowley's daughter. Other petitions to perform sealings came at a regular pace, almost daily at times. I spoke at the funeral of Edith Coats, one of our dear Granger friends, who had passed away early in the month.

June was interesting in many ways. A ward in Millcreek had done much research on and received permission to do temple work for a number of prominent individuals such as Babe Ruth, Madame Curie, and others. It was a special moment in the history of our temple. Our farm continued to produce well as we cut, baled, hauled, and stacked the first crop of hay. We continued to enjoy the horses, caring for them and riding them as often as we could. We did take a quick trip to the Boise area to visit Layne and his family. We also purchased a motor home for our use and for our children's families as well.

We continued to work the farm, getting a second crop of hay late in July, and shoeing and riding the horses and preparing for the annual trek to the High Uinta Mountains, which came late in July. Geri and I took a couple of days in the middle of the trip to attend to affairs at the temple, returning to be with the family in Black's Fork. We enjoyed the chance to be close to our posterity in a happy setting. We celebrated the July holidays in appropriate fashion with members of the family. Maintaining the farm, both in equipment and in keeping up with the crops, kept us busy on our time off during the summer months. Our grandsons were always anxious to help out with many of these chores, often making them into a party of sorts. We rode the horses and enjoyed the summer season. On one occasion with Geri, I got my horse tangled into some barbed wire, which caused her to rear and throw me. I quickly recovered, but began to feel the effects of the fall shortly thereafter.

Our experience in the Jordan River Temple presidency brought us great enjoyment and satisfaction. Many of those who labored with us shared wonderful spiritual experiences they encountered in the temple. We were blessed in the response to the stake temple days, which came with great frequency by appointment. I continued to perform many marriages. On one occasion we went to Logan to perform a sealing there. Towards the middle of August, the Jordan River Temple was closed for refurbishing. Our efforts on the farm continued to take up much of our time. We had great help from Lonnie Williams, our son-in-law in repairing some of our farm equipment, allowing us to continue our operation. We also harvested our oat crop, which was stored in the granary. Often we took rides on the horses, and family members enjoyed these outings on a regular basis. One trip took several of our family members behind Timpanogos Mountain, following the trail to Emerald Lake and back. Evidently we left our dog on the mountain, but the next day a kind person called us and informed us they had our dog, and we soon retrieved him. Our grandson Ricky Lorenzon returned from his mission to Ecuador, and we enjoyed hearing his report.

We enjoyed two missionary reunions during August, one with my former companions held at the cabin of Ray Duckworth in Oakley and the second at our home with missionaries from our time as mission president. Later in the month we flew to Anchorage, Alaska, where we spent a week with Wilson and Sonja Duffles and their family; they were dear friends who were closely associated with us in our last assignment in Brazil. One day took us north towards Denali National Park, and we enjoyed the LDS campground for Scouts and Young Women along the route. We took another trip to the Kenai Peninsula, meeting up with Mike and Jan Johnson, friends from Alpine. Mike served as the bishop of his ward there. We also went fishing for halibut, Geri catching two nice-sized ones, which were prepared and frozen for us to take back home with us. All too soon we returned home.

September found us back in the saddle with the reopening of the Jordan River Temple. The refurbishing gave a special sparkle to the building, and many commented on the loveliness of it. I continued to perform sealings of friends and extended family, almost daily at times. Our assignments to speak at stake conferences, firesides, and sacrament meetings continued on a regular basis. We had an annual review by the Area Presidency as they viewed our operation in the temple. I was also asked to perform a sealing in the Manti Temple, which was always an enjoyable experience. Stake temple days continued to provide many patrons to the temple as they participated in the various ordinances of the temple. Our efforts on the farm continued with the third crop of hay, repairs of farm equipment, working with the horses, and the purchase of a few calves to raise on our property. In the middle of all this, Geri slipped and fell, breaking her ankle, which required surgery. Over the next few weeks we moved her from a wheelchair, to a walker, to crutches, and finally to a boot. It took a couple of months for her to heal. We were saddened by the tragic news from our former neighbors Burke and Carolyn Heaton as their sons were in a terrible car accident in which Guy, their 18-year-old son, was killed and two others were seriously injured. Many of the family went with us to Malta to participate with them in the funeral. It was a sad time for all.

Just prior to the general conference in October, a special temple session of all the General Authorities was held at the Jordan River Temple. It was a pleasure to have them all with us. One of the highlights of the month was the temple work performed for the "Glory Regiment" of Civil War fame. Many spiritual incidents were recorded by patrons as they performed the work for these gentlemen. It was a very spiritual event, which we recorded in the history of the temple. A major event with the sons and grandsons was the annual deer hunt. We assisted them as much as possible in their preparations, and several were successful in their goal. Geri and I took time to celebrate our wedding anniversary, which came in the middle of the month.

November brought a flurry of marriages as the holiday season approached. Nearly every day I was involved with this marvelous activity. We continued to have special training meetings with temple workers, sealers, and members of various departments of the temple operation. The meetings were always insightful and spiritual in nature. Our son Paulo's company declared bankruptcy, and he found himself out of work. Nearly a month later he was able to obtain good employment with another company in Provo. Our annual Thanksgiving dinner gathered 40 or more of our family together for a delightful feast, prepared and presented by the various families as assigned. Activities following the meal involved riding horses and working on repairing the bathroom under renovation.

As the Christmas season approached, we found ourselves involved in many activities, including a delightful reunion with my missionary companions and their wives. We also enjoyed the annual Hamblin family Christmas party as well as a delightful time with my siblings at a lovely dinner at the governor's mansion provided by Norman and Colleen. We enjoyed a Tabernacle Choir Christmas program by special invitation. Our efforts with the temple were slowing down, even though we continued to be invited to speak at various occasions. I was asked to perform a sealing in Spanish for a family that came to the temple for that special ordinance. My sister Sarah had been suffering for some time with a bad hip and early in the month had hip replacement surgery. On Christmas morning, our son Grant called and informed us that their eighteen-month-old son Ryan was having seizures and that they were at the hospital to see what could be done. Eventually he was taken to Primary Children's Hospital where they discovered he had contracted encephalitis. The next few weeks were touch and go. He was blessed to survive the ordeal of his illness, though his struggle with it continued well into the next year.

1992

Throughout the year we found great joy in our service in the presidency of the Jordan River Temple and in the sweet association with the members of the presidency, supervisors, and workers. Our efforts included much in the way of special training meetings with various groups, such as those of the baptistry, initiatory, ordinance workers, sealers, child-care personnel, and the operational staff. Geri invited several of our grandchildren to perform musical numbers for one of these meetings, and their participation brought us great satisfaction. Often in these meetings we heard experiences of our workers expressing special spiritual influences from beyond the veil in their efforts in the temple. We held prayer meetings on a regular basis, giving instruction and receiving faithful reports from those involved. We seldom missed a day, only allowing for illness to interrupt our attendance. Year-round I was constantly involved in performing sealings for family and friends, as their children came to receive that special ordinance. Of special note was the sealing of our first grandson, Shane (Cory's oldest son) and his bride, Lara Mayo, on December 18 of this year. We also performed family sealings on a number of occasions as well. From time to time individuals or couples would come to the temple seeking counsel or a better understanding of doctrine. Some of these interviews were sad in their rehearsal of details of their lives, and others were enjoyable as doctrines were expounded and clarifications made. We continued to invite stakes in the temple district to come to the temple and spend the day in ordinance work. We invited them to take over the work in the temple if they were able, using their leaders as ordained ordinance workers to lead the sessions. In many cases the response was outstanding, with large groups representing the stake taking a major role in the temple on their assigned day. In a few cases, the response was lacking, reflecting the attitudes of the local leadership regarding emphasis on temple work.

In association with our calling, often we were invited to participate in regional and stake conferences, speaking about the importance of temple worship and inviting the membership to participate with us in these ordinances. Often General Authorities would invite us to join with them on these occasions. Speaking at these and other settings came around regularly, with seldom a week going by where either Geri or I were not involved in speaking at firesides, morningsides, seminary graduations, conventions, or sacrament meetings arranged by family or friends to hear of our joy in temple service. At one time we were invited to speak at the Snow College Forum in Ephraim. We attended general conference in April and October. Once again we saw some of our close associates join the ranks of the emeritus General Authorities as they were released from full-time Church service. We could empathize with their feelings, having passed through similar circumstances almost three years earlier. Following each general conference, our family gathered together to review the talks and spirit of the conference. This event always proved to be most rewarding to us and to our extended family.

Throughout the year we had many occasions to gather with family and friends to celebrate a number of events. In February many of my brothers and sisters and their spouses attended the Governor's Ball where my brother Norman presided as the Governor of Utah. This was his last ball as he completed his eight years in office that following December. The November elections nationally put the

Democrats in place with Bill Clinton as president of the United States and many in congress of that party. Utah elected Republicans Senator Bennett and Governor Leavitt to their respective offices. On another occasion we met once again in the governor's mansion to honor Norman prior to his departure from office.

On many occasions we participated in the baptism of grandchildren and in the constant flow of baby blessings in the continued growth of our family. Annual events such as Memorial Day and Labor Day family breakfasts brought our children and grandchildren together for a time of enjoyment and relaxation. From time to time my brothers and sisters would gather together for a meal or to celebrate a special event. One of those was the celebration of our mother's 100th birthday, she having passed away a few years ago. It was a sweet and special occasion to reflect upon her glorious life. Of special note was our annual trek to the High Uinta Mountains, following the scenic road past Kamas, over Bald Mountain Pass near Mirror Lake and then over Mount Elizabeth Pass into Black's Fork. There for nearly a week much of our immediate family gathered to enjoy the mountain air, the wide open spaces, and a chance to ride, fish, swim, and hike in a favorite spot in the mountains. These occasions became very meaningful and special to us as a family.

The fragility of our health came into focus in a dramatic way on several fronts. The year began on a very somber note with the illness of Grant and Cleadonna's son Ryan. The encephalitis he had contracted over Christmas required him to be hospitalized for more than two months and resulted in paralysis of his left side. He suffered seizures and terrible reaction to medication. For some time his life hung in the balance, and we felt that care was somewhat lacking by the hospital staff. We felt to intervene in Ryan's behalf, after which care improved significantly. After his release, he still had to have therapy to regulate his recovery. Many prayers were offered and blessings pronounced in his behalf. We attributed his recovery to the blessings of a kind Heavenly Father. I had been struggling for several months with a problem of the sciatic nerve and finally in June underwent an operation to correct the inflammation. I gradually returned to full health and strength, though the recovery process seemed to take a long time. By October I was feeling much better. My brother Blauer suffered a debilitating illness, hepatitis C, while serving with his wife, Bessie, in the Washington D.C. Temple. They had to cut their mission short to return home for him to receive appropriate treatment. Of constant concern to Geri was the care of her Aunt Arvilla, whom she had taken under her wing to assist in providing for her comfort and care.

We rejoiced in the growth and accomplishments of our children and grandchildren. Shane, Cory's son, returned from a successful mission to Portugal. In March, Cory was called and sustained as bishop of his ward. We felt blessed by two of our sons-in-law finally receiving employment after a rather extended period of unemployment. Lonnie Williams was employed with Smith's food stores, and Steve Apple began work with a firm in Lindon. Both of these we felt came in answer to prayers. Our sons Grant and Howard introduced us to the new computer program that enhanced the research of family histories and genealogical work. Other events took a good portion of our time as well. Birthdays and anniversaries were noted in due course. Other times we met with former companions of the mission field, including a group of the German-speaking missionaries. At other times we met with missionaries who served under us. We had a delightful time with a group of former South American mission presidents and their wives. Some had passed away, but their spouses represented them on these occasions. We attended the 50th anniversary of Geri's graduating class from Murray High School. She was delighted to visit with so many of her classmates, many of whom had made good progress in their lives. Wedding receptions, mostly children of friends and family, were an almost constant event. Occasionally we were saddened by the passing of old friends and relatives. Often I was invited to speak at their funerals. On September 25, Cleadonna and Grant came to the temple with Blaine Webb, who had grown up as part of their family, so that he could receive his endowment. We had lunch with Blaine and Cleadonna because Grant had to leave to go to work—his business partner, Mark Wahlquist, had passed away suddenly early in the month from a heart condition, and Grant was in a press to keep things moving in the business.

In October the wards in our stake were restructured to accommodate increased growth and provide for better meeting facilities.

Care and maintenance of our farm, autos, motor home, and yard consumed a goodly portion of our free time. Geri was mostly involved with the yard care. I considered these times most pleasant, however, enjoying the chance to be close to the earth during the different seasons of the year. We rejoiced in the beauty of our surroundings, the nearby mountains, the loveliness of the farm, and the quiet, peaceful atmosphere of our home. Visiting the American Fork Canyon to see the autumn leaves brought satisfaction and joy to our hearts. The unfolding of the seasons involved adjustments and upkeep to the farm, with much family involvement. As the seasons rolled around, we took time to can and bottle fruit and corn, helping replenish the shelves in our storeroom. Care of the horses was constant. The shoeing and the care of the equipment and corrals constantly begged for our time. Repairing fences to keep the horses out of harm's way was always a worry. There were benefits to this care, however, as we took occasion to gather children or grandchildren to participate in riding the horses up the canyon, around the farm, and on the annual deer hunt or a special trip up Mount Timpanogos with Howard and others. All of these events were enjoyable, though tiring at times. Sometimes we felt we had too many animals and so would sell off a colt here and there. We were also able to slaughter a beef to restock our freezer and that of our children.

When the temple closed down for cleaning and maintenance purposes, Geri and I would feel free to visit some of our extended family. Later on we drove to the Boise area to spend some time with Layne and Betsy and their children. As often as we could, we would drive to northern Utah to visit Duella and her family, and we helped them make the move to their new home in Farmington. As the year drew to a close, memories were rich as we reflected upon the year. We enjoyed a lovely Thanksgiving with many of our family, and then as Christmas came around, we enjoyed more frequent visits to the farm by family and friends. We appreciated meals with various members of our family in a number of settings. The grandchildren were heavily involved with snow activities around the farm, sledding behind the horses and down the hill and then making snowmen and "fox and geese" paths in the field. Our preparations for Christmas were more limited than in past years due to our heavy involvement with the temple. On Christmas day our children and grandchildren all came and paid us a visit, rejoicing in the spirit of the season. New Year's Eve brought many of them together again as we ushered in the New Year.

1993

1993 dawned with a fury as winter set in strong and hard. It snowed heavily during January, so much so that we could not ride the horses at all. The lane was filled with snow, and we had to plow it out on a regular basis. As our final year in the presidency of the Jordan River Temple rolled on, we often came to recognize the blessings of the Lord in our leadership, assisting us in our goals and desire to bring more people to the temple. Our activities and efforts connected with the temple were varied and required a certain degree of flexibility and stamina. If we were on the early shift, we would leave home close to 3:00 a.m., or sooner if the weather was bad, in order to be ready for the prayer meetings at 4:00 a.m. Our meetings with various groups serving in the temple took some coordinating, and weekly we would meet with the supervisors, baptistry worker, the organists, or other volunteers. We held special training meetings for prospective temple workers and enjoyed the association with so many who labored with us in the temple. On occasion, under the direction of the Twelve, I would invite brethren who had been sealers in other temples to perform those ordinances now in the Jordan River Temple. Those were special moments. Our regular presidency and executive meetings each Tuesday were always a delightful and inspiring time to review progress and plan for future events.

Our efforts to assign individual stakes a special day at the temple whereby they could provide the patrons, and to some extent the workers, met with varying success. Some stakes caught the vision and had several hundred members attending, and occasionally a stake would show up with only a few to participate. These stake temple days occurred almost every day. Attendance at the temple greatly increased when the Provo, Salt Lake, or Ogden Temples were closed down for cleaning or repairs. At times the sessions would be overflowing and would continue late into the night to accommodate everyone. Of particular note was the celebration of the 100th anniversary of the dedication of the Salt Lake Temple with its accompanying activities. Major mention was made of it in general conference in April. We were not in attendance due to our visit with Layne and his family in Idaho, but we listened to conference on the radio. Following the October conference, which we viewed on TV at home, we enjoyed a review session with family members. Later that month we were honored to participate in the groundbreaking ceremony of the new American Fork Temple, later named the Mount Timpanogos Temple. We took with us Elder and Sister Paul H. Dunn, also an emeritus General Authority.

Involvement with the sealing of children and grandchildren of family members and friends as well as others as occasion required continued on an almost daily basis, though it gradually dwindled to nearly weekly occurrences following our release from the temple presidency in August. In like fashion we had constant opportunities to speak at various gatherings, including area council meetings, regional and stake conferences (often in connection with one or several General Authorities), various ward sacrament meetings, firesides, devotionals, and other special occasions. At one time we were invited to participate in a special meeting of LDS Woodbadge scouters in the St. George area, and we did so with great pleasure. On another occasion we met with a large group of youth from a stake in Arizona as part of their youth conference. It was an inspiring sight. We spoke at the Orem Institute of Religion as well as at a special retreat of a stake at the Brighton resort, both of which were enjoyable. At times we were so heavily scheduled that we had to ask others of the presidency to fill in for us as we could not handle all the assignments that came our way. We were somewhere almost every week and often two or three times a week. In early January I went with Geri as she was scheduled to speak in West Jordan, and she slipped on the ice and injured her hip. She was on crutches for a couple of months, though she did not break any bones. It was difficult to see her suffering all that time. She was also protected in a special way later in May when she fell asleep at the wheel and drove off the road but regained control of the car without too much damage done. We thanked the Lord for His watchful care in each case.

Other events associated with our temple service also brought us a great deal of satisfaction and joy. Often we would be involved with counseling patrons and others about various aspects of the temple ceremonies in interviews that could only take place within the walls of the temple due to the sacred nature of the subject matter. Other counseling sessions included offended parents who were prohibited from participating in the marriage of their children due to unworthiness or not being members of the church. These were often handled with great care and tact, following a careful review of gospel principles to enlighten them more fully about the sacred purposes of the temple. On another occasion I met with Levi Geartner, one of our dear friends from Brazil, who had been excommunicated and was now seeking to put his life back in order. We had our own Brazilian missionary committee visit with us to plan and then execute a reunion where many of our missionaries came with their spouses to the temple for a special session in Portuguese, followed by a dinner and then the next day a full day at the Wheeler farm involving their families in a joint activity. It was also a special experience to meet with my German-speaking missionary companions in the temple as we enjoyed a session together and later visited in our conference room. Geri and I enjoyed a special evening in the temple with our married children as they came to perform ordinances following a nice meal together. The Young Women general board came as a group and enjoyed a lovely time together in the temple. We had a BYU leadership group come and spend time with us as did a Brazilian group, which went through a session in Portuguese. On another occasion we participated in a Spanish sealing session. Finally in mid-July we were informed that President Eliot Richards had been called to replace us in the Jordan River Temple. The transition would take place at the end of August. He and his wife paid us a visit shortly after the announcement, and we were pleased to give them an introduction to the staff and many aspects of the temple operation. About this same time, our temple recorder, Brother Gerald Wray, suffered a slight heart attack, which sidelined him somewhat during the transition period. We received an exit interview by Elder Fowler of the Area Presidency, and then following the new temple presidents' seminar, part of which we hosted in the Jordan River Temple, we effected our release. Following our release, I was asked by the Provo Temple president to assist in the training of his workers, which was a delightful experience. With the flurry of activity suddenly at an end, we felt very keenly the decrease in activity and intimate involvement in the operation of the temple. Shortly after our release, Geri and I loaded up the horses and some camping gear and made our way into the High Uinta Mountains to our favorite camping spot on Black's Fork, where we spent three glorious days enjoying the peace, solitude, and beauty of our surroundings. It was a capstone experience for our three years in the temple presidency. Though released, we continued to have some association with those with whom we had served. We had a special social for members of the presidency at our home to express appreciation to each one. We also received a special invitation to a reunion of former temple workers, which was most pleasant.

Activities Following our Release

With our release, we had more time to devote to other activities. Watching BYU football games with family members was enjoyable when they won. During the fall Geri and I did a lot of canning and preserving food for the winter months. We hosted a high priest social at our home and also paid visits to ailing friends and family members including Darlene, Geri's sister; Gene Bowers, my brother-in-law; my brother David, who was doing well in a rest home in Sandy; and Marne Tuttle, a friend of long standing. Throughout the entire year, our lives continued to revolve around efforts to maintain the farm and keep up our yard as best we could. I attempted to locate another tractor that might serve our needs but was unsuccessful at that time in locating what we needed.

Our family was involved with many of our projects around the farm, and it was always a joy to have them visit us almost daily. Family gatherings associated with one child or another drew us into their homes or brought them to ours on a regular basis. We were often involved with family baptisms, baby blessings, and special gatherings for holidays or other occasions. Often we would have them over for dinner or they would invite us to dinner at their homes. We enjoyed participating in the seminary graduation of some of our grandchildren as well as the special Alpine Days Pageant in which two of our granddaughters participated—Gerilyn and Holly. On occasion those who lived further away paid us a visit. Lonnie and Duella came with their family, and Layne and Betsy and their family came from Idaho several times, as did Peggy and Rob and their family, who in the process of the year moved from Omaha to Mountain Home in Idaho. Rob had finished his medical training, and the Air Force now required three years of his time. Duella and Lonnie also began work on a new home in Syracuse, which took up much of their spare time. They moved in just before Christmas. We stayed close to their progress during the months it was under construction. Lonnie did much of the work himself and on occasion family members, including myself, helped out. Howard also purchased a home across the river from where he lived; it included five acres of land, which he put to use housing some of our horses. They moved into that home in July.

Our annual trek to the mountains was another major undertaking, as children packed up their families and gear, and we gathered at our favorite camping spot in Black's Fork. For some reason that year, the horses always seemed to get loose, and we spent an inordinate amount of time chasing them all over the valley. Other events associated with our family came and went at regular intervals. Of special note would be individual family celebrations, such as Lee Ann and her family gathering to welcome home Greg, who had completed his mission to Russia in May. His mission report was exceptional. Cleadonna's brother Blaine received his mission call to Catania, Italy, and left in August. Some of our grandchildren also graduated from high school, and these occasions provided opportunities for us to be with them. We met with Cory and others of the family at his home for a nice BBQ on the Fourth of July. Later on our grandson Garren Apple received his Eagle award in scouting. We enjoyed an evening at the circus in Salt Lake with Grant and his family. Of special note was the special family baptism of five of our grandchildren all born within six weeks of each other eight years previously. Cory conducted the service. Nearly all members of our family were present, and each of the "Quints" as we called them were baptized—Josh Apple by his father, Steven; Jaynie Dowse by her father, Rob; Ranae Bangerter by her father, Grant; Suzanne Bangerter by her father, Layne; and Luke Bangerter, who had asked that I perform that ordinance for him. It was a sweet and lovely occasion.

In like measure we visited the far-flung children and others as occasion arose. A frequent event was for us to drive to Farmington and later to Syracuse to be with Duella and her family. We also visited with Jimmy and Beth Beene and their family who lived nearby. Beth is my wife Mildred's sister. In July we took a somewhat extended trip to Omaha to be with Peggy and her family before they moved to Idaho. Shortly after returning we made another trip to Idaho to be with Layne and his family. Following our release from the temple presidency, we were more free to take extended trips to Idaho, both to Mountain Home and to Melba to be with family.

In October Geri and I took a trip to southern Utah, through Kanab, visiting Ivan and Betty and then returning through St. George and up the back roads through Minersville. Later that month I spent a week with Layne and Rob on an elk hunt on the Middle Fork of the Salmon. It brought us no results, however. Events with the extended family and friends involved special celebrations of birthdays of one or another of my brothers and sisters. Occasionally we would gather for a meal in someone's home to renew associations and experiences. These affairs often took place every three or four months. Of particular note was our Christmas social where all of my brothers and sisters were present, excepting Glenneth, who had passed away many years ago. We treasured special visits from friends of years past, including many of our former missionaries and their wives. Duke and Alice Cowley were kind to remember us. Gary and Rose Neeleman came, along with Jim and Trelva Wilson, both of whom had served with us in the mission presidency in Brazil. Sonja and Wilson Duffles paid us a visit in July, and we were grateful for their effort as they live in

Alaska with their family. On two occasions we met with our former missionary companions to relive old memories of times past. One of those gatherings took place at the Duckworth cabin.

Geri and I had devised a plan to help keep us fit during the winter months, consisting of her jumping on a small trampoline while I walked a circuit in the basement, somewhat of a track, from bedroom to bedroom through the family room. A certain number of these rounds consisted of a mile walking, and I would spend nearly half an hour each day with this exercise. Later on we decided to go up and down the lane several times when the weather was good. This of course was in addition to the workout we received on a regular basis dealing with the animals and the farm. We felt our health was generally pretty good. We had a regular battery of tests run by our doctors, and they seemed quite positive in nature. I also had my eyes checked to see if any changes had taken place with them. When things settled down after our release, I enjoyed some extra time to read, something I had enjoyed in the past and found time to enjoy again. History and biographies had always been of particular interest to me. With more time on our hands, we also reviewed our estate with Jay Mitton, reviewing options and making decisions about the best course of action to avoid complications in later years. I also entered into a business association with Grant and his partner, which brought us fairly good returns over a short period of time. One of the challenges we faced in our advancing years was the seemingly constant flow of notices of the passing of distant relatives as well as friends of long standing. Dick Fairbourne, a lifelong friend and companion from Granger, passed away in June, and other funerals were scattered throughout the year. This served to remind us of our mortality and the temporary nature of our sojourn on earth.

As the year drew to a close, we once again rejoiced in the closeness of our family and the opportunity to be near them. Thanksgiving brought many together, with over 60 in attendance. The only gloom of the season occurred with Paulo severing his Achilles tendon during a basketball game, which required surgery to repair and left him on crutches during the next several months. Christmas time was filled with the excitement of preparations including the decorations, put in place with help from children and grandchildren alike. We had our married children come to us and spend an evening singing Christmas carols and songs in a delightful event. Just prior to the New Year, we received word that Jennifer, Cory's daughter, had received a mission call to serve in the Brazil Campinas Mission, which caused us great rejoicing.

PERIOD VIII —
The Concluding Years

Chapter 20

YEAR–BY–YEAR ACCOUNTS

"Most all of you, no doubt, have received your patriarchal blessings. These blessings come to you as personal revelation. In the beginning of the Church various members came to the Prophet Joseph Smith and said: 'What would the Lord want me to do?' Joseph Smith would ask the Lord, and he gave several revelations recorded in the Doctrine and Covenants to individuals. That could not be kept up forever, and the process of ordaining patriarchs has been instituted in part, at least, to tell us, the members of the Church, specifically and in personal terms what the Lord would like us to do and what he may have in store for us. . . . They are not all-inclusive. For example, a young man may receive a patriarchal blessing and it doesn't mention that he is going to be married. What do you do then? Does that mean you can't have a wife? Mine did not mention I was going to be married, so I went out and took care of that all by myself. It may not say that you are going on a mission. What does that mean? You can go on a mission anyway. Somebody else can call you on a mission.

"What is appropriate and important is to know that the gospel holds all the promises. Even if you don't have a patriarchal blessing, the gospel extends to every faithful member of the Church the fullness of promises including all these particulars that we have talked about. And while they are not spelled out to be so personal and specific they are nevertheless valid and we can help bring those promises and blessings to pass."[1]

---

1. Collected Works, pp. 302–303

1994

Our efforts during the year of 1994 were much different than those of years past due to the change in our assignment. Though we still had much involvement with temple work, our focus was directed more to the family and the farm. We also took several journeys, mentioned in more detail later. We were in Idaho quite a bit and often stopped in Syracuse, Utah, to see Duella and her family as we traveled back and forth to see Peggy and Layne and their families, who were living in Idaho. In early January we gathered our granddaughters together for a special breakfast and period of instruction. It was a sweet and special occasion and took place before Cory's daughter Jennifer left on her mission. Other special events included the celebration of Geri's birthday, wherein the children arranged a progressive dinner, going from one home to another for different courses of the meal. It was a delightful time to share, visit, and extend love and appreciation. Later on in March we celebrated 50 years since my marriage to Mildred with a delightful dinner and displays. We met on occasion with my brothers and sisters, often having dinner at one of the homes. These events were almost quarterly but became nearly monthly as the year drew to a close. I sometimes took time to play a round of golf with my brother Blauer or to ride horses with one of my brothers. Of course our annual party to celebrate the birthday of my youngest brother, David, united the extended family in a reunion of sorts.

My efforts in temple work continued, but at a much reduced pace. I still performed sealings for family and friends, but the regular rush of almost daily events was reduced. I now performed a sealing every other week but on occasion two or three in a week. These often took me to Salt Lake and Manti as well as other locations. On occasion I would be asked to perform the sealing in Portuguese. In order to increase activity in temple worship, our stake and ward outlined events for me to perform sealings at the Provo Temple for our members either on an assigned temple day or for family names. This was a major effort and brought about much involvement in the stake on a monthly basis. We enjoyed an occasional reunion with the former Jordan River Temple presidency, which brought us great enjoyment. Regarding our Church assignments, Geri was involved with the Young Women in the ward, and I taught the 16-year-olds in Sunday School. I felt my success in this effort was moderate at best; my hearing seemed to limit somewhat my effectiveness with them. I continued teaching that class throughout the year. In May we received an assignment to coordinate the stake family history efforts. This assignment was much more suited to our abilities. June brought about the 150th anniversary of the martyrdom of the Prophet Joseph and his brother Hyrum Smith. Several events were scheduled to commemorate this date. In November our ward boundaries were realigned, and we lost the association of many dear friends on a regular basis.

Though requested to speak at certain events, our schedule was not as heavy as in the past. We were invited to speak at the Portuguese Branch in Provo. This was a special time for us to renew our language ability. Geri and I both spoke at the Alpine Stake women's conference, which was a well-planned affair. We spoke in a ward in American Fork as well as in other sacrament meetings in different places. Of special note was an invitation from Stan and Sue Gray to fly to Stevensville, Montana, to speak to a special group involved in family history work. They flew us up and back and took care of our needs while there in a most delightful fashion. I also participated in regional training meetings.

Interesting Journeys

As mentioned before, during the year we took some significant journeys, including several trips to Idaho for various purposes, one of which was to check out a possible ranch purchase by Layne in the Mink Creek area. It did not turn into anything worthwhile as the people refused our offer. Layne seemed restless to try other employment, as he was not enjoying his association with his supervisor at work. On another occasion following the October general conference we went with Grant and Peggy and their families to the Kodachrome Basin State Park in Utah for a lovely getaway. We found it to be a most interesting and pleasant area. We also checked out property available to us in St. George.

From January 5 to 7 I took a rather extensive trip to northern Idaho with Layne to attend to his supervision in animal damage control in northern Idaho. We drove in his government pick-up, passing through Nampa, Caldwell, Payette, and Weiser and on to Midvale, where we spent about two hours with one of his trappers in his home. Then we drove on through Council and New Meadows and then down the South Fork of the Salmon River to Riggins, meeting the main river, which flowed through the country of the Nez Perce Indian Wars that took place around 100 years ago under the leadership of Chief Joseph. We stopped at some of the historical sites. From there we went on to Lewiston, Moscow, and finally Coeur d'Alene, where we had some supper and stayed the night in a motel. Layne went out with one of his trappers for several hours in the morning while I stayed in the motel, reading and writing letters. Upon his return, we drove west to Spokane; then to Pullman, the site of Washington State University; and then nine miles across the border to Moscow, the site of the University of Idaho. We left Lewiston, driving into Oregon and passing through Enterprise, La Grande, Baker City, and Ontario on our way back to his home in Kuna.

Paulo invited me to join him on a trip to the Orient from January 24 through February 2. It was an intriguing trip filled with many new vistas, marvelous luxury hotels, and more food than I should have eaten throughout. We visited Singapore and met with Paulo's business contacts, including Tony Seau, a member of the Church living in that area. We visited Kuala Lumpur in Malaysia, and then we flew back to Singapore and went to the LDS branch, which was located in a nice compound. Elder Ron Poelman and his wife were the speakers, and it was a pleasant reunion. After going to Church, we went to a ferry and took a 45-minute ride over the strait to Indonesia. The port was Batam, an island. We then flew to Hong Kong and also visited the Portuguese colony city of Macau, which we were both excited to visit. We toured some areas of the Hong Kong area, all while Paulo was taking care of his business. Of special interest to me was a visit to the temple site in Hong Kong where preparatory construction was beginning. We then returned home after a long flight. Arriving in

Salt Lake, wonderful Geri was there waiting in the car. What a thrill to be with her again.

Geri and I took a journey through Arizona from February 21 through March 1 to ease ourselves out of the heavy winter weather. Driving down Highway 89 we went leisurely and comfortably in good weather and on good roads to Kanab. We stayed the night with Ivan and Betty. Their daughters Jane and Dana were also there. The next morning we proceeded on, enjoying the beautiful scenery around the Kaibab Forest, the Vermillion Cliffs desert, Lees Ferry, the Painted Desert, and Flagstaff, where we refueled the car. We then drove on down Oak Creek Canyon, very slowly, into Sedona, an expanding city with unbelievable traffic. We drove through Cottonwood Canyon and up the mountain through Jerome to Prescott and over Yarnell Hill to Wickenburg, where we stayed at a motel for the night and enjoyed their Jacuzzi. Driving into Phoenix the next day, we visited for an hour with Warner Stevens, one of my early business partners. His mother, 95 years old and very strong, was there. From there we drove to Lowell Wilson's home for a visit in Scottsdale and back to Phoenix to stay the night with Duke and Alice Cowley. They had arranged a reception for our former missionaries. Present were Phil and Brent Brown, Yale Rogers, Robert Lovell, Darrel Bethea, Norman Thompson, Jim Allen, Wilford Cardon, and others, all with their spouses. It was a lovely evening. We visited my sister-in-law Elsie Fern Bushman at her home in Leisure World, a retirement community in Phoenix. Her brother John Schwantes and his wife, Marge, were there, preparing to return to Salt Lake. We had breakfast with them at Village Inn and spent a couple of hours together. We had invited several of our friends to accompany us into Mexico, but none of them were free to go. We stopped at the Cardon home in Mesa, and they took us to see the new estate where they would soon be moving, in the midst of a ten-acre orange grove. The house was huge. We then drove to west Phoenix and did some shopping at a salvage store. Geri bought some shoes for Howard, I found a couple of shirts, and Wilford gave me a jacket. We stayed the night with the Cardons, enjoying their children, who had grown markedly since we saw them last.

Leaving the Cardons we drove south on the number 10 freeway to Casa Grande, then west on highway 8 to Gila Bend and south to Ajo, a former large mining center but now dormant. From there we proceeded south through the Organ Pipe Cactus National Monument, a beautiful desert filled with desert plant life as well as animals and birds. We entered Mexico at Sonoyta, passing through customs and by mistake driving south for 19 miles until we were stopped at the end of the free zone for lacking a car permit. This was really a blessing because we would not have been able to go further into Mexico without the permit, which cost us $1.00 back in Sonoyta. From there we drove southwest for 50 or 60 miles to Puerto Peñasco on the Gulf of California; it was a dreary desert, though it was filled with tourists. After looking around for a couple of hours, we drove along the coast and inland a few miles and thence eastward through some very interesting country. From time to time we saw some rather massive cultivation with olives and large plantations of grapes.

Finally we came in the evening to Caborca. Our interest was to see more of the Pimería Alta, the land of Father Eusebio Kino of 300 years ago. Caborca had become at that time one of the staging missions for further expansion. It is now a large town in the center of a strong agricultural area. We found a Mexican-type motel, far from plush, but with a clean bed and a shower. We didn't find much in the way of good Mexican food. The next day we drove eastward for more than 100 miles through Santa Ana and finally to Magdalena, which had been our focal point, since it is the place where Father Kino died and was buried. His grave had been located about 30 years previously and his bones uncovered. A shrine has been built over the gravesite, and the bones are still uncovered. Some impressive murals are painted in the ceiling of the shrine. There was no one in the area that seemed to know anything of the history. Countless shops were involved in selling relics of a Catholic nature, but we found nothing really about Father Kino. We felt impressed with the greatness of his spirit and the vast work he had accomplished throughout Sonora and southern Arizona.

Refueling we drove through St. Ignatius and eastward over the mountains into the valley of Cocospera, a beautiful valley, finding the ruin of the mission of Cocospera on a hill overlooking the valley. It was very impressive. We then moved east through Cananea, a large active mining and smelting town where Mildred's uncle, John Loving, spent much of his professional career as mine superintendent. From there we drove over great grasslands to Agua Prieta and the border. We found very little that we wanted to buy in the way of souvenirs.

We crossed into Douglas and drove around the town, visiting the cemetery and finding the graves of Mother and Father Schwantes and other people we used to know 50 years ago. We saw the house where Mildred, Lee Ann, and I lived. From there we drove over the Sulpher Springs Valley to Bisbee, over the Mule Mountains to Tombstone, looking it over from the car, and then on to Tucson. We drove south of Tucson to the Mission San Xavier del Bac, where I finally found some books on Father Kino. This mission, though founded by Kino in 1692, has been rebuilt several times and is now in a magnificent state of restoration. A service was in progress with a large crowd. We stayed the night in a motel in Tucson.

The next day we arranged to attend sacrament meeting with Marina Harrison, our daughter-in-law Lissa's mother. It took us an hour to find her lovely home in northeast Tucson, and we had a brief visit. Sacrament meeting was a testimony meeting, and I spoke briefly. We then left, found a few supplies, and drove north, stopping for a picnic on the desert and then moving on into Kearny, where we visited with our daughter-in-law Gayle's parents for an hour or so. Geri drove from there to Mesa, and we stayed again with the Cardons. They had a youth fireside, and we were asked to be the speakers, speaking on the topic of "attitude." Early the next morning, we went with Wilford and Phyllis to their new estate home and picked a whole trunk full of oranges and grapefruit before departing for home.

Our route was north via Payson, Heber, and Snowflake, where we stopped for a couple of hours to visit Ray Caldwell, our first branch president in Lisbon, Portugal, and his wife, Judy. From there we drove north through the Navajo Reservation to Bluff, Blanding, and Monticello; we stayed in Moab, where we had dinner and a good motel. On March 1 we drove home via Green River, over I-70 to

Salina, through Gunnison and Nephi, arriving home about noon. The weather was excellent for farming, and I took the old tractor and began to plow in the far field, accomplishing a good piece.

From December 13 through 19, Geri and I made another trip to Arizona. We left about 2:00 p.m. and drove to Torrey, where we spent the night in a motel. We had stopped at the cheese factory in Loa. The trip was free of bad weather, although it snowed all day at home and finally left a full 12 inches there. The route over the plateau to Torrey was clear. We left Torrey at daylight and enjoyed the drive through part of the Capitol Reef National Park in the early morning. Arriving in Hanksville we stopped for gas and breakfast, visiting with the people in the restaurant. We had a beautiful morning drive south towards the Colorado River and a marvelous view of the Henry Mountains. We crossed the river at Hite Crossing and then drove eastward through the rock country towards Blanding, turning off to go to Bluff on the San Juan River. From there we went south through the Navajo Indian Reservation, through Chinle and Ganado. Continuing south we drove through Holbrook for gas and then stopped in Snowflake at the home of Ray and Judy Caldwell. He was then the mayor of Snowflake. I went with him south into the forest country to do some testing for septic tanks. We had a good dinner, a choice visit, and a good night's rest at their home.

After a good breakfast we drove on south to Show Low, then east to Springerville and Eagar, and up through the mountains to Alpine, where we paid another visit to the grave of Jacob Hamblin. We then took the Coronado Trail south through the mountains and forest, a drive of about four or five hours on winding roads through beautiful country, finally coming out at the great mines of Morenci and the mills of Clifton above the San Francisco River.

At that point we were nearly down on the desert, and we traveled across to the Gila Valley and down to Safford, thence south about 11 miles to Artesia to the home of Roland and Mae Hamblin. They welcomed us with eagerness, pressing us to stay. They had planned an evening with the group of missionaries with whom they had recently served in the Peoria and Nauvoo areas in Illinois. Roland asked me to take much of the visiting time to speak of our experiences as a

General Authority and with the temples. It was a good opportunity once again to make expression of our faith and participation in the work of the Lord. We were comfortable and had a good night's rest. The Hamblins provided us with a good breakfast and the usual seasonal gifts of shelled pecan nuts and green corn tamales, which they specialized in making. We then drove to Phoenix, passing through Safford, Thatcher, and Pima and then driving down the Gila River through Globe, Miami, and Superior and then down Queen Creek to Florence Junction, then on to Mesa, Tempe, and Phoenix. The lower desert looked fresh and beautiful. We took some time to locate Duke and Alice Cowley, as they were delayed away from home. We delivered to them a Christmas gift and then went with Duke to visit Marvin Rose, another of our missionaries. Marv, Duke, and Drew Day had come together earlier in the year to purchase for us a nice automobile, which we greatly appreciated, feeling almost overwhelmed at the devotion of these great souls after so many years. This was our first trip in this car, a 1989 Ford Crown Victoria with a limited number of miles on it, and we had enjoyed riding in it in luxury. We had a good visit with Marv and then went to stay with Lowell and Cora Wilson, my brother-in-law in Scottsdale. They provided us with a good supper. In the evening we visited with my sister-in-law Elsie Fern Bushman, who was feeling quite well.

After a nice breakfast with Lowell and Cora, we went to the temple in Mesa about noon and met with the Cowley family. Quite a number of workers in the temple remembered us, and we felt a spirit of homecoming. The wedding I performed for Suzette Cowley and Loren Tyler proceeded with a fine spirit. A large group represented both families. I had performed another marriage for her about five years before, but her first husband was very immature and the union did not endure. This new union seemed to be solid, and the families were much impressed with the spirit of the occasion. After resting for a time, we attended the family luncheon at the home of Duke and Alice Cowley, visiting with the many members of both the Cowley and Tyler families. We had reserved that evening to be with Lowell and Cora, though Cora went with her daughter to a special performance. We had a fine time with Lowell.

After a quick breakfast and hurried packing, we drove to Mesa to attend Church meetings with Wilford and Phyllis Cardon and their family with whom we had not yet had an opportunity to meet. We of course stayed the two nights with the Wilson's. Wilford urged me to remain for all of the meetings and give a presentation on the Savior to the High Priest Meeting, which I did. We met Robert Walker and his wife, daughter of President Benson. We were well received and recognized. Afterwards we stopped at the new home (estate) of the Cardons and they quickly picked a strong supply of oranges, grapefruit and tangelos from their trees. Our car was once again well loaded. We drove through Phoenix, stopping to visit with Gary Weaver. His condition is pitiful in that it is apparent that he has no grip on reality. His mental deterioration is distressing although he presents a very cheerful and positive outlook. I don't know who is really taking care of him unless it is his sister Ellen Claire and his daughter Kay. We drove north on the freeway through Flagstaff, refueling and then on across the desert to Page arriving after dark. We selected a motel which was less than impressive but rested well. Leaving Page early we drove over the Colorado River and on to Kanab where we stopped for a visit with Ivan and Betty who arranged a fine breakfast for us. We did not linger but drove on home arriving about 3 p.m. Peggy has stayed in our home during our absence.

Farm Maintenance and Family Affairs

Our work on the farm continued at a steady pace throughout the year. There were always needs for equipment repairs and upkeep of fences and ditches. A major project we performed was the re-shingling of the barn which needed it badly. The children and grandchildren were always willing to pitch in and help on each of these occasions. Geri organized regular "Rock Parties" to remove the ever present rocks that crept up out of the soil. Caring for the horses was a constant event, with shoeing and keeping up the saddles. The season had not been good to us and in the end we had to purchase hay from Idaho to see our animals through the winter. Plowing, planting and harvesting in their own times brought additional challenges with maintaining the farm equipment. We had purchased a John Deere tractor which seemed to meet our needs, but shortly began having trouble with it. It eventually cost us more than it was worth and we had to sell it. The constant need to irrigate was always foremost in our minds. Once again the boys seemed more than willing to take care of much of that for us. We planted corn and tomatoes for our own consumption and enjoyed them in their season as well as peaches and other fruit we obtained in the fall. Children and grandchildren alike seemed to come to the farm almost weekly to ride the horses. This was always a joy for us to have occasion to be with them in these outings, either up the canyon or out on the west hills.

A sad event took place in July when our daughter Peggy was separated from her husband Rob Dowse. It was a shock to the entire family and each in the family reached out to them to try to save the union. Eventually, it was determined to move Peggy's and the children's belongings to Alpine to establish a permanent home there. In January of 1995, Peggy and Rob were divorced. We secured a rental home for Peggy and her children not too far from our home, which offered her some security and peace of mind.

In April Cory's son Chad received his mission call to serve in the Brazil Recife Mission. He had always been an outstanding young man and would do well in his assignment. We were in Eastern Idaho for a moose hunt which brought no success and later on an Elk hunt near Layne's home with similar results. On one occasion we enjoyed an afternoon on Antelope Island with Lonnie and Duella. (The park was near their home in Syracuse.)

Note: Pages 475/476 and 483/484 necessitated some changes for consistency and flow, thus requiring these insertions.

Our annual journey to Black's Fork in the High Uinta Mountains was a successful event, even though it was somewhat somber due to the circumstance occasioned by Peggy's troubles with Rob. We held special breakfasts on Memorial and Labor Days, viewed the Fourth of July parade in Provo, and enjoyed the Utah State Fair events in Salt Lake City. At times in the fall we attended the BYU football games, but they were not a stellar team that year. We enjoyed our children gathering together to review each general conference at our home. We likewise attended a lovely Schwantes family reunion in Layton with extended members of that side of the family.

We mourned the passing in May of Elder Sterling W. Sill and shortly thereafter of President Ezra Taft Benson. It was hard for us to see the passing of these great and important leaders. President Howard W. Hunter was sustained as the new prophet, seer, and revelator, and I was asked to stand with the Seventies when President Howard W. Hunter was sustained in a solemn assembly in October general conference. Other acquaintances also passed away, including a cousin, several friends, and Geri's Aunt Beulah, whose remains were shipped to Utah for burial. Geri attended to those details. Our mortality seemed more and more fragile, though all our medical examinations gave us assurance of good health and vitality. My brother Samuel contracted an illness of a long duration; several ward members with whom we kept close contact also suffered physical distress. Of particular note was a lingering illness of our daughter Julie who suffered from fatigue for many months.

Our associations with former missionary companions, associates, and missionaries who served under us continued to bring us satisfaction and enjoyment. On one special meeting, arrangements were made with Duke Cowley and Wilford Cardon to begin a special fund to assist young Brazilian returned missionaries further their education. This proved to be a monumental endeavor with marvelous results. (A few years later our fund was moved into the Perpetual Education Fund of the Church.) We also had reunions with our missionaries who had served in Portugal. We had a special reunion of my companions at our Alpine home and later a more extended gathering in Idaho Falls. We went with John and Effie Dean Rich, who took us into Yellowstone Park for a portion of our time together.

We visited others of our missionaries in different settings, including Gary Garner in Idaho and several others in Arizona. We also met with and gave counsel to some of Drew Day's former missionaries in a special reunion at their home. As June approached, we were pleased to know that one of our missionaries, Elder Larry Hanks, and his wife were called to serve as mission president in Brasília. Also, Doug and Sharon Lyons (my sister Marian's daughter) were called to serve in McAllen, Texas. Geri and I also shot a round of golf with Delbert and Mabel Palmer, the scores of which were not worth mentioning. As the year drew to a close, we celebrated Thanksgiving with over 50 of our family gathered together, quickly followed by preparations for the Christmas season. Early in December we had a Christmas party with the Hamblin family and enjoyed their association. There were several wedding receptions for friends and ward members, which also came in early December. Once again around Christmas time we enjoyed another gathering of my former companions to celebrate the season. Christmas Eve found us involved with a variety of activities including ward, neighborhood, and family events. Christmas fell on Sunday, and we all attended our meetings, which were filled with Christmas music and special observances. We got to the homes of each of our children before they in turn came to our home during the day. During the holidays the boys took some of their sons on a rabbit hunt, while I enjoyed myself resting and reading at home.

1995

As we began the year, we rejoiced in the strength of our daughter Peggy as she worked through the final stages of her divorce from her husband, Rob. Others in the family also passed through trials and struggles. Grant's employment was somewhat tenuous at times, but he seemed to come out all right. We enjoyed some time later in January with Grant's family at their time share on Bear Lake. In our business efforts, we began negotiations to trade some property we owned in Orem for similar property in St. George. Our efforts with the farm involved obtaining hay from Idaho as our crop had been scanty. The weather was generally good with some snow. We continued working with the horses as well.

Our efforts in our Church assignment continued as we tried to learn the Personal Ancestral File (PAF) computer program in teaching the family history class. We also spoke in firesides and sacrament meetings from time to time. Sealings were a continuous experience, either for family or friends or for regularly scheduled sealing assignments in the Provo Temple. We noted with sadness the passing of Howard Allen, a friend and associate of over 40 years who had worked with Alex Dunn and me in the old Pioneer Welfare Region.

As February came upon us, we continued working around the farm, plowing, disking, and harrowing at various points along the way. We worked with the horses—especially the colt, Flash—and even took a ride now and then. We were able to purchase a home for Peggy and spent some time helping fix it up for her use. We had a delightful time in ordaining our grandson Jacob a teacher and blessing a new granddaughter, Olivia. In other efforts, we enjoyed having several of our children and family over for dinner and other visits. We did visit Layne, Betsy, and family in Melba, Idaho, during a slow spell in the month. A couple of our grandsons earned their Eagle Scout Award, and we participated in those ceremonies. We enjoyed a lovely time in St. George with all of my brothers and sisters and their companions, hosted by Norm and Colleen at their condo. We spoke at various firesides and sacrament meetings and maintained our efforts in sealings at the Provo Temple.

In March we prepared for a trip to Israel in June, where we would help host and speak at various sites. We also spoke at various firesides and sacrament meetings. Of special note was the ordination and sustaining of our son Grant as bishop of the Highland 8th Ward, where I was honored to perform that ordinance. This was the same ward where Glenda's husband Steven had served as bishop five years before. Grant had been serving on the high council for the past three years. This ordination was most pleasing to us. We kept busy with work around the farm, keeping things in good order, planting barley and holding rock parties. I continued to perform sealings, and on one occasion sealed the adopted daughter of my cousin Edward

Prince to him and his wife. President Howard W. Hunter passed away as his health had been delicate for some time. His tenure as prophet was the shortest in Church history. We felt deeply the loss of this marvelous, loving man.

As April general conference approached, we enjoyed the solemn assembly where President Gordon B. Hinckley was sustained as prophet, seer, and revelator. Thomas S. Monson and James E. Faust were sustained as his counselors. After the conference, we had the family come to our home for a conference review. We continued to work around the farm, cleaning ditches and working with the horses. We also prepared our yard for a reunion with my Brazilian missionary companions and spouses. These were always rewarding events. Later we were saddened by the passing of Trelva Wilson, long-time friend from our Brazil days. We attended her funeral in Walnut Creek, California. Also passing away was Robert Merchant, a former sealer in the Jordan River Temple. My mother's cousin Dorene Restowski passed away before the end of the month.

We enjoyed a trip to Goblin Valley State Park in southeast Utah with Peggy and Grant and their families during spring break. It was mostly enjoyable except for a heavy windstorm, which blew down tents and disrupted camp most of the night. We later took a trip to Las Vegas via St. George for another funeral. While in St. George, we ran into several friends and enjoyed their company for dinner. We continued to enjoy sealing sessions and also the sealings of friends and neighbors. At times we were invited to speak in sacrament meetings or firesides. Grant noted with some satisfaction the upswing in real estate due to the arrival of Micron in Lehi.

May brought several interesting developments. Farm work and horse work continued unabated. Our mare Topaz had a colt, and we cut our first crop of hay. The school board expressed an interest in some of our property for an elementary school, but it never came to fruition. Our son Grant purchased a lot in Fruitland, Utah, with the intention of building a cabin on it. We traveled to Melba, Idaho, to participate in the blessing of Layne and Betsy's new baby and then later to Vernal, Utah, for the groundbreaking of the Vernal Temple. My great-grandfather George Freestone was the first bishop there.

We were able to visit with our daughter Duella as well. Our preparations for our trip to Israel proceeded on schedule. We had visits from members of the family as well as Jason and Lindamere Souza, some of our good friends from Brazil. In other events I dictated the story of the calling of native Brazilian missionaries to members of the Church Historical Department. Our teaching of the family history class continued as scheduled, and we continued to perform sealings upon request. Jeanene Scott, wife of Elder Richard G. Scott, passed away, and we missed her sweet spirit. I began to have some concerns with my sciatic nerve, which caused me some grief.

June was full of adventure and continuing efforts on the farm, which were quite consuming. Our granddaughter Jennifer returned from her mission in Campinas, Brazil. My hip continued to give me grief, and the doctors informed me that I needed to have hip replacement surgery. I performed several sealings and enjoyed visits of friends, including Adhemar and Walkyria Damiani from Brazil. Of major interest was our trip to Israel in company with Richard and Marian Lindsay (my sister and her husband), Robert Backman, and Duff Hanks. This trip took a ten-day chunk out of the month. It was an enjoyable and interesting experience, and we visited many noted sites and spoke on various topics related to our trip. Also that month Grant and Cleadonna were able to pick up her brother Blaine from his mission in Italy. As the summer progressed, we continued our efforts with the family history class, participating in sealing sessions and speaking in Bennion on the Fourth of July on a patriotic note. Our efforts on the farm and with the animals continued, including rides up Corner Canyon and then our annual trek to the High Uintas. The water was higher than normal, and all enjoyed riding horses, hiking, fishing, and the great experience of our beloved mountains. My hip replacement surgery was scheduled for early August, so we took every occasion to fulfill our recreational desires before that time. This included an extended period of time when Layne and Betsy and their family stayed with us in anticipation of a change in his job, which did not materialize. The hip operation went as scheduled and was without pain and with little discomfort on my part. I was hospitalized for five days, and many paid me a visit, including Jim Faust and others.

I was able to speak at the Alpine Days fireside, perform sealings as normal, and follow the harvesting of grain on the farm. We did have many visits to doctors and dentists as normal for our stage of life. As September came upon us, we enjoyed a day at the Utah State Fair with the Souzas. I performed the sealing of several Ethiopian children to Harvey and Deanna Bangerter Kennard, which was a special occasion.

Many of our activities in October focused on family associations. Our semiannual conference review following general conference was outstanding, with many of our grandchildren participating. Geri and I celebrated our wedding anniversary by taking a drive around the Nebo Loop in company with Cory and Gayle. Early in the month Geri and I drove to Delta and Minersville and then down to St. George to examine apartments we had purchased and to visit family in Las Vegas. We had Bob Apple, our son-in-law Steve's father, come and paint our kitchen as well. My missionary companions and their spouses met together with us for a regular event where we enjoyed a meal together. On a sad note, Ann Labrum, my cousin, passed away at the end of the month.

In November we had several of our missionaries pay us a visit at home, and it was delightful to be with them. One of them, Rod Tolman, shared his reasoning for why he felt he needed to divorce his wife. It was a sad experience for us. We visited my brother Samuel, who was pretty much homebound due to his failing health. We did enjoy a play that Howard, Lissa, and some of their children were involved with in Lindon. We also took a quick trip to Melba, where we delivered some sheep and returned with some calves. My new hip was doing very well, for which we were grateful. We lamented the passing of my longtime friend and mission associate John Rich. More and more of our close friends were passing on it seemed.

Our Thanksgiving season was a delightful time, spent with family and friends. We had pleasant weather in December, even to the point of being able to plow the fields. Our goats all had babies, but they did not survive for some reason. We attended a wedding reception in Price for our nephew Russell Wilson's daughter. Later in the month we spoke in a ward that meets in the Joseph Smith Memorial

Building where a ward meets and Jacob de Jager served as the Bishop. We noted with sadness the passing of Geri's cousins, Jay Eyre and Adele Austin during the month. We have had close association with both of them. The Holiday season was filled with family Christmas parties involving my brothers and sisters as well as our immediate family. Another party involved my former missionary companions and their spouses. The season was relaxing and most enjoyable.

1996

The New Year introduced us to some rather severe weather, but we continued our regular activities as best we could. We spoke at different occasions, firesides on temples, the Harman Lecture Series at the BYU as well as a Priesthood Leadership Meeting in Taylorsville. We also continued our temple sealing involvement and teaching the Family History class in our ward. We enjoyed a lovely dinner with former South American Mission Presidents and spouses under the direction of Delbert and Mabel Palmer. In early February we took a trip to New Mexico and Arizona with Julie and Ramon. We enjoyed visiting with my sister-in-law Ora Mae Huish and her son Carl, plus seeing the interesting sites of the Indian Pueblo villages in Santa Fe and Taos. We then followed the old Mormon Battalion route through southern New Mexico and into Arizona. We visited with Larry and Shirley Memmott, our former missionary and spent time in Douglas, Bisbee, Tombstone, Tucson and Phoenix, Arizona where we enjoyed an evening with others of our missionaries, including Duke and Alice Cowley, Wilford and Phyllis Cardon, Kay Hamblin and his wife and Brent Brown and his wife. Brent is a Vice President at ASU and got us tickets to a basketball game which we enjoyed tremendously. We also visited another sister-in-law, Elsie Fern Bushman in Mesa as well as José and Antonietta Lombardi who were visiting their daughter. We returned through Flagstaff and the south rim of the Grand Canyon, spending the night in Kanab with Ivan and Betty Hamblin. The next day we went through Richfield before returning home. It was a delightful time. My new hip seemed to work very well. We continued our regular sealing assignment and also learned that our son Cory and his family will be moving to Brazil for three to four years where he will direct the Church Educational System there. We will miss them dearly. They would leave in July. We also learned that my brother Norman and his wife would preside over a mission in South Africa. My cousin Keith Andrus passed away after a long illness. As springtime approached our efforts around the yard and farm increased. We plowed and planted and worked the horses some. I had some health issues with swelling of my feet and legs which caused some distress. Several events occupied our time, including a special convocation at the BYU honoring Margaret Thatcher, former Prime Minister of Great Britain, to which we were invited. We also participated in an open house honoring Vern Breeze, my former counselor in the Stake Presidency. We continued to speak by special invitation to various functions and do sealings in the temple. Geri's Aunt Lucille was buried in Elsinore and we participated in that. In late April our dear friend and associate Mable Palmer passed away. She had been failing and we were saddened by her passing. We also had a quick trip to Melba, Idaho to visit Layne and his family. In April I was sustained as first assistant to our High Priest Group, an additional assignment for me. We enjoyed many of the family during the Spring Break as we travelled to Southern Utah and spent time in the Snow Canyon Area, hiking and enjoying the warm sunshine.

We did several sealing sessions in May, including ward groups and regular temple sealings. We did a large number of sealings for Gayle's family which brought her great satisfaction. We performed several sealings of friends and children of missionaries. We continued to be involved in speaking assignments at firesides and sacrament meetings. I was also asked to dedicate the war memorial at the Alpine Cemetery. Several friends young and old passed away which we accepted as the normal course of life. I had some treatment for cholesterol called chelation, recommended to me by my brother

Blauer. Several of our grandchildren graduated from seminary and high school, and we welcomed home our grandson Chad from his mission to Brazil. We ended the month by celebrating my brother David's birthday at the Granger Stake Center. He was losing his eyesight and hearing but still presented a happy countenance to all.

We continued to work the farm in the early summer, harvesting the hay and oats, and keeping things in operating order. We continued the sealing of friends and their children and held a lovely Hamblin family reunion at the Burgess Park in town. Our son Cory spent two weeks in Brazil preparing for their move in July. My brother Norman and his wife left for their mission in South Africa where they would be for the next three years. July saw Cory, Gayle, and their three youngest depart for Brazil. We participated in baptisms and birthdays of family members and enjoyed a relaxing time at Black's Fork in the High Uinta Mountains with our family. We continued to perform sealings and speak at functions upon request. For Alpine Days in August, I was asked to head a committee to honor several citizens. It turned out to be a nice affair. We were heavily involved with activities from all quarters. Geri and I spoke at a Young Women function at the Carlisle ranch in Wyoming; we joined Lonnie, Duella, and their family for a day at Lagoon; we had a reunion of the German-speaking missionaries to Brazil and another reunion with my former missionaries; we gave Peggy's children school blessings; and we continued with sealings of children of our missionaries. We also harvested corn. While our health continued to be quite good, we were saddened by the passing of my cousin Henry Bawden. On a bright note, Delbert Palmer married a woman he knew from Canada, and they seemed very happy together.

As the fall harvest came around, we enjoyed a bounteous harvest from our garden. We sold most of our straw for $2.00 a bale. We continued to speak on occasion and do sealings in the temple. BYU football took us to a couple of games, which we enjoyed. We also had a visit from our former missionary Ralph Degn, who reported to us his mission presidency in Brazil. Our nephew David Hamblin visited with us and shared his many health concerns, which have made him almost an invalid. We enjoyed a planned trip to Nauvoo with a tour group, starting in Independence and surroundings, then to Liberty, Far West, Adam-Ondi-Ahman, Nauvoo, Carthage, Hannibal, and St. Louis before returning home. It was a delightful time.

October conference brought a season of renewal and review with family members in our home as per our custom. We shortly thereafter participated in the cornerstone ceremony of the new Mount Timpanogos Temple. I was appointed a sealing supervisor of that temple. We were asked to speak about the temple in various places, one of which was in Granger. Our friend and neighbor Kyle Arnold was very ill, and we despaired for his life. He had been a good friend of many years. We took a trip to Idaho to be with Layne and his family, enjoying some time in the panhandle area of the state.

My brother Blauer and his wife Bessie invited us to join them on a cruise to the Bahamas in November, which turned into an enjoyable experience. We flew to Orlando and saw the temple site there, following which we participated in a required sales presentation to purchase a time share operation. Of course, we declined. From there we made our way to Cape Canaveral where we boarded the ship to the Bahamas. We enjoyed the chance to relax, play games, walk the decks, and enjoy shipboard entertainment, as well as swimming at various locations such as Salt Key and touring Grand Bahamas before returning to Cape Canaveral. We then visited the Epcot Center before flying back to Salt Lake.

Upon our return we learned that our granddaughter Gerilyn Beck had become engaged to Seth Merrill. Back at the temple we participated in a temple sealers' seminar, which was informative and helpful. Thanksgiving was a delightful experience with over 50 people at our home. We had our colt hit by a car but fortunately suffered no injury. My hip slipped out of joint, which was a rather painful occurrence. Our barn caught fire and burned to the ground causing the loss of much equipment and hay, amounting to over $20,000. We flew to Arizona to perform a wedding for one of Wilford Cardon's children. Seth and Gerilyn (Beck) Merrill were married on December 20. We celebrated several birthdays and parties associated with the Christmas season and decided to give each of our children $200 as a gift for Christmas and let them purchase what they needed for their use. It worked out very well. It had been an eventful year, full of involvement and a variety of activities.

1997

I spent time during January working with the insurance company concerning the loss of our barn and equipment. They made a settlement of about $16,000, which we thought would probably cover the cost of replacement. Grant helped me on the reconstruction. I designed a different roof, sloping from the front to the rear, and ordered saddles from two companies. During the month two new nice show saddles were delivered as well as a military saddle, a pack saddle, and a single harness, six bridles, and various items of equipment to shoe and groom the horses. In late January a building crew came and in three days had the new barn erected. We estimated the cost at $6,000.

Also in January Geri and I resumed our assignment at the Mount Timpanogos Temple in the sealing office. On January 18 I performed the marriage of our granddaughter Jennifer, Cory's eldest daughter, to Kevin Castle. The day before the wedding we met Kevin's family at a brunch held at Cory and Gayle's home. Kevin had stayed with us for a week or so before the wedding. We attended a breakfast in Provo with the groom's family on the day of the wedding. Jennifer and Kevin left the next day for Hawaii and then traveled on to Korea, where he was employed by the company in which Paulo and Steve were associated. Cory, Gayle, and their children had returned from Brazil for the wedding, and while they were in town, I also performed the marriage for the son of Russell Fuller, Cory's good friend. Cory and Gayle and the boys returned to Brazil on the 25th.

On the 20th Geri and I drove to St. George to spend a few days with her family, including Darlene and Noel and Dale and Lois. We stayed in our Red Rock apartment near the college, and we had plenty of food and comfortable arrangements. Ivan and Betty came over from Kanab each day. The first evening we visited with Geri's cousin La Reen, who was living with her son Merrill Kay Bradshaw, and we found that his neighbor was a cousin, Ken Hamblin, grandson of William Hamblin. On the 21st we drove around St. George and

Santa Clara, which was the birthplace of their grandfather, Wallace Hamblin; we visited the Jacob Hamblin home and the cemetery where his wife Rachel and his father are buried. We drove up to the Tuacahn Festival site and then up Snow Canyon for a picnic in fine weather. We drove up to Pine Mountain and around to Mountain Meadows. The snow was too deep to see the massacre monument, but we returned through Gunlock and the Santa Clara River. We enjoyed our evening meal and games together in the evening. The next day was spent mostly sitting together and visiting and games in the evening. We returned on the 23rd through stormy weather, though the roads were good. The remainder of the month consisted of our stake conference, which was presided over by our new Stake President, Jesse Hunsaker, who invited Geri and me to sit on the stand in the tabernacle. Duella and her family came to celebrate her birthday on the 28th. Others of the family also participated in helping around the farm.

The weather in February moderated somewhat, allowing us to begin our farming operation. I did quite a bit of plowing and working of the ground during the month. We had finished the new barn to a degree that we were able to invite the family over for a nice barn dance. Many came and enjoyed a lively time together. Geri and I continued to render service on Friday evenings at the Mt Timpanogos Temple as we directed the sealing office. We also had responsibility in the ward and stake directing the family history program, including classes in the stake center. On occasion we also spoke at firesides, and I performed a marriage nearly every week in the temples nearby. We were invited to a lovely dinner in the Jordan River Temple during which all former presidents of that temple and their spouses were recognized. Towards the end of the month Geri and I took Walt and Pat Cryer with us to Melba, Idaho, to be with Layne and his family at the baptism of their son Will. He had asked that I perform the baptism. We enjoyed a few days with their lovely family, and then we returned through Sun Valley and across the flat prairie area to Twin Falls. It was covered in deep snow.

With the wedding season upon us, I was constantly requested to perform sealings for family and friends, relatives, and others, including that of Tony and Matilde Wosnijk. Tony was a friend from Brazil, and we considered him to be almost an adopted son. We had opportunity to be with my brothers and sisters to celebrate my brother Blauer's birthday early in March. We had physical examinations and learned that Geri had gallstones and needed to have her gall bladder removed. It turned out to be a same-day surgery, and she recovered from it fairly quickly. I dislocated my hip just prior to performing a marriage in the Salt Lake Temple but was fitted with a wheelchair, allowing me to perform the ceremony and then get to a hospital to have it put back into place. We learned with sadness that Janet Sorensen, wife of my missionary companion Lynn Sorensen, was very ill with cancer, and she passed away at the end of April. My cousin Jessica Schmidt Taylor's husband, Harold, also passed away. Farming also became a major involvement during the month with planting and caring for the ground taking much of our time. We had the barn painted, nearly completing the restoration of that project. April brought general conference and the attending activities with our family as we gathered together to review the talks and events. These were always special times for us. We held a missionary reunion in Salt Lake with several of our missionaries taking time to be with us. In the middle of the month we went with many of the family to Snow Canyon to enjoy the warmer weather since many of the children had spring break. We enjoyed touring around St. George and even went down to Mt. Trumbull and to an overlook of the Grand Canyon, reviewing many places of interest relating to the early settlement of the area. Events with family and friends involved attending the play The Music Man, in which two of our grandchildren were involved—Megan Dowse and Amy Bangerter. We also enjoyed a renewed association with Delbert Palmer and his new wife, Joyce.

The month of May dawned in splendor. It was a beautiful springtime. The fields came alive with green, and the trees gave brilliance to the sweet atmosphere. We found ourselves in the most desirable surroundings in the world. The children were well and seemed to enjoy coming to the family haven. We had fields of barley and alfalfa growing with some promise. The fruit trees did not give great promise but added to the beauty of the surroundings. The horses were of deep interest to all the family and many in the family looked forward to finishing school so as to spend more time on the farm. We continued to be involved with several marriages and firesides from time to time. Our involvement with the sealing office in the temple was always pleasant. Our health seemed reasonably good, though our physical stamina seemed to drop off at times. We walked around the property as vigorously as possible so as to maintain some semblance of our physical tone. Towards the end of June we had a lovely reunion with our German-speaking Brazilian missionary companions in Bountiful. It was delightful to renew those acquaintances. We continued to tend the farm and the horses, providing delight for all of us.

July brought our annual event in the Uinta Mountains, as well as involvement with the celebration of the 150th anniversary of the entrance into the valley of the pioneers. The trek from Winter Quarters to Salt Lake had been re-enacted as part of that celebration. We took a delightful trip with Layne and Betsy to northern Arizona and enjoyed many scenes of interest associated with Jacob Hamblin and his efforts among the Indians. We returned home in time to participate in the first cutting of the hay crop. Immediately we began to irrigate in order to bring about more hay production. On August 7 I performed the sealing of Cleadonna's brother Blaine Webb and his wife, Heilala. We also enjoyed a lovely reunion at Dale and Lois Hamblin's cabin in the mountains. We visited the old homestead and remains of the cabin located at Archie's Creek, where their family had enjoyed many months of employment and recreation in the High Uinta Mountains. We also had enjoyable times with others of my siblings. We continued to be heavily involved on Fridays with the sealing office and also in performing marriages throughout the month.

September brought several important events. We joined with my brothers and sisters in a dinner party to honor my brother Blauer and his wife, Bessie, was they were leaving on a temple mission to the Santiago Chile Temple. Our granddaughter Alisa Dawn Lorenzon was married to Nathan Ries. I also performed other sealings as requested during the month. We enjoyed a lovely trip to southern Utah in company with Walt and Pat Cryer, going through small towns and areas of scenic beauty they had never seen before. October brought harvest time of tomatoes and other items from the garden. It was a fruitful season, and we added to our storehouse by canning and bottling much in the way of fruit and vegetables. General conference was special in the focus on the Restoration of the gospel and the establishment of the center of the Church in the mountains. Of special note was our daughter Julie's call to be a member of the Young Women general board. We were pleased and honored by her selection. We later on enjoyed an opportunity to spend time in Grant's cabin in Fruitland before attending the open house of the Vernal Temple.

On October 14, Geri and I celebrated our 44th wedding anniversary. We drove to Hill Field and toured the aviation museum, spending time to review in our minds those special days of World War II and the experiences of those moving times. On display were some of the airplanes I had flown in the Army air force. We saw the old biplane, open-cockpit Steerman, the primary trainer; the basic trainer, the BT 13; and the advanced trainer, the AT 6. Then there was the great B-25, in which I instructed for over 700 hours in 1944 and 1945. Great feelings and memories came as those days more than 50 years ago seemed very close.

Other events of October included the deer hunt, headed up by our son Layne. Not all the boys were successful in their attempts to get a deer. We enjoyed using the cider press to make apple cider. I had cataract surgery on my eyes during this period, which greatly improved my vision. We also enjoyed another reunion of my missionary companions during the month. November brought the beginning of winter and another flurry of marriages to perform in the temple. We had several of our grandchildren celebrating their birthdays, and we tried to make those days special for them as well. Thanksgiving was celebrated in grand style at Grant's mountain home with many of the family attending. December brought a marvelous flow of activities associated with family as we prepared to celebrate the season. These included special gatherings of our children as well as a special dinner with my brothers and sisters. We held a special meeting with our granddaughters from ages 12 through 18 in which we gave special instruction and challenges to attain goals in their lives. Of special note was the marriage of our granddaughter Audrey Jo Apple to Gordon Stock. It had been a most eventful and enjoyable year.

1998

We celebrated the New Year visiting Duella and her family and watching the Rose Parade, in which two of Grant's children (Dallan and Rachel) participated with the American Fork High School Marching Band. A couple of our grandsons came and helped with cutting and stacking wood as well as helping with the horses—riding, shoeing, and so forth. The weather was fairly mild with not too much snow. We continued our assignment at the Mount Timpanogos Temple, working the Friday afternoon shift and sometimes on Saturday mornings. We also directed the family history class in our ward. We hosted a gathering of our former Jordan River Temple presidency and enjoyed the association with them. Geri and I became nervous to go somewhere, so we decided to drive south through Price and Emery County, stopping at the museum in Castle Dale, visiting Cleveland, then driving on the dirt road to I-70 to Green River and Moab, where we spent the night. We drove to Monticello and visited with Mike Johnson and his wife Amelia, who were in charge of constructing the new temple there. We drove to Blanding for breakfast and into Mexican Hat and Monument Valley, where we enjoyed the sunshine and open skies. We drifted around that area and finally drove to Kayenta, stopping at the Betatakin ruins, passing Shonto and Kaibito, and spending the night in Page. The next day we drove across the bridge at Glen Canyon Dam and stopped in Kanab to visit with Ivan and Betty. We had breakfast with them and then drove home, arriving in the evening.

February was spent mostly around the farm and enjoying activities with the family. I plowed some ground and began getting the soil ready for planting. Later on we spent a couple of days with Grant and his family at their cabin in Fruitland. Geri and I decided to drive to Arizona to see some of our friends there. We had learned of the passing of Sister Antonietta Lombardi in Brazil, and we found that her husband, José, would be coming to Arizona to visit his daughter and her family. We stopped in St. George for the night and the next morning drove to Fredonia for sacrament meeting and then continued on over the Kaibab Plateau and Jacob's Lake through Flagstaff, arriving at the Wilford Cardon home about 5:30 in the evening in Mesa. The time in Arizona was most enjoyable. We visited several of our good friends, including Jacob and Gerta Kerns from Brazil; Elsie Fern Bushman, my sister-in-law; Lowell and Cora Wilson; Harmon Barton, a former missionary companion; and the Lombardis. Wilford insisted on getting us a new car, taking us around to several dealerships, and eventually we settled on his mother's Buick, which was in very good shape. He would not let us pay anything for it. We ended up loading the trunk full of grapefruit and oranges before driving back home through Flagstaff and Panguitch.

In March we celebrated Geri's 74th birthday in royal fashion, with several of the children helping out with the activities. In addition to our normal Friday sealing assignment, I performed several marriages for family and the children of former missionaries. I also tilled some of the fields in preparation for planting crops. We took another trip to St. George with Layne and his family, spending the night in our apartment there. The next day we toured the St. George area, including the temple, the tabernacle, Brigham Young's home, Jacob Hamblin's home, and the Santa Clara Cemetery. We then drove to Gunlock and on to Mountain Meadows to review family and Church history. We returned through Snow Canyon, enjoying a picnic before returning to the apartment in the evening.

The following day we left after breakfast and drove 70 miles south to the old community of Mount Trumbull. In 1887 the government opened up much of the Arizona Strip to homesteading, and farms and ranches blossomed throughout the area. A ward of the Church was established, and the number of members reached over 300. The community began to dwindle, and at the time of our visit there were only a few scattered ranches. A schoolhouse was built, and a portion of it is still standing as a memorial, maintained by some historical association. We drove eastward over Mount Trumbull, a fairly high mountain with a good forest on it. Much of the timber for the St. George Temple was harvested there, and we located the sawmill site.

We continued on east to the Grand Canyon, passing the old church called Tuweep. At the edge of the canyon is Toroweap Point, and it gives a spectacular view. The canyon of the Colorado is not as vast as it is further upstream, but it is possible to stand right on the edge of the canyon and see the river almost vertically below. Just below our vantage point we could see the old lava flow, which descended into the canyon from a volcano, causing large rapids in the river. We drove back north, visiting Pipe Springs and then touring the community of Colorado City, established by dissenting Mormons who still practice plural marriage. We drove back to St. George through Hurricane and enjoyed a lovely meal.

The next day we drove through Zion National Park and enjoyed the magnificence of the beautiful formations. The group took an extensive hike. We drove up through the Zion-Mount Carmel tunnel and back down again, returning for the night in St. George. The last day we cleaned the apartment and returned to Alpine, having enjoyed a lovely time with Layne and his family. Our efforts continued with the temple sealing office as well as teaching the family history class. I also gave a lesson in the high priests group meeting. We had a delightful dinner group for the Palmers, Espenschieds, Sara Paulsen, and Marne Tuttle and enjoyed a choice time together.

April brought general conference and the accompanying activities with our family. Our son Cory was home from Brazil for meetings and participated in the blessing of his grandson Cory Smith Castle as well as the ordination of his son Jed to the office of elder in preparation for his upcoming mission. We enjoyed a lovely meal at the Mandarin Restaurant in Bountiful, under the sponsorship of Lloyd Hicken, for our former missionary companions and spouses. I attended a special regional conference in American Fork, and Elder Maxwell, upon seeing me, made a point to discuss the efforts to call local missionaries in Brazil. I struggled somewhat with my health, which seemed cured by pills from the doctor. Towards the end of the month, my brother Bud (Blauer); his wife, Bessie; Geri; and I went to Boise for a few days with Layne and his family. In May, Howard was called as a bishop of a BYU ward in the stake where he had been serving as a high counselor. We also viewed the BYU ballroom dance competition in which our granddaughter Holly competed. She was preparing for a ballroom dance team tour in England, where Cory and Gayle planned to meet her. On the farm we planted half an acre of corn and over 100 tomato plants. We also continued our involvement with the sealing office at the Mount Timpanogos Temple.

In June we celebrated my 80th birthday and had much family, close and extended, come for a special breakfast. Later that day, Julie hosted a lovely catered dinner in my honor. Around the same time, Geri's Aunt Arvilla (Bill) Shelly passed away, and we took a major role in the funeral and other settlements. Cory's family began to return from Brazil for their summer break. His daughter Holly had decided to serve a mission and received her call to the Brazil Recife South Mission. His son Jed had already received his call to serve in Brazil Belo Horizonte East. Their son Chad went to Brazil to teach English for the summer. The Schwantes family held their reunion in Salt Lake, with many of the family attending. Our assignment at the temple continued as scheduled.

On the farm we struggled with the rain, losing most of the first crop due to being so wet. I struggled a little more with health concerns and even had my hip slip out of joint while irrigating. I lay on the ground for two hours, trying to attract someone's attention. Finally, our neighbor Sister Nelson heard my cries and came from over 200 yards away, then summoned help from neighbors, who helped get me to the hospital, where it was put back into place.

Our annual excursion to Black's Fork in the High Uinta Mountains served to gather much of our family together in a pleasant setting. We took several horses with us and camped in our favorite location. We rode horses, taking rides up the canyon, as well as fishing and enjoying campfires at night. All of the children did the meals and invited Geri and me to join with them at each meal. We were not allowed to do any cooking of our own. We also took a trip to Alaska with Peggy and Glenda to visit Sonja and Wilson Duffles, one of our former missionaries. We enjoyed various locations, including Seward, where the girls went fishing for halibut. Geri and I went on an excursion cruise to visit some of the nearby glaciers. The girls drove to Denali while Geri and I enjoyed the Church Welfare

Farm in Palmer, picking several choice vegetables.

In August Cory's family had shifted again. Those who had been in Brazil were back in the U.S., and those who had been stateside were in Brazil. Two of his children were also returning to Brazil as missionaries. I received a call from my cousin John Bangerter asking me to visit his son, who was being held in the Utah State Prison due to some illegal activities. I met with his son and arranged for him to contact his bishop and stake president for assistance. Eventually he was put on a work-release program in St. George, where he lived.

We continued to work the farm, getting the second crop of hay cut, raked, baled, and stacked in good order. We also harvested the oats with good results. The corn came on in good order and we harvested some, and froze it as needed. Many of the family were also able to enjoy that harvest as well. I was released from the high priests leadership, which gave us a little more freedom. We participated in mission farewells as well priesthood ordinations for our grandchildren. Geri and I attended an original German-speaking Brazilian missionary reunion, which was delightful.

In September we harvested the third crop of hay, but it was not heavy in its production. We shortly began to pasture the horses in our large field since the grandchildren were not around as much to ride the horses. We paid a visit to Layne and Betsy in Idaho, where we helped with their harvest and also in moving some of his stock. Layne was serving in the bishopric at the time. Some of my cousins—Eldon Bawden and John and Alden Bangerter—were struggling with their health, so Rulon Mackay (another cousin) and I paid them a visit, giving them blessings for their health. We took our wives with us and made an outing of it.

October brought general conference, and Layne and Betsy and their family came down to be with us. Between sessions on Saturday a lightning bolt struck the southwest corner of the barn and set the entire barn on fire again. Layne and the fire chief were able to remove the saddles and bridles, but nearly everything else was destroyed, including our entire hay crop for the year. It had been two years since we had our last fire in the barn. Grant was able to get the barn pretty well rebuilt by the end of the month.

We took a short trip to St. George to watch two grandsons participate in a football game there. On the way home we took a scenic route, going through Zion National Park, then to Bryce Canyon, and then north over the Grand Staircase National Monument to the town of Boulder. There Glenneth and Lowell Wilson's daughter Carrie lived with her husband and two children in a rather primitive but comfortable setting called a yurt. They seemed happy and content. After our return we attended a missionary reunion in President and Sister James Faust's apartment. I also performed some marriages during the month.

The most significant happening in November was the passing away of my brother Blauer L. Bangerter on Sunday, November 1, in the hospital in Provo, Utah. Geri and I went there knowing that he had surgery the day before, and with his wife Bessie we saw that he was in his extremity. With his son-in-law Jay Beck, I gave him a blessing that was almost a release from his suffering, and he passed away an hour later. The ensuing days were involved with giving support to Bessie and gathering the family for the funeral, which took place on the 5th in their stake center. I spoke, and the family was very sweet and represented themselves well.

Our apple crop came on strong, and we ground up several bushels of them to make cider. It was a great addition to the Thanksgiving feast held in our home with over 60 of our family in attendance. In December we continued our assignment in the temple, and I performed several marriages for extended family members and friends. We began a new family history study group in our ward, which was a major undertaking. We went with Paulo to St. George while he went on to Las Vegas to see the BYU game there. We returned through Minersville, taking Grant's daughter Katie with us and enjoying her bright, sweet spirit. We had family gatherings in preparation for the Christmas season with our children and also with my brothers and sisters. We also had a lovely party with my former missionary companions at the home of Asael and Ida Sorensen. Layne and Betsy and their family and spent the holidays with us. The day following Christmas, we drove with Julie and Ramon on a quick vacation to Las Vegas, and then after Church on Sunday we drove to Death Valley, where we toured the afternoon and evening, returning to Las Vegas for the night. We returned to Alpine by Tuesday.

A terrible sadness came to us on New Year's Eve. While we were having a special dinner with Glenda's family and others, Julie and Ramon came in with the news that Katie and Dallan Bangerter had met with an accident en route to Grant's cabin just beyond Daniels Summit. Katie had died in the accident, and Dallan had been taken to LDS Hospital. We had some difficulty in reaching Grant on his cell phone, but when we made contact, I had the most sorrowful talk with him, telling him and Cleadonna of the loss of their daughter. We arranged with Grant to meet them in Heber City, driving there with Ramon and Lonnie. After waiting for some time we met Grant's family at the crossroads and went to Olpin Mortuary in Heber. They had a brief view of Katie, and then we proceeded to Salt Lake and the hospital where Dallan was undergoing surgery on his left arm, which was nearly severed. Katie had died instantly in the crash. Dallan was presumed to be in a life-threatening condition, but his survival was really a miracle, with no one understanding how he was free of the crash with only minor injuries excepting his arm. The surgery saved his arm. We spent the night with the family in the hospital.

This was one of the most serious experiences in our entire family, and Grant and Cleadonna and their children were devastated. There was a great degree of comfort to Grant and Cleadonna in that he had received vivid dreams about five years earlier, witnessing just such an accident and seeing Katie would probably be taken. When the event happened he recognized his dream, and after Dallan was able to visit with him the next morning, as Grant sought to tell him that his sister had passed away (Dallan first inquired about her), Dallan said, "She is dead, isn't she?" He then said he had previously had a dream himself witnessing the scene. This came as a great comfort to the family with a realization that somehow forces beyond mortal life had entered into the happening, taking Katie's life and preserving Dallan, whose survival was miraculous. It seemed that some angelic power had lifted him from the crash and planted him on the side of the highway without his being aware of how he escaped. This event cast a heavy cloud over the family, but there was much to reassure us that Katie's time to leave mortality had been determined from on high and that Dallan had been rescued from certain death by eternal forces and beings, whom we believe to be in attendance and watching over our welfare. There was much to lead us to give our thanks to our Heavenly Father in our submission to His eternal purposes.

1999

The sad ending of 1998 moved our thoughts and feelings as we realized the reality of Katie's death and Dallan's accident and injury. The entire family was deeply saddened and touched in thinking of Katie and her sweetness and wonderful achievements. The funeral with all its arrangements was a most unhappy chore for us and especially for Grant and Cleadonna. We spent much time with them, and although they had difficulty in acknowledging the reality of her demise, they remained generally cheerful and positive. There was nothing else to do but face up to the circumstances and rely on our faith with the knowledge that she was in good condition and that the sorrow pertaining to us does not affect her happiness and well-being.

On January 2, all the adults in the family went to the Mount Timpanogos Temple. I had arranged with the temple for the family to receive Katie's endowment by proxy before her burial, and we felt great comfort in attending that session and having the great experience of knowing that Katie departed with the fullness of the blessings available in mortality. The evening prior to the funeral was spent at the viewing in the mortuary, where countless people came to visit the family and see Katie. The funeral was held on the 6th in the Highland West Stake Center. It was a beautiful expression of the family with Geri, Cleadonna, Blaine, and finally Grant giving full time to speaking of the spiritual forces that had attended Katie's life and death and the assurances they had received. The funeral lasted two and a half hours. Grant was the bishop conducting. At the cemetery, the American Fork High School Band came and played for her. Dallan was allowed to leave the hospital long enough to attend the funeral. The following day, Dallan was discharged from the hospital. Geri and I spent much time with Grant's family during this period.

Gradually our lives took on a more normal activity as we returned to our temple activity, performing sealings and working in the sealing office. I picked up a severe cold and was somewhat limited in activity for a week or so. We had our physical check-ups, and though generally in good health, were informed of increased blood pressure and cholesterol levels. My cousin Rowena Lauritzen passed away at the end of the month, and I spoke at her funeral. We also drove to Idaho to attend a high priests social, where we spoke. At the end of the month we drove to Arizona through Green River and Monticello and finally arrived in Snowflake, where we spent the night with Ray and Judy Caldwell. We then continued on down to the Gila Valley and spent two nights with Roland and Mae Hamblin and then continued on through Benson, Tucson, and Florence Junction into Gilbert. We met with several of our missionaries in a lovely reunion. We also visited Lowell and Cora Wilson, my brother-in-law and his wife, as well as Elsie Fern Bushman in Mesa. We returned through Flagstaff and Kanab, visiting with Ivan and Betty before returning home.

Into February we continued our temple activity, performing many sealings of children of friends and family. We were able to get out and ride the horses some during the warmer portions of the month. My large tractor gave me some problems, and we had to have it repaired. Our grandson Garren Apple received his mission call to Frankfurt, Germany. March brought the passing of more friends and associates from our prior temple assignment, including Gladys Heaton Walker and Winnie Bowers. Another tragic accident took the lives of the in-laws of our granddaughter Laura Lorenzon Thorpe. So the cycle of life continued with births, blessings, baptisms, sealings, and deaths. Horseback riding in the west desert with Layne and up the mountain to the north brought pleasure and relaxation to us. Grant and Cleadonna had arranged for a trip to South America along with Glenda and Steve to visit Cory and his family before their return from their assignment in Brazil. Our mare delivered a colt, whom we named Pontiac.

April involved many activities with the family, including those centered on general conference. We had missionary reunions and visits with friends from Brazil, including Adhemar Damiani, who had just been called as Area Seventy, and his wife. I also performed several weddings upon request by friends and family. Work on the farm included rock parties and horseback rides. Regarding health issues, I needed a hearing aid replacement as well as work on several of my teeth. We enjoyed a brief visit to Idaho and Layne's family to participate in the blessing of their son Eli Lewis.

At the end of the month, Delbert Palmer requested that we join them on a trip to the Mormon colonies in Mexico. We left therefore on the 26th, taking Bessie (my brother Blauer's wife) with us, and drove to Mesa, Arizona, staying overnight with Wilford and Phyllis Cardon. The next morning Delbert and his wife Joyce met us, and we began our trip to Mexico. We drove to Tucson and stopped there to visit the Pima Air and Space Museum, where we saw most of the World War II airplanes that I had flown from 1943 to 1946. We moved onward through St. David, noting the settlements by LDS people, and then visited Tombstone and the Boot Hill graveyard there. We enjoyed touring through Bisbee and the vast southwest desert and drove on to Douglas, where we spent the night at the Gadsden Hotel. The next morning we checked our visas into Mexico, arranged for automobile insurance, and finally entered Mexico about 10:30 a.m. Our journey took us east past Slaughter Ranch and through the Guadelupe Mountains, and we came out of the mountains at Janos. From there it was south for about 80 miles to Dublán and Nuevas Casas Grandes. We continued from there on to Colonia Juárez. There Bessie's niece and her husband, Brother and Sister Schmidt, provided lodging and food for us with great hospitality. We attended the new small Colonia Juárez Temple for an endowment session that evening. The following day, the 28th, after a fine breakfast, we visited the Juárez Academy hosted by Brother Whetten, the director. Leaving Juárez we visited the Indian ruins near Casas Grandes, did some shopping, and drove north to go through Columbus and Deming, New Mexico. We met with Larry and Shirley Memmott, our former missionary living in Deming. They hosted us at a diner and showed us to a motel, where we spent a comfortable night. On our return on the 29th we drove through Lordsburg and Wilcox, then down Texas Canyon and turned off at Pomerene, near Benson, where Bessie had lived and where her father was buried. This was a special stop for her, having lived in the area many years ago. We came to the Mesa area, stopping at the home of Bessie's sister-in-law, and then the Palmers took us to lunch at a restaurant they knew. We stayed the night with the Cardons. The following day we returned home, leaving Bessie at her home in Provo.

May brought about several weddings, which I performed in various temples nearby. Family events of note included the missionary farewell of Garren Apple, Glenda's son, going to Germany. Three grandchildren graduated from high school towards the end of the month. Our eldest son Cory was called and sustained as second counselor in our stake presidency nearly two months before they returned from their CES assignment in Brazil. I struggled with some health concerns, including dental worries and increased soreness in my toe. I also had my artificial hip go out, requiring me to have it put back in at the hospital. Julie and Ramon left for Europe to pick up their son Joseph, who had completed his mission in Germany.

June brought the harvest of the first crop of hay. It had been tended well by the grandsons in their irrigation turns, and we were grateful to Eugene Healey for his assistance in getting it cut and baled. Cory and his family returned from Brazil, though Cory continued to supervise the work there, traveling back and forth each month. We enjoyed the visit of one of our missionaries, Clery Pereira Bentim, and her husband, Nivaldo, who had been called as mission president to the Florianopolis mission. We continued to serve in the sealing office in the temple and also performed several weddings during the month.

July brought continued effort on the farm, preparing for the second crop of hay and the surrounding activities. It was laborious but enjoyable to work the ground and harvest the crops. We enjoyed opportunities to be with family in various settings, including Grant's cabin and other spots. Our annual trip to the Uinta Mountains was delightful as we spent nearly an entire week in that lovely setting with many of our children and grandchildren. Geri and I went to Fullerton, California, where I had been requested to rebaptize Eraldo

Soares, one of our good friends and former missionaries from our time in Brazil. He had met some difficulties in his life, but he had managed to get things back in order.

August brought several reunions with former missionaries and family. My brother Norman and his wife, Colleen, had returned from their mission in South Africa, and we enjoyed having them over for an activity. Julie, as a member of the Young Women general board, arranged for a congenial social activity for the board at our home with music and food. The farm continued to produce well with corn coming on. We also had the constant tending of the horses and the property. We also continued our efforts in the temple each Friday. Towards the end of the month we visited Layne and his family in Idaho and enjoyed watching the huge potato harvesters at work.

September found us harvesting corn and hay as well as a good crop of tomatoes. Geri was honored with Scouting's Silver Beaver Award at a large ceremony at BYU. Most of our family was present to see her receive that recognition. Our daughter Lee Ann and her family decided to purchase a home in Alpine and moved into one near Burgess Park. We seldom had a week go by without my performing a wedding for someone tied to us.

General conference found us at home, listening to the sessions on the TV. A new Conference Center was announced. After conference, we decided to make a brief tour of some of Geri's relatives and began driving to Mountain View, Wyoming, on October 5. We visited with her cousin, Myrtle, and her daughter-in-law, who is compiling family genealogy. We visited the Lyman Cemetery, finding some family members who were buried there, and after lunch we continued on to Rock Springs, then to Farson, over South Pass, and down to Lander. There we located Geri's brother, Dale and his wife, Lois, and spent the evening with them and stayed in a motel. The next morning Dale led us on a tour of his construction project, a seven million dollar prison. Our trip took us next through Riverton and Shoshoni and across the Continental Divide to Casper. In Casper we visited for two hours with Geri's Aunt Carrie. We were on the Pioneer Trail and followed it to Independence Rock and Martin's Cove. The Church had recently purchased the vast Sun Ranch, and we visited the very active visitors' center, which concentrates on the tragic experience of the handcart pioneers in 1856. Going south to Rawlins, we spent some time looking at the various landmarks associated with Geri's life while she lived there, but she did not take enough time to satisfy her. Through the evening we traveled west over the Great Divide Basin and stopped in a motel in Rock Springs, where we enjoyed supper. The next morning we left, going south from Green River over the mountains, past Flaming Gorge Reservoir and Dutch John and the Uinta Mountains down to Vernal. We attended a session in the Vernal Temple, had lunch there, and drove to Fruitland, spending the night at Grant's cabin together with his family and Lee Ann's and Glenda's families as well. Later in the month we celebrated our 46th wedding anniversary with a good Mexican dinner at Mi Ranchito.

November proved to be a rather trying time for us. I continued to perform sealings in the temple on a regular basis and also marriages as requested. Thanksgiving was celebrated at the home of Paulo and JaLayne. The day following Thanksgiving, I went with Layne to pick up a truck I had purchased in Ogden. We also visited the Aerospace Museum at Hill Field. That afternoon I developed a pain in my abdomen, and late that night Geri and Layne took me to the American Fork Hospital. After testing and diagnosis, doctors finally determined to remove my appendix, which was not the problem, but they also found that the gall bladder had ruptured and that I was severely infected. It was removed, but shortly thereafter I suffered a heart attack. This condition became very threatening, and I was transferred to the Utah Valley Hospital for special care in the ICU. I passed two days without knowing very much. Geri was with me constantly. All of the children spent time with me and gave great support. Word went through the family and the community, and many people fasted and prayed for my well-being. I spent about ten days in the hospital with special care from the doctors, especially the heart specialist, Dr. Smith. Geri was with me in the room most of the time. My heart was finally tested, and Dr. Smith advised me that I had miraculously passed the stress test on the heart and that he felt it was as sound as ever. Our feeling of thankfulness for such a wonderful blessing was overwhelming. While I was in the hospital, Delbert Palmer, who was staying in Provo, came twice a day to check on me and give me support, which was deeply appreciated. Lloyd Hicken came all the way from Bountiful to give me support and encouragement, which was reminiscent of our experience with my life-threatening illness in Brazil (see chapter 16). Following the tests on my heart, Dr. Smith advised me that I could return home the next day. We were most grateful that I had survived this near-fatal experience. While in the hospital, neighbors took it upon themselves to care for our property and horses, Conrad Teichert being in the forefront. Family members put up the Christmas decorations. Follow-up visits to various doctors pronounced me sound. We enjoyed family gatherings with my brothers and sisters as well as our children in preparation for the Christmas season. Our Christmas was rather subdued due to my recovering condition. It was a relaxing time. I also performed several weddings as time would permit during the weeks following my hospitalization. We enjoyed some time at Grant's cabin as we prepared to celebrate the New Year.

2000

As we began the New Year and the new century, it was evident how great our blessings had been. To have my health completely restored after a very close threat to my life was clearly in answer to the wonderful prayers and several blessings of my family, relatives, and many members of our ward. I did not know what the span of my life might be, but since my youth I had imagined what it would be like to live to see the year 2000, in which I would be 82 years of age. We had called on our doctors, Dr. Sundwall and Dr. Sheffield, who both declared that I was healed and well. On the 13th we had an important visit with Dr. Douglas Smith, my heart doctor. He told me how serious my attack had been, with my life resting on the brink, but again found that my heart was strong and well with no residual injury.

We resumed our efforts with the farm and animals, Cory taking two horses to his place and Howard caring for some at his. Fencing and care of the property took some of our extra time. We visited our friends Lamont and Nellie Smith in Clawson about the land we owned down there and where we had occasionally pastured our horses. We resumed our efforts in the temple and also performed several marriages. Our grandson Jacob Dowse received his endowment in preparation for his mission.

We took a trip to southern Utah with Grant and Cleadonna, stopping in Minersville at the cemetery, as well as stopping in St. George and meeting with Geri's Aunt Theo before going on to Las Vegas. There we met Lonnie and Duella, who had come in for a vacation they had won as a prize. We went to Boulder City, where we met some of Geri's cousins and toured the Hoover Dam as part of our excursion before returning home. February saw Jacob Dowse being set apart and leaving for his mission to Brazil. His father was present at the setting apart but did not participate. About the same time our granddaughter Holly, Cory's second daughter, returned from her mission to Brazil. Geri and I were asked to speak at a couple of wards nearby, sharing our experiences of past years. Our temple assignment continued unabated.

In March we finally sold our property in Clawson and then focused our attention on the work around the farm, plowing and preparing the soil. We planted barley this time. Alpine City decided to install a forced irrigation system throughout the city, taking better advantage of the water from the canyon. Towards the end of the month we took a trip into Arizona with Layne and Betsy, stopping in Minersville and seeing Old Fort Deseret. We spent the night in St. George and then drove on down through Fredonia, Jacob's Lake, and Lee's Ferry. Layne wanted to see the Indian country, so we stopped in Tuba City and Moenkopi and then drove across the desert through the Hopi villages and into Holbrook, where we spent the night. We proceeded the next day through Snowflake, Show Low, and the Salt River Canyon, stopping to visit Mae and Roland Hamblin in Safford. From there we drove past Dos Cabesas and Wilcox and into Douglas, stopping at the site of the old Douglas Air Base. We toured various sites of interest from when Mildred and I lived in the area after our marriage in 1944. We went into Agua Prieta for a couple of hours and spent the night in Douglas. The next day we left Douglas and visited Bisbee and the copper pit there, going into the Mule Mountains, the San Pedro Valley, and Tombstone. The main point of interest

there was of course the location of the famous gunfight at the OK Corral between the Earps and the Clantons. We also checked out the cemetery at Boot Hill and then continued on north, seeing the Dragoon Mountains and the Chiricahua Mountains in the distance, where Chief Cochise had his headquarters. We could easily see the Swisshelm Mountains and the Pedregosa Mountains, as well as the Peloncillos, the Tombstone Hills, the Huachuca, the Mustangs, the Whetstones, and the Galiuro Mountains. We proceeded on into the Mormon colonies of St. David and Benson. We crossed over the divide into Tucson, again visiting the San Xavier del Bac Mission. We continued along the Sonoran Desert into Chandler and Mesa, where we stayed. The next day we visited with Wilford and Phyllis Cardon, who loaded us up with oranges and grapefruit. We left for home, stopping in Kanab for dinner and driving the rest of the way to Alpine in the dark.

April general conference brought the first event in the Conference Center, and we were able to attend. We felt that the Conference Center was a marvelous achievement and indicative of the growth of the Lord's kingdom. My cousin John Bangerter passed away, and I spoke at his funeral. Geri and I spoke at a couple of nearby sacrament meetings with varied success. The family was involved with planting several rose bushes around the house, and we continued to work the farm, cleaning ditches, planting barley, and taking care of the horses. We recognized that at this point in our lives, several of our former missionaries had been called to serve as mission presidents. We noted that 35 had been called, and we felt certain that more would go. Others continued to serve additional missions in various locations. Our family continued to grow and develop. Our granddaughter Ashley, Howard's daughter, announced her engagement to McKay King from Dubois, Idaho. We spent a couple of days with Layne and his family in Melba and then appreciated the high school graduation ceremonies of three of our grandchildren: David, Rachael, and Heidi. The work on the farm continued with preparations and maintenance, and Dallan was most helpful, despite his weakened left arm, injured in the accident that took the life of his sister Katie more than a year previously. June brought a flurry of activity on different fronts. David

Tuttle organized a memorial horseback ride in Alpine to honor those missionaries who had lost their lives in the service. I celebrated my 82nd birthday without much special notice. I was in good health, but the strength of my youth was somewhat diminished. We attended the Schwantes reunion in Vallencitos, New Mexico, under the direction of Ruth Stricklin. We enjoyed the scenery of the mountains going and coming. We were saddened by a number of the younger generation who had abandoned the principles of their forefathers and had taken up loose relationships foreign to the gospel. Our grandson Jedediah returned from his mission to Belo Horizonte. We enjoyed stake conference with Loren Dunn, who presided at his last conference before being named emeritus and leaving to preside over the Boston Temple. Geri and I flew to Portland Oregon to attend and speak at a multistake singles conference, which was a delightful experience that we enjoyed very much. We continued our efforts in the temple, and I performed a marriage or two along the way. Paulo and JaLayne took their family on a Church history tour, and in the midst of it, her mother, who was quite ill from cancer, passed away. They returned early to attend the funeral.

July came with continued work on the farm, irrigating and working the hay. We harvested the first crop of hay and sold much of it as our needs were reduced. We participated in family activities such as baptisms of grandchildren and marriages of friends and relatives. The annual trek to the mountains was delightful with a lovely Sunday service conducted by Howard, who was a bishop. The children enjoyed hiking and swimming in the river at various locations. We finished the second crop of hay in August and continued the family involvement on the upkeep of the property. Our granddaughter Ashley was married to McKay King in the temple, which ceremony I performed. I also performed other marriages during the month. We became more aware of our advancing age when we were invited to the senior citizens dinner at the stake center. We certainly didn't feel old enough to be in that group, but young people of 60 years of age were also admitted. My cousin and close friend Eldon John Bawden passed away. We also learned that our neighbor Conrad Teichert had contracted cancer and was not expected to live too much longer. Our

daughter Lee Ann, under the tutelage of Julie, finished her university course recertifying her as a schoolteacher.

Paulo and JaLayne invited us to accompany them on a trip to Portugal. We left by plane on August 28th and made a brief visit to our granddaughter Gerilyn living in Detroit. We spent two days with her and her family. On the 30th we flew from Detroit to Atlanta, where we met Paulo and JaLayne and boarded a flight to Paris, France. Paulo had an upgrade fare and had me sit in first class. The adjacent seat was vacant, so he and Geri took turns with me enjoying the comforts of an overnight flight. Upon arriving in de Gaulle airport, we transferred to a flight to Lisbon, arriving about 10 a.m. on the 31st. Paulo then rented an automobile, and he toured us around Lisbon, showing us all the places he had lived in and the areas where he had worked as a missionary. We also toured Cascais and Guincho and found a motel in Estoril. On September 1 we drove around the area of Estremadura, through Sintra and our old residence. Much had changed, with better highways and much more traffic. In the evening we were hosted at the home of Antonio and Mae Leme. A few friends gathered, including the first people who had joined the Church when we opened the mission in 1974. They included Brother and Sister Amaral and the Souza family, and it was a lovely reunion.

The next day we drove north along the coast, visiting Mafra, Caldas da Rainha, Nazaré, and points in between, especially the places Paulo had known. We then traveled up to Viseu, where we stayed two nights, meeting his former landlady and several people he had been closely acquainted with. We attended Sunday meetings and gave our testimonies. Paulo wept with the richness of his memories of that place. We drove over the mountains of Caramulo and then north to Porto, looking over the city as another great place where Paulo had served. We visited the mission office and met President Soares, who had passed through the São Paulo Missionary Training Center under our direction in 1977. Returning south we visited Coimbra and stayed in Leiria.

On the 5th we drove south again, visiting the shrine of Fátima and spending more time in Lisbon to visit one of the Gonçalves daughters. We then proceeded over the long bridge to the Ribatejo and the Alentejo along the coast to the Algarve. We spent some time in Sagres, the site of the great navigator training under Prince Henry the Navigator and finally stopped in Portimão for the night. The next day, the 6th, Paulo located the Gonçalves family, and we spent half of the day visiting with them. In the afternoon we pressed eastward into Spain, passing Seville and Cadiz, and stayed the night near Gibraltar in Algeciras. On the 7th we drove to Granada, seeing the Sierra Nevada and the great Alhambra, a famous Moorish castle. The remainder of the day we drove through the great central plain of Spain, turning off to visit Toledo and its impressive setting. We then went into Madrid, having some difficulty finding a hotel. We didn't have much time to see Madrid but drove to the airport and boarded a Delta flight to New York, having much the same arrangement in first class as on our former flight. We made a brief change to a Salt Lake City flight. As it was east to west, we traveled with the sun, and it was a long day before we arrived at home again.

Back on the farm we continued our efforts to maintain the growing crops and also served in the temple, performing several weddings. Our former bishop Lloyd Carlton passed away, and we attended his funeral. October found us involved with our regular temple assignment plus several weddings performed during the month. Our farming had pretty much shut down for the season, though we continued to enjoy the horses. We had a couple of missionary reunions, one with our missionaries and another with my former missionary companions. All were then over 80 years of age, and four of our number had passed away. We also met with the former mission presidents of South America and enjoyed that association. We had two neighbors pass away, Elaine Kindred and Elvin Healey. Grant received a Distinguished Service Award in scouting, which was a joy to us—he had been serving as the Alpine district chairman. On Halloween, Geri continued her tradition of making spudnuts (donuts) for the entire family. Many came and helped with the event, and several people came to partake. November brought a continuance of weddings to perform nearly every week. We spoke at our son Howard's BYU ward as requested. The weather allowed for some outside activity, and care and repair of the farm was tackled

by members of the family. Our dear friend Conrad Teichert passed away, which cast a feeling of sadness upon the entire ward. We traveled to Idaho and helped Layne and his family move into their new home. Amanda, Grant's daughter, underwent brain surgery using a new procedure at the U of U hospital to correct recurring seizures, and it had marvelous consequences, as she became completely well from this affliction. Her ward Young Women had donated a tree at the Festival of Trees in Salt Lake in her honor. December and the Christmas season were scheduled with events of family and friends. We held a luncheon with my former mission companions early in the month. Grant and Cleadonna invited us to join them on a trip to Cancun, Mexico, and we spent a week with them. It was relaxing and enjoyable. We took a small ship ride around the great lagoon and enjoyed the lounge chairs on the beach. One day we visited the ruins at Chichen Itza and seemingly ate more than we should have. We returned on the 16th. Our preparations for Christmas continued as planned, and we enjoyed time with members of our family, taking us through the New Year.

2001

We were involved in several family activities throughout January, including an Eagle court of honor for our grandson Chris, a visit with Duella's family, watching our grandson Josh Apple play basketball and a visit to Layne's home in Idaho. Geri went through a cataract surgery, and we helped her recover at home. Our efforts with the temple and family history had only fair response. We enjoyed a dinner hosted by BYU President Merrill Bateman for a group of emeritus General Authorities.

The month of February was somewhat ordinary. We continued our activity in the temple on Fridays. I performed a couple of marriages and also participated in the blessing of Shane's third child. We had the normal trips to the dentist and doctors and attended some funerals. The weather was moderate and on the 27th I commenced plowing and disking our fields. Geri sustained a serious injury to her shoulder and spent quite a bit of time with the doctor. It was diagnosed as a rotator cuff injury.

We were scheduled to go to Arizona for a missionary reunion on March 3 and left with Julie and Ramon for Kanab. We met briefly with Ivan and Betty and spent the night in a motel. We continued on the next day to Phoenix, driving over the Kaibab and stopping at Lee's Ferry. We always enjoyed the desert, and it was beginning to come out of winter. We stayed overnight in Tempe, and the next day visited with Elsie Fern before going to the reunion at the home of Duke and Alice Cowley. About 15 or 20 of our missionaries with their wives came, and we had a good time catching up on their activities. We attended church on Sunday in Tempe and then drove to Globe and down the Salt River Canyon, which is always spectacular. We stopped to visit a missionary companion of Ramon's in Show Low and then stopped in Snowflake for a brief visit with Ray and Judy Caldwell before going to Holbrook for the night. We decided to tour the Petrified Forest National Park east of Holbrook and then drove north through the Painted Desert. From there we continued north to Canyon de Chelly. The rest of the day was spent driving through the Navajo country, continuing on to Monticello for the night. We proceeded to Arches National Park and then drove up the plateau between the Colorado and the Green Rivers in Canyonlands. This completed our sightseeing trip, and we drove home arriving late in the evening. I performed the wedding of our grandson Chad to Emily Adams on the 16th. Later that week we planted barley and alfalfa. We learned to our distress that our Elder Swenson, a former missionary living in Twin Falls, had died in an automobile accident. It was a sad time for us all.

With April came spring and a resurgence of opportunity to work the farm. Our children and grandchildren were always involved in fencing, working the ditches, and other chores. We attended a Dance Spectacular at BYU, which featured our granddaughter Holly. We had a nice reunion on the 9th and later on attended the dedication broadcast of the new temple at Winter Quarters, Nebraska. In May, we felt a lack of rain for our crops, so I decided to cut the grass that has encroached in the fields. I raked it and baled it and used it for feed. I dislocated my hip again while working in the garden and had to have a neighbor come to help get me to the hospital. They had to put me out to reset it, and I spent the night in the hospital. We enjoyed a large family celebration in honor of my brother David's 61st birthday. June allowed us to harvest the first crop of hay with the help of many of our grandsons. Our grandson Garren returned from his mission to Germany, and later on that month we had most of our children together in the temple to perform sealings. It was a wonderful time together. We had a missionary reunion with many of our missionaries attending. I was hospitalized following an angiogram as Dr. Smith cleared an area that was becoming blocked. We later drove to Idaho to participate with Layne and his family at the stake Young Women camp, which was enjoyable for us.

We had determined earlier in the year to meet with various families in a family home evening setting to instruct them in family history duties, and it met with good success. Geri and I were called as the stake family history representatives, which released us from our ward callings. We continued our efforts as scheduled in the temple as well, performing marriages and working in the sealing office. We took a quick trip to Las Vegas with Glenda and Steve and returned to a broken water pipe in our basement, which caused much damage. It resulted in new carpet, which was a benefit, and the family gathered to clean up much of it. We attended a portion of our annual trek to the mountains with many family members present. My knee prevented me from being very active.

August brought a mixed series of events. Asael T. Sorensen, a former missionary companion passed away from cancer after struggling for some months. David Apple, our grandson, left for his mission in the Philippines Tacloban Mission, and Jed, Cory's son, married Mandy Warnke of Sugar City, Idaho. This was Cory and Gayle's second wedding of the year. I also performed several other weddings during the month. More and more of our grandsons were earning their Eagle Award in scouting. The farm work quit early due to lack of water. We only got a second crop of hay. The garden produced well, however, with a variety of vegetables to spread around the family. The highway department decided to widen the highway near our place and eventually purchased about half an acre for that purpose. They took out several trees, which caused Geri some grief.

We ended the month with a lovely reunion of my former missionary companions.

September found us enjoying a tour and reception at Welfare Square, which brought back many memories of years ago when I served as chairman of the Pioneer Welfare Region. I had two angiograms under the care of Dr. Douglas Smith and assured me things would improve with my heart. I also went into the hospital for a knee replacement. I was confined for two weeks in the hospital and felt the surgery went well. September 11 was a day of great disaster when terrorists hijacked and flew airplanes into the World Trade Center in New York and into the Pentagon in Washington. This act represented the greatest threat to our society since the Second World War. It apparently was perpetrated by people from an Islamic radical group and left the country and the world frightened for our security.

In October Phyllis Reeve passed away, and we mourned her loss. She and her husband, Rex C. Reeve, were close to us in the ranks of the General Authorities and in the Jordan River Temple. We continued our experience at the temple, and I performed several weddings for family and friends. Shortly after our wedding anniversary I spoke at the Orem Institute of Religion and felt the Lord's blessing as I addressed the students.

November continued with several weddings performed as well as our efforts in the stake family history assignment. Thanksgiving was held at our home, with Geri hosting the large family gathering. December brought another wedding in Cory's family (their third this year). His daughter Holly was married to Joseph Reynolds, and they immediately took up residence in Boise, where he was in charge of building the new airport in that city. June Beck, Ramon's mother, became ill and we feared for her life, but fortunately she was able to recover in good order. We had an annual Christmas party with my brothers and sisters and their spouses. I also performed several weddings as requested. Geri had minor surgery on the skin on her chest, which caused her some discomfort. Christmas was filled with the usual delight as we visited our children living nearby. The children were always good to us.

2002

We continued our involvement at the Mount Timpanogos Temple each Friday, supervising the sealing office. I also performed several marriages for family and friends. We were pleased with the calling of our son-in-law Lonnie Williams to serve in the bishopric of his ward, and I was asked to ordain him a high priest. Geri's brother Ivan had taken a spill and injured himself, which led us to take a quick trip to Kanab and back. I had been troubled with a severe cold that caused some distress. We found that our chickens were being killed by raccoons, so we moved them to Paulo's because he had a more secure pen.

February brought the winter Olympics to Utah and it was a great success. We enjoyed watching much of it on the TV. We welcomed home our grandson Jacob Dowse from his mission and received word that another grandson, Adam Bangerter, had received his call to serve in Romania. Geri and I accepted speaking assignments at various locations, which kept us busy. In March I performed several marriages in connection with our efforts in the temple. Geri celebrated her 78th birthday. I had my hip go out again and had to spend a day in the hospital to get it back in again. We did some plowing and preparing of the soil for the season. We hosted a dinner for Rick Bangerter, a cousin called to serve as a mission president in Brazil. We also continued to speak in sacrament meetings and other occasions as requested.

In April we had a lovely reunion with our Brazilian missionaries, and then I spent another 10 days in the hospital having a section of my colon removed due to some complications discovered in an examination. This time in the hospital took the heart out of the month of April. In May our daughter Julie spoke at the BYU Women's Conference, which brought us great delight. We continued with our assignments in the temple and performed marriages on a frequent basis. Geri had been struggling with a crippling bone problem in her right foot, and she had surgery in May to help correct it. We gathered as an extended family on the 25th at Dick and Marian Lindsay's home to celebrate David's birthday. June produced even more marriages, which I was pleased to perform. We had a new fence installed along the highway since the renovation of the road took out the old one. We did our best to irrigate the farm with the small stream of water that came. We planted a garden, which did much better than the rest of the farm. I had been working with my son Grant and Gary Carson in purchasing and developing a considerable acreage in Lehi, which involved us in a mortgage of short duration. We also enjoyed a Schwantes family reunion at Mutual Dell with good participation. The Nauvoo Temple was also dedicated, and we participated in it via broadcast. I also enjoyed a chance to ride the horses, something that I had missed doing of late due to my illnesses. The summer was hot with a total lack of rain. Because our irrigation had been scanty, we were barely able to harvest two small crops of hay. We held a Hamblin family reunion at Grant's cabin in Fruitland with lovely accommodations for everyone. Our grandson Jacob Dowse was married to his sweetheart Sophia Lee on the 27th, and another grandson, Nathan Bangerter, received his mission call to the Brazil Porto Alegre South Mission. In August Geri and I visited the pageant in Castle Dale, Nathan departed for his mission, and we made a trip to California to be with Ana Wosnijk Baldwin, who had radical cancer surgery. We spent a few days in San Diego with Gerilyn and her family and also visited with friends living in the area. I also performed marriages for ward and stake members during the month.

At October general conference, we were thrilled with the calling of our daughter Julie to serve as the first counselor in the general Young Women presidency. This was a great honor and served as a major focus of our regular conference review held with our children and grandchildren. My former mission companions and I met following conference and enjoyed an evening together.

In October I began developing health problems. I lost my appetite and didn't have energy even to walk around. Geri took me to see Dr. Sundwall, who gave me a battery of tests and finally ordered a CAT scan, which showed a high count of white blood cells and very low red blood cells. These tests put me back in the hospital in American Fork. Dr. Pugh found an abscess in my stomach and small intestines, and I was treated for it while unconscious. I was medicated with concentrated doses and was released from the hospital following a two-week stay. Geri attended me constantly, and nearly all the family members spent time with me. President James Faust kept calling about my condition and twice came to the hospital to visit me and give me blessings. He said, "Well, you don't seem to be finished with your time on earth, and Heavenly Father must have more for you to do." With unusual amounts of antibiotics and medication I was stabilized, and under the care I received I began walking and finally returned home to be watched over by my sweetheart. After a week at home I felt most recovered. We had an overwhelming feeling that Heavenly Father had blessed me. I received many blessings and an unusual number of prayers.

After being released from the hospital, Geri and I decided to take a trip to Green River, Wyoming to see her brother Dale and his wife, Lois, and their son Michael, who lived in Mountain View. Our preparations for Thanksgiving centered on Paulo's home, where over 60 family members gathered for the festivities. I visited the doctors to maintain my health. Geri and I continued to spend our Friday evenings at the temple, working in the sealing office. In early December, my close cousin Rulon Mackay passed away, and later on another cousin, Phyllis McArthur, also died. They had both lived full and interesting lives. We had another gathering of my missionary companions in the Lion House. Our group was reduced from years past—we had lost Dick Platt, John Rich, Asael Sorensen, Norton Nixon, and several of the wives as well. We had several family gatherings to celebrate the Christmas season and also continued our efforts at the temple and in performing weddings for many friends and family. The entire Christmas season was lively with the presence from time to time of all the members of our family as well as our visits in their homes. Layne and Betsy came with their children at this time. For me it was an eventful year, including a great struggle for my health. We were grateful for my recovery.

2003

Having passed through a difficult experience with my surgery in the latter part of 2002, I was happy to feel good health and strength as I entered the New Year. We also felt blessed that Geraldine had enjoyed good health and strength throughout her life, and this season of holidays and celebration was very enjoyable. The weather in December and January was almost spring-like with only one storm in January.

We took a trip to Arizona with Grant and Cleadonna, leaving on January 4. We stopped overnight in Flagstaff and arrived in Mesa on Sunday in time for church meetings in the ward of Cleadonna's sister Helena. There we met with my nephew Clarence Bushman and his wife. We had dinner with Helena's family and stayed overnight with them. On the 6th we stopped by the home of Wilford Cardon. They gave us some fruit to take with us on our travels and then urged us to drive their Suburban on our tour. From there we drove through the desert from Apache Junction to Tucson, enjoying the scenery along the way. We went through part of the Saguaro Cactus Monument and visited the Desert Museum and the old Mission San Xavier de Bac. We proceeded down to Nogales on the Mexican border; we crossed over and shopped a little in Mexico, had some lunch, and drove out east to Sierra Vista, passing through the cattle country of Patagonia. That evening Grant had reserved a fine hotel. The next day we drove to Benson and then through St. David to give Grant and Cleadonna something of the history of that part of the country. From there we drove to Tombstone, mostly to visit the old Boot Hill cemetery and the site of the Earp-Clanton shootout. From there we drove to Bisbee, toured the town and the mine, and then traveled onward to Douglas. Our visit there included the home of the Schwantes family, two homes where Mildred and I had lived, the sights around the town, and a stop at the cemetery where Mildred's parents are buried. Finally we drove north past the old air base where I flew during World War II, viewed the old familiar mountains and valleys, then drove on to Safford. We stopped briefly to visit Roland and Mae Hamblin and spent at the night in a motel there. On the 8th we drove back towards Phoenix through Globe and Superior, stopped at the Cardon home to retrieve our car, and took Grant and Cleadonna to their hotel. They flew home, so Geri and I left for Flagstaff and spent the night there. The next day we drove home, stopping at Jacob's Lake on the Kaibab.

We continued our temple assignments faithfully. In February I performed several weddings, beginning with our grandson Greg and Laurie Lorenzon. We participated in the ordination of Layne's son Will to the office of teacher as well as other family events. Geri had her second cataract surgery, and all went well with that. Towards the end of the month we traveled with Grant and Cleadonna to Colorado Springs to be with Blaine and Heilala. We celebrated Geri's 79th birthday in March, with all the family except Layne in attendance. We drove to St. George to perform a couple of weddings, staying in my brother Norman's home that night. After performing the wedding, we drove to Cedar City for the wedding breakfast and then went on home. Nearing Fillmore I fell asleep at the wheel and the car went off a steep bank and through a fence on the right side, blowing out one tire. We phoned a wrecker to pull us to a station in Fillmore. We had to replace all four tires, but the car seemed to have no other damage except scratches. We drove home very thankful to our Heavenly Father for our well-being and preservation.

Julie spoke again at the general Young Women meeting and did a marvelous job. Our dear friend Morris Rowley passed away as did Mary Howells. In April, Ruth Hale, our old friend from Granger, passed away, as did Jesse Schmidt Taylor, my cousin, in May. It was sad to see so many of our friends and loved ones passing on. In May we attended baptisms of grandchildren and birthday celebrations as they came around. June brought a lovely reunion with our missionaries. We also spent time at Grant's cabin in Fruitland. Our grandson David Apple returned from his mission to the Philippines and made a great report. Our assignment was changed in the temple sealing office as Geri was released and replaced by priesthood brethren. This was a blow to her. We cut and baled our hay, which gave good results. We also enjoyed a lovely time in the mountains with the annual trek to Black's Fork.

Called as Stake Patriarch

In July we were visited by the stake presidency, and President Gottfredsen called me to be the new stake patriarch. This was a humbling expression of confidence in us. In August, Geri and I along with Julie and Cory went to President James E. Faust's office, where he ordained me a patriarch. A couple of weeks later I began giving blessings, many coming in twos and threes, mostly on Sundays. Geri was a major force behind this assignment as she would take the appointments, confirm them with the individuals beforehand, and keep the calendar of the blessings so I would not miss any. As part of this assignment, President Gottfredsen, our stake president called and set apart our daughter Lee Ann to be my personal secretary in typing up the patriarchal blessings. Glenda would type up the first draft, and then Lee Ann would format them. She worked with me to mail them out quickly to the recipients. On certain occasions I would perform a blessing in Portuguese. When that occurred, Cory would transcribe those blessings, and Lee Ann would then place them in the proper format for final copy.

That summer we visited with Duella's family and then drove to Layne's home in Melba, Idaho, where he took us boating east of town. I performed several marriages along with my regular assignment in the temple. Other friends and family continued to depart, including Grace Sheppard, who passed away in mid-August, and shortly thereafter my eldest sister Sarah passed as well. I found it somewhat trying to see these deaths take place in such rapid succession.

In October we had wonderful events to celebrate our 50th wedding anniversary. A special dinner was catered at Ramon and Julie's home, and then on another day we had another marvelous meal with our siblings and companions. We also scheduled a family home evening with each of our children and their families, giving them the story of our coming together. We celebrated the actual day of our anniversary with an endowment session in the temple, which several of our children and their companions attended. We then enjoyed a meal together in the cafeteria of the temple.

In late October Geri and I drove to southern Utah to investigate more an offer on property in which we held an interest in the outskirts of the town of Washington. Arriving there we worked our way over the hills, wondering at the vast growth of homes in the area. After viewing the property and seeing the power lines and the installation of the water line through it, we drove to Santa Clara. We visited there with Beth Tolbert, our friend and former neighbor in Alpine, and then met with Dee Atkins at the Jacob Hamblin Home. There we had a good agreement on the proposed sale of our property, which would be worked out by our other partners. It was after dark when we drove to Kanab, where we found Geri's brother Ivan and his wife, Betty, in their home, where we visited and spent the night. In the morning we went with Ivan and Betty to breakfast in the Houston Restaurant in Kanab. We refueled the car and had a leisurely drive over the mountain and up Long Valley then over the Great Basin Divide through Hatch. We turned off on Highway 12 through Red Canyon, a beautiful sight, to Bryce Canyon. We did not stop there but descended to Tropic enjoying the magnificent views. We continued through Cannonville, Henrieville, and out to Escalante, where Geri gathered much information about the Grand Staircase National Monument. Our direction was north through the magnificent rock formations and the spectacular highways up and down and around, coming to Boulder. There we turned off to visit my niece Carrie Wilson and her family, living in their tent arrangement and harvesting their crops. We went around Boulder Mountain and enjoyed the great views of the rock canyon country and the Henry Mountains, the great forests, and splendid mountain highway. Coming down from the mountain we drove through Grover and out to Teasdale and then Bicknell. At Loa we purchased some groceries and some medicine for Geri and then drove over the high plateau of Wayne County, past Fish Lake, and down the mountains through Koosharem and on to Sigurd. Geri took over the driving then, going through Salina then north to Gunnison. By the time we traveled the long stretch to Nephi, it was dark, and I drove the remainder of the trip to our home in Alpine. This journey was an outstanding experience for Geri and me. The weather was bright and clear, the scenery wonderful and varied beyond any imagination. The automobile was most comfortable and secure, and we had a great time of communion, remembrance, and companionship.

Fall brought wildfires in the San Diego area, and we were pleased with the news that our granddaughter Gerilyn and her family in the area were safe, even though they had to evacuate their home for a few days, taking with them very little—only their children, including a five-day-old baby—and staying in the Cardons' apartment. I performed several marriages during November. I also gave patriarchal blessings to Howard's two sons, Nicholas and Michael. We then drove to Melba, Idaho, where we gave Layne's son Will his patriarchal blessing.

December had us involved with many family and ward events, including a funeral, a family party at Sam and Gloria's home, and a reunion for my missionary companions at the Lion House. We had baby blessings and other family events to commemorate as well. The Christmas preparations carried on unabated, interspersed with weddings of family and friends. We had two granddaughters married: Peggy's daughter Megan to Alex Broughton on the 23rd and Julie's daughter Heidi to Daniel Shin on the 26th. We enjoyed a special sealing session with Cory and his family in which a number of Gayle's ancestors were sealed. We had a rich celebration with our family on Christmas and spent the following days surrounded by many of the family. Layne and Betsy came with their family and stayed for several days. It was a lovely time together.

2004

We began the year visiting Duella and her family as they blessed their new baby. We also enjoyed hearing the report of Lynn and Sara Paulsen Sorensen of their assignment in the Porto Alegre Temple. Geri and I decided to take a trip to southern Utah and left on the 12th, driving to St. George. We visited the Fillmore State Museum en route. We followed the Immigrant Trail west out of Cedar City through Newcastle and Enterprise then south to Santa Clara and then St. George. While at the Jacob Hamblin Home, we again visited with Dee Atkins, who was hoping to purchase the property in which we had interest in Washington. The next day after talking again with him, we drove to the Santa Clara Cemetery and then west over the old highway to Mesquite, Nevada. After lunch we went back through St. George and Hurricane to drive through Zion National Park and then over to Mt. Carmel and Kanab. In Kanab we called Ivan and Betty, and they invited us to their ward dinner in their chapel. There we met our niece Denise Bowers and her husband, Marvin Rider. We stayed the night in a motel. Our return was pleasant along highway 89 with good weather. We were saddened by the passing of Max Shirts, a good friend and missionary companion.

In February we made preparations for a trip to Brazil for the rededication of the São Paulo Temple. Julie and Ramon were to go also and much time was spent in arranging airline schedules and fares. We had been invited by Wilford and Phyllis Cardon to stay with them in São Paulo, where they were living while serving as missionaries with the Church's Perpetual Education Fund. We left Salt Lake on the 18th for Dallas and then flew overnight to São Paulo. We were met by Brothers Cardon and Oaks, former missionaries with us. We visited the Church office center and settled in the Cardons' apartment in the Morumbi area. On the 20th we visited the Missionary Training Center in Casa Verde, presided over by Allen Ostergar, another former missionary of ours. He had more than 200 missionaries in an assembly, and we all four had the opportunity to speak to them. We visited with the missionaries, shaking hands with all of them, and then had lunch together. We left the MTC driving inland about 50 or 60 miles through Jundiaí and onward to visit the Campinas Temple, built on the outskirts of that city. It was new and magnificent. The temple president, President Ichi, had us dress in white as he reverently took us on a tour of the temple, which was not in session. As we left the temple to return to São Paulo, a powerful thunderstorm burst upon us. It startled us, and soon we were in a full-fledged downpour, the kind we had experienced and enjoyed while living in Brazil. The interior of the country was sparkling green and felt like home. The cities and the expansion, however, were startling in their growth, as were the cities of Campinas and São Paulo. That evening we were invited by my cousin Rick Bangerter, presiding over the São Paulo North Mission, to dinner in a lovely churrascaria along with the Cardons. Rick's mission office was in the same house in which we lived while I served as the Area President in 1977 and 1978.

On Saturday the 21st in the Pacaembu Soccer Stadium, we attended the rehearsal of the grand pageant scheduled in connection with the rededication of the São Paulo Temple. We watched the great preparations during the day. President Hinckley and President Faust arrived and spoke to the group, as did Julie as a Church representative. The pageant itself was presented in the evening while we watched from the press box. It was more spectacular than anything we had seen, raising wonderful feelings about the nation, the people, and the Church. We were invited for dinner with President Hinckley and his company. The rededication of the temple took place on the 22nd. It had been refurbished after 25 years of use. The sessions were powerful and filled with spiritual feelings. President Hinckley asked Julie and me to speak. The choir was wonderful. In the evening we attended by invitation and spoke at the sacrament meeting in the Cardons' ward. We enjoyed a visit that afternoon with Hélio da Rocha Camargo and family and also with the José Lombardi family, who joined us in the meeting.

Wilford and Phyllis gave us every attention during the week we stayed with them. They provided meals and a comfortable room. Since it was Carnaval time, much of our activity in the city was suppressed. With Ramon and Wilford we visited downtown, took Geri and Julie to see the hospital where two of our children had been born, and looked up the two former mission homes in the Turmalina district. We also toured Vila Mariana, Bosque, and other areas of the city. It seemed so strange—the city had become so huge that we could not find our way easily. Elder Oaks arranged for a van to take us down to Santos, Guarujá, and other areas, and we really enjoyed the mountain drive in the rain. We viewed the beaches and had a nice lunch. On our return we had a flat tire. In our visit to the Church administration building, some people we met still remembered us. On two evenings past associates and friends came for a visit. On Thursday the 26th we returned to the airport to fly home. It had been a marvelous trip of sweet remembrances.

March began with an ominous tone. On a visit to Duella's home for a family dinner, Geri slipped, fell heavily, and shattered her right hip. We had an ambulance take her to the hospital in Layton, where Duella arranged for Dr. Bean to perform repair surgery the following day. Geri spent over ten days in the hospital. This was a serious disability for Geri. I continued to give patriarchal blessings and work the farm through the month of March as well as serving in the temple. Several years after divorcing her husband Gary Weaver, my sister Naomi was married to Leonard Christopherson, a long-time friend.

In April, Geri continued to recover, though it was slow. Howard and I drove out to Wyoming to promote a book he and Cory had written about the Pioneer Trail. We enjoyed seeing Martin's Cove and the South Pass area. Geri and I decided to purchase another automobile, and we settled on a 1995 Cadillac. It was a lovely car and fit our needs well. In May I continued working in the temple as well as speaking at firesides, giving blessings, and performing weddings— the foremost was that of our grandson Garren Apple to Michelle Hicks from Northern California. We were hosted at a BYU dinner for all emeritus General Authorities, which was a delightful reunion with our former colleagues. We had a family breakfast on Memorial Day with many of the family participating.

June brought more weddings, which I was glad to perform. Geri had struggled with a stiff neck for several months and had undergone some treatment for it. My heart rhythm was somewhat erratic, and upon checking it out, the doctors fitted me with a pacemaker. We continued to work the fields, cutting and baling the hay. We also visited the Hamblin reunion in Mountain View and later the Schwantes reunion as well. Geri and I took a short trip south to Manti, where we spent the night and returned the next day. We worked more with the hay and repaired the chicken coop. Lee Ann's daughter Andrea was planning a marriage, and Cory's son Nathan returned from his mission. We enjoyed a trip to Black's Fork, and while there I fell from a horse and dislocated my hip. It was replaced the next day, and we returned to the mountains to join with the large number of the family that had gathered there.

In August I continued with several patriarchal blessings and then was released from my position as director of the sealing shift at the Mount Timpanogos Temple. I then felt that it was a good time to terminate my sealing assignment since it had occupied Friday nights for eight years, and I had missed the family activities during that period. I continued to respond to requests to perform marriages. Of special note was our granddaughter Andrea marrying Abraham

Denzler. We enjoyed having our granddaughter Jan Bangerter come to live with us while working as a registered nurse in Provo. Shortly thereafter, her sister Suzanne joined us as well. During the month we were preoccupied with the tragic death of Lori Hacking, daughter of Thelma and Eraldo Soares, both of whom had served as missionaries with us in Brazil. It was later discovered that Lori's husband was the culprit. We also mourned the death of Sarah Paulsen Sorenson, who passed away the day following a reunion of my former missionary companions. The following month, Ray Duckworth, another missionary companion passed away.

We had our annual Labor Day breakfast with our family, and the same day we left to see Layne's family in Melba, Idaho. Layne then asked us to go to Blackfoot to the Idaho State Fair. It was another long ride, but we enjoyed the fair and had an opportunity to visit my sister-in-law Elsie Fern Bushman, who had been living in Idaho Falls with her son James and his wife. The next day we drove to Sun Valley for an appointment Layne had and then drove through the mountains endlessly to get back to Melba. There we attended a high school football game in which our grandson Will played. We returned home the next day since Layne and Betsy were fully occupied. We stopped along the way to visit Duella and her family.

In October we replaced the driveway, and it took two weeks to completely dry. We then had a dance on it, with Grant providing the music. Cory and I had planned a drive through Arizona for nearly a year, and so with Gayle and Geri we left on the 15th, driving in our Cadillac through Moroni, Manti, and then south to Panguitch and Kanab, where we visited briefly with Ivan and Betty and then continued over the Kaibab Mountain, also visiting Effie Dean Rich at Jacob's Lake. We drove to Lee's Ferry and back towards Page to spend the night. The next day from Page we drove to Tuba City, seeing an Indian celebration, and then we continued down to Winslow, looking at the sights where the Mormon colonists had tried settlements. We visited Joseph City and Woodruff, toured the Petrified Forest, and went into Snowflake to spend the night. The next day, a Sunday, we drove to Eagar, Springerville (where we attended church), and then to Alpine to visit the grave of Jacob Hamblin. We drove over the mountain south to visit Pima, Central, Thatcher, and Safford and made a short visit to Roland and Mae Hamblin in Artesia before driving on to Douglas, where we spent the night.

The next day we visited the places where we had lived in downtown Douglas as well as the cemetery, and then we drove out to Slaughter Ranch. Cory was enthralled and touched in making this connection with his roots. We toured Bisbee and Tombstone and then went on to Tucson, stopping at the Air Museum and staying in a hotel after visiting the San Xavier del Bac Mission. The next day we drove to Chandler to stay with Cory's daughter Jennifer and her husband, Kevin, for a couple of days. In the evening we had a party with several of our former missionaries, including Darrel Bethea, the Hamblins, the Cowleys the Spears, the Hibberts, and others. We also visited Lowell and Cora Wilson in Scottsdale. Our trip home was through Prescott, Oak Creek, and Flagstaff and then on to the south rim of the Grand Canyon, arriving home after a long drive.

In November I performed several weddings and also gave several blessings. It was a delight to have our granddaughters Jan and Suzanne living with us. They were always solicitous to our needs. One day as I was turning the horses loose, our mare Queeny rushed out and knocked me down, which gave me a terrible bruise on the face and upset my heart rhythm. It was almost a month before the rhythm returned to normal. Thanksgiving was at the home of Paulo and JaLayne, with a large number of our family present. December was once again filled with activities and celebration, including family gatherings of my brothers and sisters. My former brother-in-law Gary Weaver passed away and was buried, ending a trying life for him. We also learned that Delbert Palmer had passed away in Canada. We were not able to be at his funeral. I continued to perform weddings as we approached the Christmas season. The day was spent in visiting our children and having them visit us, as was normal. It had been an eventful year.

2005

Our dear friend Hal Johnson passed away in Idaho Falls. He had served as a mission president in Brazil and was associated with us many years ago. Also this month our friend and neighbor Mike Johnson passed away following a prolonged illness. Geri and I visited Arizona with Paulo and JaLayne, where we performed a wedding for Wilford and Phyllis Cardon's daughter. We attended a special memorial service for Delbert Palmer in Provo shortly after we returned. Our granddaughter Amy Bangerter was called to serve in the New York Rochester Mission, and I assisted in setting her apart. Then Luke, Cory's youngest son, was set apart to serve in the Tokyo North Mission—Portuguese-speaking, which came as a pleasant surprise to us all. I continued to give patriarchal blessings, many at the MTC, and also performed sealings on the Bangerter lines for persons whom Grant had extracted from the chart hanging on our wall in the hallway. I had received this family tree rendering several years ago following a visit to Switzerland. We had family members come to the temple to do those ordinances. We visited Duella and her family as well as the nearby air museum at Hill Field. Our grandson Joshua Apple received his mission call to serve in the Russia Vladivostok Mission. We visited Layne and Betsy to participate in family events there. We did a lot of work around the farm, including shoeing horses and caring for a new mare we purchased. In addition we participated in family events such as baby blessings and baptisms as they arose. On occasion we met with our former Brazilian mission companions and their spouses for an evening of enjoyment. We were invited by various groups to participate in special events. I performed the wedding of our grandson David Apple and Lisa Mitchie in the Salt Lake Temple in mid-June. Another grandson, Adam Bangerter, and Lindsey Kauffman were also married. Our annual trip to the mountains occupied much of the later part of July. In August, Cory was released and then reinstated as first counselor in their stake presidency as the presidency was reorganized.

I had several appointments with Dr. Frischknecht as my heart rhythm had been a major concern for much of the first half of the year. I had developed considerable fibrillation. Severe treatment was taken to regularize the heartbeat, and it finally returned to normal. My appetite returned finally as well. Other health concerns seemed to plague me. Dr. Saunders found a kidney infection, and I spent two days in the hospital and also suffered with knee trouble. I finally was able to leave the hospital but felt greatly restricted in walking. During the remainder of the year it gradually improved, but I was not as agile thereafter. Due to my restricted mobility, I tried not to become too active in performing weddings because it was quite a strain.

Grant was serving as branch president over the Latino Branch at the MTC, and he invited me to provide patriarchal blessings to some of his missionaries from time to time during the year because many of his missionaries had not had a patriarchal blessing or access to a patriarch. Our granddaughter Laura, Lee Ann's daughter, had divorced her husband Mike and decided to marry again. She chose to go to Hawaii and have the ceremony on the beach. Her new husband is a fine young man, by the name of Brett Alvey.

We continued to regulate our estate affairs in behalf of a limited family trust. The value of the land was somewhere near the $6 million mark. During the summer Layne brought 13 feeding calves and delivered them to Alpine. We built a corral and fed them through the summer and into the fall. Following the urging of our sons, we installed a pivot irrigation system during the summer in an attempt to reduce water consumption. We had increasing difficulties in harvesting the hay but had sufficient for the 6 horses and 13 calves. Our travels included a trip to Las Vegas before the death of Geri's Aunt Theo. We also went to Idaho to see the new ranch that Layne purchased in the Pahsimeroi Valley. We enjoyed the annual trip to Black's Fork in July. Though much of the area had been burned out by large fires in the area in the past couple of years, we still enjoyed the surroundings. It was more relaxing for us since most of the family took charge in getting things set up. In August we participated in the Alpine Days parade as I drove a tractor and flatbed with most of our family on straw bales. We also made heavy work with the hay through the summer. Later that month our son Cory received the Silver Beaver Award in the scouting program, the second of our family, following Geri, to receive that award. In September Lowell Wilson, my brother-in-law, passed away. It continued to be hard to see close friends and relatives move on to the next life. We often were invited to eat at several of our children's homes as they extended their kindness to us. We tried to keep some of the calves from getting out of their pen, and Cory took a tumble trying to bulldog one of them. Our ward was divided once again, and we remained in the same section as our granddaughter Jennifer and Kevin Castle, who had moved to Alpine from Arizona. I continued to give patriarchal blessings to members of the stake nearly every Sunday.

In October we celebrated our 52nd wedding anniversary with the family coming together. Towards the end of November, our son Paulo was called to be the bishop of his ward. We were pleased for his faithfulness and this recognition. Christmas time brought the annual family gatherings, and we enjoyed being with the family. Our annual Christmas party was held in Cory's ward meetinghouse with Lee Ann in charge. It was a marvelous time with our family. We learned of the passing of one of our missionaries, Elder Garner who lived in Clifton, Idaho. He had been a faithful member all his life. During the holidays I performed the wedding of Hugh Bangerter, my brother Blauer's son, as well as the wedding of a daughter of Roger Evershed, a former missionary of ours.

2006

With advancing age, my recording of events seemed to have diminished, and recollections of specific events are not as readily available. With the continuance of the winter season we maintained as best we could our efforts with the farm, feeding and caring for the horses and the calves in the back field. Later in January we took the calves to Layne's place in Idaho. I also performed several patriarchal blessings as requested by members of the stake. On occasion I was invited to speak at various firesides and other meetings. We enjoyed the visit of some of our former missionaries, including Drew Day, George Oaks, Fred Williams, and Tom Richards. During the month of February we had several of our family working together to complete the work spearheaded by Wilson Duffles in getting as many of my discourses published in a book form. Our intent was to have something for family and friends to refer to. We took a short trip to Las Vegas and traveled home via the Grand Canyon. I spoke at the funeral of my cousin Alice Bangerter.

In March, Cory and Howard, in connection with their book on the Willie and Martin Handcart Companies, invited me to go with them to Mossida Ranch on the south end of Utah Lake, where a group of people associated with the handcart effort at Martin's Cove discussed arrangements to provide similar services in that location for groups wanting a handcart experience for their youth. It was a pleasant day. Also that month Geri and I enjoyed a few days in Nauvoo. We appreciated hearing our daughter Julie speak at the general Young Women meeting in late March. I continued to provide patriarchal blessings for a number of our members throughout the months, often on a weekly basis. At times I would give two in a day. Around April conference time we were with friends and family and participated in the regular missionary reunions of our past association. These events were always enjoyable and informative, as we would catch up on the affairs of former missionaries and companions. Julie spoke in general conference, which was pleasing to us all. We continued our efforts to keep up the farm and take care of the animals. We took another bunch of calves to Layne's in Idaho. Glenda went with me on this occasion. We worked hard to have our tractors repaired in Spanish Fork so we could use them on the farm. I continued to perform several marriages and give patriarchal blessings.

We were saddened on May 28 with the passing of my brother Samuel. He had been ailing for a number of years, and his body finally gave out on him. I felt deeply the loss of my friend and partner of many years, knowing, however, that his condition was one of release from pain and suffering. As I experienced the effects of aging, as well as the sense of now sitting on the sidelines and watching the world go by, I was brought to the realization that there comes a time in one's life when he knows all the answers, but no one bothers to ask him the questions.

In June we took a trip to Denver with Julie and Ramon. They treated us to a ballgame with the Colorado Rockies. Carl Hansen, our nephew, had us all speak in various settings, which gave us great satisfaction. While on this trip I celebrated my 88th birthday. We returned through the Rocky Mountain State Park. Later in June, our granddaughter Suzanne married Caleb Lakey in the Salt Lake

Temple, and the reception took place at Grant and Cleadonna's home. We also enjoyed a Schwantes family reunion towards the end of the month.

In the early summer we made a trip to Idaho, where our son Layne had informed us that he could get a very good deal on a new truck for us. We were interested in seeing what options were open to us and eventually decided to purchase a new Club Cab Ford diesel pick-up truck. It was a lovely vehicle, and we enjoyed driving it for a little over one day. As we were going back into town with Layne and Betsy for a nice dinner, another pick-up truck ran a red light and hit us, totaling our vehicle on the spot. No one was injured, but we suddenly had to rethink why we needed a new truck. We got our money back and decided such an investment was not one we needed at that time.

Our annual trip to the Uinta Mountains was a delightful one, with lots of food and enjoyable campfire experiences filled with song and stories. Paulo's son Stephen Grant was baptized in the river in a special ceremony. As the summer wore on, I performed several sealings for extended family and friends. My mobility was such that I need someone to help me get dressed, and often one of my sons or grandsons was available to help perform this service. We continued working on the details for the book of my talks to be published, and it was nearing completion. By the fall we sent it to the printer and hoped for a speedy completion date for the printing. Additionally, our son Cory had taken great pains to record my life history in an autobiographical style, for which we were grateful. We hoped that it would serve as inspiration to those who read it.

August found us involved with Alpine Days, sealings, and patriarchal blessings. Our family continued to grow with several recent births. We continued to work around the farm and with the animals, mainly shoeing and feeding them. My brother-in-law John Schwantes became ill, was hospitalized for some time, and failed to improve much over the ensuing months. We began to despair for his survival. In September our son Grant received his Silver Beaver Award from the Scouts. We also took upon ourselves to request a rezoning of our property into a commercial/residential category, which we hoped would increase the potential value of the property. I continued to perform blessings each Sunday and also to visit various family members. Just prior to general conference I was asked to speak at the Brazil North missionary reunion, which was a delightful experience for us. General conference was always special, especially the as we met with our family to review the talks. During this time, BYU came to me and asked if they could use some of my World War II memorabilia in a display in the library. Eventually they used my uniform and a few artifacts of my training as well as Geri's nursing uniform. Other items of the Brethren were also featured, including items from A. Theodore Tuttle, Boyd K. Packer, and L. Tom Perry. On October 5, my sister-in-law Gloria Bangerter passed away, joining my brother Sam in the spirit world.

I continued to perform many marriages and also to assist in sealings for family members. With the weather closing in on us, we found ourselves more at home. I also gave many patriarchal blessings to missionaries at the MTC. December brought our granddaughter Amy Bangerter back from her mission to New York, and we enjoyed very much her report. Each Sunday I gave patriarchal blessings to members of the stake. As Christmas time rolled around, we held our annual family gathering at Grant and Cleadonna' s home, and many of the family attended. I was presented with a lovely cane, specially made by Orrin Olson and Hunt Willoughby. It was made from wood taken from places important to my life, including Brazil, Portugal, and the Uinta Mountains. It was a very thoughtful memento on their part. Our children and grandchildren seemed to flock around us all through the holidays, and we were most grateful for their loving kindness.

2007

The New Year saw us slowing down a little more due to the aging process. We continued to serve where we could in giving patriarchal blessings, performing sealings from time to time, and participating in special events relating to various family members. Cory invited me to officiate in a special sealing session attended by members of his stake presidency. It was a delightful time, and most of the names were from Gayle's family file. In late February their son Luke returned from his mission to Japan, Tokyo North. He also spoke Portuguese during his mission experience. He was the youngest of Cory's seven children, all of whom had served missions speaking the Portuguese language. BYU honored me in a special way in February with their special Alumni Emeritus Celebration. Many came to the open house to greet us and pay special tribute to us. Most of our children were also in attendance as were many grandchildren. About this time Cory approached us with the possibility of taking a trip into northern Mexico to do some research on the Mormon colonies for a book or an article he had been asked to write. We were anxious to be included in that effort.

In March our son Howard was called, sustained, and set apart as the president of the Highland East Stake. It was a thrill for the entire family to join him in this momentous event. We also experienced the trying circumstances of the illness of Cory's granddaughter Rebecca Bangerter (daughter of Shane and Lara), who became afflicted with an aggressive virus that nearly took her life. She was life-flighted to Primary Children's Hospital and placed in the PICU unit, where her life hung in the balance for several days. Many prayers and blessings were given in her behalf, and after a little over a month of hospital-ization she began to recover and returned to full health and strength.

In the midst of all this, general conference came with mission-ary reunions and associations. We were surprised with the pleasant news that our own daughter Julie Bangerter Beck had been called as the new general Relief Society president for the Church. This was a most wonderful event and gave us great satisfaction in recognition of her faithful service and diligent efforts over the years. About the same time, our son Cory, who had been planning to retire from the Church Educational System after 36 years of faithful and devoted service, was approached by the CES administration to accept one more assignment, that of CES coordinator in Long Island, New York. They agreed to accept the assignment and move to New York in the summer. We would miss them sorely as they departed once again to distant lands and service in the kingdom.

As somewhat of a farewell trip, Geri and I spent a little over a week in late April with Cory and Gayle as they drove us through Arizona and into northern Mexico. We enjoyed the familiar sites of Colonia Dublán and Colonia Juárez but also visited less known places such as Colonia Diaz and the mountain colonies of Colonia Pacheco and Garcia and places incidental to the establishment of the Church in that land. It was a delightful time and most rewarding for us. We returned to Scottsdale where Grant and his family had rented a condo, and we spent a few more days in comfortable settings with him, Cleadonna, and Ryan. Near the condo was an airport, and Grant noticed a B-17 and a B-25 taking off and landing. We drove over and spent a couple of hours reflecting on my time flying in Arizona as we watched those vintage planes take off and land several times. We also visited the Commemorative Air Force museum in Mesa, where we saw another B-17 among other aircraft. Grant and Cleadonna took us on a ride to the Tonto National Forest east of Phoenix. There we took note of all the native plants and cacti of Arizona with which I had become so familiar. Later we attended a baseball game with the Diamondbacks against the L.A. Dodgers. We drove home to Utah with Grant and Cleadonna.

In June several of our grandchildren graduated from high school, and we tried to participate with them. In June our grandson Nathan was married to his sweetheart, Mindy Mink from Mapleton, Utah. We took a nice trip to Layne's ranch on the Pahsimeroi River in central Idaho. Several of our family joined to participate in activities on their ranch. Our grandson Joshua Apple returned from his mission to Russia. I also continued to perform sealings and give patriarchal blessings as requested. Our efforts with the farm continued as well, feeding and caring for the animals. In late July, Cory and Gayle packed up their car and drove to New York City, where they had purchased an apartment in Queens, which was to be their home for the next three years. Nathan and his wife, Mindy, were staying in the family home.

August brought the sad news of the passing of my missionary companion and fellow servant in the kingdom, James E. Faust. He had literally worn out his life in the service of the Lord. We knew we would miss him tremendously. As the fall and winter season approached, we continued to have help in getting the farm and animals in order. The various holiday seasons came with the regular flourish. My health was somewhat tenuous, and I spent quite a bit of time confined to the house. We continued to be grateful for our lives and the lives of our family, who so graciously surrounded us in their love and affection.

2008

I slowed down on keeping records of our activities as health and other concerns took up much of our time and worry. When we did get out, it was usually for family events, even though I performed weddings from time to time. We participated in baby blessings of our great-grandchildren and in giving patriarchal blessings. Our horses found a way to get out, and we struggled to keep them in. We ran a few errands as necessary to keep the home and farm operating. Snow was heavy, and often we had to have people plow us out. We enjoyed a week-long cruise to Alaska with our children and their spouses to celebrate my 90th birthday. All but son-in-law Richard Lorenzon and Duella and her husband, Lonnie, were able to attend—Duella and Lonnie had a cruise scheduled later with his family to the same location. It was a delightful time, and much of what we saw was truly spectacular. The cruise line was first class, and all seemed to enjoy themselves. We were pleased that we could participate. In September, our son Howard received his Silver Beaver Award. He was the fourth of our family to be so honored.

2009

Our efforts to maintain some semblance of normalcy at times ran into snags as our health became more and more precarious. With the effects of my congestive heart failure and the need to be connected to an oxygen apparatus at night, our mobility was severely restricted. Our efforts in temple sealings diminished quite a bit; we occasionally performed individual ceremonies and at times family sealings, but our activity at the temple was much reduced from what we did in the past. Patriarchal blessings also slowed down, thanks in part to the ordination of Paul Mendenhall as an additional patriarch in our stake. We enjoyed having family visit us as they could, and we generally carried on a rather simple life, preparing meals, resting, using a little scooter to check on the animals, taking a myriad of pills, and striving to steady the effects of our advancing years. The results are that we get older anyway. Special events included a delightful celebration of Geri's birthday held at the Ashton cabin, where all of our children gathered in February for a few days of enjoyment and reflection. We also spent a couple of days in the Uinta Mountains in July with the large family gathering. It was a lift to our spirits to be in such glorious surroundings and with our precious family.

2010

With the dawning of a new year, the prospects of maintaining and operating our property seemed to almost overwhelm us at times. We struggled somewhat with our health, and the family stepped in to provide extra assistance each day of the week. I felt quite limited in my mobility, which was a concern to me. Many of the family rendered time and effort in maintaining a semblance of order, for which we were most grateful. Peggy worked in the yard and garden, Grant helped with the fields and watering, Layne planned to come and redo all our property in plowing and planting as soon as spring arrived. It seemed spring would never come. On March 1 we went with Ramon and Julie and their family to the Mount Timpanogos Temple, where I acted as sealer in a special session they had organized. Cory and Gayle came for general conference from New York, and Cory took me for a ride to the Oquirrh Mountain Temple and then out to Cedar Valley. It was a pleasant and enjoyable time. We had a review of general conference in April, which was a sweet and momentous time with many of the family participating.

Conclusion

Shortly after this last dictation, William Grant Bangerter began a rather rapid decline in health, stemming from dehydration and additional complications with kidney, heart, liver, and digestive system. He was admitted to the hospital in American Fork on Wednesday April 7, 2010. Following extensive examinations, he was transferred

to the Utah Valley Regional Medical Center in Provo, where his condition continued to deteriorate. Finally, on April 18, with all members of the family gathered around him in his room at the hospital
or connected by telephone, he told all that he loved them, and each
was able to hug and kiss him and express their love to him before
he took a few deep breaths and passed away quietly and peacefully,
conscious of those around him to the very end. Holly B. Reynolds, a
granddaughter, was present and recorded the following:

This has been a most spiritually enriching Sabbath, spring day.
My sweet Grandpa Bangerter passed away this morning at 5:08 a.m.
I was scheduled to work the night shift at the UVRMC pediatric unit
in Provo. Every time I work I secretly hope I'll be put on call so that
I can stay home and be with my family. I am grateful that this night
I was not put on call. . . . The tender mercies continued through the
night as I was able to visit with Grandpa at 10:30 p.m. after things
calmed down on my unit. Gratefully, my friend Jessica was the
charge nurse on Peds, and she told me to take my time downstairs
with my grandpa. When I went down, Joseph Beck was there and we
visited for a minute. I went in and gave Grandpa a kiss on the top of
his head. His bright blue eyes were open, and when I looked at him
and told him hello and that it was Holly he said, "Oh, Holly." I told
him the kiss was from Jenni and Kevin in China and Chad and Emily
in Germany. His eyes smiled, but he was obviously tired, and I didn't
stay long as I knew he slept better when not being "fidgeted" with.
I talked to his nurse for a bit and we talked about the demands his
various organs were making on each other and the fragile nature of
his condition. She was great and told me to come down anytime for
an update. Joseph and I spoke for a minute, and we both left.

At 3:15 a.m. I came back down to see how Grandpa was doing
and ran into Paulo and JaLayne at the ICU door. When asked by
Paulo how I knew to come down, I knew it was a tender mercy of
the Lord. I told him I was working upstairs and that I just wanted
to come and check on him. While the aunts and uncles started to
gather in the waiting room, I got to talk to Grandpa with Grandma. I
kissed his head and looked in his eyes and said, "Grandpa, it's Holly.
I love you!" I knew he recognized me—his eyes were wide open and

aware, and I could hear him whisper under his mask, "Oh, sweet." This phrase as well as others like "Oh, honey, sweetheart, precious" and other terms of endearment will always connect me to Grandpa and Grandma alike. I know there are many who can relate to that same sentiment.

I spoke with his nurse, who said he was ready to go. In the past couple of hours his heart was having a hard time maintaining adequate blood pressure; she had started him on his third heart medication drip, and he was quickly maxing out his doses on that. In short, his heart and other vital organs were just giving out. They were tired after 91 amazing years of serving him well. He had been asking over and over to take the mask off. The nurse had been alternating between two masks that cover his nose and mouth and force a good amount of oxygen into his airways, necessary for his blood to remain oxygenated and his organs to continue to function at any level.

He was much more alert this morning than he had been the previous day. He seemed to be aware of his surroundings, including people and the current status of his mortal life. The Spirit was warm and tender. I felt like we should have been whispering the whole time, as it was such a sacred experience for me. It felt like we were in the temple. Grandpa seemed to me to take on a childlike appearance. He wasn't the strong, handsome, confident-looking man with endless energy that I had grown to love so much. He had a look of submissiveness, meekness, and curiosity—like a young child has when he's wondering what his parents want him to do next. Just like a child, he was waiting for instruction, but the thought came to me that it was his heavenly parents who would be taking him by the hand and instructing him through this transition. I hope that makes sense. It was obvious to me that he was in the Lord's hands, and I think he felt that.

Grandma was darling, all dressed in her Sunday best (at 3 a.m.), as though she were accompanying her sweet Grant to yet another important function. And in reality she was. Grandma had a single white glove that she had brought to wear so her touch wouldn't upset Grandpa (sometimes he was sensitive to just touch). He did fine though and seemed to want her close. I told Grandma I was looking for her token curler still left in her hair. She laughed and said, "There's time yet! Give me a chance!" It was tender to watch Grandma interact with Grandpa. Here are parts of the conversation I remember. "Grant, it's your wife, Geri. I love you sweetheart. You are so precious honey. You are the love of my life, honey. We've had some great adventures haven't we! Are you ready to go home to your Heavenly Father?" Grandpa nodded yes. "Do you want to take your mask off?" (the oxygen mask that was giving him 65% forced O2). Again Grandpa looked at her and nodded his head in the affirmative. Grandma then gave Grandpa several sweet kisses on the top of his head. Uncle Grant suggested to his mom that they have a family prayer, to which Grandma agreed. Then she asked Grandpa who he'd like to say it, going through everyone's names. Finally someone decided Lonnie would offer it. He offered a beautiful prayer in behalf of all of the family and especially for Dad, offering thanks to Heavenly Father for allowing him to be a part of our lives and in living and leaving such a rich legacy. He prayed that "Thy will be done" and that Dad and Mom would have peace and comfort at this time. I must admit, I did open my eyes, sure that I would see a host of heavenly beings anticipating Grandpa's arrival into the spirit world. I didn't see any with my mortal eyes, but it was easy to imagine the likes of Mildred, Elizabeth, Katie, David, Jim Faust, and Isabelle and Wm. Henry Bangerter all there.

Peggy then helped the nurse take the mask off, which he was visually relieved to get off, and they started to put a small nasal cannula in his nostrils to give him some O2 so he could have a little bit of time to talk if he wanted. He didn't seem to want that either, but he let them put it on. Then Grandpa said clear as day, "How do I get out?" He lifted his legs a bit and his arms like he was trying to get out of bed or at least get things off of him. I've been wondering if there is a bit of a battle between the strong spirit and the weakening body that occurs as they are on the brink of separation. I know I feel like my spirit never ages. It matures, but it always feels youthful as far as energy goes. The body however goes the other direction. It matures into an overall slowing down. As I have been present at a few deaths and many births, I've felt the same sacred spirit present.

At this point everyone was tight around the bedside. Grandma at his head, Peggy, Grant with two cell phones connecting Cory and Julie on speaker phone, Cleadonna, Sonja, myself, JaLayne, Glenda, Steve, Lee Ann, Paulo holding the cell phone with Layne on speaker, Howard, Duella, and Lonnie. Each of Grandpa's children took a turn giving him a kiss on the head and expressing words of love and gratitude for being their dad. I had given Grandpa a kiss a few minutes earlier when I was in the room with just him and Grandma and said, "This is from Cory and Gayle." He looked at me with smiling eyes. Lee Ann gave him a kiss and said, "I love you, Dad. This is Lee Ann." Grandpa looked right at her and said, "Oh, Lee Ann." I think this was sweet to Lee Ann because she had told me earlier she just wanted to feel the Spirit strongly. It was suggested that we sing a few songs. We sang "High on a Mountain Top" (one of grandpa's favorite hymns), "Brasil" (the mission song, which brought tears to my eyes as I thought of the thousands of Brazilians whose lives he'd touched and whose land he had become a part of), "Encosta Tua Cabecinha," "God Be With You Till We Meet Again," and Paulo suggested we sing the "family first lesson": "Love at Home." "Love at Home" was the song sung at most FHEs growing up, and when Julie was young, she asked her dad why they had to sing the same song every FHE. He replied, "This is lesson one. When we master lesson one, we can move on to lesson two." I guess they continued to sing that "lesson" for many more FHEs. Glenda said she thought Dad was trying to sing a few words of the song.

Grandma leaned in and gave Grandpa a kiss on the lips, which was one of the sweetest things I've ever seen. She held his hand as the monitors continued to slow down. Grandpa's eyes looked straight up like they do when he's performing a certain part of the sealing ordinance, noting the presence of angels. It was clear to me that his eyes were directed upward, and then they came back down and looked around a little, and he took his last few breaths. After his last breath, his pacemaker started kicking in as his heart continued to beat but Grandpa's spirit had moved on. Paulo closed his dad's eyes, and his body looked so different to me now that his spirit had left it. I pray I won't soon forget the sweet, sacred spirit that was in that room. It was tangible, and as I thought of how literally the plan of salvation was unfolding before my eyes, I was so grateful for that testimony. I knew where Grandpa was going. I knew he was happy and that he was continuing the work of the Lord on the other side of the veil. He will probably be busier now than he ever was on Earth, which is hard to imagine. It was a gift to be there with Grandpa as we accompanied him to the veil. Today in Isaac's lunch prayer he said, "And please bless Great-grandpa that he can get a good body." Grace keeps asking, "When will we be resrected?" She still struggles with the pronunciation. I'm grateful for the real teaching opportunities to testify of the plan of salvation to my children. I hope we all take advantage of them.

Much love,
Holly

Index